Effective Human Relations

EFFECTIVE HUMAN RELATIONS

A Guide to People at Work

Fourth Edition

Catherine E. Seta
Wake Forest University

Paul B. Paulus
University of Texas at Arlington

Robert A. Baron
Rensselaer Polytechnic Institute

Allyn and Bacon
Boston   London   Toronto   Sydney   Tokyo   Singapore

Executive Editor: *Carolyn Merrill*
Series Editorial Assistant: *Sue Hutchinson*
Executive Marketing Manager: *Lisa Kimball*
Editorial Production Service: *Andrea Cava*
Composition Buyer: *Linda Cox*
Manufacturing Buyer: *Megan Cochran*
Cover Administrator: *Linda Knowles*
Photo Researcher: *Sue C. Howard*
Electronic Composition: *Denise Hoffman*

Copyright © 2000, 1996, 1991, 1985 by Allyn & Bacon
A Pearson Education Company
160 Gould Street
Needham Heights, MA 02494

Internet: www.abacon.com

Library of Congress Cataloging-in-Publication Data

Seta, Catherine E.
    Effective human relations : a guide to people at work /
Catherine E. Seta, Paul B. Paulus, Robert A. Baron.—4th ed.
        p.   cm.
    Paulus's name appears first on the previous ed.
    Includes bibliographical references and index.
    ISBN 0–205–29333–6 (hc. : alk. paper)
    1. Group relations training.   2. Interpersonal relations.
I. Paulus, Paul B.   II. Baron, Robert A.   III. Title.
    HF5549.5.G73 B37 1999
    658.3'1244—dc21   99–34613
                                                            CIP

Printed in the United States of America
10 9 8 7 6 5   RRD   05 06 07 08

Photo Credits: Photo credits appear on page 492, which should be considered an extension of the copyright page.

Contents

Preface   xiii

 Part 1   *Understanding Human Relations: Building a Solid Foundation*

1   **Understanding Human Relations: Its Nature and Scope   2**

Human Relations: A Working Definition   6

Human Relations: A Capsule Summary   9

Human Relations and Multiculturalism: Dealing with Diversity   18

Human Relations as Producer: Knowledge from Applied Research   21

Summary   27

Special Sections

Human Relations in Action

Common Sense: An Unreliable Guide to Human Behavior   8

2   **Coping with the Future: The Challenge of Change   30**

Peeking into the Future: Changes in the Workplace   33

Change: Why It's Often Resisted   36

Overcoming Resistance to Change: Some Useful Tactics   38

Change and Effectiveness: Techniques of Organizational Development   40

Opportunities for Development   46

Summary   53

Special Sections

Balancing Work and Family
Telecommuting   34

Ethics at Work
The Rise of the Disposable Worker   48

Guidelines for Effective Human Relations
Using What You've Learned   52

Case in Point
The Plan That Worked   54

Experiential Exercises
Assessing Your Managerial Style   56

Assess Yourself: Change or Stability? Are You a High or
Low Sensation Seeker?   56

 Part 2 *Understanding Yourself and Other Persons*

3 **Perception: Perceiving Other Persons
and the World around Us**   **60**

Perceiving the Physical World   63

Social Cognition: Understanding People   68

When Social Perception Fails: Common Errors in Our Efforts
to Understand Others   78

Social Perception: Its Role in Job Interviews and Performance Appraisals   79

Impression Management: Managing Perceptions of Ourselves   82

Summary   86

Special Sections

Balancing Work and Family
Initiatives at American Express   66

Human Relations in Action
Recognizing Assumptions You May Make about Human Nature   69

Ethics at Work
Self-Presentation in the Workplace: A Case Study   84

Guidelines for Effective Human Relations
Using What You've Learned   84

Experiential Exercise
Forming First Impressions: What's in a Face?   87

4 **Self and Personality: Understanding How and Why Individuals Differ   90**

Major Approaches to Personality   92
Personality: Its Impact in Work Settings   98
The Self-Concept: The Importance of How We See Ourselves   104
Personality Testing in the Workplace   109
Summary   113

Special Sections

Balancing Work and Family
Job Sharing: Do You Have the Personality That Fits?   98

Human Relations in Action
Assessing Your Own Self-Concept   105

Ethics at Work
Personality Testing in the Workplace   110

Guidelines for Effective Human Relations
Using What You've Learned   112

Part 3 *Keys to Success*

5 **Motivation: Moving Yourself and Others   116**

Motivation and Work   118
Motivation and Reward: A Double-Edged Sword   120
Needs and Motivation: The Essentials of Work   124
Process Views of Motivation: How Does Motivation Work?   128
Fairness and Motivation   133
Summary   139

Special Sections

Balancing Work and Family
Practical Suggestions from Expectancy Theory   130

Human Relations in Action
Guidelines for Setting Effective Goals   134

Guidelines for Effective Human Relations
Using What You've Learned   138

Experiential Exercise
Assessing Your Career Motivation   140

6 Communication: The Art of Getting
   Your Message Across   144

Communication: A Definition   147
Organizational Influences on Communication: Who Should (or Can)
    Communicate with Whom?   147
Electronic Communication: The Impact of New Technology   151
Personal Influences on Communication: Different Styles,
    Different Channels   156
Deceiving Others: How Is It Done and Detected?   165
Principles of Effective Communication: Some Useful Techniques   170
Summary   173

Special Sections
    Ethics at Work
    To Lie or Not to Lie: That Is the Question   168
    Guidelines for Effective Human Relations
    Using What You've Learned   172
    Human Relations in Action
    Measuring Your Own Expressiveness: A Short
    Self-Assessment   174

7 Persuasion and Power: Understanding
   Social Influence   180

Persuasion: The Fine Art of Changing Others' Minds   182
Compliance: To Ask Sometimes Is to Receive   189
Power: Beyond Influence and Persuasion   196
Organizational Politics   203
Summary   207

Special Sections
    Ethics at Work
    Subliminal Persuasion   188
    Human Relations in Action
    Measuring Your Own Power: A Quick Self-Assessment   200
    Guidelines for Effective Human Relations
    Using What You've Learned   206
    Case in Point
    Dr. Cialdini Meets Stunning Young Woman   208

Part 4

Effective Groups and Organizations

8 Group Behavior and Influence: How Do Groups Affect Us?   212

Motivation in Groups: Loafing and Facilitation   215
Social Facilitation: Motivation and Interference in Groups   219
Brainstorming: Creativity in Groups?   221
Group Decision Making: Passing the Buck   226
Summary   239

Special Sections

Human Relations in Action
Group Seekers and Avoiders: How Well-Suited Are You for Working in Groups?   226

Guidelines for Effective Human Relations
Using What You've Learned   238

Experiential Exercises
Groupthink at NBC   240

Group Processes and the Family   240

9 Teamwork and Conflict in Work Settings   244

Prosocial Behavior: Helping Others and the Organization   247
Teamwork: Working Together for Productivity   253
Conflict: Its Causes, Management, and Effects   258
Summary   271

Special Sections

Ethics at Work
Would You Blow the Whistle?   248

Human Relations in Action
Are You a Good Organizational Citizen?   252

Guidelines for Effective Human Relations
Using What You've Learned   270

Experiential Exercise
How Do You Deal with Conflict?   272

10 **Leadership: Getting the Most Out of Groups, Teams, and Organizations   276**

Who Becomes a Leader? Some Contrasting Answers   279
Leadership Styles: Contrasting Approaches to the Task of Directing Others   286
Leader Effectiveness: Who Succeeds and Who Fails?   291
New Directions in Leadership   297
Summary   303

Special Sections

Guidelines for Effective Human Relations
Using What You've Learned   302
Experiential Exercise
What Leadership Style Do You Prefer?   304

Part 5   *Effective Functioning in the Workplace*

11 **Work-Related Attitudes: Job Satisfaction and Organizational Commitment   310**

Attitudes: Components and Definition   313
Job Satisfaction: What Makes Us Happy at Work?   314
Job Satisfaction Diversity   319
Job Satisfaction: What Are Its Effects?   326
Organizational Commitment: Feeling a Part of the Organization   329
Summary   332

Special Sections

Human Relations in Action
How Satisfied Are You with Your Job? Testing Motivation-Maintenance Theory   324
Guidelines for Effective Human Relations
Using What You've Learned   330
Case in Point
Should I Stay or Should I Leave?   333

12 Interpersonal Relations: Relationships and Work   336

Interpersonal Attraction: Liking and Friendship   339

Love: What about That Special Thing?   341

Romance in the Workplace: Do Work and Love Mix?   346

Sexual Harassment: Abuse in the Workplace   350

Work and Family Relationships: The Balancing Act   354

Aggression at Work: Destructive Relationships   356

Summary   362

Special Sections

Ethics at Work
A Little Romance Can Be a Dangerous Thing   351

Guidelines for Effective Human Relations
Using What You've Learned   361

Experiential Exercise
The Experience of Sexual Harassment   362

13 Prejudice and Discrimination: Roadblocks to Traveling in a Multicultural World   368

Prejudice and Discrimination: What They Are and How They Differ   370

Explanations of Prejudice: The Origins of Hate   376

Prejudice and Discrimination: Its Guise in the Workplace   381

Reducing Prejudice and Discrimination: Complex Problems Demand Complex Solutions   388

Summary   391

Special Sections

Human Relations in Action
The Illusion of Outgroup Homogeneity   380

Ethics at Work
Gender Discrimination and Sexual Harassment   382

Guidelines for Effective Human Relations
Using What You've Learned   390

Case in Point
Not Bad, for a Woman   392

14 Stress and Burnout: Key Problems at Work   396

Stress: Its Basic Nature   399

Stress: Its Major Causes   400

Personal Factors and Stress   409

Stress: Some Important Effects   414

Managing Stress: Some Useful Techniques   421

Summary   425

Special Sections

Human Relations in Action
How Much Role Conflict Do You Have?   406

Guidelines for Effective Human Relations
Using What You've Learned   424

Experiential Exercise
Checking Your Coping Style   426

15 Career Choice and Development: Planning for Success   432

Getting Started: Choosing the Right Career   435

Career Development: Staying on Track   443

Careers: Changes over a Lifetime   452

Summary   459

Special Sections

Human Relations in Action
What Is Your Occupational Type?   438

Ethics at Work
The Negative Side of Feedback   453

Guidelines for Effective Human Relations
Using What You've Learned   458

Experiential Exercise
How Flexible Is Your Company?   460

Glossary   465

Index   475

Photo Credits   492

Preface

As we enter the twenty-first century, we can look back and appreciate the many changes that transformed the nature of business since the Industrial Revolution. Although many of the changes have been technological in nature, perhaps the most important involve how persons are considered within the context of the organization. Rather than viewing employees as "cogs in the wheel," organizations now see individuals as valued assets to be appreciated. An explosion of information about human relationships is a part of this evolution.

In *Effective Human Relations: A Guide to People at Work,* we combine the experiences and insights of three experts in human relations. Each of the authors has a broad range of research, work, and consulting experience, has taught a wide variety of courses relevant to human relations, has developed unique expertise in a number of areas, and has published widely. We have drawn on these experiences to develop a comprehensive and up-to-date treatment of human relations. This book is built as much as possible on fact, rather than opinion. We were careful, however, to evaluate the quality of the facts in creating a balanced and realistic perspective on effective human relations in the workplace.

Effective Human Relations: A Guide to People at Work is designed to provide students and employees with information and guidelines to promote effective functioning in the workplace. Today, achieving this goal requires concern for quality, teamwork, and sensitivity to a diverse workforce. It also requires a skill in balancing the demands of family and work. This book summarizes the theories and research from a variety of disciplines that are most relevant to dealing effectively with these and other issues. The material is presented in a lively fashion and related to personal and work situations by means of examples, cases, and exercises. Whenever possible, concrete suggestions and conclusions are provided, based on a critical evaluation of the adequacy and consistency of the theories and findings. Many easy or popular answers, fads, and myths exist in the field of human relations. Our aim has been to provide a useful perspective based on facts instead of our own or others' personal ideas. We have carefully documented the research basis for our statements and have provided a comprehensive and up-to-date assessment of the major issues in human relations.

This textbook is well suited for human relations courses in community colleges and four-year colleges and universities. It can also support psychology courses that deal with social science, social behavior in organizations, and management. It is a useful resource for employees and managers in any organization.

Previous editions of this book have been enthusiastically received in many colleges and organizations. Reviewers and adopters have praised these editions for the reader-friendly writing style, the comprehensive coverage, the compelling cases and experiential exercises, and the many features designed to enhance student interest and learning. These features have been maintained or enhanced in the fourth edition.

New Emphases in This Edition

A number of issues are of increasing concern to organizations as we enter the twenty-first century, including diversity in the workplace, balancing work and family, ethics, and achieving increased productivity and quality. Each of these topics has received greatly expanded treatment in this edition. Each chapter places an emphasis on increasing student awareness of cultural diversity, within and across cultures. The book includes special sections designed to develop critical thinking skills. Special sections are devoted to cross-cultural, racial, ethnic, and gender influences on human relations. We have also included special sections on balancing work and family. Many chapters contain *Ethics at Work* features that require students to evaluate ethical issues in the workplace. In addition, a number of special sections focus on productivity, quality, and teamwork.

The fourth edition again emphasizes student involvement and critical thinking about key concepts. One popular feature retained in this edition is *Human Relations in Action*. These assessment exercises, which students can use to assess themselves and others, are designed to increase students' interest in the text material and to help them better understand some of the basic issues of human relations. The *Case in Point* feature found at the end of many chapters allows students to apply the knowledge gained from each chapter to make a critical evaluation of work dilemmas they might face. *Experiential Exercises* provide instruments for self-assessment or research study. Many of the *Ethics at Work* features provide additional critical thinking experience. Finally, a *Guidelines for Effective Human Relations* section appears at the end of each chapter to help students evaluate the chapter's implications for everyday human relations. These guidelines draw conclusions that have a solid research basis and encourage students to take a broad but critical perspective on human relations in the workplace.

New to This Edition

This edition of *Effective Human Relations: A Guide to People at Work* has been thoroughly updated and enhanced by a wealth of new material. In particular, the chapters have been reorganized from the third edition. We should note, however, that we have designed each chapter so that it could be presented in any order that the instructor might choose. In this edition, the book is organized into five sections. The first part is "Understanding Human Relations: Building a Solid Foundation." It includes Chapter 1, "Understanding Human Relations: Its Nature and Scope," which presents an overview of the field of human relations, introduces the issue of multiculturalism, and describes the basic forces that impact human relations in the workplace. Chapter 2, "Coping with the Future: The Challenge of Change," deals with the need to manage change in the workplace and includes new material on developing transferable job skills. We have also added new material on the kinds of changes to be expected as we enter the new century, along with skills that we anticipate may be important keys for success.

The second part of the book is entitled "Understanding Yourself and Other Persons." Chapter 3, "Perception: Perceiving Other Persons and the World Around Us," includes new material on the basic perceptual processes as well as processes involved in perceiving and understanding other persons. This chapter also focuses on how we form impressions of others and how we may attempt to manage those impressions. Chapter 4, "Self and Personality: Understanding How and Why Individuals Differ," covers the role of personality factors in workplace behavior. Material includes the "Big Five" personality traits and testing in the workplace. New to this edition is an increased emphasis on the self-concept and how it impacts our behavior in and out of the workplace.

The third part of the book, "Keys to Success," deals with critical components for succeeding, such as motivation and effective communication. Chapter 5, "Motivation: Moving Yourself and Others," examines the role of rewards, needs, fairness, and goal setting in motivation. New to this edition is a discussion of the role of self-concepts (for example, self-efficacy) in motivation. Discussions of work quality and productivity, career motivation, and flexible benefit plans are included as well. Chapter 6, "Communication: The Art of Getting Your Message Across," considers the nature of both verbal and nonverbal communication. Deception, lie detection, and electronic communication are among the topics covered here. New material on e-mail, telecommuting, motivation for deception, and detecting lies has been added to this chapter. Chapter 7, "Persuasion and Power: Understanding Social Influence," summarizes the theories and major findings on techniques for achieving persuasion, gaining compliance, and attaining power over others. It includes material on subliminal persuasion, mindless persuasion, and resistance to unwanted influence. An extensive discussion of organizational politics and hazards to avoid in persuasion is new to this edition.

The fourth part, "Effective Groups and Organizations," covers a variety of issues related to the functioning of groups and organizations. Chapter 8, "Group Behavior and Influence: How Do Groups Affect Us?" provides insights into the factors that influence productivity and decision making in groups. New sections focus on teamwork and groupthink, and informational biases in groups. Chapter 9, "Teamwork and Conflict in Work Settings," examines how behavior in organizations can range from helping and teamwork to conflict and violence. This chapter also includes material on organizational citizenship and workplace violence. A discussion of team innovation and informational conflict has been added to this edition. Chapter 10, "Leadership: Getting the Most Out of Groups, Teams, and Organizations," examines how different leadership styles and behaviors influence effectiveness at work. New material on transactional leadership has been added to this edition.

The final part of the book, "Effective Functioning in the Workplace," deals with some of the major problems and challenges that people encounter during their careers. Chapter 11, "Work-Related Attitudes: Job Satisfaction and Organizational Commitment," discusses the factors that influence job satisfaction and describes how job satisfaction in turn affects workplace behavior. The chapter emphasizes the challenges inherent in finding fulfillment in an individual's work. The material on organizational commitment is new to this edition. Chapter 12, "Interpersonal Relations: Relationships and Work," discusses interpersonal attraction, relationship development, romance, family relationships, and violence in the context of the workplace. It provides material on sexual harassment, dual career couples, and marital status as a factor in productivity. Chapter 13, "Prejudice and Discrimination: Roadblocks to Traveling in a Multicultural World," deals with both the causes of prejudice and potential solutions to this pervasive problem. Modern racism, prejudice in the workplace, and the glass ceiling are among the topics discussed. New material on unconscious processes involved in prejudice is included in this edition.

Chapter 14, "Stress and Burnout: Key Problems at Work," highlights the factors that make life at work stressful and suggests ways to effectively manage this pressure. Chapter 15, "Career Choice and Development: Planning for Success," analyzes the factors involved in career decision making and career development. It includes material on the relationship between a person's career and his or her personal life. New material focuses on relationship skills, 360 feedback, and efforts to balance work and family.

We have organized these chapters into parts that might fit one possible course structure. Other organizational options are possible, of course. The chapters were written in such a way that they may be taught in any order.

Student Learning Aids

A number of features have been included in the chapters to enhance student learning and interest.

- **Learning Objectives.** At the beginning of each chapter, the major learning objectives are listed to aid students in organizing their study.
- **Chapter Outlines.** An outline of major topics and exercises provides an overview of each chapter.

- **Introductory cases.** Each chapter begins with a case that illustrates some of the major issues to be covered in the chapter.

- **Case in Point.** More extensive cases are presented at the end of some chapters to illustrate some of the principles discussed in the chapter. Questions are provided to stimulate discussion and to relate the course material to the case.

- **Ethics at Work.** The role of ethics in the workplace is highlighted by means of cases or discussion of some contemporary issues. Questions encourage students to assess their own ethics and value-based reactions.

- **Human Relations in Action.** Exercises in most chapters allow students to evaluate themselves or others along some important dimensions discussed in the chapter.

- **Experiential Exercises.** Additional self-assessment or evaluation exercises appear at the end of many chapters.

- **Balancing Work and Family.** New to this edition, these sections present material relevant for juggling work and family life.

- **Guidelines for Effective Human Relations.** The major conclusions relevant to effective functioning are summarized at the end of each chapter. These sections also note limitations of our present state of knowledge.

- **Summaries.** Each chapter ends with a summary that outlines the major issues and concepts discussed.

- **Margin Glossary.** Margin glossary terms and definitions are provided to aid students in reviewing and rehearsing the basic concepts or key terms presented in each chapter.

- **Glossary.** The major terms and their definitions are provided at the end of the text.

- **Illustrations.** We have used many illustrations, charts, and tables to help depict the major findings and concepts. Photographs and cartoons have been used to highlight major themes.

- **Reference Notes.** A large number of up-to-date references are provided at the end of each chapter. Both students and instructors can use these references to explore topics in greater depth.

Resource Materials for Students

A student *Study Guide*, prepared by Patrick Conley, University of Illinois at Chicago, is available to assist students in learning and reviewing the text material. It includes learning objectives, review quizzes, true-false and essay questions, lists of terms, and experiential exercises.

Resource Materials for Instructors

An *Instructor's Manual,* prepared by Patrick Conley, University of Illinois at Chicago, includes test items, discussion questions, ready-to-duplicate materials for exercises, and suggestions for lectures.

Acknowledgments

Past editions of this book benefited greatly from reviews by the following individuals: Merle Ace, University of British Columbia; Bonnie Bailey Allen, Warner Pacific College; Leanne Atwater, State University of New York at Binghamton; Patricia Baxter, Pensacola Junior College; Joseph Benson, New Mexico State University; Linda K. Davis, Mt. Hood Community College; Charles R. Flint, San Jacinto College; Frank Gault, University of Texas at Arlington; Jerry Goddard, Aims Community College; Esther Hamilton, Pepperdine University; Patrick Haun, High Point University; William Ickes, University of Texas at Arlington; Leo Kiesewetter, Illinois Central College; Jerome R. Loomis, Fox Valley Technical College; Vaugh Luckadoo, Central Piedmont Community College; Barbara M. McCaffrey, Stark Technical College; Eva McClure, Highline Community College; Howard Myers, University of Texas at Arlington; David Nakamoejo, Kapiolani Community College; Patricia J. Otto, Gateway Technical College; Thomas J. Schaughnessy, Illinois Central College; Cheryl Stansfield, North Hennepin Community College; Jacqueline Vines, Davenport College of Business; James Wilson, Pan American University; and Ursula White, El Paso Community College.

The following individuals provided helpful feedback for this revision: Susan O. Coffey, Central Virginia Community College, and Felicia Moore-Davis, Houston Community College System—Central College.

We greatly appreciate the efforts made by all of our reviewers and are most gratified by their positive reactions. Finally, we are indebted to the diligent efforts by John Seta, Leigh Paulus, Farrah Moore, and Traverse Burnett in the preparation of the original manuscript. We would like to thank our editor, Carolyn Merrill, and our former editor, Sean Wakely, for his most valuable help and support for this book.

A Concluding Comment

We have done our best to make this book an exciting and useful presentation of the literature on human relations. We hope that it will be well received by both students and instructors. Your feedback about any of the features, chapters, or sections would be most helpful in evaluating the extent to which we have met your needs. Please drop us a line. We look forward to hearing from you.

Effective Human Relations

Chapter 1

Human Relations: A Working Definition

Human Relations: Myth versus Reality

Human Relations: A Capsule Summary

Scientific Management: The Beginnings
Human Relations Emerges: Work Settings as Social Systems
Human Relations: The International Perspective
Human Relations: Application as a Guiding Principle

Human Relations and Multiculturalism: Dealing with Diversity

Dimensions of Culture: How Are We Different?

Human Relations as Producer: Knowledge from Applied Research

Experimentation: Knowledge through Intervention
The Correlational Method: Knowledge through Systematic Observation
Human Relations: Forces of Influence

Special Sections

Human Relations in Action
Common Sense: An Unreliable Guide to Human Behavior

UNDERSTANDING HUMAN RELATIONS
Its Nature and Scope

Learning Objectives

After reading this chapter, you should be able to:

1. Define the field of human relations.

2. Know the characteristics of scientific management.

3. Describe the major events and developments that led to the emergence of an independent field of human relations.

4. Summarize the basic features of individualist and collectivist cultures.

5. Explain the key methods of research in human relations.

It was Steve Landy's first day on the job in the produce department of a large grocery store. He had worked at the store for several years, starting as a carry-out clerk and later moving to cash register and stocking positions. It was a good place to earn money for college. The schedule was flexible and well suited to someone who attended classes during the day. Steve was outgoing and quite popular with his coworkers. He was also hard-working and conscientious.

The store manager, Susan Casillas, had tapped Steve as a candidate for manager training after graduation. They had discussed careers in the grocery business, and Steve thought it might be a good direction for him. He enjoyed variety in his work and dealing with people; being a manager of a grocery store would provide plenty of opportunities for both. It could also be a very stressful job, however. The hours would be long, and Steve would face constant pressure to run a profitable operation. There would always be problems to resolve with employees and customers. Opportunities for advancement would be limited, as store managers were eligible for only a few positions at the corporate level.

These thoughts periodically flitted through Steve's mind, but today he was preoccupied with learning the ins and outs of his new position. He especially looked forward to working with the produce manager, Jake Smith. Jake ran an excellent department. He expected the best of his subordinates, but he had a congenial leadership style. He motivated others by example and by gentle persuasion, encouraging his employees to come up with better ways to run the department or display the products. Even if Steve did not stay in the grocery business after graduation, he was sure that he was learning some valuable lessons while working at the grocery store.

"Hey Steve, quit dreaming," yelled Jake, with a smile on his face. "Can't you see that we need some more bananas out there?"

Steve smiled back. "I'll get right to it, boss. By the way, why don't we put another display near the checkout stands, since we got such a good deal on them this week?"

"Go ahead, if you can talk Susan into it," replied Jake. It looked like the beginning of a good relationship.

Our lives are continually changing. We change jobs, relationships, and schools, constantly encountering new people and new challenges. To some extent, such transitions can be pleasant and even exciting. There can, however, be some drawbacks. Steve was already under pressure to perform well and thus maintain his favorable image with Susan. If he decided to become a store manager, he would have to confront the difficulties and lifestyle limitations associated with this position. Nevertheless, one of his greatest assets was his ability to get along with other people, a trait that might help him become successful in this demanding career.

The study of **human relations** is concerned with the factors that help and hinder effective relationships in the work environment. Indeed, one of the most basic assumptions of human relations is as follows: To maintain an effective organization, you must provide for effective, satisfying relations among the people in it. Consistent with this point of view, human relations generally concentrates on two major goals: (1) increasing our understanding of interactions between individuals, and (2) developing practical techniques for enhancing such relations.

As you know from your own experience, human beings can interact with one another in an endless number of ways—from helping and cooperation on the one hand, to conflict and aggression on the other hand.[1] It is not at all surprising, then, that human relations is a highly diverse field. Its breadth is readily apparent in the following list, which contains a small sample of the many questions that our field currently addresses:

1. What are the best techniques for enhancing motivation?

2. What are the best techniques for persuading others and for resisting unwanted persuasive attempts?

3. How can we increase the degree of cooperation and helpfulness in work environments?

4. What type of leadership is best?

5. How can groups function most effectively?

6. What are the steps involved in career decision making?

7. How important are nonverbal signals, or body language, in communication?

8. How can individuals best handle stress?

9. What steps can we take to reduce prejudice and discrimination in work settings?

10. Do romantic relationships among coworkers interfere with productivity?

11. What makes us happy at work?

12. What are the best techniques for dealing with changes in the workplace?

human relations A field that seeks to understand work-related aspects of interpersonal relations and apply its knowledge to help organizations and individuals in facing their goals.

In this book, we will examine these questions and many others. Before turning to these intriguing topics, though, let's consider some background information—facts you will find useful in understanding this book.

First, this chapter will present a working definition of human relations. We begin in this manner for a simple reason: Such a definition will help you understand what human relations is, what it is not, and what it seeks to accomplish. Second, this chapter briefly outlines the origins of the human relations approach—where it came from and how it developed. Third, we explore cultural influences on human relations. Finally, it describes the manner in which our field attempts to discover new facts about interpersonal relations and to put such knowledge to practical use. Armed with this information, you will be ready to tackle the rest of this book, which presents a survey of the fascinating aspects of human relations in work and life settings.

HUMAN RELATIONS: A WORKING DEFINITION

As noted earlier, human relations has two major goals: increased understanding of interpersonal relations and the practical application of such knowledge to work settings. At first glance, these goals seem to provide a useful definition of the field. In fact, they do come close to meeting this need. One complicating factor, however, should not be ignored: Human relationships are extremely varied in scope. This great diversity raises an important question: Does the field of human relations seek greater understanding of all forms of interpersonal behavior, or does it focus primarily on certain key, work-related aspects of such relationships?

The answer represents something of a mixed bag. On the one hand, human relations is not restricted in its scope; it seeks knowledge about a wide range of human behavior. Given the varied nature of interactions between people in work settings, this breadth is quite appropriate. On the other hand, human relations is applications-oriented; helping to solve practical problems is its stock-in-trade. Consistent with this orientation, the field directs much of its attention to certain aspects of human relationships—aspects most directly related to the attainment of important organizational and individual goals.

A working definition of the field of human relations, then, can be stated as follows: Human relations seeks to understand those aspects of interpersonal relations most directly linked to attainment of organizational and individual goals in work settings. It also seeks to apply such knowledge to enhance these goals. In short, this field is concerned with determining how individuals can work together most effectively to achieve success and satisfaction within the workplace and with developing practical techniques for maximizing such effectiveness (see Figure 1.1).

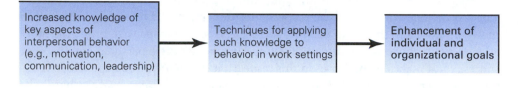

Figure 1.1 **Human Relations: Knowledge and Application**

Human relations seeks increased understanding of key aspects of interpersonal behavior. It then applies such knowledge to enhance both individual and organizational goals.

| Increased knowledge of key aspects of interpersonal behavior (e.g., motivation, communication, leadership) | → | Techniques for applying such knowledge to behavior in work settings | → | Enhancement of individual and organizational goals |

Human Relations: Myth versus Reality

Now that we know what human relations is, we should take a moment to understand what it is not. Many students taking their first course in human relations or reading a book like this one begin with false ideas about the nature of the field; that is, they believe that it offers more or less than is actually the case. Basically, three major myths about human relations exist. Each of these myths is described (and debunked) here.

Human relations provides a guaranteed formula for success. A reasonable reaction to this idea might be "Ah, if only that were true!" Unfortunately, many factors are involved in successful careers, and the ways in which they function in combination vary greatly from person to person and situation to situation. For these reasons, no simple answers and no perfect formula for success exist. Although the field of human relations can shed much light on the causes of both success and failure, it cannot solve all of our problems in this respect.

Human relations tells you how to manipulate other people, or how to get them to do what you want and share your views. Here, too, popular belief is wrong. First, although many techniques for influencing others exist and intrigue human relations specialists, none is perfect; in fact, most can readily be resisted. Second, even if such super-effective tactics for controlling others existed, teaching people to use them would hardly be a major goal of human relations. On the contrary, as this field seeks to maximize both individual satisfaction and organizational effectiveness, such steps would be contrary to its basic orientation. Thus, if you expect this text to equip you with tactics for manipulating others, you've come to the wrong place!

Human relations is just common sense. In some ways, this myth is the most dangerous. It suggests that everything you will encounter in this text and during this course is common knowledge, information you knew before studying human relations. Certainly, we learn valuable lessons from our experience. We also learn, however, that many popular ideas about human beings and human behavior are inaccurate and even misleading. For proof of the inaccuracy of common sense as a guide to understanding human behavior, see the *Human Relations in Action* section.

In summary, human relations does not offer a "yellow brick road" to success, nor will it teach you how to manipulate or control others. Instead, it will improve your understanding of the people around you, your relationships with them, and yourself. This knowledge will, in turn, help you better understand the dynamics involved in many situations in the world of work and suggest ways to cope with problems more effectively. In short, while human relations cannot guarantee personal happiness or success (and makes no promises in this respect), it can help you to cope with a complex and ever-changing social world. As such, its practical usefulness can hardly be

Human Relations in Action

Common Sense: An Unreliable Guide to Human Behavior

Common sense, as noted earlier, is often wrong. In many cases, it offers ideas or beliefs about human behavior that turn out to be false. You can readily demonstrate this fact for yourself in the following manner: Simply ask several of your friends who have not taken a course in human relations to answer the questions below. (It's also best to select friends who have not had any exposure to psychology.) Because common sense suggests a ready answer to each, your friends will probably respond quickly and confidently. After they are done, compare their answers with the ones given on page 9, which are based on the findings of systematic research. You will probably discover that your friends have done quite poorly.

You may also want to take the quiz yourself before looking at the answers. It may be interesting to take it twice—now and at the end of the course. You will almost certainly do better after reading this text and attending corresponding lectures than you do today.

Indicate whether you think each of the following statements is true or false.

_____   1. An effective way to cope with stress is to mentally or behaviorally avoid the problem.

_____   2. The greater the number of people who are aware of an illegal activity in an organization, the more likely it is that individuals feel responsible for reporting the activity.

exaggerated. At this point, you might want to take a minute to reflect on the goals that you have for this course. Figure 1.2 on page 10 provides a handy format for your reflection.

ℋUMAN RELATIONS: A CAPSULE SUMMARY

As we enter the twenty-first century, the notion that the "human side" of work is important should not surprise us. Most people, both inside and outside of business, realize that communication, motivation, and other aspects of human relations play a

_____   3. Happy workers are productive workers.

_____   4. In almost every circumstance, rewards increase motivation.

_____   5. When people brainstorm in a group, they generate more ideas than the same number of people generating ideas alone.

_____   6. A person who is a good leader will be effective in all settings.

_____   7. If a person is unhappy at work, it is likely that the person will leave the position.

_____   8. People who have different personalities or interests are often attracted to one another.

_____   9. We are better at detecting lies or deception on the part of friends than strangers.

_____   10. Striving to be the best and defining yourself in terms of your career are keys to success.

(Answer: Every statement is false.)

 **Reflecting on Personal Goals**

Now that you have learned what human relations is and is not, it may be useful to reflect on your individual goals for this course. Use the following rating scale (1 = important goal, 2 = secondary goal, 3 = not important) to assess the importance of each of the following goals. Space is also provided for you to include personal goals that are not already listed. After you have completed the course, return to this section and see how many of these goals you have met.

Rating	Goal	Rating	Goal
☐	Pass the course	☐	Learn how to interact with others more effectively
☐	Make an "A" in the course	☐	Acquire a basic understanding of human relations
☐	Learn how to be an effective leader	☐	Personal goal 1:
☐	Make new friends	☐	Personal goal 2:
☐	Learn how to manage conflict at work	☐	Personal goal 3:
☐	Prepare for changing career		

key role in the successful functioning of organizations. You may be surprised to learn, though, that this idea is relatively new. It arose only during the twentieth century and did not gain widespread acceptance among managers until the past few decades. Why did it take so long to develop? And what were its origins? We now focus on these and related questions.

Scientific Management: The Beginnings

How can businesses improve their productivity? This basic question has puzzled and enticed managers since ancient times. In one sense, the modern field of human relations can trace its roots to this issue. To understand why, we must return to the closing decades of the nineteenth century—a period of rapid industrial growth and technological advance. The prevailing view of work at that time varied little from the view maintained throughout history up to that point. According to this view, the tasks being performed were what really mattered; the people who performed them had much less importance. In accordance with this perspective, engineers worked long and hard to design the most efficient machinery possible. As they proceeded

Figure 1.3   **Scientific Management: Easier Said Than Done**

Even with all of the best equipment and machines in an office or work environment, humans may not necessarily use them efficiently or effectively. A concern with this human aspect of work was part of the scientific management approach.

with this task, however, they gradually came to a new conclusion: Although machines and equipment are important, they represent only one part of the total picture. The work process must also consider the people who run the machines (see Figure 1.3). Efforts to take this basic idea into account soon led to time and motion studies, attempts to design jobs so that they could be performed in the most efficient manner possible.

This concern with the human side of work soon paved the way for the emergence of a major new approach—**scientific management**. Although this discipline was practiced by many persons, its most noted advocate was Frederick W. Taylor. In his famous book, *The Principles of Scientific Management*, Taylor outlined the key features of this new approach.[2] In general, he remained concerned with maximizing efficiency and getting the most work possible out of employees. Scientific management therefore emphasized the importance of effective job design, planning work tasks in a systematic manner. In addition, Taylor's approach included two new features that, taken together, focused attention on employees as well as on their work.

First, Taylor suggested that employers carefully select and train workers for their jobs. In this regard, he broke with the traditional view, which held that employees are basically interchangeable cogs that can be readily shuffled from job to job. Second, Taylor recognized the importance of motivation in work settings. He firmly

scientific management An early approach to management and behavior in work settings that emphasized the importance of good job design. It also directed attention to employee motivation and to the importance of selecting and training employees for their jobs.

believed that efforts to raise worker motivation would result in major gains in productivity. His view concerning the basis of such motivation was, by modern human relations standards, quite naive; he assumed that work motivation stems mainly from workers' desire for gain—that is, their desire for money. Today, we realize that people seek to achieve many goals through their work, such as approval from others and enhanced status. Although Taylor was mistaken about the nature of motivation in work settings, he did grasp the importance of this key factor. This understanding, as we shall see, represented a major step forward.

Human Relations Emerges: Work Settings as Social Systems

As we have just noted, scientific management did direct some attention to the importance of human behavior at work. Obviously, it did not go far enough in this respect. Good job design and high motivation are indeed important factors, but they are merely part of the picture. Many other conditions also strongly affect performance in work settings, including the nature of the relations among employees, communication between them, their attitudes toward work, and the effectiveness of their leaders. Today, this fact seems obvious and easy to grasp. In the past, though, it was less so. Some dramatic research findings were required to call the social nature of work settings to the attention of practicing managers. The research that accomplished this important task, thereby stimulating the emergence of human relations, is usually termed the **Hawthorne studies.** Given its importance in the development of the modern perspective, this research is worth considering in some detail.

The Hawthorne Studies: A Brief Description.

In the mid-1920s, a series of fairly typical scientific management studies were begun at the Hawthorne plant of the Western Electric Company, a manufacturing enterprise located outside Chicago (see Figure 1.4). The purpose of the research was simple: to determine the effect of level of illumination on worker productivity. Several female employees took part in the study. One group worked in a control room where the level of lighting was held constant; another group worked in a test room where the investigators varied brightness of lighting in a systematic manner. The results proved quite baffling: Productivity increased in both the test and control rooms. Furthermore, no clear relationship existed between level of lighting and productivity. For example, output remained high in the test room even when illumination was reduced to that of moonlight—a level so dim that workers could barely see what they were doing!

Hawthorne studies   A classic series of investigations that, taken together, demonstrated the impact of social factors on behavior in work settings.

Figure 1.4   **The Hawthorne Studies: An Important Milestone**

Research at the Hawthorne plant played an important role in stimulating the emergence of the human relations field.

Puzzled by these results, Western Electric officials called in a team of experts headed by Elton Mayo. These researchers' findings had a major influence on management and on the developing field of human relations.[3] In an initial series of studies known as the Relay Room experiments, Mayo and his colleagues examined the effects of thirteen different factors on productivity. These factors included length of rest pauses, length of workday and workweek, method of payment, place of work, and even a free mid-morning lunch. Once again, the subjects were female employees working in a special test room.

Once more, the study produced mystifying results: Productivity increased with almost every change in work conditions (see Figure 1.5 on page 14). Indeed, even when subjects were returned to the standard conditions that existed at the start of the research, productivity continued to rise. What did these results mean? Why did productivity improve in this totally unexpected manner?

As if such findings were not puzzling enough, other studies soon added to the confusion. For example, in one investigation known as the Bank-Wiring Room study, members of the research team carefully observed male members of an existing

𝒥igure 1.5   The Hawthorne Studies: Some Puzzling Results

In one part of the Hawthorne studies, female employees were exposed to several changes in work conditions. Surprisingly, almost every one of these alterations produced an increase in productivity.

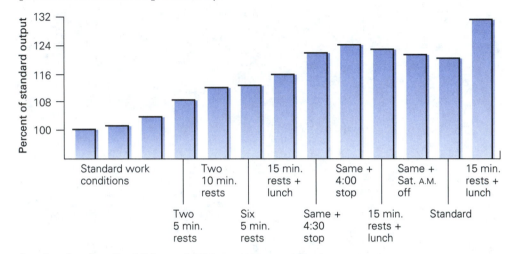

Based on data from Roethlisberger & Dickson, 1939; note 3.

work group. No attempts were made to alter the conditions under which they labored, but they were interviewed by another investigator during nonwork periods. The results of this investigation differed dramatically from those in the earlier studies. Productivity did not rise continuously. On the contrary, it became apparent that workers were deliberately restricting their output. This finding was revealed both by observations of their work behavior (for example, all men stopped work well before quitting time) and by interviews (almost all admitted that they could easily do more if they wished). Why did this behavior arise? Why did these workers consciously restrict their output, while those in the Relay Room experiments did not? Gradually, Mayo and his colleagues arrived at the answer. On the basis of the findings already described and through interviews with as many as 20,000 workers, they reached the following conclusion: Workplaces are actually complex social systems. To comprehend behavior in them, we must understand work attitudes, social relations, communication, and a host of other factors.

Armed with this insight, Mayo and his associates were soon able to interpret the puzzling findings obtained in their research. First, with respect to the Relay Room experiments, productivity rose continuously because participants reacted favorably to the special attention they received and to the relatively free supervisory climate in the test room. In short, they knew they were being observed; because they experienced positive feelings about this attention, their motivation—and productivity—rose. In contrast, output remained low in the Bank-Wiring Room study because the men in that group feared "working themselves out of a job" and raising the amount they were expected to complete each day if their productivity was too high. To avoid such outcomes, they established informal but powerful rules about behavior on the job; these rules tended to hold production down to low levels. Indeed, these employees even established punishments for "rate busters" (men who worked too hard). Such rules, which are present in virtually every task-performing or social group, are generally known as **norms.** They specify how group members should behave. In this way, they often play a key role in shaping group function.

Mayo and his colleagues concluded that social variables such as group pressure, relations between employees and management, relations among employees, and various group norms all played a role in producing the results of both sets of studies. In one case, these factors operated to enhance productivity; in the other, they acted to restrain it. In both instances, however, insight into on-the-job performance could be gained by paying attention to key aspects of human behavior.

The Hawthorne Studies: Their Lasting Influence.   By modern research standards, the Hawthorne studies were quite flawed.[4] For example, the experiments lacked essential control groups; participants knew that they were being carefully studied; and no attempt was made to ensure that they were generally representative of all workers. This last condition is necessary if the researcher hopes to extend results to large groups of employees. Controversy has also arisen about whether investigators ignored information that was inconsistent with their theoretical perspectives.[5]

Despite these drawbacks, the Hawthorne studies had an impressive overall effect. The findings called attention to the fact that work settings are actually complex social situations and that full understanding of behavior in them requires knowledge of many factors ignored by scientific management. As this basic principle gained recognition, a new perspective known as the **human relations approach** took shape.[6] This perspective devoted far more attention to human needs, motives, and relationships than had previously been the case. In addition, it recognized that lasting gains in productivity and morale can be achieved only through appropriate changes in these and related factors. In this manner, the Hawthorne studies served as the foundation for modern human relations. As this field, in turn, has exerted a major influence on modern organizations and many practices within them, one fact is clear: The workers in that long-vanished plant outside Chicago probably had greater and more lasting effects on the entire world of work than most of them would ever have dreamed possible!

norms   Rules in task-performing or social groups that indicate how members of these groups should behave.

human relations approach   An approach to work settings that pays attention to human needs, motives, and relationships.

Human Relations: The International Perspective

In recent years, human relations has adopted an international perspective.[7] This shift has involved efforts to understand differences between work settings in various nations and the effects these differences have on both employees and organizations. In addition, this perspective has included sophisticated attempts to understand how these differences relate to the culture and history of different societies.

One well-known example of the latter approach is provided by Ouchi's influential book, *Theory Z*.[8] Ouchi described several major differences between Japanese and American corporations, differences that he felt were related to contrasting levels of productivity in these organizations. Japanese companies are more likely to focus on long-range planning rather than on short-term performance. Companies often provide lifelong employment, but promotions tend to occur infrequently. Instead, individuals tend to move from one department to another, becoming familiar with a broad range of responsibilities rather than developing a high degree of specialization in one area. Workers often view companies as an extension of their family life; a strong bond of trust and loyalty forms between the company and its employees. Decision making tends to occur by means of consensus involving large groups of people, with all parties placing a stronger emphasis on quality than on quantity.

In his book, Ouchi related these differences to various cultural and historical factors; for example, Japanese industry emerged suddenly out of an essentially feudal society, and American industry developed gradually in the context of markedly different social conditions. Although strong support for his conclusions does not yet exist, Ouchi has stimulated many human relations experts to focus more attention on the role of cultural factors in human relations effectiveness.[9] As today's business world is clearly global, we cannot overestimate the importance of considering diverse perspectives. We explore cultural influences on human behavior later in this chapter.

Human Relations: Application as a Guiding Principle

The state of knowledge in most areas of human relations has significant gaps. We often have support for some general guidelines, but do not know what will happen in a variety of situations. If we wait to act until we have full scientific knowledge about a phenomenon, however, we may also lose many opportunities for improving life and productivity in work environments. Most practitioners of human relations believe that we can intervene in work environments and produce beneficial changes even in the absence of complete knowledge about the complex processes occurring therein. In short, it is possible to do some good now, even though we do not under-

Theory Z Ouchi's book contending that differences between Japanese and American management are responsible for differences in productivity levels in those countries.

stand precisely how such positive outcomes arise or what specific factors play a role in their occurrence.

Fortunately, existing evidence tends to support this optimistic point of view. The word "fortunately" is fully appropriate here. At the moment, no complete theory of human behavior in work settings exists, and none seems likely to emerge during the next few years. Thus the fact that we can produce positive changes even in the absence of such theory is advantageous, to say the least. For example, human relations practitioners have been promoting teamwork as an effective approach for productivity. Yet, as you will see, much remains to be learned about why teamwork is effective, how to increase its effectiveness, and when it is not useful.

Human relations as a field is deeply committed to applying the knowledge it obtains. Not only does it seek to understand work settings and behavior in them, but it also attempts to change these settings in ways that will enhance the satisfaction and dignity of individuals within organizations (see Figure 1.6). This idea is a major theme of human relations—perhaps *the* major theme—and one emphasized throughout this book.

Figure 1.6 Improving Work Conditions: A Major Goal of Human Relations

A major goal of the field of human relations is to enhance the satisfaction and dignity of individuals within organizations. As you can see, conditions within "sweat shops" did little to enhance either of these dimensions.

HUMAN RELATIONS AND MULTICULTURALISM: DEALING WITH DIVERSITY

Throughout this textbook, we will highlight the roles of race, ethnicity, culture, and gender in human relations. The goal is to sensitize readers to the role of cultural factors in human relationships. As we become more aware of our cultural differences and similarities, perhaps we can work together more effectively.

It is imperative that we learn to work together in our multicultural world. Facts regarding the workforce as we enter the twenty-first century make this issue a critical one for our success as a nation and as individuals. The workforce is becoming increasingly diverse in terms of gender, race, and nationality, and the lines between nations in terms of business are gradually disappearing. In addition, legal requirements make the management of diversity a matter of law. More importantly, interacting with persons of other cultures and with different perspectives can enrich your life (see Figure 1.7). Evidence also shows that, when properly managed, diverse groups and organizations enjoy advantages over those without a diverse member-

 The Multicultural World

Interacting with persons from different cultural backgrounds can enrich our lives.

ship.[10] For these reasons, we must be sensitive to the differing perspectives of persons with different cultural backgrounds. We will discuss several of these differences in this section.

Dimensions of Culture: How Are We Different?

What characteristics distinguish your racial or ethnic group from others? In thinking about this question, you will probably come up with some of the obvious factors, such as physical features, religion, cultural traditions, and language. Each of these issues may, in fact, play an important role in the identity of people of different cultures.[11] Yet, just because we know the language, religion, or cultural traditions of a group, can we accurately predict its members' behaviors, motivations, and values? Often, we cannot. As a result, investigators who have examined different cultures have attempted to find some general influential dimensions that allow us to classify cultures without regard to their language, religion, and so on.[12] One dimension that seems to clearly differentiate cultures is that of individualism versus collectivism.[13]

Cultures that are high on individualism emphasize the role of personal choice and achievement in developing one's identity. These cultures are often affluent and allow great mobility for purposes of education and employment. The United States, Canada, and Western Europe fall into this category. **Individualist cultures** stress independence, personal goals, achievement, and freedom.[14] People in individualist cultures have superficial relationships with a wide variety of people rather than close relationships within a particular group. When individual rights come in conflict with group well-being, individual rights take priority.[15]

In **collectivist cultures,** personal identity derives from the collective groups to which a person is attached, such as family, tribe, or religious group. This pattern often occurs in agrarian cultures characterized by little mobility and in which most people live in the same community their entire life. Many countries in Asia, South America, and Africa fall into the collectivistic category. Even some urban industrialized cultures are collectivistic, however. Cultures such as Japan and Israel are homogeneous in that most people share a similar cultural and religious heritage. Collectivist cultures emphasize dependence on relationships with in-group or family members, group goals, obedience, duty, and harmony. People in such cultures interact primarily with members of their in-group and make little effort to get to know individuals outside of this group.[16] When the well-being of the group conflicts with individual rights, collectivist cultures give priority to the group rather than to the individual.

Table 1.1 on page 20 summarizes the major features of individualist and collectivist cultures. Which of these two cultures best describes the one to which you belong?

individualist cultures   Cultures that emphasize individual achievement, rights, and independence.

collectivist cultures   Cultures that emphasize interdependence, obedience, group goals, and harmony.

| Table 1.1 | Collectivism versus Individualism: An Important Cultural Dimension |

Individualist cultures place much emphasis on individual rights and achievement while collectivist cultures emphasize relationships within a group.

Individualist Cultures	Collectivist Cultures
Personal choice and achievement	Identity derived from group
Independence and freedom	Interdependence with in-group
Personal goals	Group goals
Superficial relationships with a wide variety of people	Close and frequent interaction with in-group
Individual has priority over group	Group has priority over individual
High mobility	Low mobility

As you look over the characteristics of individualist and collectivist cultures in Table 1.1, you may wonder which cultural pattern is "better." As affluence and industrialization are related to individualism, you might want to vote for individualism. The fact that the United States is a highly individualistic country may bias your choice toward this type of culture. Yet it probably comes as no surprise that residents of affluent, industrialized countries are not necessarily happy. Less than one-third of former West Germans indicate that they are happy, and many Europeans reported being less happy in 1993 than they were ten years earlier.[17] Nevertheless, collectivism does not necessarily guarantee happiness. Collectivist cultures, such as Greece and Portugal, rank fairly low in satisfaction with life. Even in affluent but collectivist Japan, citizens report lower satisfaction with life than do their counterparts in most individualist countries.[18]

Thus neither individualism nor collectivism in itself is a key to personal or cultural happiness. Social support systems are a characteristic of collectivist cultures that may contribute to the well-being of members of those cultures. Other factors, such as social support, are important for happiness. For example, social support from family and friends during times of stress can help reduce the negative effects of stress. In fact, regardless of whether they are experiencing stress, individuals with strong social support networks enjoy higher levels of health and well-being.[19] On the other hand, individualist cultures are more likely to support individual needs for achievement and gender equality. People in those cultures may be more likely to reach their intellectual and creative potential.[20] Consequently, neither of these cultural types is all good or all bad. Each has benefits and drawbacks.

$\mathcal{H}$UMAN RELATIONS AS PRODUCER: KNOWLEDGE FROM APPLIED RESEARCH

Common sense, we have already seen, does not provide a very reliable guide to human behavior. Indeed, it can often lead to serious misjudgments in understanding the people around us. How, then, can we hope to uncover important facts about human relations in the world of work? How can we gain valuable insights into the way people interact with one another in work settings and organizations? Many possible answers to these questions exist, but most practitioners of human relations agree that two strategies are probably most useful: (1) adapting, generalizing, and applying knowledge acquired by related fields, and (2) doing original research focused on key aspects of human relations. Most of the information presented throughout this book was obtained by these methods.

Because human relations uncovers many intriguing facts about people and their work behavior through research of its own, it is important to have some basic knowledge of the research process. Human relations specialists decide to proceed on their own for two reasons. First, the information they require about some aspect of interpersonal relations may not be available elsewhere. Researchers in other fields may not have investigated that precise topic or question. Second, human relations experts always cast an eye toward application of the knowledge gained. They wish to use the knowledge at their disposal to help both individuals and organizations to attain their goals. As the fields on which human relations draws are often less concerned with application, additional research may be needed to determine the best ways of putting knowledge to practical use. Thus human relations experts conduct research projects designed to add to our understanding of behavior in the world of work.

You may wonder how they carry out such projects. The answer is fairly simple: by means of two techniques used in many other fields concerned with human behavior, **experimentation** and systematic observation (or the correlational method).[21] Of course, you may not wish to become a researcher or to conduct such projects yourself. Given that much of the information presented later in this book relies on studies carried out via these techniques, it is worthwhile to take a brief look at their major features.

Experimentation: Knowledge through Intervention

Suppose a human relations expert became interested in the following question: When individuals go on a job interview, how should they dress? Imagine that no firm

experimentation A method of research in which one or more factors (independent variables) are altered systematically to determine if such changes have an impact on one or more aspects of behavior (dependent variables).

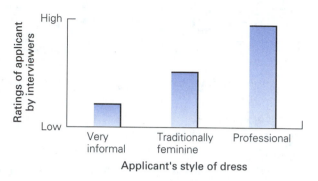

Figure 1.8 **Experimentation: A Simple Example**

In the imaginary experiment shown here, a job applicant dressed in one of three different styles when reporting for an interview. Results indicated that the applicant received highest ratings from the personnel managers who interviewed her when she dressed in a professional style.

evidence on this question exists. How could our human relations expert go about finding the answer? One possibility is that the expert could conduct an appropriate experiment in which personnel managers are exposed to different styles of dress in applicant interviews. Ratings of the applicants by managers can be used to determine the impact of applicant dress (see Figure 1.8).

Unfortunately, many people feel that experimentation is a complex and mysterious process—one well beyond their grasp. In fact, its basic logic is surprisingly simple and involves only two major steps:

1. A factor believed to affect behavior is systematically varied in either its presence or strength.

2. The researcher studies the effects of such variation on some aspect of behavior.

If the varied factor actually affects behavior, persons exposed to different levels or amounts of it should show differences in the way they act. For example, if we believe that a person in a good mood is more helpful than a person in a bad mood, we can vary subjects' moods (for example, by giving them either success or failure feedback on a task) and give them an opportunity to help (for example, ask them to do extra photocopying). If helping rates are higher for persons in good moods than for subjects in bad moods, we may infer that mood states cause changes in helping behavior. In this example, "mood" would be called an **independent variable**—a variable that is manipulated in an experiment so as to determine its effects on behavior. In this example, "helping" would be the **dependent variable**—a variable that is measured and potentially affected by the independent variable (see Figure 1.9).

independent variable   A variable that is manipulated in an experiment so as to determine its effects on behavior.

dependent variable   A variable that is measured and potentially affected by the independent variable.

Figure 1.9 **Dependent versus Independent Variables**

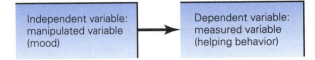

Experimenters change or manipulate independent variables, such as persons' mood states, and measure the effects of these changes on behavior, such as helping rates. The measured variables are called dependent variables.

Note that this reasoning applies only if all other factors that might also affect the behavior under study are held constant. If additional factors are allowed to vary freely, it becomes impossible to tell just why any difference in behavior occurs.

The Correlational Method: Knowledge through Systematic Observation

Experimentation is an important technique for uncovering new facts about human relations. Unfortunately, it cannot be used in all situations. Practical or ethical constraints may make it impossible for researchers to perform an appropriate experiment. For example, imagine that a human relations specialist has reason to suspect that certain styles of leadership are more effective in inducing high productivity among employees than others. Could he persuade the top executives in a large company to alter their style in specific ways, or even replace these executives at will, to vary this factor? Probably not. Similarly, imagine that a researcher believes certain types of stress lead to heart attacks among employees. Could he expose individuals to low, moderate, or high levels of such conditions to determine if such changes affect the number of employees who collapse on the job? Obviously not. In these and countless other cases, the use of experimentation is not feasible.

Researchers do not need to throw up their hands in despair, however, in these instances. They can turn to an alternative approach known as the **correlational method.** This technique involves careful observation of two or more variables to determine if they are in any way related. If changes in one are found to be consistently associated with changes in the other (for instance, if as one rises, so does the other), evidence for a link between them is obtained. Please note: In correlation, *no attempt is made to vary one of the factors in order to observe its effect on the other.* Instead, naturally

correlational method   A method of research in which two or more variables are carefully studied to determine whether changes in one are associated with changes in the other.

occurring variations in both are observed to learn whether they tend to occur together in some way.

To see how the correlational method can be applied to the study of behavior in work settings, let's return to an earlier example: the impact of a job applicant's style of dress on the outcome of a job interview. Applying basic procedures of the correlational method would be relatively simple. The researcher interested in this question would arrange to visit the employment offices of many different companies. There, she would observe the style of dress of each female job applicant and classify each applicant as dressed in an informal, traditionally feminine, or professional manner. (The researcher would probably try to make these observations in a discreet way, so that applicants would not notice.) Then, she would obtain the ratings assigned to each person by the personnel managers who interviewed them. In a final step, she would compare these two variables—applicants' style of dress and the ratings they received—to determine whether they are related. Here, the researcher would not attempt to vary the applicants' style of dress to determine the impact of such changes on the managers' ratings, nor would she attempt to intervene in the situation in any other way. Rather, she would simply observe whether a relationship exists between changes in style of dress and job interview ratings (see Figure 1.10).

As you can see, the correlational method offers several key advantages. It can readily be employed to study behavior in many different settings, including those involving work. Similarly, it can be applied to topics and issues that, for ethical or practical reasons, cannot be studied by direct experimentation. Often, this method permits researchers to uncover important relationships without affecting the organizations or the persons involved. In contrast, experimentation requires some kind of intervention or change.

Figure 1.10   **Positive Correlation between Formality of Dress and Ratings**

As you can see, as employees' dress becomes more formal, their ratings become more positive.

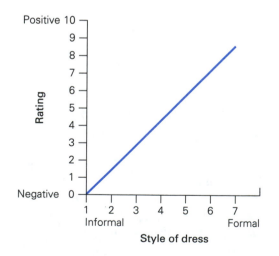

Given all of these advantages, you might wonder why human relations specialists and other researchers ever prefer to use experimentation. Doesn't it involve a lot of extra work for very little gain? Despite its many pluses, the correlational method suffers one major drawback: It is not very effective in establishing cause-and-effect relationships. Specifically, just because changes in one variable are accompanied by changes in another variable does not guarantee that changes in the first caused changes in the second. The opposite may be true or, even worse, changes in both may actually be caused by changes in some other factor not carefully observed. For example, imagine that systematic observation revealed that the greater the hair loss of male executives, the higher their salaries. One interpretation of this result is that hair loss causes promotions—not a very reasonable suggestion. Another interpretation is that promotions, with all the extra worry and pressures they involve, cause hair loss. This conclusion is a bit more convincing, but not much. Yet another possibility exists: Both hair loss and promotions are caused by another factor—more advanced age. In short, no direct link exists between these two variables; instead, both are affected by another factor.

In this example, it is easy to see that the third alternative is the most likely one. In many other instances, such a choice is more difficult. It is precisely this type of ambiguity that leads many researchers to prefer experimentation. In any case, the moral for researchers, and for consumers of research findings, is clear: Be on guard against interpreting even a strong correlation between two variables as evidence of a direct causal link between them.

Human Relations: Forces of Influence

We will conclude this chapter by giving a preview of what is to come. The field of human relations can be envisioned as covering forces that operate at the individual, interpersonal, and group levels (see Figure 1.11 on page 26). To illustrate these processes, consider the following situation:

Kelley calls her mom after supper, as usual. And as usual, their conversation turns to Kelley's problems at work. She has been employed for five years at Turnwood, Incorporated.

"I don't think I can take it anymore," says Kelley. "Every day I wake up and dread the drive into work. I feel like quitting and telling them all where they can go."

"Honey, I know you're sick of your job, but what would you and your kids live on if you did quit?" her mother replies. "Can't you find anything positive about the place? Maybe you should stop looking at the negative all the time."

"I do try to look at the positive!" Kelley says with some frustration. "You know, I really liked the job when I got it. I'd never been so happy. But now it's

𝓕igure 1.11 **Forces of Influence in Human Relations**

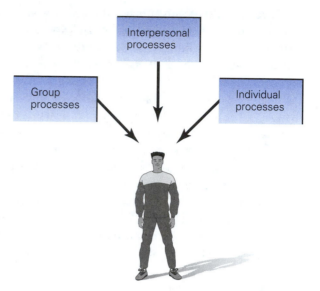

People in the workplace are influenced by (1) interpersonal processes, such as perception, motivation, and personality; (2) interpersonal processes, such as communication, prejudice, and conflict; and (3) group processes, such as teamwork and leadership. We will explore all of these forces in this book.

just the same old thing, day after day. I'm bored stiff and I'm not getting anywhere."

"Well, all I can tell you to do is to keep at it. Things will get better if you try to make them better. Maybe you don't want things to get better, because then you wouldn't have as much to complain about. When I was your age, I would have loved having a position like yours," her mother quipped.

"Okay, Mother," Kelley says with a sigh, "I know I should be happy to have any job in these tough times. But you just don't know what it's like. Maybe I'll call in sick tomorrow. I feel a cold coming on."

This sad conversation is all too common. What does it suggest about human relations at work? First, why does Kelley find her work so unsatisfying? The answer to this question points to the critical role of factors occurring at the individual level of analysis, such as employee attitudes, perceptions, motivation, and personality. Because these basic psychological factors are so important, it makes sense to study them in detail. We will consider what psychologists have learned about these and related topics in chapters dealing with social perception (Chapter 3), self and personality (Chapter 4), motivation (Chapter 5), work attitudes and job satisfaction (Chapter 11), and stress and burnout (Chapter 14).

Studying behavior at just this level would not be complete, however. People do not work in a vacuum—instead, the workplace is a social environment and the nature of our interpersonal relationships plays a critical role in determining our satisfaction and productivity at work. Thus we need to learn about the nature of these interpersonal and group processes. We will introduce the basics of these processes in the chapters on communication (Chapter 6), persuasion, power, and social influence (Chapter 7), conflict (Chapter 9), leadership (Chapter 10), interpersonal relationships (Chapter 12), and prejudice and discrimination (Chapter 13). We can also ask what is happening at the larger group level that is affecting Kelley's attitudes and behavior. Groups and organizations provide the backdrop against which behavior occurs. Similarly, as discussed earlier, we exist within a wider cultural context that determines our reactions to situations. Although Chapters 8 and 9 deal specifically with these forces, we will point out these influences where appropriate within each chapter. We also provide useful information about choosing and developing a career path (Chapter 15) and coping with the inevitable changes of the future (Chapter 2).

We find the ideas presented in this book to be interesting and presume that you will, too! At the very least, an exposure to this information will make you more sensitive to the challenges of working with other people and help you meet these challenges.

Summary

Human relations, as a field, has two major goals: (1) increased understanding of interpersonal relations in work settings, and (2) the application of such knowledge to the attainment of both individual and organizational goals. Its roots can be traced, in part, to scientific management. Although this approach was concerned mainly with enhancing productivity, it nevertheless directed some attention to the proper training of employees and to their motivation. It therefore showed more concern for the human side of work than did older, traditional views. Not until the completion of the famous Hawthorne studies, however, did widespread recognition of the social nature of work develop. These investigations concluded that behavior on the job is affected by many of the same factors that influence behavior in other contexts (for example, motivation, attitudes, and communication).

A major concern in human relations is the understanding of the role played by cultural factors. One important dimension of cultures that influences relationships is individualism versus collectivism. Although human relations readily "imports" information from related fields, experts in this field also add to our knowledge about behavior in work settings by conducting original research. In their quest for such knowledge, human relations experts employ several different techniques. The most important of these are experimentation and systematic observation (that is, via the correlational method). Human relations covers basic processes that operate at the individual, interpersonal, and group levels. Each exerts important forces that determine behavior in the workplace.

Key Terms

collectivist cultures, p. 19

correlational method, p. 23

dependent variable, p. 22

experimentation, p. 21

Hawthorne studies, p. 12

human relations, p. 5

human relations approach, p. 15

independent variable, p. 22

individualist cultures, p. 19

norms, p. 15

scientific management, p. 11

Theory Z, p. 16

Notes

1. Baron, R. A., & Byrne, D. (1994). *Social psychology: Understanding human interaction* (7th ed.). Boston: Allyn and Bacon.

2. Taylor, F. W. (1911). *The principles of scientific management.* New York: Harper & Brothers.

3. Roethlisberger, F. J., & Dickson, W. J. (1939). *Management and the worker.* Cambridge, MA: Harvard University Press.

4. Franke, R., & Kaul, J. (1978). The Hawthorne experiments: First statistical interpretations. *American Sociological Review, 43,* 623–643.

5. Gillespie, R. (1991). *Manufacturing knowledge: A history of the Hawthorne experiments.* New York: Cambridge University Press.

6. McGregor, D. (1960). *The human side of enterprise.* New York: McGraw-Hill.

7. Steers, R. M., & Miller, E. L. (1988). Management in the 1990s: The international challenge. *Academy of Management Executive, 2,* 21–22.

8. Ouchi, W. G. (1981). *Theory Z: How American business can meet the Japanese challenge.* Reading, MA: Addison-Wesley.

9. Sullivan, J. J. (1983). A critique of Theory Z. *Academy of Management Review, 8,* 132–142.

10. Cox, T. H., Lobel, S., & McLeod, P. (1991). Effects of ethnic group cultural difference on cooperative versus competitive behavior in a group task. *Academy of Management Journal, 34,* 827–847.

11. Lonner, W. J., & Malpass, R. (1994). *Psychology and culture.* Boston: Allyn and Bacon.

12. Smith, P. B., & Bond, M. H. (1993). *Social psychology across cultures: Analysis and perspectives.* Boston: Allyn and Bacon.

13. Hofstede, G. (1983). Dimensions of national cultures in fifty countries and three regions. In J. Deregowski, S. Dzuirawiec, & R. Annis (eds.), *Explications in cross-cultural psychology.* Lisse, The Netherlands: Swets and Zeitlinger.

14. Schwartz, S. H. (1994). Cultural dimensions of values: Towards an understanding of national differences. In U. Kim, H. C. Triandis, & G. Yoon (eds.), *Individualism and collectivism: Theoretical and methodological issues.* Newbury Park, CA: Sage.

15. Triandis, H. C. (1994). *Culture and social behavior.* Boston: McGraw-Hill.

16. Ibid.

17. Fedarko, K. (1993, September 13). Most happy nation. *Time*, p. 56.

18. Inglehart, R. (1990). *Culture shift in advanced industrial society.* Princeton: Princeton University Press.

19. Wills, T. A. (1991). Social support and interpersonal relationships. In M. S. Clark (ed.), *Review of personality and social psychology, Vol. 12. Prosocial behavior* (pp. 265–289). Newbury Park, CA: Sage.

20. Triandis, H. C. (1994). Culture and social behavior. In W. J. Lonner & R. Malpass (eds.), *Psychology and culture* (pp. 169–174). Boston: Allyn and Bacon.

21. Aronson, E., Ellsworth, P. C., Carlsmith, J. M., & Gonzales, M. H. (1990). *Methods of research in social psychology.* New York: McGraw-Hill.

Chapter 2

**Peeking into the Future:
Changes in the Workplace**

Change: Why It's Often Resisted
Psychological Factors: Barriers to Change
Organizational Factors: Social and
    Structural Barriers

**Overcoming Resistance to Change:
Some Useful Tactics**
Change: How to Introduce It

**Change and Effectiveness:
Techniques of Organizational
Development**
Survey Feedback: Change through
    Information
Sensitivity Training: Developing Insight
Team Building: Creating Effective
    Work Groups
Quality of Work Life: The Humanizing
    of Work and Work Settings
Effectiveness of Organizational
    Development: How Well Does It Work?

Opportunities for Development
Dual Career Ladders: A New Way to Climb
    to the Top
The "Temping" of the Workforce: Trends
    toward Temporary Employment
Transferable Job Skills: Staying Up-to-Date
Social Skills: An Important Transferable
    Quality

Special Sections
Balancing Work and Family
Telecommuting

Ethics at Work
The Rise of the Disposable Worker

Guidelines for Effective Human Relations
Using What You've Learned

Case in Point
The Plan That Worked

Experiential Exercise
Assessing Your Managerial Style

Experiential Exercise
Assess Yourself: Change or Stability? Are
    You a High or Low Sensation Seeker?

COPING WITH THE FUTURE
The Challenge of Change

Learning Objectives

After reading this chapter, you should be able to:

1. Describe the trends of change in the workplace as we move into a new century.

2. Explain why individuals often resist change at work.

3. Discuss the organizational barriers to change.

4. Indicate the best way of introducing change into an organization.

5. Define organizational development and outline several major techniques often used for this purpose.

6. Discuss the trends toward dual career ladders and temporary employment.

7. Describe the components of transferable job skills.

8. Describe some of the basic components of effective social skills for the workplace.

erry Patterson is now the new CEO of Frederick's of Hollywood, the lingerie retailer that is famous for its seductive catalog. At age 45, she moved from being president and CEO of Strauss Discount Auto. Going from a position of selling auto parts to reviving an underwear retailer is not the most expected career move. Says Ms. Patterson about dealing with change, "Nothing's sure anymore. I don't believe you're going to retire from the company you started with. There's risk all around, so security really has to be within yourself. When we make a mistake, we've got to stop walking away and saying 'I'm not going to play anymore.' Do that and you'll have a chip on your shoulder and be bitter for 50 years. What you need to do is not hold yourself back—go try something different."[1]

Ms. Patterson's advice is very sound. Today's world of work requires us to be open to change and to new opportunities. As companies struggle to keep up with brutal competition, the workforce is undergoing radical redefinitions. Massive, fast-paced changes are occurring in business today. To understand this fact, simply consider a few of the major shifts that have occurred in the world of work in recent decades: the information explosion, coupled with vastly increased use of computers; robotics and other types of automated production; and increased foreign competition and its subsequent impact upon many basic industries. All of these trends have produced major alterations in the work that people do and the way they do it. Indeed, taken as a whole, these changes are so complex and varied that we cannot yet gauge their total impact. One point, though, is already clear: Change is a basic fact of life at work.

As we enter the twenty-first century, we see an enormous change in the world of work; some have likened the current transformation of the workplace to the Industrial Revolution. It is a global phenomenon. Businesses across the world are undergoing rapid and irreversible changes. Old concepts, such as rigid hierarchical corporate structures, are giving way to more fluid structures that allow the company to react immediately to forces within the market. Individuals must also be ready and willing to change in the face of new demands. Thus the new workplace can be called "Darwinian" in that it demands adaptability and flexibility.[2]

To survive and prosper, both organizations and individuals need the ability to cope effectively with change. They must stand ready to react appropriately when change occurs. Perhaps even more importantly, they must be able to see the transformation developing and prepare in advance for its arrival. Companies that do not change or adjust to new realities may not survive. Changes are often disruptive to the personal and social lives of employees, however, so employees and some organizations often strongly resist change. In this chapter, we explore the different forces that underlie change, the factors that underlie resistance to change, and the ways to facilitate the process of change. First, let's take a brief peek into the future and explore some of the anticipated changes in the workforce.

PEEKING INTO THE FUTURE: CHANGES IN THE WORKPLACE

Of course, it is impossible to predict exactly what will happen in the future. Nevertheless, we can make some educated guesses about the challenges and changes to expect as we enter a new century. In part, these predictions reflect assumptions about the economy and productivity, but they also reflect projections about families, lifestyles, and attitudes. Just as the baby boomers and their parents exerted their own unique effect on the world of work, the members of the so-called "Generation X" who are now the young workers of today will follow a path that is different from that of their parents and grandparents. Let's get out our crystal ball and look at some trends for the future.

1. **The virtual office.** Ten years ago, fewer than 1 million employees worked away from the office via some type of computer link. Today, an estimated 11 million workers use portable electronic tools to perform work away from the traditional office setting.[3] Trends toward this type of futuristic office will continue and expand (see *Balancing Work and Family* on pages 34–35). Eventually very few employees may work at a main company campus; rather, most will work from home or from satellite centers or other form of mobile station (see Figure 2.1).[4] This trend reflects a desire to avoid stressful commutes, as well as new solutions for balancing work and family life.

Figure 2.1 **Virtual Office: A Growing Trend**

As many as 11 million workers may be working in environments such as the one depicted here. This trend is expected to increase.

2. **Flexible work schedules.** This trend is also expected to boom in the next few decades. Fewer people will work 9-to-5 jobs, and more opportunities will arise for flexible schedules. This trend reflects both the personal concerns of persons trying to balance their work and family lives and the globalization of the overall economy. That is, organizations will be required to show greater sensitivity to differences in customer needs across different time zones.

3. **Emphasis on results versus "putting in time."** As a partial consequence of flexible working conditions and schedules, businesses will continue to emphasize the bottom-line results of work efforts. The old days of just showing up for work will be history. People will be evaluated on the results, not the number of hours they spend on a task.

4. **Multiple jobs/careers.** In the relatively distant past, people expected to work at the same place of employment for their entire working life. Although this belief changed for the baby boomer generation, most of these workers nevertheless expected to work in the same vocation for their working lives. Gener-

Balancing Work and Family

Telecommuting

The U.S. federal government has taken a lead in promoting telecommuting as an impetus for promoting flexible family-friendly work arrangements. The Work and Family Program Center (a part of the U.S. Office of Personnel Management) has issued guidelines. You may contact the Office of Personnel Management for further information or e-mail *workandfamily@opm.gov.* (See also Chapter 6 for an expanded discussion of telecommuting.)

1. Formal policies and procedures should be developed to ensure and avoid misunderstanding about the terms and conditions of such employment. You can obtain a sample agreement form from the reference given as this box source.

2. The nature of the work should be suitable for telecommuting. Telecommuting is feasible for such work as data analysis, reviewing, report writing, and carrying out computer-oriented tasks (for example, word processing, data entry). Work that requires extensive face-to-face contact or cases in which employees need frequent access to material that cannot be moved from the office may not be appropriate for telecommuting.

ation X workers, on the other hand, may hold more than one job at time, dividing their work between various employers.[5] Others may switch careers several times in their lives, as their interests and economic needs change (see Chapter 15 for more information on this topic), and others may participate in various kinds of creative job-sharing programs.

5. **Diversification and globalization of the workplace.** In 1987, the Hudson Institute issued a very influential report referred to as "Workforce 2000." Its projections about the changing nature of the workforce in terms of gender, ethnic, and racial diversity drew attention to what has now become reality. The workforce is diverse and the world of business is global. These trends will continue! We will explore them in greater detail later in this chapter. At this point, we will say in the strongest way possible that workers cannot succeed in today's business world unless they can meet the challenges of communicating with persons whose cultural backgrounds result in different assumptions, values, and attitudes. Most of the chapters in this book address these issues either explicitly or implicitly.

3. Telecommuting is not suitable for situations in which on-the-job training is necessary, or for persons who thrive on interaction with coworkers.

4. Organizations should develop flexible procedures for communication and for determining the best course of action in individual situations.

Other information of which you should be aware includes the fact that telecommuting is a management option, rather than an employee benefit. Therefore, employee participation is voluntary and subject to management approval. Although this type of work is designed in part to give employees more time to devote to their families, duty time may not be used for providing dependent care. Therefore, child-care arrangements are still required. The major benefit comes from the reduction of commuting time. This kind of option is also beneficial for employees with temporary or continuing health problems who might otherwise have to retire on disability.

Source: Balancing Work and Family Demands Through Telecommuting (September 1997), United States Office of Personnel Management, Work and Family Program Center.

These trends represent just a few of the changes that we may expect in the future. The bottom line as we face a future in which change occurs quickly and frequently is that *flexibility* is the key characteristic for dealing with the world of work in the future. In the next sections, we will explore some basic reasons why people resist change.

CHANGE: WHY IT'S OFTEN RESISTED

Almost everyone wants to think of himself or herself as modern or progressive. Thus, if you stopped fifty people on the street or interviewed fifty employees at almost any company and asked them how they felt about change, most would probably express positive views. "Change," they might say, "is good. Without it, we'd just stagnate." On the basis of such sentiments, you might conclude that instituting change in work settings is a simple task. In fact, it is not. Contrary to what they may say, people often resist change—and resist it vigorously. Thus, a sizable gap often separates their attitudes and their behavior in this regard. Why does this gap exist? Why do individuals and organizations so often seek to block change? Many factors seem to play a role in this respect.

Psychological Factors: Barriers to Change

A variety of psychological factors make people resistant to change. You can probably develop your own list quite easily. Obviously, people may become quite comfortable with the way things have been and may be afraid of the potential negative consequences of change. One major reason why people resist change can be stated in a single word: uncertainty. Will the proposed changes benefit them or make their lives unpleasant? Will they help them perform their jobs, or get in the way? Often it is impossible to answer these questions in advance. Given the high stakes involved, many persons show reluctance to take the gamble and find out. Thus, fear of the unknown, of the unpredictable effects that may result from change, often serves as a major barrier to the acceptance of new policies or procedures. Researchers have found that a number of specific factors make people resistant to change in organizations:[6]

1. **Economic insecurity.** Any changes on the job could potentially threaten one's livelihood or economic security, either through the loss of a job or by a reduction in pay, and some degree of resistance to change is inevitable unless job security can be assured.

2. **Fear of the unknown.** Employees derive a sense of security from doing things the same way, knowing with whom they will work and to whom they should

answer from day to day. Disrupting these well-established, comfortable, familiar patterns creates unfamiliar conditions and a fear of the unknown, a state of affairs that is often rejected.

3. **Threats to social relationships.** As people continue to work within organizations, they form strong social bonds with their coworkers. Many organizational changes (such as the reassignment of job responsibilities) threaten the integrity of friendship groups that provide such an important source of social reward for many employees.

4. **Habit.** Jobs that are well learned and become habitual are easy to perform. The prospect of changing the way that employees perform their jobs challenges workers to relearn their jobs and to develop new job skills. This task is clearly more difficult than continuing to perform the job as it was originally learned.

5. **Failure to recognize need for change.** Unless employees can recognize and fully appreciate the need for changing things in organizations, any vested interests they may have in keeping things the same can easily overpower their willingness to accept change.

Little wonder, then, that many persons attempt to resist change with every trick and tactic at their disposal! (Most persons seem to dislike change, but not everyone shares this attitude. In fact, some people seem to seek it out and thrive on it. Where do you stand on this dimension? For an answer, see the *Experiential Exercise* on page 57.)

Organizational Factors: Social and Structural Barriers

It is probably obvious that we can't blame all resistance to change on the individual. Many individuals may be more than willing to go along with sensible change. Instead, several factors associated with the organization itself may promote resistance to change.

1. **Structural inertia.** Organizations are designed to promote stability. To the extent that employees are carefully selected and trained to perform certain jobs and receive rewards for performing them, the forces acting on individuals to perform in certain ways are very powerfully determined—that is, jobs have **structural inertia.**[7] In other words, because jobs are designed to have stability, it is often difficult to overcome the resistance created by the many forces that create that stability.

structural inertia The organizational forces acting on employees that encourage them to perform their jobs in certain ways (for example, through a reward system), thereby making them resistant to change.

2. **Work group inertia.** Inertia comes not only from the jobs themselves, but also from the social groups within which many employees work. Because strong social norms tend to develop within work groups, potent pressures exist to perform jobs in certain ways and at certain accepted rates. The introduction of change disrupts these established normative expectations, which imposes formidable barriers to change.

3. **Threats to the existing balance of power.** If changes are made with respect to who's in charge and how things are done, a shift in the balance of power between individuals and organizational subunits is likely to occur. Those units that now control the resources, have the expertise, and wield the power may fear losing their advantageous positions as a result of organizational changes.

4. **Previously unsuccessful change efforts.** Anyone who has lived through a past disaster may be understandably reluctant to endure another attempt at the same thing. Similarly, groups or entire organizations that have been unsuccessful in introducing change in the past may be unwilling to accept further attempts to introduce change in the system.

Obviously many barriers to change exist in organizations. You may wonder how one can ever overcome these barriers. Fortunately, some useful techniques have been developed, and we discuss a number of these tactics in the next section.

OVERCOMING RESISTANCE TO CHANGE: SOME USEFUL TACTICS

By now it should be apparent that many reasons exist to explain why most persons fail to greet change with open arms. A wide variety of organizational psychological factors all play roles in creating this reluctance. Whatever its specific causes, resistance to change is a serious matter. As we have noted repeatedly, the ability to adapt to changing conditions, or perhaps to foresee them, is essential for survival. In view of this fact, an important question arises: Can anything be done to overcome such resistance—that is, to encourage the acceptance of change in work settings? The answer, of course, is "yes." Several techniques for reaching this goal exist.[8] In the following section, we discuss how to introduce change in a way that facilitates its acceptance.

Change: How to Introduce It

Imagine two companies faced with the necessity of change. In one, top management examines all existing options and then simply decrees major alterations in jobs, corporate structure, and procedures. No discussions of the proposed changes are held, and no one is told why they are viewed as necessary. Employees are simply expected to comply with management's decisions. In contrast, the second company attempts to involve all of the people who will be affected in both the planning and implementation of change. Special meetings are held to discuss the necessity for change and to describe the benefits to be gained through its adoption. Then a plan acceptable to most persons involved is adopted. In which company would you expect to find more resistance to change? Obviously, in the first. The reason for this conclusion is readily apparent. Change is simply introduced in a more effective and appropriate manner in the second company. But what, precisely, does this statement mean? In essence, it involves attention to several factors that can strongly influence reactions to actual or potential change.

The first of these factors centers around the issue of participation. To maximize the acceptance of change and reduce resistance to it, it is essential that the persons affected by the new reality (or at least their representatives) participate in its planning. When a company follows this principle, employees may conclude that they have given their approval to change and even helped shape its final form. When a business ignores this principle, employees may feel that change has been shoved down their throats over their protests. Under the latter conditions, of course, they may do their best to block its implementation through passive or active means.

Closely related to the principle of participation is the need for clarity. Briefly, persons affected by proposed change should be made aware of the necessity for its occurrence and the potential future benefits. When individuals do not understand the reasons behind change, they may view it as an unnecessary annoyance, dreamed up by managers just to complicate their lives, and may see only the drawbacks associated with the change. Clearly, avoiding such reactions is important, and it validates the effort involved in explaining the necessity for change and its long-term benefits.

Another rather obvious and quite successful mechanism for facilitating organizational change is rewarding people for behaving in the desired fashion. Altering organizational operations may necessitate a modification of the kinds of behaviors that the organization needs to reward. This revision of the reward system is essential when an organization is in the transition period of introducing the change. For example, employees who must learn to use new equipment should be praised for their successful efforts. Feedback on how well one is doing not only provides a great deal of useful assurance to an uncertain employee, but also helps in shaping the desired behavior.

Finally, political variables are crucial for winning support of organizational changes. Politically, resistance to change can be overcome by gaining the acceptance of the most powerful and influential individuals. This step builds a critical internal mass of support for change. Demonstrating clearly that key organizational leaders support the change is an effective way of getting others to go along with it, either because they share the leader's vision or because they fear the leader's retaliation. Either way, political support for change will facilitate acceptance of change.

Figure 2.2   Overcoming Resistance to Change: Some Useful Tactics

Careful attention to the factors shown here can help minimize or surmount resistance to change.

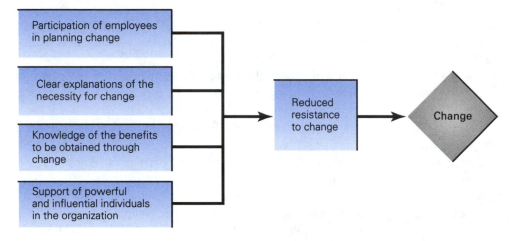

Through attention to these and several other factors (see Figure 2.2), resistance to change can often be held to a minimum. Thus careful consideration of just how change is to be introduced into a specific work setting can often yield handsome dividends in terms of its smooth and rapid acceptance. (For a concrete example of the successful introduction of change, see the *Case in Point.*)

CHANGE AND EFFECTIVENESS: TECHNIQUES OF ORGANIZATIONAL DEVELOPMENT

So far in our discussion of change, we have adopted what might be termed an "external" orientation. That is, we have focused on change in response to shifting external conditions (for example, advances in technology, increased competition). Often, though, change in work settings comes from another source: an organization's quest for excellence and effectiveness. In short, organizations actively seek change as a means of improving the ways in which they function. Such planned change is generally known as **organizational development** (OD), and a

organizational development   Techniques and procedures designed to produce planned change in an organization. Such change, in turn, is aimed at enhancing the organization's effectiveness and efficiency.

number of techniques for achieving it exist. Here, we briefly describe several of the most popular: survey feedback, sensitivity training, team building, and quality of work life.

Survey Feedback: Change through Information

Survey feedback, one widely used technique of organizational development, relies largely on the following principle: Before useful change can take place in an organization, the people in it must understand both its current strengths and its weaknesses. Flowing from this sound principle, survey feedback then proceeds through three distinct steps.[9] First, groups of employees (or perhaps even all employees) respond to a carefully designed questionnaire. This survey, which is tailored to the specific organization in question, usually seeks information on such issues as the quality and style of leadership, current organizational climate, and employee satisfaction. Second, the company reports the information obtained through the questionnaire to employees, usually in group meetings. This step requires considerable skill, for such information is often complex and allows plenty of room for misinterpretation. Also, because the survey is designed to pinpoint problems, much of the feedback offered may be negative (for example, it may indicate that some persons within the organization are performing poorly). The consultants who present the results must therefore be skilled at minimizing anxiety and other negative reactions. Third, the organization must develop specific plans for dealing with and overcoming the problems identified by the survey, again usually in sessions where open discussion is encouraged (see Figure 2.3).

survey feedback   A technique of organizational development in which information about an organization is fed back to employees and plans are then formulated for dealing with specific identified problems.

Survey feedback offers a number of major advantages. It often yields a large amount of useful information quickly. It is flexible and works in many different settings.

Figure 2.3   Survey Feedback: An Overview

As shown here, survey feedback often involves three major steps.

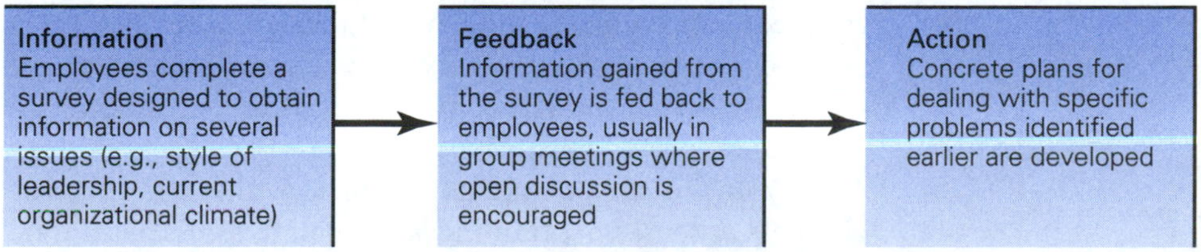

Information	Feedback	Action
Employees complete a survey designed to obtain information on several issues (e.g., style of leadership, current organizational climate)	Information gained from the survey is fed back to employees, usually in group meetings where open discussion is encouraged	Concrete plans for dealing with specific problems identified earlier are developed

In addition, the information it provides is often helpful in developing concrete plans for change. Thus, when used with skill and care, it can prove a valuable tool for helping organizations achieve enhanced effectiveness.

Sensitivity Training: Developing Insight

Sensitivity training is a method by which small, face-to-face group interaction experiences give people insight into themselves (who they are, the way others respond to them, and so on). Developed in the 1940s, sensitivity training groups (also referred to as encounter groups, laboratory groups, or T-groups) were among the first OD techniques used in organizations.[10]

The rationale behind sensitivity training is that people are usually not completely open and honest with each other, a condition that limits insights into themselves and others. When people experience special situations within which such open, honest communication is allowed and encouraged, they may gain personal insights. In this type of training, small groups (usually consisting of eight to fifteen members) meet away from the pressures of the job site for several days. An expert trainer (referred to as the facilitator) guides the group at all times, helping to ensure that the group maintains the proper atmosphere.

The sessions themselves are completely open with respect to topics discussed. Often, to get the ball rolling, the facilitator will frustrate the group members by not becoming involved initially and appearing to be passively goofing off. As members sit around and engage in meaningless chit-chat, they begin to feel angry at the change agent for wasting their time. Once these expressions of anger begin to emerge, the change agent has created the important first step needed to make the session work—he or she has given the group a chance to focus on a current event. At this point, the discussion may be guided toward examination of how each group member expresses his or her anger. Participants are encouraged to continue discussing these themes openly and honestly and not to hide their true feelings as they often do on the job. The rule is to openly and honestly share their feelings about others. For example, if a worker thinks that someone is goofing off and relying too much on his or her coworkers, the employee should say so. Participants are encouraged to respond by giving immediate feedback regarding what was said. Through sensitivity training, people presumably will come to learn more about how they interrelate with others and will become more skilled at interpersonal relations. These ideas are among the major goals of sensitivity groups.

It probably comes as no surprise that the effectiveness of sensitivity training is difficult to assess. Even if in-

sensitivity training An organizational development technique that seeks to enhance employees' understanding of their own behavior and its impact on others. Such insight can potentially reduce the interpersonal conflicts that interfere with organizational effectiveness.

terpersonal skills appear to improve, it is not always the case that people will be able to successfully transfer their newly learned skills when they leave the artificial training atmosphere and return to their jobs.[11] As a result, sensitivity training tends not to be used extensively by itself, but rather is often used along with other organizational development techniques.

Team Building: Creating Effective Work Groups

Team building represents an attempt to apply the techniques and rationale of sensitivity training to work groups. This approach asks members of a work group to diagnose how they work together and to plan how this interaction may be improved.[12] Given the importance of group efforts in effective organizational functioning, attempts at improving the effectiveness of work groups are likely to have significant impact on organizations. If one assumes that work groups are the basic building blocks of organizations, it follows that organizational change could emphasize changing groups instead of individuals.

Team building begins when members of a group admit that they have a problem and gather data to provide insight into the issue. The problems that are identified may come from sensitivity training sessions or more sensitive sources, such as production figures or attitude surveys. The data are then shared, in a diagnostic session, to develop a consensus regarding the group's current strengths and weaknesses. For this purpose, the group creates a list of desired changes, along with some plans for implementing these changes. In other words, it develops an action plan—that is, some task-oriented approach to solving the group's problems. Following this step, the group carries out the plan and evaluates its progress to determine whether the originally identified problems still remain. If the problem is solved, the process is considered complete, and the team may stop meeting. If not, it must restart the process.

Work teams have been used effectively to combat a variety of important organizational problems.[13] For these efforts to be successful, however, all group members must participate in the gathering and evaluating of information as well as in the planning and implementing of action plans. Input from group members is especially crucial in evaluating the effectiveness of the team-building program.[14] It is also important to keep in mind that because the team-building approach is highly task-oriented, interpersonal problems between group members may prove disruptive and need to be neutralized by an outside party. With such interpersonal strain out of the way, the stage is set for groups to learn to effectively solve their own problems. This transformation does not happen overnight, however. To be most effective, team building should not be approached

team building   An organizational development technique in which employees discuss problems related to their work group's performance. On the basis of these discussions, specific problems are identified and plans for solving them are devised and implemented.

as a one-time exercise undertaken during a few days away from the job. Rather, it should be envisioned as an ongoing process that takes several months (or even years) to develop. Given what a great impact effective groups can have on organizational functioning, the efforts at building effective work teams would seem to be quite worthwhile. This topic will be discussed in more detail in Chapter 9.

Quality of Work Life: The Humanizing of Work and Work Settings

How would you like to work for someone like the character in Figure 2.4? Your answer is probably something like "No way!" The reasons for this response are clear: In an organization headed by someone with this management style, employees are probably held in very low regard. Furthermore, management would probably show little concern for their feelings or welfare. What do you think would be the result of such conditions? If you guessed "poor morale and motivation, plus a corresponding low level of organizational effectiveness," you are probably correct. Fortunately, during the 1960s and 1970s, many managers became aware of these facts. They therefore sought techniques for changing this negative type of organizational climate, ways of humanizing work settings and making them more pleasant. The result of these efforts has been the emergence of yet another technique of organizational development, one that focuses primarily on the **quality of work life.**[15]

quality of work life   Techniques designed to make work more interesting and rewarding, and to make work settings better places in which to function.

Figure 2.4   **Quality of Work Life**

Most of us would not enjoy working in an environment such as the one depicted in this cartoon.

DILBERT reprinted by permission of United Features Syndicate, Inc.

This approach is not as unified or systematic in nature as the others that we have described, but it usually focuses on several major goals. First, it seeks to create a climate of mutual respect between management and employees, the opposite of what is shown in Figure 2.4. Second, it often takes advantage of work restructuring, changes in jobs designed to make them more interesting and varied. Third, it attempts to narrow the status gap between employees and supervisors. Finally, it usually recommends a participative style of decision making, in which employees are asked for their input on new policies and procedures. The ultimate goal, of course, is to attain a climate of partnership between managers and employees, in sharp contrast to the standard pattern in which they view one another as natural enemies.

Another approach to improving the quality of work life, which has become increasingly popular in recent years, has been imported from Japan—**quality circles (QCs)**. These small groups of volunteers (usually around ten) meet regularly (usually weekly) to identify and solve problems related to (1) the quality of the work they perform and (2) the conditions under which people do their jobs.[16] An organization may have several quality circles operating at once, each dealing with the particular work area about which it has the most expertise. To help them work effectively, the members of the circle usually receive some form of training in problem solving. Such large companies as Westinghouse, Hewlett-Packard, and Eastman Kodak, to name just a few, have formed quality circles.[17] Groups have dealt with such issues as reducing vandalism, creating safer and more comfortable work environments, and improving product quality. Research has shown that, while quality circles are very effective at bringing about short-term improvements in quality of work life (that is, those lasting as long as 18 months), they are less effective at creating more permanent changes.[18] As such, they may be recognized as useful temporary strategies for enhancing organizational effectiveness.

As you might imagine, many benefits might potentially result from quality of work life programs. The most direct benefit usually takes the form of increased job satisfaction and organizational commitment among the workforce. This can also bring increased productivity and increased organizational effectiveness (for example, profitability, goal attainment, and so on).[19] Achieving these benefits is not guaranteed, however. Two major potential pitfalls must be avoided to ensure successful implementation of quality of work life programs. First, both management and labor must cooperate in designing the program. Should either side believe that the program really represents merely a method of gaining an advantage over the other, the effort will fail. Second, the plan agreed to by all concerned parties must be fully implemented. It is too easy for action plans developed in quality of work life groups to become forgotten and lost amid the hectic pace of daily activities. Employees at all levels, from the highest-ranking manager to the lowest-level laborer, must take responsibility for following through on their part of the plan.

quality circles (QCs) An approach to improving the quality of work life in which small groups of volunteers meet regularly to identify and solve problems related to the work they perform and the conditions under which they work.

Effectiveness of Organizational Development: How Well Does It Work?

Although the organizational development techniques discussed here are often used by corporations, do their results justify the time, money, and effort involved? Some evidence of beneficial effects does seem to exist. For example, one review of a wide variety of techniques found that they often enhanced organizational outcomes such as profit and productivity, but evidence for positive changes at the individual level (such as job satisfaction) was relatively weak.[20] Organizational development also tends to be more effective when it involves blue-collar workers and when it uses several techniques instead of only one.[21] Organizational developments have shown much promise, but it is clear that additional research and refinements will be required to increase the effectiveness of these techniques so as to provide long-lasting positive changes for both corporations and individual workers.

OPPORTUNITIES FOR DEVELOPMENT

Dual Career Ladders: A New Way to Climb to the Top

Recent efforts at restructuring corporations involve doing away with strict hierarchies of authority. The resulting corporate structure is both more flexible and less top-heavy. With this trend, more companies are designing **dual career ladders,** allowing them to reward and promote workers without making those employees into managers. Dual career ladders involve promoting people to new titles and ranks within an organization rather than promoting them to managerial positions. These ladders offer titles and compensation based on the individual's knowledge rather than on budget and supervisory responsibilities. Thus the old view that promotions entail supervising more people is becoming obsolete. For example, Price Waterhouse, a major accounting firm in New York, promotes accountants to the position of director rather than partner.[22] This type of promotion induces talented people to stay who might otherwise leave if they did not achieve partnership.

The emergence of career ladders for professionals offers expanded growth opportunities. After several years in a department, an employee may be channeled into one of two ladders, management or professional (see Figure 2.5). Crossover between the ladders is possible, but growth occurs within a single track.

dual career ladders Promoting people to new titles and ranks within an organization rather than promoting them to managerial positions. This practice is used to restructure corporations in a way that eliminates strict hierarchies of authority.

𝓕𝓲𝓰𝓾𝓻𝓮 2.5   **Dual Career Ladders: New Paths to Success**

The growth of career ladders is a positive trend for change in the workforce. These job ladders offer titles and compensation based on expertise and knowledge. This figure illustrates a hypothetical dual career path in a customer service department.

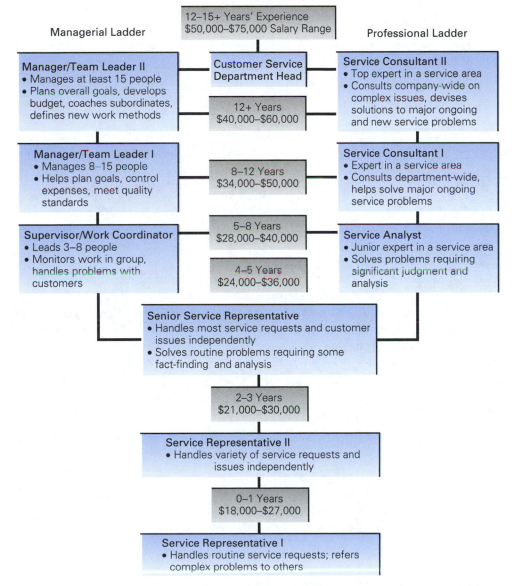

From Fuhsberg, 1993; see note 22. Reprinted by permission of Dow Jones, Inc. via Copyright Clearance Center, Inc. © 1993 Dow Jones and Company, Inc. All rights reserved worldwide.

This new trend reshapes career paths away from the traditional corporate ladder and toward a corporate lattice. It represents an alternative route to growth and change within corporate structures that deemphasize bureaucracy.

The "Temping" of the Workforce: Trends toward Temporary Employment

The restructuring of the workplace has brought a corresponding phenomenon: the rise of the temporary employee. This shift may be the most important trend in business today, and it brings with it some compelling ethical considerations (refer to the

Ethics at Work

The Rise of the Disposable Worker

As the underpinnings of mutual commitment crumble, temporary employers are becoming the rule in U.S. business. Carol is a temp in a Los Angeles accounting firm. She reports that she often feels like a second-class citizen and is ignored by the permanent workers. At lunch, she eats by herself at her desk and has made no friends, although she has worked at the firm for over a month.

"No one wants to get to know me." Carol laments. "Everyone knows I'll be gone soon, unless I'm hired permanently . . . which might mean that I take someone's job. I feel like an object here, not a person."

Carol's feelings are not unique. Temporary workers are often treated differently by others in the workplace. Consider the following questions that are raised by this trend:

1. Put yourself in the position of a temp. What are your feelings about this role?

2. What can you do as a person who works with a contingent worker to make the individual feel more accepted?

3. What are the implications of a contingent workforce for sexual harassment and discrimination issues within the workplace?

4. Is it ethical to request that an agency send out a "blonde female" for a receptionist position?

5. Is it ethical to request a temp for hazardous work on a job?

6. What are the long-term implications for an aging workforce that has served primarily in contingent work roles?

Ethics at Work section on page 48). Every day, 1.5 million temps are sent out from agencies such as Kelly Services and Manpower.[23] Another 34 million people also do some type of **contingent work.** Some of these short-term workers perform jobs that you might expect: secretarial work, sales clerking, assembly-line work. Others may be more surprising: doctors, lawyers, engineers, and bank officers.[24]

This trend essentially negates some of the work values that have been a part of American business for decades: commitment, company loyalty, esprit de corps. It also places workers in the uncomfortable position of having no pension, security, or benefit packages. A dangerous development involves the emergence of a two-tier workforce in which temporary employees are seen as second-class citizens. Their ranks are growing quickly, and businesses are not prepared to face the morale problems and conflict that will eventually occur as a result of these policies (see Figure 2.6). Nevertheless, the trend is likely to continue as companies cut costs by reducing their payrolls. U.S. employers could save as much as $800 million from payroll costs by using these tactics.[25]

As one out of three Americans has assumed a contingent work role at some point in their careers, it is likely that this trend has affected or will affect you at some point

contingent work   Temporary employment involving short-time work.

Figure 2.6   **Part-Time and Temporary Employment Can Cause Problems in the Workplace**

As shown in the widespread strike at UPS, this trend can cause conflict between workers and management.

in your own career. What can you do to improve your chances of success in this role? We offer a few suggestions:

1. Develop an entrepreneurial spirit. See your position as one that offers new challenges and opportunities.
2. Develop definable skills. Be able to state your strengths articulately, specifically, and precisely.
3. Market yourself. Once you have developed your skills, promote yourself as a specialist.
4. Realize that your position is, in reality, no more insecure than that of supposedly permanent employees.
5. Enjoy the benefits that your flexible position affords you.

We have discussed the negative side of the coin as it relates to temporary employment, but a positive side exists as well. Many people enjoy the flexibility that temporary employment offers. With the increased demands of family, temporary employment can offer a real solution to balancing work and family. Many professionals prefer the freedom of such a life. Temping provides a way to stay involved in a profession without engaging in the rat race of seven-day workweeks and pressure.

Transferable Job Skills: Staying Up-to-Date

As pointed out earlier, our crystal ball into the future reveals the fact that we are unlikely to remain in the same jobs for our entire working careers. Thus we must view learning as a lifelong enterprise; as we become more knowledgeable, we become a more valuable employee. A beneficial tactic is to view the organizations for which you work as learning institutes, as well as employers. Try to take advantage of both formal and informal opportunities for learning in the organization. Listed here are the kinds of skills that are particularly beneficial.

1. **Learn to learn.** The most important skill you can develop is an openness to learning from new experiences. Learning is indeed fundamental. It is hard to describe exactly what you should do to develop this skill, but the ability to think critically, learn from experience, analyze problems, see patterns, and play with unique solutions to problems is clearly part of the learning process (see *Guidelines for Effective Human Relations* on pages 52–53).
2. **Keep up with technology.** Of course, computer skills are a must in the world today. Stay computer-literate and take any opportunities that may become available for learning new technological skills.

3. **Develop person skills.** These skills involve your ability to communicate with other persons and relate to them in an effective manner. Often, it seems, being liked by others is a much better predictor of success than intellectual brilliance, high motivation, or other desirable qualities. Although this situation may strike you as unfair, it is a fact of life in most work settings. We now discuss this important skill in more detail.

Social Skills: An Important Transferable Quality

Given the state of affairs in today's workplace, it's important to know what factors determine whether a person is liked or disliked by others. One important characteristic is the possession of various social skills, the ability to communicate effectively with others.[26] People possessing such skills communicate well and clearly, are perceived as honest and credible, and make good first impressions.[27] Persons lacking in such skills fare poorly at interpersonal communication and are perceived negatively by the people around them.

In recent years, efforts have been made to identify the basic components of social skills. The results of such research suggest that six components are most important:

1. Emotional expressivity, the ability to express emotions nonverbally (for example, through facial expressions and gestures)

2. Emotional sensitivity, the ability to "read" the emotional and nonverbal communication of others

3. Emotional control, skill in controlling spontaneous expressions of feeling when necessary, as well as skill at feigning emotions

4. Social expressivity, the ability to speak fluently and engage others in social interaction

5. Social sensitivity, general knowledge of social norms (knowing what's considered appropriate in various situations)

6. Social control, skill at self-presentation (presenting oneself to others in a positive light) and at playing various social roles (for example, the respectful subordinate or the caring supervisor)

A questionnaire designed to measure individual differences in such skills (the Social Skills Inventory) has been devised by Riggio and colleagues; sample items from it appear in Table 2.1 on page 52.[28]

| *Table 2.1* | **Social Skills: Some Sample Items** |

Items similar to the ones presented here are used to measure individual differences in social skills.

Social Skill	Sample of Associated Behavior
Emotional expressivity	I've been told that I have an expressive face.
Emotional sensitivity	I can always tell how people feel about me.
Emotional control	I can hide my real feelings from people.
Social expressivity	I usually take the first step and introduce myself to strangers.
Social sensitivity	I often worry about making a good impression on others.
Social control	I find it easy to play different roles in different situations.

Based on data from Riggio et al., 1987; see note 28.

Training programs designed to enhance various social skills exist, some of which are quite effective. Several of these programs have become highly popular and are completed by thousands of people each year. Participation may well prove worthwhile for individuals who suspect that their careers and personal adjustment are hampered by deficits in this important dimension.

Guidelines for Effective Human Relations

Using What You've Learned

In this chapter, we examined a broad range of principles and findings related to change in the workplace. Although there are few rules that will apply to every situation, there are some general guidelines that are suggested by the various findings we have discussed. Remember, no rule works 100 percent in every situation. However, these guidelines should help you be able to deal with change in a more effective manner.

- Keep in mind that change is a necessary part of life. Look for the possibilities that changes offer you. Personal growth requires change.
- Look for signs of changes before they actually arrive, and prepare for them in advance.

Guidelines for Effective Human Relations (continued)

- Become person-oriented in your approach to others. This style will serve you well.

- Take advantage of new opportunities for advancement (for example, dual career ladders) and new ways of doing things within organizations. If you find yourself in the position of a contingent worker, don't be discouraged or surprised. Take advantage of the opportunities this position affords you.

- Keep abreast of changes in technology. Do not become a dinosaur in our technologically sophisticated world. For example, if you are not already familiar with computer technology, consider taking a course in this area. Above all, do not be afraid of technology. In most cases, it offers us a great deal.

- Assess the degree to which you may harbor psychological barriers to change. Remove these barriers and enjoy opportunities for growth.

- When you are in a position to introduce change, keep the various ways to do this most effectively in mind.

- Develop a sense of personal control over your life. If you believe you can influence your own outcomes, you will be more open to change and will avoid depression and feelings of helplessness.

Summary

Change is a fact of life in most work settings. Change arises from technological advances, shifts in social attitudes and values, and economic factors (for example, foreign competition). Many persons resist change because of their fear of the unknown, concerns over potential loss of status, and the possibility that change will endanger their jobs.

A number of tactics exist for overcoming resistance to change. Several reflect the specific ways in which change becomes introduced. In general, acceptance of change increases when the persons affected by it have an opportunity to participate in its planning, when they understand the reasons why it is necessary, and when they perceive the benefits that it will yield.

Although organizations often change in response to external pressures, they also actively seek change as a means of improving their own effectiveness. Several techniques exist for accomplishing such organizational development. Among them are survey feedback, sensitivity training, team building, and concern with the quality of work life.

Important trends for the future include dual career ladders and temporary employment. Flexibility is the key, as is attention to opportunities for developing transferable job skills.

Key Terms

contingent work, p. 49

dual career ladders, p. 46

organizational development, p. 40

quality circles (QCs), p. 45

quality of work life, p. 44

sensitivity training, p. 42

structural inertia, p. 37

survey feedback, p. 41

team building, p. 43

 *Case in Point*

The Plan That Worked

For many years *Keeping Fit,* a magazine dealing with personal health, had been a small, sleepy affair. Issues were produced only once every three months, and total circulation remained stable at about 20,000. Then came the 1980s, with rising public interest in physical fitness. Circulation began a dramatic climb and soon passed 100,000. At that point, the magazine's owners, sensing a golden opportunity, decided to switch to a monthly format and to greatly expand its length. These plans required major changes in the way *Keeping Fit* was put together.

No longer could employees enjoy the luxury of a leisurely production schedule; instead, activities at the magazine's headquarters became frenzied. And the increased circulation altered every facet of its operations—from advertising through subscriptions. Despite the vast scope of these shifts, the magazine came through with flying colors. In fact, at present, *Keeping Fit* is viewed as a model of efficiency and success by other publishers. It is for this reason that Jane Cushing, editor of another small magazine on the verge of what appears to be major growth, has come for a visit. She hopes to discover the secret of *Keeping Fit*'s success in coping with major change so that she can bring it back to her own company. She has just completed a tour of the facilities with Susan Hammon, *Keeping Fit*'s top executive, and has returned to her office. "Nice, very nice," Jane says with feeling. "You've certainly done a bang-up job of modernizing your equipment."

"Thanks," says Susan, motioning her to a seat. "We're all pretty proud of our operation. It really seems to be holding together well."

"Yes, Susan," Jane responds, "and that's why I'm here today. As you know, we're going to be facing some of the same changes you did—or, at least I hope that's the case! But I'm worried about it. We've already heard a lot of grumbling from our staff. Seems as though many of them enjoy the comfortable country club atmosphere we've developed over the years, and they're afraid of what's coming. In fact, there's even been some dark talk about sabotage. So tell me, how did you manage to do it so well? How did you avoid all these problems?"

Susan chuckles. Then, smiling, she begins. "I ought to say that's our secret! But really, there's no secret to tell. It all centered around planning. When we began to sense that a change was coming, we sat down and thought things through. One of the first points that occurred to us was this: People on the staff were going to be worried. After all, most of us are a little afraid of change, whatever we say about liking it. We don't know what it will bring, and that can be upsetting."

"Yes, I see," Jane comments. "But what did you do to handle those reactions?"

"Good question," Susan answers. "First off, we arranged a series of special meetings with everyone—from receptionist on up. We described what kinds of changes were coming, and we sought suggestions on planning the whole thing. In short, we tried to give everyone some say in how to proceed. But that's not all. We soon discovered that a lot of people couldn't see how they would benefit from a big rise in sales. They could grasp the costs, all right, but not what they had to gain."

"Ah!" Jane exclaims. "They knew there would be extra work but didn't see what that would buy them."

"Right. That's when we decided to install our bonus plan—one that would let everyone share in the rewards if circulation and profits went up. That was really the turning point. As soon as people saw how they would benefit, they become downright enthusiastic."

"Good strategy!" Jane states admiringly.

"Thanks. But we didn't stop there. We knew there were a number of popular people on the staff—you know, people everyone looks up to. Well, we made a real effort to win their support. That took some doing, but finally we got just about all of them on our side. Once they threw their weight behind us, it was smooth sailing."

"So, really, you didn't have a magic formula. It all sounds like good common sense to me. But still, it's the kind of common sense people often overlook. Thanks a lot, Susan. I really think you've been a big help. If we follow in your footsteps, I don't see how we can go wrong."

Questions

1. What do you think were the major concerns among employees at *Keeping Fit* when they first learned about the coming changes?

2. Do you think that giving employees a chance to participate in planning these changes was a good idea? Why?

3. What other tactics might Jane use in her own company to increase the likelihood of smooth and orderly change?

Experiential Exercise

Assessing Your Managerial Style

If you are presently a manager, answer the following questions in relation to your approach to your job. If you are not in this role, answer the questions with reference to how you would approach it. Choose either (a) or (b) within each question, depending upon which statement best applies to you.

1. Do you think of yourself as (a) a manager or boss or (b) a sponsor and team leader?

2. Do you (a) follow the chain of command or (b) deal with anyone to facilitate the job?

3. Do you (a) work within a set structure or (b) change structures in response to market needs?

4. Do you (a) make most of the decisions yourself or (b) include others in decision making?

5. Do you (a) keep most of the relevant information to yourself or (b) share information freely?

6. Do you think of yourself as (a) a specialist in your area or (b) a generalist who tries to

master a wide array of disciplines within your field as a manager?

7. Do you (a) demand long hours or (b) demand that your employees get results?

Go over your responses and count the number of questions that you marked (a) and the number of questions that you marked (b). If you marked more (a) responses than (b), your style may be indicative of a traditional managerial approach that is based on a hierarchical structure. If you marked more (b) than (a) responses, your style is more consistent with a new approach to management that emphasizes a flexible team approach. Chapter 10 will discuss leadership styles in more detail. For now, we want you to take a look at yourself and assess your managerial style. This exercise can help you see other approaches to human relations that may be especially useful for you. Changes in the workplace call for a flexible approach to leadership.

Experiential Exercise

Assess Yourself: Change or Stability? Are You a High or Low Sensation Seeker?

Would you ever consider skydiving for the thrills and danger it produces? Do you like to gamble? Would you enjoy leading a life like

that of Indiana Jones in "Temple of Doom"? If so, you may be a high sensation seeker—the kind of person who enjoys excitement, danger, and unpredictability. If, in contrast, the things we have just mentioned frighten you, and you prefer a life of calmness, order, and tranquility, you are probably a low sensation seeker. As you can readily guess, high and low sensation seekers also differ in their reactions to change. Persons high on this dimension tend to see change as a stimulating challenge—something to be sought out and savored. In contrast, low sensation seekers often view it as a potentially upsetting source of danger—something they would prefer to avoid if possible.

Where do you stand in this regard? Are you a high sensation seeker, a low sensation seeker, or somewhere in between? To find out, answer the following questions. For each, simply circle the letter (A or B) next to the choice that best describes your likes or the way you feel.

1. A I often wish I could be a mountain climber.
   B I can't understand people who risk their necks climbing mountains.

2. A A sensible person avoids activities that are dangerous.
   B I sometimes like to do things that are a little frightening.

3. A I would like to take up waterskiing.
   B I would not like to take up waterskiing.

4. A I would like to try surfboarding.
   B I would not like to try surfboarding.

5. A I would not like to learn to fly an airplane.
   B I would like to learn to fly an airplane.

6. A I would like to go scuba diving.
   B I prefer the surface of the water to the depths.

7. A I would like to try parachute jumping.
   B I would never want to try jumping out of a plane with a parachute.

8. A I enjoy spending time in the familiar surroundings of home.
   B I get very restless if I have to stay around home for any length of time.

9. A Sailing long distances in small sailing crafts is foolhardy.
   B I would like to sail a long distance in a small but seaworthy sailing craft.

10. A Skiing fast down a high mountain slope is a good way to end up on crutches.
    B I think I would enjoy the sensation of skiing very fast down a high mountain slope.

To obtain your score, give yourself one point for each of these answers: (1) A, (2) B, (3) A, (4) A, (5) B, (6) A, (7) A, (8) A, (9) B, (10) B. If you attained a score of 7 or higher, you are probably a high sensation seeker. If you attained a score of 3 or lower, you are probably a low sensation seeker. Please note, by the way, that there's ample room for both types in the world of work. For example, would you want to do business with a banker who was high in sensation seeking? Probably not—but you may well seek this quality in a salesperson or marketing expert. So neither orientation is better; they are just different.

Notes

1. Godfrey, N. (1998, September). Revamping a vamp. *Working Woman*, p. 36. Reprinted with the permission of MacDonald Communications Corporation. Copyright © 1998 by MacDonald Communications Corporation.

2. Sherman, S. (1993, January 25). A brave new Darwinian workplace. *Fortune*, pp. 50–56.

3. Hill, E. J., Miller, B. C. , Weiner, S. P., & Colihan, J. (1998). Influences of the virtual office on aspects of work and work/life balance. *Personnel Psychology, 51*, 667–706.

4. Herman, R. (1998). New generation changes work climate. *Furniture Design and Manufacturing, 70 (6)*, 102–103.

5. Ibid.

6. Nadler, D. A. (1987). The effective management of organizational change. In J. W. Lorsch (ed.), *Handbook of organizational behavior* (pp. 358–369). Englewood Cliffs, NJ: Prentice Hall.

7. Hannan, M. T., & Freeman, J. (1984). Structural inertia and organizational change. *American Sociological Review, 49*, 149–164.

8. Kotter, J. P., & Schlesinger, L. A. (1979, March–April). Choosing strategies for change. *Harvard Business Review*, pp. 106–114.

9. Huse, E. F., & Cummings, T. G. (1985). *Organization development and change* (3rd ed.). St. Paul, MN: West.

10. Golembiewski, R. T. (1972). *Renewing organizations: A laboratory approach to planned change*. Itasca, IL: Peacock.

11. Campbell, J. P., & Dunnette, M. D. (1968). Effectiveness of T-group experience in managerial training and development. *Psychological Bulletin, 70*, 73–104.

12. Beer, M. (1980). *Organizational change and development: A systems view*. Glenview, IL: Scott, Foresman.

13. Beckhard, R. (1972, Summer). Optimizing team-building efforts. *Journal of Contemporary Business*, pp. 23–32.

14. Vicars, W. M., & Hartke, D. D. (1984). Evaluating OD evaluations: A status report. *Group and Organization Studies, 9*, 177–188.

15. Burke, W. W. (1982). *Organizational development: Principles and practices*. Boston: Little, Brown.

16. Munchus, G. (1983). Employer-employee based quality circles in Japan: Human resource implications for American firms. *Academy of Management Review, 8*, 255–261.

17. Meyer, G. W., & Scott, R. G. (1985, Spring). Quality circles: Panacea or Pandora's box? *Organizational Dynamics*, 34–50.

18. Griffin, R. W. (1988). Consequences of quality circles in an industrial setting: A longitudinal assessment. *Academy of Management Journal, 31*, 338–358.

19. Suttle, J. L. (1977). Improving life at work— Problems and prospects. In J. R. Hackman & J. L. Suttle (eds.), *Improving life at work: Behavioral science approaches to organizational change* (pp. 1–29). Santa Monica, CA: Goodyear.

20. Porras, J. I., Robertson, P. J., & Goldman, L. (1992). Organization development: Theory, practice, and research. In M. D. Dunnette (ed.), *Handbook of industrial/organizational psychology* (2nd ed.). Chicago: Rand McNally.

21. Nicholas, J. M. (1982). The comparative impact of organization development interventions on hard criteria measures. *Academy of Management Review, 7*, 531–542.

22. Fuchsberg, G. (1993, April 21). Parallel lines: Companies create new ways to promote employees—without making them boss. *Wall Street Journal*.

23. Castro, J. (1993, March 29). Disposable workers. *Time*.

24. Ibid.

25. Ibid.

26. Riggio, R. E. (1986). Assessment of basic social skills. *Journal of Personality and Social Psychology, 51*, 649–660.

27. Friedman, H. S., Riggio, R. E., & Casella, D. F. (1988). Nonverbal skill, personal charisma, and initial attraction. *Personality and Social Psychology Bulletin, 14,* 203–211.

28. Riggio, R. E., Tucker, J., & Throckmorton, B. (1987). Social skills and deception ability. *Personality and Social Psychology Bulletin, 13,* 568–577.

Chapter 3

Perceiving the Physical World

Perception Is Organized
Perception Is Selective
Internal Factors Affecting Perception
External Factors Affecting Attention

Social Cognition: Understanding People

Social Perception and Attention: Standing
   Out from the Crowd
Person Memory
Inference: Drawing Conclusions from Social
   Information
Attribution: Understanding the Causes of
   Others' Behavior
Causal Attribution: Some Implications for
   Work Settings

**When Social Perception Fails:
Common Errors in Our Efforts
to Understand Others**

Overestimating the Role of Internal Causes:
   The Fundamental Attribution Error
The Self-Serving Bias: Taking Credit for
   Success, Avoiding Blame for Failure

**Social Perception: Its Role in Job
Interviews and Performance Appraisals**

The Halo Effect: How Overall Impressions
   Shape Judgments

Social Perception and the Job Interview
Social Perception and Performance
   Appraisal

**Impression Management: Managing
Perceptions of Ourselves**

Tactics of Self-Presentation: Self-Enhancing
   and Ingratiation Strategies

Special Sections

Balancing Work and Family
Initiatives at American Express

Human Relations in Action
Recognizing Assumptions You May Make
   about Human Nature

Ethics at Work
Self-Presentation in the Workplace:
   A Case Study

Guidelines for Effective Human Relations
Using What You've Learned

Experiential Exercise
Forming First Impressions: What's in
   a Face?

ᴘERCEPTION

Perceiving Other Persons and the World around Us

Learning Objectives

After reading this chapter, you should be able to:

1. Define perception and explain why it is an active process.

2. Describe the principles of perceptual organization.

3. Define social perception and indicate its relevance to human relations.

4. Explain how we use attribution to understand the behavior of others.

5. Describe the bases of errors in social perception.

6. Indicate how social perception can affect job interviews and performance appraisals.

7. Describe how we manage the impressions we make on other people.

I t was time for the six-month evaluation of new employees at Serve Rite Food Services Corporation. Serve Rite handles food services for a variety of companies and colleges and hires a broad range of employees, from food service clerks to managers. Kirsten Link, the regional manager, was discussing her feelings about some of her employees with Bob Olds, the personnel manager.

"I really like Ryan Dalton. He is bright and highly motivated. He came highly recommended, and he certainly has not disappointed us. I have very few problems with people in his district," Kirsten said.

Bob nodded in agreement. "He sure is a lot better than the guy he replaced. We were always getting complaints about him."

"Unfortunately, not all of our people seem to be working out," continued Kirsten. "I have heard some complaints about Vicky Hans. She has turned a lot of people off with her interpersonal style. Apparently, she really wanted to show her employees who was boss, and as result she has a morale problem. We are having a tough time keeping her locations staffed."

The Hans case was somewhat of a puzzle to Bob. Vicky had seemed quite personable in the interviews and had done well in her prior management positions. "Kirsten, do you think there might be something about that district, rather than Vicky's style, that could be responsible? In my discussions with Vicky, she has mentioned that some key people seem to resent working for a female manager. Maybe if we gave her a chance in another district, she might do well."

Kirsten shook her head in disagreement. "Bob, I think she is just using her female status as an excuse for her failure. I don't think she has the people skills to be a good manager."

*A*lthough we have constructed this hypothetical example from a hypothetical company, such conversations likely take place often in the real world. What does it tell us? First, it shows us that people may have different perceptions of the same person in the workplace. Second, it illustrates how two people can see the causes of the same person's behavior as stemming from different factors. It also demonstrates the critical role that these differences in perception make in the workplace. In this chapter, we explore the principles that underlie perception in general, and social perception in particular. We begin by discussing some basic principles of perception.

In the discussion of **perception** that follows, we first focus on this process as it applies to the physical world—

perception   The active process by which we interpret and organize information provided by our senses. It is through perception that we construct a representation of the world around us.

how it helps us understand the input received by our five senses. Next, we examine **social perception,** the process through which we seek to understand other persons. As will soon become apparent, a working knowledge of both types of perception is essential to understanding many aspects of interpersonal relations in work settings.

ᴘERCEIVING THE PHYSICAL WORLD

At any moment in time, we are literally flooded with input from our senses. Our eyes respond to wavelengths of light, our ears react to sound pitches, and so on. Nevertheless, we do not perceive the world as a random collection of sensations. Instead, we recognize specific objects and orderly patterns of events. This organization of input occurs because perception is an active process—one that imposes order and meaning on the vast array of sensations we receive. Generally, this process takes place automatically, so we are not even aware of its existence. Careful study, however, reveals that it involves strong tendencies toward selectivity and organization.

Perception Is Organized

Look at Figure 3.1c. What do you see? Do you see two separate figures, or do you see a single triangle? Most likely, you can see a triangle. How does this happen? The process by which we structure environmental input is called **perceptual organization.** We have learned much about the laws that govern perceptual organization, and it appears that the human mind comes prepared to impose order and structure on the physical world. In this case, we impose closure on the lines to create a meaningful stimulus—a triangle.

social perception The process through which we come to know and understand other persons.

perceptual organization Processes responsible for providing structure and order to our perceptual world.

Figure 3.1   **Perceptual Laws of Organization: Three Examples**

Psychologists find these three principles of perceptual grouping: similarity, proximity, and closure.

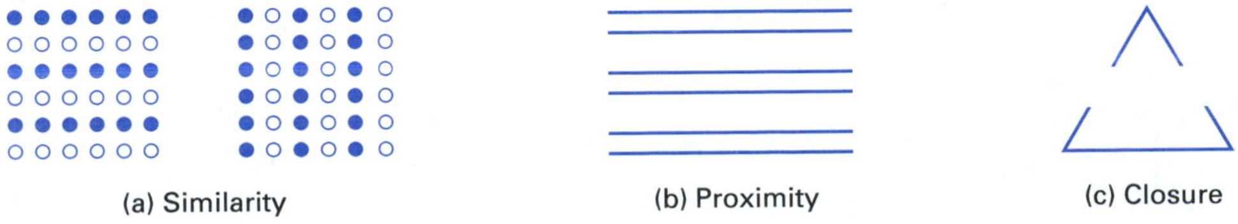

(a) Similarity   (b) Proximity   (c) Closure

Figure 3.2   **Reversing Figure and Ground**

In this illustration, you can see a white vase against a black background, or two black faces in profile on a white background. Exactly the same visual stimulus produces two opposite figure-ground perceptions.

The ease with which you are able to read the words on this page demonstrates one principle of perceptual organization, called the **figure-ground relationship.** This principle states that we organize input from our senses into stimuli (figures) that stand out against a background (ground). The black ink on this page stands out as a figure against the background of the white page. In most cases, this relationship is clear; in other cases, the relationship can be more ambiguous (see Figure 3.2). Sometimes, the figure-ground relationship can disguise objects from view in the environment (see Figure 3.3). Camouflage, for example, works by making it hard to pick out a figure from its background.

Another law of perceptual organization states that objects that are near to one another, in either time or space, tend to be grouped together—the **law of proximity.** You can see this law demonstrated in Figure 3.1b. It has implications for the assumptions we make about people in the workplace. For example, we may assume that people who work in the same office are similar to one another, simply because they work in close proximity to one another.

The final principle we will discuss is the **law of similarity**—the fact that similar items within a field tend to be grouped together (see Figure 3.1a). This law operates when we perceive both people and objects. For example, the physical similarities among men, women, or members of different ethnic, racial, or any other group make it likely that we perceive them as similar, even though many differences exist among individual members of these groups. This tendency can lead us to make broad, inaccurate generalizations. We will learn more about this error when we discuss prejudice in Chapter 13.

figure-ground relationship   A principle of perception that states that our tendency is to organize sensory input into stimuli (figures) that stand out against a background (ground).

law of proximity   A law of perceptual organization that states that objects that are near to one another, in either time or space, tend to be grouped together.

law of similarity   A law of perceptual organization that states that similar items within a field, whether people or objects, tend to be grouped together.

Figure 3.3 **Figure-Ground Relationships and Camouflage**

Natural camouflage works by making it difficult to perceive objects against the background.

Perception Is Selective

If you've ever attended a noisy party, you are already familiar with perception's highly selective nature. At such times, you can easily screen out all of the voices around you except that of the person with whom you are conversing. While the words of this individual stand out and make sense, those of all the others blend into a single background buzz. If you decide to listen to someone else, you can readily shift your attention to that person. Indeed, you can even accomplish this shift while continuing to look the first person in the eye—thus convincing him that he remains the center of your interest. In such cases, paying attention is obviously a conscious process: we decide where to direct our focus and when to do so. In many other cases attention follows a course of its own choosing. Sometimes (for example, during a dull lecture), we cannot force our attention to remain where we want it, even for a few minutes! In such cases, factors other than our own play a crucial role. But what are they? What factors lead us to pay attention to certain events or stimuli while ignoring others? In general, they fall into two major categories: *internal* and *external*.

Internal Factors Affecting Perception

One internal factor that strongly affects perception can be readily illustrated. Imagine that you are attending a business meeting. What stimuli or events will you notice? This selection depends, in part, on your current motivational state. If it is close to lunchtime and you are hungry, you may focus on the delicious smell of food entering the room from a nearby restaurant. If you are deeply concerned about your upcoming promotion, you may direct your total attention to the words and actions of your boss—the person who must go to bat for you to assure your success. In short, the places to which we direct our attention—and the stimuli that we perceive—are strongly affected by our current motives, needs, and values.

Motivation is not the only internal factor that affects attention. Our past experience plays a role in this regard as well. Imagine that three people are watching a demonstration of a new computer at a local shopping mall. One is an engineer, another an accountant, and the third a teenage boy, famous locally for his success in playing video games. What will they notice? In all probability, they will focus on very different things. The engineer's attention may be drawn to the advanced technology used in the new equipment. The accountant may focus on the excellent software—special programs she can use in recordkeeping. The teenager may notice the brightness of the colors on the screen or the score of another player. In short, each person's attention will hone in on different aspects of the same item, because past experience (or training) orients him or her in these directions.

Such differences commonly arise in many settings, including organizations. For example, in examining a competitor's product, marketing personnel may concen-

Balancing Work and Family

Initiatives at American Express

American Express is a multimillion-dollar organization that consists of five fairly independent subsidiaries. In 1987, it began a series of major initiatives with the goal of creating the "Best Place to Work." Toward this goal, the company established a "think tank" to study the challenges that would face the organization as it approached the year 2000 and to help it understand the changes occurring in the workforce. American Express saw its ability to attract and retain quality employees in the face of a shrinking labor pool as a basic problem with which it would need to deal.

One of the first steps the company took was to conduct a study of its current employees. By gaining a better understanding of the needs, values, and concerns of its current employees, the firm hoped to get better at attracting and keeping similar-quality employees in the future. American Express surveyed more than 3000 of its current employees and held focus groups at several locations. Three primary issues became very clear. First, employees were experiencing difficulties in balancing work and family responsibilities. More than half of the employees with children had taken at least one day off from work in the past few months to stay with a sick child, for example. Second, employees perceived a lack of flexibility in their work schedules. Amazingly, almost half of them had considered quitting their job because of this

trate on the materials used in the product or clever aspects of its manufacture. Engineers may take note of the technical features. Unfortunately, differences of this type can often lead to serious communication gaps, because people see different things when examining the same object. An important task for managers, then, is elucidating such differences and ensuring that they do not cause unnecessary friction between the persons involved. It is also important for organizations to recognize the needs, values, and concerns of employees. Gaps in the perceptions of senior management and other employees can produce job dissatisfaction and turnover (see the *Balancing Work and Family* section).

External Factors Affecting Attention

Attention is also often affected by external factors—various aspects of stimuli. That is, certain features of objects or events in the world around us determine whether they are more or less likely to be noticed. **Salience** is the extent to which a stimulus stands out from the others around it. The greater its salience, the more it tends to draw attention. For example, you would probably be more likely to notice a nude bather on a beach where other persons

salience The extent to which a given stimulus stands out from other stimuli surrounding it.

issue. Third, more than one-third of the employees felt that senior management did not understand and was not supportive of workers with family responsibilities.

The results were surprising to many of the members of American Express's senior management. As a result, a task force was formed to deal with many of these concerns. Among their recommendations were the following: (1) establish child-care subsidies that would provide partial reimbursement for the cost of child care; (2) establish a sabbatical program that would give employees with more than ten years of employment unpaid personal leaves or paid leaves for community service; (3) improve part-time benefits; and (4) offer flexible work arrangements that included options for such things as job sharing. We will discuss many of these kinds of programs throughout this book. For now, we simply point out that it is important to realize that differences can exist between the perspectives and perceptions of management and those of other employees, and that good things can happen for people within all levels of an organization when attempts are made to recognize these differences.

Source: Jackson, S. E. (1992). Diversity in the workplace: Human resources initiatives. New York, NY: Guilford Press.

are clothed than on a beach where every other person is also nude. Salience—and attention—are enhanced by intensity, large size, motion, and novelty. Experts in marketing are well aware of these principles; indeed, they often use them in planning effective advertisements. As the next section describes, salience also has implications for our perceptions of other persons.

SOCIAL COGNITION: UNDERSTANDING PEOPLE

Consider the following situation. You are going on a job interview. The night before, you lay in bed and think about what may happen the next day. You plan what to wear and think about the kind of impression you want to make. You anticipate the questions you may be asked and rehearse how you will answer them. In addition, you think about the questions you will ask and the information you want to gather on the interview. When you arrive at the interview, the personnel director greets you and takes you on a tour of the facility. You meet several prospective coworkers, look at the working conditions, read over the employee handbook, and have a prolonged discussion with the personnel director. Although you are tired at the end of the day, you feel things have gone well and are confident that you will receive an offer of a position. How do you decide whether you want the job? Will you like the work? Will you enjoy working with the persons employed by the company? Does management seem to be fair? Will you have a future with the company? How will the work fit into your family life?

The answers to these important questions involve inferences that you make on the basis of the available information. Research in social cognition explores how we make these inferences and seeks to explain how we make sense of ourselves and other persons. (Refer to the *Human Relations in Action* section for examples of some common assumptions people make about human nature.) Everyday ideas, theories, and ways of categorizing the social world are outcomes of social cognition processes, and, in turn, influence social perception. Three major processes are involved in social cognition: (1) attention, (2) memory, and (3) inference. Although we describe these processes as if they take place in sequence, in reality they work together at all times (see Figure 3.4).

Social Perception and Attention: Standing Out from the Crowd

Have you ever walked into a room in which you were the only female or male present? Not only do you feel as if you stand out in this context, but others also turn to notice you. This example demonstrates how attention is drawn to stimuli that stand

Figure 3.4   **Social Cognition Processes**

These three major processes are involved in social cognition. Although we talk about them separately, in reality they work together to produce our ideas, theories, and categorizations of the social world.

Human Relations in Action

Recognizing Assumptions You May Make about Human Nature

In 1992, Lawrence Wrightsman reported the results of his large research study into the assumptions people commonly make about human nature. Once such assumptions become a part of our belief system, they influence the way we perceive other people and how we behave toward those individuals. A sampling of some of the assumptions that we may make about the characteristics of people are listed here. Take a moment to reflect on which of these you may hold.

Do you assume that people are generally:

_____ Stable	_____ Unstable
_____ Selfish	_____ Unselfish
_____ Similar to you	_____ Different from you
_____ Rational	_____ Irrational
_____ Trustworthy	_____ Undependable

Now that you've reflected on these assumptions, consider how your behavior toward your coworkers might be affected by these assumptions. For example, how would you behave toward a coworker who turned in part of a project late? How does your potential behavior relate to these assumptions? Wrightsman has found that our evaluations and judgments are affected by these beliefs. For example, he found that college students who held more positive views about human nature gave higher teaching evaluations than students who held more negative beliefs. To generalize this finding to the workplace, we might all hope that our supervisor holds positive assumptions about human nature!

Source: Adapted from Wrightsman, L. S. (1992). Assumptions about human nature. Sage Press, Newbury Park, CA.

out within the immediate context. As with perception in the physical world, the term *salience* is used to describe the extent to which a given social stimulus stands out from surrounding stimuli. A person who is either unique or novel within a particular situation is salient and attracts attention. Such novelty can be based on relatively stable dimensions of people such as race, ethnicity, or gender, or it can reflect characteristics such as the clothes someone is wearing or the color of a person's hair.

Events also capture our attention when they appear to be unexpected in light of our past social experiences. For example, if someone at work who has always been aloof and cool with you suddenly treats you like his best friend, that behavior becomes salient to you. You may be likely to notice and try to explain the inconsistent behavior. Inconsistent information invites attentional focus and motivates us to try to fit the information into our impressions.

Now consider that the person whom you observe behaving in unexpected ways is your new supervisor. The fact that your work outcomes depend upon this person makes it especially likely that you will notice his behavior. Interdependence (having one's outcomes depend upon another person) focuses one's attention on that person.[1]

Why does salience matter in human relations? Capturing one's attention has several important consequences. One interesting consequence is that salient stimuli become more likely to be seen as the cause of later events (see Figure 3.5).[2] This principle also applies to people; those who stand out in a group tend to be viewed as having more influence on that group. Think about this fact when you are choosing a place to sit at a meeting or deciding what to wear to a brainstorming session.

Attention also makes our impressions of a salient person become more extreme.[3] If you have a tendency to like a person, you will like her more if she is salient. The other side of the coin is true as well; if you have a tendency to dislike a person, you will dislike her more if she stands out in the group. This fact can work for you or against you in the workplace. If you draw attention and are doing a good job, your evaluations can become more positive. On the other hand, if you make a mistake, your pratfall will really stand out. For better or worse, being noticed magnifies others' impressions of you.

Finally, salience sometimes—but not always—helps you remember more about a person or event. In many circumstances, we allocate more of our cognitive resources in processing salient stimuli. This can lead to the kind of processing that makes stimuli memorable. We discuss how memory works in the next section, making it clear that attention is necessary, but not sufficient, for good memory.

Person Memory

We have all been in the following situation one time or another. You attend a party where you don't know many people. A friend introduces you to several folks as you arrive. The introductions pass as a blur of faces, and you know you won't be able to

Salient Stimuli

People who stand out in a group tend to be viewed as influential, as shown here.

From *Wishful Thinking* by David Sipress, p. 39. Copyright © 1997 by David Sipress. Reprinted by permission of HarperCollins, Inc.

put the names and faces together. You therefore try to pay attention to each person in turn. Once you have focused on the person, will you be able to recall his name the next day? Perhaps you will. However, this possibility really depends on the goals that you have at that moment.[4] Goals determine the kind of memory strategy we use, which in turn affects how we put information into long-term memory. Let's focus on some of the goals that are important for our social memory and how you can use them to your advantage.

Although this fact may not coincide with your previous ideas, researchers have shown that the absolute worst way to remember a person is to actively try to memorize what the person does or says. Don't say to yourself, "I must remember this man." Rather, try to spend the cognitive effort to notice and form an impression of the person. If you accomplish this goal, you are likely to remember him or her. **Impression formation** goals seem to be effective because they promote the integration of new

impression formation   The process through which we combine diverse information about other persons into unified impressions of them.

| Table 3.1 | Three Important Goals for Good Social Memory |

Interaction Goal	Strategy for Social Memory
Impression formation	"What kind of person is he?"
Empathy	"How would I feel in this situation?"
Anticipated interaction	"What would it be like to work with this person?"

information into our memory system.[5] When information becomes linked in memory, more memory cues are available for recall.

Other goals work just as well or better than impression formation. One of the best ways to remember someone is to approach the person with empathy. Trying to put yourself in another's situation, or trying to imagine how she feels, really works as a memory strategy. You can also use self-reference goals in a social context.[6] For example, when you meet a new colleague, you could think about the things you have in common (Do you both have children? Are you both outgoing?). Finally, expecting to interact with that person in some meaningful way also improves memory.[7] We can conclude that the more engaging the interaction goal, the better the strategy is for our social memory. This relationship generally holds true, although an important exception exists (as discussed later in this section).

Ironically, anticipated interaction works far better in enhancing memory than actual interaction does. Can you imagine why this is the case? Think about what social interaction involves: You're listening to what is said, planning what you will say, forming an impression of the person, and so on. All of this activity competes for our limited attention and leaves very little resources for processing information. Table 3.1 summarizes the goals of these impression management strategies.

Inference: Drawing Conclusions from Social Information

We began our discussion of social cognition by describing how a person might respond to an employment interview. Then, we described factors that may influence what the job candidate attends to and remembers about her interview. Now, we explore how she may put this information together. What will determine the kinds of inferences she will make?

At first blush, one might assume that our hypothetical job candidate will base her final impression on the information she has noticed and stored. She might sit down, think about everything she has seen and heard, weigh the advantages and disadvantages of each course of action, and then come to a conclusion based upon logical reasoning. Although people might engage in this kind of deliberative processing when making important decisions, such as where to work, more often they use mental shortcuts, or **heuristics,** for drawing inferences in a rapid manner. Using heuristics help stretch our limited cognitive resources and deal with information overload in the complex social world. Let's explore several of these shortcuts and biases in information processing. Being aware of potential biases in our inferences may help us avoid serious mistakes.

Consider the case of Jack. He is very practical, likes to work with numbers, and is very precise in his speech. Would you say he is more likely to be an engineer or a construction worker? You would probably guess that Jack is more likely to be an engineer. Most people would say the same—he sounds like a typical engineer. Think about the logic involved here. The work world includes many more construction workers than engineers. Based on only purely logical grounds, your guess should therefore have been that Jack is a construction worker. Do you see this logic? The fact that you, and most people, don't make this logical choice reflects the operation of the **representativeness heuristic**—a heuristic for making judgments based on the extent to which a stimulus resembles our stereotypes.[8]

On the one hand, it makes sense that we would guess that people with certain characteristics would have certain professions, because our occupational choices often reflect our personal characteristics. On the other hand, relying on our preconceived ideas and stereotypes may lead us to overlook important types of information that may be important, such as base rates—the frequency with which certain events occur in the general population.

How might this heuristic affect behavior in the workplace? One potential influence would be in inferring that people who hold different positions within the organization have characteristics that represent our stereotypes of these roles. For example, we might assume that people who work in R&D (research and development) are flaky and flighty, that people in accounting are boring, and so on. Making such assumptions may actually give us the wrong impression of these persons, however, and perhaps lead us to make poor professional and personal decisions.

As we saw earlier, our theories and preconceptions about the world guide our thought processes. Thus it is not surprising that we are especially sensitive to information that fits with our existing ideas. This tendency also becomes manifested as the **illusory correlation,** which occurs when we perceive a stronger relationship or association between two variables than actually exists. As in our discussion about the representativeness heuristic revealed, our preconceptions about the characteristics possessed by people from various occupations will influence the inferences we make about individuals.[9] The illusory correlation takes this influence one step further, leading us to make inferences

heuristics   Mental shortcuts that allow us to make inferences in a rapid manner.

representativeness heuristic   A heuristic for making judgments based on the extent to which a stimulus resembles our stereotypes.

illusory correlation   A phenomenon that occurs when we perceive a stronger relationship or association between two variables than actually exists.

that overestimate the frequency with which various events or characteristics occur together. For example, we tend to overestimate the number of accountants who are perfectionists, the number of librarians who are quiet and timid, the number of professors who are studious and stuffy, and so on.

The illusory correlation can lead to negative forms of organizational behavior, such as sexual harassment. In one study, men who rated highly in terms of a tendency to sexually harass women were likely to see an illusory correlation between sexuality and dominance.[10] This illusory correlation would lead them to overestimate the number of occurrences in which dominant persons engage in sexual relationships with their subordinates. The implications of this finding for the business world are fairly straightforward: If a person assumes that sexual relationships between dominant and subordinate persons are commonplace, then he or she may think about sexual relationships when in a position of power. If these thoughts turn into action, sexual harassment results—a serious problem in any organizational context!

Attribution: Understanding the Causes of Others' Behavior

One question we ask repeatedly about other persons is, "Why?" Why did my boss decide to call a meeting at 4:30 P.M. on Friday? Why did my suppliers fail to deliver a major order on time? Why does Randi Helson in the accounting department always wait twenty-four hours before returning my calls? In short, we want to know why others have acted in certain ways. On closer examination, this question can be broken down into two major parts: Do their actions stem primarily from (1) internal causes (their own traits, motives, and values) or (2) external causes (factors relating to the situations in which they operate)?

To use a classic example, let's suppose that we see a man laughing at a particular movie. We want to understand whether his laughter tells us something unique about the person or whether it tells us something about the environmental entity (the movie is funny). First we want to know about the distinctiveness of his response. Does the man respond this way to all movies, or is his laughter distinctive to this particular movie? If he does not laugh at funny segments in any other movie (high distinctiveness), we would lean toward the inference that something particularly funny in this movie is making him laugh (an external attribution). But there are other factors we need to consider in this example.

We also look to see how other persons are responding in the situation. This is referred to as *consensus information*. Using our movie example, we would want to know whether other persons respond in this way to this entity (are all the persons in the theater laughing?). If the response is held in common by other persons (it is high in consensus), we are less likely to think that the person's laughter tells us something unique about him and are more likely to infer that his behavior is caused by environmental circumstances (external attribution). If he is the only person laughing, however, we're more likely to think that his laughter is caused by something unique about the person (internal attribution). We may think, for example, that he has an odd sense of humor or may be a bit weird.

We can see that high consensus and high distinctiveness are indicative of external attributions, whereas low consensus and low distinctiveness may be attributed to internal attributions (see Figure 3.6). A third source of information is important for us to be confident about either attribution. We need to know about the consistency of the person's behavior over time and modality. That is, will this person always find the movie funny (time) and will he find it funny whether he sees it at a theater or on videotape (modality)? High consistency is important for us to be sure about our internal or external attributions. For example, if the person finds the movie funny on Saturday but not on Sunday, or finds it funny only when he sees it on videotape, we

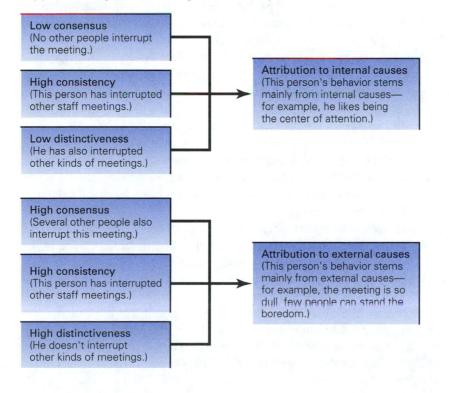

Figure 3.6

How We Answer the Question "Why?" about Others' Behavior

In deciding whether another person's behavior stems mainly from internal or external causes, we take into account three factors: *consensus, consistency,* and *distinctiveness.* Consider the question of why Jim made silly jokes during a staff meeting last week. Why did he do this?

Low consensus
(No other people interrupt the meeting.)

High consistency
(This person has interrupted other staff meetings.)

Low distinctiveness
(He has also interrupted other kinds of meetings.)

Attribution to internal causes
(This person's behavior stems mainly from internal causes—for example, he likes being the center of attention.)

High consensus
(Several other people also interrupt this meeting.)

High consistency
(This person has interrupted other staff meetings.)

High distinctiveness
(He doesn't interrupt other kinds of meetings.)

Attribution to external causes
(This person's behavior stems mainly from external causes—for example, the meeting is so dull, few people can stand the boredom.)

are less confident that the movie was the cause of his laughter or that some stable property of the person is responsible for his laughter. In essence, we become confused about why he laughed—maybe it was the result of some momentary circumstance (for example, he was just in a particularly goofy mood that day). You can see that low consistency would make it difficult to understand why he laughed.

Causal Attribution: Some Implications for Work Settings

Whether we perceive another's behavior as deriving from internal or external causes can influence several key aspects of our interpersonal behavior in work settings. First, and most generally, we tend to hold others responsible for any effects produced by their actions if these behaviors stem from their own traits or motives (that is, internal causes). If their actions are derived mainly from external causes beyond their control, however, we do not assign such responsibility. Imagine that someone in another department promises to have some work completed by a certain date. When the time comes, you find that the work is not ready. Do you blame this person for failing to keep his word? It depends. If you learn that he could not finish the job because of a serious equipment failure, you realize that it was not his fault and decide to "forgive and forget." If, instead, you find that your job is not ready because your coworker has been goofing off, you will probably react with anger and resentment. In this and many other instances, the apparent causes behind others' behavior play a crucial role in determining our relations with them.

Second, our conclusions about the causes of others' behavior can strongly affect our evaluations of their performance. To understand why, consider the following situation. You are asked to evaluate the performance of two persons, both candidates for promotion. When you examine their records, you find that both are roughly equivalent. You also know that they have attained these results in different ways. One individual is highly talented, but is coasting along, putting little effort into his work. The other has less ability but has worked very hard to attain success. To whom would you assign the higher rating? Probably to the hard worker of modest ability. Whatever your decision, you would take into account the causes of each person's behavior as well as his or her actual performance.

Research findings indicate that when we evaluate others' performance (or our own), we pay close attention to many factors relating to the potential causes of this behavior. Among the most important of these factors seem to be effort, ability, luck, and task difficulty.[11] Both effort and ability are internal causes, while luck and task difficulty are external ones. Ability and task difficulty tend to remain quite stable across time, however, while effort and luck may change greatly from one moment to the next. Thus our attempts to understand (and evaluate) the performance of others take two key dimensions into account: the internal/external dimension discussed earlier and a dimension involving stability across time (lasting causes versus temporary ones; see Figure 3.7).

Attribution and Evaluations of Others' Performance: Two Key Dimensions

In evaluating others' performance, we tend to use two dimensions: one ranging from internal to external causes of behavior and another ranging from lasting to temporary causes. The major causes of others' behavior—ability, effort, luck, task difficulty—occupy different points along these dimensions.

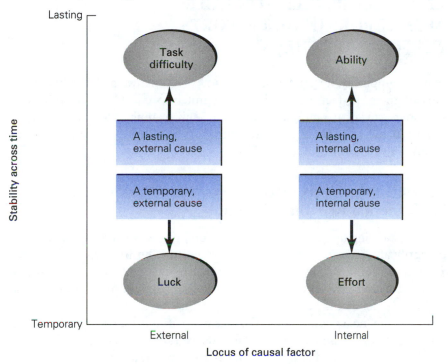

Locus of causal factor

We consider both dimensions when judging others' performance, albeit in a somewhat complex way. First, consider successful performance on some task. It is evaluated more positively when perceived as stemming from internal causes (high ability or effort) than when seen as deriving from external ones (an easy task or good luck). This evaluation makes excellent sense; after all, if someone succeeds because of talent or hard work, the worker deserves more credit than if the success reflects a lucky break. In contrast, poor task performance is evaluated more harshly when it is seen as stemming from internal causes rather than from external ones. Again, this evaluation is quite reasonable. If someone fails because of factors outside their control (for example, bad luck), we may excuse their poor showing. If they fail because of laziness, however, we have less reason to be charitable.

We also give a special edge to high effort. Thus, if two people perform at a similar level, the one who seems to be working harder often receives higher ratings.[12] This point has a practical application in your own career: If you want to receive high performance ratings, be sure to keep your effort at visibly high levels. If you do not strive to reach your goals and appear to be coasting, even good performance may fail to yield high ratings. We discuss this point in more detail later in this chapter (see "Social Perception and Performance Appraisal" on pages 81–82).

*W*HEN SOCIAL PERCEPTION FAILS: COMMON ERRORS IN OUR EFFORTS TO UNDERSTAND OTHERS

Given people's complexity, it is only reasonable to expect that we make errors in our perceptions of them. In fact, such mistakes definitely occur. Our perceptions of people around us can fail in a number of different ways, leading us to misunderstand them. Because being aware of these potential errors may help you recognize and combat them, we will now describe several.

Overestimating the Role of Internal Causes: The Fundamental Attribution Error

Suppose, while standing in a checkout line in a store, you witness the clerk on duty shouting angrily at a customer and telling him to take his business elsewhere. How would you account for this rude behavior? Your first reply might be, "It's impossible to tell." Research findings point to another answer: You would more likely conclude (tentatively, of course) that the clerk is a hostile person, best avoided. This simple example illustrates the most common form of bias in attribution: a strong tendency to view others' actions as stemming mainly from internal rather than external factors.[13] This type of mistake is termed a **fundamental attribution error.** In short, we generally perceive others as behaving as they do because they are "that kind of person." The many external factors that may have affected their actions tend to be ignored or downplayed.

As you can probably see, this error can have serious consequences. Because of it, we may expect others to behave more consistently than is justified. For example, if you see your boss act in a forgiving manner toward an employee who has made a serious error, you may jump to the conclusion that he is kind-hearted. In fact, he may have been forgiving because of external factors (for example, because the employee in question is a distant relative or the son of an old friend), not because he has a forgiving soul. If you overlook such possibilities, you may be shocked and hurt when he berates you for making the same type of error. In this and many other situations, our tendency to attribute the behavior of other persons to internal causes can lead us to reach false conclusions about them.

fundamental attribution error The term used to describe our tendency to overemphasize the importance of internal causes for other persons' behavior.

The Self-Serving Bias: Taking Credit for Success, Avoiding Blame for Failure

Another type of bias that occurs frequently in our everyday social perception is called the **self-serving bias.**[14] Briefly, this bias refers to our strong tendency to take credit for good outcomes (that is, success) while denying responsibility for negative ones (that is, failure). Both of these tendencies are easy to spot. For example, suppose you write a report for your boss, and she likes it very much. How would you account for this result? You would probably assume that it stemmed from your hard work, high level of intelligence, and innate talent. But now imagine that she rejects the report and criticizes it harshly. How would you explain this result? The chances are good that you would view it as stemming from external factors—her unreasonably high standards, the lack of clear instructions about what was needed, and so on. In short, we seem all too ready to take full credit for success but equally ready to deny personal responsibility for failure, even in work situations.

Two reasons underlie this bias. First, it allows us to protect or enhance our self-esteem—the way we feel about ourselves. Second, it permits us to present a positive public image—to appear favorably in the eyes of others.[15] Regardless of its origins, the self-serving bias can get us into deep trouble. Imagine what happens when two persons work on a task together, a common situation in work settings. Each may perceive any success attained as stemming mainly from his or her own contributions, but each will perceive failure as mainly the fault of the other person.[16] Needless to say, this problem can lead to a great deal of conflict. For this reason, we should carefully avoid the self-serving bias.

SOCIAL PERCEPTION: ITS ROLE IN JOB INTERVIEWS AND PERFORMANCE APPRAISALS

In earlier sections, you learned about some of the processes involved in forming impressions of other people and understanding their actions. These processes have a major impact on all aspects of human relations in the workplace. In this section, we focus on important situations in which these processes can influence our lives.

The Halo Effect: How Overall Impressions Shape Social Judgments

Have you ever heard the phrase "love is blind"? If so, you are already familiar with an important truth of social perception: the **halo effect.** Once we form an overall impression of another person, it tends to exert strong effects on our subsequent judgments of his or her specific traits.[17]

self-serving bias   Our tendency to take credit for positive outcomes but attribute negative outcomes to external causes.

halo effect   When our overall impressions of others spill over into and influence our evaluations of their behaviors.

Halo effects are common and powerful. For example, most organizations contain one or more young "superstars"—people with a reputation for being exceptionally talented and competent. Once they have gained such a halo, everything they do is evaluated favorably. Ideas that would be perceived as mediocre if suggested by someone else are seen as creative and brilliant when proposed by these individuals. Additionally, actions that might be viewed as risky or foolish if undertaken by others are seen as daring and bold in these "chosen" men and women. Some other people acquire a "rusty halo"—a reputation for being unable to do anything right. This impression spills over onto all their traits or behaviors, so that whatever they do or suggest is perceived in a negative light.

Obviously, halo effects carry high costs. They may lead some persons to develop an overblown view of their own merits or worth while crushing the egos of others who deserve better. Furthermore, by assigning undue influence to persons who are not ready to receive it, and by blocking recognition of hidden pools of talent, both organizations and individuals can suffer. Clearly, it is important to recognize the existence and impact of halo effects; only then can we avoid their harmful effects.

Social Perception and the Job Interview

Many companies continue to use job interviews to select employees. As the interview process involves first meetings with strangers, it is susceptible to the biases discussed in this chapter. The interviewer is trying to form impressions about the traits of the potential employee from the interactions that take place during this short period of time. First impressions are therefore likely to play an important role, and the interviewer will be tempted to make snap judgments about the suitability of applicants (see the *Experiential Exercise*). What affects these judgments? Some of the influences are summarized here:[18]

1. **The positive-negative nature of information.** Interviewers tend to place more weight on unfavorable than favorable information in the interview.

2. **Contrast effects.** An applicant's favorability is affected by judgments of the favorability of other applicants, although this influence does not seem to be very strong.

   Consider the following situation: A young woman with moderately good qualifications applies for a job with two different firms. At the first company, she is interviewed by a personnel director who has just finished speaking with two other applicants. Both competing candidates were at the top of their college classes and possess all the skills and training sought by the company. At the second firm, the interviewer is a personnel director who has just seen two other applicants, neither of whom is suitable for the job in question. From which interviewer will she receive higher ratings? The answer is obvious: She will be perceived much more favorably by the second interviewer because, in contrast to the two other applicants, she will "shine." The applicant will receive lower ratings from the first interviewer because, compared

Figure 3.8 **Good Credentials Are a Must**

Although this cartoon refers to a loan interview, we couldn't resist presenting the humorous depiction of the importance of good references and credentials in an interview setting.

to those two applicants, she will appear mediocre. This example illustrates the potential impact of *contrast effects*.[19] These effects reflect the fact that our reaction to a given stimulus (or person) is often influenced by other stimuli (people) we have recently encountered.

3. **Visual information.** The personal appearance of the applicant can affect interviewers' decisions. The primary influence of appearance seems to affect estimates of the applicant's social skills.[20] Gestures and the amount of time that the applicant spends talking also have an influence.

4. **Nonverbal cues.** Positive nonverbal cues, such as smiling and eye contact, tend to generate a good impression.[21] They have less influence, however, when the interviewer has considerable information about the applicant's qualifications.[22] Furthermore, when applicants with poor credentials give many nonverbal cues, they are often rated less favorable relative to those who do not engage in such behavior.[23] Perhaps this difference arises because interviewers attribute such actions to efforts by these applicants to shift attention away from their poor qualifications. Whatever the reason, emitting a high level of positive nonverbal cues can sometimes backfire and produce effects opposite to the ones intended. The best strategy for applicants, therefore, is the following: Practice effective nonverbal behavior and use it to your advantage during an interview, but, to achieve the best results, combine it with clear evidence of competence and excellent qualifications (see Figure 3.8).

Social Perception and Performance Appraisal

Determining who should be promoted, receive raises, or be fired is an important component of organizational behavior. If these decisions are sound, then the overall organization is likely to be sound. It would be nice if these decisions were straightforward and resulted from rational processes. In reality, these decisions are often colored by some of the processes discussed in this chapter.

The limitations of our cognitive abilities influence the accuracy of performance appraisal. We are limited in our ability to process, store, and remember information. Thus we don't always base our evaluations on all of the relevant facts. Our appraisals are also colored by our interpretations of these facts.

One major influence on these appraisals is our assumptions about why employees perform in certain ways. The reasons that we think underlie an employee's behavior play a central role in our evaluations. For example, two employees may exhibit similar performance outcomes, but our evaluations of these employees may differ. In one case, we may think that an employee's success in landing an important account results from the effort that she has put into the task; we may decide that she is hardworking, a real go-getter. In another case, we may think an employee landed an important account as a result of luck—being in the right place at the right time. It is likely that we would judge these two employees differently, despite the fact that they both landed important accounts. In the first case, our assessment of the employee's behavior is based on the assumed internal factors of hard work, talent, and dedication; we're likely to reward these qualities. In the second case, our attributions are external; we're less likely to evaluate the employee's performance positively.

Research suggests that managers use attributions during their performance appraisals. Interestingly, subordinates who are thought to be highly motivated receive higher ratings than subordinates who exhibit similar performance but whose success is attributed to talent or past experience.[24] Again, we emphasize how important it is to make others aware of your job-related efforts.

IMPRESSION MANAGEMENT: MANAGING PERCEPTIONS OF OURSELVES

The way that other people perceive us in the workplace is a critical factor to our success. Raises, promotions, and the course of our social relationships depend in large part on how others perceive us. **Impression management** is the process by which we seek to control how others perceive us. In this section, we consider some of the strategies used in managing the impressions that we make on others.

Tactics of Self-Presentation: Self-Enhancing and Ingratiation Strategies

impression management The process by which we seek to control how others perceive us.

Self-enhancing strategies are designed to improve the way we appear to others.[25] For example, "dressing for success" is a common tactic intended to make a positive impression. Having a neat and well-groomed image, how-

Table 3.2	**Impression Management Strategies**

We use various techniques to enhance ourselves in the eyes of others. Requesting feedback from others is one way to appear cooperative. Several common strategies used in requesting feedback are presented below.

Strategy	Example of the Use of This Tactic
Enhancement	"Everyone thinks this is great! What do you think?"
Entitlement	"This took me hours to put together. What do you think?"
Excuses	"I was only given two hours to put this together. What do you think?"

ever, is far more important than wearing expensive attire. You should also avoid wearing excessive perfume or cologne. Noticeable amounts may create a negative reaction—have you ever been stuck in an elevator with a person who reeks of cologne or perfume?

One interesting self-enhancement strategy involves requesting feedback from others. Seeking advice is often viewed as cooperative. The method by which you ask for feedback, however, is complicated and related to other self-enhancing strategies. It involves predicting how others will react to your requests. **Enhancement strategies** involve including statements of others' positive reactions along with your requests for feedback; for example, "John loved this idea. What do you think?" **Entitlement strategies** are designed to enhance the credit you receive for positive outcomes. Saying things like "I worked really hard on this project. What do you think?" makes it clear that you were responsible for the quality of the project and are entitled to the fruits of your labor. On the other hand, **excuses** are meant to reduce your perceived responsibility for negative outcomes. Table 3.2 summarizes these strategies.

In contrast to these impression management tactics, **ingratiation strategies** are motivated by the desire to get along with others. They enhance another person's view of you by increasing the extent to which the person likes you. Flattery and undeserved praise are common forms of ingratiation. Doing favors for a person and indicating your agreement with the other's opinions are also common.

Although these forms of self-presentation may be useful, use caution when deploying them: Excessive use of these strategies can backfire. You may be perceived as a braggart or "wimp" and may be disliked as a result of self-enhancing tactics. You may also be seen as a "brownnose," making a negative impression by using ingratia-

enhancement strategies Impression management techniques that involve including statements of praise from others along with requests for feedback.

entitlement strategies Impression management techniques that involve enhancing the credit received for positive outcomes.

excuses Impression management techniques designed to reduce the impression of responsibility for negative outcomes.

ingratiation strategies Impression management techniques that are motivated by the desire to get along with others.

Ethics at Work

Self-Presentation in the Workplace: A Case Study

Kawanda has been working at her new job with Temple for a little more than a month. She's gone far in this short period of time. Her new boss really likes her. She sees Kawanda as a hard-working and cooperative new employee. She also likes the way Kawanda shows respect for her position and authority. Every day, Kawanda praises her boss for her innovative ideas, brings her coffee, and comments on her business suit. But, if the truth was known, Kawanda's boss would have a different opinion. In reality, Kawanda dislikes her job, thinks her boss is a "hick," and loathes the small town she feels "stuck in." She's just biding her time until something better comes along.

1. How would you characterize Kawanda's behavior?
2. Do you think this behavior is appropriate in the workplace?
3. Do you think that Kawanda is wrong for acting as if she likes her job when she doesn't?
4. How do you think her boss would react if she knew Kawanda's true feelings?
5. What would you do if you were in a similar position?
6. We all engage in self-presentation. What, if anything, makes some types of self-presentation wrong and other types right?

tion. In addition, you might want to consider the ethics involved in presenting a false view of yourself through overindulgence in self-presentation (refer to the *Ethics at Work* section).

Guidelines for Effective Human Relations

Using What You've Learned

In this chapter we have examined a broad range of principles about perception. Although few rules apply to every situation, there are some general guidelines suggested by the various findings we have discussed. These are summarized on page 85 for your consideration. Remember, no rule works 100 percent in every situation. However, these guidelines should help you make better judgments and create more positive impressions.

Guidelines for Effective Human Relations (continued)

- Because perception is selective, keep in mind that others may not see things the way that you do. The motives and past experiences of others are not the same as yours. Try to consider the perspective of other people when disagreements arise. You may find that considering their viewpoint helps avoid unnecessary conflict—and you may benefit from their experience.

- Vivid and salient stimuli are more likely to attract attention and are often seen as more important. This principle applies to our perceptions of people as well. For example, we're likely to assume that the person who talks the most at a meeting is more responsible than reserved individuals. Don't let yourself fall into mindless judgments based on this illusion. Think about who is actually the best person for a critical assignment and ignore "glitz" when making an important personnel decision.

- The way other people perceive us in the workplace is a critical factor in our success. Keep in mind the various impression formation strategies we discussed. But don't overdo it; the overuse of these strategies can boomerang and create a negative impression. The best approach is to present a competent, neat, and well-groomed image. Have respect for yourself, and treat others with respect and courtesy.

- The attributions others make about the reasons for our behavior have important consequences. In performance evaluations, people give a special edge to effort. Keeping your effort at visibly high levels may help you attain high evaluations.

- Try to avoid the common errors in perceiving people. Remember that the fundamental attribution error can lead you to expect others to behave more consistently than is justified. Therefore, don't be surprised when others act "out of character."

- Self-serving biases can lead to needless conflict. Be sensitive to the fact that there is a natural tendency to take credit for success and assign blame for failure to others.

- First impressions are definitely important! Remember that halo effects are common and powerful. Before an important first meeting, spend some time planning your self-presentation strategy. Be cognizant of the impression you make on others.

- Before a job interview, practice effective nonverbal behavior, and try to use it to your advantage during an interview. For best results, combine it with clear evidence of competence.

Of course, this is not an exhaustive list of the possible pointers you could glean from this chapter. Nevertheless, you may find these suggestions useful. Perception is a process that is basic to day-to-day functioning. Your awareness of how this process operates can only be beneficial.

Summary

Contrary to common sense, we do not come to know the world around us in a simple or direct manner. Rather, we construct a picture of it through an active and complex process of perception. Perception is selective—we pay more attention to certain stimuli or events than to others. Perception is also organized—it depends on various characteristics of the stimuli in the environment.

Social perception involves our attempts to understand the people with whom we come in contact. One key aspect of such perception is attribution—the process through which we seek knowledge of the causes for others' behavior. A basic task in attribution is deciding whether other persons act the way they do because of internal or external causes. Our decision in this respect can have important effects on our evaluation of others.

Social perception is subject to a number of errors. For example, we tend to overestimate the importance of internal factors that shape others' behavior (the fundamental attribution error). A second error involves our tendency to take credit for success but to avoid blame for failure (the self-serving bias). Social perception is also subject to the halo effect; our overall impressions of another person affect or distort our evaluation of his or her specific traits or actions. In addition, our evaluation of a particular person is affected by other people we have recently encountered—the contrast effect.

Errors in social perception are important because they can lead us to make false conclusions about others and, as a result, can reduce both morale and productivity in work settings. For example, social perception affects the outcomes of job interviews, where the ratings assigned to applicants are often influenced by such factors as the nonverbal cues they emit. In addition, social perception represents an important influence on the ways we evaluate the performance of others. The reasons we assign to a person's success or failure influence our assessment of the person. We actively manage the impressions we make on other people and thus influence the way we are perceived by others. Several tactics of impression management have been identified including ways of self-enhancing through feedback requests and ingratiation strategies. In summary, perception is an important dimension of behavior in the workplace.

Key Terms

enhancement strategies, p. 83

entitlement strategies, p. 83

excuses, p. 84

figure-ground relationship, p. 64

fundamental attribution error, p. 78

halo effect, p. 79

heuristics, p. 73

illusory correlation, p. 73

impression formation, p. 72

impression management, p. 82

ingratiation strategies, p. 84

law of proximity, p. 64

law of similarity, p. 64

perception, p. 62

perceptual organization, p. 63

representativeness heuristic, p. 73

salience, p. 67

self-serving bias, p. 79

social perception, p. 63

Experiential Exercise

Forming First Impressions: What's in a Face?

Often we form impressions of people based on limited information, such as how they look, talk, or dress. To check on such impressions, we have provided pictures of four young men. Based on these pictures, give your impressions of the men. Indicate on the items below the extent to which you think the person has the characteristic listed by circling the number that best represents your impression. For example, if you think the person looks very intelligent, you would circle 1; if you think he is highly lacking in intelligence, you would circle 7; if you think he has average intelligence, you would circle 4.

Intelligent	1	2	3	4	5	6	7	Lacks intelligence
Honest	1	2	3	4	5	6	7	Dishonest
Warm	1	2	3	4	5	6	7	Cold

Compare your ratings with those made by another student. Do your general impressions agree with this person's? If they do, why do you think this agreement occurs? If some major discrepancies arise, how do you interpret them? On which trait is there the most agreement? Why is there more agreement for this trait than for the others? You might ask your teacher to collect the ratings of all members of your class so that scores can be obtained and used as another basis for discussion. Whatever the results, you will most likely find considerable agreement on one or two of the traits. If simply looking at pictures can create such a strong impression, just think how much more powerful this force is likely to be in everyday interactions.

Notes

1. Neuberg, S. L., & Fiske, S. T. (1987). Motivational influences on impression formation: Outcome dependency, accuracy-driven attention, and individuating processes. *Journal of Personality and Social Psychology, 53,* 431–444.

2. Harvey, J. H., Yarkin, K. L., Lightner, J., & Town, J. P. (1980). Unsolicited interpretation and recall of interpersonal events. *Journal of Personality and Social Psychology, 38,* 551–568.

3. Fiske, S. T., & Taylor, S. E. (1991). *Social cognition* (2nd ed.). New York: McGraw-Hill.

4. [Fiske, 1991.] See note 3.

5. Srull, T. K., & Wyer, R. S., Jr. (1989). Person memory and judgment. *Psychological Review, 96,* 58–83.

6. Klein, S. B., & Loftus, J. (1988). The nature of self-referent encoding: The contributions of elaborative and organizational processes. *Journal of Personality and Social Psychology, 55,* 5–11.

7. Devine, P. G., Sedikides, C., & Fuhrman, R. W. (1989). Goals in social information processing: The case of anticipated interaction. *Journal of Personality and Social Psychology, 56,* 680–690.

8. Tversky, A., & Kahneman, D. (1974). Judgment under uncertainty: Heuristics and biases. *Science, 185,* 1124–1131.

9. Hamilton D. L., & Rose, T. L. (1980). Illusory correlation and the maintenance of stereotypic beliefs. *Journal of Personality and Social Psychology, 39,* 832–845.

10. Pryor, J. B., & Stoller, L. M. (1994). Sexual cognition processes in men high in the likelihood to sexually harass. *Personality and Social Psychology Bulletin, 20,* 163–169.

11. Wong, P., & Weiner, B. (1981). When people ask "why" questions, and the heuristics of attributional search. *Journal of Personality and Social Psychology, 40,* 650–663.

12. Knowlton, W. A., Jr., & Mitchell, T. R. (1980). Effects of causal attributions on a supervisor's evaluation of subordinate performance. *Journal of Applied Psychology, 65,* 459–466.

13. Johnson, J. T., Jemmott, J. B. III, & Pettigrew, T. F. (1984). Causal attribution and dispositional inference: Evidence of inconsistent judgments. *Journal of Experimental Social Psychology, 20,* 567–585.

14. Mullen, B., & Riordan, C. A. (1988). Self-serving attributions for performance in naturalistic settings: A meta-analytic review. *Journal of Applied Social Psychology, 18,* 3–22.

15. Greenberg, J., Pyszczynski, T., & Solomon S. (1982). The self-serving attributional bias: Beyond self-presentation. *Journal of Experimental Social Psychology, 18,* 56–67.

16. See note 14.

17. Fisicaro, S. A. (1988). A reexamination of the relation between halo error and accuracy. *Journal of Applied Social Psychology, 73,* 239–244.

18. Schmitt, N. (1976). Social and situational determinants of interview decisions: Implications for the employment interview. *Personnel Psychology, 29,* 79–101.

19. Binning, J. F., Goldstein, M. A., Garcia, M. F., & Scattaregia, J. H. (1988). Effects of preinterview impressions on questioning strategies in same and opposite sex employment interviews. *Journal of Applied Psychology, 73,* 30–37.

20. Gifford, R., Ng, C. F., & Wilkinson, M. (1985). Nonverbal cues in the employment interview: Links between applicant qualities and interviewer judgments. *Journal of Applied Psychology, 70 (4),* 729–736.

21. Imada, A. S., & Hakel, M. D. (1977). Influence of nonverbal communication and rater proximity on impressions and decisions in simulated employment interviews. *Journal of Applied Psychology, 62,* 295–300.

22. Rasmussen, K. G., Jr. (1984). Nonverbal behavior, verbal behavior, resume credentials, and selection interview outcomes. *Journal of Applied Psychology, 69,* 551–556.

23. Riggio, R. E., & Throckmorton, B. (1988). The relative effects of verbal and nonverbal behavior,

appearance, and social skills on evaluations made in hiring interviews. *Journal of Applied Social Psychology, 18,* 331–348.

24. Baron, R. A. (1986). Self-presentation in job interviews: When there can be "too much of a good thing." *Journal of Applied Social Psychology, 16,* 16–28.

25. Baron, R. A. (1989). Impression management by applicants during employment interviews: The "too much of a good thing" effect. In R. W. Eder & G. R. Ferris (eds.), The employment interview: Theory, research, and practice. Newbury Park, CA: Sage.

Chapter 4

Major Approaches to Personality

Personality Anatomy: The Search for
Basic Traits
Learning-Oriented Theories of
Personality: Experience as a Basis
for Uniqueness
Humanistic Theories of Personality:
Accent on Growth
Cognition and Personality

Personality: Its Impact in Work Settings

The Type A/Type B Dimension: Who
Succeeds and Who Survives
Achievement Motivation: The Quest
for Excellence

The Self-Concept: The Importance of How We See Ourselves

Self-Concept: How Does It Develop?
Self-Esteem: Some Major Effects
Self-Concept: Gender Differences?
Self-Concept: Cross-Cultural Differences?

Personality Testing in the Workplace

Measuring Interests and Aptitudes:
Making the Right Career Choice
Screening, Training, and Development

Special Sections

Balancing Work and Family
Job Sharing: Do You Have the Personality
That Fits?

Human Relations in Action
Assessing Your Own Self-Concept

Ethics at Work
Personality Testing in the Workplace

Guidelines for Effective Human Relations
Using What You've Learned

SELF AND PERSONALITY

Understanding How and Why Individuals Differ

Learning Objectives

After reading this chapter, you should be able to:

1. Define personality and indicate why it is relevant to human relations.

2. Describe the trait, learning, humanistic, and cognitive approaches to personality.

3. Summarize the major characteristics of Type A and Type B individuals and indicate how these traits affect people's work and personal lives.

4. Explain how achievement motivation influences organizational behavior.

5. Explain what self-concept is and how self-concept develops.

6. Discuss cross-cultural and gender differences in the self-concept.

7. Discuss how personality testing is used in the workplace.

"*I*n a sense, jobs have personalities. Some require people who are a little more extraverted, some require those who are a little less extraverted. We want to make sure we are making the right matches." This quote is from Chuck Gaskin, Senior Vice President of Workforce Development at Branch Banking & Trust Company, of Winston-Salem, North Carolina.[1] It reflects a basic fact about success in the workplace: It is important that a person's personality matches the "personality" of the job.*

*M*aking the statement quoted above is one thing; following through on it is another. As you probably realize, human beings differ from one another in a limitless number of ways—from purely physical traits, such as height and eye color, through complex attitudes and values. A logical question therefore arises: Which of these differences are the most important—the most worthy of our attention? To study these differences scientifically, we need to be specific about what we mean by *personality*. Personality psychologists typically define **personality** as those feelings, thoughts, desires, and tendencies toward behavior that contribute to a person's individuality.

In keeping with this view, we will focus on several aspects of personality in this chapter. First, we consider a few contrasting views of personality—efforts to account for the wide range of differences among individuals. Second, we examine key work-related traits—ones that exert important effects on human behavior and human relations in work settings. Third, we address both the nature and impact of self-concept—the individual's private picture of his or her own unique traits. Finally, we discuss the role of various motives on behavior in work settings.

*M*AJOR APPROACHES TO PERSONALITY

Personality Anatomy: The Search for Basic Traits

How would you describe your best friend, your parents, your boss, or your most annoying coworker? Your list of characteristics is likely to be a long one—hundreds of ways exist to describe personality. The goal of the first theory of personality we discuss in this chapter—the trait approach—is to identify the most basic or important traits that characterize people and guide their behavior.

Gordon Allport, one of the most influential trait theorists, spent his career looking for the personality units that guide a person's actions.[2] He proposed that three kinds of traits serve this function.[3] **Cardinal traits**—traits that totally dominate a person's personality—are

personality The unique pattern of traits and behaviors that define each individual.

cardinal traits Rare traits that, when they occur, dominate a person's personality.

quite rare. Individuals who possess cardinal traits are often renowned for such characteristics, as was the case for Machiavelli, the famous philosopher. More attention has been placed on **central traits**—the relatively small number of traits that are highly characteristic of a person (for example, you might describe your mother as warm, kind, and nurturing). We might mention these traits in a letter of recommendation. All persons have a few central traits (usually between three and ten) that define aspects of their personality. The third type of traits, called **secondary traits,** are less conspicuous than central traits and are limited in their influence. Specific attitudes and tastes, such as a preference for chocolate versus vanilla ice cream, are examples of secondary traits.

We can think about traits in two ways. First, we can see traits as dimensions that allow us to compare one person with another (for example, she is friendlier than he is). This approach allows us to make relative judgments about ourselves and others. Second, we can consider how a person's traits make her unique from all others without inviting comparison. That is, the constellation of a person's traits defines her individuality. Both these viewpoints are appropriate. The study of personality requires understanding what we have in common as human beings as well as what makes us unique. We now turn our attention to the dimensions of personality that we all share.

Adult Personality Traits: The "Big Five."   A considerable amount of research has focused on identifying the basic dimensions of adult personality. Researchers agree that adults use five primary factors to describe their own and others' personalities: extroversion, agreeableness, conscientiousness, emotional stability, and openness (see Table 4.1 on page 94 for a summary of these factors).[4] These dimensions are so pervasive that they have been termed the **Big Five.** They occur across different cultures and languages, across gender, and across different occupations.[5,6] A major study that followed hundreds of men and women for six years found that both self- and spouse-personality ratings stayed remarkably stable over time.[7] These data strongly suggest that the five factors represent basic dimensions of personality.

The Big Five approach does not lack its critics. Disagreement has arisen about the structure of the Big Five.[8] Some researchers have found differences across cultures regarding how people describe personality. For example, Americans tend to use trait descriptors, like those found in the Big Five, whereas Indians tend to describe persons in action-based terms.[9] Another important criticism relates to the origins of the Big Five dimensions. Where do they come from? Why do we highlight these five dimensions? It has been suggested that an evolutionary basis underlies our propensity for judging people according to these dimensions.[10] For example, it may be argued that these dimensions provide important clues about a person's fitness as a potential partner or mate. This position is considered controversial, however, and the issue continues to inspire debate.

central traits   The relatively small number of traits that are highly characteristic of a person.

secondary traits   Relatively inconspicuous characteristics of people that are limited in influence.

Big Five   Basic personality dimensions identified as universal in human nature. They are extroversion, agreeableness, conscientiousness, emotional stability, and openness.

| *Table 4.1* | **Adult Personality: The "Big Five" Factors** |

Observer and self ratings of personality consistently reveal these five dimensions.

Dimensions of Adult Personality

I. Extroversion/ Introversion	II. Agreeableness/ Antagonism	III. Conscientiousness/ Undirectness
Outgoing ➡ Shy	Easy-going ➡ Hard to get along with	Dependable ➡ Undependable

IV. Emotional Stability/ Instability	V. Openness/ Reservedness	
Secure ➡ Insecure	Adventurous ➡ Unadventurous	

Adapted from McCrea & Costa, 1987; see note 7.

Even if the Big Five dimensions are intrinsic to personality, the importance of each factor may vary across contexts. Studies by Williams and his colleagues suggest that this variation is quite prevalent.[11] When subjects rated the importance of each of these factors in their personal relationships, "agreeableness" was rated as the most important factor. In contrast, "conscientiousness" was the most important factor when ratings were made in a work context. Thus certain aspects of personality may be more important than others in work settings. Later in this chapter, we discuss other traits that seem especially important in the world of work.

Learning-Oriented Theories of Personality: Experience as a Basis for Uniqueness

The learning-oriented view of personality implies that your personality is the sum total of all your experiences. Thus personality does not include traits or characteristics such as unconscious motives or drives. Rather, we are what we learn. Our uniqueness stems from the fact that we all have different experiences and therefore have learned different patterns of behavior.

To adequately explain this learning-oriented approach, we must first define *learning*. Generally, **learning** refers to any permanent change in behavior induced through experience. Thus, any time your behavior is altered in a relatively lasting way by some experience you have had—that is, interaction with the social or physical world around you—learning has occurred. How can this process account for the development of each of the hun-

learning   The process through which lasting changes in behavior are made through experience with the world.

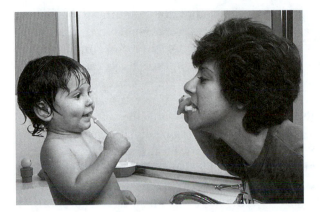

 Learning Approaches to Personality

According to this view, the child in this photo is learning to be competent and ambitious by interacting with this caregiver.

dreds of specific traits possessed by human beings? The answer is complicated, because several different types of learning exist, each of which can play an important role with respect to any given trait.

For example, one type of learning, known as *instrumental conditioning,* occurs when individuals learn to perform behaviors that yield desirable outcomes (for example, praise, money, success) or help them avoid undesirable results (for example, failure, cold, hunger).[12] Instrumental conditioning plays an important role in the formation of many traits. To illustrate this role, consider two children: One is consistently praised by his parents for showing ambition and initiative; the other is consistently criticized for competing with others or trying to "show them up." How will the two children differ as adults? Many factors contribute to the answer, but the chances are good that the first child will be active and high in achievement motivation, while the second will be passive and unambitious (see Figure 4.1).

The learning-oriented view suggests that various forms of learning may underlie even complex human characteristics. People are strongly shaped by their experiences. Thus, according to this approach, the sum total of these effects may constitute the underlying foundations of personality.

Humanistic Theories of Personality: Accent on Growth

A third group of theorists has adopted a sharply different view of personality, one known as the humanistic perspective.[13] Humanistic theories place great emphasis on positive aspects of personality. They suggest that humans possess strong tendencies toward growth and are actively motivated to maximize their personal freedom and potential. Only when environmental conditions block these growth tendencies do personal difficulties arise.

This idea has exerted a strong effect on the field of human relations. We will return to it—and to specific humanistic theories—at several points in this book. For the moment, however, we will simply call attention to some major implications of this point of view. First, according to the humanistic approach, we cannot hope to understand people or predict their behavior from knowledge of the objective conditions around them. Such observation is helpful, but it is not enough. Second, we must understand individuals' subjective points of view—how they interpret and understand their experiences. Third, and perhaps most important, the humanistic perspective takes a very optimistic view about the capacity of humans to accept responsibility, acquire new skills, and behave in constructive ways. Because individuals are strongly motivated to attain maximum growth and freedom, they will, if given a chance, continue to improve in many different ways. Thus the humanistic approach holds much appeal for many members of the human relations field.

Cognition and Personality

The final approach we discuss in this chapter represents an outgrowth of research in many areas of psychology, including cognitive psychology, learning, and motivation. Many viable theories can be labeled as "cognitive theories." This section provides an overview of the general assumptions made by this approach.

Cognitive-oriented views assume that our ideas about the world guide our perceptions, thoughts, and behaviors. We discussed this idea in some detail in Chapter 3. In applying this concept to personality, these theorists assume cognitive processes, such as memory and attention, work together with aspects of our personality to produce individuality.

One of the first and most influential of the cognitive-oriented approaches is Mischel's cognitive social learning theory. He claims that individual differences in personality can be described in terms of five "person variables":[14]

1. **Cognitive and behavioral competencies.** These variables relate to individuals' mental abilities and behavioral skills. IQ, social skills, and occupational abilities are all examples of these competencies.

2. **Encoding strategies and personal constructs.** This person variable includes individuals' ideas about their world and how it should be categorized (for example, what things belong together). It also includes individuals' beliefs about themselves, such as their ideas about their own capabilities. Other beliefs about oneself, such as "I am an outgoing person," would be included in this category as well.

3. **Subjective stimulus value.** This concept refers to the value that people assign to different outcomes. For example, for a working couple with children, day care may be a highly valued outcome of working for a particular company,

whereas this option may hold little value for an older worker whose children are in college.

4. **Self-regulatory systems and plans.** This concept refers to the knowledge that people have about the kinds of actions or strategies used in controlling their environment and their thoughts. For example, the use of delayed gratification strategies by children who give up an immediate small reward so as to obtain a larger reward at a later time is an example of a self-regulating system.

5. **Affects.** This final variable refers to the emotions and feelings we have that influence our information-processing and coping behaviors. This construct was recently added to Mischel's theory[15] and captures the "hot" nature of our thoughts and personality.

In Mischel's theory, these person variables work together to determine how we select information in our environment (attention), how we think about our world, and how we behave. The fact that people differ in terms of these person variables accounts for individual differences in our thoughts and behavior (see Figure 4.2).

Figure 4.2   **Mischel's Cognitive Social Learning Theory**

This theory proposes that individual differences in these person variables determine the way people think about and behave in their environments.

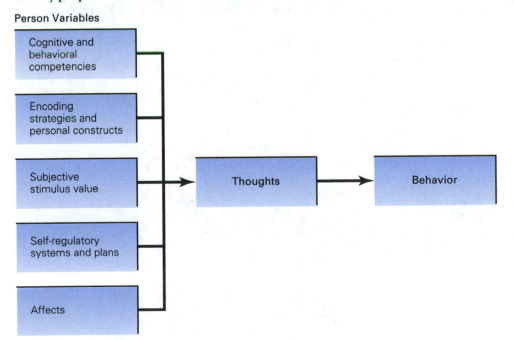

PERSONALITY: ITS IMPACT IN WORK SETTINGS

During your career, you will encounter hundreds of people. These individuals will differ from one another in countless ways. Obviously, not all of these differences affect behavior or human relations in work settings; only some have major importance in this regard. But which ones? Actually, this issue creates a tricky question, for the specific characteristics that are of greatest importance can vary widely with the type of work being performed. For example, having an outgoing, friendly personality may be closely linked to one's success in the sales field but probably has far less impact on one's performance as an accountant. Similarly, the ability to estimate length or weight may contribute to success among carpenters but has little bearing on the productivity of librarians. This variability in job requirements partly explains the increasing popularity of personality testing in the workplace. Some traits, however, have important effects on work-related behavior in a wide range of contexts. We now focus on these dimensions. (See the *Balancing Work and Family* section for discussion of the personality types that best fit in job-sharing programs.)

Balancing Work and Family

Job Sharing: Do You Have the Personality That Fits?

Job sharing is a form of part-time employment in which one position is filled by two part-time employees. For persons who cannot or do not want to commit to a full-time position but still desire to work outside the home, this kind of arrangement can provide a solution for balancing work and family. Employees, managers, and organizations can all benefit from these kinds of working arrangements. From the organizational perspective, job sharing is beneficial in that it provides the organization with the talents of two unique individuals. It also decreases the "bottom-line" cost of providing extensive overtime salary. From the employees' perspective, job sharing allows more time for children, caring for aging parents or ill family members, leisure, or the pursuit of educational opportunities. Managers or supervisors benefit from greater flexibility in managing, such as establishing work teams to meet workload surges.

This kind of arrangement is not suitable for everyone, however. The experience of people who have been a part of job-sharing teams suggests that the following characteristics are necessary. First, the job sharer must be a good communicator—effective communication between job-sharing partners is of paramount importance. Second, the job sharer must be willing to consult and cooperate—he or she must be

The Type A/Type B Dimension: Who Succeeds and Who Survives

Consider all of the people you have known. Can you recall who always seemed to work under pressure, was hard-driving and competitive, and was impatient and aggressive? Can you think of someone who showed the opposite pattern—an individual who was generally relaxed and easygoing, sociable, and not very competitive? The two persons you have in mind represent contrasting patterns of behavior labeled, respectively, the Type A and Type B personality dimensions[16] (see Figure 4.3 on page 100). Although these patterns are clearly extremes on a continuous dimension, most people fall into one category or the other.[17] Specifically, approximately 40 percent of the population shows a Type A personality, and 60 percent demonstrates Type B characteristics.

Obviously, the differences between Type A and Type B people have important implications for behavior in work settings. For example, hard-driving, competitive individuals act very differently than relaxed, easygoing ones while performing many jobs.[18] Type A and Type B persons also differ in other key respects that are less apparent. The most important of these differences involves personal health and social relations.

able to see himself or herself as a part of a team, rather than a loner in the job. Third, the job sharer must be very flexible and have the ability to deal with changing circumstances. In contrast to other kinds of positions, a job sharer does not have the same degree of control. So flexibility is a must! Fourth, the job sharer must be highly committed to the job and to making the job-sharing arrangements work.

Although this arrangement can work very well, it's not for everyone. Be sure to do some intensive and honest introspection into your personality before you make such a switch!

There are also some practical matters to consider. What financial issues should you consider when thinking about such a switch? The impact of reductions in pay must be understood, as well as considerations such as increased health insurance premiums. Discuss these issues with your supervisor and make sure that you fully understand all of the consequences. Be aware that all of your benefits will most likely be prorated if you move to part-time status.

Source: Based on suggestions in *Balancing Work and Family Demands Through Part-time Employment and Job Sharing* (Sept. 1995), United States Office of Personnel Management.

Type A Behavior: A Humorous Example

I think we can safely assume that this man is a Type A.

Take a break, Marvin! Take a break!!

From *Wishful Thinking* by David Sipress, p. 84. Copyright © 1987 by David Sipress. Reprinted by permission of HarperCollins, Inc.

The Type A Pattern and Health.   Initial research interest in the Type A/Type B dimension was inspired by an unsettling finding: People with the Type A cluster of traits appear to be more than twice as likely as those with the Type B cluster to experience serious heart disease.[19] The former individuals are also more likely to suffer a second heart attack if the first one does not prove fatal. In short, Type A individuals may pay a high price for their high-pressure lifestyle.

Additional findings help explain this phenomenon. Quite simply, Type A people respond to stress by developing more pronounced physiological reactions than do Type B individuals.[20] This fact was illustrated clearly in an investigation by Hill and her colleagues.[21] They studied the behavior of first-year medical students at three intervals: during a vacation period, during a stressful examination period, and during a second vacation period. They found that several of the typical components of Type A behavior (for example, loud, explosive speech and short response latency) increased among Type A people during the high-stress examination period (refer to Figure 4.4). Type A individuals also showed larger increases in resting heart rate than Type B students during the examination period. Apparently, during periods of stress, Type A people subject their cardiovascular systems to greater wear and tear. As the competitive, hard-driving style of Type A individuals often leads them to seek out stress-inducing challenges, it is far from surprising that their health suffers.

Type A Behavior under Stress Increased in Intensity

First-year medical students classified as Type A showed more components of the Type A behavior patterns during a high-stress examination period than during vacation periods that preceded and followed such stress.

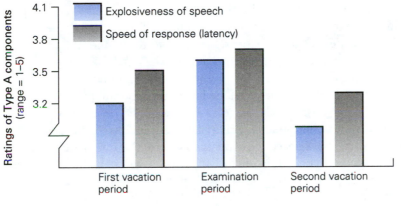

Based on data from Hill et al., 1987; see note 21.

The Type A Pattern and Performance.   Earlier, we noted that Type A and Type B people differ with respect to performance. Let's return to this important point. At first, you might expect such differences to be quite simple. Specifically, you might guess that Type A people, with their hard-driving, competitive style will always (or at least usually) surpass Type B workers.[22] In reality, the situation is much more complex. On the one hand, Type A individuals work faster on many tasks than Type Bs, even when no pressure or deadline is involved. Also, Type A people often seek more challenge in their work and daily lives than Type Bs (for example, when given a choice, they select more difficult tasks than Type Bs).[23] On the other hand, Type Bs have the edge in some situations. For example, Type A individuals frequently do more poorly on tasks requiring patience and careful, considered judgment.[24] In such cases, they may be in too much of a hurry for their own good!

More importantly, surveys reveal that most members of top management have the Type B cluster of traits, not the Type A cluster.[25] Several factors probably contribute to this surprising finding. First, Type A individuals may not last long enough to rise to the highest management levels—the health risks described earlier tend to remove them from contention at an early age. Second, the impatience of the Type A individual may be incompatible with the skills needed by top-level executives. As you know, one of the key functions performed by such persons involves decision making; the decisions involved are also far from simple. To make them effective, executives must weigh a huge amount of information. Type A workers, because of their tendency to "rush, rush, rush," are not well suited for such tasks. Finally, the impatient, aggressive style of Type A individuals may lead them to make enemies, a factor that can count heavily against them when the possibility of promotion to top-level jobs arises.

Modifications of the Type A/Type B Dimension: Four Types Rather Than Two?

Recently, researchers have refined the distinction between Type A and Type B personalities. It now appears that variations exist within the Type A and Type B categories.[26] Not all Type A people are impatient, hostile, and tense, and not all Type B individuals are calm and relaxed. Rather, some persons classified as Type A are fast-moving and charismatic, while some Type Bs are tense and inhibited.

Friedman and his colleagues have developed a more elaborate picture of these characteristics (see Figure 4.5).[27] They suggest that the quality of a person's emotional adjustment, as well as the person's activity level, should be considered within this typology. For example, fast-paced individuals who are emotionally well adjusted may be charismatic, while "hyper" individuals with poor emotional adjustment may be hostile. Research suggests that individuals with poor emotional adjustment are prone to illness regardless of their activity level.[28] Thus the emerging picture indicates that tension and impatience are the components of personality that may put us at risk. These aspects are not immune to change; when we find ourselves becoming too uptight, we owe it to ourselves and others to find ways to relax (see Table 4.2).

Table 4.2   Suggestions for Controlling "Type A" Tendencies

We have learned that Type A behavior patterns are not desirable, and may even be deadly. But how can we control these tendencies, if we have them? Here are some suggestions.

- Tell someone close to you that you have a goal to eliminate your negative attitude.
- Play to lose sometimes (even though you may find this hard to do!).
- Try to laugh at yourself and smile!
- Forget your perfectionist goals.
- Realize that you are not responsible for what other persons do.
- Record what irritates you and makes you angry. Then put these things in their proper perspective.

Adapted from Rosen, R. H. (1992). *The healthy company: Eight strategies to develop people, productivity, and profits.* New York: The Putnam Publishing Group.

Emotional Adjustment

	Good	Poor
High	▪ Charismatic ▪ Vigorous	▪ Hostile ▪ Impatient
Low	▪ Content ▪ Calm	▪ Tense ▪ Inhibited

Pace

See note 26.

Figure 4.5   **Modifications of Type A/Type B: Four Types or Two?**

Research by Friedman, Hall, and Harris (1985) suggests that emotional adjustment and pace combine to create four types of individuals.

Achievement Motivation: The Quest for Excellence

As its name suggests, **achievement motivation** (sometimes termed "the need for achievement") relates to the strength of an individual's desire to excel—to succeed at difficult tasks and to do them better than others. People rated high in such motivation share several characteristics.[29] First, they are task-oriented. That is, their major concern is accomplishing concrete goals; good relations with others are deemed of secondary importance. Second, they prefer situations involving moderate levels of risk or difficulty. Why does this preference for moderate risk arise among persons high in the achievement motive? The odds of success are good in situations involving moderate risk, but nevertheless sufficiently challenging to make the effort worthwhile. In contrast, persons low in achievement motivation tend to prefer situations involving either very low or very high levels of risk (see Figure 4.6 on page 104). With low risk, such people are almost certain to succeed; with high risk, they can attribute failure to external factors. Third, people high in achievement motivation strongly desire feedback on their performance. They can then adjust their goals to the current conditions and figure out when and to what degree they have succeeded.

Given their strong desire to excel, you would expect that persons who rate high in achievement motivation would attain greater success in their careers than individuals with lower ratings. To some extent, this statement is true; such individuals do gain promotions more rapidly than those low in motivation, at least early in their careers.[30] People with high achievement motivation may not always be good managers, however, for several reasons. First, they want to do everything themselves—they prefer not to delegate any responsibilities. This reluctance gets them into serious trouble in many organizations. Second, they desire immediate feedback on their work. Often, this response is unavailable, and its absence can interfere with their efficiency.

achievement motivation   The desire to attain standards of excellence and accomplish tasks more successfully than others.

Figure 4.6   **High Need Achievers Take Moderate Shots**

Research exploring need achievement often uses a variation of the situation depicted here. The general finding is that high need achievers tend to take shots a moderate distance from the basket whereas low need achievers shoot from either a very far or very close distance from the basket.

THE SELF-CONCEPT: THE IMPORTANCE OF HOW WE SEE OURSELVES

Suppose that you were asked to describe your most important traits—the ones that make you a unique individual and set you apart from all others. (Try this exercise in the *Human Relations in Action* section.) Would you find this task to be difficult? In all likelihood, you would not. The reason is simple: By the time we reach adulthood, most of us have a clearly developed self-concept; that is, we have a stable and (we believe) fairly accurate picture of our own personalities. We know—or think we know—whether we are bright or dull, attractive or unattractive, ambitious or complacent, and so on. Obviously, the images we hold of ourselves can exert major effects upon our lives. What is the source of these self-concepts? Are they generally accurate? And what are their effects? Research on self-concept has provided intriguing answers to these questions.

Self-Concept: How Does It Develop?

How do we come to know ourselves—to understand our own traits and characteristics? Your first answer might be that this understanding comes directly, by looking inward. This appealing solution is one accepted by most persons. After all, we have access to all of our thoughts, feelings, and behaviors, so combining them into a unified picture of ourselves should be a fairly simple task.

As it turns out, under very few instances can we come to know ourselves in this direct fashion. To understand why, consider the following question: How do you know whether you are engaging or boring? Can you tell by looking into a mirror, or by sitting in some corner and thinking quietly about yourself? Probably not. Rather, the best way

Human Relations in Action

Assessing Your Own Self-Concept

Everyone has a self-concept; of this there can be no doubt. But, as noted in this chapter, not everyone's self-concept is accurate. Some people have a good grasp of their major traits and characteristics: They see themselves much as others do. In contrast, other people's self-concepts are out of sync with their true traits or characteristics. This misperception can have serious consequences. How are your skills in this area? Is your self-concept largely accurate, or does it depart from reality in important ways? To get some preliminary insights into this crucial question, follow the procedure outlined below.

First, list on a piece of paper what you feel are your five most important traits. Then, ask at least ten people you know to do the same based on their perceptions of you. Try to get the help of friends, family, coworkers, and others—people who know you and see you regularly in different roles and contexts.

Now, compare the lists from these people with your own list. Score one point each time a trait on your own list was included by one of the people you approached. (Be sure to give yourself credit for synonyms. For example, if you described yourself as friendly, and one of the people you approached described you as sociable, score a point. Similarly, if you described yourself as ambitious and someone described you as achievement-oriented, score a point.)

If you attain a score of at least 20 (assuming you had ten people list your major traits), your self-concept is probably fairly accurate: Other people see you in the way you see yourself. If your score is 5 or less, though, there is a good chance your self-concept is inaccurate. If this is the case, you may want to give some careful thought to adjusting it to some degree.

Self-Concept: Its Basic Foundations

As shown here, our self-concept is based largely on information from four distinct sources: (1) social interaction, (2) social comparison, (3) social information, and (4) self-observation.

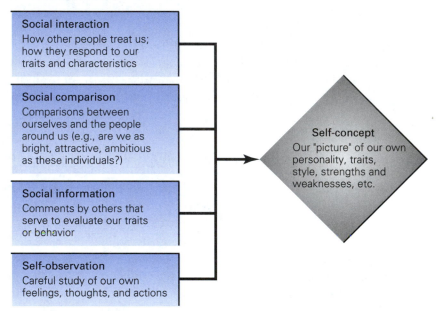

to answer this question would be through direct experience. Your interactions with the persons around you would provide the best clues. For instance, if others constantly seek your company, hang on your every word, and tell you that you are fascinating, you will probably conclude that you are, indeed, charming. If, in contrast, they cross the street to avoid conversations with you, yawn constantly as you speak to them, and tell you that you are dull, you will decide that you are not quite so charming.

In summary, contrary to what common sense suggests, we cannot really look inward to form an accurate self-concept. Rather, we usually must base our self-images on information provided by others. We can therefore state that our self-concept derives from four sources: (1) our social interactions with others, (2) comparisons of ourselves with others, (3) others' comments or statements about us, and (4) careful observations of our own feelings, thoughts, and behavior (see Figure 4.7).

Self-Esteem: Some Major Effects

Imagine two people who work for the same company. Both have similar personalities and similar job-related skills. One has a positive self-concept—he believes that he is a talented employee and a desirable human being. In short, this employee has high

self-esteem. In contrast, the other employee has a negative self-concept—he assumes that he is barely adequate in both departments. This individual possesses low self-esteem. Which one will do better work? A good guess is the employee with high self-esteem. Many studies indicate that, when individuals feel good about themselves (that is, have a positive self-concept), their morale, motivation, and productivity are all enhanced. When they hold a negative view of their self-worth, the opposite may be true.[31]

Unfortunately, this effect is only part of the total picture. Low self-esteem has other costs as well. One of the most important involves the ability of individuals to conduct an adequate job search. Research suggests that people who suffer from low self-esteem are far less effective in this crucial task than those who possess high self-esteem. Such effects are shown clearly in a study conducted by Ellis and Taylor.[32] These researchers measured the self-esteem of a large number of business school seniors, then examined the relationship between self-esteem and the success of the subjects in the actual job search. Results indicated that subjects low in self-esteem did more poorly than those high in this trait. They were less likely to make use of informal job sources (for example, friends and relatives) or sources requiring a high level of initiative (for example, direct application). As such sources are often helpful in placement, this reluctance proved a major drawback to these students. Similarly, low self-esteem individuals received lower ratings from interviewers both in interviews conducted on campus and at various companies, and they therefore received fewer job offers than those with high self-esteem.

As you can see, a negative self-concept can be costly. It can interfere with job satisfaction, motivation, performance—even with finding a good position. Thus it represents a serious problem for many persons. This fact leads to an important question: Can we help individuals suffering from low self-esteem? Fortunately, the answer seems to be yes. Assisting such people need not involve years of counseling. Instead, a growing body of evidence suggests that we can alleviate low self-esteem merely by inducing people to change how they attribute their outcomes. Often, low self-esteem people attribute successes to external causes—good luck or an easy task. In contrast, they attribute failures to internal causes ("I knew I really didn't have it in me"). If they can learn to view their failures as stemming from external causes and their successes as deriving from internal ones, their self-esteem can be improved (see Figure 4.8 on page 108).[33]

Self-Concept: Gender Differences?

Do men and women have different self-concepts? Surprisingly, little research has focused on answering this important question. Most research surrounding this issue has investigated differences between men and women in their levels of self-esteem. Although a few studies have found that men tend to have higher self-esteem than women, most research has demonstrated that self-esteem levels do not differ based on gender.[34]

> **self-esteem** An individual's positive or negative evaluation of himself or herself. A part of the self-concept.

Figure 4.8   **Self-Esteem and Attributions for Successes and Failures**

Persons low in self-esteem often demonstrate a pattern of attributions for successes and failures opposite to that of persons high in self-esteem. They blame themselves for negative outcomes and refuse to take credit for positive ones.

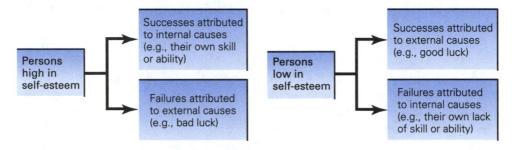

Even though men and women have similar levels of self-esteem, differences could potentially exist in their self-concepts. Men and women experience different patterns of social interaction from birth onward. For example, newborns who are given pink hair ribbons at birth are treated differently than newborns who are given blue ribbons. Because much of our self-concept derives from interactions with others (see the discussion in the previous section), these gender distinctions likely affect the development of our self-concepts in different ways. In particular, studies suggest that women are more likely than men to develop a collectivist self-concept—a self-concept in which relations with others are especially important in the formation of one's definition of self.[35] In contrast, men appear to develop an individualistic self-concept—a representation of the self as distinct from others. The origin of these differences has been debated. Some researchers have suggested that mothers and sons are likely to experience differences so as to facilitate separation from one another. Males therefore learn to emphasize and value differences. Conversely, mothers and daughters are likely to experience similarities and develop connections with one another. This emphasis may teach females to value connections and relationships. Still other researchers have argued that these differences in self-concept derive from the positions that men and women hold in society. Because women have relatively less power, they must constantly be responsive to other people. As a result, relationships become central to their self-concepts.[36]

individualistic self-concept   A cultural emphasis on defining one's self in terms of individual goals, desires, and characteristics, apart from one's group affiliations.

collectivist self-concept   A cultural emphasis on defining one's self as a part of a larger group or society.

Self-Concept: Cross-Cultural Differences?

Do differences in the self-concept exist across cultures? You already have some information about this issue. In Chapter 1, we discussed how cultures differ in terms of a **collectivist** versus **individualistic** orientation. This dis-

Table 4.3	**People Differ in Terms of Their Collectivist versus Individualist Orientation**

Cross-Cultural Variations

In a survey of IBM employees all over the world, the following cultural differences in orientation were found:

Collectivist Cultures	**Individualist Cultures**
Taiwan, Peru, Pakistan, Colombia, Venezuela	Australia, United States, United Kingdom, Canada, Netherlands

Intracultural Variations

Differences in orientation are also seen within the United States. Hispanics, Asians, and African Americans tend to be more collectivist than Anglo-Americans.

Sources: See notes 37 and 39.

tinction is especially relevant for understanding how personality may differ across cultures and within the same culture (see Table 4.3).

Recall that in individualistic cultures, such as the United States, the individual is most important. Members of such cultures tend to view the self as separate from the surrounding people and value individual prominence above all. In contrast, collectivist cultures, such as Japan, view the group as more important than the individual. To see an example of this difference, compare the American proverb, "the squeaky wheel gets the grease," with the Japanese proverb, "the nail that stands out gets pounded down."[37]

Some have argued that the boundary between the self and the world is fuzzy in a collectivist culture. For example, it has been suggested that members of the Indian collectivist culture do not have a sense of self as being separate from others.[38] In his interesting book *The Personality Puzzle*,[39] David Funder gives the example of the Japanese word for self, *jibun,* that is translated as "one's share of the shared life space." This definition captures an essential difference between collectivist versus individualist conceptions of the self.

PERSONALITY TESTING IN THE WORKPLACE

This chapter has discussed some of the ways that people differ from one another. Many of these differences are irrelevant—for instance, it makes no difference that our ears are different sizes. Other differences matter, however. Knowing our aptitudes and interests can be of value to us and to organizations that make hiring or placement decisions. This section considers how tests of these personality dimensions are used in the working world.

As we enter the twenty-first century, the use of psychological testing in the workplace is on the rise. In 1991, the Society for Human Resource Management surveyed companies about their selection processes and found that 36 percent used psychological tests as a part of their hiring procedure—a 14 percent increase over the 1985 estimate.[40] A survey conducted by the American Management Association (AMA) in 1998 found that nearly half (48 percent) of mid-sized or large companies use some form of psychological testing.[41] The trend toward greater implementation of these tests is clearly gaining momentum, and, although the use of these tests comes with some ethical questions (see the *Ethics at Work* section), chances are that you will be exposed to such tests sometime in your career.

Ethics at Work

Personality Testing in the Workplace

Everything had gone smoothly through one interview after another. Martina was sure that she had this job—and she felt lucky. Only a few members of her graduating class had found positions, and most of those jobs weren't all that great. This was a *good* position—assistant to the vice-president of a midsize company's marketing division. There would be lots of chances for advancement, and the pay was good.

As Mr. Cattell walked into the room, she was sure that he would offer her the job. "Everything looks very good so far, Martina. People were impressed with your resumé and your interviews. You seem like the kind of enthusiastic young woman that we need on our staff. There's just one more step to take before we make a decision. You'll need to fill out some questionnaires for us. Step this way, and I'll get them for you."

The "questionnaires" were a battery of psychological tests. As Martina read through the questions, she was faced with an ethical dilemma. Should she respond the way she thinks the employer would want her to respond, or should she answer the questions as honestly as possible?

1. What do you think Martina will do in this situation?
2. What would you do if you were in this situation?
3. Is there a difference between what you *would* do and what you think you *should* do?
4. What would be the consequences of not giving an honest picture of yourself? Would you feel guilty about it later? How might it affect your interactions within the company if you got the job?
5. What questions should you ask the test giver about the test?

Measuring Interests and Aptitudes: Making the Right Career Choice

Making the right choice about a career is difficult and a little scary. Although no sure way exists to predict whether a particular career is right for a specific individual, tools have been designed to provide some help in this regard.

Two types of psychological tests can be used in making a career decision—interest tests and aptitude tests. **Interest tests** measure an individual's preference for engaging in certain activities. Many interest tests have been developed, but the most common remains the Strong-Campbell Interest Inventory (SCII). This test measures the test taker's likes and dislikes for a wide range of activities. These responses are then compared to those of individuals in various fields of work. The more similar a person's responses are to those of individuals in a particular field, the more interest the test taker is assumed to have in that occupation. Individuals can use the results of this test to get some idea of their general interests and to identify specific occupations that might be of interest to them. Of course, this test should not serve as the sole basis for anyone's career choice.

Aptitude tests measure the test taker's capacity to benefit from certain types of training and indicate how well his or her abilities apply to a particular skill. For example, a person who has an aptitude for mechanical reasoning may benefit from training in engineering.

Because different jobs require different skills, obtaining information about your particular aptitudes can be helpful in making a career decision. Many aptitude tests are available. The General Aptitude Test Battery (GATB) measures several aptitudes at one time, including verbal ability, mathematical ability, motor coordination, and dexterity. As is the case with the SCII, an individual's scores on this test are compared to those of people who are successful within certain fields. The more closely an individual's score matches that of members of a specific field, the better the chance that person will be successful at the occupation. As you will see in the next section, many large companies have developed their own aptitude tests for use as screening devices.

Screening, Training, and Development

Aptitude tests are administered to see whether a potential employee has what it takes to do the job. Tests that measure assertiveness, courtesy, persistence, and other such qualities are used to assess whether an individual has a personality suited to, for example, putting up with complaining customers or making endless sales calls. Companies also use testing to find out about an individual's trustworthiness. This concern is especially important in jobs for which security is primary, such as banks and brokerage houses. Trustworthiness tests offer a way for

interest tests   Tests that measure an individual's preference for engaging in certain kinds of activities.

aptitude tests   Tests that measure a person's capacities to benefit from certain types of training.

companies to protect themselves. Incidentally, the use of lie-detector tests and drug tests is also becoming more common.

Interest and aptitude tests can range from brief, written questions to batteries of tests, such as the GATB. Higher-level positions generally require more extensive tests. In most cases, the test results are used in an appropriate manner, but they can be used improperly as a basis for employment discrimination. In the latter cases, the tests screen out groups of employees based on race, gender, disability, religion, or national origin.

When someone wants you to take an employment test, you should ask several questions. (Refer back to the *Ethics at Work* section on page 110 for further discussion of issues involved in taking these tests.) Find out (1) how the test relates to the job, (2) what feedback you will receive, (3) who will have access to the results, and (4) anything else of concern to you. If your potential employer refuses to answer these questions, seriously consider what this refusal says about the company.

Keep in mind that aptitude tests are not scored on the basis of a single response; the total pattern that emerges from a test is the important factor. A trained psychologist is best able to interpret the responses. In most cases, the test results remain highly confidential, and even you will not be able to see the results. Test results provide merely one kind of information about someone's potential, and they rarely serve as the exclusive (or even the primary) basis of hiring decisions. In addition, these tests can be as beneficial to you as to the employer; if the job does not match your interests and skills, then you will probably not be happy and successful in that work.

Guidelines for Effective Human Relations

Using What You've Learned

In this chapter we examined a broad range of principles and findings about personality. Although few rules apply to every situation, there are some general guidelines suggested by the various findings we have discussed. These are summarized below for your consideration. Remember, no rule works 100 percent in every situation. However, these guidelines should help improve your understanding of your personality as well as that of others.

■ If you are a parent (or if you intend to be some day), remember that the experiences you provide your child will shape his or her personality. It's especially important to keep in mind that your children will primarily learn by watching what you do—not by listening to what you say.

Guidelines for Effective Human Relations (continued)

- Although a great deal of our personality may be shaped by forces outside of our control, we *can* change. Strive for growth in your life, and be open to new skills and responsibilities.

- Strive to match the Type B personality profile. Your health, career, and interpersonal relationships will benefit.

- Take advantage of the interest and aptitude tests available to you. They can be valuable tools.

- Try to incorporate a positive view into your self-concept. This is especially true for success experiences. If you tend to assume your success is due to luck, avoid this tendency and accept your achievements as indications of your talent and effort.

Summary

Personality refers to the unique pattern of traits and behaviors that set each individual apart from others; this pattern remains relatively stable over time. Many theories have been advanced to account for differences in individuals' personalities. According to one such theory, the learning-oriented approach, individuals' unique experiences with the world around them account for the differences among persons. The humanistic approach emphasizes the growth potential in human nature. Trait approaches emphasize the basic units of personality. The cognitive approach emphasizes the way our thoughts and perceptions influence our personalities.

Several specific characteristics appear to be closely linked to behavior and relations in the workplace. One of these is the Type A/Type B personality dimension. Another is achievement motivation. Achievement motivation plays an important role in work situations. People high in achievement motivation have a strong desire to excel but do not necessarily make good managers.

Each of us has a self-concept—a picture of our own traits and personality. This self-concept is acquired largely from our interactions with others and from the information about us that those interactions provide. Differences have been noted in the self-concepts of men and women, and cultural differences have been identified as well. These differences are due, in part, to the divergent patterns of social interaction we experience. A positive self-concept is important for success in both work and social contexts.

Personality testing is becoming common in the workplace. Aptitude and interest tests are given to aid individuals in making the appropriate career choices. In addition, testing is used for employee screening, training, and development.

Key Terms

achievement motivation, p. 103

aptitude tests, p. 111

Big Five, p. 93

cardinal traits, p. 92

central traits, p. 93

collectivist self-concept, p. 108

individualistic self-concept, p. 108

interest tests, p. 111

learning, p. 94

personality, p. 92

secondary traits, p. 93

self-esteem, p. 107

Notes

1. Kamen, R. (1997). Psych selection. *Journal of Business Strategy, 18,* 22–27.

2. Allport, G. W. (1966). Traits revisited. *American Psychologist, 21,* 1–10.

3. Allport, G. W. (1937). *Personality: A psychological interpretation.* New York: Holt.

4. McCrae, R. R., & Costa, P. T., Jr. (1987). Validation of the five-factor model of personality across instruments and observers. *Journal of Personality and Social Psychology, 52,* 81–90.

5. John, O. P. (1990). The "Big Five" factory taxonomy: Dimensions of personality in the natural language and in questionnaires. In L. A. Pervin (ed.), *Handbook of personality theory and research* (pp. 66–100). New York: Guilford.

6. Isaka, H. (1990). Factor analysis of trait terms in everyday Japanese language. *Personality and Individual Differences, 11,* 115–124.

7. Costa, P. J., Jr., & McCrae, R. R. (1988). Personality in adulthood: A six-year longitudinal study of self-reports and spouse ratings on the NEO personality inventory. *Journal of Personality and Social Psychology, 54,* 853–863.

8. Eysenck, H. J. (1990). Biological dimensions of personality. In L. Pervin (ed.), *Handbook of Personality: Theory and research* (pp. 244–276). New York: Guilford.

9. Shweder, R. A., & Bourne, E. J. (1984). Does the concept of the person vary cross-culturally? In R. A. Shweder & R. A. Levine (eds.), *Culture theory: Essays on mind, self, and emotion* (pp. 158–199). New York: Cambridge University Press.

10. Buss, D. M. (1991). Evolutionary personality psychology. *Annual Review of Psychology, 42,* 459–491.

11. Williams, J. E., Munick, M. L., Saiz, J. L., & FormyDuval, D. L. (1995). Psychological importance of the "Big Five": Impression formation and context effects. *Personality and Social Psychology Bulletin, 21,* 818–826.

12. Hulse, S. H., Deese, J., & Egeth, H. (1980). *The psychology of learning* (5th ed.). New York: McGraw-Hill.

13. Rogers, C. R. (1977). *Carl Rogers on personal power: Inner strength and its revolutionary impact.* New York: Delacorte.

14. Mischel, W. (1982). *Personality*. New York: Holt, Rinehart and Winston.

15. Mischel, W., & Shoda, R. (1995). A cognitive affective system theory of personality: Reconceptualizing situations, dispositions, dynamics, and invariance in personality structure. *Psychological Review, 102*, 246–268.

16. Glass, D. C. (1977). *Behavior patterns, stress, and coronary disease*. Hillsdale, NJ: Erlbaum.

17. James, S. P., Campbell, I. M., & Lovegrove, S. A. (1984). Personality differentiation in a police-selection interview. *Journal of Applied Psychology, 69*, 129–134.

18. See note 16.

19. Friedman, M., & Rosenman, R. H. (1974). *Type A behavior and your heart*. New York: Knopf.

20. Holmes, D. S., McGilley, B. M., & Houston, B. K. (1984). Task related arousal of Type A and Type B persons: Levels of challenge and response specificity. *Journal of Personality and Social Psychology, 46*, 1322–1327.

21. Hill, D. R., Krantz, D. S., Contrada, R. J., Hedges, S. M., & Ratliff-Crain, J. A. (1987). Stability and change in Type A components and cardiovascular reactivity in medical students during periods of academic stress. *Journal of Applied Social Psychology, 17*, 679–698.

22. Carver, C. S., Coleman, A. E., & Glass, D. C. (1976). The coronary-prone behavior pattern and the suppression of fatigue on a treadmill test. *Journal of Personality and Social Psychology, 33*, 460–466.

23. Ortega, D. F., & Pipal, J. E. (1984). Challenge seeking and the Type A-coronary prone behavior pattern. *Journal of Personality and Social Psychology, 46*, 1328–1334.

24. Glass, D. C., Snyder, M. L., & Hollis, J. (1974). Time urgency and the Type A coronary-prone behavior pattern. *Journal of Applied Social Psychology, 4*, 125–140.

25. See note 19.

26. Friedman, H. S., Hall, H. S., & Harris, M. J. (1985). Type A behavior, nonverbal expressive style, and health. *Journal of Personality and Social Psychology, 48*, 1299–1315.

27. Ibid.

28. Friedman, H. S., & Booth-Kewley, S. (1987). Personality, Type A behavior, and coronary heart disease: The role of emotional expression. *Journal of Personality and Social Psychology, 53*, 783–792.

29. McClelland, D. C. (1961). *The achieving society*. Princeton, NJ: Van Nostrand.

30. McClelland, D. C. (1977). Entrepreneurship and management in the years ahead. In C. A. Bramlette, Jr. (ed.), *The individual and the future of organizations*. Atlanta: Georgia State University Press.

31. Mossholder, K. W., Bedeian, A. G., & Armenakis, A. (1982). Group process-work outcome relationships: A note of the moderating impact of self-esteem. *Academy of Management Journal, 25*, 575–585.

32. Ellis, R. A., & Taylor, M. S. (1983). Role of self-esteem within the job search process. *Journal of Applied Psychology, 68*, 632–640.

33. Brockner, J., & Guare, J. (1983). Improving the performance of low self-esteem individuals: An attributional approach. *Academy of Management Journal, 26*, 642–656.

34. Maccoby, E. E., & Jacklin, C. N. (1974). *The psychology of sex difference*. Stanford, CA: Stanford University Press.

35. Josephs, R. A., Marckus, H. R., & Tafarodi, R. W. (1992). Gender and self-esteem. *Journal of Personality and Social Psychology, 63*, 391–402.

36. Miller, J. B. (1986). *Toward a new psychology of women* (2nd ed.). Boston: Beacon Press.

37. Markus, H. R., & Kitayama, S. (1991). Culture and the self: Implications for cognition, emotion, and motivation. *Psychological Review, 98*, 224–253.

38. Ibid.

39. Funder, D. C. (1997). *The personality puzzle*. New York: W. W. Norton.

40. Cole, D. (1993, March). Testing for the job. *New Woman*, pp. 123–125.

41. American Management Association (1998). Job skill testing and psychological testing. New York: AMA.

Chapter 5

Motivation and Work

Defining Motivation
Career Motivation

**Motivation and Reward:
A Double-Edged Sword**

Reinforcement Approaches
Work Quality and Productivity
Intrinsic Motivation

**Needs and Motivation:
The Essentials of Work**

Maslow's Need Theory: From Deficiency
    to Growth
Maslow's Theory and Motivation at Work:
    The Crucial Links
Alderfer's ERG Theory: An Alternative
    to Maslow

**Process Views of Motivation:
How Does Motivation Work?**

Expectancy Theory: Motivation and Belief
Self-Efficacy: The Importance of Believing
    in Yourself

Fairness and Motivation

Social Equity

Special Sections

Balancing Work and Family
Practical Suggestions from Expectancy
    Theory

Human Relations in Action
Guidelines for Setting Effective Goals

Guidelines for Effective Human Relations
Using What You've Learned

Experiential Exercise
Assessing Your Career Motivation

MOTIVATION
Moving Yourself and Others

Learning Objectives

After reading this chapter, you should be able to:

1. Name the various components of motivation and career motivation.

2. Describe how rewards affect motivation.

3. Describe Maslow's need theory and discuss its implications for work motivation.

4. Describe expectancy theory and the major guidelines that can be drawn from it concerning work motivation.

5. Describe self-efficacy and understand its importance in motivation.

6. Describe how goal setting can be used to enhance motivation.

7. Explain how feelings of being treated fairly or unfairly can influence work motivation.

iamond International Corporation (DIC) introduced an employee recognition program in one of its plants when management saw major declines in worker morale, work quality, and productivity. The plan, known as the "100 Club," involved giving points to employees based on specific dimensions of their work behavior. Points could be acquired based on such things as attendance, safety, punctuality, productivity, and work quality. Each employee's goal was to earn 100 points, which would be rewarded with a jacket of recognition. According to the former personnel manager and co-owner of DIC, the basic premise was not to buy increased profits but to demonstrate management's interest and concern for its employees.[1]

The success of DIC's program (productivity soared by 14.2 percent, and quality-related mistakes declined by 40 percent) attests to the benefit of recognizing employees for positive work-related efforts and shows how programs designed to affect motivation can increase morale, work quality, and productivity. In this chapter, we explore motivation and discuss how you can use this information to increase your enjoyment and productivity at work.

MOTIVATION AND WORK

The study of motivation is one of the most important topics we will explore in this book. It has important practical and theoretical implications. From a practical standpoint, knowledge about what motivates others can help us improve productivity. In addition, knowledge about what motivates us can help us design a work environment that best suits our needs. Before considering the various aspects of motivation, we must define this concept.

Defining Motivation

We use the term **motivation** often in our everyday lives. For example, we talk about basketball players as being "motivated to win," refer to ourselves as being "motivated to succeed," and sometimes describe another's shortcomings as due to a "lack of motivation." What do we mean by these descriptions? As you will see, *motivation* captures several distinct aspects of a person's behavior.

motivation An internal force or process that energizes, guides, and maintains behavior.

Many contrasting views of motivation exist.[2] Most agree, however, on the following basic point: *Motivation is an internal force or process that energizes, guides, and maintains behavior toward a goal* (see Figure 5.1). The

Figure 5.1   **Three Components of Motivation**

Motivation involves the energization, guidance, and maintenance of behavior toward a goal.

energizing aspect of motivation is obvious and requires little explanation. Unless we are activated in some manner, we are likely to do little (or even nothing) in a given situation. Thus motivation refers in part to the force or energy that gets the "motor" of behavior running. The guiding component of motivation, too, is straightforward. As you know from your own experience, human beings do not usually flail about, performing one aimless action after another. Instead, most of our behavior is directed toward *specific goals.* It is at this point that motivation enters the picture. It does not simply get us moving; rather, this force gets us moving toward specific goals. Motivation is also important in maintaining the behavior directed at a particular goal. Most goals take time to achieve, and only those who are motivated to persist will attain them.

Of course, many physiological, psychological, and social sources contribute to motivation for our behavior. In fact, any particular behavior might be motivated by several sources. For example, a student's motivation for attending college might be the desire to learn, the need to obtain a degree that will lead to a good job, and the quest to have a good time socially. The extent to which a student is driven by her motives will determine which school or major the student chooses and how much time she spends studying and socializing. Motivation plays a key role in all aspects of human behavior—everything from attempts to satisfy basic biological urges through the appreciation of art and music or the mastery of complex skills. From the point of view of human relations, its impact on work and work settings is central.

Career Motivation

The concept of **career motivation** refers to a person's career plans, behaviors, and decisions.[3] It includes three major components, which are directly related to the definition of motivation discussed earlier. **Career resilience**—a person's ability to adapt to changing circumstances—relates to the role of motivation in maintaining behavior.

career motivation   A person's career plans, behaviors, and decisions.

career resilience   A person's ability to adapt to changing circumstances.

Figure 5.2   **Career Motivation: Career Resilience Is One Component**

Career resilience refers to a person's ability to adapt to changing circumstances. Individuals who are high in career resilience look forward to working with new people. We can safely conclude that this worker is not high in career resilience.

Individuals who are high in career resilience welcome organizational changes and look forward to working with new and different people. This component is especially important as the business world becomes increasingly global (see Figure 5.2). **Career identity** refers to the degree to which people define themselves in terms of their work; it relates to the direction of motivation. Individuals who have high career identities view themselves as professional or technical experts and express pride in their work. **Career insight** refers to the clarity of an individual's career goals and to his self-knowledge, including insight about his strengths and weaknesses. It relates to the energizing component of motivation, which encourages career planning and decision making. The *Experiential Exercise* on assessing career motivation provides some examples associated with each of these components.

Although research on this important concept remains in its early stages,[4] it is likely that individuals who rate highly in terms of career motivation are more successful in their pursuits than those who are less motivated. It is also likely that the former individuals are happier with their work roles. All three components of career motivation can be linked to on-the-job success.[5] Thus an understanding of motivation does more than account for how productive a person will be at work; it also helps us understand how positive aspects of self-identity form.

MOTIVATION AND REWARD: A DOUBLE-EDGED SWORD

career identity   The degree to which people define themselves in terms of their work.

career insight   The clarity of an individual's career goals.

It has often been said that the key task performed by managers is motivating their employees—that is, somehow building a fire underneath them so that they accomplish their work efficiently. How can this goal best be accomplished? To answer this question, we must understand the nature of motivation generally and of work motivation in particular. The viewpoints we now consider all shed light on these issues. The first concepts we explore consider how rewards influence motivation to work.

Reinforcement Approaches

Reinforcement approaches are among the oldest perspectives applied to motivate behavior. Although these approaches were developed through research conducted on the conditioning of animal behavior, we will consider their applications to motivation in the workplace. In the 1970s, psychologists who were interested in the motivational problems of employees began investigating the utility of reinforcement approaches. The major idea underlying this view is that the behavior of an individual in a work setting (or elsewhere) can be understood by considering the associations among stimuli, responses, and rewards. A **stimulus** is any event or object that summons some type of response. In the workplace, the presence of a supervisor is a typical stimulus for performance. A **response** is some measure of work performance, such as productivity. **Rewards** are things of value to an employee, such as pay or promotion. For our purposes, it is informative to discuss the relationships between rewards and responses (see Figure 5.3).

Reinforcement approaches direct us to look at the relationships that exist in the workplace between responses and rewards. In particular, we must consider whether a contingent relationship exists between responses and rewards. In a **contingent relationship,** a reward will be received only if a certain response occurs. A piece-rate method of payment offers a perfect example of a contingent reward system. A worker receives a reward (pay) in direct proportion to the level of productive effort, as when

> **stimulus**   An event or object that elicits some type of response.
>
> **response**   A measure of work performance, such as productivity.
>
> **rewards**   Things of value to an employee, such as pay or a promotion.
>
> **contingent relationship**   A relationship in which a reward will be received only if a certain response occurs.

𝒻igure 5.3   **Reinforcement: Description and Workplace Examples**

Reinforcement approaches examine how rewards are related to work performance. The three components of reinforcement strategy are depicted below. When rewards are contingent on responses, high levels of response are observed.

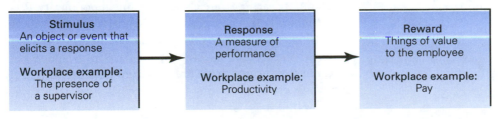

a packer receives payment according to how many boxes she fills. Salaries and hourly pay plans are examples of noncontingent reward systems; individuals are not paid in direct proportion to the quantity of their work efforts but rather are paid on a time-based system (for example, an hourly wage). Many companies use a combination of contingent and noncontingent pay systems, where employees receive a base hourly wage (noncontingent) plus a performance-based component; for example, a sales-person may receive a base salary and a bonus for each unit sold.

The reinforcement approach suggests that contingent reward systems are most effective in producing high levels of work output, because rewards are directly re-lated to responses. Response-contingent outcomes are called **reinforcers** because they "strengthen" the preceding behavior; that is, they increase the probability of those responses that produce the reward. The **law of effect** describes this phenome-non: The effect of a behavior on the environment (its consequences) will determine whether that behavior will occur again. Making pay contingent on a fixed work re-sponse, for example, increases the probability of observing that response again.

Work Quality and Productivity

The quality of performance is as important to a company as productivity. Reinforce-ment approaches have been applied primarily to affect production quantity and clearly increase the amount of effort that people expend on their work. Nevertheless, concerns arise regarding their long-term effect on people's attitudes within the workplace. Individuals who work on piece-rate schedules often report a preference for other kinds of pay systems and complain that they feel "controlled."

Many companies have found ways to reward desirable behavior in the workplace without making workers feel subject to too much control. For example, reward sys-tems can be developed that increase the self-esteem of employees and communicate management's interest and concern about their performance. The opening vignette in this chapter—DIC's 100 point club—describes one such system that uses rewards to communicate with employees, rather than controlling them. Figure 5.4 shows what can happen when an employee feels her work is unappreciated.

Performance-based pay systems seem to be the way of the future. For example, many modified systems have been adopted that reward individuals in relation to productivity and quality-related goals. Profit-sharing systems, in which employees receive payments based on corporate earnings, are also increasing in popularity. Per-formance-based compensation is not restricted to any particular level within an organization; indeed, it is likely to expand to the top levels of the corporate ladder. Be-cause the success or failure of a company usually is re-

reinforcers   Response contingent outcomes that strengthen preceding responses.

law of effect   The law stating that the conse-quences of a response determine the proba-bility of observing that response in the future.

Motivation: The Importance of Recognition

As can be seen here, motivation drops when employees feel their hard work is overlooked.

lated to the performance of senior management, the contracts of many corporate executives already include annual bonuses that are directly tied to the company's pretax profits.

Intrinsic Motivation

Common sense tells us that a person is more motivated when both extrinsic (for example, money) and intrinsic (interest) factors are present in the workplace. That is, a person is probably more highly motivated when she is paid well and engages in stimulating work. Interestingly, research on intrinsic motivation has challenged this assumption. Studies suggest that when extrinsic rewards, such as money, are tied to intrinsically interesting tasks, people find the task less interesting. This practice also reduces the likelihood that employees will engage in task-related behavior, such as choosing to perform the task again.[6] One explanation for this effect is that extrinsic rewards make people feel that external forces control their behavior. This sense of external control diminishes the feeling that the worker is performing the task because he or she likes it. Thus the feeling that "I'm doing this because I like to" (intrinsic motivation) can be curtailed.

What is the bottom line on rewards' effects in the workplace? Recent reviews of the literature suggest that rewards may not have as negative an influence on motivation within work settings as we might think from the intrinsic motivation approach.[7,8] If people are engaged in intrinsically interesting tasks, they will work hard when they receive rewards for their efforts. They may not choose to engage in this activity in their free time, however. Thus motivation may be highest when people are rewarded for their efforts and they find their work to be interesting.

NEEDS AND MOTIVATION: THE ESSENTIALS OF WORK

Another view of motivation relies on the idea that motivation is determined by the extent to which a job satisfies the basic needs of a person. In this view, jobs are seen as mechanisms for fulfilling our needs. One major question arises from this view: "What are our basic needs?" As you can see in Table 5.1, there is considerable agreement about work-related values across cultures. In this section, we consider two important need theories.

Maslow's Need Theory: From Deficiency to Growth

Mahatma Gandhi, the famous Indian patriot, once remarked, "Even God cannot talk to a hungry man except in terms of bread." In other words, when people's basic biological needs go unsatisfied, their attention will be riveted on them, and efforts to

Table 5.1   Cross-Cultural Work Values

Survey research assessed the most important work goals of more than 8,000 workers in seven nations. These are the three most important goals for individuals in each country. As you can see, there was considerable agreement about the factors of interesting work and pay.

Country

United States	Great Britain	Belgium	Japan
1. Interesting work	1. Interesting work	1. Interesting work	1. Person-job match
2. Pay	2. Pay	2. Pay	2. Interesting work
3. Job security	3. Job security	3. Job security	3. Autonomy

(Former) W. Germany	Netherlands	Israel	
1. Pay	1. Autonomy	1. Interesting work	
2. Job security	2. Interesting work	2. Interpersonal relations	
3. Interesting work	3. Interpersonal relations	3. Pay	

Data compiled by Harpaz (1990). The importance of work goals: An international perspective. *Journal of International Business, 21*, 75–93.

communicate about other matters will probably fail. This basic truth lies at the heart of a highly influential theory of human motivation, Abraham Maslow's **need hierarchy theory.**[9]

This theory begins with two reasonable assumptions:

1. Human beings have many different needs, ranging from lower-level biological needs through higher-level psychological ones.

2. These needs exist in a hierarchy—before higher-order needs can become motivators and affect behavior, lower-level needs must be at least partly satisfied.

What are these needs? Maslow offered some intriguing answers, suggesting that all human beings possess five distinct types of needs.

At the lowest or most basic level are the **physiological needs.** They include our need for food, water, and oxygen, to mention just a few. Obviously, satisfaction of these needs is essential if life is to continue. Next are what Maslow termed the **safety needs.** They involve our desire to be safe from physical or psychological harm—for example, from such threats as accident, injury, and illness. Interestingly, although modern life in the Western world is free from some of the threats that faced our ancestors (for example, famine and plague), many other dangers exist. At present, many persons fear economic depression and being assaulted by criminals in their homes or on the streets. Thus concluding that our safety needs are usually fulfilled is not entirely justified. Maslow collectively labeled the physiological and safety needs as **deficiency needs.** This term reflects his belief that unless such needs are met, an individual cannot hope to develop a healthy personality.

A third level of needs involves our desire to form friendships with others, to belong, and to be loved and accepted. These **social needs** are visible in our willingness to join various organizations and form close relationships with others. In addition, we possess two other types of needs. The first of these, the **esteem needs** (also known as ego needs), center around our desire to maintain self-respect and to gain the admiration or respect of others. Such needs are shown in our striving for prestige, achievement, and status. Finally, at the very top of the need hierarchy is the need for **self-actualization,** or self-realization. This need centers around our desire to find out who we really

need hierarchy theory   Maslow's theory asserting that five levels of human needs (physiological, safety, social, esteem, and self-actualization) exist and these are arranged in such a way that lower, more basic needs must be satisfied before higher-level needs become activated.

physiological needs   Basic biological needs, such as the need for food, water, and oxygen.

safety needs   Needs to feel safe from threats to our physical or psychological well-being.

deficiency needs   In Maslow's need theory, lower-level needs that must be at least partially satisfied before higher-level growth needs can be activated.

social needs   Needs to form friendships with others, to belong, and to love and be loved.

esteem needs   In Maslow's need theory, the need to attain self-respect and the respect of others.

self-actualization need   The need to find out who we really are and to develop to our fullest potential.

are and to develop ourselves to our fullest potential. Together, social needs, esteem needs, and self-actualization needs were termed **growth needs** by Maslow. Unless they are satisfied, personal growth cannot continue.

Maslow's Theory and Motivation at Work: The Crucial Links

By now, you are probably convinced that human beings possess many different needs. Moreover, you may agree that these needs can be arranged in order from lower-level ones through higher-level ones. But what, you may wonder, does this have to do with motivation at work? Where does knowing about all these needs and their arrangement really take us? According to many human relations experts, the answer is "pretty far."

Maslow's theory directly applies to work and work settings in several ways. It underscores the fact that companies need to be concerned with the multiple needs that people have so that workers will be satisfied and effective employees. To meet physiological needs, companies must provide adequate salaries, rest breaks, and, if possible, exercise and physical fitness programs.[10] Safety needs can be met by providing a safe and secure work environment and life- and health-insurance plans. Company social events and athletic activities may serve to satisfy social needs. Award banquets and status symbols, such as private offices and parking spots, may meet esteem needs. By allowing for individual creativity and input, companies may enable employees to find self-fulfillment in their work and satisfy self-actualization needs.

Maslow's theory also suggests that what motivates individuals may differ throughout their working lives (see Chapter 15 for a discussion of career development). Careers can be viewed as evolving through a series of stages. Early in an individual's career, she may be motivated by different needs than will be the case later in her career (see Figure 5.5). For example, early career needs are often more basic: The person needs to earn money to establish economic independence. These needs may involve finding employment that allows the individual to house and feed himself (safety and physiological needs). The workplace is also the environment where many people spend the majority of their time. Thus an individual may develop many important adult social relationships in this setting. Later in an individual's career, once the basic deficiency needs are resolved, **growth needs** may become most important. An individual may become especially sensitive to the extent to which the workplace allows for career advancement, positive self-esteem, and creativity.

Maslow's theory has not received a great deal of support regarding its view on the exact needs that exist and the order in which they are activated.[11] Can you think of exceptions? Many researchers disagree that only five basic categories of needs exist. For these reasons, other researchers have suggested

growth needs Needs for developing one's human potential.

Figure 5.5   **Career Development: Needs Change throughout the Lifespan**

Careers evolve through a series of stages. Individuals' needs will vary throughout their work lives. The younger worker in this photograph, for example, may need economic security, whereas the older worker may seek career growth.

modifications to Maslow's theory. We will discuss the most popular modification of his theory in the next section. Keep in mind, however, that Maslow's work provided an important foundation for this view.

Alderfer's ERG Theory: An Alternative to Maslow

In response to the criticisms of Maslow's theory, Clayton Alderfer proposed an alternative formulation.[12] This approach, known as **ERG theory,** is much simpler. Not only did Alderfer specify only three types of needs instead of five, but he also found that these needs are not activated in a specific order—instead, any need may be activated at any time.

The three needs specified by ERG theory are the needs for existence, relatedness, and growth. **Existence needs** correspond to Maslow's physiological and safety needs and are necessary to survive. **Relatedness needs** correspond to Maslow's social needs, which encompass the need for meaningful social relationships. Finally, growth needs correspond to the esteem and self-actualization needs in Maslow's theory—that is, the desire to develop one's potential.

Clearly, ERG theory is much less restrictive than Maslow's need hierarchy theory. It also fits better with research evidence suggesting that, although basic categories of needs do exist, they are not exactly as specified by Maslow.[13] Despite the fact that theorists are not in complete agreement about the exact number of needs and the relationships between them, they do agree that satisfying human needs is an important part of motivating behavior on the job (see Figure 5.6 on page 128).

ERG theory   An alternative theory to Maslow's need hierarchy proposed by Alderfer, which asserts that three basic human needs exist: existence, relatedness, and growth.

existence needs   Needs that are related to basic survival.

relatedness needs   Needs for meaningful social relationships.

 **Needs Theories: A Comparison of Maslow's and Alderfer's Theories**

This figure shows how Maslow's need theory relates to Alderfer's ERG approach.

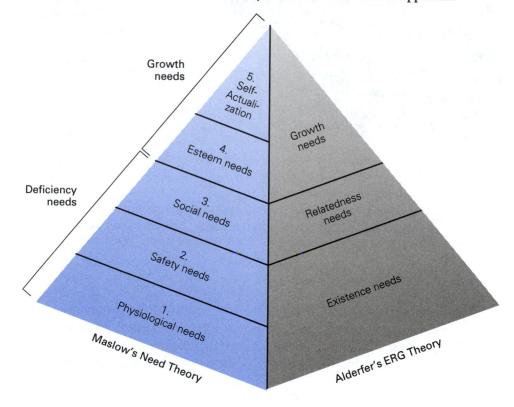

PROCESS VIEWS OF MOTIVATION: HOW DOES MOTIVATION WORK?

Process theories of motivation describe how motivation is affected by individuals' perceptions of the workplace. In general, they emphasize the importance of what people think about the workplace. A person's thoughts are critical in determining motivation. The following viewpoints take into account many of the beliefs that play a role in predicting motivation.

Expectancy Theory: Motivation and Belief

Imagine two people facing very different situations. One believes it makes little difference how hard she works; extra effort will not necessarily improve her job performance, and, even if it does, no one will notice or care. The other is certain that, if he puts out more effort, his performance will improve. He also believes that better performance will, in turn, yield many valued rewards (such as raises, promotions, and the like). Which of these two employees will be more motivated to work hard? The answer is so obvious that it hardly requires stating: the second.

Although this example is extremely simple (perhaps unrealistically so), it calls attention to a major view of motivation: **expectancy theory** (or expectancy/valence theory, as it is sometimes known).[14,15] This approach assumes that the motivation to work is strongly determined by certain beliefs or expectancies held by individuals. We have already hinted at these expectations, but it is probably useful to state them explicitly.

First, work motivation hinges on an individual's *expectancy* that increased effort will result in enhanced performance. Usually, most persons *do* believe that the harder they work, the more productive they will be. It isn't always the case, however. For example, a salesperson may believe that, if she really bears down, she'll come across as using a "hard sell" and so actually hurt her chances for success. Similarly, production workers may conclude that they can keep up with their jobs through moderate effort and that working harder will do no good; after all, the flow of parts past their stations will not increase. Expectancy theory suggests that individuals will be motivated to work only when they expect high levels of effort to improve their performance. If they do not believe that this relationship exists, they may well slack off on their jobs.[16]

Second, expectancy theory indicates that work motivation is closely linked to the view that good performance will yield rewards—that it is *instrumental*. Only when individuals believe that good performance will be recognized and rewarded will they be motivated to work more diligently. In contrast, if they feel that excellence will be ignored or overlooked, their work motivation may drop sharply or virtually disappear!

A third aspect of the theory centers around the concept of *valence*—the personal value attached by individuals to various rewards they can gain through their jobs. When these rewards are valued highly, work motivation will be high; when they lack in such value, motivation will be low. This idea makes sense; after all, why should individuals work hard to attain outcomes they don't really want?

Expectancy theory claims that motivation is a multiplicative function of all three components. That is, higher levels of motivation will result when valence, instrumentality, and expectancy are all high rather than low. The

expectancy theory   The theory asserting that workers' motivation is based on their beliefs about the probability that effort will lead to performance (expectancy), multiplied by the probability that performance will lead to reward (instrumentality), multiplied by the perceived value (valence) of the reward.

multiplicative assumption also implies that if any one of these components is zero, then the overall level of motivation will be zero. Thus, even if a worker believes that his effort will result in good performance, which will result in reward, his motivation may be zero if the valence of the reward received is zero. Figure 5.7 summarizes the components of expectancy theory and shows the interrelationships between them.

In addition, expectancy theory assumes that motivation is not equivalent to job performance. Rather, it sees motivation as just one of several determinants of job performance. In particular, the theory assumes that *skills and abilities* also contribute to a person's job performance. It is no secret that some people are better suited to perform their jobs than others by virtue of the unique characteristics and special skills or abilities they bring to their jobs. For example, a tall, strong, well-coordinated person is likely to make a better professional basketball player than a short, physically weak klutz, even if the shorter person is highly motivated to succeed.

Expectancy theory also recognizes that job performance will be influenced by a worker's *role perceptions*. How well workers carry out their jobs will depend, in part, on what they believe is expected of them. An assistant manager, for example, may be-

Balancing Work and Family

Practical Suggestions from Expectancy Theory

It is incredibly difficult to stay motivated when you are trying to meet the demands of an active work and family life. We can draw some suggestions for dealing with this problem from expectancy theory. One important suggestion gleaned from expectancy theory is to *clarify your expectations that your effort will really pay off*. Sometimes we feel that our efforts go for nothing and lose sight of the fact that what we're doing will really lead to a good level of performance at work and at home. It is important to make it clear to yourself and to other people what is expected *and* to make it possible for yourself to attain that level of performance.[17] In other words, set realistic goals for yourself and don't be afraid to set realistic goals for others around you. (It might be helpful to review the special section on setting effective goals; see *Human Relations in Action* on pages 134–135.)

A second practical suggestion from expectancy theory is to *clearly link valued rewards and performance*. This idea relates to beliefs about instrumentality—that is, make it clear to yourself exactly which job and work behaviors will lead to which rewards. For example, do you find it more rewarding to forego cooking an elaborate dinner in favor of spending time reading with your children? If so, balance your time and efforts to favor the rewarding activity as often as is possible. Expectancy theory specifies that it would be effective to do so because this balance will enhance your

Figure 5.7   Expectancy Theory: An Overview

According to expectancy theory, motivation is the product of three types of beliefs: expectancy (effort will result in performance) × instrumentality (performance will result in rewards) × valence (the perceived value of the rewards).

lieve that his or her primary job responsibility is to train employees. If the manager believes that the assistant manager should take care of the paperwork instead, he or she may be seen as a poor performer. Of course, such poor performance results not necessarily from poor motivation but from misunderstanding concerning the role one is expected to play in the organization.[19]

beliefs about instrumentality. Similarly, having realistic expectations about how your efforts at home or work will be rewarded (for example, your kids may not express appreciation for some things that you do for them) will prevent you from becoming frustrated when your efforts do not lead to rewards.

Finally, one of the most obvious practical suggestions from expectancy theory is to *seek rewards that are valued positively.* The carrot at the end of the stick must be a tasty one, according to the theory, for it to have potential as a motivator. These days, when the composition of the work force is changing so as to include increasing numbers of unmarried parents and single people, it would be a mistake to assume that all employees care about the same rewards from their companies. Some might value a pay raise, while others might prefer additional vacation days, improved health care benefits, or day-care facilities for children. With this idea in mind, an increasing number of companies are instituting *cafeteria-style benefit plans*—incentive systems through which the employees select their fringe benefits from a menu of available alternatives. Given that fringe benefits represent an average of 37 percent of payroll costs, more and more companies are recognizing the value of administering them flexibly.[18] Table 5.2 provides some examples of the kinds of flexible benefit plans that are often available. Seek out information about these kinds of plans!

Table 5.2	**Cafeteria-Style Benefits**

These are a few examples of flexible benefit plans. Others are possible.

Flexible Spending Accounts (FSAs)	Flex-Credits	Flex-Time
Allow you to set aside untaxed dollars to pay for health care expenses that are not reimbursed by your medical plan. Some also allow you to set aside untaxed dollars for dependent care.	Fixed number of benefit dollars that can be spent on the employee's choice of benefits and levels of coverage. The menu of options often includes medical, dental, life, vision, 401(k) plans, and dependent care.	Refers to options for flexible scheduling. Examples are job sharing, working at home, and choice of work hours.

Finally, expectancy theory recognizes the role of *opportunities to perform* one's job. Even the best workers may perform at low levels if their opportunities are limited. Consider the work of salespeople. Even the most highly motivated salesperson will perform poorly if opportunities are restricted—if the available inventory is low (as is sometimes the case for popular cars) or if the customers cannot afford the product (as is sometimes the case in areas heavily populated by unemployed persons).

It is important to recognize that expectancy theory views motivation as just one of several determinants of job performance. The combination of motivation with a person's skills and abilities, role perceptions, and opportunities influences job performance. To date, expectancy theory has inspired a great deal of research and has been successfully applied to understanding behavior in many different organizational settings.[20] Nevertheless, although specific aspects of the theory have been supported (particularly, the impact of expectancy and instrumentality on motivation),[21] others have not (such as the contribution of valence to motivation and the multiplicative assumption).[22] Despite its uneven popularity, expectancy theory does suggest a number of ways to motivate workers (see *Balancing Work and Family*).

Self-Efficacy: The Importance of Believing in Yourself

self-efficacy   A person's belief that he or she possesses the necessary skills and abilities to accomplish a goal.

Expectancy theory showed that our beliefs can have an important influence on our motivation. Research has also pointed to an additional type of belief that has a major impact on our motivation **Self-efficacy** refers to a per-

𝒻igure 5.8   **Self-Efficacy**

Beliefs that one "has what it takes" mediate the relationship between knowledge and action.

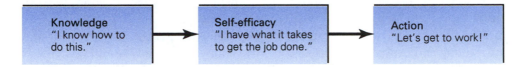

son's belief that he or she possesses the necessary skills and abilities to accomplish a goal.[23] Self-efficacy beliefs are thought to mediate the relationship between knowledge and action[24] (see Figure 5.8). If a person feels self-efficacious, he feels that he has what it takes to meet his goals. This belief leads a person to set high goals and expend the effort to obtain them. A person with high self-efficacy will pursue a goal in the face of obstacles and will set even higher goals when the original goals have been met. In contrast, individuals with low efficacy will set lower goals, abandon goals when faced with obstacles, and lower subsequent goals when they have met their original goal.

A great body of evidence supports the idea that self-efficacy beliefs play an important role in motivation. For example, research has found that persons with a higher sense of self-efficacy respond more positively to unemployment and find jobs sooner than those with low self-efficacy beliefs.[25]

Given that believing in self is so important, how do we develop self-efficacy? Research suggests that efficacy is affected by past performance—for example, the extent to which goals have been met in the past.[26] One strategy would therefore be to set high, but realistic goals for yourself and to persist in your quest even if the "going gets tough." More tips about effective techniques for goal setting appear in the *Human Relations in Action* section on pages 134–135.

𝒻AIRNESS AND MOTIVATION

At some time, all of us have had the experience of feeling "cheated"—a belief that we didn't receive the reward we deserved. When people have this feeling, their motivation decreases. We often regulate our efforts to put in a fair amount of work in a day. The next approach to the study of motivation explored in this chapter considers how perceptions of fairness or equity in the workplace influence our behavior. As you will see, perceptions of fairness are sometimes based on comparisons with other persons.

Social Equity

Sometimes, it is not the absolute amount of reward received that motivates us; rather, it is what we receive in relation to what others receive that is important. Imagine that you hold a job in a large hospital. In general, you are satisfied with your work and feel you receive a good salary. One day, you discover a disturbing fact: Another person on staff who does work similar to your own and has about the same amount of training and experience earns $5,000 more than you do! How would this knowledge affect your motivation? In all likelihood, it would decrease markedly your willingness to work. After all, you might reason to yourself, why should I work as hard as he does for less pay?

Your reaction in this respect would be quite understandable, for in our dealings with others, we all prefer to feel that we are being treated fairly. This fact lies at the

Human Relations in Action

Guidelines for Setting Effective Goals

Each of the views we have examined so far offers—or at least implies—specific steps that can be taken to increase motivation at work. These steps have been put to practical use and, in many instances, have yielded valuable benefits.[27] They are not the only techniques available, however. **Goal setting** is an important technique for enhancing motivation. In this box, we will discuss practical guidelines for setting effective goals.

Many theories of work motivation suggest that setting goals increases motivation. In fact, the process of setting goals is one of the most important motivational forces within organizations.[28] The following general conclusions from research studies may be used as effective guidelines for goal setting:

1. The first requirement of an effective goal-setting procedure is to make the goals *clear* and specific. This step gives employees something to shoot for and has been shown to increase productivity in a variety of companies.[29,30]

goal setting   The process of determining specific levels of performance for workers to attain.

2. It is best if the goals are *difficult* but attainable.[31] These goals must be seen as a realistic challenge. If the goals are seen as too difficult or unrealistic, people may simply ignore them.

heart of the **equity theory** of motivation.[34] Actually, **social equity** is more than just a theory of work motivation. It applies to a wide range of human relationships, from romantic relationships to purely economic ones. This theory has important implications for motivation in work settings, however, and we focus on these ramifications here.

Basically, equity theory suggests that people will be most satisfied with their jobs and most strongly motivated to work when they believe they are being treated fairly. How, precisely, do individuals decide whether fairness exists? The answer involves a special type of relative judgment in which we compare ourselves with others. In

equity theory   The theory stating that workers strive to maintain ratios of their own outcomes (rewards) to their own input (contributions) that are equal to the outcome-to-input ratios of other workers with whom they compare themselves.

social equity   The state in which one worker's outcome-to-input ratio is equivalent to that of another worker with whom this person compares himself or herself.

3. It helps if workers are involved in setting the goal and if the reason behind the goal is explained. Under these conditions, workers are more likely to accept the goal as reasonable.

4. Providing *feedback* about the level of performance is important in motivating people to strive for goals.

5. Money or other forms of tangible rewards may increase commitment to an accepted goal.

6. Individuals must have the ability to achieve high performance if goal setting is to have an effect on performance.

In sum, goal setting can be an effective tool for motivation. But care must be taken when setting goals or objectives. Although more research remains to be done on this important process, these guidelines can be used to increase the effectiveness of goals. You may find them useful in self-motivating, as well as in setting a motivational framework for others. Combining feedback with goal setting is the most effective way to improve the performance of individuals or groups.[32,33]

this judgment, we first examine our own **input** (everything we contribute to our jobs) and our own **outcomes** (all the benefits we derive from them). We then compare these values with the equivalent values for others. If our ratio of outcomes-to-input seems roughly equivalent to theirs, **equity** exists; we conclude that we are, in fact, being treated fairly relative to others. If our ratio of outcomes-to-input is *not* similar to theirs, **inequity** may exist. In this case, we conclude that something is "out of whack" and that fairness does not prevail. We may discover, as in the preceding example, that another person enjoys a more favorable outcomes-to-input ratio than we do: She receives higher pay for the same work. Alternatively, we may find that another person has a less favorable outcomes-to-input ratio: He receives fewer benefits for the same amount of work. In this case, the person may feel angry.

Keep in mind one important point: For equity to exist, it is *not* necessary that everyone in an organization provide the *same* input or receive the *same* rewards—far from it. Instead, it is essential that the *ratio* of outcomes-to-input remains fairly constant. Thus it is perfectly reasonable for persons who make large contributions (by virtue of their training, experience, talent, or effort) to receive larger rewards than persons who make small contributions. In fact, this matching of outcomes to contributions is central to perceived fairness in work settings.

Unfortunately, of course, equity does not always prevail. For various reasons, some persons tend to reap larger benefits than they deserve, while others get the short end of the stick and receive less than is fair. What happens in such cases? As you might anticipate, workers who are *over-rewarded* tend to feel guilty, while those who are *under-rewarded* may feel angry.

input Workers' contributions to their jobs, such as their experience, qualifications, or amount of time worked.

outcomes The rewards a worker receives from his or her job, such as salary and recognition.

equity The condition in which a worker's outcome-to-input ratio is equal to that of another person who is used for comparison.

inequity The undesirable condition in which a worker's outcome-to-input ratio is not equal to that of another person who is used for comparison. If this inequity favors a person, the result is *overpayment inequity,* which leads to feelings of guilt. If this inequity is to a person's disadvantage, the result is *underpayment inequity,* which leads to feelings of anger.

According to equity theory, people are motivated to escape the negative emotional states of anger and guilt. This theory recognizes several ways of resolving inequitable situations. In our example of underpayment inequity, the employee has several options for redressing his anger and feeling satisfied (refer to Table 5.3). For example, an underpaid person may respond by lowering his input. He may work less hard, perhaps arriving at work later, leaving early, taking longer breaks, doing less work, or performing lower-quality work. In an extreme case, he may even quit his job. He may also attempt to raise his outcomes by asking the boss for a raise or even taking home company property (such as tools or office supplies). All of these examples may be considered *behavioral* reactions to inequity, because they represent ways that people can change their existing input or outcomes.

In addition to these behavioral reactions to *underpayment inequity,* some psychological reactions are possible. Given that many workers may feel uncomfortable

Table 5.3   Possible Reactions to Inequity: A Summary

People can respond to overpayment and underpayment inequities in behavioral and/or psychological ways. A few of these are summarized here. These reactions help change the perceived inequities into a state of perceived equity.

| | *Type of Reaction* | |
Type of Inequity	**Behavioral** (What you can *do* is . . .)	**Psychological** (What you can *think* is . . .)
Overpayment inequity	Raise own input (for example, work harder), or lower own outcomes (for example, work through a paid vacation)	Convince yourself that your own outcomes are deserved based on your own input (for example, rationalize that you work harder than others and so you deserve more pay)
Underpayment inequity	Lower own input (for example, reduce effort), or raise own outcomes (for example, get a raise in pay)	Convince yourself that other's input is really higher than your own (for example, rationalize that the comparison worker is really more qualified and so deserves higher outcomes)

stealing from their employers (as they should) or would be unwilling to restrict their productivity or to ask for a raise, they may resolve the inequity by changing the way that they think about the situation. Because equity theory deals with perceived inequities, it is reasonable to expect that inequitable states may be redressed effectively by merely thinking about the circumstances differently. For example, the underpaid employee may rationalize that his coworker's input is really higher than his own, thereby convincing himself that higher outcomes are justified. For example, one study found that workers who received a 6 percent pay cut rationalized that their salary was equitable by coming to think of their work environments in more favorable terms.[35] By perceiving the situation as an equitable one, people can effectively reduce their inequity distress.

A similar set of behavioral and psychological reactions can be identified for *overpayment inequity* (see Table 5.3 for a summary of reactions). A salaried worker who feels overpaid may raise his or her input—for example, working harder or for longer hours. Similarly, workers who lower their own outcomes, such as by not taking advantage of company-provided fringe benefits, may be redressing an overpayment inequity. More commonly, overpaid persons may convince themselves psychologically that they are really worth their higher outcomes by virtue of their superior input. Workers who receive substantial pay raises may not feel distressed at all, because they already may have rationalized that the raise was warranted on the basis of their superior work and, therefore, does not constitute an inequity.

Research has generally supported the equity theory's claim that people will respond to overpayment and underpayment inequities as we have just described.[36,37] The theory's prediction that overpayment inequity will lead to increased effort, however, is less commonly obtained as predictions about underpayment inequity.[38]

In this section, we have discussed various ways that workers may deal with inequity. We should note that organizations, too, can play a role in this regard. For example, organizations can attempt to establish the fairest pay and promotion policies possible. Inequity in these procedures—either real or imagined—is a major source of unhappiness among employees in many companies. Making certain that workers are treated as fairly as possible is therefore a good way to head off possible trouble. Similarly, organizations can attempt to distribute work assignments in a balanced and reasonable manner. By doing so, instances where some persons are overworked while others are on a permanent "semi-vacation" can be reduced. Finally, organizations can attempt to disperse "perks" (perquisites, such as fancy titles or desirable offices) in a rational rather than unpredictable fashion. This approach can help hold down feelings of resentment and keep undesirable forms of organizational politics to a minimum.

Guidelines for Effective Human Relations

Using What You've Learned

In this chapter, we examined a broad range of principles and findings about motivation. Although few rules will apply to every situation, some general guidelines are suggested by the various findings we have discussed; these ideas are summarized here. Remember, no rule works 100 percent in every situation. Nevertheless, these guidelines should help improve your success in increasing your own and others' motivation.

■ Recognize that your career motivation defines an important aspect of your self-identity as well as your career success. Being aware of what motivates you, and why, gives you more control over both of these dimensions.

Guidelines for Effective Human Relations (continued)

- When using rewards to motivate, be sure to allocate rewards in ways that communicate your interest and concern about performance. Rewards that are perceived as overly controlling may decrease motivation.

- To maintain motivation over a lifetime, remember that needs vary across time. Keep Maslow's hierarchy of needs in mind when you assess your career goals.

- Make clear to those you are trying to motivate that effort will lead to performance, and that performance will lead to valued rewards.

- Keep in mind that an individual's perception of fairness in the workplace is an important component of motivation.

- When setting goals for yourself or others, be sure that the goals are clear and difficult but attainable.

Summary

Motivation is generally defined as the internal force that energizes and guides behavior. Many different theories of work motivation have been proposed. According to one perspective, contingent rewards can increase motivation. Care must be taken to ensure that individuals do not view rewards as overly controlling, lest their intrinsic motivation to work decrease. Maslow's need theory emphasizes that humans have many different needs that can be arranged in a hierarchy. Lower-level deficiency needs must be at least partly satisfied before higher-level growth needs can be activated. In contrast, Alderfer's ERG theory proposes that we are motivated by basic physiological or safety needs (existence), social needs (relatedness), and esteem needs (growth). Expectancy theory, a third approach to work motivation, suggests that individuals' willingness to expend effort on their jobs is strongly affected by certain expectancies. Among the most important of these is the expectancy that effort will improve performance and that good performance will yield valued rewards.

The belief that one has "what it takes" to accomplish one's goals in the face of adversity (self-efficacy) is another type of cognition that has been found to relate to motivation in the workplace. Still another perspective, social equity theory, indicates that work motivation will be higher when individuals believe that they are treated fairly than when they believe that they are treated unfairly. Many tactics for enhancing work motivation through goal setting have been developed. By providing clear and challenging goals, one can often enhance worker motivation, performance, and career identity.

Key Terms

career identity, p. 120

career insight, p. 120

career motivation, p. 119

career resilience, p. 119

contingent relationship, p. 121

deficiency needs, p. 125

equity, p. 136

equity theory, p. 135

ERG theory, p. 127

esteem needs, p. 125

existence needs, p. 127

expectancy theory, p. 129

goal setting, p. 134

growth needs, p. 126

inequity, p. 136

input, p. 136

law of effect, p. 122

motivation, p. 118

need hierarchy theory, p. 125

outcomes, p. 136

physiological needs, p. 125

reinforcers, p. 122

relatedness needs, p. 127

response, p. 121

rewards, p. 121

safety needs, p. 125

self-actualization need, p. 125

self-efficacy, p. 132

stimulus, p. 121

social equity, p. 135

social needs, p. 125

Experiential Exercise

Assessing Your Career Motivation

The following items are associated with different aspects of career motivation. Rate the extent to which you feel each of these items applies to you. If you are presently employed, rate each item's applicability to your feelings in your present circumstance. Otherwise, rate how you think you would feel in your work setting. Remember, there are no right or wrong answers. Use the following scale to rate each item:

Not at all applicable   1 2 3 4 5 6 7   Very applicable

Sample Item	Rating
1. Are you able to adapt to changing circumstances?	_____
2. Are you a risk taker?	_____
3. Do you welcome new job assignments?	_____
4. Do you have clear career goals?	_____
5. Do you know the things you do well?	_____
6. Do you know the things you don't do well?	_____
7. Do you define yourself in terms of your job?	_____
8. Are you involved in your work?	_____
9. Are you dedicated to your employer?	_____

Scoring: Total your ratings of items 1–3, which refer to "career resilience." The higher you rate these items, the more you may welcome organizational changes and new challenges. Now, total your ratings of items 4–6, which refer to "career insight." Higher ratings of these items mean that your career goals are clear and that you are aware of your strengths and weaknesses. Last, total your ratings of 7–9, which refer to "career identity." The higher your score on these items, the more you may define yourself in terms of your work.

Remember that this list is not a complete assessment of the various components of your career motivation. It is just a rough estimate of the aspects of your career that may be important to you at this point in time. (Items are adapted from London, 1993; see note 3.)

Notes

1. Boyle, D. C. (1992). Employee motivation that works. *Human Relations Magazine, 4,* 83.

2. Steers, R. W., & Porter, L. W. (eds.). (1989). *Motivation and work behavior* (5th ed.). New York: McGraw-Hill.

3. London, M. (1988). Organizational support for employees' career motivation: A guide to human resource strategies in changing business conditions. *Human Resources Planning, 11,* 23–32.

4. London, M. (1993). Relationships between career motivation, empowerment and support for career development. *Journal of Occupational and Organizational Psychology, 66,* 55–69.

5. Noe, R. A., Noe, A. W., & Bachhuber, J. A. (1990). Correlates of career motivation. *Journal of Vocational Behavior, 37,* 340–356.

6. Deci, E. L. (1972). The effects of contingent and noncontingent rewards and controls on intrin-

sic motivation. *Organizational Behavior and Human Performance, 8*, 217–229.

7. Wiersma, U. J. (1992). The effects of extrinsic rewards in intrinsic motivation: A meta-analysis. *Journal of Occupational and Organizational Psychology, 65*, 101–114.

8. Guzzo, R. A., Jette, R. D., & Katzell, R. A. (1985). The effects of psychologically based intervention programs on worker productivity: A meta-analysis. *Personnel Psychology, 38*, 275–292.

9. Maslow, A. H. (1970). *Motivation and personality* (2nd ed.). New York: Harper & Row.

10. Falkenberg, L. E. (1987). Employee fitness programs: Their impact on the employee and the organization. *Academy of Management Review, 12*, 511–522.

11. Wahba, M. A., & Bridwell, L. G. (1976). Maslow reconsidered: A review of research on the need hierarchy theory. *Organizational Behavior and Human Performance, 15*, 212–240.

12. Alderfer, C. P. (1972). *Existence, relatedness, and growth.* New York: Free Press.

13. Salancik, G. R., & Pfeffer, J. (1977). An examination of need-satisfaction models of job satisfaction. *Administrative Science Quarterly, 22*, 427–456.

14. Vroom, V. H. (1964). *Work and motivation.* New York: Wiley.

15. Porter, L. W., & Lawler, E. E. (1968). *Managerial attitudes and performance.* Homewood, IL: Irwin.

16. Ibid.

17. Harrell, A., & Stahl, M. (1986). Additive information processing and the relationship between expectancy of success and motivational force. *Academy of Management Journal, 29*, 424–433.

18. Foegen, J. H. (1982, October 18). Fringe benefits are being diversified too. *Industry Week*, pp. 56–58.

19. See note 15.

20. Mitchell, T. R. (1983). Expectancy-value models in organizational psychology. In N. Feather (ed.), *Expectancy, incentive, and action* (pp. 293–314). Hillsdale, NJ: Lawrence Erlbaum Associates.

21. Heneman, R. L. (1984). *Pay for performance: Exploring the merit system.* New York: Pergamon Press.

22. Miller, L. E., & Grush, J. E. (1988). Improving predictions in expectancy theory research: Effects of personality, expectancies, and norms. *Academy of Management Journal, 31*, 107–122.

23. Bandura, A. (1986). *Social foundations of thought and action: A social cognitive theory.* Englewood Cliffs, NJ: Prentice Hall.

24. Ibid.

25. Eden, D. & Aviram, A. (1993). Self-efficacy training to speed reemployment: Helping people to help themselves. *Journal of Applied Psychology, 78*, 352–360.

26. Locke, E. A. Frederick, E., Lee, C., & Bobko, P. (1984). Effects of self-efficacy, goals, and task strategies on task performance. *Journal of Applied Psychology, 69*, 241–251.

27. Campbell, J. P., & Pritchard, R. D. (1976). Motivation theory in industrial and organizational psychology. In M. D. Dunnette (ed.), *Handbook of industrial and organizational psychology.* Chicago: Rand McNally.

28. Latham, G. P., & Lee, T. W. (1986). Goal setting. In E. A. Locke (ed.), *Generalizing from laboratory to field settings* (pp. 100–117). Lexington, MA: Lexington Books.

29. Latham, G. P., & Locke, E. (1979). Goal setting: A motivational technique that works. *Organizational Dynamics, 8*, 68–80.

30. Locke, E. A., & Latham, G. P. (1984). *Goal setting for individuals, groups, and organizations.* Chicago: Science Research Associates.

31. Ibid.

32. Chhokar, J. S., & Wallin, J. A. (1984). A field study of the effects of feedback frequency on performance. *Journal of Applied Psychology, 69*, 524–530.

33. Pritchard, R. D., Jones, S. D., Roth, P. L., Stuebing, K. K., & Ekeberg, S. E. (1988). Effects of group feedback, goal setting, and incentives on organizational productivity. *Journal of Applied Psychology, 73*, 337–358.

34. Adams, J. S. (1965). Inequity in social exchange. In L. Berkowitz (ed.), *Advances in experimental social psychology*. New York: Academic Press.

35. Greenberg, J. (1989). Cognitive re-evaluation of outcomes in response to underpayment inequity. *Academy of Management Journal, 32,* 174–184.

36. Greenberg, J. (1987). A taxonomy of organizational justice theories. *Academy of Management Review, 12,* 9–22.

37. Pritchard, R. D., Dunnette, M. D., & Jorgenson, D. O. (1972). Effects of perceptions of equity and inequity on worker performance and satisfaction. *Journal of Applied Psychology, 57,* 75–94.

38. Weick, E. E., Bougon, M. G., & Maruyama, G. (1976). The equity context. *Organizational Behavior and Human Performance, 15,* 32–65.

Chapter 6

Communication: A Definition

Organizational Influences on Communication: Who Should (or Can) Communicate with Whom?

Organizational Structure and Communication: The Formal Channels

The Grapevine and Rumors: Informal Channels of Communication

Electronic Communication: The Impact of New Technology

E-mail and Internet Etiquette: Minding Your Electronic Manners

Computer-Mediated Communication: Some Consequences

Telecommuting: Work Life Away from the Office

Personal Influences on Communication: Different Styles, Different Channels

Personal Style and Communication: Why Some People Are More Effective Communicators Than Others

Verbal Communication: Speaking with Words

Nonverbal Communication: Using the Unspoken Language

Deceiving Others: How Is It Done and Detected?

A Typology of Lies and Liars: How Do We Lie?

Skill at Lying: Success in Deceit

Principles of Effective Communication: Some Useful Techniques

Personal Strategies

Listening: The Other Side of the Coin

Special Sections

Ethics at Work
To Lie or Not to Lie: That Is the Question

Guidelines for Effective Human Relations
Using What You've Learned

Experiential Exercise
Measuring Your Own Expressiveness: A Short Self-Assessment

COMMUNICATION
The Art of Getting Your Message Across

Learning Objectives

After reading this chapter, you should be able to:

1. Define the process of communication and describe its major forms.

2. Describe how the formal structure of an organization influences the nature of the communication that occurs within it.

3. Describe how informal patterns of communication operate within organizations.

4. Discuss some of the positive and negative aspects of electronic or computer-mediated communication.

5. Describe several personal factors that influence communication effectiveness.

6. Distinguish whether messages are best communicated in written or spoken form.

7. Identify and describe the impact of the most prevalent nonverbal communication cues in human relations.

8. Understand the different motivations for lying.

9. Indicate how nonverbal cues are used to deceive and how to detect deception.

10. Identify and describe measures that can be taken by individuals and organizations to improve communication effectiveness.

ewlett-Packard is a major computer manufacturing firm that has many product development teams. Some of these teams include consultants who spend most of their time on the road away from headquarters. These consultants' offices are located at homes all across the United States. The product development teams, however, need to stay in constant touch with their team members, headquarters, and customers. They are well equipped with electronic devices, such as those for sending e-mail and faxes, so as to maintain an effective team communication process. Although some problems initially cropped up when team members were learning to work effectively at a distance, company research has indicated that the consultants are more productive working from their home offices than from headquarters. An added bonus is that they get to spend more time with their families when they are not traveling.[1]

Effective communication is a necessity for effective teamwork and organizational functioning. In the past, communication in organizations took place mostly face to face, by phone, or by memo. Today, we have added other electronic means of communication, such as e-mail and faxes. Although the modern additions to the communication process can enhance organizational functioning, they can have some drawbacks, as we will see later in this chapter. In fact, although communication should be a relatively straightforward process, it is often not as effective as it should be.

Surveys indicate that practicing managers spend about 80 percent of their time engaging in a single process: **communication**.[2] That is, they spend most of their day speaking to others, listening to them, or reading what they have written. Unfortunately, much of this communication is unsuccessful; other surveys indicate that a majority of organizational communications fail in their basic purpose—to get their message across.[3]

Despite this fact, communication in the world of work is far from a total waste of time. In one sense, it can be viewed as the cement holding organizations together. To see why this is so, consider what would happen if all communication within a company was blocked. Managers would no longer be able to lead, since they could not convey their wishes to subordinates. Departments or individuals would be unable to coordinate their activities. Decisions could not be made or would be reached in the absence of essential information. In addition, the organization would be unable to react to changing conditions in a unified and effective manner. In short, total chaos would soon reign supreme.

Because communication plays such a key role in the world of work, it is essential to know something about it, or you will be hard-pressed to understand our later discussions on many other aspects of human relations. In

communication The process through which one person or group transmits information to another person or group.

this chapter, therefore, we provide you with a basic understanding of the nature of communication. To do so, we touch on several topics. First, we examine organizational influences on communication—aspects of organizations that shape its form and content. Second, we discuss different forms of electronic communication. Third, since communication often occurs between individuals, we consider some of the personal factors that can affect it. Fourth, we examine how communication can be used to deceive others and how to detect deception. Finally, we discuss several techniques for enhancing communication—tactics for facilitating the smooth and accurate flow of information between individuals or groups.

$\mathscr{C}$OMMUNICATION: A DEFINITION

A boss praises a good job by one of her subordinates. A foreman directs the activities of a construction crew. An accountant prepares a memo on the tax aspects of a proposed business deal. A young woman smiles alluringly at a man seated nearby in the company cafeteria. Probably, you will be quick to agree that all of these incidents, varied as they are, involve some form of communication. But what, precisely, does this mean? What, in short, is communication? Many definitions exist, but most agree on the following basic points.

Communication is a process in which one person or group (the **sender**) transmits some type of information to another person or group (the **receiver**).[4] In some cases, this is all that occurs: Communication is a one-way street. This process is common when top executives in a large company send directives downward to their subordinates; often, they do not expect any information in return, at least not immediately. But in most situations, there is another aspect to the process: The receiver responds in some manner. That is, the person or group who receives the initial message returns a message to the person or group who initiated the communication. The receiver provides feedback to the sender. When this occurs, communication is a reciprocal affair involving the mutual exchange of information between two or more sides.

$\mathscr{O}$RGANIZATIONAL INFLUENCES ON COMMUNICATION: WHO SHOULD (OR CAN) COMMUNICATE WITH WHOM?

Everyone communicates in organizations—it is a basic fact of life at work. It is a rare person indeed who can perform his or her job in total isolation from others. Just as clearly, however, not everyone communicates with every-

sender   The individual who initiates communication by transmitting information to one or more people.

receiver   The individual toward whom communication is directed.

one else. Production-line employees do not generally speak to the company president. Similarly, people in different departments often do not have the opportunity (or the need) to communicate with one another. Thus communication within organizations, at least at the formal level, is far from haphazard. Several factors relating to **organizational structure** and policy dictate who can or should communicate with whom. These same factors sometimes specify the form of such communication as well as its appropriate targets. Such organizational influences on communication are important and will be considered here. We should hasten to add that, where communication is concerned, they are only part of the total picture. Every work setting is also interlaced with informal networks of communication—networks having little to do with the organizational chart or formal company policy. A great deal of information is transmitted through such networks, often with amazing speed. Thus we consider these networks as well.

Organizational Structure and Communication: The Formal Channels

Consider two organizations: One is a small, high-tech company that manufactures only a few products and operates on the very edge of expanding knowledge. The other is a giant, mature business that employs thousands of people and produces, advertises, and sells a wide range of items. Will communication within these two companies differ? Of course it will. One major reason for this lies in the fact that the two organizations have very different structures. The small, high-tech firm is likely to have very few departments. Furthermore, it probably has what is termed a flat organizational structure—very few levels of management separate top people in the company from those working in production. In fact, if the company is small enough, the CEO may make frequent appearances on the factory floor and talk directly to employees.

In contrast, the giant corporation will probably possess many different divisions, departments, and subunits. It will also have a tall organizational structure—one in which many levels separate production workers from top executives. And it will almost certainly evidence a higher degree of formalization. That is, there will be many rules and policies, perhaps written down in company handbooks, governing employee behavior and outlining the responsibilities that go along with each position. (The small, high-tech business may be almost totally lacking in such formal rules.)

Considering these contrasts in organizational structure, it is not difficult to predict how communication in the two companies will differ. In the small firm, communication between people holding different jobs may be quite direct, and as a result, information will flow readily between people performing different functions. In the mature corporation, communication will be much more rigid. Most important, the direction of communication—from higher to lower levels, or vice versa—will also differ

organizational structure   The way in which an organization is put together—its departments, formal lines of communication, chain of command, and so on.

sharply.[5] In a small company, the CEO and other executives may communicate *downward* to their subordinates, yet their closeness to these people and to production may ensure that a good deal of communication flows *upward* as well. That is, top people in the company may receive a great deal of feedback about their decisions, policies, and actions from subordinates—even from people on the factory floor.

In the giant corporation, communication will be predominantly downward, from high levels to lower ones. Directives and orders will flow from the top and be communicated downward through successive steps in the chain of command. Only on rare occasions will this pattern be reversed so that communication moves upward from lower to higher levels. In fact, one classic study found that 70 percent of assembly-line workers in large companies initiated communication with their supervisors less than once a month.[6] Another study revealed that, among managers, less than 15 percent of their total communication was directed to their superiors.[7] Also, when people do communicate upward, their conversations tend to be shorter than discussions with their peers.[8]

Upward communication also tends to suffer from serious inaccuracies. One aspect of this problem is that subordinates frequently feel they must highlight their accomplishments and downplay their mistakes if they are to be looked upon favorably.[9] Another factor that limits upward communication is the tendency for some individuals to fear that they will be rebuked by their supervisors if they speak to them and that their outspokenness will threaten their superiors and thus lessen their chances for promotion.[10] This fear is not unfounded and can cause quite serious problems, as you might imagine, in jobs requiring a high degree of coordination between people. The dynamic between pilots and copilots of commercial airlines is a perfect example of this problem. Too many times, copilots are reluctant to clearly assert themselves when they fear a pilot is making an error, because norms in the cockpit dictate that a senior person should not be contradicted. Unfortunately, many fatal accidents have been directly attributed to such failures of upward communication in the cockpit.[11]

Because of the one-way nature of communication in large companies, many high-ranking executives tend to become increasingly isolated from the day-to-day realities of their business. This fact is supported by the following dramatic finding: In actual surveys, fully 95 percent of high-ranking managers reported that they understood their employees' problems; in contrast, only about 30 percent of their employees agree that this was so.[12]

Not all news that is passed along may be directly job-related. People often discuss a variety of societal issues. In this domain, they often have the opportunity to pass on good or bad news that they have recently heard or read. For example, some new crime statistics may be available for the town or city. This news can be good or bad and more or less extreme. People are more likely to pass along less extreme information, probably because it is more believable than extreme information. Likewise, people are more willing to pass along bad news than good news, perhaps because such bad news is more surprising. Interestingly, this tendency to transmit bad news depends on the topic. If the topic is a generally negative one (such as crime or disease), then there is a tendency to pass along bad news even if it is extreme. If the topic is generally positive (survival of endangered species), however, people tend to pass along positive news even if it is extreme.[13]

The Grapevine and Rumors: Informal Channels of Communication

How do people get most of their information at work? It would be comforting to answer "through official channels of communication," but in many cases, this answer is wrong. Most people working in organizations receive more information through informal channels than through formal ones. In short, they learn more about what is happening in their company—how it is doing, what changes lie ahead, and countless other issues—from coworkers than from official memos, policy statements, or announcements. This informal network of communication is generally known as the **grapevine** and is based on the friendly social relations that often develop between people who have regular contact at work.[14] Once this network is established, it seems to operate at "full speed ahead," far surpassing official channels in the volume of information it transmits.

Interestingly, the information carried by such informal networks is often quite accurate. In fact, in one well-known study, approximately 80 percent of the information transmitted through the grapevine was found to be correct.[15] That remaining 20 percent, though, can lead to serious trouble. As you probably know from your own experiences, a story can be mainly true but still be misleading, because one essential fact is omitted or distorted. For example, you may hear that someone has been promoted over another person who was more directly in line for a position. You may not know that the first person turned down the promotion because it would require a move to a distant city.

The problem of inaccuracy is clearly responsible for giving the grapevine such a bad reputation. In extreme cases, information may be transmitted by a **rumor**—a message with little or no basis in fact, usually unverifiable. Typically, rumors are based on speculation, an overactive imagination, and wishful thinking rather than fact (see Figure 6.1). Rumors race like wildfire throughout organizations, because the information they present is so interesting and ambiguous. As such, they are open to embellishment as they travel from one person to the next. Hence, even if there was, at one point, some truth to a rumor, the message quickly becomes untrue. Before you know it, almost everyone in an organization hears a rumor, and its inaccurate message is taken as fact ("It must be true, since everyone knows it").

What can be done to counter the effects of rumors? This question is difficult to answer. Some research evidence suggests that directly refuting a rumor may *not* help

grapevine An informal channel of communication based on social relations among employees.

rumor Information transmitted through the grapevine that has little or no basis in fact.

Figure 6.1   **Rumors in the Office: One Type of Informal Communication**

As rumors get passed along in organizations, they may become rather fanciful.

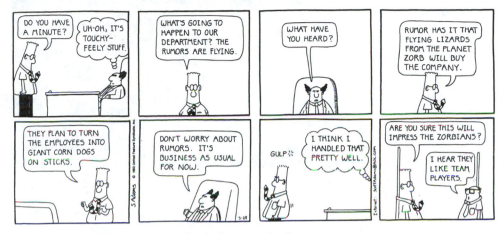

DILBERT reprinted by permission of United Features Syndicate.

counter its effects.[16] Instead, it helps spread the rumor among those who have not already heard it ("Oh, I didn't know people thought that") and strengthens it among those who have ("If it weren't true, they wouldn't be protesting so much"). What *does* help is directing people's attention away from the rumor, focusing instead on other things they know about its target. If you should ever become the victim of a vicious rumor, keep this in mind: Directing people's attention to positive things they already believe about you may be a helpful way of countering its effects. Although rumors may be impossible to stop, their impact can, with some effort, be effectively managed.

ℰLECTRONIC COMMUNICATION: THE IMPACT OF NEW TECHNOLOGY

One of the dramatic changes in the offices of the 1990s is the use of **electronic communication** (see Figure 6.2 on page 152). Faxes provide a convenient way to transmit letters and reports in a timely manner. Computer terminals can be used to transmit and receive messages by phone. This process, known as electronic mail (e-mail), is becoming a popular means of keeping in touch with colleagues or clients around the world. It has a number of distinct advantages. It is relatively inexpensive and fast. You can send similar messages to many different users

electronic communication   Recent technologic developments in communication, such as electronic mail and faxes, that provide a low-cost way to keep in touch with a broad network of individuals.

Figure 6.2 **Electronic Communication: Interaction on Computers**

Increasingly the work done in offices and at home is done by means of computers.

with simple commands. With minimal investments of time, you can also keep in touch with a broad network of people and stay abreast of the latest developments. Therefore, it can facilitate productivity in areas where these factors are important.

While there are many pluses to e-mail, some drawbacks exist as well. Some people become so enamored with it that they spend much of their day interacting with others on non-job-related issues or spend more time than necessary on job-related communication. It also increases the access that others have to our time and attention. It may not be as intrusive as telephone calls or personal interruptions, but it does require regular monitoring. For people whose effective performance requires careful time management, having to respond to the various demands of e-mail may be counterproductive. Busy executives, in particular, may cherish the insulation provided by a receptionist who controls phone calls and personal access.

E-mail and Internet Etiquette: Minding Your Electronic Manners

Most of us have experienced some of the drawbacks of e-mail. One problem that has been associated with e-mail is spamming. **Spamming** involves bulk marketing of junk e-mail to many users, most (if not all) of which holds little interest to them. A similar problem exists when one becomes overwhelmed by messages from certain user groups. Sometimes this problem may be compounded when people send their replies to the entire user group instead of a specific individual. It can become a tedious process to sort through one's mail to find the relevant message.

Although no specific rules or laws govern behavior in electronic communication, certain rules of etiquette or "Netiquette" have been suggested.[17] Some of these are as follows:

spamming   Bulk marketing of junk e-mail to many users.

1. Make messages brief and to the point.
2. Don't use e-mail for urgent messages.
3. Use group replies or mass mailings only when necessary.
4. Avoid having people read irrelevant material. The messages should be tailored to the needs of the recipients.
5. Use e-mail only as a supplement to other forms of interaction.
6. Treat people with respect, just as you would in person.
7. Respect the time and privacy of others.

For those who enjoy and benefit from e-mail, there are also some other potential problems. Coworkers or supervisors may attempt to gain access to another's e-mail. This, of course, represents a violation of privacy.[18] Supervisors may take such steps, in part to monitor the work performance of employees. In fact, monitoring performance on computers is increasingly a fact of life. It is estimated that about 40 percent of office workers are affected by computer monitoring of their work.[19] Research suggests that such monitoring may actually backfire; individuals who are informed that their performance is being monitored perform more poorly on complex solution tasks than those who are not being monitored.[20] The other important issue is worker morale. Being monitored implies a lack of trust on the part of supervisors. While this uncertainty may be justified for some employees, such knowledge might reduce job motivation for those that are intrinsically motivated (see the discussion of intrinsic motivation in Chapter 5). Some reports indicate that monitoring is related to worker stress and dissatisfaction,[21] but laboratory studies do not indicate much difference between supervisor and computer monitoring in this regard.[22]

Computer-Mediated Communication: Some Consequences

Because employees are increasingly interacting with one another via computers, a significant interest has arisen regarding how this medium influences various features of the interaction and work process. One might expect interactions to be more efficient, as less inclination may exist for getting sidetracked into non-work-related conversations. The limited face-to-face interaction, however, may inhibit the development of cohesive relationships among coworkers. Effective communication may also prove difficult because computer-mediated communication does not enable one to use the various nonverbal cues that often help us communicate our feelings.[23]

Studies comparing computer-mediated communication with face-to-face communication have found some significant differences between them.[24] The main disadvantage of computer-mediated communication appears to be that it is slower because it requires typing. As a result, it features fewer socioemotional remarks (expressions of feelings) and more task-oriented remarks. Participants are somewhat frustrated by the limitations of computer-mediated communication and often rate it and their communication partners less favorably than in the case of face-to-face communication. That is, this type of communication may produce poorer understanding of one's partner and the task.[25] It is not surprising, therefore, that in tasks requiring socioemotional conversations or interdependence (such as group judgment or negotiation), performance tends to be better in face-to-face groups. On the other hand, when groups have adequate time to adapt to the new technology, computer-mediated groups perform about as well as face-to-face groups. On intellectual tasks, such as idea generation or exchange, computer-mediated groups actually perform better than face-to-face groups.

One positive feature of computer-mediated communication is that job status or authority may appear less intimidating. Participation in group interaction tends to be more equal, with less evidence of social pressure or conformity and more uninhibited behavior. These outcomes are consistent with a reduction of potentially non-productive social barriers in organizations and a generally more participative structure. Nevertheless, the loss of social inhibitions can sometimes be a problem when it results in the sending of insults or impolite statements. Most of the studies conducted to date have used college students and not people in a work environment, so it is not clear that the same types of negative disinhibition would occur among coworkers who also engage in a considerable number of face-to-face interactions.

Computer-based communication will probably not replace face-to-face communication in work environments because of some of its limitations. Indeed, important decisions will probably always require face-to-face interactions involving an effective exchange of both intellectual and emotional information. Nevertheless, a mixture of the two forms of communication in a work environment seems to offer some real advantages in producing a fuller participation of coworkers in idea-sharing and decision-making processes. The reduction of conformity pressures and disinhibition in computer-mediated communication may also increase the chances of creative contributions and reduce the tendency toward groupthink (Chapter 8). Table 6.1 summarizes the various positive and negative consequences of the two types of communication.

Telecommuting: Work Life Away from the Office

An increasing number of jobs in this technical/computer age do not require that a worker reside in a particular location. Computer networks allow us to access and work with data from distant sites. Consequently, many employees are performing a significant amount of work at home. This phenomenon has been called **telecommuting**.[26] Among the obvious advantages of telecommuting are reduced costs for commercial office space and commuting as well as the conservation of time involved in the commuting process.[27]

telecommuting   Doing work away from the work site by means of computer.

Table 6.1	Face-to-Face and Computer-Mediated Communication Affect Social Interaction in Different Ways

Face-to-Face	Computer-Mediated
Social inhibition	Disinhibition
Better for socioemotional tasks	Better for intellective tasks
More conformity	More independence
General satisfaction	Some dissatisfaction
Positive feelings for group members	Some misunderstanding of group members
Differences in degree of participation	Increased equality of participation

Not surprisingly, most telecommuters express quite positive sentiments about their experience. They feel that they are more productive away from the central office, and many report more hours spent on work than before.[28] Some reports indicate that telecommuting can be very cost-effective for a corporation.[29] In addition, the worker's relationship with his or her family may improve. The greater flexibility in work hours allows for more active involvement in family activities and increased involvement of females in the workplace.[30] To realize such benefits, employees need to have a supportive home environment, including an understanding and cooperative family and sufficient space. To avoid interference of child-care duties with work, most companies insist that arrangements be made for child care during work hours.[31, 32]

Although telecommuting has many positive features, some disadvantages may arise as well (see Table 6.2 on page 156). Many of these drawbacks center on the limited communication and interaction with other employees and the worker's manager. In fact, an initial period of strong positive feelings is often followed by a period of reduced enthusiasm, as telecommuters experience some of the negatives of working in isolation. It appears to be particularly difficult to maintain a good rapport and level of trust with one's manager. Both the manager and the employee need to make special efforts to maintain an effective long-distance relationship and adapt their styles of interacting. When a change in management occurs, it can, of course, be quite a challenge for the telecommuter. Companies may need to institute special programs for telecommuters to overcome some of these problems and provide opportunities to build trust and rapport among employees and management. Part-time telecommuting may be the most effective arrangement, as it combines the advantages of telecommuting with those of on-site teamwork and interactions.[33]

Table 6.2   **Disadvantages of Telecommuting: A Few Problems**

Although telecommuting is an attractive work alternative, telecommuters report some of the problems listed below.

	Percent Reported
No disadvantages	35
Feeling of isolation	29
Reduced attention from coworkers	24
Managerial problems	17
Need for self-discipline	17
Technological problems	16
Reduced feelings of cohesion	14
Need to plan ahead	13

Data from a survey by Reinsch (1997); see note 31.

PERSONAL INFLUENCES ON COMMUNICATION: DIFFERENT STYLES, DIFFERENT CHANNELS

Receiving and transmitting information are basic to life at work. But, as you probably know from your own experience, all people do not accomplish these functions with equal ease. Some people find communication a simple or enjoyable task; they can easily transmit information to others either in person, over the phone, or through letters and reports. In contrast, others find communication difficult and unpleasant. In extreme cases, they may even suffer great nervousness or anxiety when faced with such tasks as giving a speech or preparing a written report. These different reactions to communication tasks call attention to a key point: Personal factors play a major role in this process. Many traits, abilities, and characteristics are important in this respect. However, most seem to fall under two major headings: personal style, and verbal and nonverbal channels of communication.

Personal Style and Communication: Why Some People Are More Effective Communicators Than Others

When groups choose one of their members to serve as a spokesperson, they do not proceed in a random fashion. Rather, they try to select an individual who is known to be effective in communicating with others. The reason for this is obvious: The better a person's communication skills, the more clearly and forcefully he or she will make the group's views known. But what factors make an individual an effective communicator? This question has been a central one in the study of persuasion—the process through which we attempt to sway others to our own way of thinking. Since we will cover persuasion in detail in Chapter 7, we will not mention all the personal factors contributing to communication effectiveness here. Instead, we will call your attention to a few that seem especially important.

The first communication strategy—whether to communicate with others in a simple or complex style—is easy to illustrate. Suppose you have to listen to two people presenting verbal reports. One speaks in short, clear sentences consisting mainly of everyday language. The other offers involved, complex thoughts expressed in sentences filled with jargon. Which would you prefer? Almost certainly, the former. While you will probably find the first speech easy to follow and understand, the second may leave you totally confused—or even with a splitting headache. The moral provided by this example is obvious: When attempting to communicate with others, it is usually best to follow the K.I.S.S. principle: Keep It Short and Simple.[34] This is true in written as well as verbal messages. Communicators who attempt to dazzle their audiences with complex, involved messages are more likely to put them to sleep or bore them to tears than to communicate successfully with them. As such, this aspect of personal style is important.

The fact that individuals respond favorably to simple messages makes eminent good sense. After all, no one likes being confused or bewildered. Now prepare for a mild surprise: Research findings also suggest that, while most persons prefer simplicity and clarity in communication, they are strongly impressed by speed, too.[35] In many cases, individuals who present verbal messages rapidly are viewed as being more effective communicators than those who deliver their messages at a slower, more leisurely pace. Specifically, fast talkers are perceived as more knowledgeable about their subject matter, more competent, and even more sincere than slow ones. And they are not simply *viewed* as being more effective; they actually are. Communicators who speak at a fast rate tend to persuade their audiences more than those who talk slowly.[36] These facts point to a straightforward and important conclusion: If you want to be effective at interpersonal communication, strive for a fast rate of delivery. Being able to present your views rapidly and without hesitation can be a major plus.

A great deal of evidence suggests that an individual's *credibility* also plays a key role in determining success at communication.[37] If an individual is viewed as high in credibility—someone who can be believed and trusted—he or she may be quite effective in transmitting information to others. If, instead, an individual is seen as low in credibility, effectiveness in communication will be sorely restricted. Thus, if you wish to be successful in getting your message across in a wide range of situations, you should be careful to protect your personal credibility. Once you are perceived as untrustworthy, your chances of getting others to listen, let alone change their minds, will be small. Successful politicians have to take these factors seriously if they want to stay in office.

Verbal Communication: Speaking with Words

Because you are reading this book, we know that you are familiar with verbal communication—transmitting and receiving ideas using words. Verbal communication can be either oral (as in face-to-face talks, telephone conversations, and tape recordings) or written (as in memos, letters, order blanks, and electronic mail). Because both oral and written communication involve the use of words, they fall under the heading of verbal communication.

What types of verbal communication are most effective? Research has shown that supervisors believe communication is most effective when oral messages are followed by written ones.[38] This combination is especially preferred under certain conditions—for example, when immediate action is required, when an important policy change is being made, when a praiseworthy employee is identified, or when a company directive is announced. General information or that requiring only future action is judged to be most effective in written form.

Apparently, oral messages are useful in getting others' immediate attention, and following up in writing helps make the message more permanent, something that can be referred to in the future. Oral messages also allow for immediate two-way communication between parties, whereas written communiqués are frequently only one-way (or take too long for a response if one is necessary). As a result, it is not surprising that researchers have found two-way communications (for example, face-to-face discussions or telephone conversations) are more commonly used in organizations than one-way communications (for example, memos).[39] One-way, written communications tend to be reserved for more formal, official messages (for example, announcements about position openings). Apparently, both written and spoken communication have their place in organizational communication.

The choice of a communication medium also greatly depends on a very important factor—the degree of clarity of the message being sent. The more ambiguous the message, the more managers prefer using oral media (such as telephones or face-to-face contact); the clearer the message, the more managers prefer using written media (such as letters or memos).[40] Most managers are sensitive to the need to use a form of communication that allows them to transfer information more efficiently.

It would be misleading to conclude this section with the idea that communication occurs only at the verbal level. Although words are a very important part of communication, they represent only one way of transmitting messages. A great deal of what is communicated is done in the absence of words—nonverbally.

Nonverbal Communication: Using the Unspoken Language

You have probably heard someone say that we communicate more with our bodies than with words. Do you think this statement is true? In one way, it probably makes a lot of sense. Our faces, gestures, posture, and movements help us express emotions that accompany our verbal statements as well as form a substitute for such statements. Sometimes, a frowning stare can change the inappropriate behavior of a child or even an employee.

Many times, you may find it difficult to interpret someone's nonverbal behavior. When people stare at you, what does that mean? Do they find you attractive or strange looking? Or are they simply "spaced out"? When people look you straight in the eye while trying to sell you an automobile, does that mean they are being honest or just pretending to be to take advantage of you? As you can see, the role of nonverbal behavior in communication can be complicated. There are some general principles, though; research has shown that **nonverbal communication** functions primarily to convey interpersonal feelings of like or dislike, degree of interest in the communication process, and the relative status of the communicator. Let's see what we actually do know about this interesting way of communicating.

One of the bodily cues that can convey messages is posture. When someone slumps in his or her chair during a meeting, it may be a sign of boredom or depression. If this individual sits up straight, it may signify interest or elation. Similarly, if two people lean toward each other while holding a conversation, this is often a sign that they like one another; if they lean away, less favorable reactions probably exist.

Unmasking the Face: Reading Facial Expressions.

Perhaps the most obvious nonverbal cues are provided by facial expressions. The people around us smile, frown, clench their teeth, and display many other facial actions. Research on these expressions has yielded many interesting facts, but among these, two seem most important. First, although the number of different expressions individuals demonstrate seems infinite, all are based on combinations of only six different emotions: happiness, sadness, surprise, fear, anger, and disgust.[41] Second, facial expressions are, by and large, universal. That is, no matter where you are in the world, a smile is interpreted as a sign of happiness or friendliness, and a frown is a sign of sadness or annoyance.

But if facial expressions are universal and based on only a few underlying emotions, why are they so often misleading? Why do they sometimes give a false impression about others' true feelings? The answer is simple: Individuals often attempt to conceal their real feelings and emotions. Thus they alter or manage their outward expressions to mislead others. There are many reasons for this. First, they may not wish to reveal their true feelings to others either because it would be embarrassing or because they do not feel comfortable about disclosing this information. Second, concealing their feelings may be part of their job or role. For example, negotiators must avoid tipping their hands to their opponents, and they usually try to do this by maintaining a "poker face." Similarly, physicians attempt to hide worry or concern from their patients to avoid upsetting them. Third, many people actually earn their living from skilled manipulation of their facial expressions—actors, salespersons, and politicians, to name a few.

nonverbal communication   A silent form of communication involving facial expressions, eye contact, body movements, or dress.

Smiling: What's in a Smile?   What do you think when you see someone smiling? You probably presume that this person is happy. In fact, we may smile for many different reasons. We may smile with relief after an exam or with anxiety just before giving a speech. Have you ever noticed all of the smiling faces at a funeral? Presumably, these smiles reflect some emotion other than enjoyment. Smiles of enjoyment appear to be somewhat different physiologically than other smiles. Muscles that surround the eye are involved in smiles of enjoyment, but not other smiles.[42]

When others smile, don't you sometimes feel like smiling as well? Smiles are one of the most potent nonverbal cues. People who smile are not only seen as being happy, but they are also rated as more attractive, sociable, sincere, and competent.[43] Even more important, people who smile stimulate smiling in those around them. (Fortunately, when people frown, others do not tend to frown as well.[44]) Women smile more often and are smiled at more than men. While this may reflect a generally positive social disposition on the part of women, others interpret it as reflecting gender status differences. Low-status people may use smiles to ingratiate themselves with high-status individuals. Since women have generally been relegated a lower status in many cultures than men, they tend to smile more at men than vice versa. Consistent with the role of status in smiling, individuals applying for jobs tend to smile more than those who are conducting the interview. However, this effect was observed primarily in men; female smiling was only marginally affected by this status difference.[45] So, while status differences are related to smiling, it may not be the reason women smile more than men.

Obviously, smiling can help contribute to a positive work environment, but does it contribute to a person's success at work? As part of a pleasant disposition, it will certainly evoke favorable personal evaluations and help contribute to a positive atmosphere. In fact, there appears to be a **smiles-leniency effect** in that people who have done something wrong but smile are treated more leniently than those who do not smile. In one study, students were shown pictures of students who were taught to express different smiles.[46] A felt smile is one that expresses true positive feelings. A false smile involves appearing happy when one feels no emotion. A miserable smile involves smiling despite unpleasant circumstances.[47] The students in the photos were judged as to the likelihood that they had engaged in academic dishonesty and the severity of action to be taken. No differences were noted in perception of guilt, but those who smiled were recommended for more lenient actions than those with a neutral expression (see Figure 6.3). Even though smiling may have some positive results at work, smiles are not likely to compensate for persistent job-related deficiencies, such as lack of organization and tardiness. There is also the potential problem of being seen as phony if a smile is inconsistent with other behavior. If someone is generating false rumors about you at work, his smile may actually increase your negative feelings about him. By all means, project a sunny and pleasant disposition—but make sure it is accompanied by consistent actions.

smiles-leniency effect   Smiling wrongdoers are treated less severely than nonsmiling ones.

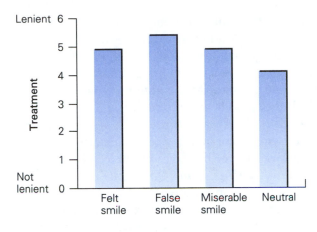

 Smiles: Getting a Break

When students smiled, they were given more lenient treatment for academic dishonesty than if they did not smile.

Gazes and Stares: Are the Eyes the Key to the Soul?   How comfortable are you when you look a stranger in the eye? You probably quickly avert your gaze when direct eye contact is made. In fact, with strangers, mutual gazes tend to last about a second. Why are we so sensitive about eye contact? Maybe because it makes us very self-aware, which tends to be a generally unpleasant state. While we limit mutual eye contact, nonmutual gazing at others is important in the communication process and in regulating interactions.

What does it mean when someone looks at you? The meaning of eye contact appears to vary with the situation or the relationship. In romantic situations, eye contact appears to indicate the degree of attraction of the partners for one another. However, people may also have intense eye contact when they are angry. So, eye contact may demonstrate the intensity of one's feelings, whether they are positive or negative.

In work or performance situations, eye contact is perceived as reflecting competence. If you maintain eye contact while speaking or being interviewed for a job, you are seen as more competent than those who do not. In fact, those who maintain eye contact in work or speaking situations are seen as more dominant or more powerful. In general, it is to your advantage to maintain eye contact in most interactions, as it will yield more favorable perceptions. Of course, this can be overdone; people who stare inappropriately tend to make others uncomfortable.[48]

It would be difficult for most of us to have comfortable interactions with others if we were not able to meet their gaze. Shifting of gazes helps cue people to regulate their conversations. For example, a long gaze at the end of a statement may indicate a desire to have the other person take a turn. We also use eye contact when we attempt to control individuals: to persuade them, gain their approval, or take control of an interaction. Here again, it is important to be moderate since obvious "overgazing" may be seen as an attempt to manipulate. The result will be either increased resistance or attempts to escape rather than compliance.[49]

Physical Contact in Interactions: That Personal Touch.   In the course of our daily interactions, we often touch people in various ways. We may shake hands with a new acquaintance, give a pat of encouragement to an employee, or hug a friend that we have not seen for a while. These gestures are a natural part of our lives and may help amplify our verbal statements and the associated emotions. However, people differ greatly in the extent to which they tend to touch other people. In some cultures, touching is a frequent part of all types of interactions, while in other cultures individuals are more restrained.[50] It is important to understand the norms of different cultures so we do not offend people unknowingly. For example, a big fuss was made when the Australian prime minister touched the Queen of England on the back. Royal etiquette forbids such a gesture by nonroyalty.

Women are more likely to touch others than men.[51] This trend is consistent with their tendency to be more expressive in a variety of ways. Men may, in fact, misinterpret touching by women as indicating sexual interest when it is simply intended to reflect friendliness.[52] Another interesting pattern is that men are more likely to initiate touch with women than the reverse. However, for all ages, females still initiate touch more than males.[53] What does this all mean? Some have suggested that the perceived status difference between men and women in late teens through middle age is responsible. The Tailhook scandal, in which Navy officers "manhandled" female officers in the hallway of a hotel, represents a shameful example of the role of touching to exploit status differences. If women in a culture are seen as having lower status, they may feel more inhibited than men in initiating touches in male/female interactions. Thus, while touching may be a natural part of interaction at work, we obviously have to be sensitive to the meaning people attach to it. You certainly would not want to put your arm casually around the shoulder of your boss unless this person had encouraged this type of friendly interaction. Nor should a boss abuse his or her status by initiating unwanted touches with employees. Extreme versions of this problem can be seen as sexual harassment (see Chapter 12). Finally, men need to learn that female touching is not necessarily an indicator of sexual intent. With a little common sense, it is possible to have a pleasant and natural work environment where people can express themselves openly without offending one another.

Communication through Dress: Do the Clothes Make the Person?   You are probably already aware of the importance of dress as a vehicle of communication. This is especially the case in organizations where, as self-styled "wardrobe engineer" John T. Malloy reminds us, what we wear communicates a great deal about our competence as employees.[54] Organizational researchers are increasingly conscious of the importance of dress as a communication vehicle (see Figure 6.4).[55]

What we communicate by the clothing we wear is not a simple matter. We cannot make up for the absence of critical job skills by simply putting on the right clothes. People who are qualified for jobs, however, may communicate certain things about

Figure 6.4   **Dressing for Success: Communication with Clothes**

Which of the people below would you like? Why?

themselves via the way they dress. Clearly, one of the key messages sent by the clothes people wear is their understanding of the appropriate way to present themselves for a job. Generally speaking, the most positive images are communicated when people are dressed appropriately for the occasion.[56] An important reason for this appears to be that people who do so tend to feel better about themselves; they project higher levels of self-confidence. In one study, for example, student job candidates appeared for interviews wearing either their informal street clothes (for example, T-shirts and jeans) or conservative garb (for example, suits with shirts and ties). Those in formal clothing not only felt they made a more positive impression than those dressed casually, but also tended to express this more positive self-image by requesting a starting salary that was, on average, $4,000 higher.[57]

In our culture, individuals may have stereotypes about people who dress in a certain way. Those who dress conservatively tend to be seen as more forceful, self-reliant, dynamic, aggressive, and decisive than those wearing softer, more casual clothing.[58] Thus it is important to be sensitive to the image you need to project for a certain job and to choose a mode of dress consistent with that image. Clothing may be a powerful vehicle of communication, not just because of what it connotes about you, but also because it changes the way you feel about yourself.

Another important characteristic that can be communicated by dress is sexual intention. A person wearing revealing clothes may be seen as having interest in sexual activity. This interpretation is particularly common in men; women who wear revealing clothes are judged as more sexy and seductive than those who do not.[59] Of course, if this type of impact is intended, it is fine (assuming that it doesn't lead to problems at work). If you want to be judged on your professional competence, however, it may backfire, leading to unwanted advances or sexual harassment. When you dress for work, think about the image you want to project there. If you are not sure whether certain clothing is appropriate, you might seek the feedback of trusted coworkers.

Cultural Differences.   We have noted a variety of cultural differences in nonverbal communication. You might have wondered whether there were any general principles to explain such differences. It appears these may, in fact, exist. Hall has proposed that cultures are either high or low context. In a **low-context culture** such as the United States, speech is explicit, and the message is conveyed fairly directly by the words spoken.[60] Nonverbal cues are of secondary importance in these cultures. In a **high-context culture,** the meaning of a message must be determined by examining its context carefully. Context can include past knowledge about the communicator, the setting in which the communication is taking place, and various nonverbal cues, such as eye contact and tone of voice. Many countries in Asia and the Middle East can be classified as high context cultures. For example, the Japanese rarely say no. Instead, they may frown, take a deep breath, and say, "That is difficult."[61] There appears to be a close link between low/high context and the individualism/collectivism dimension discussed in Chapter 1.[62] Individualist countries tend to be direct or explicit in their communication (low context), while communication in collectivist countries is indirect with emotional communication playing an important role (high context).

Even though there are considerable variations in communication styles across cultures, a number of patterns of nonverbal communication appear to be similar worldwide. Basic emotions are expressed in a similar fashion in most cultures. There is high agreement when individuals from one culture are asked to determine the feelings expressed in pictures of individuals from another culture.[63] Certain facial expressions appear to be universal, such as a quick raise of an eyebrow in a greeting or a wrinkled nose to show contempt. Smiles are interpreted across the world as a submissive, nonthreatening gesture. In most cultures, acquaintances maintain closer physical distance than strangers.[64] We do not yet know why nonverbal communication patterns across cultures are so similar in some ways and so different in others. Possibly, some of these patterns are a remnant of evolutionary development, while others are the result of societal differences. Whatever the reason, it is important for all of us to be attuned to both verbal and nonverbal channels of communication to be successful in cross-cultural relationships.

low-context culture   A culture in which the meaning of communication comes primarily from the words spoken rather than nonverbal or other contextual factors.

high-context culture   A culture in which the meaning of a communication depends greatly on nonverbal factors, such as eye contact and tone of voice.

Nonverbal Communication: Some Practical Uses.   By now, you are probably convinced that individuals communicate with one another through nonverbal cues such as facial expression, eye contact, body language, and dress. But what are the practical implications of all this? Growing evidence suggests that the way individuals use and interpret this silent language can have important effects on their lives and careers.

First, research shows that being expressive—using nonverbal cues freely and effectively—can contribute to success in several different fields. In one study, clients at a large clinic who typically saw different doctors were asked to rate them.[65] It was found that the doctors who were expressive—those who showed a high level of nonverbal communication with clients—were the most popular. In the same investigation, a group of highly successful salespersons were studied. As you might expect, they too were found to be high in expressiveness. The message in these findings is clear: In some professions, at least, being able to communicate with others nonverbally can be a big plus.

Skill in nonverbal communication can also yield handsome results from interviews.[66] Persons who are able to transmit positive cues to the interviewer receive higher ratings than those who do not communicate in this manner. For example, in one investigation, subjects played the role of interviewer and conducted a brief job interview with another person who played the role of applicant for an entry-level management job. The applicant behaved in one of two ways: In one condition, she emitted many positive nonverbal cues: She leaned toward the interviewer, smiled frequently, and maintained a high level of eye contact. In the other, she refrained from demonstrating these positive cues. After the interview, subjects rated the applicant on several dimensions relating to her qualifications for the job and personal traits. She received higher ratings when she emitted positive nonverbal cues than when she showed more neutral behavior.[67]

These and related findings suggest that being aware of the process of nonverbal communication and being able to use it effectively can yield important benefits. Thus, there are strong reasons for developing our skills in this subtle but important area of human relations. (How expressive are you? For some insight into this intriguing question, refer to the *Experiential Exercise* section.)

DECEIVING OTHERS: HOW IS IT DONE AND DETECTED?

We do not always want others to know our true feelings. We may want to persuade someone to buy a product even though we do not like it ourselves. We may not want our bosses or teachers to know that we don't like them. Have you ever told someone you liked them when you did not? Did you feel uncomfortable doing so, or was it rel-

Lying: Truth or Consequences

President Clinton's lying about his relationship with Monica Lewinsky had serious consequences for the lives of many people.

atively easy for you? Some people have a difficult time not showing their true feelings, while others find it easy to act contrary to their emotions. Of course, some deceptions may be minor, as when we don't let someone know we did not like a dish he or she cooked.

How do we find out how much people really do lie? Of course, the most straightforward way is to ask them, hoping that they won't lie about lying. This approach has been tried in several studies. If we can believe these reports, people report lying about once or twice a day.[68] All of us have probably lied on occasion. Sometimes they are only "little white lies," such as telling someone you already have a date when you really do not. Such lies help us deal with situations in which we are uncomfortable in telling the truth, such as "I really don't like you, and I wish you would leave me alone." We seem to have a reasonable degree of tolerance for such lying, since many of us have coped with a variety of situations in this manner. Other forms of deception are seen as more serious. Lying about past drug abuse, sexual activity, employment, or income on a tax return can have serious repercussions (see Figure 6.5).

A Typology of Lies and Liars: How Do We Lie?

Although most of us agree that lying is wrong, some scholars have suggested that lying is an important part of maintaining effective social interactions. Most of us want to feel good about ourselves and in our interactions. Sometimes lying enables us to achieve such aims. Lies can also be used to manage our impressions or emotions. In that sense, they may be no different than many of the other behaviors we use for that purpose (Chapter 3). For example, if a friend asks whether we like her hideous dress, we will tend to say "yes" so as to maintain good relations with her and avoid an unpleasant conflict. Most people see these types of lies as not very serious and express little regret over them.[69]

Lies can be categorized as being **self-centered** or **other-oriented.** Self-centered lies are primarily designed to maintain a positive impression with others or to get our way. A salesperson might say that he really likes the look of a suit on someone simply to make a sale or a student may tell a teacher that she really studied hard for an exam when she did not. Other-oriented lies are motivated by a concern for maintaining pleasant interactions or enhancing social relationships. For example, we may indicate agreement with a friend's views even though we disagree. We may say we really look forward to a lunch with our boss even though we actually find it difficult to talk with him or her.[70]

Of course, some people lie much more than others. Those who lie frequently tend be very concerned about the impressions they make on others. They may be quite sociable but also quite manipulative. When most of their lies tend to be self-serving, they report less satisfaction in their relationships. This result may arise partly because they have difficulty in developing genuine relationships with people based on real feelings. On the other hand, those whose lies are other-oriented tend to enjoy fairly good relationships.[71] These types of lies tend to occur more often with friends than with strangers.

Lying at work seems to be governed by the same principles as lying in general. Lies at work may be motivated by self-interest in advancing oneself in the organization. We want to impress our coworkers and supervisors, so we tend to monitor carefully what we say to key people. We may give false compliments and publicly agree with actions or positions that we know are favored by key people. Role conflicts are another significant source of lies in work environments. Workers often must attempt to balance the demands of different departments, family, and outside interests. Someone may say he needs to leave early for a doctor's appointment when he is really attending his daughter's swim meet. A worker may say that she has been working hard on a project when she has really been focusing on the demands of another division.

Is honesty always the best policy? Lying can be a serious problem. If people lie about significant issues, they can be fired or destroy relationships. Thus honesty is important for developing trust at work and with one's friends and family. Honest expressions of feelings and thoughts can help relationships grow and work environments improve. The failure to express our true thoughts or opinions in groups can often lead to bad decisions (Chapter 8). In contrast, conflicts produced by honest differences of opinion can stimulate deeper thinking and creativity (Chapter 9). Clearly, honesty appears to be a good policy in most cases. Nevertheless, we must recognize that in many informal social interactions, the feelings of others

self-centered lies   Lies designed to maintain a positive impression.

other-oriented lies   Lies that are motivated by a concern to maintain pleasant interactions.

can be served best by not being ruthlessly honest about issues that are in most cases of minor importance (for example, whether we like a dinner someone has prepared or a certain piece of music someone has played). (See the *Ethics at Work* feature.)

Skill at Lying: Success in Deceit

When dealing with people in personal and work situations, it is often important to know whether they are telling the truth. Sometimes, a background check can provide confirming evidence, but often we have to rely on a person's word. In that type of sit-

Ethics at Work

To Lie or Not to Lie: That Is the Question

Anita Primrose is filling out an application for a position as student recruitment co-ordinator at Ekberg College. She has worked for six years as an assistant coordinator at Fairmont Junior College. She also has a bachelor's degree in personnel management. She has a positive outlook on life and generates much enthusiasm in those who work with her. All of these qualities and qualifications make her a strong candidate for the position. However, when Anita comes to the questions about personal background, she is faced with a dilemma. During her sophomore year in high school, she ran around with a group of kids who were involved in drugs. She was having some problems at home and found comfort in the acceptance provided by these friends. Not surprisingly, she joined in some of the drug-taking sessions. Her grades suffered, and she was in danger of dropping out of school. However, when one of these friends committed suicide, she was shocked into reevaluating her lifestyle. With the help of some counseling, she was able to develop better relations with her parents and a stronger self-concept. She has not been involved in drugs since that time.

1. Should Anita admit to having used drugs in the past, or should she deny it?
2. Do you think such questions are relevant for a job evaluation? Do employers have the right to ask them?
3. How do you think admitting past drug use will affect her chances for getting the job?
4. If she is hired, do you think knowledge of past drug use by superiors will affect her work relationships?
5. What about Anita's right to privacy?
6. What is right or wrong in this situation?

uation, how do you determine whether someone is telling the truth? Do you try to look him straight in the eye to see if he avoids your gaze? Do you watch for signs of nervousness? Such techniques can be useful in detecting lies. For example, dilated pupils, frequent self-touching, body movement, frequent blinking, high vocal pitch, lack of spontaneity, negative verbal statements, hesitation in speech, and reduced smiling are just some of the characteristics that have been associated with lying.[72] Personality is not a good predictor of lying. Lying often seems to be motivated by situational factors, such as the rewards or approval that might be gained or the need to cover up inconsistencies. Some people are better at lying than others. People who have a high degree of social skill (that is, they are expressive and socially tactful) are particularly successful at deceiving others. Men are more skilled at lying than women.[73] Not surprisingly, socially anxious or unskilled individuals are not very successful liars.[74] Table 6.3 provides a summary of the nonverbal cues for detecting lying.

Highly motivated liars, possibly because they have a lot to gain from their lies, may try a little too hard to appear sincere. Observers can often detect this, especially when they have access to nonverbal behavior such as body movements, facial expressions, and tone of voice.[75] However, liars tend to manipulate their facial expressions to appear honest, so it is sometimes easier to detect deception when we do not have access to facial cues.[76] When liars fear being caught or feel guilty about lying, it may be easier to detect their lies. However, some people appear to be natural liars who have little personal difficulty in lying and are quite successful at it. These individuals

---

Table 6.3   Cues Associated with Lying and Deception

People who lie have certain nonverbal characteristics. However, these are not necessarily the same as those traits observers associate with lying.

Cues Associated with Lying	Cues Interpreted by Observers as Indicating Deception
Lack of spontaneity	Less sustained eye contact
Negative verbal statements	Less smiling
Less smiling	More posture shifts
Dilation of pupils	Longer response times
Hesitation in speech	Slower rate of speech
Self-touching	More speech errors
Body movement	More speech hesitations
Blinking	Higher pitch
High vocal pitch	Unusual nonverbal behaviors

apparently have been successful in deceiving others since childhood and may be quite confident of their deception abilities.[77]

Our ability to detect lies is only slightly better than chance.[78] Women are somewhat better at spotting untruths than men.[79] We tend to use a certain set of cues to determine whether someone is lying. Someone who avoids our gaze, hesitates in her speech, or displays unusual nonverbal behavior, such as staring and arm raising, is likely seen as trying to deceive us.[80] The trouble is, good liars can manipulate these cues quite easily, while people who are honest but socially anxious may be seen as untruthful.[81] Since the face can be manipulated in many different ways, it is an effective means of deceiving; your body or tone of voice is more likely to give you away than your face.[82] How do these observations square with your experience? Of course, access to a wide variety of cues makes it impossible for us to know which of these is critical in a successful deception.

PRINCIPLES OF EFFECTIVE COMMUNICATION: SOME USEFUL TECHNIQUES

Personal Strategies

What can you do to become a more effective communicator? You may want to take one of the many courses that are offered to increase your communication skills. One advantage of such courses is that they provide practice in techniques in a group setting. The feedback and support derived during such practice may give you the confidence required to become a more effective communicator. Among the drawbacks of such courses are they sometimes present overly simple solutions to complex problems, and they usually do not include practice with those individuals that are part of the communication problem. The sensitivity training movement provides a case in point.

Sensitivity training is the outcome of a movement designed to increase interpersonal openness and accuracy of communication in groups.[83] Individuals often inhibit their true feelings because they fear evaluation or negative reactions. Sensitivity training sessions provide a nonthreatening environment in which to communicate feelings honestly. Only when our real feelings are expressed can we obtain useful feedback from others about the accuracy of those feelings. For example, you might not like people who chew gum, but you are unlikely to tell them this to their face. In a sensitivity training group, you are free to express this feeling to the group members. They, in turn, might ask you why you feel this way or give their reactions to this comment. You might discover that

sensitivity training A group-interaction technique designed to increase interpersonal openness and communication accuracy.

others agree with you, or that those who chew gum do so not to irritate you but to take their mind off their desire for a cigarette. As a result, you may learn much about yourself and others.

Most participants in these sessions feel they have benefited from the experience.[84] Studies indicate that sensitivity training may increase empathy for others and reduce prejudice.[85] It may also help people become more forthright in expressing their feelings. Unfortunately, this may not go over well at home or at work if others have not been similarly sensitized. Successful attempts at improving communication in the workplace and at home should involve the entire work or family unit if at all possible.

Listening: The Other Side of the Coin

Have you ever had the following experience? You are introduced to someone at a party or meeting. You speak with her for a few minutes, and then another person joins you. You are about to introduce your new acquaintance when you discover—much to your chagrin—that you have already forgotten her name! Why do such events occur? It might be comforting to blame it on the frailty of human memory, but in fact, the reason is even simpler: Often, we just don't listen.[86] Instead of paying careful attention to what others say, we allow our minds to wander. We daydream, we think about what we are going to say when it is our turn to talk, or we mentally argue with the speaker and so fail to follow all his remarks. Obviously, if we do not listen carefully to what others say, communication with them suffers. In extreme cases where we have managed to totally tune another person out, it may cease altogether. For this reason, learning to be a good listener is essential to becoming an effective communicator.

One problem with listening is that we typically take a passive role. This makes sense, since the other person is doing the talking. We may relax a bit and, if it is not critically important to listen (for example, for directions on a test), our minds may wander to more pressing issues. Of course, this is impolite and potentially embarrassing when it is your turn in the conversation. Another reason we may not listen carefully is that we do not respect the opinion of the speaker. This may not be lost on the victim of your inattention. Since good listening is a fairly rare commodity, you will make a very good impression on both friends and strangers by showing a sincere interest in what they have to say. One way to overcome the poor listening habit is to become an active listener.[87] **Active listening** involves responding to a speaker's message by giving him or her feedback about your reactions. This can be in the form of questions, interpretations, clarifications—any response that indicates you are interested and in tune with the message.

> **active listening**   Attentive listening in which the listener reacts to communication with questions, feedback, or requests for elaboration.

Guidelines for Effective Human Relations

Using What You've Learned

In this chapter, we examined a broad range of principles about communication in human relations. Although few rules will apply to every situation, there are some general guidelines suggested by the various findings we discussed. These are summarized below for your consideration. Remember, no rule works 100 percent in every situation. However, these guidelines should help improve your success at communicating in a wide variety of situations.

- Present your message as simply as possible in a pleasant but forceful manner.

- Maintain your credibility by being honest and straightforward in your communications.

- Dress appropriately, especially if you are in a subordinate position.

- Follow up your oral communications with written ones, especially if the message is a complex one.

- Be aware of your nonverbal behaviors, and use them to enhance your communication skills. A smiling or pleasant demeanor and appropriate use of eye contact can enhance the impact of your message. In general, the more expressive you are and the more pleasant your nonverbal expressions, the more effective you will be in human relations.

- Be attuned to the cues that indicate deception, such as lack of spontaneity and hesitation in speech. Although these and other cues are not foolproof indicators of lying, they should alert you to possible problems in your relationship.

- Take the time and effort to listen. Best of all, become an active listener.

Suppose that you follow all of the principles described in this chapter. Will it mean you are guaranteed to succeed—to get your message across to others? Not at all. Even under the best of conditions, communication is an iffy proposition. Too many factors enter into the picture for it to ever be perfect. But there is one additional principle that can prove helpful in many cases: redundancy. This involves transmitting your message several times, in different forms or through different channels. For example, a message delivered in person one day could be reinforced with a written memo the next. Similarly, telephone conversations can be followed up

Guidelines for Effective Human Relations (continued)

with letters. And when communicating face-to-face with others, appropriate nonverbal cues can be employed to drive home your point.

To conclude: By means of approaches outlined on page 172, you can greatly improve your communication skills. The costs of implementing some of these steps are high; much effort is involved. But the rewards, too, are substantial. Not only can effective communication further your career, but it can also lead to enhanced coordination with others, improved morale, effective leadership, and improvement in overall productivity within your work group. Given these rewards, it is hard to imagine a process more deserving of our attention.

Summary

Communication is a process in which one person or group (the sender) transmits information to another person or group (the receiver). Within an organization, communication often proceeds through formal channels dictated by an organizational chart. Such communication tends to be mainly downward, from higher to lower levels of the company. In addition to formal channels, all organizations possess an informal network of communication known collectively as the grapevine. Communication through these systems can be accurate and rapid; however, the grapevine often transmits rumors—information based solely on speculation or imagination.

Electronic communication is increasing the frequency and ease of communication among people in and outside of organizations. E-mail has become a common method of communication but requires a certain etiquette for it to be most effective. Although computer-mediated communication can be efficient and may reduce conformity pressures, the inability to effectively communicate feelings by this medium limits its overall effectiveness. Telecommuting is increasingly popular and can increase flexibility of lifestyle. On the other hand, it limits communication among employees and with managers.

A number of personal factors influence communication in work settings. Individuals who present information in a simple manner, who speak rapidly, and who are viewed as being high in credibility are more effective communicators than those who do not demonstrate these characteristics.

In addition to communicating verbally through spoken or written language, we also transmit much information to one another nonverbally. Such communication involves facial expressions, eye contact, and body movements. Nonverbal cues play an important role in attempts to deceive others about our real feelings. Although lie detection is difficult, attention to certain nonverbal cues may increase our accuracy in this regard.

Effective communication may require a nonevaluative atmosphere in which we can express our true feelings and receive useful but nonthreatening feedback. It is also important to listen effectively and to employ redundancy (repeating a message through another channel or in a different form).

Key Terms

active listening, p. 171

communication, p. 146

electronic communication, p. 151

grapevine, p. 150

high context culture, p. 164

low context culture, p. 164

nonverbal communication, p. 159

organizational structure, p. 148

other-oriented lies, p. 167

receiver, p. 147

rumor, p. 150

self-centered lies, p. 167

sender, p. 147

sensitivity training, p. 170

smiles-leniency effect, p. 160

spamming, p. 152

telecommuting, p. 154

Experiential Exercise

Measuring Your Own Expressiveness: A Short Self-Assessment

A high level of expressiveness—the emission of many clear nonverbal cues—can often come in handy. This is more likely to be the case in some jobs than in others, but in general it can be a useful skill to possess. As you probably already realize, though, individuals differ greatly in terms of expressiveness. Some are very high in this dimension, others are very low, and most fall somewhere in between. Where do you stand in this respect? Are you relatively expressive or relatively lacking this trait? To find out, answer each of the questions listed on page 175.

To what extent is each of the following statements true or false about you? Indicate your answer by writing a number from 1 (not at all true of you) to 9 (very true of you) in the space next to each statement.

_____   1. When I hear good dance music, I can hardly keep still.

_____   2. My laugh is soft and subdued.

_____   3. I can easily express emotion over the telephone.

_____   4. I often touch friends during conversations.

_____   5. I dislike being watched by a large group of people.

_____   6. I usually have a neutral facial expression.

_____   7. People tell me that I would make a good actor or actress.

_____   8. I like to remain unnoticed in a crowd.

_____   9. I am shy among strangers.

_____   10. I am able to give a seductive glance if I want to.

_____   11. I am terrible at pantomime and in games like charades.

_____   12. At small parties, I am the center of attention.

_____   13. I show that I like someone by hugging or touching that person.

You have just completed the Affective Communication Test (ACT) (see note 65), a questionnaire designed to measure individual differences in expressiveness. To obtain your score, proceed as follows: (1) Add your answers from items 1, 3, 4, 7, 10, 12, and 13. (2) Reverse the scores of items 2, 5, 6, 8, 9, and 11. For example, if you entered 3 for item 2, now enter 6; if you entered 9, now enter 1. (3) Add the numbers you obtained in (1) and (2). This is your total score.

If you obtained a total score of 87 or greater, you are quite expressive; most people fall below this level. If, instead, you obtained a score of 54 or lower, you are fairly low in this dimension. Research findings indicate that persons scoring high in expressiveness are more likely to have had certain types of experiences than persons scoring low in expressiveness. For example, they are more likely to have held an elected office or to have given a lecture to a group. Can you remember any experiences you have had that are consistent with your own level of expressiveness?

Notes

1. Fisher, K., & Fisher, M. D. (1998). *The distributed mind: Achieving high performance through the collective intelligence of knowledge work teams.* New York: AMACOM.

2. Roberts, K. H. (1984). *Communicating in organizations.* Chicago: Science Research Associates.

3. Reber, R. W., & Terry, G. E. (1975). *Behavioral insight for supervision.* Englewood Cliffs, NJ: Prentice-Hall.

4. See note 2.

5. Hawkins, B. L., & Preston, P. (1981). *Managerial communication.* Santa Monica, CA: Goodyear.

6. Walker, C. R., & Guest, R. H. (1952). *The man on the assembly line.* Cambridge, MA: Harvard University Press.

7. Luthans, F., & Larsen, J. K. (1986). How managers really communicate. *Human Relations, 39,* 161–178.

8. Kirmeyer, S. L., & Lin, T. (1987). Social support: Its relationship to observed communication with peers and superiors. *Academy of Management Journal, 30,* 138–151.

9. Read, W. (1962). Upward communication in industrial hierarchies. *Human Relations, 15,* 3–16.

10. Glauser, M. J. (1984). Upward information flow in organizations: Review and conceptual analysis. *Human Relations, 37,* 613–643.

11. Foushee, H. C. (1984). Dyads and triads at 35,000 feet: Factors affecting group processes and aircrew performance. *American Psychologist, 39,* 885–893.

12. Likert, R. (1959). Motivational approach to management development. *Harvard Business Review* (July/August): 75–82.

13. Heath, C. (1996). Do people prefer to pass along good or bad news? Valence and relevance of news as predictors of transmission propensity. *Organizational Behavior and Human Decision Processes, 68,* 79–94.

14. Baskin, O. W., & Aronoff, C. E. (1989). *Interpersonal communication in organizations.* Santa Monica, CA: Goodyear.

15. Walton, E. (1961). How efficient is the grapevine? *Personnel, 28,* 45–49.

16. Thibaut, A. M., Calder, B. J., & Sternthal, B. (1981). Using information processing theory to design marketing strategies. *Journal of Marketing Research, 18,* 73–79.

17. See note 1.

18. Pettit, J. D., Jr., Vaught, B., & Pulley, K. J. (1990). The role of communication in organizations: Ethical considerations. *Journal of Business Communications, 27,* 233–249.

19. Bylinsky, G. (1991, November). How companies spy on employees. *Fortune,* pp. 131–140.

20. Aiello, J. R., & Svec, C. M. (1993). Computer monitoring of work performance: Extending the social facilitation framework to electronic presence. *Journal of Applied Social Psychology, 23,* 537–548.

21. Irving, R. H., Higgins, C. A., & Safayeni, F. R. (1986). Computerized performance monitoring systems: Use and abuse. *Communications of the ACM, 29,* 794–801.

22. Griffith, T. L. (1993). Monitoring and performance: A comparison of computer and supervisor monitoring. *Journal of Applied Social Psychology, 23,* 549–572.

23. Straus, S. G., & McGrath, J. E. (1994). Does the medium matter? The interaction of task type and technology on group performance and member reactions. *Journal of Applied Psychology, 79,* 87–97.

24. Bordia, P. (1997). Face-to-face versus computer-mediated communication: A synthesis of the experimental literature. *The Journal of Business Communication, 34,* 99–120.

25. See note 23.

26. Katz, H. C. (ed.) (1997). *Telecommunications: Restructuring work and employment relations worldwide.* Ithaca, NY: ILR Press.

27. Baruch, Y., & Nicholson, N. (1997). Home, sweet work: Requirements for effective home working. *Journal of General Management, 23,* 15–30.

28. Ibid.

29. Parks, B. (1998). Telecommuting brightens the future for Florida Power and Light. *Employment Relations Today* (Winter): 65–72.

30. Feldman, D. C., & Gainey, T. W. (1997). Patterns of telecommuting and their consequences: Framing the research agenda. *Human Resource Management Review, 7,* 369–388.

31. Reinsch, Jr., N. L. (1997). Relationships between telecommuting workers and their managers: An exploratory study. *Journal of Business Communication, 34,* 343–369.

32. See note 27.

33. See note 31.

34. Borman, E. (1982). *Interpersonal communication in the modern organization* (2nd ed.). Englewood Cliffs, NJ: Prentice-Hall.

35. Miller, N., Maruyama, G., Beaber, R. J., & Valone, K. (1976). Speed of speech and persuasion. *Journal of Personality and Social Psychology, 34,* 615–624.

36. MacLachlan, J. (1979). What people really think of fast talkers. *Psychology Today, 13,* 113–117.

37. Rajecki, D. W. (1990). *Attitudes: Themes and advances.* Sunderland, MA: Sinauer Associates.

38. Level, D. A. (1972). Communication effectiveness: Methods and situation. *Journal of Business Communication, 10,* 19–25.

39. Klauss, R., & Bass, B. M. (1982). *International communication in organizations.* New York: Academic Press.

40. Daft, R. L., Lengel, R. H., & Trevino, L. K. (1987). Message equivocality, media selection, and manager performance: Implications for information systems. *MIS Quarterly, 11,* 355–366.

41. Buck, R. (1984). *Nonverbal behavior and the communication of affect.* New York: Guilford Press.

42. Frank, M. G., Ekman, P., & Friesen, W. V. (1993). Behavioral markers: Recognizability of the smile of enjoyment. *Journal of Personality and Social Psychology, 64,* 83–93.

43. Reis, H. T., Wilson, I., Monestere, C., Bernstein, S., Clark, K., Seidl, E., Franco, M., Gioioso, E., Freeman, L., & Radoane, K. (1990). What is smiling is beautiful and good. *European Journal of Social Psychology, 20,* 259–267.

44. Hinsz, V. B., & Tomhave, J. A. (1991). Smile and (half) the world smiles with you, frown and you frown alone. *Personality and Social Psychology Bulletin, 17,* 586–592.

45. Deutsch, F. M. (1990). Status, sex, and smiling: The effect of role on smiling in men and women. *Personality and Social Psychology Bulletin, 16,* 531–540.

46. LaFrance, M., & Hecht, M. A. (1995). Why smiles generate leniency. *Personality and Social Psychology Bulletin, 21,* 207–214.

47. Ekman, P., & Friesen, W. V. (1982). Felt, false, and miserable smiles. *Journal of Nonverbal Behavior, 6,* 238–252.

48. Kleinke, C. L. (1986). Gaze and eye contact: A research review. *Psychological Bulletin, 100,* 78–100.

49. Ellsworth, P. C., & Langer, E. J. (1976). Staring and approach: An interpretation of the stare as a nonspecific activator. *Journal of Personality and Social Psychology, 33,* 117–122.

50. Argyle, M. (1988). *Bodily communication* (2nd ed.). New York: Methuen & Co., Ltd.

51. Major, B., Schmidlin, A. M., & Williams, L. (1990). Gender patterns in social touch: The impact of setting and age. *Journal of Personality and Social Psychology, 58,* 634–643.

52. Abbey, A., & Melby, C. (1986). The effects of nonverbal cues on gender differences in perceptions of sexual intent. *Sex Roles, 15,* 283–298.

53. Hall, J. A., & Veccia, E. M. (1990). More "touching" observations: New insights on men, women, and interpersonal touch. *Journal of Personality and Social Psychology, 59,* 1155–1162.

54. Malloy, J. T. (1975). *Dress for success.* New York: Warner Books.

55. Forsythe, S., Drake, M. F., & Cox, C. E. (1985). Influence of applicant's dress on interviewer's selection decisions. *Journal of Applied Psychology, 70,* 374–378.

56. Riggio, R. E., & Throckmorton, B. (1988). The relative effects of verbal and nonverbal behavior, appearance, and social skills on evaluations

made in hiring interviews. *Journal of Applied Social Psychology, 18,* 331–348.

57. Solomon, M. R. (1986, April). Dress for effect. *Psychology Today,* pp. 20–28.

58. See note 56.

59. Abbey, A., Cozzarelli, C., McLaughlin, K., & Harnish, R. J. (1987). The effects of clothing and dyad sex composition on perceptions of sexual intent: Do women and men evaluate these cues differently? *Journal of Applied Social Psychology, 17,* 108–126.

60. Hall, E. T. (1976). *Beyond culture.* New York: Doubleday.

61. Triandis, H. C. (1994). Culture and social behavior. In W. J. Lonner & R. Malpass (eds.), *Psychology and culture* (pp. 169–173). Boston: Allyn & Bacon.

62. Gudykunst, W. B., Ting-Toomey, S., and Chua, E. (1988). *Culture and interpersonal communication.* Newbury Park, CA: Sage.

63. Ekman, P. (1972). Universal and cultural differences in facial expression of emotion. In J. Cole (ed.), *Nebraska symposium on motivation* (Vol. 19). Lincoln: University of Nebraska Press.

64. Keating, C. F. (1994). World without words: Messages from the face and body. In W. J. Lonner & R. Malpass (eds.), *Psychology and culture* (pp. 175–182). Boston: Allyn & Bacon.

65. Friedman, H. A., Prince, L. M., Riggio, R. E., & DiMatteo, M. R. (1980). Understanding and assessing nonverbal expressiveness: The affective communication test. *Journal of Personality and Social Psychology, 39,* 333–351.

66. Imada, A. S., & Hakel, M. D. (1977). Influence of nonverbal communication and rater proximity on impressions and decisions in simulated employment interviews. *Journal of Applied Psychology, 62,* 295–300.

67. Baron, R. A. (1984). Self-presentation in job interviews: When there can be "too much of a good thing." *Journal of Applied Social Psychology, 16,* 16–28.

68. DePaulo, B. M., Kashy, D. A., Kirkendol, S. E., Wyer, M. M., & Epstein, J. A. (1996). Lying in everyday life. *Journal of Personality and Social Psychology, 70,* 579–995

69. Ibid.

70. DePaulo, B. M., & Kashy, D. A. (1998). Everyday lies in close and casual relationships. *Journal of Personality and Social Psychology, 74,* 63–79.

71. Bell, K. L., & DePaulo, B. M. (1996). Liking and lying. *Basic and Applied Social Psychology, 18,* 243–266.

72. Grover, S. L. (1997). Lying in organizations: Theory, research, and future directions. In R. A. Giacalone & J. Greenberg (eds.), *Antisocial behavior in organizations* (pp. 68–84). Thousand Oaks, CA: Sage.

73. Zuckerman, M., DePaulo, B. M., & Resenthal, R. (1981). Verbal and nonverbal communication of deception. In L. Berkowitz (Ed.), *Advances in experimental social psychology* (Vol. 14). New York: Academic Press.

74. Riggio, R. E., Tucker, J., & Throckmorton, B. (1987). Social skills and deception ability. *Personality and Social Psychology Bulletin, 13,* 568–577.

75. DePaulo, B. M., LeMay, C. S., & Epstein, J. A. (1991). Effects of importance of success and expectations for success on effectiveness at deceiving. *Personality and Social Psychology Bulletin, 17,* 14–24.

76. See note 73.

77. Ekman, P., & Frank, M. G. (1993). Lies that fail. In M. Lewis & C. Saarni (eds.), *Lying and deception in everyday life.* New York: Guilford Press.

78. See note 73.

79. McCornack, S. A., & Parks, M. R. (1990). What women know that men don't: Sex differences in determining the truth behind deceptive messages. *Journal of Social and Personal Relationships, 7,* 107–118.

80. Bond, C. F., Jr., Omar, A., Pitre, U., Lashley, B. R., Skaggs, L. M., & Kirk, C. T. (1992). Fishy-looking liars: Deception judgment from expectancy violation. *Journal of Personality and Social Psychology, 63,* 969–977.

81. See note 77.

82. Ekman, P., & Friesen, W. V. (1975). *Unmasking the face.* Englewood Cliffs, NJ: Prentice-Hall.

83. Aronson, E. (1999). *The social animal.* New York: W. H. Freeman and Company.

84. Dunnette, M., & Campbell, J. (1968). Effectiveness of T-group experiences in managerial training and development. *Psychological Bulletin, 70,* 73–104.

85. Rubin, I. (1967). The reduction of prejudice through laboratory training. *Journal of Applied Behavior Science, 3,* 29–50.

86. Rowe, M. P., & Baker, M. (1984, May/June). Are you hearing enough employee concerns? *Harvard Business Review,* pp. 127–135.

87. Richter, J. W. (1980, September). Listening: An art essential to success. *Success!* p. 26.

Chapter 7

Persuasion: The Fine Art of Changing Others' Minds

Persuasion: Pathways to Success
Two Paths to Success: Mindless and
    Mindful Persuasion

Compliance: To Ask Sometimes Is to Receive

Multiple Requests: The Old One-Two
    Punch Strikes Again
Resisting Unwanted Influence: Learning
    How to Say No

Power: Beyond Influence and Persuasion

Individual Power: Its Basic Sources
Hazards to Avoid in Your Attempts to
    Persuade and Influence

Organizational Politics

Tactics of Influence

Special Sections

Ethics at Work
Subliminal Persuasion

Human Relations in Action
Measuring Your Own Power: A Quick
    Self-Assessment

Guidelines for Effective Human Relations
Using What You've Learned

Case in Point
Dr. Cialdini Meets Stunning Young
    Woman

PERSUASION AND POWER
Understanding Social Influence

Learning Objectives

After reading this chapter, you should be able to:

1. List several of the factors that determine whether attempts at persuasion will succeed or fail.

2. Distinguish between peripheral and central routes to persuasion.

3. Discuss individual differences in susceptibility to influence.

4. Describe the foot-in-the-door and door-in-the-face strategies for gaining compliance and explain why each succeeds.

5. Define power and list some of the major sources from which it derives.

6. Describe several tactics for gaining and using power in organizational settings.

Amway Corporation manufactures household and personal care products, which its representatives then sell on a door-to-door basis. The growth of this company has been remarkable, as it has grown from a small organization into a billion-dollar business today. In the manual used to instruct Amway's salespeople, the company describes a technique called BUG.[1] This technique involves leaving the customer with sample products for a trial period. The salesperson then returns in a few days to pick up orders that the customer may want to place. This technique is remarkably effective. In the words of a distributor: "Unbelievable! We've never seen such excitement. Product is moving at an unbelievable rate, and we've only just begun...."[2] The effectiveness of this technique is based on a well-known principle of persuasion called the reciprocity rule, *which describes the sense of indebtedness we feel to repay what another person has given us.*

You have undoubtedly been exposed to this technique—in supermarkets, for example. In our everyday lives, we both use and are the recipients of such tactics on countless occasions. Attempts at influence are one of the most common forms of behavior in the world of work. For this reason, you should understand the nature of influence and know how to guard against it. This chapter examines both of these topics, plus several others. We begin with a discussion of persuasion attempts by one person to change the behavior or attitudes of others through convincing appeals and arguments. Second, we examine a mixed bag of tactics that are useful in attaining compliance as well as techniques that may prove helpful in getting others to agree to your requests. Finally, we turn to power—the strongest and most impressive form of influence.

PERSUASION: THE FINE ART OF CHANGING OTHERS' MINDS

You attend a meeting in your department and hear two people arguing for different policies. You watch TV and are numbed by a seemingly endless string of commercials. Your spouse tries to talk you into taking your vacation at the seaside rather than in the mountains. What do all of these incidents have in common? They all involve communication efforts by one or more people to transmit information to others (refer to Chapter 6). Going beyond this basic fact, they also share another feature: All involve attempts at persuasion. In each scenario, one or more people tried to change your behavior by getting

reciprocity rule   A societal norm that makes us feel a sense of indebtedness to repay what another person has given us.

you to see the world the way they do and to share their views. **Persuasion** involves communication for a specific purpose: to change someone's mind. More precisely, it is the effort by one or more persons to alter the beliefs or behavior of one or more other people through convincing appeals and arguments. Of course, the arguments presented are sometimes far from logical and the facts anything but accurate. Generally, though, these flaws are concealed, and persuasion maintains at least an outward appearance of reason and authority.

Persuasion is an oft-encountered form of influence, perhaps the most common one in use.[3] Each day you are sure to be subjected to persuasive efforts as everyone—from your boss to politicians and advertisers—attempts to change your behavior in various ways. Most of these efforts will fail; only a small fraction of the persuasive appeals we receive manage to alter our views or our actions. This fact raises an intriguing question: Why do some attempts at persuasion prove effective, while others fail?

Persuasion: Pathways to Success

Many factors play a role in determining the success of persuasive appeals. The most important of these factors tend to fall under two major headings: (1) the characteristics of the person doing the persuading (often termed a *communicator*), and (2) the various aspects of what the communicator says, or the features of the persuasive appeal.

Characteristics of Would-Be Persuaders: Attractiveness, Style, and Credibility.
Suppose that your job involves ordering supplies for your company. In this role, you receive visits from two salespeople representing competing firms. The first is well groomed and attractive. When describing her company's products, she speaks in an eloquent, forceful, and enthusiastic manner. Finally, she helps you choose the products that your company needs most, not the ones that will yield her the largest commission. In contrast, the second salesperson is sloppy, poorly groomed, and unattractive. He speaks in a halting and unconvincing manner. He consistently tries to get you to order the most expensive products on his list just to increase his own gains. Which of these two people will be more successful in affecting your decisions? The answer is obvious: the first. Of course, this vignette presents a simple and extreme case. Nevertheless, it highlights three of the most important factors in determining the success of attempts at persuasion: a communicator's attractiveness, his or her style of presentation, and his or her credibility.

With respect to attractiveness, communicators we like (either because of their appearance or personality) are much more effective in changing our views and our behavior than ones we don't like (see Figure 7.1 on page 184).[4] The following reason explains why: When we like people, we tend to lower our defenses and interpret much of what they say in a favorable light. Little wonder, then, that they are effective in exerting influence upon us.

persuasion Attempts to change the behavior or attitudes of others through convincing appeals and arguments.

Communicator Characteristics: Useful in Advertising

Advertisers make use of the fact that we are persuaded by people we like or admire.

In terms of personal style, a number of different factors affect persuasion. One of the most important is a communicator's rate of speech. Research studies indicate that would-be persuaders who speak rapidly are more successful in changing listeners' views or behavior than ones who speak at a more leisurely pace.[5] When people speak quickly and smoothly, we interpret such eloquence as a sign of underlying knowledge; that is, we assume that they really know their subject. In contrast, if they speak slowly, we conclude that they really don't know much about the subject of their presentation. Regardless of the mechanism involved, it is clear that, where persuasion is concerned, fast talkers definitely have an edge.

A communicator's credibility, too, is important. **Credibility** refers to the perception that a communicator can be believed or trusted. As you might guess, people with high credibility are much more effective at persuasion than those with low credibility. Two factors play a key role in shaping such judgments. First, communicators who are high in expertise are viewed as more credible than ones who are low in ex-

pertise. Second, communicators who do not seem to gain anything from influencing others or who appear to take others' interests into account are seen as having higher credibility than ones who seem to operate entirely out of

credibility The perception that a communicator can be believed or trusted.

Figure 7.2   **Effective Persuasion: Some Key Factors**

As shown here, several personal characteristics contribute to success at persuasion.

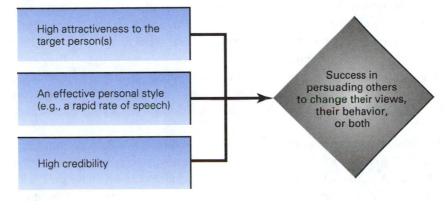

self-interest. Thus a salesperson who seems concerned about a customer's well-being will be higher in credibility, and therefore more successful at persuasion, than one who focuses only on maximizing her or his commissions.

To summarize, several factors contribute to effectiveness at persuasion. If you want to maximize your own success at this important task, you should take steps to (1) enhance your attractiveness; (2) improve the smoothness, speed, and eloquence of your delivery; and (3) increase your image of credibility. To the extent that you can accomplish these goals, you may well enhance your ability to change the views and actions of the people around you (see Figure 7.2). This capability, of course, can be an important plus, both in your career and in life away from work.

The Contents of Persuasive Appeals: What You Say Matters.   The success of a persuasive appeal depends on its content as well as its source. In short, what is said, as well as who says it, is important. What, precisely, should go into attempts at persuasion so as to maximize their effectiveness? Because each persuasive appeal deals with a unique set of issues, it is not possible to specify the exact content; it will depend on the specific situation. Research findings, however, point to several general guidelines that are helpful in constructing almost any persuasive message. By paying close attention to them, you can enhance the impact of your own attempts at persuasion, whether they are delivered directly to one person or to a larger audience.

First, it is often useful to present **two-sided** rather than **one-sided arguments.**[6] Specifically, you should not simply offer support for your own view; you should also

two-sided argument   A persuasion technique wherein you mention and refute opposing positions as well as offer support for your own view.

one-sided argument   A persuasion technique wherein you present only support for your own view.

mention and then refute opposing positions or suggestions. By following this course of action, you not only build up enthusiasm for your own position, but also weaken the positions supported by others. As a result, your chance for successful persuasion may increase.

Second, it helps to build an emotional element (for example, mild anxiety) into your appeals. Specifically, you should suggest that failure to adopt your suggestions will lead to negative outcomes and then subsequently offer concrete ways of avoiding these unpleasant results. If members of your audience become worried, they may quickly adopt the actions you recommend. Such **fear appeals,** as they are termed, are effective in many contexts.[7] Take care, however: Don't overdo it. If you paint too frightening a picture, the process may backfire and actually reduce your persuasiveness.

Third, tailor your appeals to the people you are addressing. Be sure that your comments do not go over their heads. One major reason why even carefully planned persuasive messages fail is that the people who hear them don't always have the background or technical knowledge to understand them. Of course, if they don't comprehend what's being said, the chances of influencing them drop to nearly zero. Also, avoid stating views that are radically different from those held by the audience. A large amount of research on persuasion indicates that when individuals are presented with views sharply different from their own, they tend to reject them out of hand because they find those positions extreme or outlandish and feel that they are not worthy of attention. In contrast, if the audience receives appeals containing views only moderately different from their own, they may consider them carefully and be influenced.[8] Where persuasion is concerned, moderation—not extremity—is usually more effective.

Two Paths to Success: Mindless and Mindful Persuasion

We could continue with our discussion of factors that influence persuasion, as many play a role in its success. Instead, we note that research on this process has taken a somewhat different path in the past few years. Rather than asking what kinds of messages produce the most attitude change, recent studies have focused on which cognitive processes determine whether someone will or will not be persuaded. In other words, efforts have been made to tie the process of persuasion to current knowledge about human and **social cognition,** or the manner in which we process, store, and remember social information (refer to Chapter 3).

Attitude change occurs in two distinct ways.[9] In the first, we think about the arguments presented in a careful, rational manner. They remain at the center of our attention, and we are persuaded because, logically, they make

fear appeals   Suggestions that failure to adopt your position will lead to negative outcomes.

social cognition   The manner in which we process, store, and remember social information.

| *Figure 7.3* | **Persuasion: Two Basic Mechanisms** |

Research findings indicate that persuasion can occur through two distinct processes. In the first (the central route), persuasion takes place because target persons direct careful attention to arguments that are convincing and logical. In the second (the peripheral route), it occurs because target persons are distracted by other stimuli or events and do not notice that the arguments presented are weak and unconvincing.

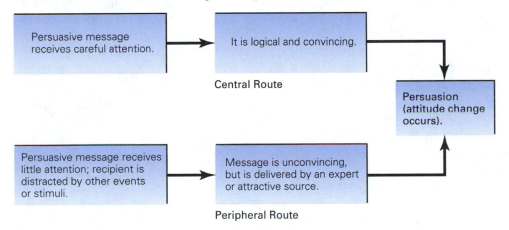

sense. This avenue is known as the **central route to persuasion.** This route is also referred to as *mindful* persuasion, because it is based on the quality of arguments provided in the message.

A second form of persuasion can be referred to as *mindless* persuasion, because it involves little thought or reasoning. (We are not referring to subliminal persuasion here; see the *Ethics at Work* section on pages 188–189 for a discussion of this issue.) In this form of persuasion, we are aware of the message or request for compliance but do not give the arguments our full attention. Instead, we may be distracted by other events or perhaps by the style or appearance of the would-be persuader. Here, persuasion occurs in a kind of automatic manner; it is referred to as the **peripheral route to persuasion.**

Both kinds of persuasion occur in organizational settings. An example of persuasion by the central route is provided by a situation in which, because of a convincing and fact-filled presentation by an individual from marketing, a group of executives decides to change their company's product mix for the coming year. An example of persuasion by the peripheral route occurs when a buyer for a large company is swayed to place an order with one potential supplier because the salesperson from that supplier is witty and charming. Figure 7.3 provides an overview of these two distinct routes to persuasion.

central route to persuasion   Persuasion that is accomplished through the impact of information. Involves thinking about the issue.

peripheral route to persuasion   Persuasion that is accomplished through the impact of cues unrelated to the issue. Sometimes called "mindless" persuasion.

What determines which route to persuasion will be taken? Research on this issue has uncovered a number of variables that affect this process. People appear to be more likely to think about a message (use the central route) when they are highly involved in an issue. When people are not able to think about the message or are uninvolved in an issue, they are likely to be influenced by peripheral cues, such as the attractiveness of the communicator.[10] A person's mood also affects the effectiveness of these two routes. Individuals who are in a positive mood tend not to scrutinize the quality of messages. Thus they are more likely to be swayed by peripheral cues, such as source expertise, than by argument quality. In contrast, persons in neutral moods may be swayed more by the strength of arguments used to advocate a position.[11] The general conclusion of the research on this issue is that techniques that stimulate

Ethics at Work

Subliminal Persuasion

In the 1950s, subliminal persuasion became a source of controversy when it was claimed that flashing the words "Eat popcorn" very quickly on a movie screen could persuade people to buy more popcorn. A considerable outcry followed this claim, both from the public and from researchers. In response to this criticism, the use of subliminal persuasion dwindled in the 1960s, but since the 1970s, its use has increased dramatically. Subliminal messages show up in advertisements with hidden erotic images, in horror movies (moviemakers are said to maximize scary scenes by flashing images such as death masks on screen), and in Muzak recordings (for example, recordings of "Be honest" in stores are designed to reduce shoplifting).

Subliminal persuasion is based on the idea that people are sensitive to information that is presented below the threshold of awareness—that the message can make an impact at an unconscious level. There is considerable controversy about the validity of this claim, yet many businesses are profiting from sales of tapes that contain subliminal messages. For example, one company earned $50 million in subliminal tape sales in a single year. This trend is increasing.* Audiotapes usually contain some type of soothing sound, such as waves or New Age music, that masks the subliminal message. The messages usually contain self-help themes such as "eat less," "stop smoking," or "I am a worthwhile person." Videotapes flash similar messages at a rate so fast that they cannot be detected (around 1/30th of a second or less).

The market for the use of subliminals appears to be broadening. For example, computer programs

> **subliminal persuasion**   Persuasion that is accomplished by presenting a message to a person's subconscious.

thinking tend to make messages based on strong arguments more persuasive. Techniques that minimize a person's scrutiny of a message, such as distraction, increase the effectiveness of peripheral cues (see Figure 7.4 on page 190).

*C*OMPLIANCE: TO ASK SOMETIMES IS TO RECEIVE

Suppose you want another person to do something for you—anything from helping you with your work to scratching your back (figuratively or literally). How would you persuade this individual to comply? The most direct approach, of course, is to

have reportedly been designed that flash subliminal messages during TV shows, and vacation resorts use them to help their guests relax. Given this rising trend, it may be time for us to consider some of the ethical issues raised by subliminals. Below, we present a few of these issues for your consideration:

1. Is it ethical to present subliminal messages to people without their knowledge?

2. Is there an ethical difference between presenting subliminals designed to be pro-social (for example, preventing shoplifting) versus commercial (for example, "buy our product")?

3. Given the controversy about whether subliminals are effective, is it ethical to advertise subliminal self-help tapes?

4. Does the use of subliminals to help provide a quick-fix solution prevent a person from seeking more traditional solutions to his or her problems?

5. Should subliminal messages be treated in a manner similar to drugs and be regulated according to tests of their effectiveness and potential harmful effects?

6. Is it ethical to expose children to magazine ads with hidden subliminal messages?

*Rajecki, D. W. (1990). *Attitudes: Themes and advances.* Sunderland, MA: Sinauer Associates.

Figure 7.4   **Two Routes to Persuasion: Which Path to Follow**

Research findings indicate that several factors influence whether the central or peripheral route to persuasion will be effective. Several of these factors are depicted here.

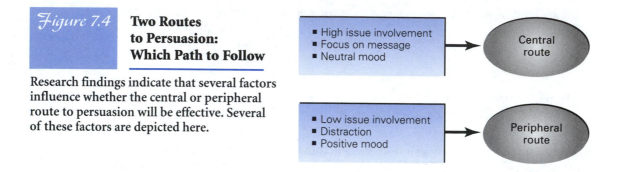

simply ask for the favor. This type of influence is called a *compliance-gaining strategy.* As you know from your own experience, it is a common tactic. Individuals do frequently make direct requests to others, and in many circumstances, individuals comply in an almost mindless fashion.

An interesting study conducted by Harvard social psychologist Ellen Langer demonstrates the often mindless nature of compliance.[12] Langer asked different people waiting in line to use an office copier whether she could use it first. When asked this simple question, a number of people complied with her request. When she gave a specific reason for using the machine ("May I use the copier because I'm in a rush?"), a majority of individuals let her use it. These results probably aren't especially surprising to you; most people will help you out when you're logjammed at the office. What happened in a third situation, however, might surprise you. When she asked, "May I use the office copier because I have to make copies?" nearly all agreed, even though no real reason for her request was given! Using the single word *because* was sufficient to trigger an automatic compliance response.

Robert Cialdini has termed this automatic tendency a "click, whirr" response and has investigated many of the techniques that produce it.[13] His research has taken him into the world of compliance-gaining professionals (salespeople, fund-raisers, and others), where he disguised his identity to observe such techniques from the inside. Much of what he observed involved conscious attempts to influence people by taking preliminary steps to tip the balance in the practitioners' favor—in short, they try to "soften up" the targets. Many different tactics can be used for this purpose, and several have proved highly effective. (It should be noted that compliance-gaining professionals aren't the only ones who use these techniques: We all employ them—and fall for them—at some time in our lives.)

self-presentation   The effort to create a desired impression on others.

One such tactic involves impression management or **self-presentation**—efforts by ingratiators to create a desired impression on a target person. This approach can involve enhancing one's personal appearance through dress and grooming,[14] presenting information that suggests that the persuader has desirable characteristics (such as sincerity, competence, intelligence, or friendliness), or merely associating oneself with positive people or events. In the latter instance, ingratiators might name-drop (link themselves to important or respected people) or casually introduce evidence of their past accomplishments into the conversation. Additional tactics include **self-deprecation,** providing negative information about themselves to promote an image of modesty, and **self-disclosure,** offering personal information, even if it isn't requested, to foster the impression that they are honest and like the target person. A growing body of evidence suggests that, when used with skill and care, these tactics work.[15]

Be careful about how you use these tactics. They can backfire and have very negative consequences on how others view you. At the end of this chapter, we discuss how ingratiation techniques can lead to perceptions of you as a "slime."

Multiple Requests: The Old One-Two Punch Strikes Again

Often, when people want others to do something for them, they do not begin with their main request. Instead, they use a kind of one-two punch designed to enhance their chances of success. The idea behind this approach is simple: One request can serve as a kind of setup for another; that is, it can help soften up a target person so that he or she is more likely to comply with a second, and perhaps more important, request. Two such strategies are the foot-in-the-door and the door-in-the-face techniques.

The Foot-in-the-Door: Small Request First, Large Request Second.

An old saying goes, "Give them an inch, and they'll take a mile." It refers to the fact that individuals seeking compliance with their wishes often begin with a small or trivial request. Once this favor has been granted, they escalate to a larger or more important one. This approach, known as the **foot-in-the-door technique,** can be observed in many different settings. For example, salespeople often begin by asking potential customers to accept a free sample or a brochure describing their products. Only later, after these requests have been granted, do they try to close an order. Similarly, individuals seeking help with their work often start with trivial requests (for example, to lend a pencil or answer a simple question). After these requests are granted, they move to more and more involved tasks. In these and other instances, the

self-deprecation Providing negative information about oneself to promote an image of modesty.

self-disclosure Offering personal information, even if it isn't requested, to foster the impression that one is honest and like the target person.

foot-in-the-door technique A tactic for enhancing compliance by beginning with a small request and, when it is granted, moving to a larger one.

basic strategy is the same: Get another person to agree to a small initial request and thereby increase the chances that he or she will later agree to larger favors.

Does this strategy really work? Does beginning with a small request and then shifting to a larger one actually increase the chances that this second favor will be granted? A large body of research findings indicates that it is an effective strategy.[16] For example, consider a famous study conducted by Freedman and Fraser.[17] In this investigation, hundreds of people were telephoned by an experimenter who identified himself as a member of a consumers' group. Some were called only once and were hit with the large request "cold." Other subjects were called twice, and so exposed to the foot-in-the-door tactic. The small request was simple: Would the subject answer a few questions about the soaps used in the home? The second request, made several days later, was much larger. In this case, the experimenter asked if his organization could send a five- or six-person crew to the subject's home to conduct a thorough inventory of all products on hand. It was explained that the survey would take about two hours, and that the crew would require complete freedom to search through the house, including all closets, cabinets, and drawers. Obviously, this request was truly a gigantic favor. Yet, among those subjects called twice, fully 52.8 percent agreed! In contrast, only 22.2 percent of the individuals called only once consented.

Additional research offers an explanation for why the foot-in-the-door tactic works. Apparently, once individuals agree to a small initial request, they undergo subtle shifts in self-perception. Specifically, they come to see themselves as the kind of person who "does that sort of thing," or the kind of person who agrees to help others when they request it. Thus, when contacted again and asked for a second favor, they agree so as to be consistent with their changed (and enhanced) self-image.[18] The desire to be consistent with this image can lead them to comply with requests they would rather refuse (see the *Case in Point* on pages 208–209).

Of course, the foot-in-the-door technique does not succeed under all conditions. For example, as you might guess, it often fails when the second request involves actions that are costly or very unpleasant (would you loan $1,000 to a friend just because you loaned her $1 a few days ago?). In many settings and with respect to many target actions, however, beginning with a small request and shifting to a larger one can be highly effective. For this reason, you are sure to encounter it in your own life, both on and off the job, on many occasions.

The Door-in-the-Face: Large Request First, Small Request Second.   Although the foot-in-the-door technique is quite successful, the opposite strategy may also succeed. In this case, people start by asking for a large favor—one that the target person is almost certain to refuse. When he or she does, they shift to a smaller request—the one they really wanted all along. This approach, known as the **door-in-the-face technique** (referring metaphorically to the door that is, at first, slammed in the requester's

door-in-the-face technique   A tactic for enhancing compliance by beginning with a large request and, when it is rejected, backing down to a smaller one.

**Multiple Requests:
The Door-in-the-Face Technique**

As shown here, individuals sometimes start with a large request—one that other people are almost certain to refuse—and switch to a smaller request (the one they wanted all along). This technique is often successful.

© King Features Syndicate.

face!), is also very common (refer to Figure 7.5).[19] For example, consider the following scenario, which occurs in many companies on a regular basis.

An individual in the sales department has closed a big order and wants to make sure it is shipped on time. Her customer would like to receive it in about two weeks, so she calls the shipping department and indicates that she wants the order out of the warehouse by the end of the week. The shipping manager reacts with an agonized shriek and shouts that it can't possibly be done in less than a month. The caller counters with a request that it be shipped in ten days to two weeks. The shipping manager, somewhat mollified, indicates that he will do what he can to meet this deadline. Thus, by beginning with a large request—one she really didn't want—the salesperson has managed to get the desired outcome. She has, in short, used the door-in-the-face tactic to good advantage.

Research evidence lends support to the effectiveness of this strategy.[20] The "start big–shift small" approach does often yield more compliance than beginning with the true request itself. Moreover, the reason for its success is clear. When an individual starts with a large request and then backs down to a smaller one, it puts pressure on the person with whom he is dealing to make a similar concession: "How can I refuse to meet him halfway?" Another aspect involves concern about self-presentation, or portraying ourselves in a favorable light to others. If we refuse a large and unreasonable request, the refusal appears justified and our image doesn't suffer. If we then reject a much smaller request from the same source, however, we may appear unreasonable. We may therefore yield to the door-in-the-face tactic because of our concern that failing to do so will make us look rigid.[21]

Multiple Requests: Foot-in-the-Door and Door-in-the-Face Tactics

The order in which we make requests influences compliance. These are two common forms.

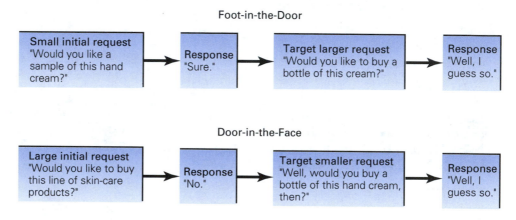

The moral, then, is clear: Beware of persons who begin with unreasonable demands and then back down to smaller ones. They may be setting you up for the kill with a carefully developed strategy for gaining compliance.

Figure 7.6 summarizes the two multiple request techniques.

Resisting Unwanted Influence: Learning How to Say No

We are bombarded with persuasion attempts every day. We receive piles of junk mail designed to sell us everything from magazines to furniture to insurance. Commercials occupy a major portion of our TV time. Memos from various people in our company are aimed at changing our views. Friends, coworkers, bosses, advertisers, and politicians attempt to shape our behavior in various ways. It is unreasonable to expect that we will not be influenced to some degree by these appeals.

It is harmful, financially and psychologically, to be persuaded by every appeal we receive. Ideally, we would like to accept influence based on education, reasoning, and scrutiny. This disciplined approach is not always possible, however. Even though we like to think of ourselves as rational decision makers, our discussion so far suggests that people are often persuaded in mindless ways. Simply thinking that we are immune to persuasion does not mean that we are immune.

How can we counteract attempts to persuade us? One method is suggested by the common saying, "forewarned is forearmed." That is, if we are aware that a persuasion attempt will be made, we will be less receptive to it. Research suggests that **forewarning** does decrease the impact of persuasive messages.[22] Why does it work? One reason is that forewarning induces us to play "**attitudinal politics**."[23] Aronson and Pratkanis coined this term to describe the goal of holding an opinion so as to secure some strategic purpose.[24] For example, our goal may be to appear independent and not easily influenced. Forewarning may invoke this goal and, regardless of the merits of the message, we may resist its appeal. At other times, our goal may be to appear open to the opinions of others. In this case, forewarning might be expected to result in more rapid compliance.[25]

The resistance to persuasion afforded by playing attitudinal politics may, however, be only temporary. As our goals change, our defenses against persuasion weaken. Thus we may resist the persuasive appeal when it is given but succumb to its influence at a later time,[26] because we may remember only the arguments made in the message and not the goal of resistance.

Forewarning can provide a stronger defense against influence. When we are forewarned, we often formulate possible rebuttals against the upcoming persuasion attempt. For example, we may think of counterarguments and reasons to resist, or we may prepare ourselves to examine the upcoming arguments in detail. This cognitive mindset provides an effective defense against persuasion. It leads us to consider other options and allows us to make decisions based on how well a persuasive message stands up to scrutiny.

We should be aware, however, that several factors decrease the likelihood that "forewarned is forearmed." For example, if we are distracted from thinking about a message, forewarning does not result in resistance: Remember our discussion of mindless persuasion! In addition, sometimes we simply do not care enough about an issue to muster our defenses. When we are not involved in an issue or do not believe that the topic is important, forewarning alone will not induce us to allocate the time and effort to scrutinize persuasive messages. This finding has important implications. It suggests that we can, in fact, be persuaded by messages that we might otherwise resist if we cared about the issue.[27]

What will provide us with a good defense against unwanted influence? Our discussion so far suggests that what matters is how we react to and evaluate persuasive messages rather than prior knowledge that a persuasion attempt will be made. One strategy in formulating a tactical defense is to play "devil's advocate,"[28] by pretending to advocate the opposite position and approaching the persuasive message with healthy skepticism. We should ask ourselves questions that help us diagnose the intent of the

forewarning Advance knowledge of the persuasive intent of a spoken, written, or televised message. When individuals know that attempts at persuasion are forthcoming, their ability to resist such appeals is often increased.

attitudinal politics Holding an opinion so as to secure some strategic purpose.

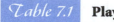**Table 7.1**   **Playing Devil's Advocate**

Some suggestions for developing a mindset that limits susceptibility to influence are listed here.

What does the person have to gain from persuading me?

Why is the message being presented to me in this way?

What other options are available to me?

What would happen if I didn't take the course that is recommended by the message?

What are the arguments against following the recommended course?

What are the arguments for taking an alternative position?

What other information do I need to make an informed decision?

Adapted from Pratkanis & Aronson, 1991; see note 23.

influencing agent and determine the options that are open to us. Table 7.1 lists some suggestions for playing devil's advocate. They should help you develop the kind of mindset that leads to informed, rather than mindless, persuasion.

POWER: BEYOND INFLUENCE AND PERSUASION

Imagine the following scene: An office supervisor is trying to persuade an employee to come to work on Saturday so as to finish a big job. The employee refuses, stating that he has better things to do with his weekends. The supervisor tries every persuasive trick at his disposal. He appeals to the employee's loyalty, describes the serious problems that will arise if the job isn't finished on time, and praises his excellent past work. All is to no avail—the employee still refuses. Just then, the head of the division strolls by and asks what's happening. The supervisor explains the situation, and the division head turns to the reluctant employee. "Jones," he says in a deep voice, "I want you to come in on Saturday." "Well, if you really need me . . . " the target murmurs weakly. The matter is closed, the employee will report for duty bright and early Saturday morning.

This incident illustrates the basic difference between influence and power. As you can readily see, the difference is largely one of degree. While **influence** refers to the capacity to change others' behavior in some desired man-

influence   The capacity to change others' behavior in some desired manner. In contrast to power, influence involves the consent of the target.

ner, **power** refers to the ability to do so regularly and strongly. In fact, according to some experts, power is the ability to control others' actions, even without their consent, against their will, or without their knowledge and understanding, so as to promote one's own goals.[29] In short, power is influence carried to its ultimate extreme.

As you know from your own experience, power is a desirable commodity and something that many people seek and enjoy. This perception is far from surprising. Power comes closer than any other form of influence to the daydream of total control over others. Another aspect of it is **status**—and lots of it. Powerful people, as a rule, enjoy high levels of respect and prestige. Moreover, they usually have many desirable privileges not shared by others. Little wonder, then, that power is sought by many. The following is also true, however: While many successful persons have a strong drive for power, possession of this motive does not seem essential for good job performance. In fact, research suggests that a high need for power may interfere with efficiency and can produce low morale among subordinates.[30] Thus the link between power motivation and effectiveness is complex.

What, precisely, is the origin of power? Why was the division head in the earlier example able to command obedience from the employee, while the office supervisor was not? How can individuals attain such influence? We now focus on these major questions.

Individual Power: Its Basic Sources

Power can stem from many different sources—everything from inherited royalty, on the one hand, to sheer brute strength, on the other. Careful analysis suggests, however, that it usually derives from five distinct sources.[31]

Reward Power: Control over Valued Resources.

One major source of personal power involves control of valued rewards or resources. Individuals who are able to determine who gets raises, promotions, or various perks usually can exert tremendous influence over others. In fact, with a little practice, they can usually get subordinates to jump through hoops! The reason behind this influence is simple: Only by doing what the power holder wants can individuals hope to attain valued rewards. **Reward power** offers a good explanation for the reactions of the employee in the earlier example. He probably realized that the head of the department could determine the size of his next

power   The ability to affect the behavior of others regularly and strongly, and even against their will.

status   The level of respect, prestige, and privilege assigned to a specific individual by other members of his or her group or organization.

reward power   Power stemming from the ability to control various rewards sought by others.

raise and whether he would be promoted. It is not surprising that he quickly yielded to the request (or demand) that he work on Saturday.

Coercive Power: Control over Punishments.   The other side of the coin from reward power involves the ability to inflict punishments of various kinds, a capacity known as **coercive power.** This form of power plays mainly on fear. Subordinates realize that if they do not behave as the power holder wishes, they will suffer unpleasant outcomes or events. For example, people holding coercive power can fire employees, lower their pay, criticize them publicly, or give them poor references. The open use of coercive power is frowned upon in work settings, and for good reason. Exposing employees to strong punishment or censure can lead them to nurse a grudge. Needless to say, this development can be devastating to morale. As such, coercive power is generally used as sparingly as possible. When it is employed, it is often concealed behind a velvet glove. Even then, however, it is readily recognized by most people and can have important effects on their behavior.

Legitimate Power: Control Based on Rank.   Have you ever seen thousands of people bow down before a queen, king, or religious leader? If so, you are already familiar with a third basis for power. Such people, as well as top executives, elected government officials, and even sports coaches, exercise authority over others by virtue of the jobs or titles they hold. In short, individuals obey their directives because it is considered appropriate and legitimate for chief executive officers, presidents, and head coaches to be in charge. Because authority stemming from **legitimate power** is viewed as justified, it is less likely to stir up resentment among those who must obey.

Referent Power: Control Based on Attraction.   Earlier, we noted that individuals are more willing to accept influence from someone they like than from someone they dislike. This situation points to a fourth major source of power: authority based on attraction. When individuals are greatly admired by others, they can often exert a tremendous amount of influence. In fact, exercising such **referent power** may be easy, for many persons are both willing and eager to obey directives from those they admire. Dramatic examples of referent power in action are provided by charismatic political leaders, sports heroes or heroines, and movie stars. This type of power can also be observed in work settings, where popular executives often inspire great respect—and willingness to obey—

coercive power   Power stemming from control over punishments and negative outcomes. The use of coercive power is discouraged in most work settings.

legitimate power   Power based on an individual's position or rank.

referent power   Power based on the personal attractiveness of the individual who possesses it.

among their staff. In short, where power is concerned, being liked is a major step toward being able to exert considerable control over others.

Expert Power: Control Based on Knowledge.

A final source of power, that deriving from expertise, can be readily illustrated. Suppose that you visit your accountant. After examining your records, he recommends that you send a huge payment to the government at once. Will you comply? Probably, you will. Painful as this action is, you realize that your accountant knows best where tax matters are concerned. The fact that you follow her directions demonstrates the impact of **expert power**—the ability of people with special knowledge to exert strong influence over others. In most cases, expert power is restricted to issues or behaviors related to the expert's knowledge. In some instances, however, it spills over into additional areas, perhaps because a high degree of expertise often confers high status. Advertisers use this knowledge when they seek endorsements by celebrities or athletes who may actually know little about the car, cereal, or sneaker they're touting. In any case, technical skill or expertise can serve as a major source of power.

Various Bases of Power: Independent or Linked?

Before concluding this discussion of the various types of power (see Table 7.2 for a summary), we should consider one final question: Are these sources independent or closely linked? The answer is clear: In many instances, they are highly interdependent. Different types of power tend to occur in combination—for example, individuals high in reward power are often high in coercive power as well. Also, the presence and use of one type of power often affects other types. For example, use of coercive power may reduce a person's referent power, because people usually dislike those who

expert power   Power based on the possession of special knowledge or skill.

Table 7.2	**Power: Five Distinct Sources**

Individuals may derive power in an organization from the sources described here.

Type of Power	Description
Reward power	Based on the ability to control valued resources or needs.
Coercive power	Based on the ability to inflict punishments.
Legitimate power	Based on an individual's position or rank within an organization.
Referent power	Based on the personal attractiveness of a person.
Expert power	Based on the possession of special skills or knowledge.

punish them. Similarly, because legitimate power is often associated with high status, its presence can enhance attraction toward those who hold it and so increase their referent power. We could describe many other examples, but the main point should be clear: While power can stem from many different sources, the different types tend to be intricately linked.[32] (How much power do you possess? For a quick overall estimate, see the *Human Relations in Action* section.)

Human Relations in Action

Measuring Your Own Power: A Quick Self-Assessment

Now that you have examined the major sources of power, you may find yourself wondering, "How much power do I have?" Answering this question is no simple task. Power, to a large extent, is in the eye of the beholder. Thus it's not simply what you can do to—or for—other people that counts; what they *believe* you can do is important, too. You can gain at least a degree of insight into your own power (either at home or at work) by answering the questions below. Check one space for each question:

1. **Reward power:** To what extent can you influence the rewards of other persons—their promotions, raises, job assignments, or emotional well-being?

   _____ Not at all

   _____ Somewhat

   _____ Very much

2. **Coercive power:** To what extent can you influence the negative outcomes received by others—dock their pay, fire them, give them poor references, and the like?

   _____ Not at all

   _____ Somewhat

   _____ Very much

3. **Legitimate power:** To what extent does your position or title give you the authority to tell others what to do?

   _____ Not at all

   _____ Somewhat

   _____ Very much

Hazards to Avoid in Your Attempts to Persuade and Influence

Lest we leave you with the impression that persuasion and influence might follow a "cookbook" path, we note that psychologists are not the only people who are aware of influence strategies. As lay psychologists, we are aware that people are constantly

4. **Referent power:** To what extent do other people like or admire you and so show willingness to do what you want?

_____ Not at all

_____ Somewhat

_____ Very much

5. **Expert power:** To what extent do other people seek your advice or suggestions concerning technical matters or special skills that you possess?

_____ Not at all

_____ Somewhat

_____ Very much

Scoring

Give yourself 1 point for each "Not at all" answer, 5 points for each "Somewhat" answer, and 10 points for each "Very much" answer. Then add all your scores together.

Interpretation

If you scored 40 or higher, welcome to the "power elite"; you seem to exert considerable power or influence over others. If you scored between 20 and 35, you have a moderate degree of power over others. If you scored between 5 and 15, your power quotient is low. If this is the case, though, don't despair. Instead, read the _Guidelines for Effective Human Relations_ section on page 206, which presents specific hints for increasing your personal power and social influence.

trying to influence our attitudes and behavior. Our influence attempts can also have unexpected effects on our own as well as other individuals' behavior. We point out some of these "hazards" here.

1. **The slime effect.** Most of us are quite aware that people engage in self-presentational strategies, such as ingratiation. Research suggests that we especially dislike persons whom we perceive as behaving in this manner. One interesting study conducted in the Netherlands found that people who appeared especially likable toward superiors and dislikable toward subordinates ("licking upward–kicking downward") were viewed very negatively and "slimy."[33] This "slime effect" seems to derive from our general tendency to be suspicious of the ulterior motives of people who behave very positively in the presence of their superiors; this suspicion is confirmed when we observe the same people behaving negatively to their subordinates.[34] As a general rule, we may automatically look to the situation as a cause for likable behaviors. This tendency may undermine influence techniques that rely on people behaving in likable ways.

2. **Reactance: A boomerang effect of persuasion.** It is a fact of human nature that people don't like to be pushed around. In fact, when we feel that someone is trying to control or change our behavior, we often lean over backward to do just the opposite. This tendency is called **psychological reactance.**[35] Both adults and children experience this phenomenon. (Actually, my mother tells me she used a reverse-reactance strategy to get me to eat green beans as a child: She told me that I couldn't have them and, of course, I wanted them more!) When exposed to persuasive appeals, we can usually tell that someone is trying to influence us. The existence of reactance is a major roadblock along the path to persuasion. To minimize its effects, don't be too pushy and threaten individuals' freedom to choose. Always provide the person you wish to influence with room to maneuver, and also provide at least an illusion of free choice. Moreover, you should avoid showy, blatant, and tacky signs of power (see Table 7.3 for examples).

3. **Metamorphic effects of power and persuasion.** Although most research has concentrated on the effects of attitude change techniques on the targets of influence, some evidence suggests that they may also change the attitudes and values of the users of these techniques. Surveys show that husbands, wives, and business managers who use strong and controlling tactics of influence come to view the people they influence in a less favorable light.[36] This kind of effect, which has been labeled a **metamorphic effect of power,** describes the transformation in a persuader as a function of his or her success

psychological reactance   Going out of one's way to perform the behaviors that someone is trying to control or change.

metamorphic effect of power   The transformation that occurs in a persuader as a function of his or her success in changing others.

Table 7.3   **Tacky Power**

The following are a few tacky forms of power you should avoid:

1. Larger-than-necessary offices and special privileges, such as special dining rooms, parking places, and bathrooms.

2. Layers of office staff and "cronies" hanging around you.

3. Formal titles; don't be afraid to use your first name.

4. Specialized vocabulary: Remember, you're trying to communicate, not impress!

in changing others.[37] One interesting example of this effect is seen in laboratory-controlled research comparing the reactions of persuaders using foot-in-the-door, door-in-the-face, and rational persuasion techniques.[38] Persuaders who used either the foot-in the-door or door-in-the face techniques viewed their targets of persuasion as less competent than persuaders who used the rational technique; they also reported less enjoyment in using these strategies. Be forewarned: The mind you change may be your own!

ORGANIZATIONAL POLITICS

In the best of all possible worlds, organizations would be totally fair places in which to work. Promotions, raises, and other rewards would be distributed solely on the basis of merit or past performance, and major decisions related to policy and other matters would rely on careful examination of all available data. Unfortunately, reality departs greatly from this picture of perfection (see Figure 7.7 on page 204). Work settings are not always governed by principles of fair play and rationality. In fact, they are often highly political in nature, with individuals and groups constantly jockeying for position and power. The rules of this game, generally known as **organizational politics,** are complex and ever-changing.[39] Yet the stakes are so high that, sooner or later, nearly everyone must play. Although the cast of characters shifts over time, the major focus remains the same: gaining and using power.

Unfortunately, organizational politics play a major role in most work settings. Indeed, who you know, who you can count on as an ally, and who owes you a favor are often more important in determining the fate of your ca-

organizational politics   Tactics for gaining, holding, and using power in organizations.

Figure 7.7   Organizational Politics: A Reality of the Workplace Environment

DILBERT reprinted by permission of United Features Syndicate.

reer than your actual performance. Furthermore, the winners in this game tend to be the individuals who control an organization, regardless of what the formal organizational chart says. Given the obvious importance of this political process, we wish we could arm you with a firm set of guidelines for dealing with organizational politics. Unfortunately, this goal is far easier to state than to attain. The situations involved are complex, and each work setting is, in a sense, unique. Nevertheless, we can give you a sense of where organizational politics are most likely to occur and describe tactics that are used commonly to gain advantages.

Although politics are widespread within organizations, they are more prominent in certain places within organizations. In general, politics are most likely in upper and middle management than in production and blue-collar domains.[40] These differences relate more to organizational factors than to any characteristics of the individuals who occupy these positions. More specifically, characteristics of positions that have a high level of role ambiguity and unclear performance evaluation systems foster organizational politics.[41]

Tactics of Influence

It is impossible to offer a short list of techniques guaranteed to work in organizational politics. We can, however, provide a summary of general tactics—ones that fit with what we know about power and influence. In addition, these tactics seem relatively benign, compared with many of the nasty forms of politics that are often encountered in the real world. If you use them with care, they may contribute to your success in the political maneuvering you are sure to encounter. As you are likely to encounter most of these tactics in the years ahead (even if you don't use them yourself), being familiar with them may be helpful in itself.

1. **Cultivate the right allies.** Having allies who will support your views and positions is a must. It is important to muster mutual support as quickly as possible—but choose your partners carefully. You may find yourself in a position of owing the wrong persons favors if you partner with the wrong persons!

2. **Count on reciprocity.** As a general rule, it is helpful to do favors for others. You can call in these IOUs when it will do you the most good.

3. **Project an image of competence and confidence.** It has long been said that nothing succeeds like success. In organizational politics, this axiom seems to be true with a vengeance. If you always appear to be on top of your job and to know just what you are doing, you may soon develop a "halo." Keep your image as bright and shiny as possible.

4. **Remember that being liked is a plus.** Although some kinds of power are hard to attain on your own (such as reward or legitimate power), referent power can be cultivated. Through careful use of social skills, you can increase your appeal to key people in your organization. Being liked by such individuals may give a big boost to your career.

5. **Be persuasive.** Forceful arguments, eloquently stated, are often highly effective in swaying others. Take great pains to develop your persuasive skills to the highest degree. The payoff for doing so may be substantial.

6. **Make a good first impression.** First impressions do count, so it is important to look good on any project or assignment from the start. Important people in your organization will tend to remember this positive impression, and your position in the political arena may improve greatly.

If the tactics just outlined strike you as duplicitous or manipulative, consider that they are mild and benevolent in comparison to another group of strategies known as "dirty tricks."[42] These less savvy tactics include (1) spreading false rumors about opponents, (2) channeling communication so that opponents fail to receive vital information, and (3) conducting meetings according to a hidden agenda so that you, but not your opponents, are prepared to discuss certain topics. These procedures are clearly unethical and violate the basic principles of fair play and justice; we certainly don't recommend them here. The world of work, unfortunately, has its share of unprincipled persons. For your own protection, you should be familiar with such tactics and prepared to defend against them. You will then have a good chance of surviving in the complex and often harsh arena of organizational politics.

Guidelines for Effective Human Relations

Using What You've Learned

In this chapter, we examined a broad range of principles and findings about persuasion and power. Although there are few rules that apply to every situation, there are some general guidelines suggested by the various findings we discussed. These are summarized below for your consideration. Remember, no rule works 100 percent in every situation. However, these guidelines should improve your social power and increase your resistance to unwanted influence.

- It is important to make an attractive and credible impression on those you seek to influence. It is also important to improve the smoothness, speed, and eloquence of your delivery.

- Remember that what you say matters as much as how you say it. Tailor your appeals to the individuals you hope to influence. Presenting two sides of an issue is often effective.

- Do not appear too pushy. Individuals react against blatant attempts to persuade.

- Be aware that persuasion is often mindless. Guard yourself against mindless social influence by playing devil's advocate. Do not automatically yield to pressure without considering the potential undesirable consequences.

- Remember that cultural stereotypes about susceptibility to persuasion are often incorrect. Do not underestimate those you seek to influence.

- Beware of those who set you up with overly small or large requests. They may be intentionally softening your resistance to later requests.

- Develop positive sources of power. Stay clear of the use of coercive power in the workplace and elsewhere.

- Be aware of the existence of organizational politics. Learn to play the game in ways that do not compromise your sense of self or your ethical principles.

Social influence is a necessary part of our lives. Cooperation and effective human relations require that we both influence and are influenced by others. A little caution, sensitivity, and common sense, however, should be exercised. Excess use of power and persuasion as well as excess susceptibility to influence are dangerous to your psychological, social, and financial health.

Summary

We often wish to change the behavior of others. Many techniques exist for accomplishing this goal. One of the most effective approaches is persuasion, in which we attempt to change others' minds (and hence their actions) through persuasive appeals. The effectiveness of such efforts is strongly affected by the characteristics of the people doing the persuading (such as their attractiveness, style, or credibility). It is also influenced by the contents of the persuasive message. Two paths to persuasion exist: the "mindless," or peripheral route, and the "mindful," or central route.

Additional techniques for exerting influence focus on compliance—getting others to agree to various requests. Efforts to enhance our appeal to other persons are often successful in this regard. Another tactic for attaining compliance involves multiple requests (such as the foot-in-the-door and the door-in-the-face techniques). In this approach, we begin with one request and then shift to the one we really desire.

Power is the ability to change the behavior of others regularly, strongly, and even against their will. It stems from several different sources, including control over rewards and punishments, expertise, legitimacy, and personal attractiveness. These sources interact so that possession of one type of power affects the possession or use of others. Organizations are highly political in nature, with various individuals and groups constantly jockeying for power. Several methods exist for dealing with organizational politics, such as courting the right allies, projecting an image of competence, being persuasive, and creating a positive first impression.

Key Terms

attitudinal politics, p. 195

central route to persuasion, p. 187

coercive power, p. 198

credibility, p. 184

door-in-the-face technique, p. 192

expert power, p. 199

fear appeals, p. 186

foot-in-the-door technique, p. 191

forewarning, p. 195

influence, p. 196

legitimate power, p. 198

metamorphic effect of power, p. 202

one-sided argument, p. 185

organizational politics, p. 203

persuasion, p. 183

peripheral route to persuasion, p. 187

power, p. 197

psychological reactance, p. 202

reciprocity rule, p. 182

referent power, p. 198

reward power, p. 197

self-deprecation, p. 191

self-disclosure, p. 191

self-presentation, p. 190

social cognition, p. 186

status, p. 197

subliminal persuasion, p. 188

two-sided argument, p. 185

 *Case in Point*

Dr. Cialdini Meets Stunning Young Woman

Everyone is subject at some time to the tactics of compliance. Robert Cialdini is a noted psychologist who has done extensive research on the psychology of influence. His findings illuminate the ways in which the automatic tendency to maintain consistency can lead to poor choices. As is true for all of us, Professor Cialdini has himself fallen prey to this weapon of influence. Below, we present Cialdini's encounter with a "stunning young woman" who appeared on his doorstep several years ago, purportedly taking a survey.

STUNNING YOUNG WOMAN: Hello. I'm doing a survey on the entertainment habits of city residents, and I wonder if you could answer a few questions for me.

CIALDINI: Do come in.

SYW: Thank you. I'll just sit right here and begin. How many times per week would you say you go out to dinner?

C: Oh, probably about three, maybe four times a week. Whenever I can, really; I love fine restaurants.

SYW: How nice. And do you usually order wine with your dinner?

C: Only if it's imported.

SYW: I see. What about movies? Do you go to movies much?

C: The cinema? I can't get enough of good films. I especially like the sophisticated kind with the words on the bottom of the screen. How about you? Do you like to see films?

SYW: Uh . . . yes I do. But let's get back to the interview. Do you go to many concerts?

C: Definitely. The symphonic stuff mostly, of course; but I do enjoy a quality pop group as well.

SYW (*writing rapidly*): Great! Just one more question. What about touring performances by theatrical or ballet companies? Do you see them when they're in town?

C: Ah, the ballet—the movement, the grace, the form—I love it. Mark me down as *loving* the ballet. See it every chance I get.

SYW: Fine. Just let me recheck my figures here for a moment, Mr. Cialdini.

C: Actually, it's Dr. Cialdini. But that sounds so formal; why don't you call me Bob?

SYW: All right, Bob. From the information you've already given me, I'm pleased to say you could save up to $1,200 a year by joining *Clubamerica!* A small membership fee entitles you to discounts on most of the activities you've mentioned. Surely someone as socially vigorous as yourself would want to take advantage of the tremendous savings our company can offer on all the things you've already told me you do.

C (*trapped like a rat*): Well . . . uh . . . I . . . uh . . . I guess so.

Questions

1. Dr. Cialdini reports that this encounter took place long before he began his study of compli-

ance tactics and that his response would be quite different today. What do you think his new response would be?

2. What would be your response to the SYW? Would you buy the entertainment package?

3. What tactics of compliance did SYW use?

4. What were the specific pressures that SYW tried to place on Dr. Cialdini?

5. What could you say to the SYW to counteract these pressures?

From *Influence: Science and Practice*, 3rd ed., by Robert B. Cialdini. Copyright © 1993 by HarperCollins College Publishers. Reprinted by permission.

Notes

1. Cialdini, R. B. (1993). *Influence: Science and practice.* 3rd ed. New York: HarperCollins College Publishers.

2. Ibid, p. 28.

3. Rajecki, D. W. (1990). *Attitudes: Themes and advances.* Sunderland, MA: Sinauer Associates.

4. Kiesler, C. A., & Kiesler, S. (1969). *Conformity.* Reading, MA: Addison-Wesley.

5. Miller, N., Maruyama, G., Beaber, R. J., & Valone, K. (1976). Speed of speech and persuasion. *Journal of Personality and Social Psychology, 34,* 615–624.

6. See note 3.

7. Mewborn, C. R., & Rogers, R. W. (1979). Effects of threatening and reassuring components of fear appeals on physiological and verbal measures of emotion and attitudes. *Journal of Experimental Social Psychology, 15,* 242–253.

8. See note 3.

9. Petty, R. E., & Cacioppo, J. T. (1986). *Attitude change: Central and peripheral routes to persuasion.* New York: Springer-Verlag.

10. Petty, R. E., Cacioppo, J. T., & Goldman, R. (1981). Personal involvement as a determinant of argument-based persuasion. *Journal of Personality and Social Psychology, 41,* 847–855.

11. Worth, L. T., & Mackie, D. M. (1987). Cognitive mediation of positive affect in persuasion. *Social Cognition, 5,* 76–94.

12. Langer, E., Blank, A., & Chanowitz, B. (1978). The mindlessness of ostensibly thoughtful action: The role of "placebic" information in inter-

personal interaction. *Journal of Personality and Social Psychology, 36,* 635–642.

13. See note 1.

14. Baron, R. A. (1986). Self-presentation in job interviews: When there can be "too much of a good thing." *Journal of Applied Social Psychology, 16,* 16–28.

15. Avery, R. D., & Campion, J. E. (1982). The employment interview: A summary and review of recent research. *Personnel Psychology, 35,* 281–322.

16. Beamon, A. L., Cole, M., Preston, M., Klentz, B., & Steblay, N. M. (1983). Fifteen years of foot-in-the-door research: A meta-analysis. *Personality and Social Psychology Bulletin, 9,* 181–186.

17. Freedman, J. L., & Fraser, S. C. (1966). Compliance without pressure: The foot-in-the-door technique. *Journal of Personality and Social Psychology, 4,* 195–202.

18. DeJong, W., & Musili, L. (1982). External pressure to comply: Handicapped versus nonhandicapped requesters and the foot-in-the-door phenomenon. *Personality and Social Psychology Bulletin, 8,* 522–527.

19. See note 13.

20. Cialdini, R. B., Vincent, J. E., Lewis, S. K., Catalan, J., Wheeler, D., & Darby, B. L. (1975). Reciprocal concessions procedure for inducing compliance: The door-in-the-face technique. *Journal of Personality and Social Psychology, 31,* 206–215.

21. Pendleton, M. G., & Batson, C. D. (1979). Self-presentation and the door-in-the-face technique for inducing compliance. *Personality and Social Psychology Bulletin, 5,* 77–81.

22. Freedman, J. L., & Sears, D. O. (1965). Warning, distraction, and resistance to influence. *Journal of Personality and Social Psychology, 1,* 262–266.

23. Pratkanis, A. R., & Aronson, E. (1991). *Age of propaganda.* New York: W. H. Freeman & Co.

24. Ibid.

25. Cialdini, R. B., Levy, A., Herman, C. P., Kowalski, L. T., & Petty, R. E. (1976). Elastic shifts of opinion: Determinants of direction and durability.

Journal of Personality and Social Psychology, 34, 663–672.

26. See note 23.

27. See note 9.

28. See note 23.

29. Grimes, A. J. (1978). Authority, power, influence, and social control: A theoretical synthesis. *Academy of Management Review, 3,* 724–735.

30. Cornelius, E. T., III, & Lane, F. B. (1984). The power motive and managerial success in a professionally oriented service industry organization. *Journal of Applied Psychology, 69,* 32–39.

31. French, J. R. P., & Raven, B. (1959). The bases of social power. In D. Cartwright (ed.), *Studies in social power* (pp. 150–167). Ann Arbor: University of Michigan Press.

32. Green, C. N., & Podsakoff, P. M. (1981). Effects of withdrawal of a performance contingent reward on supervisory influence and power. *Academy of Management Journal, 24,* 527–542.

33. Vonk, R. (1998). The slime effect: Suspicion and dislike of likeable behavior toward superiors. *Journal of Personality and Social Psychology, 74,* 849–864.

34. Ibid.

35. Brehm, J. W. (1966). *A theory of psychological reactance.* New York: Academic Press.

36. Kipnis, D. (1976). *The powerholders.* Chicago: University of Chicago Press.

37. Ibid.

38. O'Neal, E. C., Kipnis, D., & Craig, K. M. (1994). Effects of the persuader on employing a coercive influence technique. *Basic and Applied Social Psychology, 15,* 225–238.

39. Mayes, B. T., & Allen, R. W. (1977). Toward a definition of organizational politics. *Academy of Management Review, 2,* 672–678.

40. Gandz, J., & Murray, V. V. (1980). The experience of workplace politics. *Academy of Management Journal, 23,* 237–251.

41. Fandt, P. M., & Ferris, G. R. (1990). The management of information and impressions: When

employees behave opportunistically. *Organizational Behavior and Human Decision Processes,* (Feb.): 140–158.

42. Cavanagh, G. F., Moberg, D. J., & Velesquez, M. (1981). The ethics of organizational politics. *Academy of Management Review, 6,* 363–374.

Chapter 8

**Motivation in Groups:
Loafing and Facilitation**

Social Loafing: How to Get Less
 Out of More

**Social Facilitation: Motivation
and Interference in Groups**

Theories of Social Facilitation:
 Arousal and Evaluation

**Brainstorming: Creativity
in Groups?**

Factors That Inhibit Effective
 Brainstorming
Improving Group Brainstorming

**Group Decision Making:
Passing the Buck**

Group Polarization
Information Biases in Groups: A Focus
 on Commonalities

Groupthink: Defective Decision Making
 in Groups
Evaluation of the Groupthink Model
Teamwork and Groupthink: Problems
 of Self-Management

Special Sections

Human Relations in Action
Group Seekers and Avoiders: How Well-
 Suited Are You for Working in Groups?

Guidelines for Effective Human Relations
Using What You've Learned

Experiential Exercises
Groupthink at NBC
Group Processes and the Family

GROUP BEHAVIOR AND INFLUENCE

How Do Groups Affect Us?

Learning Objectives

After reading this chapter, you should be able to:

1. Discuss how social loafing can affect group performance.

2. Describe the phenomenon of social facilitation and why it occurs.

3. Identify the major factors that influence the performance of brainstorming groups.

4. Discuss the factors that underlie the group polarization effect.

5. Describe the information biases in groups.

6. Describe the basic characteristics of groupthink.

7. Know the rules for good group decision making.

ohnny Carson had been a 30-year fixture on late-night television and an important financial asset to the NBC television network. In 1991, he was close to retirement, and a group of NBC executives in Burbank, California, were faced with deciding on a successor. They had to choose between David Letterman, who hosted a successful late-night program that followed the Carson show, and Jay Leno, who had been a permanent guest host for five years. The decision was difficult because each of the candidates had strong positive characteristics and the network was under constant scrutiny by the press regarding its choice. Whichever candidate was chosen, the group was likely to get some criticism and the other candidate would likely sign with the rival CBS network. The executives decided to hire Leno, and Letterman subsequently signed with CBS. Instead of having two top hosts in its line-up, NBC lost one of its top talents. To add insult to injury, Letterman won the ratings war, bumping NBC from its longstanding top spot in the late-night ratings.[1]

roups and organizations are constantly confronted with decisions that have important consequences. It is therefore important for groups to evaluate carefully all of the relevant facts and perspectives before making decisions. What has been your experience in groups? Do you think they typically make good decisions? Research suggests that groups often fall short in the decision-making department. The decision by NBC was an initial disaster because it lost not only its rating lead, but also one of its top talents. It has been suggested that NBC executives succumbed to "groupthink" by not following good decision-making procedures.[2] In this chapter, we analyze groupthink, as well as other group phenomena and principles that have important implications for our life at work and in other organizations. Many studies have suggested that groups have a strong impact on our behavior. Some of these effects may be quite counterproductive. We will look carefully at the variety of factors that play a role in group behavior and at how these factors can lead to either positive or negative results for groups. First, we briefly discuss some basic characteristics of groups.

What is a **group?** We usually think of a group as consisting of two or more individuals with some common bond, goal, or task. Sometimes groups are simply temporary collections of people, such as groups at spectator events. Some groups, such as clubs, churches, and families, may have strong bonds and maintain long-term relationships. Although there are obviously many types of groups, we can formally define a *group* as a collection of two or more interacting individuals who share common goals, have a stable relationship, and see themselves as a

group A collection of two or more interacting individuals with a stable pattern of relationships between them, who share common goals and who perceive themselves as being a group.

group.[3] Unless some degree of verbal or nonverbal interaction takes place among group members, a sense of group identity is not likely to exist.

A group typically has some degree of stability in that it is not constantly changing but has a core group of members. Most groups exist because they share common goals or interests. This makes it likely that group members will see themselves as a distinct group. Fraternities and sororities reflect this idea quite nicely. There is likely to be much social interaction among members. Although there is always some turnover, the change in membership is gradual and provides some degree of stability. The members share common goals about the importance of social life on campus and have strong perceptions of their group identity.

$\mathcal{M}$OTIVATION IN GROUPS: LOAFING AND FACILITATION

Do you like to work alone or in groups? Your answer probably depends on the task you are doing. Sometimes we may want the social stimulation or motivation that others can provide, but at other times we may work best alone. Of course, often there is little alternative, as in the case of participation on some sports teams. Research has shown that groups can affect our motivation to work hard on a task. Sometimes we may loaf when we are in groups, but other times groups may make us work more diligently. However, increased motivation does not always translate into better performance. In this section, we consider when groups bring out a person's best performance and when they do not.

Social Loafing: How to Get Less Out of More

When groups make people feel less accountable or responsible, individuals seem to be less motivated in work situations. One of the first such observations was made by Ringlemann, who noted that as the number of individuals in a group pulling on a rope increased, the amount of force each individual exerted was reduced. Doesn't this finding contradict what you might have expected? It would seem natural for people in the group to be motivated to work harder for the group goal. Yet recent research has demonstrated that motivation losses in groups, called **social loafing,** do occur whenever efforts of individuals are combined into a group product (see Figure 8.1 on page 216).[4]

Research has shown that social loafing can occur on a variety of tasks. The basic characteristic of these tasks is that they are additive. On **additive tasks,** individuals in the group do their own individual task, and the sum of

social loafing   The tendency for group members to exert less individual effort on an additive task as the size of the group increases.

additive tasks   Group tasks in which the individual efforts of several persons are added together to form the group's product.

Figure 8.1   Social Loafers: Doing Less in Groups

Sometimes given members of groups tend to have reduced motivation for working on a task.

all of the individual efforts is the group product. This is typical of many work situations, such as telemarketing, car sales, and painting, in which individuals may work independently within a group. Social loafing has been found in studies in which individuals were asked to clap, shout loudly, or generate uses for a simple object.

When do we loaf the most? From your experiences, you probably remember times when it was hard to be motivated to do your share of the work. At other times, you were likely highly motivated to contribute to a group effort. The degree of loafing that occurs depends on a number of situational and personal factors.[5] Loafing is most likely to occur when group members do not strongly value the task they are performing. It may be uninteresting or the group may have felt little choice in selecting their work. We are more likely to loaf when we do not know the other group members very well or when we expect them to loaf. The larger the group, the more people will loaf, especially in all-male groups. People from Western cultures, such as the United States or Canada, are more prone to social loafing than people from Eastern cultures such as China or Japan.

Why do we loaf? A number of reasons explain why individuals tend to loaf in groups. One major reason seems to be the fact that in many such situations, people may not be individually identifiable because their performances are combined into a group score. Under such conditions, people may feel little concern about the quality of their performance. Identifiability is important mainly because it allows the individual's performance to be evaluated.[6] When individual performance can be evaluated by others, people seem to be motivated to exert more effort on a task. This probably makes sense to you, as you may tend to work harder when the boss or the manager is around to observe your work than when he or she is not.

A somewhat broader perspective is that social loafing occurs when individuals feel that their contributions to the group are not rewarded, are not needed, or are too costly.[7] Most of us want some type of personal reward or benefit from our efforts. If working in a group reduces the extent to which we can gain those types of outcomes, we will tend to work less hard on the group task.

Karau and Williams have developed a **collective-effort model** that highlights this concern with personal rewards.[8] They note that the link between our efforts and desired outcomes is likely to be more uncertain in groups. It is suggested that we will work hard in groups only when two conditions are satisfied. First, we must expect that our efforts will have an impact on the group's performance. Second, high levels of group performance should lead to desired outcomes, whether they be personal, social, or financial. Thus computer programmers are likely to work more diligently as members of a group that needs their unique skills or talents and when the collective group effort will likely result in a very useful new product. They are likely to work less diligently when much overlap in skills occurs and they have little confidence that the group's efforts will lead to a significant result.

Counteracting Social Loafing.   There appear to be a number of ways to counteract people's tendency to loaf in large work groups. One is to increase *accountability* by making sure that each person's performance can be assessed or evaluated.[9] This can be done in a variety of ways that depend to a large extent on the type of work situation. For example, procedures could be designed to keep track of the work each person accomplishes. This approach can be seen in factories that pay on the basis of the amount of work done by each individual (piece rate) and stores that pay on a commission basis.

It may also be useful to complement the accountability strategy with one focusing on the intrinsic merits of the task. Studies have shown that when people feel that the task on which they are working is unique or challenging, they may not loaf even if their performance is pooled with that of the group. Under such conditions, people may be motivated by the opportunity to make a unique contribution or to test their skills.[10]

> **collective-effort model**   A theory of social loafing that proposes that it occurs because of the uncertain connection between our efforts and outcomes in groups.

Another way of overcoming social loafing might be called *group pride.* If people feel that the performance of their group can be compared with that of others, they may be motivated to work hard so that their group will do well relative to the other groups. This can be seen most clearly when one team competes with another. In the same way, stores or companies may have competitions with one another. This effect has been shown in several studies in which groups whose members' performance was pooled were provided with either an objective standard of ideal performance or the average performance of previous participants. In both cases, the social loafing effect was eliminated.[11]

Since social loafing is likely when individuals see their contributions as unrewarded, unneeded, and too costly,[12] individuals can be motivated to work hard in groups by counteracting these perceptions. Essentially, when there are external or personal rewards to be obtained from working on a group task, social loafing can be minimized. Table 8.1 summarizes the factors that influence the degree of social loafing in groups.

One interesting aspect of social loafing is that it can be contagious. Seeing some members of the group loafing may stimulate other group members to do likewise.[13] However, it is also possible that group members will compensate for failure of the other members to perform. This *social compensation* will occur if the task is one that is meaningful or important to the group member, and if it is evident that the co-worker is unable or unwilling to try to do well.[14] You have probably done this your-

Table 8.1   **Social Loafing: Some Ways to Overcome It**

The extent to which social loafing will occur or will be reduced or prevented depends on a variety of factors.

Factors That Increase Loafing	Factors That Reduce Loafing
Lack of identifiability	Individual identifiability
No individual evaluation	Individual or group evaluation
No individual or group standards of evaluation	Individual or group standards of evaluation
Task is easy, boring, or the same as others'	Task is difficult, interesting, or different from others'
Individual contributions not necessary	Individual contributions essential
No individual or group incentives	Individual or group incentives
Large group	Small group
Unfamiliar group	Familiar group

self in situations in which achievement of the group goal was important to you, but other group members were not doing their fair share.

Applicability of Social Loafing.   Although there is much evidence for social loafing in laboratory studies, little evidence has been gathered thus far for the role of this factor in real-life working situations. Your own experience probably suggests that it does play a role in such situations. The fact that economies based on the socialistic system of pooling individual contributions (for example, communes or collective farms or industries) have not been very productive is consistent with a social loafing perspective. In any case, anyone concerned with achieving a high level of productivity out of a group should be aware of the potential problems caused by social loafing and the ways it can be avoided.

SOCIAL FACILITATION: MOTIVATION AND INTERFERENCE IN GROUPS

Even though much evidence exists for the loss of motivation in groups, you probably are aware of situations in which you have been strongly motivated in group situations. If you have participated in team sports, taken part in recitals, or competed in games, you know that in these types of situations your adrenaline may really start going. This phenomenon has been studied for a long time with both animals and humans. These studies have generally led to a consistent pattern of results. Whenever we are in the presence of another person who is either observing our performance or doing the same task, the performance of simple or well-learned behaviors or tasks is facilitated and the performance of complex or poorly learned tasks is hindered. For example, when people are jogging, they jog faster when others are watching, but when people are trying to solve arithmetic problems they do poorly when others are watching.[15] These findings have important implications for work situations. Menial or fairly simple work may be done best in groups or while being monitored. Complicated jobs that involve learning and creativity might be done best in isolation. Why is this the case? Many ideas have been proposed and examined. We will briefly discuss a number of them.

Theories of Social Facilitation: Arousal and Evaluation

Some researchers have argued that the presence of other members of the same species increases one's level of excitation or *arousal*.[16] This enhanced state of excitation in turn enhances the occurrence of *dominant* or strong responses and hinders the occurrence of *subordinate* or weak ones. On simple or well-learned tasks, the correct responses are presumably dominant—that is, they have become strongly trained or automatic. On complex or poorly learned tasks, the correct responses are fairly weak or subordinate. Many studies support this **arousal model.** For example, in one study subjects were asked to do a complex motor task over a period of trials either alone or in front of an audience. On the initial learning trials, the incorrect responses were presumably dominant, and audience presence should have interfered with performance. As the trials progressed, the correct responses should have gained in strength and eventually become dominant. At that point, they should have been facilitated by audience presence. This is exactly what was found.[17]

Although the arousal model accounts fairly well for many of the findings obtained in this area of study, a number of other proposals have been generated about the factors that underlie the observed effects. It is rather obvious that many of the group situations we have discussed involve an element of *evaluation* or competition. When we are being observed by others while doing some task, we may be concerned about what the observers think of our performance. When performing a task in a group, we may be concerned about how well we are doing relative to the other group members. This concern over evaluation may be an important factor in the occurrence of excitation or arousal. Research has generally supported the importance of evaluation as a factor in task performance.[18] However, it also appears that in situations involving little opportunity for evaluation, effects of others' presence can still be observed.[19]

Why does the presence of others have an effect even when no evaluation is possible? Perhaps whenever people are around us, we have a need to monitor them because we never know for sure what is going to happen. This state of enhanced preparedness or monitoring may be the basis for enhanced arousal in the presence of others.[20] At work, performance of our various tasks may be influenced both by the mere presence of coworkers and by their potential evaluation of us. Of course, whether this is beneficial for productivity depends on the complexity of the task. For example, in one study students were examined doing a computer task either alone or in the presence of someone doing a different task.[21] Students who were experienced on computers had higher scores when someone else was present than when they were alone. The computer task may have been fairly simple for them. For inexperienced students, the effects of having others present depended on their gender. Inexperienced females had lower scores with someone present than when alone. Inexperienced males performed better with someone present than alone. Thus only females showed the poorer performance expected when the task was novel for students. It appears that part of the reason may be differences in expectations of success. Inexperienced females

arousal model of social facilitation   A theory stating that the presence of others increases arousal, which increases people's tendencies to perform the dominant response. If that response is well learned, performance will improve; if it is novel, performance will be impaired.

generally do not expect to do as well on computer tasks as inexperienced males. When females do have positive expectations about their performance, the presence of others did not have such a negative effect.[22]

BRAINSTORMING: CREATIVITY IN GROUPS?

When groups or organizations are trying to decide on some new courses of action or solutions to problems, they often resort to some version of a technique called **brainstorming**.[23] It typically involves the free exchange of ideas in a group so as to come up with novel ideas. It is assumed that group brainstorming will stimulate its members to generate many novel ideas. You have probably participated in groups of that sort. How successful were they? Very likely, it may have appeared that you generated quite a few good ideas and that the group was a success. The problem with such observations is that they do not take into account what you might have been able to do if the group members brainstormed by themselves. This issue has been carefully examined in research on brainstorming.

Studies on brainstorming emphasize a number of rules for the group to follow in generating ideas. Group members should feel free to express any or all ideas, no matter how unusual. There is an emphasis on number of ideas, with the more ideas the better. There should be no criticism or evaluation of ideas while they are being generated, and group members are encouraged to build on each other's ideas.

Contrary to early enthusiasm for the effectiveness of brainstorming, it now appears that brainstorming in groups is *not* particularly effective. When such brainstorming is compared with the efforts of the same number of individuals brainstorming alone, the groups of individuals (called *nominal groups*) almost always outperform the real groups in terms of both number and quality of ideas.[24]

Factors That Inhibit Effective Brainstorming

Why do brainstorming groups fare so poorly? A number of factors appear to be responsible. Even though there is an emphasis on being noncritical, there is still likely to be a concern with what others are thinking of one's ideas. As we have seen with the social facilitation phenomenon, such *evaluative concerns* will inhibit the performance of creativity tasks. People in brainstorming groups may also be prone to *free ride* or *loaf* because they may feel that their efforts are dispensable and no clear accountability for performance exists. While both of these factors do seem to be involved to some extent, some research suggests that the most impor-

brainstorming   A technique designed to enhance creativity in problem-solving groups by emphasizing the free exchange of novel ideas. These groups are not as effective as commonly thought.

tant factor is the interference or *blocking* that occurs when one person is trying to think up ideas while listening to those of others.[25]

Another factor that seems to play a role in brainstorming groups is a social comparison process. Individuals interacting in groups can compare their performance with that of others. There may be a tendency to shift one's performance level in the direction of others in the group. The least productive members may increase their performance somewhat and the most productive members may decrease their performance. As a result, there is a tendency for group members to perform similarly to others in their group. The strongest trend in laboratory groups seems to be for the more productive members to move in the direction of the least productive ones. This downward comparison process may be one reason that interactive groups perform more poorly than nominal groups. Interestingly, the group's level of performance may become somewhat of a norm and carry over to subsequent sessions. High-performing groups continue to be high performing, and low-performing ones carry on their low performance level. As a number of factors inhibit performance of groups (for example, evaluation, loafing, blocking), groups may develop a relatively low norm. In fact, it turns out that groups typically stop generating ideas before the time period allotted is over, even though they have not run out of ideas. When a group is given information about how much a group of individuals can generate, they greatly increase their output of ideas.[26]

Although groups do not perform well, individuals in groups tend to judge their performance more favorably than do those who work alone. This **illusion of productivity** also appears to be related to social comparison.[27] Individuals in groups can compare their performance with that of others. Since there is a tendency toward similarity of performance in groups, they should find that their performance is not too discrepant from that of others. Those performing alone do not have such an opportunity to compare and may be a bit unsure about the adequacy of their performance. (See Figure 8.2 for a summary of the social influence model of group brainstorming.)

Improving Group Brainstorming

A number of procedures have been suggested to improve the performance of brainstorming groups. Prior practice with brainstorming seems to help.[28] It can aid the group in becoming better coordinated in the generation of ideas in a group. To optimize the fact that individuals may more efficiently generate ideas in isolation than in a group, a procedure in which individuals first generate ideas alone, then share these ideas in a group, and then brainstorm again as individuals may be optimal. This type of procedure is employed in the *nominal group technique*.[29] This technique involves presentation of the topic to the group, individ-

illusion of productivity   The tendency of individuals in brainstorming groups to perceive their performance favorably even though they typically perform more poorly than individuals in nominal groups.

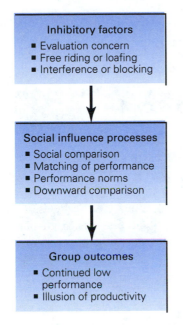

Inhibitory factors
- Evaluation concern
- Free riding or loafing
- Interference or blocking

Social influence processes
- Social comparison
- Matching of performance
- Performance norms
- Downward comparison

Group outcomes
- Continued low performance
- Illusion of productivity

Figure 8.2 **Brainstorming: A Social Influence Model**

Research has shown that group brainstorming is not very effective when compared to individual brainstorming, but perceptions of performance in groups can be quite favorable. This appears to be related to the factors outlined here.

Based on ideas from Paulus and Dzindolet, 1993; see note 13.

ual generation of ideas, and subsequent sharing of them in the group in sequence, allowing for clarification but not critiquing of the ideas presented. The ideas are then discussed and subsequently ranked individually.

Several techniques have been designed to allow for sharing of ideas in a way that avoids the problems of verbal group interaction such as blocking. In the technique of *brainwriting,* group members share their ideas on pieces of paper without talking. With this approach, one can generate ideas at will and examine the ideas from others as they are passed along. This procedure can prove quite effective in generating large numbers of ideas in groups.[30]

Another structured approach that appears to be fairly effective is called *synectics.*[31] The main concern of this approach is to increase divergent thinking and to come up with unusual ideas. Groups have a tendency toward convergent thinking or coming up with fairly expected or uncontroversial ideas. To promote divergent thinking, synectics emphasizes a spectrum policy, which holds that few ideas are all good or all bad and that it is important to look at all sides of an issue. During dry spells, when few ideas are being generated, the group is asked to use metaphors, analogies, or fantasy to generate further ideas.

Recently, there has been much interest in a computer-based idea-generation technique called *electronic brainstorming.* It is part of a computerized group decision

Figure 8.3   Group Decision Support: Computer Group Dynamics

Group decision support systems like the one shown here are used to facilitate brainstorming and decision making by the use of controlled interaction through computers.

support system that is designed to aid groups through a series of stages—idea generation, idea organization, idea ranking, and generation of ideas for implementation.[32] This system has been used by many major corporations (see Figure 8.3). Electronic brainstorming typically involves groups of three to eighteen people generating ideas on individual computers about a particular issue. Whenever they wish, they can request access to ideas generated by others in the group. A certain number of these ideas are then displayed at the bottom of the screen. Ideas may also be projected on a monitor at the front of the room. The suggestions generated by the group are collected by a central computer. One presumed advantage of this computerized system is that individuals are not identified with their ideas, which should lessen evaluation apprehension. Production blocking is also reduced because idea generation by one person does not interfere with the ability of another to generate ideas. Furthermore, it is not possible for one person—particularly someone who has high status in the group—to dominate the idea-generation process. It is possible to tap the full potential of the group without the inhibitions and interference involved in typical group interaction.

Studies have shown that electronic brainstorming is more effective than the typical interactive brainstorming in generating ideas and yields positive reactions from participants.[33] Nevertheless, electronic brainstorming groups often do not generate more ideas than the same number of individuals who brainstorm individually. Thus no evidence suggests that any mental stimulation occurs because of exposure to the ideas of others. One reason may be that group members may be too engrossed in generating their own ideas to pay much attention to the ideas from others on their screen. When group members are motivated to attend to those ideas, it can stimulate them to come up with even more ideas.[34]

Clearly, brainwriting and electronic brainstorming appear to be preferable to conventional verbal group brainstorming in generating large numbers of novel ideas. In most group situations, however, interaction or idea sharing takes the verbal form. Should we completely avoid this type of brainstorming? A number of reasons suggest that this course of action may not be necessary. Face-to-face verbal brainstorming may increase positive group feelings or cohesiveness and a feeling of commitment to the ideas finally decided on by the group. Unfortunately, little research exists on actual work groups. Cohesive work groups that are highly motivated to solve work-related problems may actually be quite productive.[35] Table 8.2 summarizes ways that brainstorming can be made more effective.

Verbal brainstorming can also be made more productive by following certain procedures, though groups may need some training to help them become more efficient.[36] Members may otherwise veer off on tangents or needlessly elaborate their ideas. Most importantly, groups should supplement their group brainstorming with individual brainstorming sessions in which they have an opportunity to more fully integrate and utilize the ideas they encountered in the group session.[37] It also appears best to use small groups or pairs if possible. Working with only one other person would limit many of the negative effects of groups but still give a person the benefit

Table 8.2	**Better Brainstorming: Some Techniques**

Although group brainstorming may not be as effective as individual brainstorming, there are some ways to optimize the effectiveness of brainstorming groups.

First practice with group brainstorming.
Alternate individual and group brainstorming.
Use spectrum policy—look at all sides of an issue.
Use small groups or pairs.
Have groups with a variety of perspectives, talents, and knowledge bases.
Give the groups some goals for which to aim.
Use group brainstorming with less socially anxious individuals.
Use electronic brainstorming or brainwriting.

of being stimulated by another person's ideas. Finally, some people may be more comfortable in group interaction. For example, individuals who are high in social anxiety tend to be more stressed in social performance situations and more concerned with the impressions they make on others.[38] Groups composed of highly socially anxious individuals perform poorly on a brainstorming task. Those composed of less socially anxious individuals tend to perform about as well in groups as alone.[39] (See also the *Human Relations in Action* section.)

GROUP DECISION MAKING: PASSING THE BUCK

It seems that in our democratic society, practically every major decision is made by a group of individuals. Judges, juries, legislatures, committees, and task forces are just some of the groups that dominate decisions in our society. Most universities have

Human Relations in Action

Group Seekers and Avoiders: How Well-Suited Are You for Working in Groups?

While some of us enjoy group activities and working in groups, others prefer solitary activities or working alone. There may be many factors that underlie this difference in orientation. The items below represent some of these and are designed to determine how you feel about groups in general. Simply write Y (yes) or N (no) for each of the following statements.

_____   1. I usually feel uncomfortable with a group of people that I don't know.

_____   2. I enjoy parties.

_____   3. I do not have much confidence in social situations.

_____   4. I am basically a shy person.

_____   5. I like going on job interviews.

_____   6. I usually feel anxious when I speak in front of a group.

_____   7. Large groups make me nervous.

committees that are responsible for major decisions, and corporations are run largely on the basis of staff and board meetings. Of course, there are cases where strong and fairly independent leaders make crucial decisions by themselves, but these seem to be the exceptions rather than the rule.

Even though the idea of group decision making fits with the democratic aspirations of many nations, how effective is this process? Do groups generate high-quality solutions? How effective are groups in making decisions? As with brainstorming, the basis of comparison used for judging group decision making is the performance of a group of individuals.

A major problem with group decision making is that the group tends to be disorganized in its approach to the problem. Unless a formalized structure is imposed by some outside force or by a group leader, most groups do not attempt to develop a system for approaching the problem or the decision. Basically, groups seem to go with the flow, which is usually the first plausible idea presented. As soon as this idea is accepted by a majority of the group, the group rarely reverses itself. This has been called the *strength in numbers effect*. The theory is that decisions tend to go in the

_____   8. I would rather work on a group project than an individual project.

_____   9. I am basically a loner.

_____   10. I find that groups bring out the best in me.

To score your questionnaire, count the number of times your answers coincided with the following answer pattern: 1 = Y, 2 = N, 3 = Y, 4 = Y, 5 = N, 6 = Y, 7 = Y, 8 = N, 9 = Y, 10 = N. If you come up with a score of 8 or higher, you would probably prefer to avoid most group situations—that is, you may be a group avoider. If you have a score of 2 or lower, you probably seek out group situations and activities—that is, you are a group seeker. Unfortunately, it is not always possible to choose your preferred situation. When people do get into situations that conflict with their preferences, they may not function as well as they would otherwise. For example, group avoiders may not do as well as group seekers on group tasks like brainstorming or group decision making. If you find this is true for you, you might try to match your activities and work with your group preference style.

direction of the largest subgroup that agrees on a particular course of action.[40] This same phenomenon underlies two other interesting group decision phenomena—group polarization and groupthink.

Group Polarization

Think about the groups to which you belong. Why do you belong to them? What are the members like? Most likely, you belong to groups whose members are similar to you in many ways. People tend to join groups composed of members who have values and opinions similar to their own. This is obvious in the case of political and church groups, but it is also characteristic of more informal social and work groups. When group members get together, they often discuss their opinions on various issues. Given the degree of similarity among group members, they are likely to be in general agreement on many issues. Interestingly, such discussions may lead them to become even more strongly convinced of their general point of view about an issue.

Early studies of this type of situation noticed that groups tended to become less cautious after group discussion in comparison to the feelings expressed by the individuals before the discussion. This intrigued scholars because it had been expected that group decision making would be more cautious than individual decisions. Yet soon it was found that groups could shift toward caution as well as toward risk. Later studies demonstrated that shifts toward more extreme positions could be obtained for a wide variety of issues, and the phenomenon came to be known as **group polarization.**[41,42] What produces this polarization in groups?

One critical factor appears to be whether the group was already leaning in one direction or another from some neutral position. When the group members who are already of the same mind on some issue come together to discuss it, the comparison of views (*social comparison*) and exchange of ideas (*information*) seem to generate more momentum in an already favored direction.[43] When views are compared in such a group, individuals may discover that others hold the position either as strongly as or more strongly than they do. Because they supposedly value being extreme on this issue (for example, being conservative or liberal), they may change their opinions somewhat to more strongly reflect the valued direction. The information exchanged has another effect: Group members hear new arguments that provide additional support for their favored position. In fact, the arguments in support of the generally favored direction greatly outnumber those in support of the opposite direction. Under such circumstances, then, people would begin to feel even more strongly about an issue.

This group polarization phenomenon has been demonstrated with laboratory groups using many types of issues. It obviously has important implications for any group situation where like-minded individuals (for ex-

group polarization   A process that occurs when groups of like-minded individuals discussing issues become more extreme in the direction of their initial attitudes and beliefs.

ample, judges, corporations, political parties, and gangs) gather to discuss issues. In fact, individuals in extremist groups appear to show increased polarization as they become more involved with such groups. One clear example of this type is a study by Myers and Bishop that examined polarization on racial issues.[44] Groups of white students were assessed for their attitudes about a number of issues related to the integration movement (for example, forced busing, black power). On the basis of this questionnaire, they were assigned to groups that were all pro-integration, all anti-integration, or mixed. They were given an opportunity to discuss one particular topic related to the race issue, and then the attitudes of group members were reassessed. As expected, the mixed group members showed little change, but the members of the other groups became more extreme in their favored direction. The anti-integration group members became more so, while the pro-integration groups became more pro-integration. Groups that discussed issues unrelated to race showed little change in racial attitudes.

Because we choose most of the groups to which we belong on the basis of similarity of interests, opinions, or values, it seems likely that group polarization is a common experience in many groups. It is therefore important for us to be aware of the group polarization effect and to avoid blind acceptance of extremist positions. The world has suffered much from leaders or groups who have championed extremist positions. This phenomenon is often associated with intergroup discrimination and violence. We should never forget the lessons of Nazi Germany! Yet polarization is also important for understanding the workings of informal and work groups. We can assume that there is usually little harm in groups' feeling strongly about a particular position or cause. As individuals, however, we should always make sure that we are not being driven to make decisions or to take actions that we will later regret. It appears that such bad decisions are, unfortunately, not uncommon, as we will see in our discussion of groupthink.

Information Biases in Groups: A Focus on Commonalities

In many group situations, members must share information so as to make sensible decisions. In deciding on an advertising or marketing campaign, for example, it is important to have much relevant information about different aspects of a product. An accurate diagnosis of the cause of an illness may require input from a number of different medical specialists. Group members may differ in the extent to which they have unique information or expertise. That is, some may possess much more knowledge in a particular area than others. One advantage of group decision making is the opportunity to share this unique knowledge or information. Unfortunately, groups do not seem to take full advantage of this type of diversity.

One problem with the group sharing process is **sampling bias.** In face-to-face discussions, group members tend to focus on information or knowledge that they share or have in common. With this type of bias, groups are unlikely to make a good decision based on a full understanding of the many different issues.[45] How can we overcome this sampling bias? Several procedural interventions may prove helpful. Instructing each group member to mention only items that have not been shared might increase the likelihood that unshared information will come to light. Having groups rank various alternatives, rather than simply picking out the best, also increases the exchange of unshared information.[46] Apparently, this ranking procedure stimulates a fuller discussion of the issues. Another useful technique is to inform the group about which individuals have expertise in which areas. Group members may then defer to the experts and not repeat information from their domains, and the group may explore in more detail its full range of informational resources.[47]

Leadership style also seems to be influential in overcoming sampling bias. Groups with participative leaders appear more likely to discuss both shared and unshared information than those helmed by directive leaders. This finding certainly makes sense in that participative leaders attempt to obtain as much group member involvement as possible. Directive leaders, however, are more likely to repeat information especially if it is unshared information. They may therefore take a more active role in ensuring that group members are made aware of the unshared information.[48]

When group members do mention unique or unshared information, this information is less likely to be repeated in the group discussion than shared information. This development is known as the **common knowledge effect.**[49] In fact, the group decision appears to be determined primarily by the prior opinions or knowledge that the group shared rather than the information exchanged during the group discussion. Why does unique or unshared information have so little impact on group decision making? One reason may be that the group cannot easily determine the validity or correctness of unique information. Most of us feel more confident about our opinions when others agree with them. Thus information that is shared and repeated by others may be seen as more valid by the group. Individual group members may, in fact, feel uncomfortable in sharing unique information because they may anticipate this credibility problem. If individuals appear quite confident when they share their unique or expert information, however, they may have a greater impact on the group.[50] If individuals are perceived to be experts, then their unique information is more likely to be repeated and remembered. The leadership style of the groups may also be important in this respect. Directive leaders are more likely to share unique information and lead the group to the best decision than participative leaders.[51]

sampling bias The tendency of groups to focus on information or knowledge that they have in common.

common-knowledge effect In group discussion, unique or unshared information tends to be repeated less than shared information.

Table 8.3	**Counteracting the Common-Knowledge Effect and the Sampling Bias**

Force group members to mention only unique information.

Rank alternatives.

Assign expertise.

Include confident experts.

Include directive leaders.

Table 8.3 summarizes the various ways in which the sampling bias and the common-knowledge effect can be counteracted.

Why is it important to know about the sampling bias and the common-knowledge effect? These two tendencies often prevent groups from making full use of all of the ideas and information offered by their members. As a result, any decisions made by the group may be flawed because critical information was not shared. This concern is just one of the many problems that inhibit effective decision making in groups.[52] These types of problems are highlighted even more by the phenomenon of groupthink, which is discussed in the next section.

Groupthink: Defective Decision Making in Groups

Many of you probably have vivid memories of the tragic explosion of the *Challenger* shuttle seventy-four seconds after launch on January 28, 1986. Seven astronauts, including teacher Christa McAuliffe, lost their lives (see Figure 8.4 on page 232). This terrible tragedy was a real shock to the United States. We have always taken great pride in our space program, and it seemed to be a constant source of successes. This program apparently could do no wrong. The last *Challenger* mission was highly publicized because it was the first flight in which a civilian participated. The leaders of the program therefore faced a lot of pressure to put their best foot forward. Not only was the whole nation watching; this was an important opportunity to generate more enthusiasm for additional funding for the program.

Unfortunately, the weather would not cooperate. The temperature dropped to freezing and the launch had to be delayed. Conditions soon improved, but they were still below those recommended by engineers. In cold weather, the O-rings that connected the different sections of the shuttle tended to become brittle and not function

Groupthink: Sometimes a Recipe for Disaster

Groupthink may have been responsible for a number of bad group decisions, including the decision to launch the *Challenger* despite unusually cold weather.

properly. Some problems with these rings had already been encountered in prior launches. The engineers from the company that designed the O-rings objected to the impending launch. However, they were overruled by higher-level officials in their company and in the space program, who felt that they were being overly cautious. After all, there had not been any serious problems, and minor variations from the standards probably would not be a problem. Besides, continual delays in the launch would not look good from a public relations point of view. The high-level officials did not think the concerns were serious enough to pass on to the top official in the project. Unfortunately, they were wrong.[53]

The *Challenger* disaster highlights the unfortunate consequences that can result when groups do not carefully evaluate alternative courses of action. Janis has analyzed a number of well-known examples of this type and has labeled the overall process **groupthink**.[54] Some historic examples include the Bay of Pigs fiasco, which was an unsuccessful attempt to invade Cuba after Castro's revolution, the failure of generals to prepare for possible Japanese attacks on Pearl Harbor, and the escalation of the Vietnam War. The decision to select Jay Leno over David Letterman as a replacement for Johnny Carson, as highlighted at the beginning of the chapter, can also be seen as an instance of groupthink.[55]

groupthink   The tendency of groups to make decisions without carefully evaluating alternative courses of action.

| Figure 8.5 | **Leader Pressure: One Factor in Groupthink** |

Leaders may make it clear that they want the group to agree with their position.
Not doing so may have negative consequences for the group members.

Of course, it is always easy to play "Monday-morning quarterback" after any wrong
decision. Yet wrong group decisions are not necessarily a result of groupthink, and
most decisions that groups make are fairly straightforward and reasonable.[56] Groupthink happens primarily when a group is more concerned about agreement than
about a careful assessment of alternative courses of action, and it is a potentially serious problem in cases of complex decisions that will have significant consequences.

Concurrence Seeking.   The driving force of groupthink is called **concurrence
seeking.** Members of many groups like to get along with one another and come to
some concurrence or agreement on important issues. Otherwise, there would be
conflict and possible hostilities among group members. Concurrence seeking is especially important for groups that are already highly cohesive. Such groups have
strong interpersonal bonds and probably have similar opinions and values on many
issues. (Remember our discussion of group polarization.) So it would seem only natural that they would want to minimize conflict. In addition to group cohesiveness,
Janis has proposed that a number of factors lead to a strengthening of the concur-
rence-seeking tendency. If the group is insulated from other groups, it is unlikely to
have the benefit of alternative views. If it does not have systematic procedures to
search out and appraise information and alternative positions, it is likely to approve
the first reasonable idea. If the leader of the group pres-
sures the group to come to a decision or to support a particular course of action, there is an increased tendency
for premature agreement (see Figure 8.5). Finally, if there
is a lot of pressure to come up with a decision and little

concurrence seeking   The tendency of group
members to strive for agreement on important issues.

sense that a better solution than the one being proposed by a leader or influential group member will be found, there will be a strong tendency to seek a quick concurrence among the group. These features unfortunately characterize many decision-making groups in government and industry. As a result, many decisions primarily reflect a premature group consensus rather than a careful consideration of alternatives.

Symptoms of Groupthink.   In his study of cases of groupthink, Janis found that groups prone to groupthink were characterized by certain features or symptoms. First, such groups evidence a significant amount of *pressure to uniformity.* There is *direct pressure* by group members on dissenters to go along with the group consensus. Because of concerns about reaction to dissension, group members practice *self-censorship* by not expressing reservations they have about an impending decision. Certain members of the group may act as *mindguards* to keep people in line with the group consensus or to keep dissenting information from reaching the group. As a result of the lack of public dissension, the group may develop an *illusion of unanimity.* A second major feature associated with groupthink is considerable *misperception* or distortion of the actual state of affairs. Third, the group may feel invulnerable and morally superior to other groups. Groups in conflict with one's own group may be viewed negatively. Fourth, once consensus has been developed, the group may *rationalize* away any information that does not fit with the decision. These four factors often can be found at the basis of decisions by countries to go to war or to engage in certain battles. They can also be important factors in the underestimation of competitors in business, as in the case of the U.S. automakers' underestimation of the ability of their Japanese competitors to develop a competitive automobile industry.

Defective Decision Making.   Groups that are engaging in groupthink tend to use a number of decision-making procedures that help lead them to defective decisions. They do a generally poor search of information relevant to the decision. They do not engage in a complete survey of alternatives and objectives and fail to examine sufficiently the risks involved in the preferred choice. The available information is processed in a biased fashion: The group emphasizes information supporting the decision and ignores or deemphasizes inconsistent information. The group also fails to reappraise or evaluate the alternatives once a preliminary consensus has been reached, and does not work out contingency plans to be used in case the proposed course of action fails (see Table 8.4 for a summary). As you can see, this approach to group decision making is a recipe for disaster. Of course, not all groups do such a poor job at decision making, but careful examination of poor decisions in business and government often reveals the existence of many of the factors emphasized in the groupthink model.

Table 8.4 Groupthink: Some Major Symptoms

A summary of the groupthink model.

Symptoms of Groupthink	Symptoms of Defective Decision Making
Illusion of invulnerability	Incomplete survey of alternatives
Collective rationalization	Incomplete survey of objectives
Belief in morality of the group	Failure to examine risks of favorite choice
Stereotyping of outgroups	Poor information search
Direct pressure on dissenters	Selective bias in processing available information
Self-censorship	
Illusion of unanimity	Failure to reassess alternatives
Mindguards	Failure to work out contingency plans

Adapted from Janis, 1982; see note 54.

Evaluation of the Groupthink Model

The ideas proposed by Janis are certainly provocative and may fit with our personal experiences.[57] However, most of the evidence thus far has come from case studies.[58] This type of evidence can, of course, be used to fit with a variety of models; it does not provide clear evidence for the central role of the processes outlined by Janis. Careful laboratory studies have provided only mixed results. Other factors not specified by Janis are likely to influence the quality of group decision making as well. Some have argued that political considerations, feelings of group efficacy, and fear of rejection tend to lead groups to make poor decisions.[59] For example, when groups have an inflated perception of their competence or efficacy, they may be prone to carelessness in the procedures they employ for decision making.[60] Similarly, groups that are concerned with maintaining a positive group identity may be more concerned about group relations than the quality of their decision making.[61] To fully understand group decision making will probably require a broader model than the one suggested by Janis.[62] Nevertheless, the groupthink model is useful in sensitizing us to a range of factors that can lead to poor decisions in groups.

Avoiding Groupthink.   Fortunately, there are some simple steps that groups can take to avoid falling into the groupthink trap. First, it is important that the group make a commitment to coming up with the best decision possible rather than simply reaching consensus with a minimum of conflict. The leader of the group can play an important role by promoting such an approach to group decision making and by not pressuring the group to adopt a particular point of view. To make the best possible decision, the group should use a number of procedures. There should be a broad-ranging and nonevaluative search of information relevant to the decision. Brainstorming may be useful at this stage. If feasible, several independent groups should be formed with different leaders. These groups might, in turn, subdivide periodically into smaller subgroups. These subgroups should represent a reasonable cross section of the group in terms of skills and perspectives. This procedure would increase the opportunity for diverse views to be aired and evaluated in the different groups. If all of the groups come to a similar consensus, you could have a reasonable degree of confidence in the decision. If not, it would stimulate the groups to carefully assess the basis for their differences and come to a carefully considered final decision.

At this point, some input from knowledgeable outsiders who are not subject to the pressures of an existing group may prove helpful. These people may be able either to provide further support for the decision or to challenge some of the assumptions on which it is based. Finally, for important decisions, second-chance meetings should be scheduled. At these meetings, the members of the group can air any second thoughts or doubts that have arisen since the decision was made.

Although these steps will not ensure that good decisions will always be made, they will prevent bad decisions resulting from groupthink. In any case, you should always be alert for elements of groupthink in groups you are involved in and be ready to make suggestions for counteracting them. Based on our discussion of group decision making, we can suggest a number of guidelines that are important for good decision making; these ideas appear in Table 8.5.

Table 8.5   Rules for Good Decision Making

If you follow these rules in groups, you are likely to make better decisions.

Set a good decision-making goal.

Organize the procedures for decision making.

Do a systematic search for information held by group members.

Make group members accountable for sharing information needed for making a good decision.

Have a diversity of views and expertise in the group.

Use second-chance meetings to reevaluate the decision.

Teamwork and Groupthink: Problems of Self-Management

Today, many work teams have considerable freedom in making decisions that were once traditionally made by management. Teams that have this type of freedom of choice are often called **self-managed teams.** Such teams may have the power to specify the distribution of work assignments, conduct team meetings, decide on compensation, and resolve interpersonal or work-related problems. A number of features of such teams, however, may render them susceptible to groupthink. The teams may become quite socially cohesive and perhaps insulate themselves from other groups or individuals. In addition, they tend to develop similar values or beliefs. Teams may not have norms that require methodical decision making, and they may experience time pressure in making important decisions. In essence, self-managed teams may exhibit many of the symptoms of groupthink and therefore may not function as effectively as they should.[63]

Of course, one can use the suggestions provided previously to minimize groupthink in teams. Some additional approaches may be helpful in preventing groupthink in teams as well.[64] Teams should develop appropriate decision-making practices or norms, which may require some training. They should be constantly exposed to different perspectives by rotating team members or encouraging interaction with outsiders or members of other teams. Team members should be highly trained in self-leadership skills so that group members will be encouraged to fully share their views and expertise. Finally, only some types of people may function effectively in teams. People who do not value independence may not take full advantage of the potential of self-managed teams and may be easily swayed by group pressures. Table 8.6 summarizes the four major factors that are important for avoiding groupthink in teams.

self-managed teams   Teams that have much freedom of choice in the conduct of their work.

Table 8.6	**Avoiding Groupthink in Self-Managing Teams: Four Strategies**

Develop effective decision-making norms and practices.

Increase interaction with new or outside members.

Train self-leadership skills.

Select team members with a desire for independence.

Based on Moorhead et al., 1998; see note 63.

Guidelines for Effective Human Relations

Using What You've Learned

In this chapter, we examined a broad range of principles and findings about groups. Although few rules will apply to every situation, there are some general guidelines suggested by the findings we have discussed. These are summarized below for your consideration. Remember, no rule works 100 percent in every situation. However, these guidelines should help improve your success in groups in a wide variety of situations.

■ In groups, it may be best to make sure that individuals are accountable for their work to prevent social loafing.

■ When you are performing a complex task or learning a new one, you should seek private circumstances, if possible. When you are performing simple tasks, you may want to work in group situations.

■ Idea generation should be done in private, if possible. Group brainstorming should be limited to small groups and may be most useful if combined with individual brainstorming.

■ In decision-making groups, it is important to resist the pressure to come to consensus before a careful consideration of all options and unshared information. Using two or more independent decision-making groups and having second-chance meetings are ways to avoid bad decisions.

One of the most important lessons of this chapter is that when groups are not appropriately managed or controlled, serious problems can occur for the group members and the organization. It is important for group members to be aware of the forces that influence group functioning. When both leadership and group members make a commitment to work together to optimize group functioning, it becomes possible for groups to reach significant achievements. This will involve each individual's taking responsibility for the welfare of the group and its effective functioning. Group norms should support effective communication among group members and the right of members to challenge the direction in which the group is going. Finally, effective group functioning will require good leadership (see Chapter 10). There is no way to ensure that groups will meet their potential, but groups that follow these guidelines are likely to be successful.

Summary

A group is defined as a collection of two or more interacting individuals with a stable pattern of relationships between them, who share common goals and who perceive themselves as being a group. Many interesting processes can take place in groups. When people perform tasks in groups, lessened feelings of responsibility may be reflected in lowering of performance or social loafing. Sometimes, however, motivation is increased. Individual productivity is influenced by the presence of other group members. As a result, a person's performance may improve in the presence of others when the job he or she is doing is well learned, but decline in the presence of others when the job is novel. This phenomenon is known as social facilitation. Its effects have been attributed to the mere presence of others and to the evaluation apprehension caused by others.

Groups are often asked to brainstorm by exchanging ideas freely about some problem or issue. Research indicates that these groups actually produce fewer ideas than a comparable number of individuals brainstorming alone. However, a number of techniques can be used to enhance the generation of ideas in groups, such as synectics or the nominal group technique.

When groups discuss problems or issues, they may demonstrate a tendency toward polarization. Groups that are already inclined in a particular direction may move even more strongly in that same direction after group discussion. This effect seems to be the result of the exchange of information and the social comparison of views that occur during the discussion. Groups also tend to focus on information or knowledge that they have in common rather than unique or unshared information.

The failure of groups to carefully evaluate alternative courses of action when they make decisions has been termed groupthink. Groupthink results from the desire of group members to get along with each other and to come to an agreement or concurrence on important issues. Fortunately, a number of procedures can be employed to eliminate or limit the occurrence of groupthink.

Key Terms

additive tasks, p. 215

arousal model of social facilitation, p. 220

brainstorming, p. 221

collective-effort model, p. 217

common-knowledge effect, p. 230

concurrence seeking, p. 233

group, p. 214

group polarization, p. 228

groupthink, p. 232

illusion of productivity, p. 222

sampling bias, p. 230

self-managed teams, p. 237

social loafing, p. 215

⚡ *Experiential Exercise*

Groupthink at NBC

We have briefly discussed the controversy about NBC's decision to replace Johnny Carson with Jay Leno. Several important decisions were made at this time. Read the interesting analysis of these decisions by Christopher Neck (see note 2). Given the present situation in late-night television (in terms of ratings and competition), do you think NBC still made a bad decision? Can you come up with some other cases where television executives made bad decisions and some cases where they made very good ones? Is there any indication that the quality of the decision-making process played a role in these outcomes? On the basis of this chapter, list good decision-making procedures that television executives should follow in setting their programming.

⚡ *Experiential Exercise*

Group Processes and the Family

In this chapter, we highlighted many principles that influence group functioning. These principles mostly related to groups in work environments. One other important group in our lives is the family. Families do tasks together, make decisions, brainstorm, and sometimes work as a team. Can you select some principles of group processes that seem to apply to your experience with families? Do you think some of the principles of good practices for work groups would be helpful in helping families function more effectively? If so, which ones? If not, why not?

Notes

1. Carter, W. J. (1990). *The late shift: Letterman, Leno, and the network battle for the night.* New York: Hyperion.

2. Neck, C. P. (1995). Letterman or Leno: A groupthink analysis of successive decisions made by the National Broadcasting Company (NBC). *Journal of Managerial Psychology, 11*, 3–18.

3. Forsythe, D. L. (1990). *An introduction to group dynamics.* Monterey, CA: Brooks/Cole.

4. Latane, B., Williams, K., & Harkins, S. (1979). Many hands make light of work: The causes and consequences of social loafing. *Journal of Personality and Social Psychology, 37*, 822–832.

5. Karau, S. J., & Williams, K. D. (1993). Social loafing: A meta-analytic review and theoretical integration. *Journal of Personality and Social Psychology, 65,* 681–786.

6. Harkins, S. (1987). Social loafing and social facilitation. *Journal of Experimental Social Psychology, 23,* 1–18.

7. Shepperd, J. A. (1993). Productivity loss in performance groups: A motivation analysis. *Psychological Bulletin, 113,* 67–81.

8. See note 5.

9. Weldon, E., & Mustari, E. L. (1988). Felt dispensability in groups of coactors: The effects of shared responsibility and explicit anonymity on cognitive effort. *Organizational Behavior and Human Decision Processes, 41,* 330–351.

10. Harkins, S. G., & Petty, R. E. (1982). Effects of task difficulty and task uniqueness on social loafing. *Journal of Personality and Social Psychology, 43,* 1214–1229.

11. Harkins, S. G., & Szymanski, K. (1989). Social loafing and group evaluation. *Journal of Personality and Social Psychology, 56,* 934–941.

12. See note 7.

13. Paulus, P. B., & Dzindolet, M. T. (1993). Social influence processes in group brainstorming. *Journal of Personality and Social Psychology, 64,* 575–586.

14. Williams, K. D., & Karau, S. J. (1991). Social loafing and social compensation: The effects of expectations of co-worker performance. *Journal of Personality and Social Psychology, 61,* 570–581.

15. Geen, R. G. (1989). Alternative conceptions of social facilitation. In P. B. Paulus (ed.), *Psychology of group influence* (pp. 15–51), 2nd ed. Hillsdale, NJ: Erlbaum.

16. Zajonc, R. B. (1980). Compresence. In P. B. Paulus (ed.), *Psychology of group influence* (pp. 35–60). Hillsdale, NJ: Erlbaum.

17. Martens, R. (1969). Effect of an audience on learning and performance of a complex motor skill. *Journal of Personality and Social Psychology, 12,* 252–260.

18. Seta, J. J., Crisson, J. E., Seta, C. E., & Wang, M. A. (1989). Task performance and perceptions of anxiety: Averaging and summation in an evaluative setting. *Journal of Personality and Social Psychology, 56,* 387–396.

19. Schmitt, B. H., Gilovich, T., Goore, N., & Joseph L. (1986). Mere presence and social facilitation: One more time. *Journal of Experimental Social Psychology, 22,* 242–248.

20. Guerin, B. (1986). Mere presence effects in humans: A review. *Journal of Experimental Social Psychology, 22,* 38–77.

21. Robinson-Staveley, K., & Cooper, J. (1990). Mere presence, gender, and reactions to computers: Studying human–computer interaction in the social context. *Journal of Experimental Social Psychology, 26,* 168–183.

22. Ibid.

23. Osborn, A. F. (1957). *Applied imagination.* New York: Scribner.

24. Diehl, M., & Stroebe, W. (1987). Productivity loss in brainstorming groups: Toward the solution of a riddle. *Journal of Personality and Social Psychology, 53,* 497–509.

25. Ibid.

26. See note 13.

27. Paulus, P. B., Dzindolet, M. T., Poletes, G., & Camacho, L. M. (1993). Perception of performance in group brainstorming: The illusion of group productivity. *Personality and Social Psychology Bulletin, 19,* 78–89.

28. Bouchard, T. J. (1972). Training, motivation, and personality as determinants of the effectiveness of brainstorming groups and individuals. *Journal of Applied Psychology, 56,* 324–331.

29. Delbecq, A. L., Van de Ven, A. H., & Gustafson, D. H. (1975). *Group techniques for program planning: A guide to nominal group and delphi processes.* Glenview, IL: Scott, Foresman.

30. Paulus, P. B., & Yang, H. Y. (1999). *Idea generation in groups: A basis for creativity in organizations.* Unpublished manuscript, University of Texas at Arlington.

31. Prince, G. (1970). *The practice of creativity.* New York: Harper & Row.

32. Nunamaker, J. R., Jr., Dennis, A. R., Valacich, J. S., Vogel, D. R., & George, J. F. (1991). Electronic meeting systems to support group work. *Communications of the ACM, 34,* 40–61.

33. Nunamaker, J. F., Jr., Dennis, A. R., Valacich, J. S., & Vogel, D. R. (1991). Information technology for negotiating groups: Generating options for mutual gain. *Management Science, 37,* 1326–1346.

34. Yang, H. (1998). *The effectiveness of cognitive stimulation in electronic brainstorming.* Unpublished master's thesis, University of Texas at Arlington.

35. Zaccaro, S. J., & Lowe, C. A. (1987). Cohesiveness and performance on an additive task: Evidence for multidimensionality. *Journal of Social Psychology, 128,* 547–558.

36. Putman, V. L. (1998). *Effects of facilitator training and extended rules on group brainstorming.* Unpublished master's thesis, University of Texas at Arlington.

37. Paulus, P. B. (in press). Groups, teams and creativity. *Applied Psychology: An International Review.*

38. Leary, M. R., & Kowalski, R. M. (1993). The interaction anxiousness scale: Construct and criterion-related validity. *Journal of Personality Assessment, 61,* 136–146.

39. Camacho, L. M., & Paulus, P. B. (1995). Social and procedural factors in brainstorming: The role of social anxiousness. *Journal of Personality and Social Psychology, 68,* 1071–1080.

40. Stasser, G., Kerr, N. L., & Davis, J. H. (1989). Influence processes and consensus models in decision-making groups. In P. B. Paulus (ed.), *Psychology of group influence* (pp. 279–326), 2nd ed. Hillsdale, NJ: Erlbaum.

41. Moscovici, S., & Zavalloni, M. (1969). The group as a polarizer of attitudes. *Journal of Personality and Social Psychology, 12,* 125–135.

42. Myers, D. G. (1982). Polarizing effects of social interaction. In H. Brandstatter, J. H. Davis & G. Stocker-Kreichgauer (eds.), *Group decision making* (pp. 125–161). London: Academic Press.

43. Zuber, J. A., Crott, H. W., & Werner, J. (1992). Choice shift and group polarization: An analysis of the status of arguments and social decision schemes. *Journal of Personality and Social Psychology, 62,* 50–61.

44. Myers, D. G., & Bishop, G. D. (1970). Discussion effects of racial attitudes. *Science, 169,* 778–779.

45. Stasser, G. (in press). The uncertain role of unshared information in collective choice. In L. Thompson, J. Levine, & D. Messick (eds.), *Shared knowledge in organizations.* Mahweh, NJ: Erlbaum.

46. Hollingshead, A. B. (1996). The rank-order effect in group decision making. *Organizational Behavior and Human Decision Processes, 68,* 181–193.

47. Stasser, G., Stewart, D. D., & Wittenbaum, G. M. (1995). Expert roles and information exchange during discussion: The importance of knowing who knows what. *Journal of Experimental Social Psychology, 31,* 244–265.

48. Larson, J. R., Jr., Foster-Fishman, P. G., & Franz, T. M. (1998). Leadership style and discussion of shared and unshared information in decision-making groups. *Personality and Social Psychology Bulletin, 24,* 482–495.

49. Gigone, D., & Hastie, R. (1993). The common knowledge effect: Information sampling and group judgment. *Journal of Personality and Social Psychology, 72,* 132–140.

50. Hinsz, V. B. (1990). Cognitive and consensus processes in recognition memory performance. *Journal of Personality and Social Psychology, 59,* 705–718.

51. See note 48.

52. Winquist, J. R., & Larson, J. R., Jr. (1998). Information pooling: When it impacts group decision making. *Journal of Personality and Social Psychology, 74,* 371–377.

53. Moorhead, G., Ference, R., & Neck, C. P. (1991). Group decision fiascoes continue: Space shuttle *Challenger* and a revised groupthink framework. *Human Relations, 44,* 539–550.

54. Janis, I. L. (1982). *Groupthink* (2nd ed.). Boston: Houghton Mifflin.

55. See note 2.

56. Paulus, P. B. (1998). Developing consensus about groupthink after all these years. *Organizational Behavior and Human Decision Processes, 73,* 362–374.

57. Aldag, R. J., & Fuller, S. R. (1993). Beyond fiasco: A reappraisal of the groupthink phenomenon and a new model of group decision processes. *Psychological Bulletin, 113,* 533–552.

58. Tetlock, P. E., Peterson, R. S., McGuire, C., Change, S., & Feld, P. (1992). Assessing political group dynamics: A test of the groupthink model. *Journal of Personality and Social Psychology, 63,* 403–425.

59. See note 56.

60. Whyte, G. (1998). Recasting Janis's groupthink model: The lead role of collective efficacy in decision fiascoes. *Organizational Behavior and Human Decision Processes, 73,* 185–209.

61. Turner, M. E., Pratkanis, A. R., Probasco, P., & Leve, C. (1992). Threat, cohesion, and group effectiveness: Testing a social identity maintenance perspective on groupthink. *Journal of Personality and Social Psychology, 63,* 781–796.

62. See note 57.

63. Moorhead, G., Neck, C. P., & West, M. S. (1988). The tendency toward defective decision-making within self-managing teams: The relevance of groupthink for the 21st century. *Organizational Behavior and Human Decision Processes, 73,* 327–351.

64. Ibid.

Chapter 9

Prosocial Behavior: Helping Others and the Organization

Intervention: To Blow the Whistle or Not?
Helping Behavior: Do We Care?
Organizational Citizenship Behavior: Being a Good Citizen
Spontaneous Behaviors: Taking the Extra Step

Teamwork: Working Together for Productivity

Team Productivity: Beyond the Hype
Innovation in Work Teams: Can Teams Be Creative?
Team Effectiveness: How to Get the Most Out of Groups

Conflict: Its Causes, Management, and Effects

Informational Conflict: Differences of Opinion
Personal Conflict: Opposing Interests

Managing Personal Conflicts
Conflict: A Look at Its Major Effects
Culture and Conflict Management: Some Differences in Style

Special Sections

Ethics at Work
Would You Blow the Whistle?

Human Relations in Action
Are You a Good Organizational Citizen?

Guidelines for Effective Human Relations
Using What You've Learned

Experiential Exercise
How Do You Deal with Conflict?

TEAMWORK AND CONFLICT IN WORK SETTINGS

Learning Objectives

After reading this chapter, you should be able to:

1. Discuss the prosocial behaviors that can occur in organizations.

2. Know the factors that influence each of the organizational prosocial behaviors.

3. Describe the different types of teams or work groups in organizations and their effectiveness.

4. Explain the factors that enhance team innovation.

5. Summarize the ways to increase team effectiveness.

6. Know the ways groups deal with informational conflict.

7. Describe the major causes of personal conflict within organizations.

8. Discuss the positive as well as negative effects of conflict.

9. Indicate several techniques through which personal conflict can be managed or resolved.

ristol-Myers Squibb is a major chemical company that was formed by a merger. The company was experiencing many problems in getting the employees to work well together. Top management decided that changing the company to a teamwork structure would be an effective way to increase cooperation and productivity. Unfortunately, management did not effectively communicate its expectations and vision. Managers also did not make the necessary changes in the organizational structure to facilitate team development and functioning, and team members were not trained in the skills necessary for effective teamwork. The company quickly discovered that its teams were not working out very well. With the assistance of a human relations and teamwork expert, changes were made in the organizational culture and employees were given the appropriate training. Soon teams were working with a low level of conflict and high level of efficiency.[1]

Most of us belong to a variety of groups and have had experiences in which one of our groups got into conflict with another one. It may have started over a rather minor incident, but quickly escalated into a full-scale conflict. Conflicts can happen not only between groups, but also among members of the same group and can be very destructive to the overall harmony and functioning of the group. In this chapter, we discuss maintaining positive relationships and cooperation among individuals and groups and how we can manage conflicts when they do arise.

All the persons and units within an organization are interdependent: What happens to one affects what happens to the others. If the organization prospers, there are rewards for everyone; if it does poorly, however, no one is likely to benefit (except, perhaps, competitors!). Given these facts, it seems only reasonable to assume that cooperation or helpfulness should be the byword in all work settings. All units and individuals within an organization should work together as closely and smoothly as possible.

As incidents such as the one outlined above suggest, though, this ideal is not always attained. Just "throwing groups together" as teams does not ensure that they will work together effectively and cooperatively. Sometimes different units or persons in a business ignore one another or fail to coordinate their actions in basic ways. In other cases, they may actually compete, seeking to attain certain goals at the expense of other people or groups. In even more extreme cases, open conflicts or violence may develop. Obviously, such events can greatly reduce an organization's efficiency, productivity, and morale.[2]

The broad range of behaviors encountered in organizations varies in the extent to which individuals are working together harmoniously (see Figure 9.1). At one extreme are those who do their best to help their fellow workers or corporation. At the

Figure 9.1   **The Prosocial/Antisocial Dimension:
The Good, the Bad, and the Ugly**

Behaviors in an organization fall along a continuum from helpfulness to conflict.

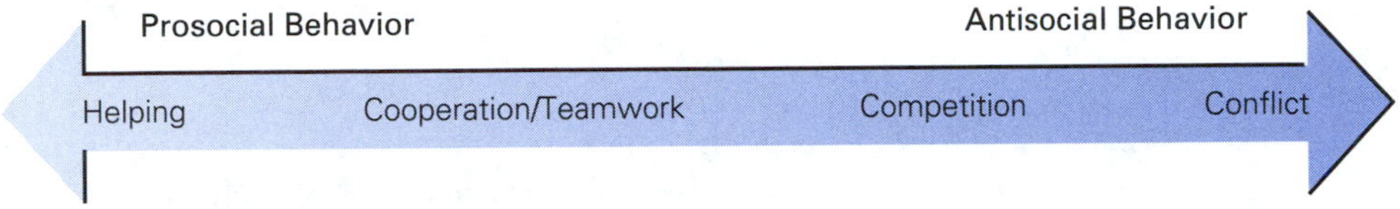

Prosocial Behavior		Antisocial Behavior	
Helping	Cooperation/Teamwork	Competition	Conflict

other extreme are those who instigate conflict with their bosses or other employees. Cooperation involves working with others for a common goal. Both helping and cooperation can be seen as prosocial behaviors because they are motivated to benefit others. Competition and conflict are antisocial behaviors because they are motivated by a desire to take advantage of or hurt another person. We will examine the processes that underlie some of the behaviors along the prosocial/antisocial dimension.

PROSOCIAL BEHAVIOR: HELPING OTHERS AND THE ORGANIZATION

It is apparent that people differ in the extent to which they are concerned with their own selfish gains or the welfare of others. In fact, some people make a career of helping professions, such as medicine and social work, while others are concerned with making lots of money. As businesses by definition are designed to make money, selfish orientations are likely to predominate. The investors want a good return on their investments, the executives want to be highly paid, and employees want to get a fair share of the profits. While it is possible to meet all of these needs in some companies, the desires of these different groups may not be compatible, because high levels of reward to one group may mean depriving others. For example, union contracts are designed to make sure that the rank-and-file workers will not be taken advantage of because of their low power status.

Because of the individualistic concerns in most corporations, employees are mostly concerned with doing their assigned jobs and do little to promote the welfare of others or the company that is not in their job description. They may ignore conditions or activities that should be rectified, fail to help other employees who are having difficulties in their jobs, and show little concern for the broader well-being of the company or organization. That is, they may show little **prosocial behavior**—behavior that is designed to further the welfare of others or the

prosocial behavior Behavior designed to further the welfare of others or the organization. Helping behavior, organizational citizenship behaviors, and spontaneous behaviors are examples of such behavior.

organization.[3] This may involve helping others in need, setting a positive cooperative example to others, or contributing to the overall success of the company or organization in ways not required by one's job. We will discuss briefly interventions, helping behavior, organizational citizenship behavior, and spontaneous behavior.

Intervention: To Blow the Whistle or Not?

In most organizations, activities occur that are contrary to the formal or informal rules. Individuals may sneak extra coffee breaks, take small items such as pens and tablets home for their personal use, or be involved in sexual harassment. Sometimes explicitly illegal activities take place, such as insider trading, inflating appraisals, rigging bidding procedures, or confiscation of company funds. Brokerage houses on Wall Street, savings and loans organizations, and defense contractors have been much in the news for these types of illegal activities. There is often pressure to look the other way when we observe such activities. However, they may be very destructive to the organization and the society at large. Therefore it is important for employees periodically to put the interest of the company and/or society ahead of their selfish interests and blow the whistle on such activities (see *Ethics at Work*).[4]

Ethics at Work

Would You Blow the Whistle?

Imagine you are working in the dairy department of a local grocery store. You have been working there for about a year. You have flexible hours, enjoy your work, and get along with the other employees. It is a great job to have while you are going to school.

Charley Noll is the manager of a grocery store. He is generally well liked by the employees and treats them fairly. However, recently he has been a bit down. He is going through a divorce and has begun drinking heavily. Things are becoming financially a bit tough for him.

Some nights you work the late shift and help close the store. You notice that Charley puts a couple of six-packs of beer in a bag and takes them out as the two of you leave the store. You know that he has not paid for them. This same routine is repeated on a number of occasions.

What would you do? Would you confront him directly? Would you just ignore what is happening? Or would you call the regional manager to let him know what is going on? What are some of the factors that go into making a choice among these alternatives? Do you think these same issues also affect others who find themselves in similar situations?

Whistle-blowing encompasses a broad category of behaviors that can have different motivations. Sometimes the motivations can be selfish or antisocial.[5] For example, an employee may reveal some illegal activities to get a reward from some government agency. Antisocial whistle-blowing is intended to harm the organization, involves unfair procedures, and causes extensive damage to an organization. For example, one employee revealed that his company was violating national security rules without first going through appropriate organizational channels. Moreover, he delayed his whistle-blowing so as to increase the amount of reward he would receive.[6] Prosocial whistle-blowing, on the other hand, is intended to benefit the organization and involves the use of fair procedures.

Retaliation is a common reaction to whistle blowers, because they may be perceived as violating organization norms of "mutual trust" and because coworkers and supervisors may fear the potential harm to the organization and their jobs. Retaliation is most likely if a person has low status or power and has little support from management. In contrast, whistle-blowing is most likely to be effective if the whistle blower enjoys a high power position and has some personal credibility.[7]

Reasons for Not Intervening.   In many instances, those who observe violations do not intervene. There is a large body of evidence about intervention in emergencies that may suggest some reasons for this. The inappropriate activities may be known by quite a few employees, so each of these individuals shares the responsibility for reporting them. Yet **diffusion of responsibility** may be at work: Each person's sense of responsibility is reduced to the extent that others (for example, management) are perceived to be equally or even more responsible. Also, any blame for not intervening will be shared by all of those who had knowledge of the activities. For example, evidence has shown that the more bystanders at an emergency, the less likely that a particular bystander will intervene.[8]

Another reason for not intervening is the costs associated with such an action.[9] Intervention may be disruptive to many of the interpersonal relationships at work and may lead to ostracism by those who have looked the other way. It may be easier to deal with the discomfort of ignoring the activities than to intervene.

Finally, if most of your coworkers seem to accept or ignore what you consider inappropriate behavior, you may reevaluate your own opinions. You may decide that your own values or opinions are out of line and change them to be more consistent with those of other employees. Thus for a long time, members of the Tailhook group in the Navy looked the other way when women were sexually molested in a traditional drunken gauntlet.[10] They may have justified the activity as "boys will be boys," especially when they were drinking. Even the high-level brass who were aware of the event did not deem it to be a serious problem. It took a number of brave women officers to finally stand up and expose this event to stimulate a reevaluation in the armed services about the appropriateness of these traditions.

diffusion of responsibility   The tendency of individuals to assume that others will take responsibility for needed actions.

Increasing Interventions in Organizations.   Few of us would disagree that it is important to minimize inappropriate or illegal behavior in organizations. But how can we ensure that employees will be motivated both to behave in an appropriate manner and to react when others do not? Probably the most important factor here is leadership. Unless those in positions of leadership clearly uphold the corporate values and are supportive of others who do, employees may have little motivation to go out of the way to be good citizens. Management should also create an atmosphere that is supportive of individuals intervening when they see inappropriate behavior. Interveners should be valued and protected. It may be necessary to set up procedures so that individuals can intervene without being identified. The one drawback of such a system is that it may place individuals in a competitive relationship with one another. This can have negative consequences, as we will discuss later in this chapter. One way to counteract this problem is to emphasize teamwork and group decision making. Inappropriate behaviors can then be handled and rectified in an informal manner at the level of the group, perhaps before they become a significant problem.

Helping Behavior: Do We Care?

In the cold everyday working world, we may not often have strong feelings of responsibility for our fellow workers. We may be willing to dish out advice or provide some emotional support, but we typically stay out of the lives of our fellow workers. When they experience significant losses or life changes, we assume that it is the responsibility of family and close friends to help them cope. However, many workers may not have family living nearby and may not have developed a strong network of friends. They may have to rely on their fellow employees for support and assistance.

Factors Influencing Helping.   Not everyone at work is equally disposed to be helpful to fellow employees. Apparently one important factor is the extent to which one is able to empathize with the problems the person is experiencing.[11] If you have recently lost a loved one, you should be especially aware of the emotional needs of another person who has had the same experience. There may also be informal norms that have developed at work about getting involved with fellow employees. In some work environments, individuals may keep their social distance. They may be friendly at work and go to lunch, but they do not get involved in each others' affairs after work. In other environments, there may be a strong tradition of being involved in activities with fellow workers outside of the job. There may be parties, involvement in a bowling league, and social visits in each others' homes. In this kind of work environment, workers are more likely to be involved in each others' lives at times of need and be a source of social support. This can be important for health and well-being (Chapter 14). On the negative side, relationship problems that develop outside the work environment may be brought to work.

Mood and Helpfulness.   One important predictor of helpfulness is the mood of the individual.[12] When people are in a good mood, they are more likely to be helpful than when they are in a neutral mood. Why? Part of the reason appears to be that we like to maintain positive moods, and helping others may be one way to do this.[13] Good moods also are associated with positive thoughts and positive feelings toward other people, and they make it more likely we will act positively toward others. Therefore, we would expect that when employees are generally happy or satisfied at work, they will be more likely to be helpful to others.[14] In fact, even just having a manager who is in a good mood has been found to lead to helpfulness in employees and increased sales performance of employees in retail stores.[15]

So it appears that helpfulness at work is greatly influenced by emotional factors. If we are empathetic and in a positive mood, we are likely to be helpful to other employees and customers. Organizational programs that increase empathy and job satisfaction may increase not only the cooperative atmosphere at work but also productivity.[16]

Organizational Citizenship Behavior: Being a Good Citizen

Are you always on time at work? Do you seldom use your sick days? Do you volunteer to help with company-sponsored events on your day off? Do you help people who have been absent catch up with their work? If so, you are a good organizational citizen. You are the kind of person who does those extra things that are not required or compensated but that are important if an organization is to run effectively. The acts that go beyond the formal job requirements are called **organizational citizenship behaviors.**[17] Organ cites five different categories of such behaviors. *Altruism* is those voluntary behaviors that help some person with an organizational task or problem. *Conscientiousness* is carrying out some of the job or role requirements considerably beyond the minimal requirements. (In some circles, conscientious individuals might be called "rate busters.") *Sportsmanship* involves not complaining or making a big deal of minor grievances or problems. *Courtesy* involves keeping those who are affected by your actions or decisions informed about them before they happen. The president of the United States typically does this when Congress is informed prior to some military action. Finally, *civic virtue* consists of being actively involved in the life of the organization. This might involve attending meetings, being involved in discussions, and making helpful suggestions.

What factors are responsible for motivating organizational citizenship behavior? Not surprisingly, the most important factor is job satisfaction.[18] A critical factor in this satisfaction appears to be whether employees trust

> **organizational citizenship behaviors** Behaviors that are important for organizations to run effectively but that are not required or compensated. Some categories of these behaviors are altruism, conscientiousness, sportsmanship, courtesy, and civic virtue.

that the company will continue to deal with them fairly in the future.[19] Without such an expectation, employees are unlikely to invest much beyond what is required by their jobs. Degree of emotional commitment to the organization also seems to be quite important.[20] One important factor that may influence job satisfaction, commitment, and organizational citizenship behavior is cohesiveness. *Cohesiveness* is the extent to which individuals are attracted to and identify with their work group. In fact, one study found that cohesiveness was particularly important in increasing the extent of courtesy displayed by employees.[21] Courtesy, as noted earlier, involves being sensitive to the problems and rights of one's fellow employees.

There are also likely to be considerable individual differences among employees in the extent to which they will exhibit citizenship behavior when they are highly satisfied. Some people may simply have a value system that requires them to be good citizens at work and in other contexts. Which kind of person are you? Take the organizational citizenship test in the *Human Relations in Action* section and see.

Human Relations in Action

Are You a Good Organizational Citizen?

For the following items, indicate whether you regularly engage in the behaviors described where you work by marking yes (Y) or no (N).

_____   I make innovative suggestions.

_____   I volunteer for tasks that are not required.

_____   I help others who have been absent.

_____   I help orient new people.

_____   I help others who have heavy work loads.

_____   I do not take extra breaks.

_____   I do not coast toward the end of the day.

_____   I do not spend a lot of time in idle conversations.

_____   I am punctual.

_____   I do not take unnecessary time off work.

If you answered yes to 8 or more, you are most likely a solid corporate citizen. If you marked 5 or fewer, you may need to adjust your behavior to improve your citizenship image.

Adapted from a scale developed by Smith, Organ, and Near, 1983; see note 23.

Spontaneous Behaviors: Taking the Extra Step

Prosocial behavior and organizational citizenship behaviors are examples of behaviors that are helpful to the organization and involve doing something extra. Another term for some of these behaviors is **organizational spontaneity.** These active behaviors promote the survival and effectiveness of the organization and go beyond the roles prescribed by the job.[22] This category of behaviors excludes passive behaviors as well as those that are expected as part of the job (for example, attending meetings). Spontaneous behaviors include helping one's coworkers, protecting the organization from threats (such as thefts or hazards), making constructive suggestions, developing oneself (such as through learning new skills), and spreading goodwill about the organization.[24] It appears that positive moods at work are important for the occurrence of such spontaneous behaviors. These positive mood states can come from working conditions or the atmosphere in one's work group, or they can carry over from experiences outside the work environment.[25] It is also important for individuals to accept or internalize the corporate values or objectives as their own. Interestingly, some of the factors that increase general task productivity may inhibit spontaneous behaviors. For example, setting goals or providing incentives may increase task performance but reduce the willingness of individuals to help others.[26] The moral of the story may be that individuals need to be motivated to be concerned with the general welfare of the organization as well as the attainment of their individual goals. Such a cooperative atmosphere may be important to the success of organizations.

Prosocial behavior, organizational citizenship behavior, and spontaneous behaviors represent slightly different perspectives about the types of behaviors that involve taking some extra initiative to help the organization and fellow employees to be successful. Research suggests that positive attitudes, job satisfaction, and positive mood states are important for the occurrence of such behaviors. Therefore, it makes sense for corporations to develop procedures and programs that produce a positive work atmosphere and motivate individuals to do their specific jobs well. This may not be easy, but the success of a corporation may depend on it. As discussed in the next section, teams or quality circles may be one approach that could achieve those goals in some corporations.

TEAMWORK: WORKING TOGETHER FOR PRODUCTIVITY

One of the major changes on the work scene in the past ten years has been the increased use of teams of workers. **Teams** can be considered a type of cooperative group, as their focus is on achieving a common goal. In some cases, teams are necessary because a variety of skills are required

organizational spontaneity Active behaviors that promote the survival and effectiveness of the organization and that go beyond the roles prescribed by the job.

teams Cooperative work groups that emphasize employee involvement and responsibility. Quality circles and self-managing teams are two examples of such work groups.

to complete a task, as with medical or surgery teams. They are also part of a human relations movement that stresses the importance of employee involvement and responsibility.[27] Of course, the major reason they are so popular is the assumption that they will increase worker productivity. By giving workers increased responsibility and choices, their level of motivation to do high-quality work should be increased. Teams also give each group member a chance to contribute fully their various talents and skills.

Surveys indicate that most corporations today employ some type of teamwork or participative or collaborative work group.[28] Teamwork is found on factory floors and in management suites of many major corporations, such Saturn, Xerox, and Corning.[29] Many work tasks are difficult to accomplish without careful coordination with one's fellow workers. For example, developing complicated software packages requires groups of talented programmers to work as teams on various aspects of the program. These teams, in turn, must coordinate their activities carefully with one another to ensure that the developments remain compatible.[30] To take full advantage of diversity of perspectives or skills, some workers are part of **cross-functional teams.** These teams typically involve collaboration by people from different departments or areas of an organization. They can help increase coordination among the different parts of the organization and possibly develop innovations that are not possible with work groups that focus on only one aspect of the organization. In one study of such management teams in hospitals, these teams were found to suggest many interesting innovations.[31]

Team Productivity: Beyond the Hype

Although teams are very popular, are they really effective? Because teams differ so much in their nature, task, and organization, it is difficult to derive simple conclusions about their functioning and effectiveness. We will briefly discuss two common ones.

Quality Circles.

Quality circles are small work groups that come together periodically to identify and resolve work-related problems. Japanese companies have used such groups to increase or maintain product quality and overall productivity. In the United States, such groups are usually part of a change in organizational culture intended to focus on the quality of work life (QWL). Quality circles are used to develop more positive worker attitudes. A review of quality circle effectiveness has found little evidence for increased productivity.[32]

Although quality circles may prove beneficial for brief periods of time or with participative management, the general conclusion is that quality circles do not have a

cross-functional teams Teams that involve collaboration of members from different areas of an organization.

quality circle A small work group that comes together periodically to identify and resolve work-related problems. These groups are often part of a focus on the quality of work life in organizations.

long-lasting benefit on productivity.[33] In retrospect, this finding is not entirely surprising. Quality circles involve only a modest change in the nature of the work environment. Groups provide consultation and feedback services, but the work structure remains essentially the same. That is, most of the work is done independently without reliance on other team members. A more radical change in the structure of work involves the use of **self-managing work teams.**

Self-Managing Teams.   In some companies, groups of employees are allowed to manage themselves.[34] Such self-managing teams or semiautonomous work groups control their own work assignments and monitor and evaluate each others' performance. They are typically responsible for a particular task or product in an organization. The focus is on cooperative interaction, with opportunities to learn a variety of different jobs.

Comparisons of self-managing teams with other types of teamwork indicate that self-managing teams may be quite effective at increasing job satisfaction and productivity.[35] What aspects of self-managing teams make them so effective? One important factor may be motivation. Because the group has a great deal of freedom in its various activities, its members may have a high level of motivation.[36] In addition, self-managing teams may do a better job of matching group member skills with the various group tasks. Self-managing groups typically involve the development of a wide range of skills so that individuals can perform a variety of tasks. By experimenting with different work arrangements, the team may discover how best to take advantage of the talents of the group. The task variety that is provided by such teamwork may also make the work more interesting and reduces the chance of burnout (see Chapter 14).

Although self-managing teams may sound like the ideal work form, there are those who disagree with this idea. Some have pointed out that the research evidence is still rather tentative about the superiority of self-managing teams.[37] Others have suggested that teams are simply a fad that has been forced upon workers, even in situations where work coordination is not necessary (for example, in telemarketing).[38] Another perspective is that teams can be effective but that they require certain types of knowledge, skills, and abilities.[39] Some of these skills involve interpersonal issues, such as conflict resolution, collaborative problem solving, and communication. Others encompass self-management skills, such as goal setting, planning, and task coordination. To optimize teamwork, individuals should be selected who have the appropriate sets of knowledge, skills, and abilities or members should receive the necessary training in these areas. It is also important to understand that different types of teams may require different types of skills or support. For example, autonomy is not related to positive outcomes in project teams that come together only for a limited time to accomplish a particular task or solve a problem. Possibly, members of such teams already have considerable autonomy in other aspects of their work.[40]

self-managing work teams   Teams that have much control over and responsibility for the conduct of their work.

Innovation in Work Teams: Can Teams Be Creative?

Today's fast-paced world is characterized by an ever-present clamor for new ideas. Entrepreneurs are constantly promoting new devices or approaches to make our lives more efficient or comfortable. With the increasing complexity of technology and science, however, it is difficult for a solitary individual to come up with new developments. Instead, innovations increasingly require the contributions of a wide range of experts.[41] Many times such experts are organized into work teams to coordinate the innovation activities. As we learned in our discussion of groups (Chapter 8), group interaction can often inhibit productivity. Individuals in groups may loaf because they feel less accountable, or they may feel inhibited because others may not approve of or accept their ideas. When group members have different backgrounds or expertise, effective communication and mutual understanding may be lacking.[42]

How can we maximize innovation and creativity in teams? Most scholars agree that some level of diversity of knowledge or expertise is important. To avoid problems of communication, groups might be structured to have a moderate level of diversity so that group members can understand and relate to each other's ideas and concerns. Certain team members may have the expertise to communicate the ideas and findings of their group to other teams. For example, a team of microbiologists might include a member who has a strong background in chemistry; this member might interact with a team of biochemists to facilitate developments requiring contributions from both teams. It is also important to ensure organizational and team support for innovations or risk taking. Otherwise, groups may tend to stick with safe ideas or ideas that are consistent with existing practice or ideology.

Although diversity and support for innovation are important in enhancing creativity in teams, a number of other factors can play a role as well. The major factors that facilitate innovation are as follows:[43–45]

- Moderate levels of diversity
- Support for innovation from the organization and team
- Constructive and thoughtful resolution of conflicts among ideas
- Group members who employ innovative thinking styles
- Leaders who encourage innovation and whose style encourages the participative activities of teams
- High levels of **reflexivity** or thoughtful and careful analysis, planning, and action in the course of team activities
- Some degree of experience and maturity as a team, which enable the group to develop cohesion, organization, and a clear sense of mission

reflexivity   Thoughtful and careful analysis, planning, and action in the course of team activity.

In summary, creative products do not inevitably flow from team interaction. Team innovation and creativity require thoughtful efforts and coordination among the group members, leaders, and the organization.[46]

Team Effectiveness: How to Get the Most Out of Groups

As you learned in Chapter 8, although working in groups can be fun, they often are not very effective ways of accomplishing tasks. Research on teams provides a similar picture. Cooperative teamwork with one's coworkers does lead to positive feelings and impressions of effectiveness. However, we know that impressions and reality may be quite different.[47] For teams to be effective, it appears that some of the following conditions need to exist:[48,49]

1. **Participative management.** Unless management is willing to share its responsibility with workers, it will be difficult for a corporation to effectively harness the potential of work teams. If teams are allowed to make only token decisions or if their decisions are not accepted by upper management, members may quickly lose their enthusiasm for teamwork.

2. **Group cohesiveness.** It is important that there exist harmonious relationships among group members. Conflicts and jealousy will inhibit the ability of the group to function effectively in a cooperative manner.

3. **Group structure and training.** In the absence of external leadership, the group must develop procedures and norms to govern its functioning. This step may require some extensive training in effective group interaction and problem solving and the help of a trained facilitator.[50]

4. **Feedback and rewards.** It is important that groups get feedback about their performance and receive recognition and rewards for their achievements.

5. **Goals and performance norms.** It is important for the group to have a goal or a mission to motivate the group. Teams that develop high performance norms are more likely to meet such goals.

6. **Complementarity of skills.** Teams are most likely to be effective if their task requires coordination of a set of skills. If everyone is doing the same task or has the same skills, there may be little need for the coordination involved in teamwork.

It is apparent that just allowing employees to function as teams does not ensure success. The corporation and employees will require extensive preparation and training. Groups must learn to work together effectively. The costs of this type of training can be considerable and need to be taken into account when evaluating whether the benefits of teamwork outweigh the costs.[51] Furthermore, teamwork may not be the best solution for all types of work or organizations. Until we have more definitive evidence on the subject, it is best to be cautious and well prepared before jumping on the teamwork bandwagon. Nevertheless, research on teams has provided some evidence for the benefits of cooperation among employees and between employees and management in increasing productive work environments.

CONFLICT: ITS CAUSES, MANAGEMENT, AND EFFECTS

Have you ever been part of a group that has not had some conflicts? Probably most of your experiences in groups have involved some degree of conflict. These groups could include your family, friends, social groups, or work groups, and the conflicts might involve disagreements about ideas, rules, or fairness. Most of us don't like conflict—so why does it arise so often?

The basic reason flows from the fact that most groups include some degree of **interdependence.**[52] That is, the behaviors, actions, or ideas of group members will have important implications for each other. So what you do or say will have an impact on the other group members, and vice versa. Interdependence exists for both *information* and *outcomes.* **Information dependence** exists when group members must exchange information so as to make decisions or complete a task. This situation can lead to conflicts when group members do not fully share information or argue about the facts or their validity and relevance. **Outcome interdependence** exists when group members have a mutual interest in the division of some scarce resources. When these interests overlap or are similar, group members are in a cooperative relationship.

When some difference of interest occurs, however, group members maintain a competitive relationship and conflicts may arise. Therefore, **conflict** can be defined as disagreements that occur because of differences in opinions or interests. We will discuss each type of conflict and explain how it is managed.

Informational Conflict: Differences of Opinion

When conflict about ideas or opinions arises, group members can deal with the conflict in essentially two ways—avoidance and reduction.[53] As most of us don't like conflict, avoidance would seem to be a likely strategy. In fact, it

interdependence A state that exists when the actions, behaviors, and ideas of group members have important implications for one another.

information dependence A relationship in groups in which group members must exchange information to make decisions or complete a task.

outcome interdependence A relationship in which group members have a mutual interest in the division of some scarce resources.

conflict Disagreements that occur because of differences in opinions or interests.

| *Figure 9.2* | **Informational Conflict: Key Elements** |

Informational conflict can be associated with three different reactions.

Based on Levine and Thompson, 1996; see note 53.

is used quite frequently. Avoidance does not resolve the basic differences, however, so attempts at conflict reduction would seem more useful in the long run. Ironically, sometimes group members go out of their way to create conflict so as to attain their goals. We will describe each of these three strategies (see Figure 9.2).

Conflict Avoidance.   One way to avoid conflict is to persuade oneself or others that one's thoughts or ideas are really in agreement. This type of thought control may prove rather difficult to achieve when individuals have strong feelings about the relevant issues or ideas. A more common approach is simply to withhold the expression of true feelings. This type of conflict avoidance is part of groupthink (see Chapter 8).

Groups may also use decision rules that specify how group decisions will be made.[54] A *majority* rule, which requires a simple majority of the group to agree, is probably the most common solution, because it seems democratic and allows for the resolution of conflicts without getting unanimous agreement. On the other hand, the *unanimity* rule, in which all members must come to an agreement on a decision, actually tends to lead to higher levels of satisfaction, because it ensures that all group members have a full hearing by the group. Of course, unanimity may be difficult to achieve, especially when the group is dealing with important issues. Group members are most likely to *compromise* by moving their opinions or beliefs to some middle position that all group members can accept.

Conflict Reduction.   When conflicts occur, it is necessary to reduce the conflicts if the group is to continue functioning effectively. Typically, the group will include a number of factions that support different options. Most research suggests that the faction that has the most members or even a majority will have the greatest influence in determining how the conflict is reduced (see Chapter 8). Groups tend to move in the direction of the majority view, especially when the majority is quite strongly committed to its views. This movement may be partly motivated by a desire to receive approval from the majority, called **normative influence.** When group members actually become convinced that the majority represents the correct view, **informational influence** has occurred.[55]

Sometimes a group cannot come to an agreement about an issue, because members refuse to compromise their opinions. In that case, the group may redefine its boundaries. That is, some group members may be expelled from the group by the majority or they may leave voluntarily.[56] In work situations, this step typically occurs when a persistent disagreement makes it difficult for the group to attain its goals.

Conflict Creation.   Although conflict avoidance and reduction are the most common ways of reacting to differences in opinions or feelings, sometimes group members intentionally try to produce conflict (see Figure 9.3 for an example). This case may arise when members of some subgroup feel very strongly about their position or believe that conflict avoidance and reduction are harmful to the group. Indeed, sometimes it is important to air differences in perspective so as to develop a more accurate picture of reality or to make better decisions.[57] When a company is deciding on the best way to market a product, for example, it should get the honest perspectives of people from different parts of the company or those with different backgrounds. In a meeting on marketing, therefore, all participants should fully air their opinions. Someone may even play "devil's advocate" to stimulate an honest and frank exchange.

normative influence   Movement in the direction of a group majority that is motivated by a desire to seek approval.

informational influence   Movement in the direction of a group majority that is based on a belief that the majority view is correct.

**Conflict Creation in Groups:
Disagreement for Its Own Sake**

Sometimes groups seem to create conflict on purpose. Although the interaction depicted seems rather negative, sometimes disagreement can have positive effects.

When some subgroup that is in a minority feels very strongly about its position or ideas, its members may purposely create conflict to highlight their point of view and to prod the majority into thinking more deeply about the issues. This strategy does seem to work, in that strong, persistent presentations of opinions by a minority can produce opinion changes in majority group members. Nevertheless, minorities are seldom able to sway the majority to switch to the minority position unless some objective way exists to demonstrate the correctness of the minority position.[58]

Groups do appear to benefit from cognitive conflict if it is handled effectively. Group decision making is often improved, for example, because conflict can induce a careful analysis of information and opinions.[59] In a similar fashion, conflict can improve individual problem solving and creativity. For example, group members who are exposed to minority opinions tend to provide more creative responses in subsequent situations.[60]

Thus cognitive conflict can be a double-edged sword. On the one hand, it can produce disharmony in work groups and pressure members to adopt uniformity as their creed. On the other hand, it can make group members more careful in evaluating their alternatives and may lead to more creative solutions. Although most of us would like to work in a conflict-free environment, periodic conflicts about important issues may actually be important for the effective functioning of groups and organizations. Therefore, it is not surprising that top management teams limit emotional or interpersonal conflict but are likely to engage in cognitive conflict.[61]

Personal Conflict: Opposing Interests

Although much conflict centers around differences in opinions or ideas, a variety of conflicts may stem from the personal relations among coworkers. As mentioned earlier, these conflicts often center around opposing interests when resources are scarce. We now examine this and several other bases for personal conflicts.

The Problem of Limited Resources: "We've Got to Get Our Share."   Unfortunately, no organization, no matter how successful, has unlimited resources. Space, money, materials, labor—all must be conserved and used to the greatest advantage. But what division of these resources among various departments or individuals is best? Not surprisingly, bitter disputes about this issue often erupt. Each unit tends to ask for more than the others feel is fair, and each strives to ensure that it doesn't receive the short end of the stick. Indeed, from the perspective of organizational politics, supervisors who succeed in such disputes are perceived as effective, and they often gain in power and status. Those who bring home less than their subordinates believe is fair are viewed in a much more negative light. Whatever the final outcome, though, this continuous struggle within organizations for a share of available resources is clearly a major cause of confrontation and conflict.

Reward Structures: Building Conflict into the System.   Suppose that at a particular company, bonuses and raises are distributed to production-line staff on the basis of total output: The higher the overall production, the more reward they receive. Similarly, imagine that among service personnel—people who must deal with customer complaints—a somewhat different reward system operates. Here, the lower the total costs of service during a given period, the greater the raises and bonuses. Is there a potential basis for conflict in this setup? You bet there is! From the point of view of production workers, faster is better—the more they produce, the higher their pay. In a sense, conflict between these two groups is practically ensured. The reward system adopted by their company pits the interests of one group directly against those of the other. The moral in this example is simple: When planning reward systems, carefully avoid such problems. Serious conflict may be fostered in situations in which, with a little care, it might have been avoided.

Interpersonal Relations and Conflict: From Grudges to Criticism.   The causes of conflict we have considered so far all relate to aspects of organizations themselves. But conflict actually occurs between individuals. In fact, it is specific persons who decide to threaten or thwart others' interests—not departments or other organizational units. This fact calls attention to another cause of conflict in work settings: faulty interpersonal relations between key individuals.

There are many sources of conflict in interpersonal relations. First, consider the impact of lasting *grudges*. When individuals are angered by others, and especially when they lose face (look foolish publicly), they may develop strong, negative attitudes toward the persons responsible for these outcomes. As a result, they may spend considerable time and effort planning or actually seeking revenge for these wrongs. Unfortunately, such grudges can persist for years, with obvious negative effects for the organizations or work groups in question.

Second, conflict often stems from or is intensified by faulty *attributions*—errors concerning the causes behind others' behavior. When individuals find that their interests have been hindered by another person, they generally try to determine *why* this person acted this way. Was it a desire to harm them or give them a hard time? Or did the provoker's actions stem from factors beyond his or her control? When people infer some negative motive, anger and subsequent conflict are more likely and more intense than when they assume that this is not the case.[62]

A third interpersonal factor of considerable importance in generating instances of organizational conflict might be termed *faulty communication*. This refers to the fact that individuals often communicate with others in a manner that angers or annoys them, even though they do not intend to do so. Such faulty communication often involves a lack of clarity—for example, a manager is certain that she communicated her wishes clearly to a subordinate, when in fact, the subordinate is confused about exactly what he is supposed to do. When the manager later finds that the task has not been completed, she is annoyed. And the subordinate, in turn, is angered by what he considers to be unfair treatment. In other cases, faulty communication centers around inappropriate *criticism*—negative feedback delivered in a manner that angers the recipient instead of helping this person to do a better job. The negative effects of such destructive criticism have been demonstrated clearly in research.[63]

In sum, considerable evidence suggests that conflict in work settings often stems from the relations between individuals as well as from underlying structural (organization-based) factors. At first glance, this finding might appear to be quite pessimistic in its implications for the reduction or management of such conflict; after all, it adds several potential causes to the ones that have traditionally been viewed as important in this respect. In fact, it can actually be interpreted as being quite optimistic in this regard. Interpersonal behavior can readily be modified. Indeed, in many cases it may be easier to change than organizational structure, and easier to modify than built-in underlying conflicts of interest. For this reason, understanding the interpersonal causes of organizational conflict may offer important and practical benefits.

Managing Personal Conflicts

As with cognitive conflicts, people may employ a variety of strategies in dealing with personal conflicts. Among these are conflict avoidance, conflict reduction, and conflict creation (see Figure 9.4).

Conflict Avoidance.   Personal conflict is often avoided because most group members see it as threat to the group. It may hinder the attainment of group goals[64] or may reduce group perceptions of harmony or cohesion.[65] Not all groups, however, are equally motivated to avoid conflict. Groups can vary in the strength of their "ingroup" bonds and the perceived value of the group to outsiders. Ingroup bonds re-

 Personal Conflict: Key Elements

Personal conflict can be associated with three different reactions.

Based on Levine and Thompson, 1996; see note 53.

Figure 9.5 **Conflict Avoidance and Type of Group**

Groups are most likely to avoid conflict if they have both strong intragroup attraction and high outside respect (inner-circle groups).

Based on Thompson et al., 1994, see note 66.

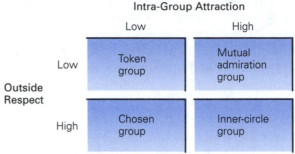

flect the degree of attraction among group members. Perceived value indicates the respect that the group commands from others. Groups that have both of these characteristics are termed *inner-circle groups*. Those that have neither of these characteristics are *token groups*. Groups that are high on ingroup attractiveness but low on outside respect are *mutual admiration groups*. Those with low attraction but high respect are *chosen groups*. Groups are probably motivated to maintain both their intragroup attraction and external respect. Conflict, of course, could harm both attraction and respect. As you might expect, inner-circle groups appear to work more assiduously to avoid conflict, as they have the most to lose (see Figure 9.5).[66]

How do groups avoid personal conflict? One way is to simply do nothing—that is, to avoid the issue or contact with the persons involved. You might not bring up the subject at meetings or refuse to go to the lunchroom. Organizations often avoid conflict by setting up rules or regulations that allow groups to deal with potential problem issues before conflicts arise. For example, a company might establish rules to ensure fair distribution of pay increases or special privileges so as to make sure they are seen as equitable by all group members (see Chapter 5).

Conflict Reduction.   Often conflict may occur or persist in despite efforts to avoid it. If allowed to continue, it will ultimately exert a disruptive influence on an organization. After all, while a conflict persists, valuable resources better used elsewhere will be committed to it. Even worse, growing evidence suggests that the more each side has invested in a conflict—the more losses the group members have experienced as a result of their disagreement—the more difficult it is for them to bring it to an end. Thus strong reasons exist for attempting to resolve existing conflicts as quickly as possible. How can this be accomplished? Fortunately, a number of tactics for attaining this goal seem effective. We consider several of these briefly.

By far the most common tactic used for resolving organizational conflicts is **bargaining** or negotiation.[67] As

bargaining   A process in which two or more sides exchange offers, concessions, and counteroffers in an attempt to resolve their disagreement; also called negotiating.

you probably already know, this process consists of a mutual trading of offers, counteroffers, and (with luck) concessions between the parties involved or their representatives. If the process is successful, a solution acceptable to both sides is attained, and the conflict is brought to a close. The catch, of course, is that often the process is *not* successful. Negotiations frequently deadlock, with the result that conflict is intensified rather than reduced. A major question concerning bargaining, then, is this: What factors either increase or reduce the likelihood of its success? Research findings point to some intriguing answers.

First, open and direct communication between the opposing sides is beneficial, especially if this continues throughout the entire process.[68] Only one type of contact between opponents should be avoided: implicit or explicit *threats*. When these are used, tempers tend to flare, and the chances of an agreement can be sharply reduced. Second, willingness to make concessions, even small ones, is extremely helpful. When one side to a conflict makes such a move, the rule of reciprocity (acting toward others as they behave toward us) dictates that the other should do likewise. In this way, a path is opened to further, mutual steps toward compromise. This fact points to another interesting conclusion about bargaining: In general, it is best to begin with a position you do not really expect to attain. By doing so, you leave yourself room for maneuvering and for a number of small concessions. But beware of starting with too extreme an offer: It can anger your opponent and stiffen his or her resistance.

Despite the best efforts of both sides, negotiations sometimes deadlock. When they do, the aid of a third party, someone not directly involved in the dispute, is often sought. Such *third-party intervention* can take many different forms, but the most common are **mediation** and **arbitration**. In mediation, the third party attempts, through various tactics, to facilitate voluntary agreements between the disputants. Mediators have no formal power and cannot impose an agreement on the two sides. Instead, they seek to clarify the issues involved and enhance communication between the opponents. Mediators sometimes offer specific recommendations for compromise or integrative solutions; in other cases, they guide disputants toward developing such solutions themselves. In sum, their role is primarily that of *facilitator*—helping the two sides toward agreements they both find acceptable. In contrast, arbitrators do have the power to impose (or at least strongly recommend) the terms of an agreement.

Both mediation and arbitration can be helpful in resolving organizational conflicts. However, both suffer from certain drawbacks. Because it requires voluntary compliance by the parties to a dispute, mediation often proves ineffective. Indeed, it may simply serve to underscore the depth of the differences between the two sides. Arbitration suffers from several potential problems. First, it may exert a *chilling effect* on negotiations, bringing

mediation   A form of third-party intervention in disputes in which the intervening person does not have the authority to dictate an agreement. Mediators simply attempt to enhance communication between opposing sides and to provide conditions that will facilitate acceptable agreements.

arbitration   A form of third-party intervention in disputes in which the intervening person has the power to determine the terms of an agreement.

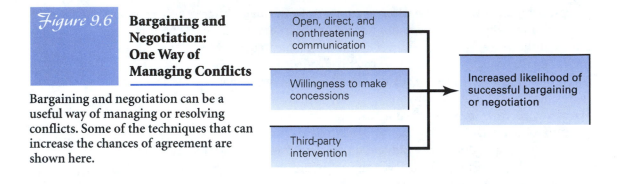

Figure 9.6   **Bargaining and Negotiation: One Way of Managing Conflicts**

Bargaining and negotiation can be a useful way of managing or resolving conflicts. Some of the techniques that can increase the chances of agreement are shown here.

voluntary progress to a halt. Because both sides know the arbitrator will resolve the dispute for them, they see little point in engaging in serious bargaining, which, after all, is hard work. Second, one or both sides may come to suspect that the arbitrator is biased. The result: Disputants become increasingly reluctant to agree to arbitration. Finally, there is some indication that commitment to arbitrated settlements is weaker than commitment to directly negotiated ones.

By taking these factors into account, groups or individuals participating in bargaining can increase the likelihood of an agreement and avoid some key pitfalls (see Figure 9.6). Thus, under appropriate conditions, bargaining can be a highly effective technique for resolving even bitter and prolonged conflicts.

Another useful strategy for resolving conflicts lies in the establishment of some **superordinate goals.** That is, conditions can be arranged so that the two sides no longer compete; rather, they must work together to attain a goal of interest to both. The benefits of superordinate goals have been demonstrated in classic research by Sherif and his associates. These investigators found that when opposing groups had to work together to achieve common goals, their perceptions of each other improved and conflict decreased.[69] In sum, it appears that either reminding the parties to a conflict of their shared goal (for example, the overall success of their organization) or actually establishing such objectives can be a highly effective means for resolving confrontations.

Conflict Creation.   Why would a group want to create personal conflict? In most cases it is probably not a good idea, as conflict can have many negative side effects for groups and may escalate. Sometimes, however, a little personal conflict can yield positive results for the group as a whole. When some people are not receiving fair treatment, actions taken to confront those in power about these issues may lead to some positive changes.[70] Conflict may also bring about a feeling of unity or cohesion within groups.[71] One can often see such a development when unions go on strikes or even

superordinate goals Goals shared by all members of an organization. When the parties to a conflict are made aware of these goals, the conflict may be resolved or lessened.

when countries engage in international conflicts. Conflict can, in fact, be seen as an indication of group strength because it requires some confidence in one's group and it positions the group to confront other groups.[72]

Conflict: A Look at Its Major Effects

So far, we have discussed different types of conflicts and suggested ways of dealing with them. In this discussion, it probably became clear to you that conflict is really a double-edged sword. Depending on what happens and how conflict occurs, it can yield either harmful or beneficial outcomes. In this section, we review those end results mentioned previously and add a few others.

The Negative Side of the Coin.
Some of the negative effects of conflict are readily obvious. For example, conflict often generates strong negative feelings among the parties concerned, interferes with communication among them, and all but eliminates any coordination with their activities. In these ways, of course, it can seriously impair effective organizational functioning.

Other effects of conflict, though, are a bit more subtle. First, it has been found that when groups experience conflict, their leaders often shift from democratic to autocratic practices (see Chapter 10).[73] The reason for this seems to be straightforward: Groups experiencing stress require firm direction from their leaders. Thus, when conflict develops, these persons shift to more authoritarian tactics—tactics that are accepted without protest by their subordinates. Groups experiencing conflict therefore tend to be far less pleasant to work in than groups not encountering such stress.

Conflict also increases the tendency of both sides to engage in *negative stereotyping*. The members of each group emphasize the differences between themselves and their opponents and come to perceive others in an increasingly negative light. "You know what marketing people are like" and "All those staff people are the same" are just two statements that capture the essence of such thinking. In short, conflict tends to heighten our tendency to divide the world into two opposing camps—"us" and "them"—with all the unfortunate outcomes this division implies.

Finally, conflict leads the sides to close ranks and emphasize loyalty to their own department or group. This effectively prevents opponents from taking each other's perspective and tends to lessen the chances for an effective, satisfactory compromise. As you can readily see, conflict has a number of unfortunate, costly effects.

The Positive Side of the Coin.
Nevertheless, the total picture is not entirely bleak. While conflict often exerts a disruptive effect upon organizations and work settings, under certain conditions it can actually be helpful.[74] First, conflict can serve to bring problems that have previously been ignored out into the open. In this way, it can facilitate their solution. All too often, unpleasant issues are swept under the corporate rug. As a result, they tend to persist. Once open conflict breaks out, however, this approach is no longer possible, and problems that require attention may finally receive

it. Second, conflict can sometimes lead to the consideration of new ideas and approaches. Once conflict erupts, an organization cannot go on conducting business as usual. Instead, new solutions or policies may be needed. To the extent that conflict facilitates their emergence, it can indeed be useful. Third, the careful consideration of information and ideas expressed during conflict can help groups make better decisions.[75] Fourth, the expression of conflict may increase feelings of group unity or cohesion. Finally, it may encourage the opposing sides to carefully monitor each other's performance—a process that increases effort and productivity on both sides. In these ways, conflict can actually contribute to effective organizational functioning.

Of course, it is important to note that these positive effects will be seen only when conflict is carefully managed or controlled. If conflicts are allowed to become extreme and intense, strong negative feelings may be generated on both sides. Then, rationality and the potential benefits just described may fly quickly out the window! If such pitfalls can be avoided, however, conflict can play a useful role. Indeed, it can turn out to be an effective tool for inducing positive organizational change. (See Figure 9.7 for a summary of the potential negative and positive effects of conflict.)

Figure 9.7   **Conflict: Mixed Effects**

As shown here, conflict can produce beneficial as well as harmful effects.

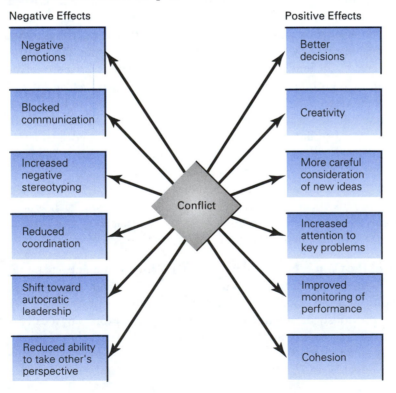

Negative Effects		Positive Effects
Negative emotions		Better decisions
Blocked communication		Creativity
Increased negative stereotyping		More careful consideration of new ideas
Reduced coordination	Conflict	Increased attention to key problems
Shift toward autocratic leadership		Improved monitoring of performance
Reduced ability to take other's perspective		Cohesion

Culture and Conflict Management: Some Differences in Style

You have probably noticed that conflict management can vary according to culture and subculture. As discussed in Chapter 1, some cultures are individualist, focusing on personal rewards, achievements, and independence; other cultures are collectivist, being primarily concerned with the rewards gained from being interdependent as part of a family, group, or collective.

Collectivist cultures tend to use an approach to conflict that can be labeled *harmony*.[76] They focus on low competitiveness, suppression of negative emotions, and avoidance of conflict. Their main concern, therefore, is the maintenance of group harmony and avoidance of conflict. This type of conflict management dominates in such countries as Japan, Korea, and China.

In contrast, individualist cultures may have one of two different conflict management styles. Some such cultures emphasize reasoning and focusing on the facts and tend to use a *confrontational* approach. They are likely to support competitive work environments, expression of negative emotions, and use of confrontation and compromise. The main concern in individualist cultures is reason and fairness. The confrontational style tends to be found in English-speaking countries. Some other individualist cultures emphasize general rules and universal values that govern behavior and resolution of conflicts. This is called the *regulative* approach. There is low competition due to the extensive use of rules and procedures and a focus on equality. Although negative emotions are expressed, conflict is avoided primarily by using bureaucratic procedures based on the general rules and values of the culture. This approach tends to be common in Eastern European countries and some Western European countries such as France and Germany.[77] Table 9.1 summarizes the three cul-

---

Table 9.1   **Conflict Management Styles: Variations across Cultures**

Three general styles of management can be found in different cultures. Each of these styles varies in how conflict is expressed and handled.

	Conflict Management Style		
	Harmony	**Confrontational**	**Regulative**
Emphasis	Harmony	Reason, fairness	Rules, equality
Competitiveness	Low	High	Low
Expression of negative emotions	Suppression	Expression	Expression
Behavior	Avoidance	Confrontation and compromise	Avoidance

Based on Kozan, M. K. (1997). Culture and conflict management: A theoretical framework. *International Journal of Conflict and Management, 8,* 338–360.

tural approaches to conflict. How do these conclusions about conflict management style fit with your experience? If you have acquaintances from these countries, you might want to see to what extent they agree with this perspective.

Guidelines for Effective Human Relations

Using What You've Learned

In this chapter, we examined a broad range of principles and findings about teamwork and conflict in human relations. Although few rules will apply to every situation, there are some general guidelines suggested by the various findings we have discussed. These are summarized below for your consideration. Remember, no rule works 100 percent in every situation. However, these guidelines should help you increase cooperation and reduce conflict in work environments.

- Be aware of those factors that inhibit your helpfulness and that of your coworkers. Management that treats employees fairly and high degrees of job satisfaction increase the likelihood that employees will exhibit helpful and responsible behavior at work. In particular, it is important to promote positive feelings in employees.

- Effective teamwork requires cohesion, participative management, a group goal, and some degree of structure.

- Be aware of the factors that lead to conflict, such as limited resources, competing reward structures, and negative interpersonal factors. In resolving conflicts, try to focus on the benefits of negotiation. Focus on the interests you have in common rather than those that divide.

- People often demonstrate a tendency to avoid conflict. Organizations or groups that develop procedures for effective airing of conflicts can benefit by resolving important differences, making better decisions, and increasing their creativity.

In general, any factor that increases positive emotional states and cooperation among workers should have positive consequences for job satisfaction and productivity. There are many features of work environments that produce negative reactions and conflict, such as competing reward systems. It is important for management to develop a cooperative and caring atmosphere that will motivate the employees to resolve conflict effectively, both for their own sake and for the benefit of the organization.

Summary

The degree to which individuals in an organization cooperate or coordinate their efforts may be very important to its success. At one end of the scale, individuals may engage in helpful or cooperative behavior; and at the other end, conflict may occur. Behaviors that are designed to further the welfare of the organization are prosocial behaviors. Intervening to prevent illegal or destructive behaviors, helping other employees who are in need of assistance, and being a good organizational citizen are some examples of such prosocial behavior.

Cooperative groups, such as quality circles and self-managing teams, have been used to increase productivity in organizations. Quality circles do not appear to be very effective, but self-managing work teams are often associated with high levels of productivity and satisfaction. Teams composed of members with diverse expertise in a supportive environment can prove quite innovative. To maximize the effectiveness of work teams, certain conditions such as participative management and group structure and training are required.

Conflict occurs when groups or individuals have disagreements based on differences of opinions or interests. Conflict about differences of opinions—that is, informational conflict—is often avoided or can be reduced when those holding a minority view move in the direction of the majority. Well-managed interpersonal conflict can lead to better decision making and increased creativity. Personal conflicts over differences in interests may arise over limited resources, competitive reward systems, and faulty interpersonal relations. Such conflicts can be reduced through bargaining and negotiation, third-party intervention, and the induction of superordinate goals. Interpersonal conflict can lead to negative stereotyping and ineffective communication. Under some conditions, this type of conflict may have positive effects, by leading to consideration of new ideas or procedures and bringing important organizational problems into the open.

Key Terms

arbitration, p. 265

bargaining, p. 264

conflict, p. 258

cross-functional teams, p. 254

diffusion of responsibility, p. 249

information dependence, p. 258

informational influence, p. 260

interdependence, p. 258

mediation, p. 265

normative influence, p. 260

organizational citizenship behaviors, p. 251

organizational spontaneity, p. 253

outcome interdependence, p. 258

prosocial behavior, p. 247

quality circle, p. 254

reflexivity, p. 256

self-managing work teams, p. 255

superordinate goals, p. 266

teams, p. 253

Experiential Exercise

How Do You Deal with Conflict?

All of us deal with conflict in different ways. Some of us try to avoid or minimize conflict at all costs; others may thrive on conflict and may be very difficult people with whom to negotiate. A third group may see conflict as a necessary evil and try to make the best of such situations. The following questionnaire is designed to determine your conflict style. Place a *T* next to the items with which you agree and an *F* next to those with which you disagree.

Conflict Style Scale

_____ 1. When there is a conflict among groups, I like to be right in the middle of it.

_____ 2. I find conflicts among people or groups very uncomfortable.

_____ 3. When I'm involved in a conflict, I don't let it linger but get to work to try to resolve it.

_____ 4. Sometimes I try to produce a conflict in a group on purpose just for the excitement of it.

_____ 5. I enjoy helping people or groups resolve their conflict.

_____ 6. Whenever I have a conflict with someone, I tend to withdraw into my own shell and ignore that person.

_____ 7. I usually try to get my own way in most situations.

_____ 8. I hold grudges for long periods of time.

_____ 9. I avoid criticizing people for their mistakes and try to help them avoid their mistakes in the future.

_____ 10. I tend to let others have their way just to minimize conflicts.

_____ 11. I often find myself involved in resolving conflicts between friends.

_____ 12. I tend to keep my feelings to myself if I think they might produce some conflict.

If you marked *T* for items 2, 6, 10, and 12, you have an *avoidant style* of dealing with conflict—you try to avoid it if at all possible. If you marked *T* for items 1, 4, 7, and 8, you are a *conflict seeker*. You tend to enjoy conflicts and may even try to generate them. If you marked *T* for items 3, 5, 9, and 11, you take a *problem-solving* approach to conflict. You try to find ways to help people and groups deal with conflicts. Although from the perspective of this chapter, the problem-solving approach may be most helpful for groups, sometimes the other styles may be beneficial as well. Groups that have become lethargic may need some conflict to energize them. When important issues are not on the line, avoidance of conflict is certainly desirable.

Notes

1. Sheriton, J., & Stern, J. L. (1997). *Corporate culture–team culture: Removing the hidden barriers to team success.* New York: AMACOM.

2. Deutsch, M. (1990). Sixty years of conflict. *International Journal of Conflict Management, 1,* 237–263.

3. Brief, A. P., & Motowidlo, S. J. (1986). Prosocial organizational behaviors. *Academy of Management Review, 11,* 710–725.

4. Dozier, J. B., & Miceli, M. P. (1985). Potential predictors of whistle-blowing: A prosocial behavior perspective. *Academy of Management Review, 11,* 823–836.

5. Miceli, M. P., & Near, J. P. (1997). Whistle-blowing as antisocial behavior. In R. A. Giacalone & J. Greenberg (eds.), *Antisocial behavior in organizations* (pp. 130–149). Thousand Oaks, CA: Sage Publications.

6. Naj, A. K. (1992, December 7). Federal judge awards ex-GE staffers record amount in whistleblower case. *Wall Street Journal,* p. A5.

7. See note 5.

8. Latane, B., & Nida, S. A. (1981). Ten years of research on group size and helping. *Psychological Bulletin, 89,* 308–324.

9. Piliavin, I. M., Piliavin, J. A., & Rodin, J. (1975). Costs, diffusion and the stigmatized victim. *Journal of Personality and Social Psychology, 32,* 429–438.

10. O'Dell, L. (1993, August 18). Officer gives graphic testimony on Tailhook assault. *Fort Worth Star-Telegram.*

11. Batson, C. D., Fultz, J., & Schoenrade, P. A. (1987). Distress and empathy: Two qualitatively distinct vicarious emotions with different motivational consequences. *Journal of Personality, 55,* 19–39.

12. Carlson, M., Charlin, V., & Miller, N. (1988). Positive mood and helping behavior: A test of six hypotheses. *Journal of Personality and Social Psychology, 55,* 211–229.

13. Clark, M. S., & Isen, A. M. (1982). Toward understanding the relationship between feeling states and social behavior. In A. H. Hastorf & A.

M. Isen (eds.), *Cognitive social psychology* (pp. 73–108). New York: Elsevier Science.

14. Isen, A. M., & Baron, R. A. (1991). Positive affect as a factor in organizational behavior. *Research in Organizational Behavior, 13,* 1–54.

15. George, J. M., & Betenhausen, K. (1990). Understanding prosocial behavior, sales performance, and turnover: A group level analysis in a service context. *Journal of Applied Psychology, 75,* 698–709.

16. George, J. M., & Brief, A. P. (1992). Feeling good—doing good: A conceptual analysis of the mood at work-organizational spontaneity relationship. *Psychological Bulletin, 112,* 310–329.

17. Organ, D. W. (1988). *Organizational citizenship behavior: The good soldier syndrome.* Lexington, MA: Lexington Books.

18. Organ, D. W. (1990). The motivational basis of organizational citizenship behavior. In B. M. Staw & L. L. Cummings (eds.), *Research in organizational behavior* (Vol. 12, pp. 43–72). Greenwich, CT: JAI Press.

19. Konovsky, M. A., & Organ, D. W. (1996). Dispositional and contextual determinants of organizational citizenship behavior. *Journal of Organizational Behavior, 17,* 253–266.

20. Van Dyne, L., Cummings, L. L., & Parks, J. M. (1995). Extra-role behaviors in pursuit of construct and definitional clarity (a bridge over troubled waters). *Research in Organizational Behavior, 17,* 215–285.

21. Kidwell, R. E., Jr., Mossholder, K. W., & Bennett, N. (1997). Cohesiveness and organizational citizenship behavior: A multilevel analysis using work groups and individuals. *Journal of Management, 23,* 775–793.

22. See note 16.

23. Smith, C. A., Organ, D. W., & Near, J. P. (1983). Organizational citizenship behavior: Its nature and antecedents. *Journal of Applied Psychology, 68,* 453–463.

24. Katz, D. (1964). The motivational basis of organizational behavior. *Behavioral Science, 9,* 131–146.

25. See note 16.

26. Wright, P. M., George, J. M., Farnsworth, S. R., & McMahan, G. C. (1993). Productivity and extra-role behavior: The effects of goals and incentives on spontaneous helping. *Journal of Applied Psychology, 78*, 374–381.

27. Hackman, J. R., & Oldham, G. R. (1980). *Work design.* Reading, MA: Addison-Wesley.

28. Cohen, S. G., & Bailey, D. E. (1997). What makes teams work: Group effectiveness research from the shop floor to the executive suite. *Journal of Management, 23*, 239–290.

29. Appelbaum, E., & Batt, R. (1994). *The new American workplace.* Ithaca, NY: ILR Press.

30. Cusumano, M. A. (1997). How Microsoft makes large teams work like small teams. *Sloan Management Review* (Fall): 9–20.

31. West, M. A., & Anderson, N. R. (1996). Innovation in top management teams. *Journal of Applied Psychology, 81*, 680–693.

32. Barrick, M. R., & Alexander, R. A. (1987). A review of quality circle efficacy and the existence of the positive-findings bias. *Personnel Psychology, 40*, 579–591.

33. Cotton, J. L. (1993). *Employee involvement.* Newbury Park, CA: Sage.

34. Pearce, J. A., & Ravlin, E. C. (1987). The design and activation of self-regulating work groups. *Human Relations, 40*, 751–782.

35. See note 28.

36. Amabile, T. M. (1996). *Creativity in context.* Boulder, CO: Westview Press.

37. See note 28.

38. Sinclair, A. (1992). The tyranny of a team ideology. *Organization Studies, 13*, 611–626.

39. Stevens, M. J., & Campion, M. A. (1994). The knowledge, skill, and ability requirements for teamwork: Implications for human resource management. *Journal of Management, 20*, 503–530.

40. See note 28.

41. Liedtka, J. M., Haskins, M. E., Rosenblum, J. W., & Weber, J. (1997). The generative cycle: Linking knowledge and relationships. *Sloan Management Review* (Fall): 47–58.

42. Schein, E. H. (1996). Three cultures of management: The key to organizational learning. *Sloan Management Review* (Fall): 9–20.

43. West, M. A. (in press). Sparkling fountains or stagnant ponds: Work groups as sources of innovation. *Applied Psychology: An International Review.*

44. Janz, B. D., Colquitt, J. A., & Noe, R. A. (1997). Knowledge worker team effectiveness: The role of autonomy, interdependence, team development, and contextual support variables. *Personnel Psychology, 50*, 877–904.

45. Hyatt, D. E., & Ruddy, T. M. (1997). An examination of the relationship between work group characteristics and performance: Once more into the breech. *Personnel Psychology, 50*, 553–585.

46. See note 1.

47. Paulus, P. B., Dzindolet, M. T., Poletes, G. W., & Camacho, L. M. (1993). Perception of performance in group brainstorming: The illusion of group productivity. *Personality and Social Psychology Bulletin, 19*, 78–89.

48. Hayes, N. (1997). *Successful team management.* London: International Thomson Business Press.

49. Syer, J., & Connolly, C. (1996). *How teamwork works: The dynamics of effective team development.* London: McGraw-Hill.

50. Swezey, R. W., & Salas, E. (eds.). (1992). *Teams: Their training and performance.* Norwood, NJ: Ablex Publishing.

51. See note 38.

52. Kelley, H. H., & Thibaut, J. W. (1978). *Interpersonal relations: A theory of interdependence.* New York: Wiley.

53. Levine, J. M., & Thompson, L. (1996). Conflict in groups. In E. T. Higgins & A. W. Kruglanski (eds.), *Social Psychology: Handbook of Basic Principles* (pp. 745–776). New York: Guilford Press.

54. Miller, C. E. (1989). The social psychological effects of group decision rules. In P. B. Paulus (ed.). *Psychology of group influence* (2nd ed.) (pp. 327–355). Hillsdale, NJ: Erlbaum.

55. Deutsch, M., & Gerald, H. B. (1955). A study of normative and information social influences

upon individual judgment. *Journal of Abnormal and Social Psychology, 51,* 629–636.

56. Levine, J. M., & Moreland, R. L. (1985). Innovation and socialization in small groups. In S. Moscovici, G. Mugny, & E. Van Avermaet (eds.), *Perspectives on minority influence* (pp. 143–169). Cambridge, UK: Cambridge University Press.

57. De Dreu, C., & Van De Vliert, E. (eds.) (1997). *Using conflict in organizations.* London: Sage Publications.

58. Wood, W., Lundgren, S., Ouellette, J. A., Busceme, S., & Blackstone, T. (1994). Processes of minority influence: Influence effectiveness and source perceptions. *Psychological Bulletin, 115,* 323–345.

59. Amason, A. C., & Sapienza, H. J. (1997). The effects of top management team size and interaction norms on cognitive and affective conflict. *Journal of Management, 23,* 495–516.

60. Nemeth, C. (1992). Minority dissent as a stimulant to group performance. In S. Worchel, W. Wood, & J. A. Simpson (eds.), *Group process and productivity* (pp. 95–111). Newbury Park, CA: Sage.

61. See note 59.

62. Baron, R. A. (1988). Attributions and organizational conflict: The mediating role of apparent sincerity. *Organizational Behavior and Human Decision Processes, 41,* 111–127.

63. Baron, R. A. (1988). Negative effects of destructive criticism: Impact on conflict, self-efficacy, and task performance. *Journal of Applied Psychology, 73,* 199–207.

64. Zander, A. (1968). Group aspirations. In D. Cartwright & A. Zander (eds.), *Group dynamics: Research and theory* (pp. 418–429). New York: Harper & Row.

65. Mullen, B., & Copper, C. (1994). The relation between group cohesiveness and performance: An integration. *Psychological Bulletin, 115,* 210–227.

66. Thompson, L., Kray, L., & Lind, A. E. (1994). *The bright and dark side of group identity.* Paper presented at the meeting of the Society of Experimental Social Psychology, Lake Tahoe, Nevada.

67. Thompson, L. (1998). *The mind and heart of the negotiator.* Upper Saddle River, NJ: Prentice Hall.

68. Lewicky, R. J., Saunders, D. M., & Minton, J. W. (1997). *Essentials of negotiation.* Chicago: Richard D. Irwin.

69. Sherif, M., Harvey, O. J., White, B. J., Hood, W. R., & Sherif, C. W. (1961). *Intergroup conflict and cooperation: The robbers' cave experiment.* Norman: University of Oklahoma Press.

70. Lind, E. A., & Tyler, T. R. (1988). *The social psychology of procedural justice.* New York: Plenum.

71. Pruitt, D. G., & Rubin, J. (1996). *Social conflict: Escalation, stalemate, and settlement.* New York: Random House.

72. See note 53.

73. Fodor, E. M. (1976). Group stress, authoritarian style of control, and use of power. *Journal of Applied Psychology, 61,* 313–318.

74. Robbins, S. P. (1974). *Managing organizational conflict.* Englewood Cliffs, NJ: Prentice Hall.

75. See note 57.

76. Kozan, M. K. (1997). Culture and conflict management: A theoretical framework. *International Journal of Conflict and Management, 8,* 338–360.

77. Ibid.

Chapter 10

Who Becomes a Leader? Some Contrasting Answers

The Trait Approach: In Search of "Born Leaders"

The Situational Approach: Technical Skill versus Charisma

The Interactionist Approach: Leadership as a Two-Way Street

Gender and Leadership: Where Have All the Women Gone?

Minority-Group Members and Leadership: Another Bias?

Leadership Styles: Contrasting Approaches to the Task of Directing Others

Person-Oriented versus Production-Oriented Leaders: Showing Consideration or Initiating Structure

Gender and Style

Cultural Differences in Style

Leader Effectiveness: Who Succeeds and Who Fails?

Fiedler's Contingency Model: Matching Leaders and Tasks

Transactional Leadership: An Exchange Process

Charismatic or Transformational Leaders: Important in Times of Need

New Directions in Leadership

Teamwork: Sharing the Power

Leadership and the New Technology: New Styles for a New Age

Leadership Development: Making Good Leaders

Self-Leadership: A Style for Today's Worker?

Leadership versus Management: Some Important Differences

Special Sections

Guidelines for Effective Human Relations
Using What You've Learned

Experiential Exercise
What Leadership Style Do You Prefer?

*L*EADERSHIP

Getting the Most Out of Groups, Teams, and Organizations

Learning Objectives

After reading this chapter, you should be able to:

1. Define *leadership*.
2. Discuss the trait, situational, and interactionist approaches to leadership.
3. Outline how gender and minority-group membership affect leader emergence.
4. Describe person- versus production-oriented dimensions of leader behavior.
5. Discuss how gender and culture affect leader style.
6. Summarize the main points of the major theories of leadership.
7. Indicate how leaders' relations with their subordinates can affect subordinates' performance and careers.
8. Describe the characteristics of charismatic or transformational leaders.
9. Discuss how to manage teamwork effectively.
10. Understand some new trends in leadership.

ary Kay Cosmetics is one of the most successful companies in its industry. Like many successful companies, it has an inspirational leader, Mary Kay Ash, and a dedicated management group. They work hard to harness what they see as the untapped potential for success in women. The company provides its "partners" with a vision, realistic goals, training and coaching, and independence in their jobs. Each year the partners gather at a convention to undergo training, to celebrate success, and to receive rewards. At these very joyful affairs, many inspirational stories are shared. The Mary Kay system appears to work. In the 1980s, it had more women earning high incomes than any other company in the world.[1]

*Y*ou are probably quite familiar with Mary Kay Cosmetics and its system of rewarding its employees for success in sales. The "secret" of Mary Kay's success is probably shared by many other successful corporations. Part of this secret is effective leadership that empowers employees to attain a high level of success in their work. In this chapter, we examine the factors that are related to this type of effective leadership.

When we use the term **leadership,** we refer to the exercise of a special type of influence—that exerted by one member of an organization (or group) over one or several other members. In work settings, formal leaders are generally appointed to their positions. Thus specific persons are named office manager, director of sales, or vice president for human resources. In other contexts, though, leaders may be chosen by members of their groups or may emerge in an informal manner. Regardless of how they gain their authority, leaders usually play a key role in the groups they head. Indeed, if they are suddenly removed through illness or transfer to another job, both productivity and morale may suffer greatly. In extreme cases, groups or work units may become incapable of carrying out their major functions until a new leader is obtained. Because leadership plays a key role in many organizational settings, it is important for you to gain a basic understanding of this process. In short, it is essential for you to know something about leaders—who they are, how they operate, and what effects they produce. To provide you with such knowledge, we focus on three major topics. First, we consider the question of *who becomes a leader*—why certain persons rise to positions of power and influence. Second, we describe several *leadership styles*—contrasting approaches adopted by leaders in their efforts to influence other persons. Then we turn to *leader effectiveness* and consider several factors that determine the degree to which leaders are successful in directing their groups or subordinates. Finally, we consider a variety of new directions in leadership.

leadership   The exercise of influence by individuals within work or social groups over other members.

278

*W*HO BECOMES A LEADER? SOME CONTRASTING ANSWERS

Few people become leaders. In fact, the vast majority of human beings spend their lives following rather than issuing directives. Relatively few attain even modest authority over others. And only a tiny number rise to positions from which they can exert influence over thousands or even millions of persons. These facts lead to an intriguing question: What factors set such persons apart from the rest of us? In other words, why do they and not others become leaders? Many answers to this puzzle have been offered. Most, though, attribute leadership to (1) something about the *persons* in question (that is, their possession of special traits), (2) something about the *situations* in which they find themselves, and (3) a *combination* of these factors. Gender and minority-group membership also appear to influence leadership.

The Trait Approach: In Search of "Born Leaders"

Are some people born to lead? Common sense seems to suggest that this is so. Great leaders such as Joan of Arc, George Washington, Winston Churchill, Mikhail Gorbachev, and Martin Luther King, Jr., do seem to differ from ordinary human beings in several ways. They also appear to share certain traits, such as iron wills, boundless energy, and driving ambition. To a lesser degree, even leaders lacking such worldwide fame seem different from their followers. Top executives, many politicians, and even sports celebrities often seem larger than life and possess an aura that sets them apart from other persons (see Figure 10.1). On the basis of such observations, early re-

---

Figure 10.1   **Leadership Traits: Some People May Be Born Leaders**

Some people seem to have a natural knack for effective leadership.

DILBERT reprinted by permission of United Features Syndicate.

searchers interested in leadership formulated a view known as the **great person theory.** According to this approach, all leaders possess key traits that set them apart from most other persons. Furthermore, these traits remain the same across time and across different groups. Thus all leaders have similar traits regardless of the time period in which they live and the type of group they lead. Consistent with this view, the central task of leadership research was seen as that of identifying these traits, and many researchers launched energetic efforts to accomplish this task.

Unfortunately, this work generally failed. Try as they might, supporters of the great person theory were unable to develop a short list of traits that produce leadership ability. In fact, after several decades of work on this topic, there seemed to be almost as many different lists of key leadership traits as there were individual investigators! More recent efforts to determine whether leaders and followers differ in measurable ways have been a bit more successful. For example, it has been found that persons who possess certain patterns of motives, such as a high need for power and low need for affiliation with others, tend to be more successful in leadership roles than persons who do not show these patterns.[2]

Similarly, it has been observed that political leaders tend to be higher in such traits as self-confidence, need for achievement, and dominance than nonleaders.[3] Traits have been used to predict the effectiveness of U.S. presidents. Not surprisingly, achievement drive and intelligence are related to a perception of greatness. Interestingly, being overly tidy was related to being rated as less effective, possibly because this trait is related to being pacifistic. Taller presidents and less attractive ones were also rated more favorably.[4,5] However, student leaders tend to be more attractive and have more mature faces.[6] Finally, some leaders are viewed as being charismatic because they are willing to go against the status quo, have a strong vision or goal, and are willing to take risks.[7]

It is important not to misunderstand this concept: None of these findings suggests that all leaders share the same traits, or that possession of these characteristics is required for leadership for all times and in all places. However, they do suggest that personal factors *can* play a role in leadership in some cases, and that in this respect, at least, there may be a grain of truth in the great person perspective.

The Situational Approach: Technical Skill versus Charisma

great person theory The view that leaders possess special traits that set them apart from others and that these traits are responsible for their assuming positions of power and authority.

Imagine the following scene: The top executives of a giant corporation are on their way to an important meeting. It is being held far out in the desert, at an estate owned by the president of another company with which they plan to merge. On the way, their limousine breaks down, many miles from any town. Who takes charge? Surprisingly, it is the driver—the only person who knows enough about motors to get the car started again. As he oversees repairs, he gives direct orders to vice presidents, members of the board, and other top officials. They willingly obey his commands without a murmur. Later, when they arrive at the meeting, the driver surrenders his authority and becomes an obedient subordinate once again.

While it may seem a bit farfetched, this incident actually illustrates an important point about leadership—one totally overlooked by the trait approach just described. Briefly, it is this idea: In many cases, the person most likely to act as a leader is not necessarily the awe-inspiring great woman or man whose charisma, charm, or power hypnotizes others into blind submission. Rather, it is the individual whose skills and competence happen to be most useful to the group in a given context. According to this view, often known as the **situational approach,** different persons may well rise to positions of authority under different conditions. What is crucial in determining who will take charge is the contribution each person can make to the group and its current needs. Thus, under appropriate circumstances, even normally meek, shy, and retiring individuals may come forward to direct the actions of others if they are best able to meet the group's requirements.

In addition, the situational approach suggests that when one individual remains in a position of leadership over time, this person *must* adjust his or her behavior to shifts in situational factors. In short, leaders must be flexible and take account of changes in important variables, such as their subordinates' motivation, confidence, and ability to perform their jobs.[8,9] Only if leaders show such flexibility will their effectiveness remain high.

In sum, the situational view argues that external pressures and factors, *not* personal characteristics or traits, are of central importance in determining who will become a leader and how successful such persons will be in performing this role. According to this view, the key question we should ask about leadership is not, What kind of person becomes a leader? Rather, it should be, What skills, knowledge, or abilities are needed by a group in a given situation, and who can best provide them? If we can answer these questions, the situational view contends, we can accurately predict who will lead at a given time and with what degree of success.

The Interactionist Approach: Leadership as a Two-Way Street

The trait and situational approaches described above offer sharply contrasting views of leadership. Yet they are similar in one key respect: Each presents a relatively simple answer to the question, Who becomes a leader? The trait approach replies that those persons possessing special characteristics emerge as leaders. The situational

situational approach   A view suggesting that the person who becomes the leader of a specific group is determined largely by situational factors (for example, the technical skill or knowledge needed for a particular task).

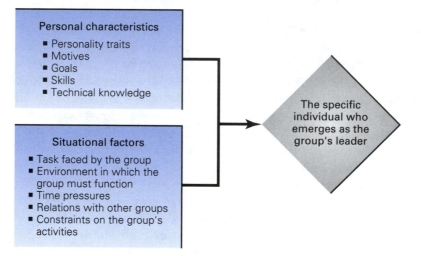

Figure 10.2   **Leadership: The Interactionist Approach**

According to the interactionist approach, which member of a group becomes its leader is determined both by personal characteristics and by situational factors. Thus, an individual with one set of traits or skills may rise to leadership under one set of conditions, while another person with very different traits may attain this position under other circumstances.

Personal characteristics
- Personality traits
- Motives
- Goals
- Skills
- Technical knowledge

Situational factors
- Task faced by the group
- Environment in which the group must function
- Time pressures
- Relations with other groups
- Constraints on the group's activities

The specific individual who emerges as the group's leader

approach points to those individuals whose skills are most useful to a group in a given context. Simple answers are always appealing, and these are no exception. At present, though, most experts on leadership have concluded that neither, by itself, is sufficient. Instead, they believe that both personal and situational factors must be taken into account—the **interactionist view.** In other words, they believe that it is the *interaction* between the traits possessed by individuals and situational conditions that determines who will rise to positions of power or influence (see Figure 10.2). Perhaps some concrete examples will help illustrate the nature of this key point.

First, consider a team of experts assembled by a large consulting firm and assigned the task of solving a problem posed by one of the firm's clients. Which member will assume leadership in this context? Probably, the one who is most creative—that is, most successful in proposing new avenues of attack on the problems or most effective in pulling the diverse skills of various team members together. In this context, then, creativity and an ability to combine diverse points of view may be the most important factors determining leadership. This oc-

interactionist view   A view contending that how a particular member of a group becomes its leader depends both on the personal characteristics of the individual and on many situational factors.

curs because in this particular situation these skills are the most desirable ones. Now, in contrast, consider a group of assembly-line workers in a large furniture factory. Who will emerge as the leader here? Perhaps in this case it will be the person who is most vocal in presenting complaints to the foreman. Or it may be the worker with the greatest seniority. It might even be the one who is most sociable. In any case, the characteristics related to leadership in this group would almost certainly be different from those in the first.

By now, the major point should be clear. According to the interactionist view, there is no simple answer to the question, Who becomes a leader? Rather, this approach realizes that different kinds of persons possessing different patterns of traits will rise to positions of authority in different situations. Clearly, this view is more complex than the trait or situational theories outlined earlier. However, it offers two major advantages over these older approaches. First, it is almost certainly more accurate. Thus, while it is not as simple or easy to grasp, it is closer to the truth. Second, it is optimistic in its implications about who can become a leader. Briefly, the interactionist approach suggests that almost anyone, possessing practically any combination of traits, can become a leader in *some* context. Thus, if any individual is not viewed as leadership material in a particular job or career, he or she can move to another position in which the traits he or she possesses are highly valued. Of course, certain traits seem to contribute to leadership in almost any situation, such as intelligence, ambition, decisiveness, and self-assurance. But aside from these basics, a wide range of personal skills and characteristics can contribute to success and influence in different careers. As we will note in Chapter 15, effective career planning or development should involve two crucial steps: (1) trying to identify your own major traits, and (2) selecting a career in which these will be valued and used to the fullest. Together, these steps will help ensure that you reach the highest level of success and leadership you are capable of attaining. (See Chapter 15 for further discussion of career development and planning.)

Gender and Leadership: Where Have All the Women Gone?

You have probably noticed that women are generally less likely to be leaders in organizations. In fact, even though women now fill about one-third of all management positions, they generally serve in low-level positions with relatively low pay.[10] Women account for considerably less than 10 percent of top executive positions.[11] Why do you think this is so? Is it because men and women have different interests or skills? Or is there some systematic exclusion of women based on unwarranted prejudices? As you might expect, there are a broad variety of reasons, such as differences in style, societal influences, and organizational biases.[12] One factor that is particularly problematic is the role of societal stereotypes.

Figure 10.3

Perceptions of Women Leaders: A Personal Bias

Individuals with conservative attitudes about female roles tend to rate women leaders most positively when these leaders are task-oriented. Individuals with liberal attitudes rate women leaders most positively when they are relation-oriented.

Based on Forsyth et al., 1997; see note 15.

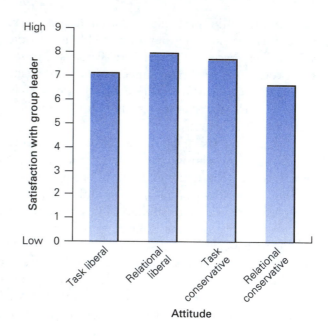

Sex role socialization in our society and the associated expectations and stereotypes may be partly responsible for gender-based differences in leaders. In particular, people tend to have **leadership prototypes**—that is, assumptions about the behaviors, traits, and abilities of effective leaders.[13] These prototypes tend to be more consistent with male roles than female roles, perhaps in part because people are more familiar with seeing men in leadership positions. The prototypical male role is to be task-oriented or directive, and the prototypical female role is to be more relationship-oriented. As a result, the task-oriented role may be more strongly associated with a perception of leadership. Therefore, it may not be surprising that both men and women have a preference for male bosses.[14] Interestingly, reactions to male and female leaders with these two different styles depend on whether people have a liberal or conservative attitude about women's roles. In one study involving groups led by women leaders, those who showed conservative perspectives toward female roles felt that the task-oriented leader was most effective, but those who had liberal attitudes responded positively to those with a relational style (see Figure 10.3).[15]

Even though stereotypes about leadership may be biased against women, no convincing evidence exists that men are better leaders than women.[16] Many women leaders have successfully overcome the societal obstacles.

leadership prototypes   Assumptions we hold about the characteristics of effective leaders.

Women who achieve high corporate positions often put off marriage and having children, or do without them.[17] They tend to be self-confident and have a high level of expertise.[18] So women can overcome the various barriers that exist, but they may have to make extra efforts to do so.

Minority-Group Members and Leadership: Another Bias?

We have documented that women are underrepresented in management and leadership positions in our society. Unfortunately, the situation with minority-group members' representation in management is as bad or worse.[19] Some surveys have indicated that minorities hold less than 10 percent of all management positions. It seems likely that many of the same factors we have discussed with regard to gender may account for this fact. The cultural and educational backgrounds of different ethnic groups may make them prefer positions not likely to lead to promotions or positions of power. For example, those who are strongly identified with black culture may have difficulties adjusting in an organization patterned after the needs of white men.[20] Differences in educational background do not seem to fully account for differences in management level or pay.[21] There is evidence that discrimination based in part on stereotypes about suitability for management may play a role.[22] The historical role of the white male in leadership positions in the United States may have led to leader stereotypes in favor of this type of person. There are also systematic barriers in organizations that limit the mobility of certain groups. For example, the in-group of white male managers may want to maintain their status at the expense of the groups of female or minority-group subordinates by promoting continuation of these group boundaries. As a result, these subordinates may not know what is going on in the organization or be involved in a network that makes them aware of opportunities. There may also be fewer opportunities to develop the mentor relationships with superiors that could aid the eventual promotion process.

How can the barriers to advancement by women and members of minority groups be overcome? Most corporations have developed affirmative action procedures to seek out and promote qualified women and minority-group members. Those who carry out these programs need to be careful to avoid the perception of tokenism. If it is evident that the person was selected solely on the basis of gender or racial/ethnic group, there are likely to be negative feelings on the part of the recipient, those who were not selected, and coworkers.[23] It is important that the procedure be fair and that it not be perceived as a quota system.[24] Special management training programs that provide women and minorities with the challenging opportunities required for promotion will be helpful.[25] Provision of mentors and support groups is also beneficial.[26] It may be necessary to provide incentives to top executives for working effectively to increase diversity in management. Diversity and fairness in the workplace should not be left to chance. Specific procedures or programs need to be instituted to ensure that racial, ethnic, and gender biases are minimized or eliminated as factors in career advancement.

LEADERSHIP STYLES: CONTRASTING APPROACHES TO THE TASK OF DIRECTING OTHERS

While leaders do not seem to differ from followers in a small number of easily stated ways, they *do* differ markedly from one another. Different leaders possess different motives and seek sharply contrasting goals. In addition, they use different techniques for exerting influence over other persons and directing their activities. Since such differences in leadership style strongly affect the atmosphere and functioning of groups, they are important and worth considering with care.

In one sense, there are probably as many unique styles of leadership as there are individual leaders. Each determines what works best for him or her and then uses this approach in a fairly consistent manner. But most differences between leaders seem to relate to two key dimensions. These vary from primary concern with output or productivity through primary concern with people and positive human relations.

Person-Oriented versus Production-Oriented Leaders: Showing Consideration or Initiating Structure

Have you ever seen a film or stage version of Dickens's *A Christmas Carol*? If so, you are already familiar with the extremes along two dimensions of leader behavior. Prior to his night with the spirits, Scrooge was interested in only one thing: carrying out his business in the most efficient and profitable manner possible. He had little interest in establishing friendly relations with his subordinates. After visits from the Ghosts of Christmas Past, Present, and Future, though, his focus changed. Scrooge's major concern became furthering the welfare of his long-suffering clerk, Bob Cratchit. Efficiency and profit were less important, and took a back seat to friendly human relations.

While few people ever experience such radical shifts in style as Dickens's character, evidence suggests that leaders differ greatly along both of these dimensions.[27] Some are *production-oriented* and focus mainly on getting the job done. Others are lower on this dimension and show less concern with attaining high levels of output or efficiency. Similarly, some leaders are *people-oriented* and show deep concern with establishing good relations with their subordinates. In contrast, others are low on this dimension and don't really care much about the quality of their relations with such persons.

At first glance, you might assume that these two dimensions (often termed **initiating structure** and **showing consideration**) are closely linked. That is, you might well guess that persons high on one must necessarily be low on the other. In fact, however, this is not the case. The two dimensions actually seem to be independent, so that a given manager can be high on both, high on one and low on the other, or low on both. This basic fact was emphasized some years ago by Blake and Mouton, in well-known research on management style.[28] They developed a special questionnaire designed to measure managers' positions along both dimensions. On the basis of answers to this questionnaire, individuals are assigned two numbers, one representing their position on concern with production and the other representing their position on concern with people. In both cases, scores can range from low (1) to high (9). For example, a manager who shows little concern with either production or people would receive a score of 1,1. Blake and Mouton describe this orientation as an *impoverished style* of management, and this term seems appropriate; indeed, it is hard to see how a person with this style could serve as an effective leader. In contrast, a manager who shows high concern with production but little concern with people would receive a score of 9,1. This orientation is termed *task management* and is obviously a common approach in work settings. The opposite pattern is one in which a manager shows high concern with people but low concern with production (1,9). It is described as the *country-club* style of management. As a final example, consider a manager who shows moderate concern with both people and production. Such a person would receive a score of 5,5—a pattern Blake and Mouton term *middle-of-the-road* management. Of course, other scores, too, are possible (for example, 3,9; 7,4; 9,5; 2,8). In fact, since concern with people and concern with production are measured on 9-point scales, 81 different combinations exist. All these patterns can be represented on a grid such as the one shown in Figure 10.4 on page 288. Examine it now, being sure to note the positions of the styles discussed above (such as the country-club and task management styles).

Now let us turn to a very practical question. Given that leaders vary greatly in their concern for production and their concern for people, what combination of these styles is best? This turns out to be a difficult question to answer for two major reasons. First, as you might guess, concern for people affects mainly morale or job satisfaction, while concern for productivity affects mainly output or efficiency. Thus, there tends to be a degree of tradeoff between them: High concern with people raises

initiating structure A style of leadership focused mainly on productivity or successful task accomplishment. Leaders who rate highly on this dimension often engage in such actions as organizing work activities, setting deadlines, and assigning individuals to specific tasks; also called task orientation.

showing consideration A style of leadership focused mainly on the establishment of positive relations between the leader and other group members; also called people orientation.

The Managerial Grid: A Useful Technique for Representing Leadership Style

Grids such as this one are often used to represent a manager's position on two key dimensions: concern for people and concern for production.

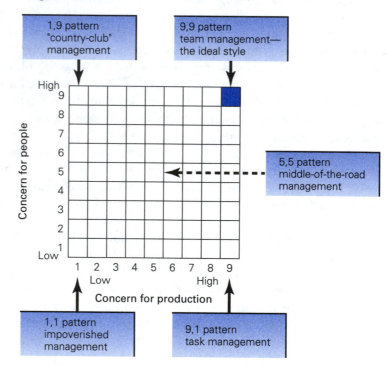

Based on a figure developed by Blake and Mouton, 1978; see note 28.

morale but may lower output, while high concern with productivity may enhance output but lower job satisfaction. Second, there are complex interactions between these factors. For example, a high level of people-concern on the part of a manager can yield a favorable work atmosphere and so enhance productivity as well as morale. Similarly, a high level of concern for productivity can sometimes enhance morale, especially when a work group faces stressful conditions and needs strong direction from its leader.[29] Because of such effects, there can be no simple answer to the question, Which pattern is best? It depends on the specific situation faced by a group. Having pointed out the complexities, though, we can now add that in many situations, leaders who are high on *both* dimensions (those showing the 9,9 pattern) seem to be the most effective.[30] (Blake and Mouton call this *team management*.) Apparently, the high concern for subordinates shown by such leaders encourages commitment and positive feelings among these persons, while their high concern with productivity converts this positive morale into good, efficient performance. In many cases, then, interest in people and interest in productivity are not incompatible approaches. On the contrary, they may combine to yield highly desirable results.

A long-term research program in Japan has yielded quite a bit of evidence for such an outcome. Misumi and his associates have used the terms *performance-oriented* and *maintenance-oriented* in distinguishing leader types.[31] The performance orientation is focused on goal achievement and problem solving. The maintenance orientation is concerned with the preservation and strengthening of the group. It appears that a leader style that combines both performance and maintenance orientation is most effective (a PM style).[32] Leaders who combine these orientations effectively tend to be moderately but not extremely high in performance and maintenance orientation. There are two reasons for the effectiveness of the combined performance and maintenance style. Performance-oriented leadership is seen as pressure and control in the absence of maintenance behaviors. When maintenance behaviors are present, performance behaviors are seen as helpful planning and the provision of expertise.

Not all of us react the same way to different leadership styles. To check on how your own preferences may play a role, see the *Experiential Exercise* on page 305.

Gender and Style

One additional factor that seems to affect managers' leadership style is gender. Research findings indicate that, in general, females are more participative or democratic than males.[33] For example, a study of female executives found that women lead by building relationships, sharing information, and fostering an atmosphere of inclusion. That finding does not mean, however, that women leaders can be pushed around. In fact, they tend to be intellectually competent, assertive, and confident.[34]

The gender difference in leadership style may be the result of gender-role socialization.[35] In general, women are expected to be *communal* in orientation. They are supposed to be friendly, emotionally expressive, unselfish, and concerned with the welfare of others. Men, on the other hand, are expected to be *agentic* in orientation. They are supposed to be independent, assertive, and competent. These orientations presumably derive in part from the different roles they have typically occupied in family and occupational settings. Women do a disproportionate amount of the child rearing and domestic work and have tended to be in gender-typed occupations, such as secretary or nurse. Differences in social behavior of men and women may be results of people's trying to act consistently with their gender roles. In groups, this may be reflected by men being task-oriented and women being socially oriented.[36] Males are also more likely to provide negative feedback than females.[37]

A number of studies have examined leadership emergence in leaderless groups. These studies indicate that degree of participation in groups is strongly related to being perceived or selected as a group leader.[38] In fact, the frequency of participation may be more important than the quality of one's participation.[39] This may be in part because a high participation level is seen as indicating a strong motivation to contribute to the group.[40] Given their sex-role socialization, men can be expected to dominate in mixed-sex groups and emerge as leaders. This seems to be particularly evident in classrooms, where men are more likely to talk than women are.[41] The gender bias in favor of men is primarily evident when leadership measures focus on task-oriented behaviors. When leadership measures focus on social contributions, such as helping with interpersonal problems or group morale, women emerge more often as leaders. Interestingly, the general tendency of men to emerge as leaders becomes reduced the longer the group members interact. Apparently, increased time together allows members to discover each other's real abilities and to rely less on gender-based expectations. It is certainly a positive sign that in real-world groups that work together for extensive periods of time, stereotypes based on gender, race, or ethnic group may be overcome by the evidence of actual competencies of the group members.

One factor in favor of women leaders is the fact that many organizations are changing to a team-oriented structure. This type of structure involves more participation in decision making by employees and a flatter organizational hierarchy. In fact, organizations that recently made one top 100 list for best organizations tended to exhibit "feminine" qualities, such as concern for the individual, family orientation, sharing, and collaboration.[42] The feminine style of leadership may be better suited for a team-based organization than the masculine style is. This type of organization needs a cooperative approach that involves collaboration, empathy, and ability to listen. The future therefore appears bright for both men and women who possess these skills.

Cultural Differences in Style

There appear to be significant differences in the leadership styles that tend to be dominant or preferred in different cultures. There is little doubt that in the United States, the person-oriented style is preferred. This style appears to be less important for Germans. They appear to be more tolerant of task orientation on the part of leaders and coworkers.[43] Furthermore, in Asia, superiors are obligated by the cultural mores to be effective leaders. This may involve being concerned about the personal and family life of the employee. For example, in India, the mostly male leaders are expected to take a fatherly role and treat the employees as family. In the United States, a more objective and impersonal style of leadership is expected.[44] Therefore, managers who deal with international work groups have to be sensitive to the different expectations of these group. A style that works well with one group may result in negative reactions from another group. The best policy is probably to be sensitive to the reactions of a particular group and to adjust the leadership style to fit with its needs and expectations.

$\mathcal{L}$EADER EFFECTIVENESS: WHO SUCCEEDS AND WHO FAILS?

Most groups have a leader. Yet not all groups perform effectively or attain their major goals. One reason for this basic fact centers on differences in leader effectiveness. All leaders, it appears, are *not* created equal. Good ones assist their groups in many ways and help ensure their success. But poor ones, like the proverbial lead weight, drag the groups they head down to failure and despair. Differences in leader competence, then, are important and have a wide range of practical implications. But what factors cause a leader to be effective or ineffective? Why, in short, are some persons so successful in this role and others so disappointing? Our discussion of leadership would be sadly incomplete without some attention to these matters. We therefore focus on a framework that offers valuable insights into the nature and causes of leader competence: Fiedler's *contingency theory* of leader effectiveness.

Fiedler's Contingency Model: Matching Leaders and Tasks

Leadership, we have noted, does not occur in a vacuum. Rather, leaders attempt to exert their influence on group members within the context of specific situations. Given that these can vary greatly along many dimensions, it seems reasonable to expect that no single style or approach to leadership will always be best. Rather, the most effective strategy will vary from one situation to another.

This basic fact lies at the heart of a theory of leader effectiveness developed by Fiedler.[45] Fiedler describes his model as a **contingency theory,** and this term seems apt, for the basic assumption of the theory is this: The contribution of a leader to successful performance by his or her group is determined both by the leader's traits and by various features of the situation in which the group operates. To fully understand leader effectiveness, the theory contends, both factors must be taken into account.

With respect to characteristics possessed by leaders, Fiedler has focused most attention on what he terms *esteem for the least preferred coworker* (or *LPC* for short). This refers to leaders' tendency to evaluate the person

contingency theory   A theory suggesting that leader effectiveness is determined both by characteristics of the leader and the degree of situational control this person can exert over subordinates.

with whom they find it most difficult to work in a favorable or unfavorable manner. Leaders who perceive this person in negative terms (low LPC leaders) seem primarily motivated to attain successful task performance. In short, they are primarily production-oriented. In contrast, leaders who perceive their least preferred coworker in a positive light (high LPC leaders) seem concerned mainly with establishing good relations with their subordinates; they are primarily people-oriented.

But which of these two types of leaders is more effective? Fiedler's answer: It depends. And what it depends on is several situational factors. Specifically, Fiedler suggests that whether low LPC or high LPC leaders prove more effective depends on the degree to which the situation provides the leader with *control* or *influence* over group members. This, in turn, is determined largely by three factors: the nature of the leader's *relations with group members* (the extent to which he or she enjoys their support and loyalty), the *structure of the task* faced by the group (ranging from unstructured to highly structured), and the leader's *position power* (his or her ability to enforce the compliance of subordinates). Combining these three factors, the leader's situational control can range from very high (positive relations with members, a highly structured task, high position power) to very low (negative relations with members, an unstructured task, low position power).

Now that we have examined both the leader characteristics and situational factors Fiedler views as most important, we can return to the central question: When are different types of leaders most effective? Fiedler suggests that low LPC leaders (those who are task-oriented) will be superior when situational control is either low or high. However, high LPC leaders (those who are people-oriented) will shine when situational control is moderate (see Figure 10.5). The reasoning behind these predictions can be summarized as follows.

Under conditions of low situational control, groups need considerable direction and structure to accomplish their tasks. Since low LPC leaders, with their focus on task performance, are more likely to provide this than high LPC leaders, they will usually be superior in such cases. Similarly, low LPC leaders will also have an edge in situations that offer the leader a *high* degree of situational control. Here, low LPC leaders realize that their goal of task accomplishment is likely to be met. As a result, they may relax and adopt a hands-off style—one that aids their groups in this context. In contrast, high LPC leaders, realizing that they already enjoy good relations with their followers, may shift their attention to task performance. As a result, they may begin behaving in ways their subordinates perceive as needless meddling!

Turning to situations offering the leader *moderate* control, a different set of circumstances prevails. Here, conditions are mixed, and attention to positive human relations is often needed to smooth ruffled feathers and ensure good performance. High LPC leaders, with their people orientation, often have an important edge in such situations—especially since low LPC leaders may be worried about attaining good performance and tend to act in directive, autocratic ways.

𝒻igure 10.5   **Contingency Theory: Some Major Predictions**

Fiedler's contingency theory predicts that low LPC leaders (those who are primarily task-oriented) will be superior to high LPC leaders (those who are primarily people oriented) when situational control is either very low or high. The opposite will be true when situational control is moderate.

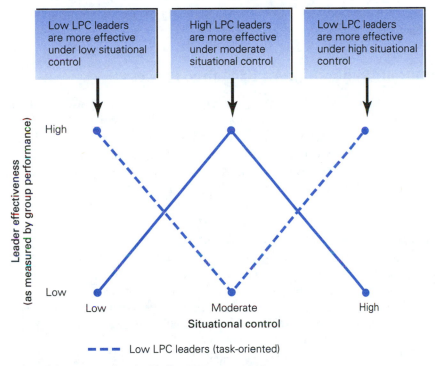

Adapted from suggestions by Fiedler, 1978; see note 45.

To summarize: Fiedler predicts that low LPC leaders, with their focus on task performance, will prove more effective under conditions of either low or high situational control. In contrast, high LPC leaders, with their focus on personal relations, will have a major edge under conditions where such control is moderate.

How has the theory fared when put to actual test? The results of some studies lend support to the theory, but not all findings have been consistent with it. While laboratory studies have tended to support Fiedler's view, field investigations (those carried out with existing groups operating in a wide range of contexts) have not been as favorable.[16] Such investigations have sometimes yielded results contrary to what contingency theory would predict. The theory has been criticized on several bases. For example, a degree of ambiguity exists with respect to classifying specific situations along the dimension of situational control. Unless situations can be accurately classified as very low, low, moderate, and so on in this regard, predictions concerning leader effectiveness are difficult to make. Similarly, some critics have questioned the adequacy of the questionnaire used to assess leaders' standings on the LPC dimension. In particular, the reliability of this measure does not seem to be as high as that of other widely used tests.[47] Despite these problems, Fiedler's theory is widely recognized as one that has added much to our understanding of the factors influencing leader effectiveness.

Transactional Leadership: An Exchange Process

A group or organization exists because it has certain goals. Leaders can be seen as those individuals who are charged with motivating people to achieve these goals. One way to accomplish this task is to control the reward process. **Transactional leadership** models assume that effective leadership is based on a give-and-take process in which the leader provides various rewards in return for a subordinate's accomplishments.[48] Thus leaders may respond to a subordinate's commitment to a task, loyalty, or ingenuity by giving the person more freedom or responsibility, emotional support, and attention.

An important aspect of transactional leadership is goal setting.[49] Instead of specifying a particular behavior, leaders may specify desired outcomes. For example, a car dealer may set a goal of selling a certain number of cars in one month for each employee. Research on goal setting suggests that the most effective goals are specific, difficult but not impossible, and accepted by the subordinates. Goal setting increases motivation and results in increased self-confidence or self-efficacy when the goals are attained.[50]

Although this process may sound fairly straightforward, goal setting is actually a bit more complicated. The major problem is, How do leaders persuade their subordinates to accept challenging goals? When leaders have the respect of their followers and a relationship exists between achieving the goal and receiving rewards, the followers may take the goals provided by the leader quite seriously. Others suggest, however, that goals should be set in a participatory manner[51] to ensure that subordinates will accept the goal. Which approach do you think is the correct one? Possibly both have some merit. When we can establish our own goal, we will probably feel a high degree of commitment to it. If we are not highly motivated, however, we might be tempted to set a rather low goal so that we can be sure to achieve it.[52] Externally set goals—that is, goals dictated by a supervisor—may be seen as a challenge and may motivate us to a higher level of achievement than we would have set for ourselves. When such goals are subsequently achieved, they certainly will have a strong positive effect on our self-esteem.[53]

transactional leadership   A leadership style based on providing rewards for accomplishments of subordinates.

One type of leader who is able to motivate people to achieve beyond their expectations is a charismatic or transformational leader.[54]

Charismatic or Transformational Leaders: Important in Times of Need

One of the continuing searches in our society is for strong and dynamic leaders who will help us overcome our problems and lead us to prosperity. There have been many instances in history of such leaders who have had a tremendous impact on their country and the world (for example, Hitler, Napoleon, Gandhi). In the business world, individuals such as Ross Perot and Bill Gates probably come to mind. Analyses of **charismatic leaders** suggest that they share certain characteristics.[55,56] They have a clear vision about where they want to go and how to get there. Of course, it is one thing to have a vision and quite another to inspire followers about one's vision. One way the latter is accomplished is by relating this vision to the needs and values of the followers. Herb Kelleher, CEO of Southwest Airlines, has inspired his employees by his vision for a company that provides inexpensive, low-frill travel but allows maximal employee involvement in company operations and is sensitive to employees' needs. The charismatic leader uses unconventional behaviors to achieve the group's goals. Kelleher has his airplanes painted in bright colors, served connections ignored by other airlines, and used a first-come-first-served policy instead of assigned seating. Additional characteristics of charismatic leaders are a willingness to take risks and make personal sacrifices, sensitivity to the needs and feelings of others, self-confidence, and a high level of energy.[57]

Charismatic leadership can also be seen as part of the broader style of **transformational leadership**.[58] Bass and his colleagues have developed a Multifactor Leadership Questionnaire (MLQ) to assess the various components of this type of leadership.[59] Transformational leaders possess three characteristics in addition to charisma. They provide inspirational motivation by sharing a vision and communicating high expectations. They intellectually stimulate followers to be innovative and creative by questioning old assumptions and approaches to problems. They give individualized consideration to each follower's needs for growth and achievement by offering supportive mentoring and coaching. Studies of this type of leadership in industry, the military, and educational settings have shown that transformational leaders are rated as being more effective and providing a more satisfying work environment than transactional leaders or laissez-faire leaders. In addition, studies using objective indicators such as church attendance, financial success, and military performance have found that trans-

charismatic leaders Leaders who exert powerful effects on their followers and to whom several special traits are attributed (such as possession of an idealized vision or goal, willingness to engage in unconventional behaviors to reach it).

transformational leadership A leadership style that involves inspiration, intellectual stimulation, and individual consideration.

Figure 10.6   **Women as Managers: Transformational Leaders**

A study of middle- and upper-level managers of *Fortune* 500 companies found that women were rated higher than men by their subordinates on the four components of transformational leadership.

Based on Bass and Avolio, 1994; see note 60.

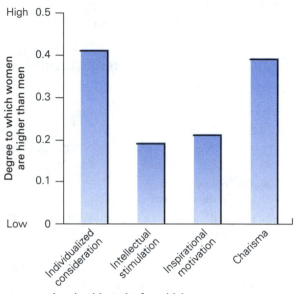

Leadership traits for which women surpass men

formational leadership can be linked to greater effectiveness or success. As some bias exists against women leaders, as noted earlier, you may be surprised that female managers or supervisors are rated as being higher than men on transformational leadership (see Figure 10.6).[60]

Why do transformational leaders stimulate their followers to attain high levels of performance? We do not have a definitive answer, but a number of reasonable possibilities have been suggested. One important factor appears to be the high level of trust that followers have for transformational leaders.[61] Transformational leaders also influence the self-concept of their followers. Their followers have increased self-esteem, believe that their work and life is meaningful, and identify strongly with the leader and the group.[62] As a result, they are likely to be very devoted or loyal to their leader, excited about the leader's idea, and willing to make significant personal sacrifices for the broader goal or vision outlined by the leader.[63]

Although transformational leadership can be very positive in developing or rejuvenating corporations, some potential negatives exist. Transformational leaders may be so tightly wedded to their vision that they fail to adapt to changing circumstances. Such leaders may also ignore the needs of their followers and encourage them to attempt unreasonable goals.[64] There are many examples of groups being led in destructive directions by charismatic leaders of countries or organizations. Thus it is not just important to have strong and dynamic leadership; leaders also need to have values that help build positive relationships among individuals and groups and that are focused on the broader welfare of society and the environment. It is interesting to see that increasing numbers of organizations are projecting images of themselves as good citizens of society as well as generators of profit. Possibly, we are finally learning that where leaders take us may be the most important issue for the survival of our planet and the ability of its diverse populations to live in harmony.

NEW DIRECTIONS IN LEADERSHIP

It is hard to say what is changing more rapidly—technology or the way that organizations function. The constant change in technology has transformed the nature of many jobs. Indeed, many people now work at home and thus quite independently from others in the organization. How does that separation affect the role of the leader or manager? On the other hand, corporations are relying increasingly on work teams that have a high degree of authority in managing their own affairs (see Chapter 9). Do these groups still need leaders or managers? We will examine some of the ways that leadership practices have evolved to adapt to these new realities.

Teamwork: Sharing the Power

In recent years, there has been an increased use of teams in organizations as part of a move toward participative management. (See Chapter 9.) These work groups typically allow employees to be involved in decision making.[65] This shared power can range from just having input into decision making to actually sharing the decision power. There is some evidence that participative decision making increases commitment, morale, and profitability.[66] However, sharing decision making and power does not always lead to positive outcomes.[67] If recommendations or decisions are not received positively by upper management, team members may become discouraged. Managers may also need special training to effectively implement shared decision making. Many may resist giving up part of their power, especially if they are held accountable for the results. However, the experience and expertise gained by group members who are allowed participative decision-making roles may allow top management to focus on the broader developmental concerns of the organization. Firms such as Southwestern Bell and General Electric have instituted procedures to ensure that top managers will delegate as much power as possible to subordinates.[68] So in a way, effective leadership from that perspective becomes effective delegation and sharing of one's power with others. Although those who have a strong desire for power may resist this move, the ability of corporations to compete effectively may depend on it.

In some organizations, explicit efforts are made to give as much authority and power as possible to those in the lowest ranks. This approach is called **empowerment.**

empowerment The practice of giving as much authority and power as possible to those at the lowest ranks of the organization.

It is assumed that employees will be more motivated and challenged under such a system than in cases where the authority resides mostly in upper management.

It appears that the participative management style would be the most comfortable one when working with teams or sharing power. But if a manager has a more directive or task-oriented style, how can he or she be trained to effectively share power and deal with teams? Working with effective models or mentors may be helpful. If high-level executives model the sharing of power, lower-level executives may follow their lead. Simulations that involve role playing may also be useful.[69] Unfortunately, the research on leadership style and team performance has not been very definitive about the style that is best for teams. There is some evidence that teams with autocratic and socially distant leaders perform best.[70] Possibly these types of leaders help keep teams focused on their task better than democratic and socially close leaders. Maybe having a democratic team and a democratic leader may be too much of a good thing. However, as with most of the other findings on leadership, it will probably depend on the type of task and team. It is quite possible that the best leader may be one who has both a positive personal style and task orientation, as suggested by Blake and Mouton's managerial grid.[71]

There are some general guidelines for increasing the effectiveness of team leaders.[72,73]

1. All members should know who the team leader is and should respect this person's authority.
2. Team leaders should keep the group focused on the task. They should clearly verbalize the team goal.
3. Team leaders should be good communicators. They need to keep the team members informed, ask for input, and discuss areas of concern.
4. Team leaders should recognize the importance of both task and team skills.
5. Team leaders should obtain training to develop the appropriate leadership skills for teamwork.
6. The organization needs to provide rewards and information for effective functioning of the team.

Leadership and the New Technology: New Styles for a New Age

Today, an increasing amount of work is done on computers. As much of this work can be performed at home or in locations distinct from the physical location of a corporation, workers may have limited face-to-face interaction with their supervisors. Consequently, the leader's personal style may have a somewhat limited influence on his or her subordinates. This constraint may frustrate those leaders who enjoy personal relations with their employees or those who are very task-oriented and like to monitor subordinates closely. So what is a leader to do?

Leaders can still have a considerable effect by communicating with their distant employees. For example, when groups must work on various tasks using computers, leaders can send comments and suggestions to the group. One study has examined whether the transformational or transactional style is more effective in this situation. In this study, the transactional leader emphasized specific goals and rewards related to the tasks. This type of leader expressed confidence in the group and emphasized the importance of working together, learning, and creativity. In general, transformational leadership was related to group feelings of effectiveness and these feelings led to more effectiveness in the task of writing a group report. On the other hand, transactional leadership was related to greater effectiveness when the task involved generating ideas.[74] Possibly some mixture of transactional and transformational leadership may prove most beneficial when groups are working in a distributed or distant fashion. Specific goals may help groups to complete specific tasks (for example, generating ideas), and feelings of group effectiveness may provide the motivation to achieve success on broader group projects or goals (such as writing a group report).

Leadership Development: Making Good Leaders

Although we have discussed many different perspectives about leadership, researchers have made several rather consistent findings. Those who have surveyed the literature suggest that some general rules or principles of good leadership exist:[75–77]

1. Leaders need a clear and compelling vision to motivate their followers.
2. Leaders must be perceived as trustworthy and competent.
3. Leaders must develop a relationship with followers that inspires them to attain group and organizational goals.
4. Leaders need to use the resources of the followers effectively by employing strategies appropriate to the environment or situation.

How do we develop these types of qualities and others that make us effective leaders? Achieving effective leadership is a difficult and complex task. Executives and managers need a broad variety of skills to deal with their employees effectively. They must know how to best motivate their employees and how to optimize their productivity and satisfaction. Obviously, most of us could use some help in developing such skills. Leadership development programs are intended to fill that gap.

Leadership development programs are designed to increase specific competencies of leaders. These competencies, of course, vary from one organization to another. For example, AT&T lists continuous learning, strategic thinking, building partnerships, and creating a climate for success as some of the characteristics that its leaders should strive to attain.[78] Personal values and missions have been emphasized at some other organizations.[79]

How do we go about leadership development? A broad range of techniques are available.[80] Multirater feedback (also known as 360 feedback; discussed in Chapter

15) from coworkers, managers, subordinates, and customers may provide useful information on how well a person is achieving her goals, especially if this feedback is rather consistent. If the leader values this information and feels that change is possible, he or she may be motivated to make some modifications or look for training. Leaders may seek the assistance of coaches who provide one-on-one training in a specific area. For example, coaches can help leaders develop competencies in the use of computers, conflict management, and time management. Another popular option includes action learning programs, structured sessions in which people work together to solve specific problems. They may involve team-building exercises; some emphasize overcoming physical and mental challenges in outdoor settings. Sometimes leaders attend formal programs at a university or institute that focus on particular leadership skills. Finally, much development may occur on the job. For example, Executive Vice President of Operations for American Airlines, Bob Baker, has worked in practically every part of that airline during his 30-year career. He feels that it has given him "a unique ability to see things from multiple sides."[81]

How effective are these leadership development programs or experiences? Unfortunately, the research conducted to date does not allow us to reach a definitive conclusion.[82] Coaching and action learning programs often receive favorable reviews from the participants, but the positive response does not necessarily mean that they actually enhance leadership development. It probably takes a combination of experiences over an extended period of time to produce significant and long-lasting results. Most importantly, leaders must be motivated to improve their capabilities if any of these leadership development programs is to have much effect.

Self-Leadership: A Style for Today's Worker?

The typical work situation has undergone many changes in the past few decades. More people work collaboratively in teams, and in many cases these team members may work fairly independently or in different locations (Chapter 9). Although a need still exists for some sort of supervision or accountability, an external leader may no longer serve as an important source of motivation. Instead, workers may need to develop the ability of **self-leadership**.[83] That is, they may need to inspire themselves through self-direction and self-motivation to perform their jobs. Self-leadership focuses on the intrinsic rewards or value of a person's own work and the strategies the worker can employ to increase his or her self-leadership.

Three types of strategies are available to enhance self-leadership. *Work context strategies* focus on making the environment more conducive to intrinsic motivation—for example, making it more pleasing both aesthetically and socially or finding the right environmental conditions for doing a particular task. For instance, some difficult tasks should probably be tackled with minimal distraction, while other tasks might benefit from some social stimulation.[84] *Task per-*

self-leadership Being self-directed and motivated in your job.

formance strategies attempt to increase the intrinsic motivation for the task itself—for example, by the worker having more freedom or self-control in doing his or her job and by the establishment of subgoals that the worker can achieve by completing a particular task. *Thought self-leadership strategies* focus on developing constructive ways of thinking that increase a person's optimism and sense of self-efficacy.[85] This effort may rely on positive self-talk and mental imagery. For example, if you are going to give a speech, you might tell yourself, "I can do this," and imagine yourself giving a successful talk. With enough repetitions of these types of thought processes, you may become truly confident about your ability to give a good speech. Of course, it will also be important to achieve the necessary subgoals involved in preparing for the speech (task performance strategies) and find the best situation to prepare for it (work context strategies). Figure 10.7 summarizes the three self-leadership strategies.

How do we develop self-leadership skills? Training for self-leadership usually involves guided practice in the three different strategies over a period of weeks.[86,87] The main aim of the training process is to develop skills that allow the individual to adjust effectively to different work situations. This effort will require careful self-observation and assessment and the use of the appropriate strategies to motivate the person to a high level of performance. Some people may benefit more from this type of training than others do. Individuals who have low self-confidence, are not open to new experiences, and are not very conscientious may find it difficult to acquire these types of skills. Of course, those types of people are precisely the individuals who would potentially benefit the most from self-leadership training. Other people may already have a high level of the skills required for self-leadership and therefore derive very little benefit from training.[88]

Figure 10.7 **Self-Leadership: Three Effective Strategies**

Self-leadership can be enhanced by certain strategies.

Based on Neck et al., 1995; see note 83.

Self-leadership skills are particularly important when people work in teams that have considerable freedom in conducting their activities.[89] Although teams may have informal leaders and face some supervision by external authorities, they seem to work best when they are allowed to manage their own duties (see Chapter 9). If team members have high levels of self-leadership skills, the team is likely to function more effectively. Team members need to have skills in self-control and self-management so that they will be intrinsically motivated, effective in goal setting, and able to take corrective actions when necessary.

Leadership versus Management: Some Important Differences

This chapter has discussed leadership in general terms, using the term "leader" to refer to any type of leader, whether inside or outside of organizations. A fairly common leadership position in organizations is that of manager over some group of employees. The functions of leadership and management can be quite different. In many cases, the function of management is to maintain order and efficiency. This function involves such tasks as planning, budgeting, organizing, staffing, monitoring, and problem solving. In contrast, the aim of leadership is to produce useful change.[90] This function involves developing a vision, communicating this vision, and motivating others to follow. The services of managers are, of course, needed to achieve the vision and goals that are espoused by the leader. Thus organizations need both roles.

The number of managers and leaders needed will vary from organization to organization. More complex organizations may need more managers, and organizations that require considerable change or undergo continual changes may need more people with effective leadership skills.

Guidelines for Effective Human Relations

Using What You've Learned

In this chapter we examined a broad range of principles and findings about leadership. Although few rules apply to every situation, there are some general guidelines suggested by the various findings we have discussed. These are summarized on page 303 for your consideration. Remember, no rule works 100 percent in every situation. However, these guidelines should help improve your success as a leader in a wide variety of situations.

Guidelines for Effective Human Relations (continued)

- If you want to be a leader, you will need self-confidence and assertiveness.

- If you are in a management position, your best leadership style may be one that shifts from person-oriented to production-oriented as the need arises for different styles.

- Effective leadership involves having a vision and inspiring followers with this vision.

- Team leaders need special leadership skills. They need to communicate effectively with team members and clearly outline the task and goal.

- If you are not inclined to be a leader, you can help make a leader successful by being a motivated and responsive follower. However, it is important to maintain a sense of independence. Leaders do not always know best or have your best interests in mind. Make sure the leader's motives are consistent with yours and that of the organization. If not, you may provide an important service to yourself and the organization by asserting your independence and providing corrective feedback. Remember, where you are being led is often more important than how you are being led.

Summary

In most groups, one individual exerts more influence than any of the others. Such persons are generally termed *leaders,* and they play a crucial role in the groups or organizations they head. At one time, it was assumed that all leaders share certain traits and that they rise to positions of authority because of these special characteristics. Now, however, it is realized that situational factors (for example, the tasks faced by a group, the environment in which it must operate) are also important. Thus, according to the modern interactionist perspective, different individuals possessing different patterns of traits will tend to become leaders in different situations.

Leaders differ greatly in terms of their concern with production and their concern with people. Some evidence suggests that leaders who rate highly on both of these dimensions may be the most effective in a wide range of situations. Women tend to be more participative in their style than men.

Many factors determine a leader's effectiveness. According to Fiedler's contingency theory, both the leader's characteristics and several aspects of the situation are crucial in this respect. Specifically, this theory contends that production-oriented leaders are more effective than people-oriented ones under conditions in which the leader has either high or low control over the group. In contrast, people-oriented leaders are more effective under conditions in which the leader has moderate control over the group.

Charismatic leaders sometimes motivate group members or organizations to high levels of effectiveness. Teamwork allows employees to share the decision making in organizations. Team leaders need special skills to help teams be productive. Team members and those who work at home may need self-leadership skills. Leadership development programs may be useful in helping individuals develop the appropriate leadership skills.

Key Terms

charismatic leaders, p. 295
contingency theory, p. 291
empowerment, p. 297
great person theory, p. 280
initiating structure, p. 287
interactionist view, p. 282
leadership, p. 278

leadership prototypes, p. 284
self-leadership, p. 300
showing consideration, p. 287
situational approach, p. 281
transactional leadership, p. 294
transformational leadership, p. 295

Experiential Exercise

What Leadership Style Do You Prefer?

We have discussed different styles of leadership. The major styles are (1) directive and production-oriented and (2) participative and people-oriented. These styles may be differentially effective in various work situations. One factor that may influence the effectiveness of a particular leadership style is the attitude of the potential followers. Some may strongly prefer a participative or people-oriented approach, others a directive and task-oriented style. Which of these contrasting styles do you think you prefer? To gain some insight into this issue, respond to the statements on page 305. If you agree with the statement, write *Y.* If you disagree, write *N.*

_____ 1. I like to know exactly what is expected of me at work.

_____ 2. I like a leader who monitors workers closely.

_____ 3. Leaders should primarily be concerned with promoting worker morale.

_____ 4. One of the most important characteristics of a leader is willingness to listen to subordinates.

_____ 5. The most important quality for a leader is the ability to get the job done.

_____ 6. It is more important for a leader to have good relations with workers than to constantly focus on productivity.

_____ 7. Leaders should keep their distance socially from their employees.

_____ 8. People will take advantage of leaders who are friendly and oriented toward having good relations with employees.

_____ 9. Employees should play an important role in management decisions.

_____ 10. It is important for leaders to show a personal interest in employees.

If you answered *Y* to three or more of items 1, 2, 5, 7, and 8 and *N* to three or more of items 3, 4, 6, 9, and 10, you are probably direction-oriented. That is, you are probably best suited for work situations oriented to productivity and formal leader/follower relations. If you answered *Y* to three or more of items 3, 4, 6, 9, and 10 and *N* to three or more of items 1, 2, 5, 7, and 8, you are participation-oriented and probably would work best in situations where there is likely to be a focus on developing positive and informal leader/follower relations. If you do not show a definite pattern in one direction or the other, you may do well under either type of leadership situation.

Notes

1. Kotter, J. P. (1990). *A force for change: How leadership differs from management.* New York: Macmillan.

2. Spangler, W. D., & House, R. J. (1991). Presidential effectiveness and the leadership motive profile. *Journal of Personality and Social Psychology, 60,* 439–455.

3. Costantini, E., & Craik, K. H. (1980). Personality and politicians: California party leaders, 1960–1976. *Journal of Personality and Social Psychology, 38,* 641–666.

4. McCann, S. J. H. (1992). Alternative formulas to predict the greatness of U.S. presidents: Personological, situational, and zeitgeist factors. *Jour-*

nal of Personality and Social Psychology, 62, 469–479.

5. Simonton, D. K. (1987). *Why presidents succeed: A political psychology of leadership.* New Haven, CT: Yale University Press.

6. Cherulnik, P. D., Turns, L. C., & Wilderman, S. K. (1990). Physical appearance and leadership: Exploring the role of appearance-based attribution in leader emergence. *Journal of Applied Social Psychology, 20,* 1530–1539.

7. Conger, J. A., & Kanungo, R. N. (1987). Toward a behavioral theory of charismatic leadership in organizations. *Academy of Management Review, 12,* 637–647.

8. Hersey, P., & Blanchard, K. H. (1982). *Management of organizational behavior* (4th ed.). Englewood Cliffs, NJ: Prentice Hall.

9. Graeff, C. L. (1983). The situational leadership theory: A critical review. *Academy of Management Review, 8,* 285–291.

10. Hymowitz, C., & Schellhardt, T. D. (1986, March 24). The glass ceiling. *Wall Street Journal,* pp. 1D, 4D–5D.

11. Morrison, A. M., & Von Glinow, M. A. (1990). Women and minorities in management. *American Psychologist, 45,* 200–208.

12. Ragins, B. R., & Sundstrom, E. (1989). Gender and power in organizations: A longitudinal perspective. *Psychological Bulletin, 105,* 51–88.

13. Lord, R. G., & Maher, K. J. (1991) *Leadership and information processing: Linking perceptions and performance.* Boston: Unwin Hyman.

14. Eagly, A. H., & Karau, S. (1991). Gender and the emergence of leaders: A meta-analysis. *Journal of Personality and Social Psychology, 60,* 685–710.

15. Forsyth, D. F., Heiney, M. M., & Wright, S. S. (1997). Biases in appraisals of women leaders. *Group Dynamics: Theory, Research, and Practice, 1,* 98–103.

16. Eagly, A. H., Karau, S., & Makhijani, M. (1995). Gender and the effectiveness of leaders: A meta-analysis. *Psychological Bulletin, 117*(1), 125–145.

17. Fierman, J. (1990, July 30). Why women still don't hit the top. *Fortune,* pp. 41–62.

18. See note 12.

19. See note 11.

20. Thomas, D. A., & Alderfer, C. P. (1989). The influence of race on career dynamics: Theory and research on minority career experiences. In M. Arthur, D. Hall, & B. Lawrence (eds.), *Handbook of career theory.* Cambridge, UK: Cambridge University Press.

21. Cabezas, A., Shinagawa, L. H., & Kawaguchi, G. (1989). Income and status differences between white and minority Americans: A persistent inequality. In S. Chan (ed.), *Persistent inequality in the United States.* Lewiston, NY: Edwin Mellen Press.

22. Larwood, L., Szwajkowski, E., & Rose, S. (1988). Sex and race discrimination resulting from manager-client relationships: Applying the rational bias theory of managerial discrimination. *Sex Roles, 18,* 9–29.

23. Turner, M. E., & Pratkanis, A. R. (1994). Affirmative action as help: A review of recipient reactions to preferential selection and affirmative action. *Basic and Applied Social Psychology, 15,* 43–70.

24. Nacoste, R. B. (1994). If empowerment is the goal . . . : Affirmative action and social interaction. *Basic and Applied Social Psychology, 15,* 87–112.

25. McCall, M. W., Jr., Lombardo, M. M., & Morrison, A. M. (1988). *The lessons of experience.* Lexington, MA: Lexington Books.

26. See note 11.

27. Halpin, A. W., & Winer, B. J. (1957). A factorial study of the leader behavior descriptions. In R. M. Stogdill & A. E. Coons (eds.), *Leader behavior: Its description and measurement.* Columbus: Ohio State University, Bureau of Business Research.

28. Blake, R., & Mouton, J. (1978). *The new managerial grid.* Houston: Gulf.

29. Fleishman, E. A. (1973). Twenty years of consideration and structure. In E. A. Fleishman & J. G. Hunt (eds.), *Current developments in the study of leadership.* Carbondale: Southern Illinois University Press.

30. Blake, R. R., & Mouton, J. S. (1985). *The managerial grid III.* Houston: Gulf.

31. Misumi, J. (1985). *The behavioral science of leadership: An interdisciplinary Japanese research program.* Ann Arbor: University of Michigan Press.

32. Smith, P. B., & Peterson, M. F. (1988). *Leadership, organizations and culture: An event management model.* London: Sage.

33. Eagly, A. H., & Johnson, B. T. (1990). Gender and leadership style: A meta-analysis. *Psychological Bulletin, 108,* 223–256.

34. Astin, H. S., & Leland, C. (1991). *Women of influence, women of vision: A cross-generational study of leaders and social change.* San Francisco, CA: Jossey-Bass.

35. Eagly, A. H. (1987). *Sex differences in social behavior: A social-role interpretation.* Hillsdale, NJ: Lawrence Erlbaum Associates.

36. Eagly, A. H., & Karau, S. J. (1991). Gender and the emergence of leaders: A meta-analysis. *Journal of Personality and Social Psychology, 60,* 685–710.

37. Brewer, N., Socha, L., & Potter, R. (1996). Gender differences in supervisors' use of performance feedback. *Journal of Applied Social Psychology, 26,* 786–803.

38. Driskell, J. E., & Mullen, B. (1990). Status, expectations, and behavior: A meta-analytic review and test of the theory. *Personality and Social Psychology Bulletin, 16,* 541–553.

39. Sorrentino, R. M., & Boutillier, R. G. (1975). The effect of quantity and quality of verbal interaction on ratings of leadership ability. *Journal of Experimental Social Psychology, 11,* 403–411.

40. Mullen, B., Salas, E., & Driskell, J. E. (1989). Salience, motivation, and artifact as contributions to the relation between participation rate and leadership. *Journal of Experimental Social Psychology, 25,* 545–559.

41. Sadker, M., & Sadker, D. (1986). Abolishing misperceptions about sex equity in education. *Theory in Practice, 25,* 219–226.

42. Kram, K. E., & Hampton, M. M. (1998). When women lead: The visibility-vulnerability spiral. In E. B. Klein, F. Gabelnick, & P. Herr (eds.), *The psychodynamics of leadership* (pp. 193–217). Madison, CT: Psychological Press.

43. Friday, R. (1989). Contrasts in discussion behaviors of German and American managers. *International Journal of Intercultural Relations, 13,* 429–446.

44. Brislin, R. (1993). *Understanding culture's influence on behavior.* Orlando, FL: Harcourt Brace Jovanovich.

45. Fiedler, F. E. (1978). Contingency and the leadership process. In L. Berkowitz (ed.), *Advances in experimental social psychology* (vol. 11). New York: Academic Press.

46. Peters, L. H., Hartke, D. D., & Pohlman, J. T. (1985). Fiedler's contingency theory of leadership: An application of the meta-analysis procedures of Schmidt and Hunter. *Psychological Bulletin, 97,* 274–285.

47. Ashour, A. S. (1973). The contingency model of leadership effectiveness: An evaluation. *Organizational Behavior and Human Performance, 9,* 339–355.

48. Graen, G., & Scandura, T. A. (1987). Toward a psychology of dyadic organizing. *Research in Organizational Behavior, 9,* 175–208.

49. Locke, E. A. (1991). *The essence of leadership: The four keys to leading successfully.* New York: Macmillan.

50. Locke, E. A., & Latham, G. P. (1990a). *A theory of goal setting and task performance.* Englewood Cliffs, NJ: Prentice Hall.

51. Sims, H. P., Jr., & Lorenzi, P. (1992). *The new leadership paradigm: Social learning and cognition in organizations.* Newbury Park, CA: Sage.

52. Larey, T. S., & Paulus, P. B. (1995). Social comparison and goal setting in brainstorming groups. *Journal of Applied Social Psychology, 25,* 1579–1597.

53. Chemers, M. M. (1997). *An integrative theory of leadership.* Mahwah, NJ: Lawrence Erlbaum Associates.

54. Bass, B. M. (1998). *Transformational leadership: Industry, military, and educational impact.* Mahwah, NJ: Lawrence Erlbaum Associates.

55. Bass, B. M. (1985). *Leadership and performance beyond expectations.* New York: Free Press.

56. See note 7.

57. Shamir, B. (1992). Attribution of influence and charisma to the leader: The romance of leadership revisited. *Journal of Applied Social Psychology, 22,* 386–407

58. See note 1.

59. Avolio, B. J., Bass, B. M., & Jung, D. I. (1997). *Replicated confirmatory factor analyses of the multifactor leadership questionnaire.* Binghamton, NY: Center for Leadership Studies, Binghamton University.

60. Bass, B. M., & Avolio, B. J. (1994). *Improving organizational effectiveness through transformational leadership.* Thousand Oaks, CA: Sage.

61. Shamir, B., House, R. J., & Arthur, M. B. (1993). The motivational effects of charismatic leadership: A self-concept based theory. *Organizational Science, 4,* 577–594.

62. House, R. J., & Shamir, B. (1993). Toward the integration of transformation, charismatic, and visionary theories. In M. M. Chemers & R. Ayman (eds.), *Leadership theory and research: Perspectives and directions* (pp. 81–108). San Diego: Academic Press.

63. Ibid.

64. Conger, J. A. (1989). *The charismatic leader.* San Francisco: Jossey-Bass.

65. Goodman, P. S., Devadas, R., & Hughson, T. L. (1988). Groups and productivity: Analyzing the effectiveness of self-managing teams. In J. P. Campbell & R. J. Campbell (eds.), *Productivity in organizations* (pp. 295–327). San Francisco: Jossey-Bass.

66. Burke, W. W. (1986). Leadership as empowering others. In S. Srivasta & Associates (eds.), *Executive power: How executives influence people and organizations* (pp. 51–77). San Francisco: Jossey-Bass.

67. Schweiger, D. M., & Leana, C. R. (1986). Participation in decision making. In E. A. Locke (ed.), *Generalizing from laboratory to field settings* (pp. 147–166). Lexington, MA: Heath.

68. Hollander, E. P., & Offermann, L. R. (1990). Power and leadership in organizations. *American Psychologist, 45,* 179–189.

69. Thornton, G. C., & Cleveland, J. N. (1990). Developing managerial talent through simulation. *American Psychologist, 45,* 190–199.

70. Morgan, B. B., Jr., & Lassiter, D. L. (1992). Team composition and staffing. In R. W. Swezey & E. Salas (eds.), *Teams: Their training and performance* (pp. 75–100). Norwood, NJ: Ablex.

71. See note 28.

72. Hackman, J. R., & Walton, R. E. (1986). Leading groups in organizations. In P. S. Goodman (ed.), *Designing effective work groups* (pp. 72–119). San Francisco: Jossey-Bass.

73. Swezey, R. W., & Salas, E. (1992). Guidelines for use in team-training development. In R. W. Swezey & E. Salas (eds.), *Teams: Their training and performance* (pp. 75–100). Norwood, NJ: Ablex.

74. Sosik, J. J., Avolio, B. J., & Kahai, S. S. (1997). Effects of leadership style and anonymity of group potency and effectiveness in a group decision support system environment. *Journal of Applied Psychology, 82,* 89–103.

75. Bennis, W., & Nanus, B. (1985). *Leaders: The strategies for taking charge.* New York: Harper & Row.

76. See note 49.

77. See note 53.

78. Hollenbeck, G. P., & McCall, M. W., Jr. (1998). Leadership development: Contemporary practice. In A. K. Kraut & A. K. Korman (eds.), *Changing concepts and practices for human resources management: Contributions from industrial/organizational psychology.* San Francisco: Jossey-Bass.

79. Covey, S. R. (1989). *The 7 habits of highly effective people.* New York: Simon & Schuster.

80. See note 78.

81. Seely, S. (1998). Three decades of experience. *Flagship News 54,* 3.

82. See note 78.

83. Neck, C. P., Stewart, G. L., & Manz, C. C. (1995). Thought self-leadership as a framework for enhancing the performance appraisers. *Journal of Applied Behavioral Science, 31*(3), 278–302.

84. Paulus, P. B. (1983). Group influence on individual task performance. In P. B. Paulus (ed.), *Basic group processes* (pp. 97–120). New York: Springer-Verlag.

85. Neck, C. P., & Manz, C. C. (1996). Thought self-leadership: The impact of mental strategies training on employee cognition, behavior, and affect. *Journal of Organizational Behavior, 17,* 445–467.

86. Ibid.

87. Stewart, G. L., Carson, K. P., & Cardy, R. L. (1996). The joint effects of conscientiousness and self-leadership training on employees' self-directed behavior in a service setting. *Personnel Psychology, 49,* 143–155.

88. Williams, S. (1997). Personality and self-leadership. *Human Resource Management Review, 7,* 139–155.

89. Cohen, S. G., Chang, L., & Ledford, G. E., Jr. (1997). A hierarchical construct of self-management leadership and its relationship to quality of work life and perceived work group effectiveness. *Personnel Psychology, 50,* 275–308.

90. See note 1.

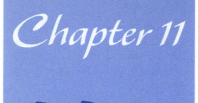

Chapter 11

Attitudes: Components and Definition

Job Satisfaction: What Makes Us Happy at Work?
Focus on Work Settings: External Causes of Job Satisfaction
Focus on Individuals: Internal Causes of Job Satisfaction

Job Satisfaction Diversity
Stage of Career and Occupational Differences
Cultural Differences: Career Success versus Quality of Life
Gender Differences
Motivation-Maintenance Theory: From Satisfaction to Motivation
Social Exchange Theory: Why We Often Stay in Jobs We Dislike and Leave Jobs We Like

Job Satisfaction: What Are Its Effects?
Job Satisfaction, Absenteeism, and Turnover
Job Satisfaction and Life Satisfaction: Is There a Spillover?
Job Satisfaction and Personal Health

Organizational Commitment: Feeling a Part of the Organization
Producing Organizational Commitment

Special Sections
Human Relations in Action
How Satisfied Are You with Your Job? Testing Motivation-Maintenance Theory

Guidelines for Effective Human Relations
Using What You've Learned

Case in Point
Should I Stay or Should I Leave?

WORK-RELATED ATTITUDES

Job Satisfaction and Organizational Commitment

Learning Objectives

After reading this chapter, you should be able to:

1. Define *attitude* and list the components of an attitude.

2. Discuss external and internal causes of job satisfaction.

3. Discuss stage-of-career and occupational differences in job satisfaction.

4. Discuss cultural, ethnic, and gender differences in job satisfaction.

5. Indicate how satisfaction and motivation are related.

6. Outline the major effects of job satisfaction in work settings.

7. Describe the relationship between job satisfaction and life satisfaction.

8. Describe the relationship between job satisfaction and personal health.

9. Discuss the factors that produce commitment to an organization.

*I*magine this. . . . *You read the morning paper and talk with your kids as you're driven to work in a company-sponsored van. When you arrive, you drop your children off at the company's day-care center and deposit your dry-cleaning at the company-sponsored cleaners. You go to your office and call the masseur for a relaxing massage to start your day. Next, you check your calendar to see when you will have a chance to go downstairs and work out in the company-sponsored gym. On your calendar, you see that today is your sister's birthday and call the company concierge to arrange to send her flowers. Now you're ready to begin an exciting day at work.*

Is this scenario a fantasy? Not in many of today's most influential companies.

*F*ortune magazine's list of the 100 Best Companies to work for in America[1] found that many companies are coming up with exciting ways to make your life at work more pleasant. For example, massages are available at Eddie Bauer and many Silicon Valley companies. Many well-known companies, such as General Mills and Johnson & Johnson, offer dry-cleaning service. Starbucks and Honda of America have personal concierge services, and on-site day-care centers are becoming more common.

Why do these companies spend money on such amenities for their employees? The answer is clear: It makes their employees happy! These goodies communicate to the employees that the company values them and cares about their well-being. (Table 11.1 describes some other ways in which companies communicate their appreciation to their employees.) In other words, they promote a positive attitude about the organization. It is only reasonable to assume that individuals who hold mainly positive at-

Table 11.1 **Examples of How Several Companies Show Employee Appreciation**

- Jan Carlzon, president of Scandinavian Airlines, sends personally written "thank you" notes to employees when they excel.
- There is a reserved parking space at the front door for the "employee of the month" at Phoenix Textiles.
- American Airlines has a program in which it gives coupons redeemable for gifts or trips to employees who excel.
- Xerox initiated a "You Deserve an X Today" program in which any employee can give anyone else a $25 gift certificate.

From Rosen, R. H. (1991). *The healthy company: Eight strategies to develop people, productivity, and profits.* New York: Putnam Publishing.

titudes toward their jobs or their companies will often behave very differently from employees who hold negative views in these respects, and a large body of research supports this idea.[2] In this chapter, we learn why attitudes are important in the workplace. We begin by exploring exactly what an attitude is and learn some techniques for promoting attitude change. We then look into one of the most important kinds of work-related attitudes: job satisfaction. We also explore what makes a person committed to an organization.

ATTITUDES: COMPONENTS AND DEFINITION

If asked how you feel about your job, you might say that you love your work, think it is challenging, and are committed to the company. On the other hand, you might admit that you hate your work, think it is boring, and hope to find a better position soon. In either case, you would be expressing the basic components and definition of attitudes. **Attitudes** are relatively stable clusters of feelings, beliefs, and predispositions to act directed toward some specific or abstract concept.[3]

Let's explore the definition in depth. Attitude includes three components (see Figure 11.1). The first component is affective: Feelings are associated with the things about which we hold attitudes. For example, you may love your work, hate broccoli, and adore ice cream. This affective component is the "hot" aspect of an attitude. Second, attitudes have a cognitive component: We hold certain beliefs about things we have attitudes about. You may believe that your employers are fair or you may believe that they

attitudes Relatively stable clusters of feelings, beliefs, and predispositions to act directed toward some specific or abstract concept.

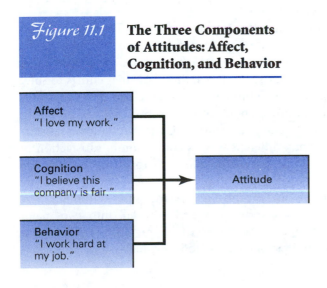

Figure 11.1 **The Three Components of Attitudes: Affect, Cognition, and Behavior**

Affect
"I love my work."

Cognition
"I believe this company is fair."

Behavior
"I work hard at my job."

Attitude

don't have your best interests in mind. Third, attitudes have a behavioral component: We have predispositions to act in certain ways toward attitudinal objects. As discussed later in this chapter, sometimes we act in ways that are consistent with our attitudes (for example, we stay at jobs we like), but in other circumstances we may act in ways that are inconsistent with our attitudes (for example, we may leave jobs we like). For now, let's ignore this complication and simply conclude that we do have behavioral intentions that are related to attitudinal objects.

Our definition also takes into account the fact that attitudes are relatively stable; that is, the feelings or beliefs are not fleeting. Attitudes tend to persist over time, although they can certainly change. Last, attitudes are formed about specific objects (for example, you may have a very positive attitude about chocolate ice cream) or they can refer to abstract concepts, such as "democracy" or "justice." As applied to the workplace, work-related attitudes consist of the lasting feelings, beliefs, and behavioral intentions associated with the various components of our job—including the setting, the nature of our work, the people with whom we work, and the entire organization. We now turn our attention to one of the most important work-related attitudes: job satisfaction.

*J*OB SATISFACTION: WHAT MAKES US HAPPY AT WORK?

Job satisfaction varies greatly from individual to individual, and from organization to organization. While some persons report mainly positive reactions to their work, others offer nonstop gripes about real or imagined problems. Furthermore, while morale and satisfaction are high in some companies, they are low or almost nonexistent in others. Why do these differences arise?

What factors contribute to job satisfaction or dissatisfaction? The answer to this question has obvious practical value, for if we understand the causes of job satisfaction (or dissatisfaction), we can take appropriate steps to increase positive attitudes among employees. You will not be surprised to learn, therefore, that efforts to solve this particular puzzle have continued without pause for several decades. The results of this ongoing work have revealed much about job satisfaction. Taken as a whole, however, they point to the following general conclusion: Understanding job satisfaction is a complex task because many different factors contribute to satisfaction or dissatisfaction among employees. In fact, so many of these factors exist that it would be impossible to examine all of them here. Instead, we focus on only the most important causes. Although these are highly diverse, they generally fall into two major groups: factors relating to the characteristics of work settings and factors relating to individuals.

job satisfaction   Individuals' degree of positive attitudes toward their current position or work.

Focus on Work Settings: External Causes of Job Satisfaction

Most research on the causes of job satisfaction has focused on various aspects of work settings themselves—that is, on conditions faced by employees that either increase or reduce their satisfaction with their jobs. Everything from the nature of the work being performed to reward systems and relations with coworkers and supervisors appears to play a role (see Figure 11.2).

With respect to the work itself, job satisfaction is enhanced by tasks that are mentally challenging and interesting, but not too tiring. In short, people like to be challenged, but not overwhelmed.

Another group of factors affecting employees' attitudes toward their jobs centers on the reward system used by an organization—that is, the procedures followed in distributing such benefits as raises, bonuses, and promotions. Growing evidence indicates that greater job satisfaction is observed when systems are fair and afford individuals a feeling of control—allowing them to believe that they can influence the rewards they receive. In contrast, systems that omit this condition tend to produce lower levels of reported satisfaction among employees.

General working conditions, too, can strongly affect positive or negative attitudes toward one's job. In most cases, a work environment that is comfortable, that is

> ### *Figure 11.2* **Positive Relationships: One Factor That Promotes Job Satisfaction**

Our satisfaction with our jobs is enhanced by positive relationships with our coworkers and supervisors. Do you think that the two different employees have different levels of job satisfaction?

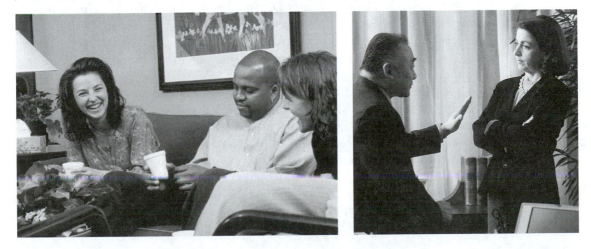

characterized by relatively low physical and psychological stress, and that facilitates the attainment of work goals will tend to produce high levels of satisfaction among employees.[4] In contrast, environments that are uncomfortable, are characterized by high stress, or prevent achievement of work goals tend to lead to low levels of reported job satisfaction.

It should be noted, however, that workers' perceptions about whether favorable job conditions result from the actions of the organization or from other sources will also influence the extent to which these favorable conditions lead to optimal positive attitudes about the workplace.[5] For example, favorable working conditions that result from the actions of a union strike may increase persons' satisfaction with their work without influencing their perceptions that the organization is committed to them as workers. On the other hand, unfavorable conditions that are perceived to be beyond the control of the organization (for example, poor economic times that lead to low company profits) may not always produce negative attitudes about the workplace. Rather, the extent to which employees believe that favorable and unfavorable conditions result from the discretionary actions of their employers plays an important role in shaping their work-related attitudes.[6] Thus workers' attributions about the causes of workplace events are clearly important for understanding behavior in the workplace (see Chapter 3).

Focus on Individuals: Internal Causes of Job Satisfaction

Some persons seem to be easy to please—they appear to be satisfied under almost any conditions that life happens to bring their way. Similarly, some individuals are almost never happy, no matter how many benefits they enjoy. Probably you have known persons of both types. This fact points to another major set of factors affecting job satisfaction: personal characteristics possessed by individuals. Support for the important role that personality factors play in job satisfaction comes from a number of sources. For example, research has shown that personality factors measured in childhood predict work satisfaction in adulthood.[7] In short, people carry certain traits or perspectives with them from situation to situation that may strongly affect their degree of satisfaction with any given job.

First, individuals who are high in self-esteem or who possess a positive self-image appear to be more satisfied with their jobs than persons who are low in self-esteem or who possess a negative self-image.[8] Perhaps this difference arises because persons with high self-esteem tend to perceive everything they do in a favorable light. Alternatively, they may be actually more competent and successful than others are. Whatever the reason, the better an individual's self-image, the more likely he or she is to report being happy and satisfied on the job. Second, persons who are high in the ability to withstand stress tend to report higher job satisfaction than persons low in this ability.[9] Third, individuals who believe that they can alter or control their own outcomes tend to report higher job satisfaction than those who feel that such outcomes remain outside their personal influence.[10] Fourth, persons who are high in status and seniority often report higher levels of satisfaction than do their counterparts who are low in status or seniority.[11] Such findings probably stem, at least in part, from the fact that persons in the former group actually enjoy better working conditions than do those in the latter group. They may also reflect the fact that people who are happy in a given job or organization tend to remain in it and thus achieve a higher status and seniority as a result of their positive attitudes.

Furthermore, individuals with positive expectations about their jobs—especially about the job's ability to satisfy their basic needs—appear to be higher in satisfaction than those lacking in such expectations. Evidence for this intriguing conclusion is provided by a study carried out by Pulakos and Schmitt.[12] These researchers asked graduating high school seniors to rate the importance of various outcomes they hoped to attain from their future jobs (such as good pay, security, and new skills and knowledge) and to rate the likelihood that their jobs would provide these outcomes. Then, at nine months and again at twenty months after graduation, the same individuals completed a measure of job satisfaction. The results were clear: The more positive the participants' initial expectations about their future jobs, the higher their reported satisfaction after they had gained employment. These findings and those of other studies suggest that positive expectations may often be fulfilled, at least with respect to job satisfaction. Definite limits exist for this relationship, however. Positive expectations may foster high levels of job satisfaction as long as such expectations are realistic and have some chance of being met. If they are unreasonably high, bitter disappointment may result, and satisfaction may, in the long run, be reduced.[13] For this reason, organizations should avoid building up false hopes among prospective employees. If they do, they may well be setting the stage for disillusionment and other negative reactions. As long as these pitfalls are avoided and expectations about one's job remain realistic, however, a positive, hopeful approach may be a major plus.

Finally, and not surprisingly, it appears that people who enjoy good personal adjustment away from work tend to report greater satisfaction with their jobs than those whose personal lives are marked by stress and unhappiness (see Figure 11.3 on page 318). Perhaps the same skills that help well-adjusted persons succeed in their personal lives are also useful to them in work settings (such as the ability to get along with others and a high degree of self-confidence). Whatever the reason, individuals who are happy and well adjusted off the job tend to be satisfied on it as well.[14]

Some intriguing but controversial evidence suggests that job satisfaction has a genetic basis. Researchers studied 34 pairs of monozygotic (identical) twins who were separated at an early age and reared apart.[15] This special circumstance allows researchers to estimate the influence of genes on behavior. Because these twins were raised in different environments, the extent to which their attitudes are similar provides an estimate of the degree to which genetics influenced their attitudes. The researchers found that genetics accounted for about 30 percent of their job satisfac-

Personal Adjustment Away from Work: One Internal Cause of Job Satisfaction

Individuals who enjoy good personal relationships away from work tend to report higher levels of job satisfaction. On the other hand, those whose personal lives are marked by stress and unhappiness are not as happy with their jobs.

tion. Most likely, this similarity reflects their common motor skills and physical abilities. Nevertheless, this interesting result highlights the fact there are limits to which we can improve a person's satisfaction by changing environmental conditions; these limits are set by the personal characteristics of the individual.

What is the bottom line concerning the causes of job satisfaction? Is a person's happiness at work a product of the work environment or the individual's disposition? As you may have already concluded, as with most issues in psychology, the answer appears to be "both." Measures of job satisfaction remain stable over long periods of time, and this stability is due to both job characteristics and personality dispositions.[16] Table 11.2 summarizes the internal and external causes of job satisfaction.

Table 11.2   Job Satisfaction

External Causes	Internal Causes
■ Mentally challenging and interesting work that is not too tiring	■ High self-esteem
■ Reward systems that are fair and provide a sense of control	■ High status or seniority
■ Good relationship with coworkers	■ Positive and realistic expectations
■ Positive working environment	■ Good personal adjustment away from work
■ Low physical and psychological stress	■ Genetic determinants

JOB SATISFACTION DIVERSITY

An important fact concerning job satisfaction is that it varies greatly across different groups of employees. These variations can be seen between people who are at different stages in their careers and between people in different occupations. Some interesting differences between men and women in their levels of job satisfaction have been noted as well. In addition, the importance of working is not the same across all cultures, and not all workers consider the same factors to be important in their work.

Many researchers have sought to identify why individuals differ in job satisfaction and work values. Environmental factors, such as early family experiences[17] and occupational socialization,[18] have been suggested as causes of these individual differences. Interestingly, some recent evidence suggests that genetic factors may also be associated with differences in work values.[19] Some of the similarities and differences among persons on these dimensions are discussed in this section.

Stage of Career and Occupational Differences

As you might expect, managers, technical and professional workers, and self-employed people generally report higher satisfaction than blue-collar personnel do. Interestingly, this finding tends to hold across many cultures.[20] Similarly, older workers often report greater satisfaction with their jobs than younger ones. One popular explanation for these findings claims that professionals and older workers gain more prestige from their jobs. It has also been assumed that they are involved in more challenging job activities and have more control over their positions than do younger workers and members of the rank-and-file. These assumptions may not be justified, however.[21] For example, highly successful male executives who are in mid-life often report doubts about their career, value conflicts, and job dissatisfaction; in particular, these managers say that they feel a sense of alienation from their careers.[22]

During mid-career, usually between the ages of thirty-five and fifty, individuals are faced with career dilemmas that were not present earlier in their careers. For example, they are no longer viewed as "learners" within the organization, and their mistakes carry greater consequences. Reaching a mid-career plateau can present a crisis that may result in a sense of job dissatisfaction. During this stage, many individuals leave their occupations and redefine their career goals. Thus developmental factors and changes in what one wants from the workplace can override the attraction of objective measures of success such as more money and more prestige.

Cultural Differences: Career Success versus Quality of Life

Recall from Chapter 1 that cultures differ in terms of having an individualist or collectivist orientation. Hofstede has identified another difference among cultures that is especially important to our understanding of job satisfaction. He draws a distinction between cultures that emphasize career success and those that prize quality of life.[23] Cultures that emphasize **career success** stress the acquisition of material possessions and individual assertiveness, whereas countries that emphasize **quality of life** emphasize relationships among people, concern for others, and life enjoyability as most important. It probably does not surprise you that the United States rates highly along the career-success dimension. Scandinavian countries, Japan, and Austria are examples of cultures that emphasize quality-of-life values.[24] Adler relates an interesting example of how these differences in orientation can lead to misunderstandings about employee commitment.[25]

As Adler notes, Swedish policy allows parents to take maternity or paternity leave whenever they desire. When the policy was first introduced, the managing director of the Swedish Postal Service created tumult when he announced his intention to take off several months to stay at home with his newborn. The press picked up on his decision, and he explained that executives, like other workers, need to balance their work and family lives. Likewise, Adler notes, such a misunderstanding may occur when Swedish business people surprise their international clients with their intentions of ending the workweek at 5:00 P.M. on Friday, regardless of whether the project is complete. Rather than understanding their strong commitment to quality of life, their clients may interpret this behavior as reflecting a low commitment to the project.

As you can infer from this example, differences in quality-of-life versus career-success orientation can lead to differences in the bases of job satisfaction across cultures. Cultures that emphasize quality of life stress social needs over productivity, whereas cultures that emphasize career success tend to place a greater emphasis on individualistic ego needs, such as self-actualization and self-esteem.[26] We must therefore consider the frame of reference for understanding differences in cultural values.

Gender Differences

Gender differences have also been noted in the kinds of work that men and women value. Research has shown that men consistently value job dimensions that relate to status, prestige, and high incomes. On the other hand, women value job dimensions relating to helping others and social relations.[27–30] Although the research doesn't suggest that this statement applies to every male or female, that women don't value money, or that men don't value relationships, it does suggest the existence of important differences in emphasis between genders. For example, males may be less dissatisfied with a job that does not provide positive social relations than females are. In one investigation on this topic, Varca, Shaffer, and McCauley measured job satisfaction among 400 college graduates (half male, half female).[31] Important differences between

career-success orientation An orientation found in cultures that emphasize acquisition of material possessions and individualism.

quality-of-life orientation An orientation found in cultures that emphasize relationships among people and concerns about life quality.

men and women were uncovered, at least with respect to satisfaction with pay and opportunities for promotion. Among individuals holding relatively high-level jobs (such as marketing manager), men reported greater satisfaction than women did. Among those holding low-level jobs, the pattern was reversed; women reported greater satisfaction with their current jobs than did men. One explanation for these differences is that males in "higher-level" jobs derive fulfillment from their higher earnings and prestige, whereas females felt more satisfied in "lower-level" jobs that traditionally are more person-oriented. These differences also may result from a disparity in pay and promotion opportunities for men versus women in upper-level positions (see Figure 11.4).

An interesting and potentially controversial perspective on these issues has recently emerged. This view suggests that gender differences in attraction to various occupations reflect the extent to which the occupations serve to maintain or enhance individuals from the dominant social group (that is, men) or serve to favor oppressed groups within a society (that is, women).[32] Pratto and her colleagues have found that males are overrepresented in occupations that maintain the existing social structure (for example, law, law enforcement, military), whereas females are overrepresented in occupations that serve oppressed members of society (for example, social workers, civil law attorneys). She suggests that these choices in part reflect differences in males' and females' desires to support dominant versus subordinate groups in society.[33,34]

Regardless of the source of these cultural and gender differences, it is important to keep in mind that persons within a given culture and across cultures may differ in their work-related attitudes. To live in a global or domestic multicultural society, we must learn to recognize and appreciate these differences.

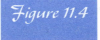

Gender Differences in Job Satisfaction

Evidence indicates that women report lower levels of satisfaction with their jobs than men. It has been suggested that this difference results from women's comparisons of their pay and promotion opportunities with men holding similar positions. Since there is often a disparity in favor of men, women's job satisfaction may be reduced.

Motivation-Maintenance Theory: From Satisfaction to Motivation

So far, our discussion suggests that job satisfaction and job dissatisfaction are simply two sides of the same coin. That is, certain conditions either increase job satisfaction or decrease job satisfaction, depending on the extent to which they are present in work settings. According to a theory offered by Herzberg,[35] this idea is not true. Rather, theorists claim that job satisfaction (plus high levels of work motivation) and job dissatisfaction (along with low levels of such motivation) spring from somewhat different sources. You may find it interesting to learn how Herzberg reached this surprising conclusion.

Herzberg conducted a study in which more than 200 engineers and accountants were asked to describe times when they felt especially satisfied or dissatisfied with their jobs. (This approach is sometimes known as the **critical incident technique.**) Careful analysis of their answers then pointed to an intriguing pattern of results. When describing incidents in which they felt dissatisfied, most persons mentioned conditions surrounding their jobs rather than the work itself. For instance, they commented on such factors as physical working conditions, pay, security, and their relationships with others. To the extent that these conditions were positive, feelings of dissatisfaction were prevented. Given their role in preventing such negative reactions, Herzberg termed these factors **hygiene or maintenance factors.** When describing incidents in which they felt especially satisfied or happy with their jobs, subjects usually mentioned factors relating more directly to the work they performed. For example, they spoke about the nature of their jobs and daily tasks, achievement in them, promotion opportunities, recognition from management, increased responsibility, and the chance for personal growth. Because such factors contributed to job satisfaction, Herzberg termed them **motivators.** Figure 11.5 summarizes both motivators and hygiene factors.

As already noted, motivators seem to be linked to the job an individual performs, while hygiene factors relate to conditions surrounding one's work. Another way of viewing these two groups of factors exists as well. As you may recall from our discussion of Maslow's hierarchy of needs (see Chapter 5), people seem to have both lower-level deficiency needs (physiological, safety, and social) and higher-level growth needs (esteem and self-actualization). Hygiene factors involve the satisfaction of lower-level deficiency needs, while motivators involve the satisfaction of higher-level growth needs. Recall that hygiene (or maintenance) factors involve such conditions as the pay one receives, social relations with others, and physical working conditions. Obviously, these factors are related to physiological, safety, and social needs. In contrast, mo-

critical incident technique A procedure used to study job satisfaction in which participants describe times in which they felt especially satisfied or dissatisfied with their jobs.

hygiene or maintenance factors Work factors related to conditions surrounding jobs, such as working conditions and pay.

motivators Work factors related to characteristics of the work itself, such as the growth opportunities it provides.

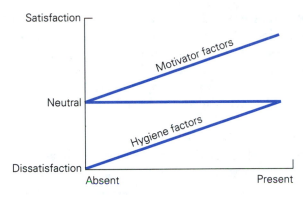

Motivator and Hygiene Factors

According to Herzberg's motivation-maintenance theory, job satisfaction is produced by the presence of motivator factors, such as opportunities for growth. The presence of hygiene factors, such as pay, prevents job dissatisfaction.

tivators involve such conditions as opportunities for growth, increased responsibility, and promotion. Here, self-esteem and self-actualization needs seem more central.

Taking Herzberg's theory and related research findings into account, the bottom line seems to go something like this: To the extent that individuals satisfy their basic deficiency needs at work, feelings of dissatisfaction will be prevented. Nevertheless, the fulfillment of such needs, by itself, cannot produce high levels of satisfaction or motivation. To attain these positive results, opportunities for the fulfillment of higher-level needs, too, must be provided. In sum, the key to high morale and high productivity at work seems to lie not simply in offering employees good pay, job security, and pleasant working conditions, but also in ensuring that they have ample opportunities to grow. (See the *Human Relations in Action* section on pages 324–325.)

Social Exchange Theory: Why We Often Stay in Jobs We Dislike and Leave Jobs We Like

Will a person with a salary of $1 million be satisfied or dissatisfied with her job? Will she choose to stay in the position or leave? At first glance, you may be tempted to answer "satisfied" and "stay" to these questions. Would your answer be different if you knew that the person made $2 million last year and was just offered a position at XYZ Corporation at $4 million per year? This information might change your appraisal of the person's level of satisfaction with her present job. It would also change your estimate of the likelihood of the person's leaving the job that pays $1 million per year.

These considerations form the basis of exchange theory.[36] Taking these possibilities into account, this theory introduced the term **comparison level (CL)** to indicate how satisfied a person will be with a certain outcome resulting from an interaction, including an employment relationship. The CL is the outcome that people think they deserve from a certain relationship. It is influenced

comparison level (CL) The outcome that people think they deserve in a relationship.

by all outcomes known to the person by either direct experience or by his or her imagination. Thus the amount of compensation received in the past can establish a CL that is used to evaluate present outcomes. When the outcome from a present relationship—for example, a job—exceeds the person's comparison level, he or she will be satisfied with the present relationship. On the other hand, when present outcomes fall below the person's CL, he or she will be dissatisfied with the relationship (see Figure 11.6 on page 326).

Will the satisfied person stay at, and the dissatisfied person leave, his or her present job? Social exchange theory points out that satisfaction does not solely determine whether an individual will remain in an interaction. Instead, it states that a person's **comparison level for alternatives (CL$_{alt}$)** is an important factor in determining the stability of the relationship. The value of the CL$_{alt}$ depends on the outcome that the individual thinks can be

comparison level for alternatives (CL$_{alt}$) The outcome that people think can be obtained from the best available alternative.

Human Relations in Action

How Satisfied Are You with Your Job? Testing Motivation-Maintenance Theory

Many students work while they go to college or during vacation periods. Some of the features of these jobs may be quite positive, while others may be somewhat negative. For the items listed below, indicate whether you are dissatisfied or satisfied with these in your present job. (If you do not have a job now, rate your last job.)

		satisfied	dissatisfied
1.	Pay	____ satisfied	____ dissatisfied
2.	Job security	____ satisfied	____ dissatisfied
3.	Promotion opportunities	____ satisfied	____ dissatisfied
4.	Recognition for good work	____ satisfied	____ dissatisfied
5.	Physical working conditions	____ satisfied	____ dissatisfied
6.	Relations with other workers	____ satisfied	____ dissatisfied
7.	Opportunity for growth or learning	____ satisfied	____ dissatisfied
8.	Degree of responsibility	____ satisfied	____ dissatisfied
9.	Company policies	____ satisfied	____ dissatisfied
10.	Quality of supervisors	____ satisfied	____ dissatisfied

obtained from the best available alternative interaction. This outcome could be another position or unemployment, for example.

According to social exchange theory, comparisons of present outcomes to the CL_{alt} determine whether a person will remain in his or her present position or will leave. When the CL_{alt} exceeds his or her present outcomes, the person is likely to leave; when the CL_{alt} is below the present outcomes, the person is likely to stay.

Social exchange theory provides us with a straightforward way to understand relationships between job satisfaction and job stability. Different kinds of comparisons determine (1) how satisfied a person is with a job and (2) whether a person will stay in the position. They help us understand why people may remain in relationships that make them unhappy and why people leave relationships that make them happy. The theory also explains why job turnover and job satisfaction may be only slightly related. (See the *Case in Point* section on page 333 for further consideration of these issues.)

11. Nature of work   ____ satisfied   ____ dissatisfied
12. Opportunities for achievement   ____ satisfied   ____ dissatisfied

Motivators Score   *Maintenance Score*

____ Satisfied   ____ Satisfied

____ Dissatisfied   ____ Dissatisfied

Scoring

Add the number of times you checked "satisfied" and the number of times you checked "dissatisfied" on items 3, 4, 7, 8, 11, and 12. Write these numbers under "Motivators Score." Do the same for items 1, 2, 5, 6, 9, and 10, and write the scores under "Maintenance Score." Do these scores relate to your job satisfaction, as suggested by Herzberg's motivation-maintenance theory? If you are satisfied with your job, you probably have a high satisfaction score for motivators. If you are very dissatisfied, you probably have a high dissatisfaction score for maintenance. You can ask your instructor to collect this information from all students in the class to see what percentage of the time the predictions fit with motivation-maintenance theory.

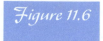 **Social Exchange Theory: Perspectives on Organizational Satisfaction and Job Stability**

According to this view, people compare the outcomes they are presently receiving from a job with their comparison level (CL). This comparison determines their satisfaction with their jobs. They also compare their present outcomes with comparison level alternatives (CL_{alt}). This comparison determines whether the person will stay or leave.

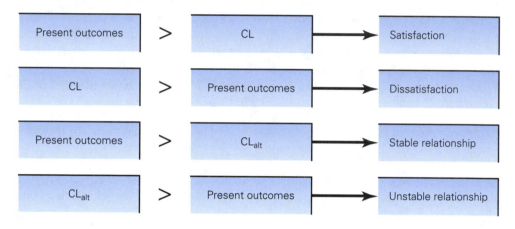

JOB SATISFACTION: WHAT ARE ITS EFFECTS?

Throughout the discussion to this point, we have made an important implicit assumption—that job satisfaction exerts strong effects upon behavior in work settings. On the face of it, this suggestion seems eminently reasonable. After all, the way people feel and think about their jobs should influence the way they perform them. But is this really the case? We will see that the influence of job satisfaction on work behavior is not always easily identified. In fact, it is sometimes quite puzzling!

Why is this the case? Part of the answer lies in the fact that job satisfaction is an attitude (or, perhaps, a cluster of related attitudes). Attitudes, in turn, do not always affect behavior in a simple or clear-cut way. As we learned in the discussion of social exchange theory, sometimes attitudes direct our words and deeds—but sometimes they do not. Many factors (such as the strength of our views or their degree of specificity) seem to determine which of these outcomes prevails. For example, many people continue to smoke despite knowing that this practice is harmful to their health. Most of us have occasionally said things we don't really believe because good manners or common sense requires us to do so. Given the complex link between attitudes and behavior, it is not surprising that job satisfaction affects work settings in a far from simple manner. Keep this fact in mind as we examine some of its major effects.

Job Satisfaction, Absenteeism, and Turnover

Imagine two employees, both of whom hate to get up in the morning and dislike fighting their way through the morning rush hour to work. One likes her job very much, but the other dislikes it. Which worker is more likely to call in sick or miss work for other reasons? The answer is obvious: the one who dislikes her job. Job satisfaction's effect on absenteeism has been documented in many investigations. In general, these studies report that the lower an individual's satisfaction with his or her job, the more likely that person is to miss work.[37] The strength of this relationship, though, is quite modest. That is, while job satisfaction affects absenteeism to some extent, its influence is far from overpowering.

Similar findings have been obtained with respect to turnover. That is, the lower an individual's level of satisfaction with his or her job, the more likely that person is to resign and seek other opportunities. Again, however, the strength of this association is modest.[38] This fact, in turn, raises an interesting question: Why aren't the links between job satisfaction and both absenteeism and turnover even stronger? Social exchange theory provides one answer to this question. These behaviors—as well as others relating to work—are affected by many factors. Job satisfaction is only one among these influences. For example, absence from work is probably affected by weather, traffic conditions, and the distance employees must travel to work, as well as by their attitudes toward their jobs (see Figure 11.7 on page 328). Similarly, turnover may reflect general economic conditions and alternative employment opportunities, as well as job satisfaction.[39] Given the existence of so many factors, it is not surprising that such a modest relationship exists between job satisfaction and turnover or absenteeism. Indeed, it would be far more surprising if these links were extremely powerful.

Job Satisfaction and Life Satisfaction: Is There a Spillover?

Work is an important part of our daily lives. In fact, for most of us, it forms a central aspect of our self-concept. We define ourselves, at least in part, by our careers or professions. While fantasies of a life of total leisure are intriguing, to say the least, few people can really imagine a full or satisfying life that does not involve some type of productive work. Given these facts, it makes sense to ask the following question: Does satisfaction with one's career or job spill over into one's personal life?

Absenteeism: Affected by Many Factors

Absenteeism is affected by many factors, including traffic conditions and distance from work. How would you feel about facing this kind of traffic on a Monday morning?

Research findings suggest that the answer to this question is "yes." A number of studies indicate that satisfaction on the job is, indeed, related to satisfaction with one's life in general.[40] Moreover, at least one investigation suggests that this link is a causal one;[41] that is, changes in job satisfaction appear to cause changes in general **life satisfaction.** (Evidence suggesting that general life satisfaction affects job satisfaction is somewhat weaker.) The findings on so-called spillover suggest that efforts to enhance employees' satisfaction with their jobs and reduce their stress may yield handsome rewards.[42] Not only will they improve the quality of life at work, but these benefits may also enhance the quality of life in general. Certainly they are worth pursuing.

Job Satisfaction and Personal Health

Before concluding, we add one final bit of icing to the cake: Evidence suggests that job satisfaction can contribute to personal health. First, such satisfaction has been linked to longevity: Persons satisfied with their jobs actually tend to live longer than those who are dissatisfied with work do![43] Second, high levels of job satisfaction are associated with several aspects of mental well-being, such

life satisfaction   Individuals' level of satisfaction with their lives away from work.

as reduced anxiety, high self-esteem, and good social adjustment.[44] If managers or organizations needed any further inducement for paying close attention to the satisfaction of their employees (as well as their own), these intriguing results provide it.

ORGANIZATIONAL COMMITMENT: FEELING A PART OF THE ORGANIZATION

So far, we have discussed attitudes related to our feelings and beliefs about our jobs. We now turn to another important work-related topic: organizational commitment. This attitude refers to the extent to which an individual identifies with and feels a part of the organization of which he or she is a member and desires to remain employed by that organization.

Organizations want to foster this type of attitude in their employees. Committed employees are less likely to leave the organization and they have lower rates of absenteeism.[45] In addition, committed employees perform better in their jobs than do employees who lack this attitude. Employees who feel attached to their organization are willing to make personal sacrifices and share with others for the good of the organization.[46]

Not only is organizational commitment good for the company, but it also has positive consequences for persons who have this attitude. Individuals with this type of positive attitude tend to have successful careers and are happier in their lives in general.[47]

Producing Organizational Commitment

Given that organizational commitment is a desirable attitude, a question then arises: How can we foster organizational commitment? Recently, it has been suggested that two types of organizational commitment exist.[48] **Continuance commitment** refers to an individual's inclination to continue to work for the organization because he or she cannot afford to leave. **Affective commitment** refers to a person's desire to stay with the organization because he or she agrees with its policies and wants to remain affiliated with the business. Different factors are associated with each type of commitment.

Affective commitment seems to be associated with aspects of work that make employees feel competent and efficacious (remember the importance of self-efficacy for motivation?).[49] Not surprisingly, continuance commit-

continuance commitment   An individual's inclination to continue to work for the organization because he or she cannot afford to leave.

affective commitment   A person's desire to stay with the organization because he or she agrees with its policies and wants to remain affiliated with the business.

Table 11.3   **Factors Associated with Increased Organizational Commitment**

Many factors are related to individuals' commitment to their organizations. We have not separated these factors into continuance and affective dimensions. You can probably make an educated guess as to which of these factors are related to each dimension, or both.

Job Characteristics

> High levels of responsibility
>
> Opportunities for promotion
>
> Job autonomy: having freedom to plan, schedule, and carry out work
>
> Importance of the work undertaken

Personal Characteristics

> Length of time the person is employed by the company
>
> Age (related to employment longevity)
>
> Personal growth needs

Company Policies

> Employee ownership (for example, stocks) of company
>
> Clear organizational values
>
> Vigorous recruitment
>
> Clear newcomer orientation procedures

ment appears to be linked to economic factors such as job benefits and salary. There are several other factors related to organizational commitment as well; Table 11.3 summarizes these factors.

Guidelines for Effective Human Relations

Using What You've Learned

In this chapter, we examined a broad range of principles and findings about job satisfaction. Although few rules will apply to every situation, there are some general guidelines suggested by the various findings we have discussed. Remember, no rule works 100 percent in every situation. However, these guidelines should help improve your satisfaction with your job.

Guidelines for Effective Human Relations (continued)

- Take advantage of opportunities you may have to express your opinions about your job (for example, gripe sessions). Use these opportunities constructively. Don't let your emotions get out of hand! Remember that in most cases employers are interested in the morale of their employees.

- Emphasize the positive as well as the negative aspects of your job when discussing problems. Suggest ways of dealing with the issues.

- When considering a new position, assess the characteristics of the work setting itself. General working conditions have a strong influence on our long-term job satisfaction.

- Seek out work that is challenging and interesting, but not overwhelming. Too much challenge in work can produce burnout.

- Try to maintain positive relations with your coworkers and supervisors. The social climate of the workplace has a great deal of influence on job satisfaction.

- Remember that your attitude about yourself has as much to do with your job satisfaction as any other factor. Develop and maintain a positive self-image and learn to take control of your life.

- Expect positive things to happen . . . and often they will! Research indicates that those who hold positive expectations about their work are more satisfied with their jobs than those who hold negative expectations. But remember to be realistic in your expectations.

- Do not ignore other dimensions of your life at the expense of your work. Job satisfaction cannot compensate for a lack of life satisfaction. If you enjoy good personal adjustment away from work, it is likely that you will also enjoy greater satisfaction with your job.

- If you feel something is missing at work, assess the presence or absence of the hygiene and motivation factors we discussed. They may help you determine whether you are truly dissatisfied with your job or whether your position is not providing you with sufficient motivation factors. This assessment may be useful in deciding a course of action.

- Remember that job satisfaction is likely to change across our career stages. Use these changes as opportunities for growth.

- Do not underemphasize the importance of your job satisfaction. It has significant implications for your happiness and your personal health.

Summary

Our attitudes affect how we feel about the workplace as well as how we perform. Attitudes are composed of three factors: feelings, beliefs, and behavior. They remain relatively stable and are formed about specific or general concepts. A wide range of factors influences job satisfaction. Some involve various aspects of work settings, such as the work itself, the reward systems employed by an organization, and general work conditions. Others involve characteristics of individual employees, such as their self-esteem, personal adjustment, and expectations about their jobs. Intriguing, but controversial, evidence suggests that job satisfaction may have a genetic component.

Contrary to popular belief, most individuals report a fairly high level of satisfaction with their jobs. In addition, people often stay in jobs they dislike and leave positions they like. Social exchange theory helps us understand the circumstances that affect these decisions. According to this view, a person compares his or her present outcome to a comparison level (CL) and comparison level alternative (CL_{alt}). When a present outcome exceeds a CL, the individual has a positive attitude about her job; when the present outcome is below a CL, she is unhappy with her job. When the present outcome exceeds a CL_{alt}, an individual will leave a job even if he has a positive attitude about the job; when the present outcome is below a CL_{alt}, he will stay in the job even if he is unhappy.

Job satisfaction also differs across various groups of employees. It is higher among professional and technical workers than among blue-collar ones, and higher among older employees than among younger ones. Cultural and gender differences in job satisfaction also exist. For example, persons in some cultures are more oriented toward quality of life; members of other cultures are oriented toward career success dimensions. There are, however, many similarities among individuals from different cultures in terms of what they need from their work.

Herzberg suggests that different factors affect job satisfaction and job satisfaction. Job satisfaction and high levels of motivation are related to motivators—factors having to do with opportunities to grow within the workplace. Job dissatisfaction and low levels of motivation are related to hygiene or maintenance factors—factors having to do with conditions surrounding jobs, such as working conditions and pay.

A relationship exists between job satisfaction and both employee turnover and absence from work. High levels of job satisfaction appear to spill over into general life satisfaction and may even enhance personal health.

Organizational commitment is an important work-related attitude, and one that organizations want to foster in their employees. Committed employees are less likely to leave the organization and they have lower rates of absenteeism. In addition, committed employees perform better in their jobs than do employees who do not have this attitude. Employees who feel attached to their organization are willing to make personal sacrifices and share with others for the good of the organization.

Key Terms

affective commitment, p. 329

attitudes, p. 313

career-success orientation, p. 320

comparison level (CL), p. 323

comparison level for alternatives
(CL$_{alt}$), p. 324

continuance commitment, p. 329

critical incident technique, p. 322

hygiene or maintenance factors, p. 322

job satisfaction, p. 314

life satisfaction, p. 328

motivators, p. 322

quality-of-life orientation, p. 320

Case in Point

Should I Stay or Should I Leave?

Tiffany Carpenter has a dilemma . . . a dilemma that many of us might think we would welcome. She's just been offered a position earning 50 percent more than her present job, with double the fringe benefits! She's been working for five years at her hometown newspaper as a reporter. While investigating a number of rip-offs by unethical insurance salespersons, she found evidence of consumer fraud at a national level. Her series on this story was picked up by the Associated Press and now the *New York Times* has offered her a staff position.

That's the good news. Here's the bad news: Taking the position would mean a complete change in her life. It would mean leaving a job with which she's been very happy, moving away from all her family and friends, changing her lifestyle, and causing her husband to leave his job (or deal with a commuter marriage). Moving from a small town to a large city also seems a little scary to her.

As Tiffany contemplates her decision, she receives a call from her former roommate,

Claire. Claire is overwhelmed with surprise that Tiffany is even thinking of declining the offer.

"Are you crazy?" Claire exclaims. "You'd have to be out of your mind to give up this chance. Why would you even think of staying at a hick newspaper when you can work at the top?"

After this conversation, Tiffany is more confused than ever. She feels that maybe she has no ambition, and maybe she's a wimp to be wary of moving. And so what if her career interferes with her husband's career?

What do you think? Is there a clear-cut solution to her dilemma? What factors should she consider? How much should she consider the implications of moving for her family's life? Should career or family come first in her life? How can she find a balance? If she decides to stay in her present position, should she feel that she lacks ambition? How should she deal with Claire in this case? If she decides to leave, how should she deal with the conflict that may be produced by uprooting her family?

Notes

1. Fisher, A. (1998). The 100 best companies to work for in America. *Fortune, 137*(1), 68–70.

2. Locke, E. A. (1976). The nature and causes of job satisfaction. In M. Dunnette (ed.), *Handbook of industrial and organizational psychology.* Chicago: Rand McNally.

3. McGuire, W. J. (1985). Attitudes and attitude change. In G. Lindzey & E. Aronson (eds). *Handbook of social psychology* (3rd ed., Vol. 2, pp. 233–346). New York: Random House.

4. Sundstrom, E. (1986). *Workplace.* Cambridge, UK: Cambridge University Press.

5. Eisenberger, R., et al. (1997). Perceived organizational support, discretionary treatment, and job satisfaction. *Journal of Applied Psychology, 82*(5), 812–820.

6. Ibid.

7. Staw, B. M., Bell, N. E., & Clausen, J. A. (1986). The dispositional approach to job attitudes: A lifetime longitudinal test. *Administrative Science Quarterly, 31,* 56–77.

8. See note 2.

9. Scheier, M. F., Weintraub, J. K., & Carver, C. S. (1986). Coping with stress: Divergent strategies of optimists and pessimists. *Journal of Personality and Social Psychology, 51,* 1257–1264.

10. Andrisani, P. J., & Nesetl, C. (1976). Internal-external control as a contributor to an outcome of work experience. *Journal of Applied Psychology, 61,* 156–165.

11. See note 6.

12. Pulakos, E. D., & Schmitt, N. (1983). A longitudinal study of a valence model approach for the prediction of job satisfaction of new employees. *Journal of Applied Psychology, 68,* 307–312.

13. Wanous, J. P. (1980). *Organizational entry: Recruitment, selection, and socialization of newcomers.* Reading, MA: Addison-Wesley.

14. Cole, R. E. (1979). *Work, mobility, and participation.* Berkeley: University of California.

15. Avery, R. D., Bouchard, T. J., Segal, N. L., & Abraham, L. M. (1989). Job satisfaction: Environmental and genetic components. *Journal of Applied Psychology, 74,* 187–192.

16. Steel, R. P., & Rentsch, J. R. (1997). The dispositional model of job attitudes revisited: Findings of a 10-year study. *Journal of Applied Psychology, 82*(6), 873–879.

17. Holland, J. L. (1973). *Making vocational choices.* Englewood Cliffs, NJ: Prentice Hall.

18. Kaufman, D., & Fetters, M. J. (1980). Work motivation and job values among professional men and women: A new accounting. *Journal of Vocational Behavior, 17,* 251–262.

19. Keller, L. M., Bouchard, T. J., Arvey, R. D., Segal, N. L., & Dawis, R. V. (1992). Work values: Genetic and environmental influences. *Journal of Applied Psychology, 77,* 79–88.

20. Tannanbaum, A. S. (1980). Organizational psychology. In H. C. Triandis & R. W. Brislin (eds.), *Handbook of cross-cultural psychology* (Vol. 5, pp. 281–334). Boston: Allyn & Bacon.

21. Poole, M. E., Langan, J., & Omodei, M. (1993). Contrasting subjective and objective criteria as determinants of perceived career success: A longitudinal study. *Journal of Occupational and Organizational Psychology, 66,* 39–54.

22. Korman, A. K., Wittig-Berman, U., & Lang, D. (1981). Career success and personal failure: Alienation in professionals and managers. *Academy of Management Journal, 24*(2), 342–360.

23. Hofstede, G. (1980). *Culture's consequences: International differences in work-related values* (p. 25). Beverly Hills, CA: Sage.

24. Adler, N. J. (1997). *Organizational behavior.* Cincinnati, OH: South-Western College Publishing.

25. Ibid, p. 57.

26. Ibid.

27. Chusmir, L. H., & Parker, B. (1991). Gender and situational differences in managers' values: A look at work and home lives. *Journal of Business Research, 23,* 325–335.

28. Parker, B., & Chusmir, L. (1990). A generational and sex-based view of managerial work values. *Psychological Reports, 66,* 947–950.

29. Erez, M., Borochov, O., & Mannheim, B. (1989). Work values of youth: Effects of sex or sex role

typing? *Journal of Vocational Behavior, 34,* 350–366.

30. Perron, J., & St.-Onge, L. (1991). Work values in relation to gender and forecasted career patterns for women. *International Journal for the Advancement of Counseling, 14,* 91–103.

31. Varca, P. E., Shaffer, G. S., & McCauley, C. D. (1983). Sex differences in job satisfaction revisited. *Academy of Management Journal, 26,* 348–353.

32. Pratto, F., Sidanius, J., Stallworth, L. M., & Malle, B. F. (1994). Social dominance orientation: A personality variable relevant to social roles and intergroup relations. *Journal of Personality and Social Psychology, 67,* 741–763.

33. Pratto, F., Stallworth, L. M., Sidanius, J., & Siers, B. (1997). The gender gap in occupational role attainment: A social dominance approach. *Journal of Personality and Social Psychology, 72,* 37–53.

34. See note 32.

35. Herzberg, F. H. (1968). One more time: How do you motivate employees? *Harvard Business Review,* 53–60.

36. Thibaut, J. W., & Kelley, H. H. (1959). The social psychology of groups. New York: Wiley.

37. Porter, L. W., & Steers, R. M. (1973). Causes of employee turnover: A test of the Mobley, Griffeth, Hand, and Meglino model. *Journal of Applied Psychology, 67,* 53–59.

38. Mowday, R. T., Koberg, C. S., & McArthur, A. W. (1984). The psychology of the withdrawal process: A cross-validational test of Mobley's intermediate linkages model of turnover in two samples. *Academy of Management Journal, 27,* 79–94.

39. Carsten, J. M., & Spector, P. E. (1987). Unemployment, job satisfaction, and employee turnover: A meta-analytic test of the Muchinsky model. *Journal of Applied Psychology, 72,* 374–381.

40. Rice, R. W., Near, J. P., & Hunt, R. G. (1980). The job satisfaction/life satisfaction relationship: A review of empirical research. *Basic and Applied Social Psychology, 1,* 37–64.

41. Chacko, T. I. (1983). Job and life satisfactions: A causal analysis of their relationships. *Academy of Management Journal, 26,* 163–169.

42. Crouter, A. C., Perry-Jenkins, M., Huston, T. L., & Crawford, D. W. (1989). The influence of work induced psychological states on behavior at home. *Basic and Applied Social Psychology, 10,* 273–292.

43. Palmore, E. (1969). Predicting longevity: A follow-up controlling for age. *Gerontologist, 9,* 247–250.

44. Kornhauser, A. W. (1965). *Mental health of the industrial worker: A Detroit study.* New York: Wiley.

45. Shore, L. M., & Martin, H. J. (1989). Job satisfaction and organizational commitment in relation to work performance and turnover intentions. *Human Relations, 42,* 625–638.

46. Randall, D. M., Fedor, D. B., & Longenecker, C. O. (1990). The behavioral expression of organizational commitment. *Journal of Vocational Behavior, 36,* 210–225.

47. Romzek, B. S. (1989). Personal consequences of employee commitment. *Academy of Management Journal, 39,* 649–661.

48. Meyer, J. P., Allen, N. J., & Gellatly, I. R. (1990). Affective and continuance commitment to the organization: Evaluation of measures and analysis of concurrent and time-lagger relations. *Journal of Applied Psychology, 72,* 710–720.

49. Alle, N. J., & Meyer, J. P. (1990). The measurement and antecedents of affective, continuance, and normative commitment to the organization. *Journal of Occupational Psychology, 63,* 1–18.

Chapter 12

Interpersonal Attraction: Liking and Friendship

Propinquity and Familiarity: The Benefits of Closeness
Attractive Features: Can We Make a Deal?
Similarity: The Glue of Relationships

Love: What about That Special Thing?

Theoretical Perspectives: The Different Faces of Love
An Integrative Perspective: Putting It All Together

Romance in the Workplace: Do Work and Love Mix?

Office Romance: Some Basic Features
Romance and Job Performance: Pluses and Minuses
Handling Work Romance: Some Guidelines

Sexual Harassment: Abuse in the Workplace

Environment and Harassment: The Organizational Context
Dealing with Sexual Harassment: Minimizing the Problem

Work and Family Relationships: The Balancing Act

Dual Career Couples: Are Two Better Than One?
Marital Status and Quality of Life: Are Pairs Happier Than Singles?
Single Parents: Extra Demands
Work and Home: The Spillover Effect

Aggression at Work: Destructive Relationships

The Causes of Violence: Why?
Personal Characteristics and Violence: Who?
Controlling Violence: What Can We Do?

Special Sections

Ethics at Work
A Little Romance Can Be a Dangerous Thing

Guidelines for Effective Human Relations
Using What You've Learned

Experiential Exercise
The Experience of Sexual Harassment

INTERPERSONAL RELATIONS
Relationships and Work

Learning Objectives

After reading this chapter, you should be able to:

1. Describe the major factors that lead to liking and friendship.

2. Understand the different theories of love.

3. Discuss the major findings on romance in the workplace.

4. Summarize research on the occurrence and perception of sexual harassment.

5. Outline the influence of the major family variables, such as marital status and dual careers, on health and well-being.

6. List the personal and situational factors that can cause violence.

7. Discuss the ways in which violence can be controlled.

*R*ebecca was an MBA student who worked for a major corporation. She typically had the weekends free to pursue her own activities. She had worked for several months on plans for a fiftieth birthday party for her mother that was to be held this Saturday morning. She had coordinated the plans with friends and family, reserved a restaurant, organized some group gifts, and prepared for a follow-up party at her own house. She was really excited about the special day that was about to unfold. Then came the call! Early that Saturday morning her boss called to say that Rebecca had to work that day. She began to explain her plans for the day, but her boss interrupted, "I don't want your excuses. I need you to come to work." Rebecca felt she had no choice but to go. The party went on as planned while she worked for the entire day. What made the experience even more painful was Rebecca's discovery that there was no real emergency at work, and her boss could have easily managed without her.

*T*his true story was reported to a professor who was motivated to write about this practice as being typical of many "abusive organizations."[1] Such organizations expect their employees to make work their number one priority at all times. They have very little concern about employees' family needs and make very little effort to accommodate these outside demands. Employees often feel trapped in such companies because of limited alternatives in their region.

Rebecca's dilemma reflects only one of many types of relationships that can affect our work life. Sometimes, fellow employees may become attracted to each other and begin dating. They may even fall in love and decide to get married. This can present problems at work, especially if one of the partners has management responsibility. Other employees may be concerned about favoritism or may be jealous. Thus, the issue of interpersonal relations in the workplace is important, since effective work environments require compatible interpersonal relations. In this chapter, we analyze interpersonal relations in general and try to understand the implications of this knowledge for relations in work environments. First, we examine the factors that lead us to become attracted to other individuals and to fall in love with them. Then we examine the development of relationships, the role of romantic relationships in the workplace, and balancing of work and family relations.

INTERPERSONAL ATTRACTION: LIKING AND FRIENDSHIP

Propinquity and Familiarity: The Benefits of Closeness

One obvious factor in friendships is the need to be in close proximity to each other. Whether because of residential location, seating position, configuration of work sites, or involvement in various groups, we tend to come into contact with certain people. We may not particularly like some of them, but we may be attracted to others. Not surprisingly, most friendships and romantic relationships start with people who work or live close to each other. A casual reading of the marriage or engagement section of your newspaper will show that many of the couples went to the same university or high school or worked at the same company.

One reason for our attraction to people in close proximity is that we are attracted more to familiar people than to strangers. Studies have shown that the more frequently we encounter strangers, the more favorably we feel about them. This was first shown in carefully controlled laboratory studies where interaction was restricted lest the tone of the interaction overwhelm the effects of incidental exposure. In other words, familiarity appears to breed attraction and not contempt. This is particularly true if the stimuli to which we are exposed are fairly complex and our initial reactions are neutral, as is presumably the case with most strangers.[2] It appears that the familiarity effect is also used with considerable success by politicians and advertisers. We certainly encounter a lot of advertising and political campaigns that focus primarily on brand or name familiarity.

Attractive Features: Can We Make a Deal?

Of course, just because someone is nearby and familiar does not mean that he or she will be liked. One important factor determining our choice of friends is their characteristics. We tend to like people who have attractive features—intelligence, a good personality, good looks, talent, and attractive possessions. In romantic friendships, it appears that looks are particularly important. We are strongly attracted to individuals who are physically attractive and may be more affected by this factor than by others, such as intelligence and personality, in initial encounters. Unfortunately, we tend to assume that individuals who are above average in physical attractiveness are also above average in social competence, intelligence, mental health, and happiness.[3] There is little evidence that supports such ideas. Physically attractive people are more socially skilled and more popular, but this is likely a result of being treated more positively in social interactions. However, it should be noted that our self-perceptions of attractiveness have a stronger influence on our personal characteristics than our attractiveness as judged by others.[4] So, even if you are not blessed with Hollywood-style good looks, a positive self-image can help you be a success socially. Last but not least, smile! People who smile are rated as being considerably more attractive than those who do not.[5]

One example of the impact of attractiveness in the work environment comes from a study of MBA graduates conducted over a span of ten years.[6] Men who were rated as more attractive in school yearbook photos received higher starting salaries and continued earning higher salaries over the ten-year period. Attractive women did not receive higher starting salaries but earned more in subsequent years. Being one point higher on a five-point attractiveness scale resulted in $2,600 more earnings for men and $2,150 more for women in the ten-year period. The study did not provide evidence about the mechanisms that might underlie this effect. Possibly, more attractive graduates were perceived as being more competent. Alternatively, higher self-confidence on the part of more attractive graduates may have translated into better performance or impressions.

Although we are often drawn to physically attractive people, we may not actually seek them out as friends or dates. Here, choices seem to be governed by reality, in that we tend to select people who are similar in physical attractiveness (see Figure 12.1).[7] In fact, people seem to follow an economic perspective in selecting prospective romantic partners. We may roughly determine our own value on the dating market by taking into account looks, education, income, job, and other personal assets and look for partners with an equivalent value. In this way, wealthy old men may end up marrying beautiful young women. This may be seen as a fair trade. Of course, we might take a little risk and try for someone slightly above our own estimated value. Who knows? We might get lucky.

𝒥igure 12.1   **Physical Attractiveness: Romantic Couples Are Often Similar in Their Attractiveness**

Similarity: The Glue of Relationships

Not only do people strive for similarity in terms of overall "worth," but they also are attracted to people who are similar in values, opinions, race, socioeconomic level, and personality. Laboratory studies have shown our liking for others is increased to the extent that their opinions are in agreement with ours.[8] Studies of friends and romantic partners have also found evidence for the important role of similarity. Friends in high school may select among themselves on the basis of their activities or involvement in drugs or alcohol.[9] Marriage partners tend to be similar in a variety of personality traits, such as extroversion and dominance.[10] Even more important, similarity is important to satisfaction with relationships. When college students were asked to indicate the reasons for the breakup of romantic liaisons, they frequently cited boredom and differences in interests, sexual attitudes, background, and marriage ideas. In the case of marriage, success rates also tend to be higher for couples who have more in common (such as education and age).[11]

Do Opposites Attract?   Contrary to the evidence cited so far, it has often been suggested that opposites attract and even make better marriage partners. One basis for this idea is that individuals with different characteristics complement each other's weaknesses.[12] Thus, the shy accountant wife can keep the financial aspect of the family in order, while the sociable salesperson husband can arrange the social activities. While this kind of complementarity may have some merit, basic differences in social inclinations are more likely to cause problems in a relationship. For instance, how can this couple ever agree on how to spend their spare time? So, it is not surprising that similarity rather than complementarity is the main determinant of marital success.[13] This does not mean that differences along some dimensions can't be useful (for example, one person prefers outside housework and the other inside housework), but contrasting personalities or values are likely to lead to continual conflict in a relationship.

*L*OVE: WHAT ABOUT THAT SPECIAL THING?

They say that love makes the world go 'round. Certainly, if you listen to the songs on the radio, you would begin to believe it. It is the focal point of many contemporary songs, books, plays, and television shows. Why all the fuss? Is love such a special phenomenon? Well, if it is, psychologists were slow to look at it scientifically, but now there is an increasingly sophisticated body of research.

Theoretical Perspectives: The Different Faces of Love

Although we use the word **love** to describe special feelings associated with a variety of relationships (for example, romantic or family relationships), we no doubt realize that the nature of love varies among relationships and even within the same relationship. We will briefly examine some of the different perspectives that have been developed about love and its variations.

Reinforcement-Affect Model.   You have probably seen the bumper sticker on cars that says, "If it feels good, do it!" This sentiment is the basis of a hedonistic approach to life, which is concerned primarily with satisfaction of one's needs. Events that satisfy such needs are often called rewards or reinforcements and produce positive emotional reactions. To the extent that a relationship is associated with these rewards, strong positive feelings can develop. These rewards can come directly from the relationship—affection, attention, and praise—or from pleasant events that accompany the relationship—parties, movies, or a romantic evening. This principle underlies the Byrne-Clore reinforcement-affect model of attraction.[14] This model focuses on similarity of opinions and values. Since agreement from others serves to validate our view of the world, it serves as a powerful reward and produces positive feelings or affects. From this perspective, love is simply a strong degree of liking produced by rewards associated with a relationship (see Figure 12.2).

love A strong, affectionate relationship between people.

Figure 12.2   **Reinforcement-Affect Model of Love**

One influential theory of attraction is the Byrne-Clore reinforcement-affect model, which suggests that like and dislike are derived from positive or negative feelings associated with rewarding or punishing events in a relationship.

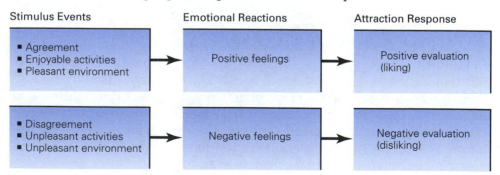

Exchange versus Communal Relationships.   So far, our discussion may make fairly good sense to you. Certainly, you wouldn't fall in love with someone unless you had many positive feelings about him or her. But receiving rewards may not be sufficient to produce a compatible love relationship. Another important factor is equity (see Chapter 5) of rewards. That is, individuals supposedly seek a fair balance or exchange of rewards in a relationship. If one partner is providing most of the rewards or benefits (such as affection or housework), this partner is likely to become dissatisfied, and the relationship may break up.[15] However, moderate differences among the partners in how much they bring to the relationship may not be a serious problem in relationships that involve strong caring and affection. These are sometimes called communal relationships, in which the partners are concerned primarily with satisfying each other's needs rather than with a fair balancing of rewards.[16]

Liking versus Loving.   Are reinforcement and equity all there is to love? Recent developments suggest that there is much more. First, loving and liking are actually somewhat distinct states. Friendship or liking involves a primarily positive evaluation of another person. Love, on the other hand, may involve a number of other factors. Rubin developed a scale indicating that love consisted of three components: (1) a strong need for affiliation or dependency—"I just can't do without him"; (2) a desire to be helpful—"I would do almost anything for her"; and (3) a sense of exclusiveness about the other person—"I feel very possessive about him."[17] This scale is a good predictor of desire to get married or otherwise commit to a romantic relationship, so it probably gives a fairly valid glimpse of this state called love.

Passionate Love.   One feature that often characterizes falling in love is a high level of emotionality or excitement. You have just found this wonderful and attractive new person and can't get her out of your mind. This level of excitement and arousal may be both positive and negative. The attention, sexual excitement, and process of getting to know someone new may all contribute to a generally positive feeling; yet, there is also a sense of uncertainty about the future of the romance. Will it last? Does the other person love you as much as you love her? You may be frustrated by separation, or you may experience feelings of jealousy.

The arousal and excitement aspect of love is the central focus of Walster and Berscheid's three-factor theory of love.[18] According to this model, passionate love requires (1) an appropriate and desirable love object, (2) culturally based beliefs and expectations about love, and (3) a heightened level of emotional arousal. Supposedly, when we are strongly aroused in the presence of an attractive person, we may interpret this emotional state as love. We do this in part because, in our culture, we have learned to associate love with such emotional states. The high level of arousal or excitement may actually be the result of sexual attraction or some other element of the

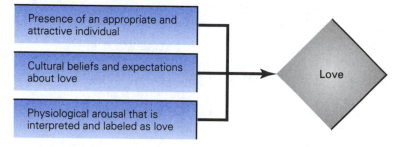

Figure 12.3 **Passionate Love: A Three-Factor Model**

The three-factor theory of passionate love proposes that love involves an attractive person, cultural beliefs about love, and interpretation of emotional arousal as love.

relationship, such as anxiety or uncertainty (see Figure 12.3 for a summary of this model). It can also come from sources outside of the relationship. Any factor that causes us to be aroused in the presence of an attractive individual, even the threat of shock, may lead to the inference of love.[19] For example, one study compared the reactions of men to an attractive female interviewer after they had crossed either an unstable bridge over a deep gorge or a stable bridge close to the ground. Those who crossed the scary bridge responded with sexual answers to ambiguous pictures and were most likely to try to contact the interviewer at a later time.[20] It appears that these men misinterpreted the arousal produced by the bridge as sexual attraction to the female interviewer.

The transfer of excitement from one source to another may explain why love and hate sometimes go together.[21] The sexual arousal and excitement of a love relationship may *transfer* to the anger produced in relationships by conflicts or jealousies. Some of the violent outbreaks that accompany attempts by one person to break off a relationship while the other is still passionately in love may be related to this factor. So, it is probably best to go slowly in winding down or cooling relationships.

It appears that the passionate phase of love lasts only a few months for most couples. It is difficult to maintain a high level of excitement about the relationship as the couple becomes more familiar with each other. Some of the initial uncertainty is gone, and there is no longer the thrill of discovery inherent in any new relationship. There may still be strong sexual attraction, but there is likely to be less of the idealization that was part of the early phase of the relationship. However, strong feelings of affection and caring may persist, as well as a sense of commitment. This is called the companionate love phase.[22]

An Integrative Perspective: Putting It All Together

The story of love appears to be complex. There are different types of love and different factors involved in the love experience. Sternberg has proposed that the different types of love relationships can be understood as varying on three basic dimensions—passion, intimacy, and decision/commitment.[23] Passion represents the emotional and arousal factors involved in love. Intimacy is the feeling of closeness and attachment. Decision/commitment is the decision that one is in love and that one is going to try maintain the relationship for a long period of time. Table 12.1 shows how different types of love relationships can be understood as varying on these three dimensions. For example, if only intimacy is present, one is experiencing liking, while passionate love (infatuation) would involve passion but little intimacy or commitment. A combination of passion and intimacy is romantic love. Companionate love involves intimacy and commitment but little passion. The ultimate or complete love that many strive for in romantic relationships comes from a combination of all three components—passion, intimacy, and commitment. Some evidence exists for this model, but more research is needed to determine its ability to account for love relationships in comparison to other models.[24] How many of the types of love listed in Table 12.1 have you experienced?

Table 12.1   **Love: An Integrative Approach**

Sternberg proposed that different types of love are based on different degrees of passion, intimacy, and decision/commitment. How these contribute to different types of love is shown here.

	Love Components		
Type of Love	**Passion**	**Intimacy**	**Decision/ Commitment**
Liking	No	Yes	No
Infatuation	Yes	No	No
Romantic	Yes	Yes	No
Companionate	No	Yes	Yes
Consummate	Yes	Yes	Yes

Based on suggestions by Sternberg, 1987; see note 23.

ROMANCE IN THE WORKPLACE: DO WORK AND LOVE MIX?

There have been drastic changes in the proportion of men and women in the workplace over the past few decades. Although women still dominate some job categories, such as secretaries and nurses, increasing numbers now hold a wide variety of professional and corporate positions. As a result, men and women find themselves working as colleagues in such areas as sales, research, and management (see Figure 12.4). While these changes are certainly positive ones from the standpoint of advancing the equality of women in the workplace, they also have provided more opportunities for the development of romance. Is this a positive or negative development? Certainly, those who have found a romantic partner through work channels may view it positively. But what about their fellow workers and bosses? What happens to their effectiveness at work? Does romance interfere with job performance and produce conflicts among employees, or does it provide an added reason to be highly motivated at work? These questions have drawn increased attention from researchers in the past few years.

Office Romance: Some Basic Features

Romantic involvement seems to be a common occurrence at work, with about 70 percent of workplaces having at least one reported romance.[25] The likelihood of romance may be partly facilitated by the proximity factor. Working together provides opportunities for communication and interaction. As noted earlier, we tend to like

Figure 12.4 **Workplace Romance: An Increasingly Common Phenomenon**

Today, men and women find themselves colleagues in a wide variety of work settings. This has increased the frequency of workplace romance.

people who are more familiar, and working together provides additional opportunities for communication and interaction. People therefore have more chances to discover similarities in values and opinions. Many jobs tend to attract employees who share fairly similar outlooks on life. For example, people working for a U.S. automobile manufacturer are likely to agree about the need for strong restrictions on the importation of foreign-made automobiles. In addition, when supervisors give their subordinates positive performance feedback or appraisal, the positive feelings produced in the subordinates may increase their liking for the supervisors.[26]

While shared similarities may aid the attraction process, romantic couples in the workplace often differ in a number of ways. The men in a relationship tend to be older, better educated, and of higher status.[27] This could be viewed as an exchange process, in that the higher status of the man is balanced by the youthfulness of the woman. The exchange does not appear to be based solely on the attractiveness of the woman, since the partners tend to be similar in physical attractiveness.[28] Thus, attraction in the workplace develops in about the same way as it does in most other situations. This attraction may develop into romance or love, especially if an individual has a positive attitude toward workplace romance, the organizational culture is tolerant of this type of romance, and the person has a lot of freedom or autonomy in his or her work.[29]

Workplace romances may have the same features or bases as the love relationships we have already discussed. A number of different motivations, however, affect the decisions to become romantically involved at work—love, ego, and job.[30] Love motivation involves a sincere desire for romance and long-term companionship. Those motivated by ego are interested in excitement, adventure, and sexual experiences. Job-motivated people are interested in the work-related benefits provided by the relationship, such as security, power, improved job conditions, and advancement.

Of course, the partners in a work romance may have similar or different motives for the relationship. As a result, there are many different types of romances.[31] In some, both partners may be motivated by love and ego, resulting in a passionate love relationship. This is the most common type found in the workplace. In others, when both partners are motivated primarily by love, a companionate relationship is likely to develop. A fling is the result of two people motivated exclusively by ego. Sometimes, the male in a relationship is motivated primarily by a desire for job power and control. He may seek out a female who has greater influence or power than he does to further these goals. This form of relationship, which involves a man with ego and job motives and a woman with love and job motives, is called a male-dominated utilitarian relationship. When the woman is motivated by ego and job but the male only by ego, a female-dominated utilitarian relationship exists. (This typically involves women with low status or power forming relationships with older, high power men.) As you can see, workplace romances can vary greatly in terms of motivation. We have summarized these and their reported frequency in Table 12.2 on page 348. How many of these motivations have you observed or experienced?

Table 12.2   Job Romance: Three Basic Motives

On the basis of the three basic motives for work romance (love, ego, and job), five different types of relationships are possible.

Partners	Motives	Relationship	Frequency
Male	Love, ego	Passionate love	36%
Female	Love, ego		
Male	Love	Companionate love	23%
Female	Love		
Male	Ego	Fling	19%
Female	Ego		
Male	Ego, job	Male-dominated utilitarian	8%
Female	Love, job		
Male	Ego	Female-dominated utilitarian	14%
Female	Ego, job		

Adapted from Dillard and Segrin, 1987; see note 31.

Romance and Job Performance: Pluses and Minuses

While work romances may fulfill a number of different needs for the participants, they are not without controversy. Some have suggested that such relationships interfere with the effective functioning of organizations.[32] The participants may be less productive at work because of their increased preoccupation with one another. Gossip, suspicion, and jealousy may negatively affect the work atmosphere. If the romance involves managers or takes place between people of different rank, the ability to manage effectively may be hurt, because credibility and objectivity in the eyes of the other employees may be lowered. Certainly, managers will not be able to objectively appraise the performance of the romantic partner. Also, once romances end, bad feelings among the participants may persist. This situation can lead to development of sexual harassment when one partner still wants to maintain the relationship or an embittered partner attempts to harm a former partner's career.[33]

Surveys indicate that most people perceive workplace romance in a negative manner. Such romances are seen as reducing productivity and job involvement.[34] In fact, this perception tends to be true in the early phases of the relationship when individuals may invest too much time and energy in the relationship during work hours. Later, as the relationship stabilizes, the couple may experience increased interest and motivation for work.[35] Positive effects on productivity and job involvement are most likely for those who start a workplace romance with a love motive. These people may be trying to impress their supervisors and thereby avoid negative reactions to such a romance.[36] Romances involving people of different status are more likely to negatively affect productivity and morale than romances between those of equal status, in part because of the negative reactions of peers to such romances. There may be feelings of jealousy, concerns about fairness, and a general awkwardness in work relationships.[37]

The picture for workplace romance is thus a bit mixed, with both positive and negative effects observed. A concrete example of this type of pattern is shown in Figure 12.5. In the study depicted in this figure, researchers found a slight tendency for people involved in organizational romance to arrive late or leave early, to complain more, or to have increased absence from work. However, there was also a strong increase in enthusiasm for work.[38] The people most likely to show an improvement in job performance were women who were love motivated.[39] Possibly, positive feelings about the love relationship spill over into positive feelings about the job. So, while there may be some drawbacks to office romance, there may be some positive effects as well. These positive effects appear most often with love-motivated employees and during the later phases of equal-status relationships.

Figure 12.5   **Effects of Workplace Romance: Not Always Negative**

Individuals involved in organizational romance may show a variety of changes in work behavior. While there is some tendency for more complaints, absenteeism, and tardiness, there is also increased enthusiasm for the job.

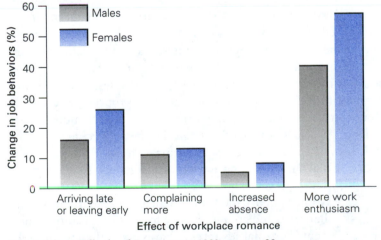

Adapted from Dillard and Broetzmann, 1989; see note 38.

Handling Work Romance: Some Guidelines

It is apparent that the effects of work romance can be varied. Sometimes work romance can be disruptive and interfere with job performance. At other times, it can create increased enthusiasm for the job. Because it is difficult to develop a single policy for every situation, it probably does not surprise you that the most common way of dealing with work romance is to do nothing.[40] This may not always be the best policy, however. Management needs to be sensitive to the motives that lie behind such romances and the varied effects they can have. Prohibiting the development of romantic relationships may not be feasible and may cut off the potential for relationships that are positive both for the participants and for the corporation. In particular, relationships motivated by love may be least problematic.[41] However, relationships that are exploitative or disruptive should not be ignored. The participants should be counseled about the impact of their relationship on the workplace, and steps should be taken to minimize the negative effects. They may have to limit their interaction at work, or they may need to be moved to different departments. If the relationship continues to be a problem, one or both of the partners may have to leave.

Do you think romantic involvement in the workplace is appropriate or unethical? What do you think about the dilemma outlined in the *Ethics at Work* section?

*S*EXUAL HARASSMENT: ABUSE IN THE WORKPLACE

One aspect of relations in the workplace that is a definite problem is sexual harassment. Have you ever experienced unwanted advances or requests from those with whom you work? Have you ever felt pressured to go out on a date or become involved with a supervisor? Have you ever been threatened with loss of your job if you did not go along with the request? If you can answer affirmatively to these questions, you have experienced sexual harassment. **Sexual harassment** can be defined as any unwanted sexual act or communication. These acts may fall into one of five categories. *Gender harassment* is the use of sexual or sexist remarks designed to convey insulting or degrading attitudes. *Seductive behaviors* are inappropriate attempts to initiate a romantic or sexual relationship. *Sexual bribery* involves attempts to gain sexual favors by means of promises of rewards. *Sexual coercion* is forcing sexual activity by way of threat. *Sexual assault* involves forced sexual contact.[42]

Studies indicate that sexual harassment occurs with considerable frequency. The percentage of women who report being harassed ranges from 35 to 90 percent.[43]

sexual harassment   An unwanted sexual communication or act.

Women report more experiences of sexual harassment than men and are more likely to consider insulting comments or sexual advances as harassment than men.[44] One study comparatively rated degree of sexual harassment based on the five categories described earlier. Not surprisingly, the more severe the behavior, the higher the harassment rating. Women were generally higher in their ratings, particularly for gender harassment and seductive behavior (see Figure 12.6 on page 352). When the harasser was a supervisor, the behavior was seen as more severe than when the person was a subordinate or coworker.[45] Sexual harassment is a worldwide problem and may be especially severe in cultures where women have very little power and status.[46]

Unfortunately, women report to others only about 10 percent of the instances of sexual harassment.[47] Moreover, even those events that have been objectively defined as sexual harassment may not be labeled so by those who experience them.[48] Studies indicate a range of perceived harassment from 5 percent to 36 percent in different work environments. However, reports of the occurrence of behaviors that fall into one of the five objectively defined categories range from 10 percent to 90 percent. Possibly, women do not see commonly defined harassment behaviors as being

Ethics at Work

A Little Romance Can Be a Dangerous Thing

Brenda is a supervisor in the accounting department of McKelvey Finance. She oversees about twenty-five men and women and has a good rapport with her subordinates. She has a pleasant personality and takes a personal interest in the lives of the employees. She has recently hired several new people and is spending some extra time with them to make sure they learn the ropes. She is particularly impressed with Manuel. He is bright and personable and has quickly fit into the social network. She discovers that they have quite a few interests in common. They both like to camp, bike, and sail. They even belong to the same religious denomination. Brenda has been divorced for about three years and has had a difficult time finding compatible men. Her social life has been close to nil. Now, here in her own "backyard," she has come across an ideal person with whom to have a relationship. Too bad that he works for her! She knows the company frowns on relationships between supervisors and their subordinates. "But what would it hurt if we went for a casual biking date?" she thinks to herself. "We could keep things at an appropriate, nonromantic level. No one would have to know. At work we could just act like nothing is going on. I could make it clear to him that we would have to set limits on our relationship."

What do you think? Is Brenda deluding herself? What sorts of problems are likely to occur? What would happen if other employees and management found out? Do you think it is ever appropriate for someone to date a subordinate? Why or why not? If you think it is appropriate, are there some rules or regulations that should govern such relationships?

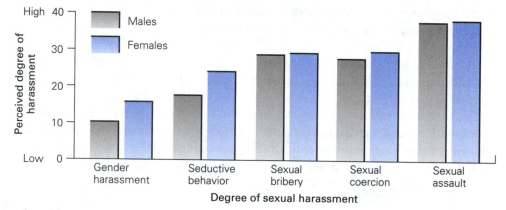

Figure 12.6   **Sexual Harassment: Different Perceptions**

Ratings of the degree of sexual harassment experienced by men and women are based on the different types of behaviors.

Adapted from Tata, 1993; see note 43.

inappropriate, or they may subjectively redefine it as not harassing to minimize the emotional cost involved in dealing with such incidents. Also, personal characteristics, such as a general negativity to sexual matters, may motivate individuals to ignore instances of harassment.[49] What are your experiences with sexually inappropriate behavior? How do you feel about them? You may wish to fill out the sexual harassment survey in the *Experiential Exercise* section on page 363 to compare your experiences and feelings with those of others.

What are the consequences of sexual harassment? Obviously, they depend on the severity of the harassment and the personal characteristics of the victim. Some victims may be better able to put harassers in their place, but others may lack the confidence or power to do so. In general, sexual harassment appears to have very significant consequences for job satisfaction, psychological problems, and physical health. Females who have experienced sexual harassment report high levels of psychological distress, which are in turn related to health problems. These women also have higher rates of absenteeism and a strong desire to leave their jobs.[50]

Environment and Harassment: The Organizational Context

When sexual harassment occurs, we tend to focus on the harassers and their personal characteristics. Two features of organizations, however, strongly influence the occurrence of sexual harassment in the workplace.[51] The first feature is organizational climate. Some organizations are simply more tolerant of sexual harassment than others. They do not take complaints seriously, complaining may lead to reprisals, and the alleged harassers are rarely punished. A second important feature comprises the gender context, with male-dominated workplaces being associated with higher levels of sexual harassment.

Sexual harassment features can also be common to a job or workgroup. These features may include off-color jokes, the presence of sexual reading materials or pictures, and pressures to go to sexually oriented clubs for after-work gatherings. Moreover, people may be aware of sexual harassment experiences of their coworkers, either by direct observation or through the grapevine. This indirect exposure to sexual harassment has been termed *ambient sexual harassment;* like direct sexual harassment, it is related to organizational tolerance of sexually harassing behavior. The ambient aspect of harassment has negative effects above and beyond those of direct harassment on psychological problems, job satisfaction, and health.[52]

Dealing with Sexual Harassment: Minimizing the Problem

What should be done about sexual harassment? The most important factor is for top management to make it clear that this type of behavior will not be tolerated. The behaviors that constitute sexual harassment should be clearly outlined to all employees, and there should be a procedure for reporting and dealing with them. Among major companies, about three-fourths have developed sexual harassment policies. In most cases, the harasser is reprimanded, and 20 percent of the time firing is the result.[53] There are, however, many factors that inhibit reports of sexual harassment. Given the confusing array of social norms among different groups, it may not be clear what is appropriate or inappropriate in different contexts. There may be a tendency to give the offender the benefit of the doubt. Our desire for social acceptance may lead us to put up with a variety of behaviors that we find personally inappropriate. It also may be emotionally easier to ignore the relatively minor forms of harassment (such as sexist remarks) than to confront the offenders or go through the complaint process. Concerns about privacy and keeping jobs may lead some not to report inappropriate behavior.[54]

To minimize sexual harassment in the workplace and help employees confront the problems as they occur, the following guidelines are suggested:[55]

1. There should be a clear policy statement that explains what constitutes sexual harassment and that such behaviors will not be tolerated.
2. Specific procedures for dealing with sexual harassment should be outlined.
3. Informal procedures that protect the privacy of the employees are preferred. A mandatory formal investigation policy may inhibit reporting. In most cases, the offenders may not have been aware that their behavior was offensive, and the problem may be easily rectified.

4. Informal assistance from a third party, such as the human resources manager, should be available. Since bosses are often the perpetrators of sexual harassment, employees should not be required to go through their supervisors as part of the process.

5. A formal process for fact finding and action should be available if needed.

6. Counseling should be available to help individuals directly confront the harasser either in person or in written form. It may be possible to resolve the problem in this manner without involving other parties.

7. The department involved should attend a training program on the detection and prevention of sexual harassment.

WORK AND FAMILY RELATIONSHIPS: THE BALANCING ACT

Although we tend to separate life at work and at home in our minds, they are often very much related. Problems at work can carry over to our family relationships, and family problems can affect our functioning at work.[56] Many companies are aware of this relationship, and some have programs to ease family burdens, such as child-care facilities and family counseling. We now discuss in further detail some of the problems for families that are derived from careers.

Dual Career Couples: Are Two Better Than One?

For increasing numbers of couples, both partners have jobs or careers. This may be due to economic necessity or preference. Only 11 percent of all families fit the traditional mold of working father and mother at home with the children.[57] Dual careers may yield economic benefits and a sense of fulfillment for both partners. However, there are likely to be some problems. All of the home and family chores need to be completed after work hours. Women tend to get stuck with a disproportionate amount of such chores.[58] Men whose wives work tend to have poorer mental and physical health, possibly because of the increased pressures on the family.[59,60] Both husbands and wives show similar stress reactions to work-related problems.[61] These emotional reactions can be contagious, so that the emotional state of one partner can influence that of the other.[62] Finally, there is the issue of obtaining quality day care.[63] There may be guilt about leaving young children for large parts of the week in day-care facilities, and it may be difficult to find quality time for interaction with the children.

The various job-related strains have led some couples to get off the fast track and seek simpler lives.[64] One way to do this is by job sharing. Some companies allow two employees to share the same job. Although this option reduces an employee's income and benefits, the increased flexibility may be well worth the price. Furthermore, the employee can keep involved in a meaningful and well-paying career. This is certainly preferable to the alternative of low paying part-time or temporary positions.

Marital Status and Quality of Life: Are Pairs Happier Than Singles?

Although there are pluses and minuses to being a dual career couple, what about being married itself? Is marriage good for our well-being? Can satisfying marital relationships compensate for the negative aspects of our careers? There is, in fact, considerable evidence that married people are happier and healthier than singles.[65] There are a variety of possible reasons for this finding. Couples enjoy each others' social support and may encourage each other to seek medical treatment and health-promoting behaviors. Singles may lead riskier lives, in part because they do not have a strong feeling of responsibility to a significant other. They may also experience loneliness, and single parents have the added demands of raising children alone. However, marriage is not always the best option. Individuals in distressed marriages have poorer mental and physical health. Some lifestyles and personalities may be best suited to being single. Single individuals may also have greater flexibility in adjusting to job demands.

Single Parents: Extra Demands

About 6 percent of the workforce are single parents.[66] They have a particularly demanding lifestyle. Furthermore, if these individuals are divorced or widowed, they may suffer from relatively poor health.[67] As discussed earlier, this may result from feelings of loneliness and lack of social support. There is also the continual concern with child care. Income of single parents is often limited, and it may be difficult to afford quality child care. Sometimes, children must be left at home without supervision for long periods of time. This gives them more opportunities to get into trouble. These children may also lack the parental involvement in their schoolwork that may be important for encouraging achievement.

One solution to the child-care dilemma may be to involve children in after-school programs. They can keep kids from getting into trouble as well as provide encouragement for doing homework. Organizations can help single parents by providing flexible scheduling. Flex-time allows the employee to adjust his daily work schedule to fit with personal needs. Instead of having all employees work the same schedule, some employees can begin earlier or later in the day or work four ten-hour days per week. Some jobs can be performed at home as well as at the office. Telecommuting involves transferring work by computer hook-up to the office. This arrangement can provide increased flexibility, reduce distractions, and reduce commuting time. It also enables parents to be available for child care if needed. However, the child-care duties can interfere with work and produce conflicts. Working at home also isolates employees from coworkers and may inhibit opportunities for promotion.

Although single parents face numerous challenges, they may have little choice but to make the extra efforts required. However, by fully utilizing the opportunities available to them in the community and at work, they may be able to effectively manage these obstacles. Moreover, children of single parents may develop a greater sense of personal responsibility and self-esteem because of their greater independence.[68]

Work and Home: The Spillover Effect

Whatever the nature of one's home life, it is likely to spill over into work. People report that parenting, community involvement, and recreation have positive effects on their functioning at work.[69] Alternatively, one's career may provide rewards that are lacking at home. The resulting satisfaction and sense of well-being could carry over to one's family life. However, some feel that being successful in one domain requires sacrifice in another. So, a successful home life may necessitate less investment into one's career, while a successful career may limit one's ability to share quality time with one's spouse and children and to share fairly in the home responsibilities.[70] Each of these scenarios probably occurs to some extent in different families and for different personalities. Which one best fits your situation or your type of personality? The most important lesson from this line of research is that work and family life do influence one another. Thus, both employees and management need to be sensitive to ways in which to increase satisfaction and success in both spheres of life.

AGGRESSION AT WORK: DESTRUCTIVE RELATIONSHIPS

Although we may make many friends at work, we may also make some enemies. In fact, one major problem at work is an increase in aggressive or violent incidents. Aggressive behavior includes any behavior that is intended to harm another person. It can range from negative comments to physical violence. Because physical violence is dramatic and serious, statistics about these types of incidents have been much in the news. The number of U.S. workers killed on the job every year has more than doubled since 1989.[71] Homicides rank as the number one cause of traumatic deaths that occur at work.[72] Some of these events may involve romantic conflicts in which one partner wishes to vent his or her anger about interpersonal conflicts. The work environment may be the only place where he or she can locate the partner with certainty.

A large number of such cases involve jealous husbands or ex-husbands who attempt to kill their wives. It is, of course, difficult to anticipate or prevent these incidents unless one knows ahead of time what is going to happen—which is usually not the case.

Another type of violence that is increasing in the workplace involves disgruntled employees who seek revenge for perceived wrongs by a supervisor. Hundreds of these cases occur every year. Some of the most highly publicized ones have involved postal employees. In addition to assaults, a significant number of rapes, thefts, and robberies occur in the workplace. It is estimated that the total yearly violent incidents at work in the United States number about 1 million. This is about 15 percent of all of the acts of violence experienced by U.S. residents.[73]

Of course, many more aggressive incidents at work do not result in fatalities. Surveys of workplace violence have noted the occurrence of fistfights, stabbings, assaults with weapons, and sexual assault. Sexual harassment and work harassment (unfair or insensitive treatment) are also significant problems in some workplaces and can be viewed as a form of aggression. Sabotage, vandalism, and theft may also have an aggressive basis.[74] Why does this violence and aggression occur, and how we can prevent it? Unfortunately, conducting scientific research on these spontaneous events is problematic. Nevertheless, a large body of evidence on aggression gives us some clues.[75,76]

The Causes of Violence: Why?

Many causes of violent or aggressive behavior at work have been identified. One major factor appears to be frustration, which results from the failure to achieve some desired goal. Promotions, raises, approval from supervisors or coworkers, good working conditions, job satisfaction, and fair treatment by others are just some of the goals to which people aspire at work. When faced with increasing pressure to enhance their productivity and downsizing, many employees experience increased levels of stress (Chapter 14), lower levels of job satisfaction (Chapter 11), and increased frustration. The combination of these negative experiences with specific unpleasant incidents or encounters in the workplace may provoke aggressive or violent incidents. Such aggression is typically accompanied by strong feelings of anger or hostility, hostile or aggressive thoughts, and increased levels of physiological and psychological arousal.

As you probably know from personal experience, people often have aggressive feelings and thoughts without acting on them. Why? Various mental processes appear to intervene between the instigating events and the potential aggressive behavior. First, individuals appraise or evaluate the incident to determine whether aggressive feelings or thoughts are justified. They may evaluate whether the action was intentional and whether serious harm was done. Second, individuals evaluate their options. Although aggression may seem like a natural response, it can lead to loss of one's job, friends, and freedom. Most people therefore consider alternative ways of dealing with their problems or frustrations. They may try to talk things out, ask someone to serve as a mediator, or simply leave for a better situation.

What are the specific factors that lead to violent or aggressive actions? Employees may have conflicts over division of labor, promotions, and work procedures. However, it appears that problems with supervisors are most likely to produce violence. Employees may feel that the supervisor has not been fair in assigning jobs, giving raises, or suggesting promotions. Highly stressful work conditions and authoritative supervision may also contribute to the level of negative emotionality experienced. In a similar vein, authoritative or rigid parenting styles have been related to aggressive behavior in children.[77] Angry or dissatisfied employees are unlikely to be very productive or reliable and may be fired. Loss of one's job is, of course, a major emotional event and will probably greatly increase the negative emotions. It is therefore not surprising that much work-related violence involves those who have recently been dismissed.

Personal Characteristics and Violence: Who?

You have probably been angry and frustrated at work many times and have never expressed these feelings in a violent way. In fact, violence occurs in only a small number of such cases. But even one case of violence at work is too many. Can we predict who is likely to blow up or act out violently? We cannot predict with any level of certainty how a particular person will react, but there are some general characteristics that increase the chances of someone's behaving in an aggressive or violent manner. Men are involved in much more violence than women. Although some have suggested a biological basis for this difference, much evidence suggests that the reason for this lies in the cultural socialization of males. Cultural norms and traditions reward males for being tough and acting aggressively when they are wronged. This may have been useful in the past for survival for some groups, such as those who guarded herds. Some of this culture of violence may have been carried on in societal traditions and norms. This seems to be particularly evident in the southern United States.[78] Films and television also glorify violence by men.

There appears to be considerable consistency in violence-proneness. Males who were aggressive in childhood (for example, at age 9) are more likely to have been convicted of a violent crime by age 32.[79] Some of this aggression may be instrumental in nature. Individuals may seek a certain goal (dominance, valued possessions, and so on) and may calmly seek to attain it, even by violent means if necessary. However, much violence may involve strong emotional reactivity.[80] One group that tends toward such emotional reactivity is people with the Type A personality. Some of these individuals may react with anger or hostility to situations that frustrate their competitive drives.[81] Individuals with a low level of mental development may also tend to react violently to provocations,[82] as might those who consume alcohol.[83] Both of

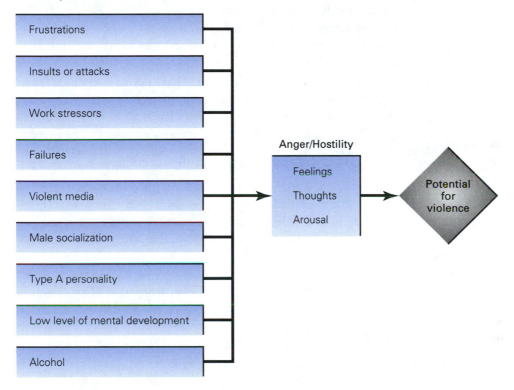

| *Figure 12.7* | **Causes of Aggression: Feeding the Anger** |

A variety of factors influence the occurrence of violent behavior.

these factors may lead individuals to misread social cues and reduce their sensitivity to potential negative consequences of aggression.[84] Figure 12.7 summarizes the factors that have been associated with increased levels of violence.

Controlling Violence: What Can We Do?

There are many common-sense solutions to violence. One is that when people are able to vent their aggressive feelings by expressing them, it will reduce their aggressive inclinations in the future. So kicking the furniture, hitting a punching bag, or yelling at someone should help reduce the feelings of anger. Actually, evidence suggests that this is *not* the case. Acting out aggressively seems to actually maintain or increase the aggressive impulses.[85] For example, couples who tend to verbally express their hostile feelings are also those who tend to be involved in more physical violence.[86] It seems to be quite clear that in most cases, violent behavior is more likely to stimulate further violence than to reduce it.[87] So what does work, you ask? Several techniques appear to have some value in curtailing violence:[88–90]

1. **Screening for aggressive tendencies.** Some people are more likely to act out aggressively than others. This tendency can be discovered by checking behavior in past jobs, using tests that assess tendencies to be aggressive, and conducting person interviews.

2. **Training.** Aggression-prone individuals tend to have poor social skills. Training these individuals to deal effectively with a variety of potentially frustrating situations may be useful. Teaching skills in conflict management, interpersonal communication, and stress management may also offer benefits. In addition, employees can be trained to recognize the behavioral characteristics of violence-prone individuals (for example, a tendency toward anger, blaming others).

3. **Developing perceptions of justice.** It is important for individuals to feel that procedures and actions at work are fair. Management needs to ensure that employees understand the basis for decisions and that the same standards of fairness are used with everyone.

4. **Reducing emotionality.** Since much of violence is emotion-based, it is important to find ways to lower the emotional level without venting or acting out. Relaxation techniques may be helpful, but recent approaches have also used self-instructional training.[91,92] This involves getting the angry person to revise his or her thinking processes about events that are the cause of the anger.

5. **Producing incompatible responses.** Have you ever felt angry at someone but found it hard to maintain this anger when something amusing happened? Apparently, angry feelings can be reduced when competing emotions are produced.[93] So taking someone who is angry to a funny movie or some other pleasant event may at least temporarily defuse the anger. When the person is in a less angry state, he or she may be able to think more calmly and rationally about the cause of the anger.

6. **Dealing with the causes of the anger.** Although acting out may stimulate more aggression, it is important not to let anger fester. Some people may hold in their frustrations for a long time before blowing up and committing a violent crime. Supervisors should be alert to employees who seem to be upset about some aspect of their work situation. Talking things out in a calm and controlled manner as problems occur may help prevent individuals from building up their negative emotions.[94,95]

7. **Applying person-oriented leadership.** Supervisors should be sensitive to the needs of their workers. While it is important to maintain high productivity, a supervisor who maintains good relationships with employees and is sensitive to employee input is likely to minimize the build-up of aggressive feelings. Employees also will feel free to discuss their feelings with such a supervisor.

Guidelines for Effective Human Relations

Using What You've Learned

In this chapter, we examined a broad range of principles and findings about inter-personal relations. Although few rules will apply to every situation, some general guidelines are suggested by the various findings we have discussed. These are summarized below for your consideration. Remember, no rule works 100 percent in every situation. However, these guidelines should improve your success in interpersonal relations.

- Don't put too much emphasis on physical attractiveness in your relationships. Similarity in important characteristics and values is more important for success of relationships.

- For love relationships to last, it is important to maintain a high reward level in addition to maintaining intimacy and commitment.

- Romance in the workplace can create a number of problems. If you do get involved in such a relationship, you should minimize your interaction during work hours. Romantic involvements with subordinates are most problematic.

- Be aware of the different sensitivities of males and females about behaviors that may be seen as sexual harassment. The best policy is to treat members of either sex with respect. Pressuring a subordinate to become involved sexually is inappropriate and can lead to serious sanctions at work.

- Be aware of how your family status affects your work performance. A marital partner can provide emotional support, but dual careers can put additional strains on a relationship.

- It is important to deal with strong negative emotions or anger when they occur. Person-oriented leaders who emphasize cooperation are likely to minimize the occurrence of violent outbursts.

It is clear that we need people and that involvement with others has many benefits. However, if we make inappropriate choices in our relationships, we may pay a significant price. It is best to be cautious in developing relationships. This will minimize the potential for becoming involved in coercive situations as well as allow for mutual discovery before personal commitments are made. Our search for love and relationships can yield a beautiful harvest, but it can also lead to pain. Caution, sensitivity, and common sense may allow you to avoid much of the pain.

Summary

We tend to like people who are familiar or who have attractive features. Contrary to common expectations, we are attracted most to those who are similar to us in such dimensions as opinion and personality.

Love is based partly on positive emotions related to the exchange of rewards. There are many types of love, ranging from passionate to companionate. It has been proposed that the different love relationships vary on three basic dimensions: passion, intimacy, and decision/commitment. Workplace romance is an increasingly frequent phenomenon. People become involved in such romances due to a wide variety of motives. While such romances may have some negative effects on job performance, these may be counteracted in part by an increase in enthusiasm for the job.

Sexual harassment can be a serious problem. It is important to institute procedures to eliminate its occurrence.

One's family situation can influence work performance and careers. Dual career couples and single parents may have a particularly difficult time balancing work and family life.

Violence in the workplace is an increasing problem. Violence seems to be related to a variety of situational and personal factors. However, there are a number of approaches that appear to be effective in reducing the occurrence of violent behavior.

Key Terms

love, p. 342
sexual harassment, p. 350

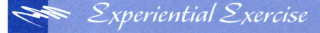 Experiential Exercise

The Experience of Sexual Harassment

For the following items, indicate whether you have experienced this type of behavior at work. Then indicate whether you feel this type of behavior constitutes sexual harassment.

1. Sexist remarks or jokes that are degrading.

    Experienced   Yes _____ No _____

    Harassment   Yes _____ No _____

2. Inappropriate or unwanted attempts to initiate romantic or sexual relations.

    Experienced   Yes _____   No _____

    Harassment   Yes _____   No _____

3. Promises of rewards for sexual favors or relations.

    Experienced   Yes _____   No _____

    Harassment   Yes _____   No _____

4. Threats of punishment or retaliation to obtain sexual favors or cooperation.

    Experienced   Yes _____   No _____

    Harassment   Yes _____   No _____

5. Forced sexual contact.

    Experienced   Yes _____   No _____

    Harassment   Yes _____   No _____

Ask your instructor to obtain this information from all of the students in the class. The more severe behaviors will probably be experienced less frequently but will be seen as harassing by a higher percentage of students. Female students should have more experience with these behaviors and be more likely to see them as harassing than male students.

Adapted from a scale developed by Fitzgerald et al., 1988; see note 42.

Notes

1. Powell, G. N. (1998). The abusive organization. *Academy of Management Executive, 12*, 95–96.

2. Bornstein, R. F. (1989). Exposure and affect: Overview and meta-analysis of research, 1968–1987. *Psychological Bulletin, 106,* 265–289

3. Eagly, A. H., Ashmore, R. D., Makhijani, M. G., & Longo, L. C. (1991). What is beautiful is good, but . . . : A meta-analytic review of research on the physical attractiveness stereotype. *Psychological Bulletin, 110,* 109–128.

4. Feingold, A. (1992). Good-looking people are not what we think. *Psychological Bulletin, 111,* 304–341.

5. Mueser, K. T., Grau, B. W., Sussman, S., & Rosen, A. J. (1984). You're only as pretty as you feel: Facial expression as a determinant of physical attractiveness. *Journal of Personality and Social Psychology, 46,* 469–478.

6. Frieze, I. H., Olson, J. E., & Russell, J. (1991). Attractiveness and income for men and women in

management. *Journal of Applied Social Psychology, 21,* 1039–1057.

7. Berscheid, E., Dion, K., Walster, E., & Walster, G. W. (1971). Physical attractiveness and dating choice: A test of the matching hypothesis. *Journal of Experimental Social Psychology, 7,* 173–189.

8. Byrne, D., Clore, G. L., & Smeaton, G. (1986). The attraction hypothesis: Do similar attitudes affect anything? *Journal of Personality and Social Psychology, 51,* 1167–1170.

9. Kandel, D. B. (1978). Similarity in real-life adolescent friendship pairs. *Journal of Personality and Social Psychology, 36,* 306–312.

10. Buss, D. M., & Barnes, M. (1986). Preferences in human mate selection. *Journal of Personality and Social Psychology, 50,* 559–570.

11. Cate, R. D., & Lloyd, S. A. (1988). Courtship. In S. W. Duck (ed.), *Handbook of personal relationships* (pp. 409–427). New York: John Wiley.

12. Winch, R. F. (1958). *Mate selection: A study in complementary needs.* New York: Harper & Row.

13. Meyer, J. P., & Pepper, S. (1977). Need compatibility and marital adjustment in young married couples. *Journal of Personality and Social Psychology, 35,* 331–342.

14. Byrne, D., & Clore, G. L. (1970). A reinforcement-affect model of evaluative responses. *Personality: An International Journal, 1,* 103–128.

15. See note 11.

16. Clark, M. S., & Mills, J. (1979). Interpersonal attraction in exchange and communal relationships. *Journal of Personality and Social Psychology, 37,* 12–24.

17. Rubin, Z. (1970). Measurement of romantic love. *Journal of Personality and Social Psychology, 16,* 1243–1246.

18. Walster, E., & Berscheid, E. (1974). A little bit about love: A minor essay on a major topic. In T. L. Huston (ed.), *Foundations of interpersonal attraction* (pp. 356–400). New York: Academic Press.

19. Kenrick, D. T., & Cialdini, R. B. (1977). Romantic attraction: Misattribution versus reinforcement explanations. *Journal of Personality and Social Psychology, 35,* 381–391.

20. Dutton, D. G., & Aron, A. P. (1974). Some evidence for heightened sexual attraction under conditions of high anxiety. *Journal of Personality and Social Psychology, 30,* 510–517.

21. Zillmann, D. (1971). *Connections between sex and aggression.* Hillsdale, NJ: Erlbaum.

22. Hatfield, E. (1982). Passionate love, companionate love, and intimacy. In M. Fisher & G. Stricker (eds.), *Intimacy* (pp. 267–292). New York: Plenum.

23. Sternberg, R. J. (1987). Liking versus loving: A comparative evaluation of theories. *Psychological Bulletin, 102,* 331–345.

24. Acker, M., & Davis, M. H. (1992). Intimacy, passion and commitment in adult romantic relationships: A test of the triangular theory of love. *Journal of Social and Personal Relationships, 9,* 21–50.

25. Dillard, J. P., & Miller, K. I. (1988). Intimate relationships in task environments. In S. W. Duck (ed.), *Handbook of personal relationships* (pp. 449–466). New York: John Wiley.

26. Pierce, C. A., Byrne, D., & Aguinis, H. (1996). Attraction in organizations: A model of workplace romance. *Journal of Organizational Behavior, 17,* 5–32.

27. Miller, K. I., & Ellis, B. H. (1987, May). Stereotypical views of intimate relationships in organizations. Paper presented at the Annual Meeting of the International Communication Association, Montreal.

28. Dillard, J. P., & Witteman, H. (1985). Romantic relationships at work: Organizational and personal influences. *Human Communication Research, 12,* 99–116.

29. See note 26.

30. Quinn, R. E. (1977). Coping with Cupid: The formation, impact, and management of romantic relationships in organizations. *Administrative Science Quarterly, 22,* 30–45.

31. Dillard, J. P., & Segrin, C. (1987, May). Intimate relationships in organizations: Relational types,

illicitness, and power. Paper presented at the Annual Meeting of the International Communication Association, Montreal.

32. Collins, E. G. C. (1983). Managers and lovers. *Harvard Business Review, 83,* 142–153.

33. Pierce, C. A., & Aguinis, H. (1997). Bridging the gap between romantic relationships and sexual harassment in organizations. *Journal of Organizational Behavior, 18,* 197–200.

34. Anderson, C. I., & Hunsaker, P. L. (1985). Why there's romancing at the office and why it's everybody's problem. *Personnel, 62,* 57–63.

35. See note 26.

36. Dillard, J. P. (1987). Close relationships at work: Perceptions of the motives and performance of relational participants. *Journal of Social and Personal Relationships, 4,* 179–193.

37. Mainiero, L. A. (1986). A review and analysis of power dynamics in organizational romances. *Academy of Management Review, 11,* 750–762.

38. Dillard, J. P., & Broetzmann, S. M. (1989). Romantic relationships at work: Perceived changes in job-related behaviors as a function of participant's motive, partner's motive, and gender. *Journal of Applied Social Psychology, 19,* 93–110.

39. Dillard, J. P. (1987). Close relationships at work: Perceptions of the motives and performance of relational participants. *Journal of Social and Personal Relationships, 4,* 179–193.

40. See note 30.

41. See note 38.

42. Fitzgerald, L. F., Shullman, S. L., Bailey, N., Richards, M., Swecker, J., Gold, T., Ormerod, M., & Weitzman, L. (1988). The incidence and dimensions of sexual harassment in academia and the workplace. *Journal of Vocational Behavior, 32,* 152–175.

43. Tata, J. (1993). The structure and phenomenon of sexual harassment: Impact of category of sexually harassing behavior, gender, and hierarchical level. *Journal of Applied Social Psychology, 23,* 199–211.

44. Gervasio, A. H., & Ruckdeschel, K. (1992). College students' judgments of verbal sexual harassment. *Journal of Applied Social Psychology, 22,* 190–211.

45. See note 43.

46. Menon, S. A., & Kanekar, S. (1992). Attitudes toward sexual harassment of women in India. *Journal of Applied Social Psychology, 22,* 1940–1952.

47. Gutek, B. A., Nakamura, C. Y., Gahart, M., & Handschumacher, I. (1980). Sexuality and the workplace. *Basic and Applied Social Psychology, 1,* 255–265.

48. Barak, A., Fisher, W. A., & Houston, S. (1992). Individual difference correlates of the experience of sexual harassment among female university students. *Journal of Applied Social Psychology, 22,* 17–37.

49. Ibid.

50. Fitzgerald, L. F., Drasgow, F., Hulin, C. L., Gelfand, M. J., & Magley, V. J. (1997). Antecedents and consequences of sexual harassment in organizations: A test of an integrated model. *Journal of Applied Psychology, 82,* 578–589.

51. Ibid.

52. Glomb, T. M., Richman, W. L., Hulin, C. L., Drasgow, F., Schneider, K. T., & Fitzgerald, L. F. (1997). Ambient sexual harassment: An integrated model of antecedents and consequences. *Organizational Behavior and Human Decision Processes, 71,* 309–328.

53. Gibbs, N. (1991, October 21). Office crime. *Time,* pp. 52–64.

54. Kremer, J. M. D., & Marks, J. (1992). Sexual harassment: The response of management and trade unions. *Journal of Occupational and Organizational Psychology, 65,* 5–15.

55. Niven, D. (1992, March/April). The case of the hidden harassment. *Harvard Business Review,* pp. 12–22.

56. Kabanoff, B. (1980). Work and nonwork: A review of models, methods, and findings. *Psychological Bulletin, 88,* 60–77.

57. Friedman, D. E. (1987). Work vs. family: War of the worlds. *Personnel Administrator, 32,* 36–39.

58. Atkinson, J., & Huston, T. L. (1984). Sex role orientation and division of labor early in marriage. *Journal of Personality and Social Psychology, 46,* 330–345.

59. Haynes, S. G., Eaker, E. D., & Feinleib, M. (1983). Spouse behavior and coronary heart disease in men: Prospective results from the Framingham heart study. *American Journal of Epidemiology, 110,* 1–22.

60. Kessler, R. C., & McRae, J. A., Jr. (1982). The effect of wives' employment on the mental health of married men and women. *American Sociological Review, 4,* 216–227.

61. Barnett, R. C., Marshall, N. L., Raudenbush, S. W., & Brennan, R. T. (1993). Gender and the relationship between job experiences and psychological distress: A study of dual-earner couples. *Journal of Personality and Social Psychology, 64,* 794–806.

62. Hatfield, E., Cacioppo, J. T., & Rapson, R. (1992). The logic of emotions: Emotional contagion. In M. S. Clark (ed.), *Review of personality and social psychology* (Volume 14) (pp. 151–177). Newbury Park, CA: Sage.

63. Zedeck, S., & Mosier, K. L. (1990). Work in the family and employing organization. *American Psychologist, 45,* 240–251.

64. Castro, J. (1993, April 8). The simple life. *Time,* pp. 58–63.

65. Burman, B., & Margolin, G. (1992). Analysis of the association between marital relationships and health problems: An interactional perspective. *Psychological Bulletin, 112,* 39–63.

66. See note 57.

67. Verbrugge, L. M. (1979). Marital status and health. *Journal of Marriage and the Family, 41,* 267–285.

68. Barbar, B. L., & Eccles, J. S. (1992). Long-term influence of divorce and single parenting on adolescent family- and work-related values, behaviors, and aspirations. *Psychological Bulletin, 111,* 108–126.

69. Kirchmeyer, C. (1992). Perceptions of nonwork-to-work spillover: Challenging the common view of conflict-ridden domain relationships. *Basic and Applied Social Psychology, 13,* 231–249.

70. See note 63.

71. Kelleher, M. D. (1996). *New arenas for violence: Homicide in the American workplace.* Westport, CT: Praeger.

72. *Fort Worth Star Telegram* (1993, June 1). Mindless violence: Workplace killings at an unacceptable level, p. 15.

73. Bachman, R. (1994). Violence and theft in the workplace. *Crime Data Brief.* Washington, DC: U.S. Department of Justice.

74. Neuman, J. H., & Baron, R. A. (1997). Aggression in the workplace. In R. A. Giacalone & J. Greenberg (eds.), *Antisocial behavior in organizations* (pp. 37–67). Thousand Oaks, CA: Sage Publications.

75. Baron, R. A., & Neuman, J. H. (1996). Workplace violence and workplace aggression: Evidence of their relative frequency and potential causes. *Aggressive Behavior, 22,* 161–173.

76. Baron, R. A., & Richardson, D. R. (1994). *Human aggression* (2nd ed.). New York: Plenum.

77. Baumrind, D. (1973). The development of instrumental competence through socialization. In A. D. Pick (ed.), *Minnesota symposia on child psychology,* Vol. 7 (pp. 3–46). Minneapolis: University of Minnesota Press.

78. Nisbett, R. E. (1993). Violence and U.S. regional culture. *American Psychologist, 48,* 441–449.

79. Farrington, D. P. (1978). The family backgrounds of aggressive youths. In L. Hersov, M. Berger, & D. Shaffer (eds.), *Aggression and antisocial behavior in childhood and adolescence* (pp. 73–93). Oxford, UK: Pergamon.

80. Berkowitz, L. (1993). *Aggression: Its causes, consequences, and control.* New York: McGraw-Hill.

81. Strube, M. J., Turner, C. W., Cerro, D., Stevens, J., & Hinchey, F. (1984). Interpersonal aggression and the type A coronary-prone behavior pattern: A theoretical distinction and practical implications. *Journal of Personality and Social Psychology, 47,* 839–847.

82. Pulkkinen, L. (1987). Offensive and defensive aggression in humans: A longitudinal perspective. *Aggressive Behavior, 13,* 197–212.

83. Taylor, S. P., & Leonard, K. E. (1983). Alcohol and human physical aggression. In R. G. Geen & E. Donnerstein (eds.), *Aggression: Theoretical and empirical reviews, Vol. 2: Issues in research* (pp. 77–101). New York: Academic Press.

84. See note 80.

85. Ibid.

86. Straus, M. A., Gelles, R. J., & Steinmetz, S. K. (1980). *Behind closed doors: Violence in the American family.* Garden City, NY: Anchor Books.

87. Widom, C. S. (1989). Does violence beget violence? A critical examination of the literature. *Psychological Bulletin, 106,* 3–28.

88. Fix, J. T., & Kleiner, B. H. (1997). Workplace violence: Assessing the risk and implementing preventive measures. *Employment Relations Today,* Spring, 75–85.

89. See note 71.

90. See note 74.

91. Novaco, R. W. (1975). *Anger control: The development and evaluation of an experimental treatment.* Lexington, MA: Lexington Books.

92. Goldstein, A. P. (1988). *The prepare curriculum: Teaching prosocial competencies.* Champaign, IL: Research Press.

93. See note 76.

94. Deffenbacher, J. L. (1988). Cognitive-relaxation and social skills treatments of anger: A year later. *Journal of Counseling Psychology, 35,* 234–236.

95. See note 92.

Chapter 13

Prejudice and Discrimination: What They Are and How They Differ

Stereotyping: The Basis of Prejudice
Discrimination: Prejudice in Action

Explanations of Prejudice: The Origins of Hate

Intergroup Conflict: Competition as a
    Basis for Bigotry
"Us" versus "Them": Social Categorization
    as a Basis for Prejudice
The Role of Social Learning: Early
    Experience as a Basis for Prejudice
The Roots of Prejudice: Summing Up

Prejudice and Discrimination: Its Guise in the Workplace

Discrimination Based on Gender:
    Subtle but Significant
Sexism in Work Settings: Some
    Positive News
Modern Racism: Some Bad News

Reducing Prejudice and Discrimination: Complex Problems Demand Complex Solutions

Breaking the Chain of Bigotry:
    On Learning Not to Hate
Increasing Intergroup Contact:
    The Positive Effects of Acquaintance

Special Sections

Human Relations in Action
The Illusion of Outgroup Homogeneity

Ethics at Work
Gender Discrimination and Sexual
    Harassment

Guidelines for Effective Human Relations
Using What You've Learned

Case in Point
Not Bad, for a Woman

PREJUDICE AND DISCRIMINATION

Roadblocks to Traveling in a Multicultural World

Learning Objectives

After reading this chapter, you should be able to:

1. Define and distinguish between prejudice and discrimination.

2. Describe how stereotypes can lead to prejudice.

3. Explain how "tokenism" represents a subtle form of discrimination.

4. Describe three explanations of prejudice.

5. Describe how prejudice and discrimination affect behavior in the workplace.

6. Distinguish between old-fashioned and modern racism.

7. Explain how we can apply what we've learned about gender discrimination to other forms of bias and prejudice.

8. Describe several techniques for reducing or eliminating prejudice.

Throughout this book, we have pointed out that today's business world is a multicultural and global environment. Progressive organizations recognize this fact. In the recent past, many of these organizations have developed programs that are aimed at celebrating diversity and creating an atmosphere devoid of prejudice and discrimination. The programs are aimed toward creating an organizational climate that is hospitable to women and minorities. For example, Digital Equipment Corporation maintains a Core Groups program in which employees meet voluntarily to learn about one another and to discuss their similarities and differences. The goal of the program is to enhance positive relationships among employees and to break down potential barriers between groups. Similar programs have been developed at Pepsi-Cola International, Xerox, Harris Semiconductor, and General Electric.[1]

Even after several decades of social change, prejudice and discrimination persist in the workplace. This negative side of human behavior exerts a major effect on people within the workplace. As the world of work takes on an increasingly international perspective, more companies will be doing business in multiple countries, and we will be working with people from many different backgrounds. To be competitive and successful at work, we must eliminate prejudice from the workplace. Prejudice and discrimination therefore warrant careful attention.

In this chapter, we consider several aspects of prejudice and discrimination in the world of work. First, we define prejudice more precisely and distinguish it from discrimination. Second, we consider the bases from which it springs—that is, the possible origins of hatred and intolerance. Third, we focus on several important domains in which prejudice can arise—job interviews, promotions, and sexual harassment. Finally, we review several steps that can be taken, both by individuals and by businesses, to overcome prejudice's negative effects.

PREJUDICE AND DISCRIMINATION: WHAT THEY ARE AND HOW THEY DIFFER

prejudice A negative attitude toward members of a social group.

In newscasts and magazine articles, the terms *prejudice* and *discrimination* are often used as synonyms. Human relations experts who study these topics, however, distinguish between them. They use the term **prejudice** to refer to a special type of attitude—generally, a negative one—toward the members of some distinct social group. They use the term **discrimination** to refer to specific negative actions directed against these individuals. This chapter will draw the same distinction.

Human relations experts view prejudice as a special type of attitude. More precisely, they often define it as an attitude toward the members of some specific group that leads the person who holds the attitude to evaluate group members negatively, simply because they belong to that group. Thus, when we say that a given person is prejudiced against members of some social group, we mean that he or she tends to reject these members or evaluate them negatively merely because they belong to that group.[2] Their individual behaviors, skills, or characteristics make little difference to the prejudiced person and rarely enter the picture.

Like other attitudes, prejudice consists of three basic components: cognitive, affective, and behavioral aspects. (Do you remember these distinctions from Chapter 4?) The cognitive component of prejudice refers to the beliefs and expectations held about the members of particular groups. These beliefs and expectations are extremely important because, once formed, they exert several powerful effects. First, they lead individuals who accept them to assume that all members of a given group possess the same traits or behave in the same manner. Second, they often distort social perception, so that no matter how individuals act, their behavior is interpreted as lending support to these preconceived beliefs. Third, our expectations often demonstrate an unsettling, self-fulfilling nature.[3] Once we believe that members of a given social group possess certain traits, we tend to treat them as if these beliefs were true. This treatment may then cause those people to act in ways that confirm our beliefs. For example, consider a manager who believes that workers older than age fifty-five simply can't cut it—that is, that they are far less productive than younger workers. Because of this belief, she tends to assign older workers to relatively easy tasks and sets very low goals for them. These individuals, recognizing the manager's low expectations, experience a drop in self-confidence. This development, in turn, impairs their ability to perform competently. The result: The manager's initial, false beliefs bring about their own confirmation! Figure 13.1 on page 372 illustrates this process.

The affective component refers to the feelings or emotions that people experience when they are in the presence of members of specific groups or when they merely think about them. Several studies designed to assess emotional reactions to members of one's own and a different racial group have provided direct evidence for such reactions. Their results indicate that many people do actually experience greater anxiety and emotional arousal when interacting with persons belonging to another race than when interacting with members of their own racial group.[4]

The behavioral aspect of prejudice involves tendencies to act in negative ways toward the persons or groups who are the object of such attitudes. When these tendencies spill over into overt actions, they constitute discrimination.

discrimination   Negative actions directed toward an individual based on his or her group membership.

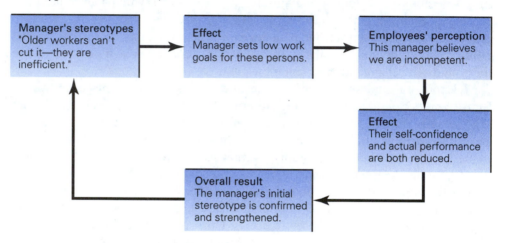

Figure 13.1   **Stereotypes: Their Self-Fulfilling Nature**

Because a manager expects older workers to be inefficient and incompetent, she assigns them easy tasks and sets low goals for them. The employees recognize her low expectations and so suffer reductions in self-confidence. This impairs their ability to perform well, and so tends to confirm the manager's initial false beliefs (that is, her stereotype of older workers).

Stereotyping: The Basis of Prejudice

In Chapter 3, we discussed the fact that we view the world through our mental concepts and cognitive structures. We also view group members in this way. Our beliefs and expectations about a person are colored by our conceptualization of the social groups to which the individual belongs. The term *stereotype* refers to a person's beliefs and expectations about an individual based on the individual's group membership.

Stereotypes play a major role in social behavior and serve to make the social world more stable and predictable. They guide the impressions we form of the individuals whom we encounter in our day-to-day lives; these impressions, in turn, often guide our interactions with others (see Figure 13.1 for an example). Using stereotypes to form impressions of others often results in assumptions that a set of stereotypic attributes are characteristic of most members of a social group.[5] For example, a common stereotype is that redheads and Italians have fiery tempers; in fact, this trait is not characteristic of all redheads and all Italians. Considerable evidence shows, however, that these kinds of beliefs will persist even though our interactions with specific members of groups disagree with our general beliefs.

descriptive stereotype Beliefs concerning how most people in a group behave and what they prefer.

It is useful to distinguish between two aspects of stereotyping in describing how they affect our beliefs. First, a **descriptive stereotype** indicates how most people in the group supposedly behave and what they prefer.

This component informs us about the abilities of members of the stereotyped group. For example, the descriptive stereotypes associated with African Americans claim that they are good athletes; those associated with women claim that they are good secretaries but poor leaders. These stereotypes are controlling because they provide the basis for expectations that members of the stereotyped group will conform to these characteristics. They therefore limit the possibilities that an individual will act outside the boundaries of these expectations.[6]

The other dimension of stereotyping can be even more controlling. A **prescriptive stereotype** tells certain groups how they should think, feel, and behave (see Figure 13.2).[7] For example, women should be sociable, and males should be rough and tough. Society often demands that an individual conform to these beliefs, and the penalties for nonconformance can be severe. Consider the fate of a boy who does not match gender stereotypes and prefers playing with dolls to playing baseball.

> **prescriptive stereotype** Controlling attitudes that tell members of groups how they should think, feel, and behave.

Figure 13.2   **Stereotypes: Prescriptions for Behavior**

As can be seen in this cartoon, gender stereotypes dictate certain kinds of knowledge.

From *Wishful Thinking* by David Sipress, p. 26. © 1987 by David Sipress. Reprinted by permission of HarperCollins, Inc.

 **The Stamp of Stereotypes**

Stereotypic beliefs often create a system in which the stereotype stamps itself upon the perceptions of other people. In this study, stereotypes influenced subjects' judgments even when they were offered substantial incentives for accuracy.

Data from experiment 2, Nelson et al.; see note 8.

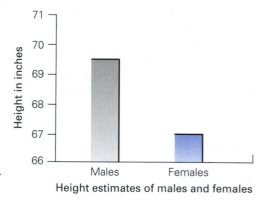

Height estimates of males and females

Stereotypic beliefs often lead us to form the wrong perceptions. They also stamp themselves upon the perceptions of other people. An impressive series of studies has demonstrated the potency of this "stamp."[8] Encouraging research participants to be accurate, discouraging them from relying on stereotypic cues, and even offering a substantial financial incentive for accuracy have not prevented subjects from using stereotypes in their judgments of the height of males and females. In the study depicted in Figure 13.3, participants were asked to judge the height of males and females based on a number of photographs. They were told that "for every woman of a particular height, somewhere in the booklet there is also a man of the same height" and were explicitly instructed not to rely on the person's gender in making their judgments. In addition, the subjects were offered a $50 prize for being the best judge of height. Despite these warnings and inducements, the participants estimated that males were taller than females.

Disturbing evidence also exists that positive attitudes toward minority groups may not always prevent prevailing negative cultural stereotypes from influencing perceptions of the behaviors of those group members.[9] Stereotypes also influence what we remember about other people.[10–12]

Our day-to-day interactions with individuals from a wide array of social groups provide us with considerable evidence that our stereotypes may be wrong. Nevertheless, our stereotypes can prove highly resistant to change; observations of behavior of group members that deviates from our stereotypes don't seem to alter our belief in those stereotypes. When we observe an individual who does not conform to our stereotype, we often consider that person an exception to the rule[13] and maintain our stereotypic beliefs about the group as a whole.

Recently, research has suggested that our ability to generate compensatory expectations may play a role in the maintenance of stereotypes.[14] **Compensatory expec-**

compensatory expectations Expectations that members of groups will "make up" for their stereotypically inconsistent behavior or the inconsistent behaviors performed by other group members.

tations are beliefs that a member of a stereotyped group will perform behaviors in the future that make up for or balance observed inconsistencies. In one study that investigated this process, participants were presented with behaviors that contradicted their stereotypes of clergy members. In one case, the behavior was mildly inconsistent (the minister was described as having read sexually explicit magazines for his own pleasure). In another case, the behavior was extremely inconsistent (the minister was described as having had an affair with a married woman and having sexually assaulted a seven-year-old child). When participants were exposed to mildly inconsistent actions, they expected the minister to perform deeds in the future that made up for this inconsistent action. This compensatory behavior allowed the individuals to maintain their stereotypes that ministers behave in prosocial ways. Most interestingly, when individuals were presented with extreme inconsistency, they ceased to expect that the deviant member would behave in prosocial ways. At the same time, they expected another minister, who was unaware of the deviant minister's actions, to perform deeds that balanced out the observed inconsistency. Thus one way that we may maintain our stereotypes in the face of disconfirming evidence is by predicting that members of groups will compensate for observed inconsistency. Coupled with our tendencies to subtype group members who behave in stereotypically inconsistent ways, the generation of compensatory expectations may lead to a powerful one-two punch that reinforces existing stereotypes.

On the surface, it might seem to be maladaptive for our cognitive structures to remain so resistant to change. Consider, however, what would happen if our beliefs did not structure our encounters with others. Every new social circumstance and every new person we meet would represent an unexplored frontier—a considerable amount of cognitive effort would be required to carry out this exploration. We would be overwhelmed by events that deviate even slightly from our prior encounters and rendered motionless in a social world that requires action. In short, we do not easily change our beliefs because relying on these beliefs provides us with a sense of prediction and control that is critical to our functioning. The negative side of this coin is that social categorizations can create stereotypic beliefs that control other people and produce discrimination and bias. When this result occurs, the price is incalculable and intolerable.

Discrimination: Prejudice in Action

Attitudes are not always reflected in overt actions. In fact, a large gap often separates the views held by individuals and their actual behavior. Prejudice is no exception to this general rule. In many situations, persons holding even strong negative views about the members of various racial or ethnic groups cannot express that hatred directly. Laws, the fear of retaliation, and social pressure combine to prevent them from engaging in openly negative actions against the targets of their hatred. In other cases, such restraining forces are absent and the negative beliefs, feelings, and behavior tendencies that constitute prejudice may find expression in overt actions. Such behaviors are known as discrimination.

Discrimination can take many different forms. At relatively mild levels, it may involve simple avoidance: Prejudiced persons avoid contact with the groups they dislike—at work and in their personal lives. At stronger levels, it can involve exclusion: Members of disliked groups may be prevented from living in certain neighborhoods, sending their children to certain schools, and joining certain social organizations (such as clubs and churches). In extreme cases, discrimination can involve direct physical assaults, hate crimes, or even the mass murder of one group by members of another.

Needless to say, all of these forms of discrimination are important and can exert harmful effects on the targets of the prejudice. Of concern to many human relations experts, however, are several practices that are collectively known as **job discrimination.** Job discrimination includes the reluctance to hire persons belonging to certain groups, failure to promote them, and attempts to pay them less than other employees are paid for their job or specialty. In the past, practices of this type were quite widespread, with the victims including racial and ethnic minorities, women, older workers, and sometimes young workers. Fortunately, this situation has changed greatly in recent decades, largely because legislation has made such actions illegal. In its more blatant forms at least, such discrimination definitely seems to be on the wane. But it has far from totally vanished, and the struggle to eliminate it from all work settings is a continuous process. In addition, several subtler forms of job discrimination persist. These tactics include the withholding of aid or assistance from persons belonging to certain groups, so that their job performance suffers, and tokenism, the hiring or promotion of a few "show" women, African Americans, or Hispanics in order to comply with the letter, if not the spirit, of the law. Such subtler forms of discrimination are often more difficult to spot than the obvious practices of the past, but they continue to exert negative effects on the persons toward whom they are directed.

$\mathcal{E}$XPLANATIONS OF PREJUDICE: THE ORIGINS OF HATE

Where does prejudice come from? Why do individuals so often hold strong negative attitudes toward members of groups other than their own? Answering these important questions about the origins of prejudice may help us to develop effective strategies for overcoming its impact in work settings. Unfortunately, prejudice is far too complex to permit us the luxury of finding simple answers. Instead, it appears to stem from several different sources, none of which should be ignored. Among the most important of these are intergroup conflict, social categorization, and early learning experiences.

job discrimination   Practices including a reluctance to hire, promote, or pay fairly based on a person's group membership.

Intergroup Conflict: Competition as a Basis for Bigotry

In recent decades, a growing number of Cubans have moved to the United States. Most have settled in southern Florida, turning Miami into virtually a bilingual city. Indeed, in many locations, Spanish—not English—is the language in daily use. Because these immigrants came seeking political freedom, and because Cuba and Florida have enjoyed a great deal of trade and commerce in the past, we might expect that this immigration would have gone smoothly. In fact, it has not. Many long-time residents of Miami have objected strongly to this sudden influx of "foreigners." And many have voiced negative attitudes about Cubans in general. In short, prejudice has arisen in an area previously more famous for its palm trees and tropical climate.

Why has the influx of Cubans created such a stir? According to one explanation for the occurrence of prejudice, the answer is competition. As more and more Cubans arrived, they began to compete with the previous residents for jobs, housing, and schools. This competition, in turn, stimulated the development of anti-Cuban attitudes. One major explanation for the occurrence of prejudice, therefore, suggests that it often stems from direct economic competition between distinct social groups; an idea known as *realistic conflict theory.*

Unfortunately, the validity of this theory has been confirmed by both systematic research and careful observation of events occurring in many societies. Researchers have found that when groups are placed in direct competition for valued rewards, they come to dislike and disparage one another.[15] They label one another as "enemies," view their own groups as morally superior, and draw the boundaries between themselves and their opponents ever more firmly. Simple competition, originally free from animosity and hatred, gradually develops into full-scale, emotion-laden prejudice. Prejudice and job discrimination appear to increase when economic conditions are poor and jobs are scarce.[16] It therefore seems reasonable to conclude that one important basis for the emergence of strong intergroup prejudice is direct economic competition (see Figure 13.4. on page 378).

"Us" versus "Them": Social Categorization as a Basis for Prejudice

A second factor contributing to prejudice is, in some respects, even more disturbing because it seems to be built directly into our perceptions of the social world. Briefly, a growing body of evidence indicates that human beings have a strong tendency to divide all people around them into two distinct groups.[17] Either individuals are similar to themselves in key respects and are seen as part of their own *ingroup,* or they are viewed as different and are assigned to the *outgroup.* If this tendency to divide the social world into these distinct categories—known as **social categorization**—stopped there, it would have little practical significance. Unfortu-

social categorization   Tendency to divide people into groups.

Figure 13.4   **Competition: One Source of Prejudice**

According to realistic conflict theory, prejudice sometimes develops out of competition for scarce resources.

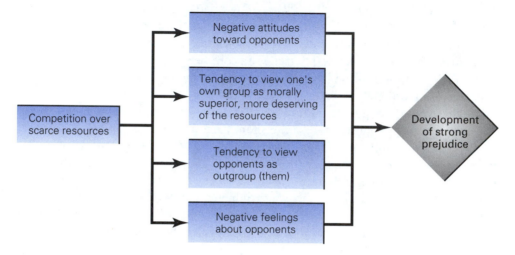

nately, though, this is not the case. Instead, sharply contrasting feelings and beliefs are usually attached to members of the ingroup and members of the outgroup. While persons in the former ("us") category are viewed in highly favorable terms, those in the latter ("them") category are seen in a more negative light. Members of the latter category are assumed to possess undesirable characteristics and are often strongly disliked or at least mistrusted. In addition, they are seen as much more similar to one another than persons in our ingroup.[18] In short, while individuals belonging to our own group are known to differ in many respects, outgroup members are viewed as being very much alike. "You know what they're like" is a phrase that captures the essence of this view. (You can demonstrate this unsettling tendency for yourself by performing the exercise in the *Human Relations in Action* section on pages 380–381.)

Unfortunately, this inclination to divide the world into "us" and "them" appears to be very powerful. Indeed, it seems to occur even when only a flimsy basis for such distinctions exists. Similarly, our tendency to hold more positive attitudes toward members of our ingroup than toward members of various outgroups is very strong. Why? One possibility is that individuals seek to enhance their self-esteem by identifying with specific social groups. This tactic can succeed only to the extent that the persons involved perceive these groups as somehow superior to other, competing groups.[19] As all individuals are subject to the same forces, the final result is inevitable: Each group views itself as somehow better than its rivals, and prejudice arises out of this clash of social perceptions (see Figure 13.5). This process, known as social competition,[20] may set the stage for strong discriminatory actions in work settings and elsewhere.

> ### *Figure 13.5*   Ingroup Identification: One Potential Source of Prejudice
>
> Prejudice sometimes arises out of social competition. Individuals may attempt to enhance their self-esteem by identifying with groups they view as superior to others. Since the members of many groups have the same desire, conflict between them occurs. Prejudice then follows this clash of social perception.

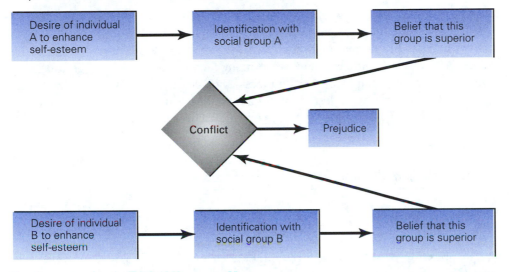

Based on suggestions by Tajfel, 1982; see note 20.

The Role of Social Learning: Early Experience as a Basis for Prejudice

Heroines and heroes may be born, but bigots are clearly made. Few persons would suggest that children enter the world with racial hatreds, sexist attitudes, or techniques of job discrimination firmly in place. Rather, such reactions must be acquired. The social learning view of prejudice incorporates this fact. According to this view, individuals acquire prejudice toward various groups because they hear such views expressed by parents, friends, teachers, and others and because they are directly rewarded (with praise and approval) for adopting them.

The mass media also seem to play a major role in inspiring prejudice. For example, until recently, the members of racial and ethnic minorities, as well as women, were presented in a negative light on television and in films. Specifically, they were depicted as unintelligent, unambitious, and suited only to simple or low level jobs. Fortunately, this situation has changed somewhat in recent years in the United States, Canada, and other nations. Members of various minority groups and females are now shown in a wider range of roles and in higher-status jobs than was true in the past. Even today, however, room for improvement exists (see the *Guidelines for*

Effective Human Relations section on pages 390–391). Until such change occurs, and all traces of racism, sexism, and other forms of bigotry disappear from the mass media, their potential for contributing to such reactions will remain.

The Roots of Prejudice: Summing Up

As this brief discussion suggests, prejudice stems from many different causes. Direct economic competition, training on our parents' knees—or in front of the TV set—and basic ways of perceiving the social world around us all play a role in its occurrence. At first glance, the existence of so many factors may strike you as confusing and their identification as perhaps unnecessary. Actually, this knowledge has great practical value. Only by understanding the roots of prejudice can we hope to devise effective techniques for reducing its impact and occurrence. Later in this chapter, we

Human Relations in Action

The Illusion of Outgroup Homogeneity

Earlier, we noted that one basis for prejudice seems to lie in our tendency to perceive all members of any group other than our own as similar. This is sometimes known as the **illusion of outgroup homogeneity**, and it is, in fact, an illusion: There is no reason to believe that people in other groups are any more alike than people in our own group. Yet, despite this fact, our tendency to jump to such conclusions is quite strong. You can demonstrate its impact for yourself by obtaining the help of several friends and following the directions below. (Be sure to choose friends who have not read this book or taken a course in human relations.) Work with one person at a time.

First, tell each of your friends that you are going to ask him or her to estimate how much the people in various groups differ from one another. Explain that he or she will do this by writing a number from 1 to 7 on a piece of paper you will supply. If your friend feels that the people in the group you name vary only a little (they are all pretty much the same), he or she should enter the number 1. If, in contrast, your friend thinks that these people vary a great deal, he or she should enter the number 7. Numbers in between, of course, reflect different degrees of perceived variability.

Now present your first example. Read this statement: To what extent do people in (name a foreign country; for example, England if you live in the United States) vary in their political views?

illusion of outgroup homogeneity   The tendency to view persons belonging to other groups as varying less than persons in our own group. In short, outgroup members are all perceived as being very much alike.

will draw on the information presented in this section. Before doing so, we examine one specific form of prejudice—a type that plays a key role in many work settings and that has recently been the focus of a great deal of political, legislative, and research interest: prejudice based on gender.

PREJUDICE AND DISCRIMINATION: ITS GUISE IN THE WORKPLACE

Prejudice and discrimination remain prevalent within today's society, despite the rapid social changes that occurred during the twentieth century. Therefore, it is not surprising that these negative elements also infect the workplace. Some of the mani-

Next, read the following statement: To what extent do people in (name your own country) vary in their political views?

In each case, remind your friend to enter a number from 1 to 7.

Now present your second example. Read this statement: To what extent do (name your friend's own age group; for example, people in their twenties) vary in physical fitness?

Then read this statement: To what extent do middle-aged people vary in physical fitness?

At this point, you are ready to examine your results. First, obtain an average score for each item. (Add together the numbers selected by each of your friends and then divide by the number of persons who participated.) Now, compare these numbers. You will probably find that for both items your friends assigned a higher number to their own groups than to other groups. That is, they perceive more variability among persons in their own country or age group than among persons in some other country or age group. This tendency to view people in other groups as more alike than people belonging to our own group is, in a sense, the entering wedge of prejudice. If the members of some group are perceived as all being pretty much alike, there is no reason to bother with them as individuals or to take account of their personal needs and traits. By encouraging such false beliefs, the illusion of outgroup homogeneity, which might seem neutral in itself, can play a destructive role in human relations.

festations are subtle and some are blatant, as you can see from the account of a woman's experiences within the workplace (see the *Ethics at Work* section). In all guises, however, prejudice and discrimination have harmful effects within organizations.

First, when employees react to their coworkers based on stereotypic beliefs, they effectively limit their coworkers' potential to act as individuals. Stereotyped individuals become confined to the roles that are dictated by the stereotype and, therefore, lose a great deal of their freedom to develop their individuality. Much human potential is lost in this way. The careers of persons who are stereotyped may be damaged by various forms of discrimination with respect to hiring, promotion, pay, and appraisal of their work. When talented individuals are overlooked because of their group membership, organizations may ignore precious human resources.

Second, prejudice can be a source of friction and conflict within organizations. Us-versus-them attitudes create unnecessary divisions in the workplace, hindering the development of a positive sense of company identity and cooperation. This result can have a devastating effect on company efficiency and climate.

Ethics at Work

Gender Discrimination and Sexual Harassment

The following account is a real-life example from a lawsuit that was filed by a woman against her employers. This account was taken from a report written by the social psychologist who served as an expert witness on this case (Fiske, 1993; see note 6).

Lois Robinson was a welder in a shipyard in Jacksonville, Florida. The work in this shipyard was dangerous and tough—requiring repairs of large ships in drydock. Women made up less than 5 percent of the craftworkers, and there was likely to be only one woman on each shift.

The shipyard was described as a boys' club or man's world. There were work trailers that had "Men Only" painted on the side. Open hostility by some men toward women existed within this atmosphere. For example, it was reported that one worker carved the handle of a tool in the form of a penis and waved it in front of a woman's face; another put a flashlight in his pants to show how well-endowed he was; and another was reported to say: "There's nothing worse than having to work around women." Off-color jokes (including a frequent joke about death through rape) were routine parts of the work atmosphere. Calendars showing women in various states of undress and sexually explicit poses were posted along many walls of the shops.

The female workers were frequently called demeaning names ("honey," "dear," "baby," "sugar," and so on) and were also called sexually explicit names. They were often touched, propositioned, and teased.

Although most of the research on prejudice in the workplace has concentrated upon racism and sexism, other forms of prejudice exist as well: prejudice based on age, prejudice based on sexual orientation, and a growing form of prejudice—that directed toward HIV-positive employees. Although important differences exist among all of these forms of prejudice and discrimination, we will concentrate on prejudice and discrimination based upon gender within the workplace. We choose to focus on this form because more research has been conducted on this issue than on other forms of bias. In addition, the lessons learned about gender discrimination are easily extended to other forms of discrimination.

Females constitute a majority of the world's population. Despite this fact, they have been treated very much like a minority group in most cultures throughout history. Women have been largely excluded from economic and political power. They have been the object of pronounced negative stereotyping. And they have often suffered overt discrimination; for example, they have been barred from many jobs, certain types of training, and various social organizations. Fortunately, such overt discriminatory practices appear to be decreasing, at least in many places and to some

Lois Robinson constantly complained about these working conditions but was brushed off. Eventually, she filed a lawsuit alleging sex discrimination due to sexual harassment in a hostile work environment. She won her case at the trial court level.

Consider the following issues:

1. What does this case have to do with stereotyping and discrimination?

2. Why were some men so openly hostile toward the female workers?

3. Why does the presence of sexually explicit pin-ups constitute a form of sexual harassment?

4. How did the behavior of these men limit the ability of women in the workplace to attain their potential as craftpersons?

5. What would you do as a female within this setting?

6. What would you do as a male within this setting?

Opening the Door for Women

Women are increasingly entering professions once dominated by men—as in the case of Supreme Court Justice Sandra Day O'Connor, shown here.

degree (see Figure 13.6). Furthermore, the past decade has witnessed major shifts in beliefs about the traits of men and women and the supposed differences between them. As you probably know, such shifts have generally been in the direction of realizing that males and females are not nearly as different in many respects as society once assumed.[21] Nevertheless, discrimination based on gender (or *sexism,* as it is often termed) persists in many settings, including businesses and other organizations. Given the negative effects produced by such prejudice and the major social changes that have stemmed from efforts to overcome it, this timely topic clearly has important implications for human relations. Thus we will consider it here in some detail.

Discrimination Based on Gender: Subtle but Significant

Why do women continue to lag behind men economically in many ways? Although laws and court rulings have significantly reduced direct discrimination against women, there still exist a number of subtle factors that work to keep women as second-class citizens in the world of work.

One such force involves the persistence of traditional views about the characteristics supposedly possessed by men and women. Such views (often known as gender-role stereotypes) suggest that men tend to be aggressive, forceful, persistent, and decisive, while women tend to be passive, submissive, dependent, and emotional. Evidence indicates that such differences are largely false: Men and women do not differ as consistently or to as large a degree in these ways as these stereotypes suggest. Nevertheless, such beliefs persist and continue to play a role in organizational settings. One reason is that the traits attributed to men by these stereotypes are ones that seem consistent with managerial success, while the traits attributed to women are ones that seem inconsistent with such success. As a result, women are perceived as less suited for managerial positions, even when they possess the appropriate credentials for them.

Evidence for the operation of such gender-role stereotypes has been obtained by Heilman and her colleagues in a series of studies.[22] In these experiments, the researchers repeatedly found that women are perceived as less suited for jobs traditionally filled by men and that any characteristics that serve to emphasize or activate female gender-role stereotypes tend to intensify such negative effects. For example, women who are physically attractive are perceived as being more feminine and, therefore, as less suited for managerial roles than are less physically attractive women. Interestingly, the impact of gender-role stereotypes can be countered by clear evidence of a woman's ability or competence. In such cases, women applying for traditionally male-dominated jobs (such as sports photographer) actually receive higher ratings than men.[23] Apparently, they are perceived as a special subgroup—one that is even more competent than men for such jobs. In general, though, traditional gender-role stereotypes tend to operate against success and advancement by women in work settings.

Devaluing Female Achievement: Luck, Skill, or Effort?

When individuals perform some task, the success or failure they achieve can be attributed to several potential causes. Specifically, a given level of performance can be viewed as stemming mainly from internal factors, such as ability and effort, or from external factors, such as luck or low task difficulty. As you might guess, in most cases good performance related to ability or effort is viewed as more deserving of recognition than similar performance deriving from luck or the accomplishment of an easy task.[24] For this reason, raises, promotions, and other corporate rewards are frequently dispensed to persons who apparently succeeded because of high ability or outstanding effort. In contrast, persons who are seen as having succeeded because of luck or an easy job receive such rewards far less frequently.

This distinction probably strikes you as quite reasonable, and to a degree it is. But consider the following fact: A growing body of evidence suggests that many persons attribute successful performance by men and women to different factors. Briefly, success by men is often attributed to their ability or effort. In contrast, similar levels of performance by women are often viewed as stemming mainly from luck or an easy task.[25] In short, if a man succeeds, it is assumed that he worked very hard or that he possesses a high level of ability. If a woman attains the same success, however, it is often assumed that she "lucked out" or that the task she faced really wasn't very hard.

These tendencies work against the advancement of women in business settings. After all, even when they attain the same level of achievement as their male colleagues, their success may be discounted or devalued. Fortunately, recent evidence indicates that such bias may be decreasing, at least in some business settings.[26] To the extent that it persists, it can prove quite damaging.

Sexism in Work Settings: Some Positive News

Clearly, women have suffered significantly from various forms of prejudice based on gender. Yet women have also made significant strides in a wide variety of areas in terms of educational and career achievements. Even more encouraging, sexist attitudes seem to be weakening. Recent studies indicate a lessening of bias in on-the-job evaluations, job interviews, and evaluations as leaders.[27,28] Thus major shifts seem to be reducing gender discrimination in the world of work. Women are apparently receiving more equitable treatment now than in the past.

Of course, we do not mean to imply that sexism is no longer of major importance in work settings. On the contrary, women and other disadvantaged groups continue to face serious problems in this regard. It does appear, however, that at least some types of prejudice are on the wane and are less influential—and harmful—than they were in the past. We can only hope that such trends continue and that sexism and other forms of prejudice eventually vanish in work settings—and in all other contexts.

Modern Racism: Some Bad News

We tend to associate *racism* with Ku Klux Klan rallies, segregated lunch counters, and race riots. Such blatant forms of deep-seated prejudice are, fortunately, rare. But is racism actually gone from our society? Unfortunately, the answer to this question is "no." The images of racism that come to mind when we read about lynch mobs and slavery refer to **old-fashioned racism**—blatant forms of prejudice characterized by the belief that discrimination against persons based on their racial or ethnic group membership is appropriate. Although this form of racism may be less prevalent now than in the past,[29] it has been replaced by a more subtle demon—**modern racism**.[30] Modern racism arises in indirect ways—when it is easy to rationalize and socially acceptable. For example, many persons profess to believe in racial equality but in practice oppose racially symbolic practices such as interracial marriages.

The most disturbing fact about modern racism is that we often remain unaware of its existence, even though

old-fashioned racism Obvious forms of prejudice and discrimination, such as slavery and lynch mobs.

modern racism The subtle and indirect forms of prejudice and discrimination that are characteristic of today's world.

it has an adverse effect on its victims. The subtleties of this influence can be seen in a job-interview study conducted by Word and his associates.[31] These researchers were disturbed by the fact that African Americans seem to perform more poorly on job interviews than Euro-Americans. Given that African Americans have the same qualifications as other job candidates, they wondered if social factors might explain this difference. In the first part of this study, all applicants were trained by the researchers on interview skills so that they were virtually identical. These applicants were then taped being interviewed by white male college students. The question of interest was whether the interviewers behaved differently when they interviewed African American versus Euro-American applicants. The answer was yes—unwittingly, the interviewers sat further away, made less eye contact, and made more speech errors (low-immediacy behaviors) when interviewing African American applicants. The interviews were also significantly shorter with African American applicants.

In a second phase of this study, the tables were turned so that Euro-American participants served as applicants. These subjects talked with white interviewers who were trained by the experimenters to use either the behavioral style typically seen in "African American interviews" (low-immediacy behaviors) or that employed in "Euro-American interviews" (high-immediacy behaviors). The taped interviews were assessed by independent observers. Applicants interviewed in the low-immediacy style were judged to be less capable than those interviewed in the high-immediacy style. A disturbing finding was that the applicants interviewed in this manner also saw themselves as less capable and more nervous. This research shows that very subtle (and often unconscious) social factors can create a disadvantage for victims of modern racism.

More disturbing evidence comes from a study that investigated unconscious influences of racial stereotypes on social behavior. In this study, Bargh, Chen, and Burrows presented participants with subliminal pictures of either African American or Euro-American faces.[32] The participants performed a very boring task and then were told that the computer had lost their data and that they would have to perform the task again. While the researchers informed the participants of this fact, they videotaped the subjects' faces. Later, persons who were unaware of whether the participant had been exposed to either African American or Euro-American pictures rated the amount of hostility exhibited by participants. Results showed that persons who were exposed subliminally to African American pictures expressed more hostility in their facial expressions than did persons exposed to Euro-American pictures. This unsettling result suggests that negative stereotypes about African Americans can exert an unconscious influence on our social behavior.

The bottom line on racism within the workplace can be characterized as a "good news–bad news" situation. The good news is that blatant forms of old-fashioned racism have largely decreased. The bad news is that modern racism persists and that negative stereotypes may have an unconscious influence on our social behavior. This possibility is disheartening for the victims of modern racism and for the business world as a whole. Clearly, the demands that we face us within a world dominated by international competition dictate that we erase any vestige of prejudice and discrimination from our workplace.

REDUCING PREJUDICE AND DISCRIMINATION: COMPLEX PROBLEMS DEMAND COMPLEX SOLUTIONS

Prejudice and discrimination create tremendous problems both for individuals and for entire societies. Because of their presence, basic rights are often violated, injustice is incurred, and valuable pools of talent are wasted. Given these major costs, efforts to overcome the negative impact of prejudice and discrimination seem well justified. But do techniques for accomplishing this valuable goal exist? Can prejudice and discrimination actually be overcome? Fortunately, the answer to both questions appears to be "yes." When used with skill and care, several strategies can reduce prejudice and eliminate the discriminatory practices it often breeds. Several of these strategies are described in this section. Note that none, by itself, offers a perfect solution to the problem of prejudice. Rather, because prejudice stems from several different sources, a combination of tactics is probably needed to make serious dents in its armor.

Breaking the Chain of Bigotry: On Learning Not to Hate

Earlier, we noted that prejudice, like other attitudes, is learned. Children acquire their hatred of various groups largely through training provided by their parents, teachers, friends, or the mass media. Given this fact, it is apparent that one means for countering the impact of prejudice is by somehow breaking this chain of bigotry—that is, by preventing youngsters from acquiring such negative views early in life.

This goal can be accomplished in several different ways. First, educational campaigns can call parents' attention to the important future costs attached to these attitudes. Second, teachers and schools can make special efforts to counteract the training in prejudice many children receive at home. Third, the contents of television shows and other forms of the mass media can be changed to present positive, rather than negative, views of minorities, women, the aged, the handicapped, and other groups that have often been the targets of discrimination. Of course, none of these steps is easy, and all require careful planning. A growing body of evidence, however, suggests that such procedures can help. For example, when children view television programs showing women in a positive light, their acceptance of negative gender stereotypes declines.[33] Such findings indicate that systematic efforts to circumvent prejudice may well yield impressive, beneficial results.

Increasing Intergroup Contact: The Positive Effects of Acquaintance

One major source of prejudice seems to lie in our tendency to divide the social world into two opposing camps: "them" and "us." Closely associated with this classification process is our belief that people belonging to various outgroups (ones other than our own) are markedly different from ourselves. To the extent that prejudice stems from these factors (and considerable evidence indicates that it does), another tactic for reducing its occurrence is suggested: increased contact with members of outgroups. If we actually meet such persons and interact with them on a regular basis, several beneficial changes may occur.[34] First, we may realize that they are much more similar to ourselves than we initially assumed. This growing recognition of similarity, in turn, may increase our liking for them. Second, as we get to know individual members of other groups, stereotypes about them—especially negative ones—are likely to be shattered. After all, it is hard to assume that all members of some group are alike when we learn through direct experience that they are not. Third, increased contact with members of other groups may promote more positive views of them simply because repeated exposure to almost any person or stimulus tends to produce such results—a development known as the **mere exposure effect**. In sum, several reasons explain why increased contact with members of other groups may enhance our attitudes toward them, and so overcome prejudice (see Figure 13.7).

> **mere exposure effect**   Increased attraction to a stimulus based on repeated presentations of or exposure to the stimulus.

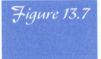 **Intergroup Contact: The Basis for Its Beneficial Effects**

As shown here, increased contact among different social groups can reduce prejudice in several ways.

Table 13.1	**Beneficial Conditions in Which Contact Might Reduce Prejudice between Groups**

1. Equal status (social, economic, and/or task-related)
2. Informal contact
3. Cooperative situation

For such effects to occur, however, certain conditions must prevail.[35,36] First, intergroup contact must take place in a context where the two groups involved are approximately equal in social, economic, and task-related status. If they differ in these respects, communication between them may prove difficult, and prejudice can actually increase. Second, the two groups must engage in relatively informal contacts. Formal or restricted communication does not seem helpful in countering stereotyping beliefs. Finally, the groups must meet under cooperative conditions, where they can work together rather than against one another. When such conditions exist, direct contact between members of different racial or ethnic groups can sharply reduce prejudice. In short, under these circumstances, getting to know others better can serve as a useful step toward viewing them in more positive ways. Table 13.1 summarizes these points.

Guidelines for Effective Human Relations

Using What You've Learned

In this chapter, we examined a broad range of principles and findings about prejudice and discrimination. Although few rules will apply to every situation, there are some general guidelines suggested by the various findings we have discussed. Remember, no rule works 100 percent in every situation. However, these guidelines should help improve your ability to succeed in our diverse society.

- Respond to individuals as *individuals*, rather than as representatives of their social group. Avoid assumptions that persons will conform to your group-based expectations.
- Avoid interpreting a person's behavior as supporting your preconceived beliefs.

Guidelines for Effective Human Relations (continued)

- Examine your stereotypic beliefs and try to assess where they come from. Devote a night of TV watching to identifying the stereotypes this medium conveys. Think about how these portrayals may have influenced your beliefs.

- Avoid the tendency to see competitors as enemies. Competition is a fact of life, but it doesn't require seeing others as negative and ourselves as morally superior. Recognize that these tendencies are exaggerated under times of adverse economic conditions and job scarcity.

- Recognize that there is no reason to believe that people in other groups are more alike than people in our own group. The illusion of outgroup homogeneity can be dangerous.

- Make it a point to engage in personal interactions with diverse members of society. This helps break down categories and helps you to perceive others as individuals.

- When arranging workgroups, set up cooperative activities that are designed to achieve superordinate goals. When individuals cooperate to meet higher-order goals, boundaries break down.

- Do not tolerate blatant or subtle forms of prejudice and discrimination. Speak up and establish the social norm of cooperation and mutual respect in your environment.

Summary

Prejudice may be defined as a negative attitude toward the members of some group held by members of another group. Discrimination refers to negative actions against the objects of prejudice, ranging from simple avoidance, to exclusion of or even direct assaults against persons belonging to a disliked group. Job discrimination involves such behaviors as reluctance to hire persons from certain groups, failure to promote them, and attempts to pay them less than they deserve.

Prejudice seems to stem from several different sources. It can result from the application of stereotypes to individuals. Sometimes it derives from direct economic competition between different groups. It is also encouraged by our strong tendency to divide the social world into two basic categories: "us" (our ingroup) and "them" (outgroups). Finally, children often acquire prejudiced attitudes from their parents, friends, teachers, and the mass media.

We can use the lessons learned about gender discrimination to understand the factors involved in other forms of discrimination. Although they constitute a majority of the world's population, females have often been treated as a minority group. They have been excluded from economic and political power, have suffered overt discrimination, and have served as the objects of stereotyping. Today, blatant forms of discrimination against women in work settings seem to be decreasing, though more subtle forms of bias against them persist, such as a tendency to devalue their achievements and a tendency to discount the competence of female leaders.

Several different strategies may be effective in reducing prejudice. First, educational campaigns may help prevent the formation of prejudiced views early in life. Second, increased contact among members of different groups may help eliminate negative stereotypes and improve relations among them.

Key Terms

compensatory expectations, p. 374

descriptive stereotype, p. 372

discrimination, p. 371

illusion of outgroup homogeneity, p. 380

job discrimination, p. 376

mere exposure effect, p. 389

modern racism, p. 386

old-fashioned racism, p. 386

prejudice, p. 370

prescriptive stereotype, p. 373

social categorization, p. 377

 Case in Point

Not Bad, for a Woman

Carla Parker is up for evaluation and possible promotion. Eighteen months ago, she joined UBX Systems, Inc., as its first female engineer. Now, three people—Jack Feldman, her supervisor; Bob Rollins, head of employee relations; and Steve Johnson, chief engineer—are going over her record. Putting aside her folder and leaning back in his chair, Jack begins: "She looks pretty good on paper," he remarks. "In fact, I think she's doing a real fine job for us. I

have to admit that, at first, I was a bit surprised. We've never had a woman in that job before, and I had some doubts. But I don't anymore. I think she's a good, solid performer. Let's give her a merit raise."

Steve Johnson looks doubtful. "Well, I agree that her record looks pretty strong, Jack, but there's one thing that bothers me. Since she's been with us, she's never really had any tough jobs or emergencies. Everything's been pretty easy and pretty routine. How do we know what she'll do when the going gets rough? It's one thing to do well when everything's going smoothly, and another to deliver in the crunch. I have some concerns about that."

"I don't agree," replies Jack. "That AMPAD job was pretty sticky, but she handled it real well. And after all, we don't get that many special problems or emergencies these days anyway."

"Maybe so, maybe so," Steve admits with some reluctance. "But there's another thing, too. One of the people who works for her came to me the other day to complain. Seems he didn't like her style. I haven't been able to pinpoint the problem yet, but there does seem to be something going on that the old-timers don't like."

"Ha! I know who that was," exclaims Bob. "It must have been Mike Haggerty. And I know what's eating him, too. He just doesn't like having a woman boss. He just can't adjust—too old, I guess. You know, I've watched Carla in action a lot of times and I think she's doing just fine. In fact, I don't see that she really does anything different from Tom Bellasco, the person she replaced."

"Well," Steve answers, "I wouldn't like taking orders from a woman, myself." Then, smiling in an unpleasant way, he continues: "But I guess it wouldn't be so hard to take from Carla. Yeah, she's a real cutie, all right. And nice legs, too—I think I could get along with her just fine. . . ."

At these comments, Bob grows angry. "Hey, come off it, Steve! That stuff is way out of line. We're here to talk about her work, not her sex appeal. It's a good thing some of our female employees can't hear you; you'd be in big trouble—and you'd deserve it, too."

Steve is taken aback, and looks slightly embarrassed. But he recovers quickly. In fact, he, too, grows angry: "OK, OK, let's stick to the point. And my feeling is that taking everything into account, she's not ready for promotion or a bonus raise. She's doing OK, for a woman, but I'm not going to approve any special rewards for her yet. Let's give her another six months or a year and see what happens. I'll bet she folds in the end."

Questions

1. Which of the three people present at this evaluation qualifies for the booby prize as "head chauvinist"?

2. What forms of bias against women can you spot in this meeting?

3. What forms of bias against older people can you identify?

4. How might these be reduced or eliminated?

5. Suppose that Carla is not promoted and fails to receive a merit raise. Should she lodge a formal complaint or grievance?

Notes

1. Jackson, S. E. (1992). *Diversity in the workplace: Human resources initiatives.* New York: Guilford.

2. Katz, P. A. (ed.). (1976). *Toward the elimination of racism.* Elmsford, NY: Pergamon.

3. Skrypnek, B. J., & Snyder, M. (1982). On the self-perpetuating nature of stereotypes about women and men. *Journal of Experimental Social Psychology, 18,* 277–291.

4. Stephan, W. G., & Stephan, C. W. (1988). Emotional reactions to interracial achievement outcomes. *Journal of Applied Social Psychology, 19,* 608–621.

5. Fiske, S. T., & Taylor, S. E. (1991). *Social cognition,* 2nd ed. New York: McGraw-Hill.

6. Fiske, S. T. (1993). Controlling other people. *American Psychologist, 48,* 621–628.

7. Ibid.

8. Nelson, T., Biernat, M., & Manis, M. (1990). The robust effects of everyday base rates (sex stereotypes) on the assessment of individual targets. *Journal of Personality and Social Psychology, 59,* 664–675.

9. Devine, P. G. (1989). Stereotypes and prejudice: Their automatic and controlled components. *Journal of Personality and Social Psychology, 56,* 5–18.

10. Pryor, J. B., & Ostrom, T. M. (1981). A cognitive organization of social information: A converging operations approach. *Journal of Personality and Social Psychology, 54,* 203–218.

11. Seta, C. E., & Seta, J. J. (1990). Identifying the sources of social actions: The role of cues in person memory. *Journal of Personality and Social Psychology, 5,* 779–790.

12. Seta, C. E., & Hayes, N. S. (1994). The influence of impression formation goals on the accuracy of social memory. *Personality and Social Psychology Bulletin, 20,* 93–101.

13. Weber, R., & Crocker, J. (1983). Cognitive processes in the revision of the stereotypic beliefs. *Journal of Personality and Social Psychology, 45,* 961–977.

14. Seta, J. J., & Seta, C. E. (1993). Stereotypes and the generation of compensatory and noncompensatory expectations. *Personality and Social Psychology Bulletin, 19,* 722–731.

15. Sherif, M., Harvey, O. J., White, B. J., Hood, W. R., & Sherif, C. W. (1961). *Intergroup conflict and cooperation: The Robbers' Cave experiment.* Norman: University of Oklahoma Press.

16. Hepworth, J. T., & West, S. G. (1988). Lynchings and the economy: A time-series reanalysis of Hovland and Sears (1940). *Journal of Personality and Social Psychology, 55,* 239–247.

17. Locksley, A., Ortiz, V., & Hepburn, C. (1980). Social categorization and discriminatory behavior: Extinguishing the minimal intergroup discrimination effect. *Journal of Personality and Social Psychology, 39,* 773–783.

18. Schaller, M., & Maass, A. (1989). Illusory correlation and social categorization: Toward an integration of motivational and cognitive factors in stereotype formation. *Journal of Personality and Social Psychology, 56,* 709–721.

19. Turner, J. C., & Oakes, P. J. (1989). Self-categorization theory and social influence. In P. B. Paulus (ed.), *Psychology of group influence.* Hillsdale, NJ: Lawrence Erlbaum.

20. Tajfel, H. (1982). *Social identity and intergroup relations.* Cambridge, UK: Cambridge University Press.

21. Helmreich, R. L., Spence, J. T., & Gibson, R. H. (1980). Sex-role attitudes: 1972–1980. *Personality and Social Psychology Bulletin, 8,* 656–663.

22. Heilman, M. E., & Martell, R. F. (1986). Exposure to successful women: Antidote to sex discrimination in applicant screening decisions? *Organizational Behavior and Human Decision Processes, 37,* 376–390.

23. Heilman, M. E., Martell, R. F., & Simon, M. C. (1988). The vagaries of sex bias: Conditions regulating the undervaluation, equivaluation, and overvaluation of female job applicants. *Organizational Behavior and Human Decision Processes, 41,* 98–110.

24. Mitchell, T. R., & Kalb, L. S. (1982). Effects of job experience on supervisor attributions for a subordinate's poor performance. *Journal of Applied Psychology, 67,* 181–188.

25. Stevens, G. E., & DeNisi, A. S. (1980). Women as managers: Attitudes and attributions for performance by men and women. *Academy of Management Journal, 23,* 355–361.

26. Peters, L. H., O'Connor, E. J., Weekely, J., Pooyan, A., Frank, B., & Erekrantz, B. (1984). Sex bias and managerial evaluations: A replication and extension. *Journal of Applied Psychology, 69,* 349–352.

27. Goktepe, J. R., & Schneier, C. E. (1989). Role of sex, gender roles, and attraction in predicting

emergent leaders. *Journal of Applied Psychology, 74,* 165–167.

28. Graves, L. M., & Powell, L. M. (1988). An investigation of sex discrimination in recruiters' evaluations of actual applicants. *Journal of Applied Psychology, 73,* 20–29.

29. Schuman, H., Steeh, C., & Bobo, L. (1985). *Racial attitudes in America.* Cambridge, MA: Harvard University Press.

30. Gaertner, S. L., & Dovidio, J. F. (1986). The aversive form of racism. In J. F. Dovidio & S. L. Gaertner (eds.), *Prejudice, discrimination and racism: Theory and research* (pp. 61–89). Orlando, FL: Academic Press.

31. Word, C. O., Zanna, M. P., & Cooper, J. (1974). The nonverbal mediation of self-fulfilling prophecies in interracial interaction. *Journal of Experimental Social Psychology, 10,* 109–120.

32. Bargh, J. A., Chen, M., & Burrows, L. (1996). Automaticity of social behavior: Direct effects of trait construct and stereotype activation of action. *Journal of Personality and Social Psychology, 71,* 230–244.

33. Liebert, R. M., Neale, J. M., & Sprafkin, J. (1982). *The early window: Effects of television on children and youth,* 2nd ed. New York: Pergamon.

34. Pettigrew, T. F. (1981). Extending the stereotype concept. In D. L. Hamilton (ed.), *Cognitive processes in stereotyping and intergroup behavior* (pp. 303–331). Hillsdale, NJ: Erlbaum.

35. Cook, S. W. (1985). Experimenting on social issues: The case of school desegregation. *American Psychologist, 40,* 452–460.

36. Miller, N., & Brewer, M. B. (eds.). (1984). *Groups in contact: The psychology of desegregation.* New York: Academic Press.

Chapter 14

Stress: Its Basic Nature

Stress: Its Major Causes
Work-Related Causes of Stress

Personal Factors and Stress
Life Events and Stress: The Potential Costs
    of Change
The Hassles of Our Lives: The Costs of
    Daily Stressors
Individual Differences in Resistance to
    Stress: Variations in Susceptibility
Gender and Ethnic Differences
Attitudes and Stress: Is Attitude
    Everything?

Stress: Some Important Effects
Stress and Health: The Silent Killer
Stress: Its Effects on Our Mental States
Stress and Behavior at Work
Burnout: When Stress Consumes

**Managing Stress: Some Useful
Techniques**
Lifestyle: Actions Speak Loudly
Coping with Stress: Getting a Handle on
    Your Problems
Getting Control of Emotions

Special Sections
Human Relations in Action
How Much Role Conflict Do You Have?

Guidelines for Effective Human Relations
Using What You've Learned

Experiential Exercise
Checking Your Coping Style

STRESS AND BURNOUT
Key Problems at Work

Learning Objectives

After reading this chapter, you should be able to:

1. Discuss the basic characteristics of stress.

2. Describe several major work-related causes of stress.

3. Discuss how life events and daily hassles are related to stress.

4. Explain how reactions to stress are affected by personality characteristics.

5. Discuss gender and ethnic differences in stress response.

6. Describe the impact of stress upon personal health and task performance.

7. Define burnout and indicate why it occurs.

8. Describe several techniques for managing stress.

*L*aurie Elwell is in her third week in her new position as head of the electronics department at Allmart. She is in charge of three other employees who help stock and sell the products. She received a much-needed raise with this promotion. This will help greatly as she, a single parent, tries to raise her two children. However, there are many extra responsibilities, and she now has to work longer hours than before. She also has to be ready to come in any time there is some special problem or one of the employees fails to show up. There is considerable pressure to help generate profits by promoting high-markup items. She is not sure the extra pressure and time investment are justified by the additional salary. She is having trouble sleeping at night and has been getting migraine headaches. She is also not able to be home for dinner with the kids on many evenings. She misses spending time with them after school. Her son Chris is having problems with his schoolwork and needs some extra attention. Yet when she gets home, she is so tired physically and mentally that she just wants to lie down and go to sleep. "Maybe I shouldn't have taken the promotion," she thinks to herself. "I enjoyed just being able to come in for my forty hours a week and then go home and forget about my job. Now it's always on my mind."

*Y*ou have probably faced situations similar to Laurie's. All of us periodically *have* to deal with pressures at home, at work, and at school. At times we may feel like we can't handle any more. We may feel tense or depressed, have trouble sleeping, and reach a stage of physical and emotional exhaustion. If you've ever had this type of experience, you've encountered one of the most common problems of the twentieth century—**stress.**

Unfortunately, such conditions are far from rare in the world of work or in modern life generally. Even worse, when they occur, they often exert far-ranging negative effects on the persons exposed to them. For these reasons, stress is a timely topic, fully deserving of our close attention. This chapter focuses on stress and on the closely related topic of burnout. First, we examine the nature of stress. Then we consider several causes of stress—factors that lead to its occurrence. Next, we will examine the effects of stress and how personal factors such as optimism, gender, and ethnic group influence the experience of stress. Since burnout is one of the most serious of these stress-related effects, it will be discussed separately. Finally, we turn to several techniques for managing stress—tactics for reducing or countering its negative impact.

stress The physical, psychological, and behavioral reactions experienced by individuals in situations where they feel that they are in danger of being overwhelmed—pushed beyond their abilities or limits.

$\mathscr{S}$TRESS: ITS BASIC NATURE

How would you describe the experience of stress? Most people think of stress as an unpleasant emotional state accompanied by high levels of arousal. To a degree, such descriptions are accurate. Stress does indeed involve a subjective, emotional component. However, experts on this subject now agree that this is only part of the total picture. To fully understand stress and its many effects, we must understand three related issues.[1]

First, we must consider *physiological aspects* of stress. According to Selye, a leading expert on this topic, these can be divided into several distinct stages.[2] When first confronted with any threat to our safety or well-being, we experience an immediate and vigorous *alarm reaction*. Arousal rises quickly to high levels, and many physiological changes that prepare our bodies for strenuous activity (as in flight or combat) take place. This initial reaction is soon replaced by a second stage known as *resistance*. Here, activation remains relatively high but drops to levels that are more sustainable over relatively long periods of time. Finally, if stress persists, the body's resources may become depleted, and a final stage known as *exhaustion* occurs. At this point, the ability to cope (at least physically) decreases sharply, and severe biological damage may result if stress persists.

Second, in order to fully understand stress it is necessary to consider the external events or stimuli that induce it—the nature of various **stressors.** What is it about these stimuli that produces stress? What do they have in common? It appears that many events we find stressful share the following properties: (1) They are so intense in some respect that they produce a state of *overload*—we can no longer adapt to them; (2) they evoke simultaneous incompatible tendencies (for example, tendencies to both approach and avoid some object or activity); and (3) they are uncontrollable—outside our ability to change or influence.

Perhaps most important of all, stress involves the operation of several cognitive factors. The most central of these is the individual's *cognitive appraisal* of a given situation or potential stressor. In simple terms, stress occurs only to the extent that the persons involved perceive that (1) the situation is somehow threatening to their important goals, and (2) they will be unable to cope with these potential dangers or demands.[3] In short, stress does not simply shape our thoughts; in many cases, it derives from and is strongly affected by them.

To understand the nature of stress, therefore, it is necessary to consider the emotional and physiological reactions it involves, the external conditions that produce it, and the cognitive processes that play a role in its occurrence.[4] Taking all these factors into account, we can define stress as follows: *It is a pattern of negative emotional and physiological reactions occurring in situations where individuals perceive threats to their important goals that they may be unable*

stressors Various aspects of the world around us that contribute to stress.

to meet.[5] In short, stress occurs when individuals feel, rightly or wrongly, that they may soon be overwhelmed by events or circumstances that exceed their personal resources.[6]

STRESS: ITS MAJOR CAUSES

Stress and work—somehow, the two words seem to go together. And the reason for this is obvious: Most of us experience at least some degree of stress in our jobs. In fact, like Laurie in our opening example, we are exposed to many different events and conditions that cause us to feel pressured or in danger of being pushed to our personal limits. Factors contributing to stress at work vary greatly in their nature and scope. Most, however, fall into two major categories: ones relating to our jobs or organization, and ones relating to our personal characteristics.

Work-Related Causes of Stress

What aspects of jobs or organizations contribute to stress? Unfortunately, the list is long. Here, we will consider several of the most important of these sources of strain and discomfort.

Working Conditions.   Today most work environments appear to be quite pleasant. Most offices are air-conditioned and have only a moderate level of noise. Although there may be a lack of privacy in some open offices, there is usually sufficient space to carry out one's task. But you probably have experienced work situations that are a bit unpleasant. Factories can be hot and noisy, as can construction sites. When heat and noise reach high levels, stresslike effects do occur.[7] Work performance declines under such conditions, and inferior performance effects can even carry over to other environments.[8] One major problem with noisy and hot conditions is that tempers may begin to flare. Aggressive behavior is much more likely to occur when people work under noisy and hot conditions.[9] Crowded working environments may also produce stress reactions among employees and lead to reduced performance levels.[10,11] Obviously, we can't take our work environments for granted. To get the best performance out of employees, it is important to provide a comfortable work environment (see Figure 14.1).

Social conditions at work can also strongly affect levels of stress. Organizations characterized by high levels of politics and uncaring or unsupportive work environments are associated with increased reports of physical symptoms.[12] Work environments that discriminate based on gender and that involve sexual harassment are especially likely to have negative emotional effects.[13]

$\mathcal{F}igure\ 14.1$ **Working Conditions: One Source of Stress**

Work environments can be a source of stress. Do you think these environments are likely to differ in the stress they produce in workers?

Occupational Demands: Some Jobs Are More Stressful Than Others. Think about the following jobs: production manager, librarian, emergency room physician, janitor, firefighter, college professor, airline pilot. Do they differ in degree of stressfulness? Obviously, they do. Some jobs, such as those held by emergency medical service workers, firefighters, and police, expose the persons who hold them to periods of high stress.[14] Others, such as college professor, janitor, and librarian, do not. This basic fact—that some jobs are much more stressful than others—has been confirmed by the results of a careful survey involving more than 130 different occupations.[15] Results of this survey indicate that several jobs (for example, physician, office manager, foreman, waitress or waiter) are quite high in stress. In contrast, others (for example, maid, craft worker, farm laborer) are much lower in this regard. The amount of stress can, of course, vary on a daily basis. Air traffic controllers have more health complaints and negative moods when the air traffic workload is heavier. Occasionally, jobs change in the amount of stress involved. For example, working for the post office used to be considered a fairly easy job. However, with changes in technology and increased pressure for productivity, the job of postal worker has become much more stressful.[16]

Why are some jobs more stressful than others? It appears that several features of jobs are indeed related to the levels of stress they generate.[17] For example, the greater the extent to which a given job requires (1) decisions, (2) the constant monitoring of devices or materials, (3) repeated exchange of information with others, (4) unpleas-

Figure 14.2   **Job Characteristics: Contributing to Stress**

Certain characteristics of jobs tend to make them stressful. The ones shown here all
seem to contribute to the stress quotient of various jobs. Note that the higher the
values shown, the greater the contribution of each job characteristic to stress.

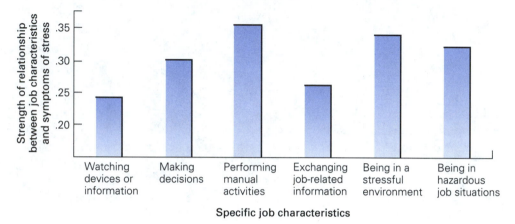

Based on data from Shaw and Riskind, 1983; see note 17.

ant physical conditions, and (5) performing unstructured rather than structured
tasks, the more stressful it tends to be (see Figure 14.2). Moreover—and this is the
most important point—such features were found to be quite general in nature. Thus,
the greater the extent to which virtually any job possesses these characteristics, the
higher the level of stress it produces among persons holding it, regardless of the specific tasks being performed. Also, any feature of a job that creates problems for one's
relationships at home is also likely to be associated with stress. For example, jobs that
require a lot of travel and time away from home create significant difficulties for
marital and family relationships.[18]

These findings and related evidence in other studies indicate that one major
source of stress at work involves the nature and demands of various jobs. For this reason, it is probably wise to take two key factors into account whenever you consider a
career in some field, or a job in a specific company: the level of stress it will involve
and your own ability to handle such pressures. Given the powerful impact of stress on
our physical and mental well-being (effects we will soon review), this may be one case
where it really pays to look before you leap. (For specific suggestions on how to assess
various aspects of different careers, see Chapter 15.)

Multiple Roles: Benefits and Drawbacks.   Most of us play multiple roles in life.
We may be spouses, parents, workers, and members of community, social, and religious organizations. All of these roles make demands on our time and energy, and it

is possible to become overloaded with responsibilities. Interestingly, family stressors appear to be related more strongly to symptoms of psychological distress for women than for men. The reverse is true for work stressors, with these having more impact on men.[19] Why is this so? Clear evidence is lacking, but it appears that women may take more responsibility in family matters and thus suffer more from problems that occur in that area.[20] Of course, both men and women who have to deal with problems at work, in the home, and in other organizations may find themselves experiencing quite high levels of stress. In fact, when both members of dual earner couples were interviewed, it was found that they were equally affected by job experiences or job quality.[21] The stress experienced in one role can even spill over to one's other roles. Someone who is having problems at home may not function well at work, and someone who is experiencing difficulties at work may be less able to cope effectively with home responsibilities. One fact is quite clear. The more conflict that arises between the demands of work and the family, the lower a person's satisfaction with his or her job and life in general.[22]

Yet having multiple roles is not necessarily a problem. Much evidence suggests that having multiple roles can actually reduce stress. Women who work have fewer mental and physical problems than those who do not. This is particularly true for those who view their job as a career.[23] Other studies indicate that both men and women who occupy more roles have higher levels of well-being.[24] Of course, it is possible that well-adjusted people get involved in more roles rather than more roles producing better adjustment. However, studies that have examined this possibility suggest that having multiple roles in and of itself may be the critical factor.[25]

Why would multiple roles lead to lower levels of stress? You have probably gotten involved in some activities to get away from problems you were experiencing in other areas of your life. Teenagers may take on a job to gain more independence from their parents and to meet some other sources of interpersonal support. Women may similarly find satisfaction and support in their work that they do not receive from their roles as wives or mothers. The extent to which a role provides positive benefits may depend on the extent to which one has control over the tasks or activities involved. In the family role, women often have little choice about the tasks they are expected to perform, and they may deal with people who can be difficult to control (children and husbands). In many careers, they may experience more freedom of choice and have more control. In most work environments, lines of authority and responsibility are clearly outlined. However, at home there may be constant conflict over responsibilities and areas of authority.

Our discussion has painted a somewhat negative picture of the family role. It should be noted that those who are involved in a family role have higher levels of well-being than those who are single.[26] This finding fits with the general idea that having multiple roles is healthy. Being involved in a family has many benefits, such as social support, companionship, and social structure. The reason multiple roles are healthy may be that one role can compensate for what is lacking in the other roles. Of course, if one gains a tremendous amount of satisfaction out of one role, one may shun other roles. Some people commit themselves to religious careers that prohibit marriage and limit other community involvements. Some may find the family role sufficiently rewarding that they are not interested in developing a career. The benefits of multiple roles also depend on the relationships that exist in each of these roles. The mental health benefits of working are evident for wives only when husbands share the family work.[27] Clerical workers who had nonsupportive bosses were at greater risk for heart disease than those who had supportive ones.[28]

Role Conflict: Differences in Expectations.

Having multiple roles can lead to role conflict when one role makes it difficult to effectively carry out other roles. Being a single parent and working a night job is one obvious example of such a conflict. Role conflicts, however, also develop in other ways. A **role** can be defined as expectations that are held about a particular position by the person who is in that position and relevant others inside and outside the organization.[29] Whenever these expectations come into conflict, a person may experience stress. For example, if your boss expects you to work overtime and your family expects you to spend more time at home, serious role conflict arises. The type of conflict that occurs when a person is faced with the incompatible expectations of people from different areas of one's life is called **inter-role conflict.** Sometimes a conflict occurs between our own expectations and that of others. This type of mismatch is called **person-role conflict.** For example, a job may require a person to simply follow orders and not allow that individual to achieve a goal of having leadership responsibility. A third type of conflict, **within-role conflict,** involves incompatible expectations from people in one domain of one's life.[30] For example, some of your coworkers may expect you to provide clear feedback about their performance, but others may not.

Obviously, if you experience a lot of conflict in these different areas, your stress level may be rather high. You may want to check how you stack up in the area of role conflict by completing the items in the *Human Relations in Action* section on pages 406–407.

Overload and Underload: Doing Too Much or Too Little.

When the phrase *job stress* is mentioned, most people conjure up an image of someone caught in the trap of trying to do too much in too little time. In this case, common belief is not far off the mark, for overload is in fact a major cause of stress at work. Actually, a distinction is often made between **quantitative overload**—a situation in which an individual is confronted with more

role   Expectations that are held about a particular position.

inter-role conflict   Conflict that occurs when people from different parts of an individual's life have conflicting expectations about that person's role.

person-role conflict   Conflict between our own expectations and the expectations of others.

within-role conflict   Conflict that occurs when people in one area of an individual's life have different expectations.

quantitative overload   A situation in which individuals are confronted with more work than can be completed in a given period of time.

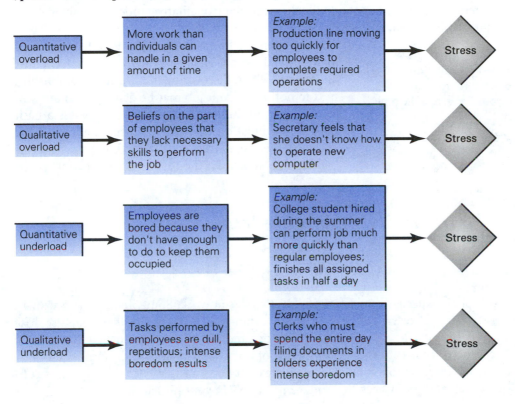

𝓕𝑖𝑔𝑢𝑟𝑒 14.3   **Overload and Underload: Contrasting Patterns**

Both overload and underload can serve as sources of stress at work. Two distinct patterns (quantitative and qualitative) exist for each.

work than can be completed in a given period of time—and **qualitative overload**—the belief by an employee that he or she lacks the skills or abilities required to perform a given job. Both types of overload are unpleasant, and research findings suggest that both can lead to high levels of stress.[31,32] Figure 14.3 summarizes the stressful impact of underload and overload.

But overload is only part of the total picture. While being asked to do too much on one's job can be stressful, so, too, is the opposite—being asked to do too little. In fact, there seems to be considerable truth to the following saying: "The hardest job in the world is doing nothing—you can't stop and take a break." Such underload (or underutilization) leads to boredom and monotony. In this respect, it can be quite stressful.[33] Again, a distinction be-

qualitative overload The belief of an employee that he or she lacks the skills or abilities required to perform a specific job.

tween **quantitative underload** and **qualitative underload** is often drawn. Quantitative underload refers to the boredom that results when employees have so little to do that they find themselves sitting around much of the time. In contrast, qualitative underload refers to the lack of mental stimulation that accompanies many routine, repetitive jobs. Thus an individual experiencing qualitative underload can be doing quite a bit but still be bored to tears.

quantitative underload   A situation in which individuals have so little to do that they find themselves sitting around much of the time.

qualitative underload   The lack of mental stimulation that accompanies many routine, repetitive jobs.

Most persons find either type of underload stressful, and for good reason. First, everyone wishes to feel useful and needed. Thus, discovering that we are accomplishing next to nothing on our job may be damaging to our self-esteem. Second, human beings seem to possess a basic need for stimulation. Contrary to what common sense suggests, their preferred state is definitely *not* staring blankly into space. On the contrary, most people prefer

Human Relations in Action

How Much Role Conflict Do You Have?

We often experience a variety of role conflicts at work. Some involve disagreement between roles or expectations at work (within-role conflict). Conflicts may also arise between our job and our outside interests and activities (inter-role conflict). Some conflicts occur because of a mismatch of our characteristics and those required by the job (person-role conflict). To what extent do you experience these types of conflicts at your job? Check those items that apply in your present situation.

Within-Role Conflict

_____   1. My coworkers have conflicting expectations of me.

_____   2. I often have difficulty in prioritizing the tasks given to me by my superior.

_____   3. Some of my coworkers desire feedback but others do not.

_____   4. Some of my coworkers do not follow company policies and expect me to support their behavior.

Inter-role Conflict

_____   5. My job gives me little time for my hobbies.

_____   6. I neglect my personal interests because of my job.

to be active and to be doing interesting things at least part of the time. For these reasons, jobs that demand too little can be as stressful as those that demand too much. In sum, it appears that, with respect to the amount of work or effort demanded from individuals by their jobs, the middle course is best. The most desirable and least stressful jobs seem to be those that keep their holders busy but do not overtax their abilities or lead them to feel unable to cope.

One reason that both overload and underload are stressful is that they involve a loss of control. Feelings of loss of control over some aspects of a person's life or job can be critical factors in determining how the experiences and demands of life affect that individual. Feelings of choice or autonomy at work are important not only for job satisfaction but also for their ability to buffer the effects of the stress experienced.[34]

Responsibility for Others: Often, a Heavy Burden.   In any organization, there is a division of responsibility. Some persons deal primarily with financial matters such as

_____   7. It is difficult to have time for family life because of my job.

_____   8. My job makes it difficult to have a social life.

Person-Role Conflict

_____   9. My work prevents me from achieving my personal goals.

_____   10. My values and the values in my workplace differ.

_____   11. My job does not help me achieve my ambitions.

_____   12. My training and expertise are not used effectively in my job.

If you checked more than half of these items, you are experiencing a significant amount of role conflict. If this conflict is contributing to your level of stress, you might consider making some adjustments. Of course, if the level of role conflict is very high, you might consider looking for a more compatible job.

Based on Pandy, S., & Kumar, E. S. (1997). Development of a measure of role conflict. *The International Journal of Conflict Management, 8,* 187–215.

budgets, others handle the flow of supplies or maintenance equipment, and still others deal primarily with people. Are there any differences in the level of stress associated with these contrasting types of responsibility? Research suggests that there are. In general, people responsible for other people—those who must deal with, motivate, and make decisions about others—experience higher levels of stress than persons who handle other aspects of a business.[35] Such persons are more likely to report feelings of tension and anxiety and to demonstrate physical symptoms of stress, such as ulcers and hypertension, than their counterparts in finance, supply, and so on. The basis for this difference is obvious. Supervisors and managers must witness the pain of persons who are fired or passed over for promotion. As you can imagine, such experiences are often very stressful. Being responsible for other persons *is* often a heavy burden, and one that exacts a toll in terms of job-related stress.

Lack of Social Support: The Costs of Isolation.   You have probably noticed that often when people are under stress, they seek out *support* and comfort from others. While support and comfort may make them feel better, do they actually reduce the effects of stress? In general, the answer seems to be "yes." When individuals believe that they have the friendship and support of others at work, their ability to resist the adverse effects of stress seems to increase. For example, one investigation examined managers at a large public utility who were experiencing high levels of stress. The managers who felt they had the support of their immediate supervisors reported fewer physical symptoms associated with stress than managers who did not feel that they enjoyed such support.[36]

How does social support assist individuals in dealing with stress? Several mechanisms may play a role. First, having friends they can turn to in time of difficulty may help individuals to perceive stressful events as less threatening and more under their control than would otherwise be the case. Second, such persons can suggest useful strategies for dealing with sources of stress. Third, they can help reduce the negative feelings that often accompany exposure to stressful events.[37]

Unemployment: The Stress of No Work.   Since having a job can be a source of stress, one obvious way to reduce the stress is not to have a job at all. Of course, this is not an option for most adults. Even those who have sufficient resources often choose to work for the many rewards provided by their job. But what happens when people lose their jobs? With the ever-changing world and national economies, there are continual changes in the job demands in different sectors of the economy. So job changes and unemployment are a fact of life. Becoming unemployed can have significant negative effects on a person's health.[38,39] The unemployed are confronted with uncertainty about their future and the potential loss of valuable resources such as their homes and cars. Their self-esteem is also lowered since much of their self-concept may have been derived from their work.[40] They may feel the embarrassment of others knowing of their situation. The anxiety and stress of those who are laid off or have some degree of job insecurity may even spill over to their children.[41] If attempts to find a job are not fruitful, the unemployed person may become depressed and develop feelings of helplessness. Unfortunately, this makes it less likely that the individual will aggressively seek new opportunities or project himself or herself in a positive manner. Depression for the unemployed is lifted when they get what they are seeking in subsequent time periods. For some this is a new job, for others this may be losing a disliked job, and for some it may be not wanting a new job. Thus, having something go their way may give them a more positive perspective on life.[42]

PERSONAL FACTORS AND STRESS

Let's begin this section with two basic facts: (1) What happens to people off the job often affects the way they behave at work, and (2) the characteristics people bring with them to their jobs can strongly affect the ways they react to stress. In the context of these points, another fact becomes clear: If we wish to fully understand stress in work settings, we must take into account personal as well as organizational factors. That is, we must consider the current lifestyles, attitudes, and characteristics of the persons in question. Some of these personal factors will now be considered.

Life Events and Stress: The Potential Costs of Change

Movies and plays often suggest an important link between events in one's life and personal health. Specifically, they often show individuals who have experienced traumatic events (for example, the death of a loved one, divorce) pining away until they become seriously ill or even die. This suggestion of a link between stressful life events and health is intriguing and has important implications for behavior in work settings. After all, employees who are suffering from ill health or deep depression are unlikely to be effective at their jobs. But is this picture accurate? The answer appears to be "yes." Many studies indicate that when individuals undergo stressful changes in their lives, their personal health does indeed suffer.[43,44] Some of the events related to such changes are listed in Table 14.1 on page 410. As you can see, events near the top of the table are very upsetting and stressful, while ones farther down are only mildly stress inducing. (Note that death of a spouse is assigned 100 points, while other life events receive smaller values that reflect their degree of stressfulness relative to this shattering event.) Research suggests that the greater the number and intensity of stressful life events individuals experience, the greater their likelihood of developing serious illness. For example, persons who report life events totaling 150 to 300 points have about a 50 percent chance of becoming seriously ill during the next year. Those

Table 14.1   **Life Events: Some Are More Stressful Than Others**

When asked to assign arbitrary points (1 to 100) to various life events according to the degree of readjustment they required, a large group of individuals provided these values. The higher the numbers shown, the more stressful the events listed.

Event	Relative Stressfulness
Death of a spouse	100
Divorce	73
Marital separation	65
Jail term	63
Death of a close family member	63
Personal injury or illness	53
Marriage	50
Fired from job	47
Retirement	45
Pregnancy	40
Death of a close friend	37
Son or daughter leaving home	29
Trouble with in-laws	28
Trouble with boss	23
Change in residence	20
Vacation	13
Christmas	12

Based on data from Holmes and Masuda, 1974; see note 45.

who experience events totaling more than 300 points have a 70 percent chance of experiencing such an outcome.

For example, in one study on this topic, Holmes and Masuda asked patients at a university medical center to report all significant life changes (events) during the past eighteen months.[45] Persons who experienced events totaling 300 points or more showed a much higher incidence of illness during the next nine months than those with 200 points or less (49 percent versus 9 percent).

It probably makes sense to you that the life events that are perceived by individuals in a negative way would have the most impact on health. In fact, such stressors seem to weaken our resistance to infectious agents such as the viruses responsible for the common cold.[46]

The Hassles of Our Lives: The Costs of Daily Stressors

Traumatic life events are relatively rare. Many persons live for years or even decades without experiencing any of them. Unfortunately, the daily lives of most of us are filled with countless minor sources of stress that seem to make up for their relatively low intensity by their high frequency of occurrence. That such *daily hassles* are an important cause of stress is suggested by the findings of several studies by Lazarus and his colleagues.[47] These researchers have developed a *Hassles Scale* on which individuals indicate the extent to which they have been "hassled" by common events during the past month. Items included in this scale deal with a wide range of everyday events (for example, having too many things to do at once, shopping, concerns over money). Scores on the Hassles Scale are related to both reports of psychological symptoms and physical health. The more stress people report as a result of such daily hassles, the poorer their psychological and physical health. Indeed, some findings suggest that stress induced by daily hassles has stronger effects on health than those resulting from traumatic life events.[48] This result may be due in part to the fact that we are less likely to receive social support for our hassles than we are for major life events.[49]

In sum, while traumatic life events such as the death of a loved one or the loss of one's job are stressful and exert adverse effects on health, the minor hassles of daily life—perhaps because of their frequent, repetitive nature—may sometimes prove even more crucial in this respect. Whatever their relative importance, both traumatic life events and daily hassles are important sources of stress for many persons. And since this stress is often carried into the workplace by the persons involved, it is certainly worth noting in this discussion of stress and its effect in work settings.

Individual Differences in Resistance to Stress: Variations in Susceptibility

You have probably observed that individuals differ greatly in their resistance to stress. Some suffer ill effects after exposure to brief periods of relatively mild stress, while others are able to function effectively even after prolonged exposure to much higher levels of stress. How do such persons differ? There appear to be several characteristics that play important roles.

Optimism: A Buffer against Stress.

One personal factor that seems to play an important role in determining resistance to stress is the familiar dimension of **optimism-pessimism**. Optimists, of course, are people who see the glass as half full; they are hopeful in their outlook on life, interpret a wide range of situations in a positive light, and

optimism-pessimism The personality dimension based on the outlook that individuals have on life. Those with a positive outlook are optimists, and those with a negative outlook are termed pessimists.

tend to expect favorable outcomes and results. Pessimists, in contrast, are individuals who see the glass as half empty; they interpret many situations negatively and expect unfavorable outcomes and results. Recent studies indicate that, as you might well guess, optimists are much more stress-resistant than pessimists. For example, optimists are much less likely than pessimists to report physical illness and symptoms during highly stressful periods such as final exams and the first semester of college and to recover more quickly after surgery.[50] Optimists and pessimists seem to adopt sharply contrasting tactics for coping with stress. Optimists engage in *problem-focused coping*—making and enacting specific plans for dealing with sources of stress. In addition, they seek *social support*—the advice and help of friends and others—and they refrain from engaging in other activities until current problems are solved and stress is reduced. On the other hand, pessimists tend to adopt different strategies, such as giving up in their efforts to reach the goals the stress is interfering with and denying that the stressful events have even occurred[51] (see Figure 14.4). Needless to say, the former strategies are often more effective than the latter.

 **Optimists and Pessimists:**
Different Ways of Coping with Stress

Optimists and pessimists adopt different strategies for coping with stress. In general, those chosen by optimists are more effective.

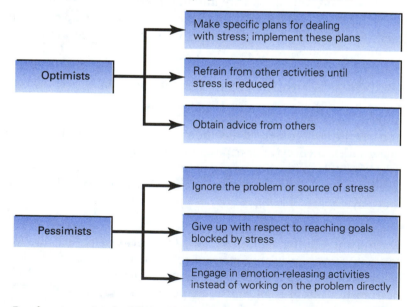

Based on suggestions by Scheier, Weintraub, and Carver, 1986; see note 51.

Gender and Ethnic Differences

It is probably evident to you that stress does not respect gender or ethnic "boundaries." All of us experience stress, but there is some evidence that some groups are more susceptible than others. We have already pointed to some of the factors that underlie the higher levels of stress that women may experience in our society because of their disproportionate responsibilities in the home. Therefore it is probably not surprising to you that women report higher levels than men of depression and psychological symptoms of distress, such as discomfort and mental disorganization.[52] Interestingly, women also report higher levels of happiness and life satisfaction.[53] How can this be? Women appear to be more emotionally expressive than men and more sensitive to their emotional states. Therefore, they are more likely to report stronger positive *and* negative emotions. The gender difference in positive well-being occurs primarily for those who are married. So even though some aspects of the marital role may be stressful and lead to periodic negative emotions, women still appear to find many satisfactions in this role.

There also appear to be some racial and ethnic differences in the experience of stress. African Americans have higher levels of hypertension (elevated blood pressures) than whites. Some research suggests that this may in part be due to a higher reactivity of blacks to physical and social stressors.[54] Although genetic factors may be involved, sociocultural factors such as the black experience and social and economic status in the United States and characteristics of the African American culture may be more important. However, other studies indicate little difference in the extent to which blacks and whites respond with psychological distress to life changes or in the ways in which they cope with job stress.[55,56] Research with Mexican American working mothers also demonstrates the importance of cultural factors. These mothers felt a mental health benefit when their husbands helped with housework but not when they helped with child care. The reverse has been found with other populations. Possibly, the role of mother may be more important to Mexican American women than to those from other ethnic groups.[57] However, clear explanations for ethnic differences in the experience of stress and the degree to which there are differences in actual susceptibility to stress will have to await further research.

Attitudes and Stress: Is Attitude Everything?

We have highlighted just a few of the characteristics associated with people who vary in their ability to deal with stress. Research has provided evidence for a host of other characteristics that are related to the ability to tolerate or handle stress well, such as sense of humor and one's perspective on life.[58] Research supports the conclusion that it is not so much what happens to us but our attitudes toward these events that determine the degree to which we experience negative effects in response to generally stressful events. For example, recent studies indicate that people who are strongly religious may be able to cope better with life stressors than others.[59] It is, of course, difficult to know precisely why this is the case. Religious people may lead a somewhat healthier lifestyle involving social interaction, support, and limited use of alcohol. Religion also provides people with a way of giving meaning to life and its many stressors.[60]

On the basis of a broad range of studies, it appears that people who have the following attitudes or orientations are highly prone to the negative effects of stressful conditions:

1. They take everything seriously and do not discriminate between what is important and unimportant.
2. They are pessimistic, assume the worst, and worry about everything.
3. They are easily angered and have little tolerance for frustration.
4. They have a negative attitude toward others and are judgmental.
5. They evaluate life from the narrow perspective of the present; they see life as generally meaningless.
6. They blame themselves for events beyond their control.
7. They have no sense of humor.

In contrast, people who are able to handle stressors quite well are those who:

1. Are easy-going, go with the flow, and discriminate between the important and unimportant.
2. Are optimistic and act upon this optimism.
3. Are slow to anger and tolerant of frustration.
4. Approach others with a positive attitude.
5. See life from the broad perspective of the outside observer; they see life as generally meaningful.
6. Are realistic and understand that some events are beyond one's control.
7. Have a sense of humor.

STRESS: SOME IMPORTANT EFFECTS

By now, you are probably convinced that stress derives from many sources and is quite common at work. What you may still not fully realize, though, is just how powerful and far-reaching its effects can be. Systematic research on this topic indicates that stress influences our physical well-being, our psychological states, our personal adjustment, and many aspects of our behavior. In fact, there is hardly any aspect of our lives that it does not affect. If you would like to know more about the specific nature of these effects, read on; information about them follows. But be prepared for some intriguing—and unsettling!—surprises.

Stress and Health: The Silent Killer

Here comes the first of the surprises we promised: At the present time, most medical experts believe that *from 50 percent to 70 percent of physical illnesses are related to stress.*[61] Moreover, included among these stress-related diseases are some of the most serious and fatal ones known to medical science. We have already touched on evidence linking stress to heart disease (see the discussion on the Type A personality pattern in Chapter 4). Here, we will simply add that high levels of stress are also linked to the following major health problems: high blood pressure, arteriosclerosis (hardening of the arteries), ulcers, diabetes, and the common cold.[62] Recent evidence suggests that stress may exert negative effects in part because it diminishes the effectiveness of the immune system, which allows us to resist diseases.[63] In short, stress is implicated in the occurrence of some of the leading causes of death among human beings. If you needed any further basis for giving it careful consideration in your own life, this fact should provide it!

Stress: Its Effects on Our Mental States

At present, most behavioral scientists believe that mind and body are closely connected. Events and conditions affecting one often affect the other. Given this view, it is not surprising to learn that as stress affects our basic bodily processes, it also influences our psychological states. Several such effects have been uncovered. First, as you might well expect, exposure to stress often induces negative changes in mood or emotions. Persons experiencing stress frequently report such feelings as anxiety, depression, irritation, and fatigue. Second, exposure to stress—especially stress relating to one's job—may result in lowered self-esteem.[64] This seems to stem from the fact that persons experiencing stress often feel unable to cope with their jobs. This, in turn, affects feelings of competence and self-worth and reduces self-esteem. Third, and perhaps most important, stress is often associated with reductions in job satisfaction.[65] Considering the negative and unpleasant nature of intense, continued stress, this is far from surprising. In any case, given the important links between job satisfaction and key forms of behavior at work (reviewed in Chapter 11), the effect of stress on such attitudes has important practical implications.

When people experience stress for a long period of time, they may come to have a sense of helplessness.[66] This feeling is often associated with feelings of depression

Table 14.2   **The Stressors of Police Work: Some Subjective Ratings**

Police work can be very stressful, which can lead to a variety of negative mental and physical problems. When some police officers were asked to rate the stressors they experience, they provided the following results.

Killing someone in the line of duty	79.4
Fellow officer killed	76.7
Physical attack	71.0
Battered child	69.2
High-speed chases	63.7
Shiftwork	61.2
Use of force	61.0
Accident in patrol vehicle	59.9

Adapted from Paton and Violanti, 1996; see note 14.

and even suicide. For example, police have a higher suicide rate than the general population, which could related to the stress and traumas that they often experience (see Table 14.2).[67]

Stress and Behavior at Work

How does stress affect the quality of your job performance? When you are under high pressure, deadlines, or increasingly close supervision, you may actually work harder and complete your tasks more quickly. But what will happen to the quality of your work? Evidence suggests that for simple tasks such as stuffing envelopes and loading trucks, performance quality may not suffer. On more complicated tasks, such as developing computer programs or doing financial analyses, the quality of performance may decline.[68] For example, in one study researchers asked a large group of nurses to describe their own levels of work-related stress. Ratings of their actual job performance were then obtained from supervisors or coworkers. Results indicated that the higher the nurses' feelings of stress, the lower their job performance.[69]

Decision making can also be affected by stress. When individuals are under time pressure, attempt to process a great deal of information, and try to handle several tasks or issues at the same time, the effectiveness of decision making is likely to suffer. The focus of attention may narrow to only a part of the relevant information, and simpler decision strategies may be used. When the decision is an important one, the consequences of poor decision making can be serious. For example, in 1988 the naval ship *USS Vincennes* shot down an Iranian airliner, killing all those aboard the plane. The decision makers had concluded that the airliner was a military aircraft heading directly toward the *Vincennes*. Subsequent analyses have discovered that a number of flaws in the information-gathering and decision-making processes played a significant role in this unfortunate action.[70] In Chapter 8, we provided additional examples of poor group decision making in high-pressure situations.

Task performance is not the only aspect of work behavior influenced by stress. Stress is also modestly related to absenteeism and turnover.[71] This is hardly surprising, for when individuals find their jobs highly stressful, they may well seek to avoid them. High levels of job stress are also linked to alcoholism and drug abuse.

Burnout: When Stress Consumes

When most people begin their careers, they are full of hope, enthusiasm, and energy. They have exciting plans and look forward to a bright, if not dazzling, future. All too often, though, these early dreams of success, contributions, and achievement rapidly fade. Individuals find that they cannot change things very much, that many of the activities they must perform are boring, and that each day they must cope with a number of unpleasant and stressful events. For most persons, the result of this collision between youthful dreams and reality is a period of adjustment. After it is complete, they continue with their careers in an orderly and usually satisfying manner. For others, though, the outcome is much less positive. Such persons become greatly dissatisfied with their work. They experience mental and physical fatigue. They develop negative feelings about their jobs and about life in general. They become **burnout** victims.[72] People who suffer from burnout demonstrate several distinct characteristics.[73]

First, victims of burnout suffer from *physical exhaustion.* They have low energy and feel tired most of the time. In addition, they report many symptoms of physical strain, such as frequent headaches, nausea, poor sleep, and changes in eating habits (for example, loss of appetite). Second, they experience *emotional exhaustion.* Depression, feelings of helplessness, and feelings of being trapped in one's job are all part of the picture. Third, persons suffering from burnout often become cynical about others and hold negative attitudes toward them. This is termed *depersonalization.* They may also derogate themselves, their jobs, their organizations, and even life in general. To put it simply, they come to view the world around them through dark gray rather than rose-colored glasses. So they often report feelings of *low personal accomplishment.* Persons suffering from burnout conclude that they haven't been able to accomplish much in the past, and they assume that they probably won't succeed in this respect in the future, either. In sum, burnout can be defined as a *syndrome of emotional, physical, and mental exhaustion coupled with feelings of low self-esteem or low self-efficacy, resulting from prolonged exposure to intense stress.*

burnout A syndrome resulting from prolonged exposure to stress, consisting of physical, emotional, and mental exhaustion plus feelings of low personal accomplishment.

Burnout: Some Major Causes.   What are the causes of burnout? As we have already noted, the primary factor appears to be prolonged exposure to stress. When we experience role conflict, role ambiguity, overload, and lack of social support over a period to time, we may start experiencing the symptoms of burnout.[74,75] These may come about in part because of the way an organization functions. If a work unit (supervisor and persons under his or her control) lacks clear rules and procedures (lack of standardization), and supervisors are not able to make their own decisions (centralization), burnout is likely. Burnout is also more likely in an organization if there is little formalization in the relationships among different units or poor coordination among them.[76]

In general, job conditions implying that one's efforts are useless, ineffective, or unappreciated seem to contribute to burnout.[77] This is consistent with the concept of equity discussed in Chapter 5. When people receive fewer benefits (for example, appreciation, compensation) than they feel are fair given their efforts, they will feel underbenefited. If they receive more than is fair, they will feel overbenefited. Interestingly, both of these types of inequitable outcomes are related to measures of burnout (see Figure 14.5).[78] Under such conditions, individuals develop the feelings of low personal accomplishment that are an important part of burnout. Similarly, poor opportunities for promotion and the presence of inflexible rules and procedures lead employees to feel trapped in an unfair system and contribute to the development of negative views about their jobs.[79]

Another important factor contributing to burnout is the *leadership style* adopted by supervisors. Apparently, the lower the amount of consideration demonstrated by supervisors (that is, the lower their concern with employees' welfare or with maintaining friendly relations with them), the higher employees' reported levels of burnout.[80]

Some Personal Factors in Burnout.   Some people may be more susceptible to burnout than others. Those who take their work and other roles seriously are more likely to suffer burnout than those who take a rather casual approach to their work.

Jobs that require interpersonal involvements and commitments to other individuals as part of one's work, such as nursing, teaching, and social work, may be particularly likely to lead to burnout. Individuals in these jobs often make significant investments of their time and emotions into these relationships without receiving clear rewards or appreciation for their efforts. In these jobs, it may help to have a *communal orientation*.[81] Individuals who are high in communal orientation are concerned about the needs of others and obtain satisfaction from meeting those needs. For example, leaders of self-help groups that deal with such issues as bereavement and cancer may experience burnout because of their extensive involvement in the problems of others. When these types of leaders are high in communal orientation, they experience more of a sense of personal accomplishment and less depersonalization.[82] This type of person is less likely to react negatively to investing more in a relationship

| *Figure 14.5* | **Fairness and Burnout: Negative Effects of Under- and Overbenefits** |

Therapists rated the degree to which they received benefits from their clients. When they reported being either underbenefited or overbenefited, they experienced high levels of emotional exhaustion and depersonalization.

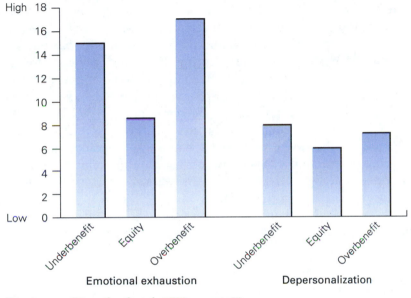

Based on van Dierendonck et al., 1996; see note 78.

than he or she receives in return. In a study of nurses, it was primarily those who were low in communal orientation who experienced depersonalization, low personal accomplishment, and emotional exhaustion when they perceived an imbalance between what they invested and what they received.[83] In contrast, nurses who reported having significant coping resources, such as physical stamina, social relationships, and spiritual or philosophical beliefs, appeared to be less prone to burnout.[84]

Burnout: Some Major Effects.   Whatever the precise causes of burnout, once it develops, it has important consequences. First, it may lead individuals to seek new jobs or careers. In one study concerned with the impact of burnout, several hundred teachers completed a questionnaire designed to measure their burnout and the extent to which they would prefer to be in another job or career.[85] As expected, the greater the teachers' degree of burnout, the more likely they were to prefer another job and to be actively considering a change of occupation.

Second, persons suffering from burnout may seek administrative roles where they can hide from jobs they have grown to hate behind huge piles of forms. While this pattern certainly occurs, it appears to be relatively rare. Most victims of burnout seem either to change jobs or to withdraw psychologically and mark time until retirement.

Burnout: Countering Its Effects.   If our discussion so far has left you slightly depressed, don't give up hope. Growing evidence suggests that burnout can be reversed. With appropriate help, victims of burnout can recover from their physical and psychological exhaustion. If ongoing stress is reduced, if individuals gain added support from friends and coworkers,[86] and if they cultivate hobbies and other outside interests, at least some persons, it appears, can return to positive attitudes and renewed productivity. Exercise, meditation, power naps, and brief one- or two-day breaks may provide some temporary relief or stress reduction.[87] One example of such an effect occurs when people who have experienced burnout take a vacation. Unfortunately, burnout tends to return once the person goes back to work. This pattern was observed in a study of clerical workers who took a two-week vacation and was somewhat stronger for women than for men (see Figure 14.6).[88]

To really deal effectively with burnout requires active efforts designed to overcome burnout and to change the conditions from which it develops.

Figure 14.6   **Burnout and Vacation: Relief That Does Not Last**

When clerical workers took a vacation, their feelings of burnout were reduced. Those feelings returned, however, when they came back to work.

Based on Westman and Eden, 1997; see note 88.

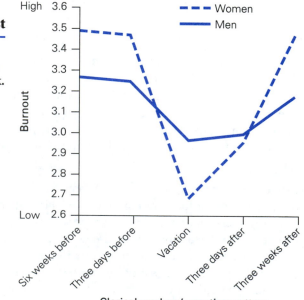

Clerical workers' vacation pattern

There are a number of key steps involved in getting burnout under control.

1. **Reorder your priorities and goals.** You should eliminate or reduce those activities that are of secondary importance in your life. This should give you more time and energy for what is really important.

2. **Accentuate the positive.** Focus on the rewarding aspects of your work and learn to take pride in your accomplishments and skills. Also be sure to seek out positive experiences outside the job, such as hobbies, sports, and brief vacations.

3. **Get involved in a social support network.** Those who suffer from burnout may feel isolated from others. They need friends who can listen to their problems, provide emotional support, and provide positive feedback and encouragement. This is particularly important for extroverts.[89]

4. **Compartmentalize your life.** Try to leave the problems from work there so that you can enjoy your time and relationships off the job.

5. **Restore feelings of equity.** Feelings of burnout tend to be high if individuals feel that they are not receiving appropriate rewards for their work efforts. Burnout can be reduced by reducing work efforts, getting more rewards, developing expectations more in line with reality, or leaving the job.[90]

Through these and related steps, individuals can turn the tables on burnout. Instead of being its helpless victims, they can circumvent or even convert it into a basis for personal growth. In short, when tedium and burnout are handled effectively, they can actually leave individuals stronger, wiser, and more in touch with their own basic values than was true initially.

If these efforts fail to produce positive results, though, don't give up. Instead, seek the help of counselors or other professionals specially trained to assist individuals in overcoming such problems.[91]

$\mathcal{M}$ANAGING STRESS: SOME USEFUL TECHNIQUES

Stress derives from many sources. For this reason, it is probably impossible to completely eliminate it from work settings. While it cannot be totally removed, it can be managed. We will now describe several techniques for accomplishing this task.[92]

Lifestyle: Actions Speak Loudly

What is your lifestyle? Are you a loner, couch potato, aficionado of fatty foods, and a smoker? If so, you may be endangering your health in addition to reducing your physical and emotional ability to handle stress. Evidence suggests that being married or having the social support of one or more close friends or relatives is related to well-being and the ability to withstand the negative effects of stress.[93] Regular physical exercise can help minimize the physical deterioration that can result from stress.[94] In fact, exercise may reduce one's reactivity to various stressors.[95] Avoidance of unhealthy dietary and other habits, such as smoking and alcohol abuse, is also important for increasing one's resistance to stress.

As the link between physical fitness and health has become increasingly clear, many companies have added *employee fitness programs.* These programs are run and funded by organizations to improve the physical fitness of their employees. Such programs are based, in part, on the assumption that improved physical fitness increases individuals' resistance to the adverse effects of stress. However, their growing popularity also derives from findings suggesting that physical fitness reduces absenteeism and enhances productivity and that employee fitness programs contribute to commitment and other positive attitudes among employees.[96,97] Given these important benefits, it is not all surprising that such programs have grown in popularity and are now widespread throughout industry.

Coping with Stress: Getting a Handle on Your Problems

Even if we lead the right lifestyle, we can't avoid experiencing stress. However, we can control how we deal or cope with stress. What is your style of coping? Does stress make you feel hopeless, or does it stimulate you to deal with the problems that produced the stress? There are many effective ways of coping with stress.[98]

Emotional coping involves trying to reduce the negative feelings associated with the stress experience. You may try to relax yourself in preparation for a speech or performance or reduce the sadness of a loss by doing some distracting activities or going to a funny movie. Of course, these strategies do not change the actual event or situation that is causing the stress. To do this will require some form of either mental or behavioral coping.

Mental coping involves changing one's perspective or attitude about the stressor. This is known as cognitive reevaluation. It is especially useful if there is nothing that can be done to actually change the situation. People cannot reverse the loss of a loved one and may decide it was God's will or that this person would want us to go on and live a productive and useful life. If it is necessary to speak in front of groups as part of a job that you cannot afford to lose, you may convince yourself of your capabilities relative to those in the audience in order to reduce your fear or anxiety.

In many cases, the most effective way of dealing with stress is active behavioral problem solving.[99] Conflicts at work or at home, an overload of demands on one's time, and a variety of daily hassles are probably handled best by changing the situation or behavior patterns responsible for the problems. Learning how to say no, organizing one's time more efficiently, changing problematic habits, and attempting to change

Figure 14.7   The Stressful Lifestyle: Learning to Cope

Families often have to learn to deal with stress both at work and at home.

the behaviors of others that are causing stress are just a few examples. This may be easier said than done, but the alternative is the persistence of a stressful lifestyle (see Figure 14.7).

There is probably not a single best approach for dealing with stress. It will depend on the person and the situation. One thing is clear, though: Coping by avoiding the problem mentally and behaviorally or blaming oneself is the worst alternative. This way of coping is ineffective in the long run and is associated with the most negative results.[100] In general, your best policy is to heed the suggestions that follow.

1. Assess the problem and the alternatives for dealing with it. Is it temporary or long-term, controllable or uncontrollable? Do you have the personal resources for dealing with the problem, or do you need help? What needs to change—you, others, the situation, your attitude, or all of these?

2. On the basis of your analysis, decide on the best course of action for dealing with the problem. If you decide it cannot be handled or solved directly, you may have to leave the situation or relationship.

3. Develop attitudes and strategies that help you deal with unavoidable stressors. Learn to look at the positive side of things and different ways of relaxation.

Getting Control of Emotions

Many techniques of stress management center on a common theme: teaching individuals special procedures for replacing strain and tension with relaxation. One of the most popular of these is **relaxation training.** Here, individuals learn how to relax their muscles in a systematic

relaxation training Special training in which individuals learn to relax one group of muscles at a time. This, in turn, often causes them to experience a reduction in tension.

manner (for example, from the feet upward to the head). Such relaxation feels good and does seem helpful in reducing emotional tension. A related tactic involves learning to breathe in a deep and regular manner. Such breathing, too, can lower tension. A third and somewhat different technique is known as **meditation**. Individuals practicing meditation assume a comfortable position, close their eyes, and attempt to clear all disturbing thoughts from their minds. Then, they silently repeat a single syllable, or *mantra,* over and over again. When performed correctly, such meditation seems to produce feelings of relaxation and well-being. It also affects basic bodily functions in a way suggestive of relaxation (for example, it lowers oxygen consumption and produces brain-wave patterns indicative of a calm mental state).[101]

A final tactic for replacing strain with relaxation is known as *biofeedback.* In this approach, individuals are connected to sensitive equipment that can detect small changes in their bodily functions (for example, increases or decreases in blood pressure). Whenever these functions exceed target levels (for example, whenever blood pressure is too high), a tone sounds or a light flashes. Individuals then attempt to stop the tone or light by lowering their blood pressure, slowing their pulse, and so on. Surprising as it may seem, most persons are able to master this technique, although they cannot report precisely *how* they manage to produce these effects.

Through relaxation training, meditation, biofeedback, and related techniques, individuals can learn to manage stress. They can stop acting as their own worst enemies and can take an active role in enhancing both their health and their careers.

meditation   A technique for inducing relaxation in which individuals clear disturbing thoughts from their minds and then repeat a single syllable (mantra) over and over again.

Guidelines for Effective Human Relations

Using What You've Learned

In this chapter we examined a broad range of principles and findings about stress. Although few rules will apply to every situation, there are some general guidelines suggested by the various findings we have discussed. These are summarized below for your consideration. Remember, no rule works 100 percent in every situation. However, these guidelines should help you avoid or deal with stress more effectively.

■ Jobs that involve decisions, repeated exchange of information with others, unpleasant physical conditions, responsibility for others, and unstructured tasks are the most stressful. If these features are a problem for you, avoid jobs that have these characteristics.

Guidelines for Effective Human Relations (continued)

■ Multiple roles and role conflict can increase stress, but often multiple roles can give increased meaning to one's life. It is probably healthy to develop multiple interests and activities, but do not get involved in so many different roles that you become overloaded.

■ Jobs that provide about the right amount of challenge are preferred. Avoid jobs that would overtax your abilities or ones that require so little effort that they would be boring.

■ Major life events can be a significant source of stress, but the hassles of daily life may have even more negative impact. You should find ways to minimize these daily problems.

■ Develop an optimistic perspective on life. Optimists cope more effectively with stress.

■ Develop stress-resistant attitudes. Take a broad perspective and don't blame yourself for things that are beyond your control.

■ To avoid burnout, it is important to set priorities in life and to be involved in a social support network.

■ It is best not to ignore or avoid stress-producing conditions but to actively attempt to change them.

Summary

When individuals perceive that their ability to cope may soon be overwhelmed, they often experience stress. Stress stems from many causes. Several of these relate to work itself (for example, demands of a given job, multiple roles, overload, unemployment). Others involve personal characteristics of individuals, such as major events in their lives, optimism, gender, and attitudes.

Stress exerts harmful effects on health. In addition, it can produce depression, lowered self-esteem, and reduction in job satisfaction. The relationship between stress and performance appears to be complex and may depend on such factors as the complexity of the tasks performed and the specific stressors involved. Prolonged exposure to intense emotional stress can lead to burnout. Persons suffering from this reaction experience physical, emotional, and mental exhaustion and may be unable to cope with their jobs or personal lives. Some victims of burnout leave their fields, while others seek refuge in administrative positions. Still others mark time until retirement and so become "deadwood." Fortunately, several techniques for preventing or reversing burnout exist.

Individuals can manage stress by enhancing their physical fitness, using effective coping strategies, or by engaging in tactics designed to substitute relaxation for tension.

Key Terms

burnout, p. 417

inter-role conflict, p. 404

meditation, p. 424

optimism-pessimism, p. 411

person-role conflict, p. 404

qualitative overload, p. 405

qualitative underload, p. 405

quantitative overload, p. 404

quantitative underload, p. 405

relaxation training, p. 423

role, p. 404

stress, p. 398

stressors, p. 399

within-role conflict, p. 404

Experiential Exercise

Checking Your Coping Style

How do you cope with stressors in your life? The following statements reflect different coping strategies. Choose some problem that has been a major source of stress for you this past month. Write it out in the space below. Then indicate to what extent you have dealt with the problem in the following ways. Rate each of these using the scale below.

0   not at all
1   yes, once in a while
2   yes, sometimes
3   yes, fairly often

_____   **1.** Discussed the problem with friends.

_____   **2.** Tried to put it out of my mind.

_____   **3.** Developed a plan to deal with the problem.

_____   **4.** Kept my feelings to myself.

_____   **5.** Tried to distract myself from thinking about it.

_____   **6.** Looked at the positive side of things.

_____	7.	Accepted the problem as part of life.
_____	8.	Tried to reduce tension by drinking, eating, relaxing, or exercising.
_____	9.	Tried different solutions.
_____	10.	Took an objective view of the whole situation.
_____	11.	Avoided being with people.
_____	12.	Prepared myself for the worst.
_____	13.	Expressed my feelings openly.
_____	14.	Sought the help and guidance of someone I trusted.
_____	15.	Took my feelings out on others.
_____	16.	Saw the problem as a learning experience.
_____	17.	Decided to take things one day at a time.
_____	18.	Told myself things to make me feel better.

Add the scores for items 1, 3, 9, 13, 14, and 17. This will indicate the degree of active behavioral coping.

Add the scores for items 6, 7, 10, 12, 16, and 18. This will give the degree of active mental coping.

Add the scores for items 2, 4, 5, 8, 11, and 15. This will provide the degree of avoidance coping.

For which coping style do you have the highest score? If you score 5 or 6 for any of the coping styles, you probably have a strong tendency to deal with stressors with this style.

Notes

1. Kahn, R. (1992). Stress and behavior in work settings. In M. D. Dunnette (ed.), *Handbook of industrial and organizational psychology* (2nd ed.). Chicago: Rand McNally.

2. Selye, H. (1976). *Stress in health and disease.* Boston: Butterworths.

3. Lazarus, R. S., & Folkman, S. (1984). *Stress, appraisal, and coping.* New York: Springer.

4. Lazarus, R. S., Delongis, A., Folkman, S., & Gruen, R. (1985). Stress and adaptational outcomes: The problem of confounded measures. *American Psychologist, 40,* 770–779.

5. See note 1.

6. McGrath, J. E. (1976). Stress and behavior in organizations. In M. D. Dunnette (ed.), *Handbook of industrial and organizational psychology.* Chicago: Rand McNally.

7. Sundstrom, E. (1986). *Work places: The psychology of the physical environment in offices and factories.* New York: Cambridge University Press.

8. Repetti, R. L. (1993). Short-term effects of occupational stressors on daily mood and health complaints. *Health Psychology, 12,* 125–131.

9. Evans, G. W., & Cohen, S. (1987). Environmental stress. In D. Stokols & I. Altman (eds.), *Handbook of environmental psychology* (pp. 571–610). New York: John Wiley & Sons.

10. Baum, A., & Paulus, P. B. (1987). Crowding. In D. Stokols & I. Altman (eds.), *Handbook of environmental psychology* (pp. 533–570). New York: John Wiley & Sons.

11. Oldham, G. R. (1988). Effects of changes in work-space partitions and spatial density on employee reactions: A quasi-experiment. *Journal of Applied Psychology, 73,* 253–258.

12. Cropanzano, R., Howes, J. C., Grandey, A. A., & Toth, P. (1997). The relationship of organizational politics and support to work behaviors, attitudes, and stress. *Journal of Organizational Behavior, 18,* 159–180.

13. Goldenhar, L. M., Swanson, N. G., Hurrell, J. J., Jr., Ruder, A., & Deddens, J. (1998). Stressors and adverse outcomes for female construction workers. *Journal of Occupational Health Psychology, 3,* 19–32.

14. Paton, D. P., & Violanti, J. M. (1996). *Traumatic stress in critical occupations: Recognition, consequences and treatment.* Springfield, IL: Charles C. Thomas.

15. National Institute for Occupational Safety and Health. (1978). Department of Health, Education, and Welfare. Washington, DC: Government Printing Office.

16. Carlson, M. (1989, December 25). Mailroom mayhem. *Time,* 30–31.

17. Shaw, J. B., & Riskind, J. H. (1981). Predicting job stress using data from the position analysis questionnaire. *Journal of Applied Psychology, 68,* 253–261.

18. Vormbrock, J. K. (1993). Attachment theory as applied to wartime and job-related marital separation. *Psychological Bulletin, 114,* 122–144.

19. Dytell, R. S., Pardine, P., & Napoli, A. (1985). *Importance of occupational and nonoccupational stress among professional men and women.* Paper presented at the meeting of the Eastern Psychological Association, Philadelphia.

20. Baruch, G. K., Biener, L., & Barnett, R. C. (1987). Women and gender in research on work and family stress. *American Psychologist, 42,* 130–136.

21. Barnett, R. C., Marshall, N. L., Raudenbush, S. W., & Brennan, R. T. (1993). Gender and the relationship between job experiences and psychological distress: A study of dual-earner couples. *Journal of Personality and Social Psychology, 64,* 794–806.

22. Kossek, E. E., & Ozeki, C. (1998). Work-family conflict, policies, and the job life satisfaction relationship: A review and directions for organizational behavior–human resources research. *Journal of Applied Psychology, 83,* 139–149.

23. Verbrugge, L. M. (1988). Role burdens and physical health of women and men. In F. Crosby (ed.), *Spouse, parent, worker: On gender and multiple roles.* New Haven, CT: Yale University Press.

24. Thoits, P. (1983). Multiple identities and psychological well-being. *American Sociological Review, 48,* 174–187.

25. See note 23.

26. Wood, W., Rhodes, N., & Whelan, M. (1989). Sex differences in positive well-being: A consideration of emotional style and marital status. *Psychological Bulletin, 106,* 249–264.

27. Kessler, R. C., & MCrae, J. A. (1982). The effects of wives' employment on the mental health of men and women. *American Sociological Review, 47,* 216–227.

28. Haynes, S. G., & Feinleib, M. (1982). Women, work, and coronary heart disease: Results from the Framingham 10-year follow-up study. In P. Berman & E. Ramey (eds.), *Women: A developmental perspective* (Publication No. 82-2298, pp. 79–101). Bethesda, MD: National Institutes of Health.

29. Pandy, S., & Kumar, E. S. (1997). Development of a measure of role conflict. *International Journal of Conflict Management, 8,* 187–215.

30. Ibid.

31. Daniels, K., & Guppy, A. (1997). Stressors, locus of control, and social support as consequences of affective psychological well-being.

Journal of Occupational Health Psychology, 2, 156–174.

32. Marshall, N. L., Barnett, R. C., & Sayer, A. (1997). The changing workforce, job stress, and psychological distress. *Journal of Occupational Health Psychology, 2,* 99–107.

33. Johnson, G. J., & Johnson, W. R. (1997). Perceived overqualification, emotional support, and health. *Journal of Applied Social Psychology, 27,* 1906–1918.

34. See note 32.

35. McLean, A. A. (1980). *Work stress.* Reading, MA: Addison Wesley.

36. Oullette Kobasa, S. C., & Puccetti, M. C. (1983). Personality and social resources in stress resistance. *Journal of Personality and Social Psychology, 45,* 839–850.

37. Costanza, R. S., Derlega, V. J., & Winstead, B. A. (1988). Positive and negative forms of social support: Effects of conversational topics on coping with stress among same-sex friends. *Journal of Experimental Social Psychology, 24,* 182–193.

38. Feather, N. T., & O'Brien, G. E. (1986). A longitudinal study of the effects of employment and unemployment on school-leavers. *Journal of Occupational Psychology, 59,* 121–144.

39. Hamilton, V. L., Hoffman, W. S., Broman, C. L., & Rauma, D. (1993). Unemployment, distress, and coping: A panel study of autoworkers. *Journal of Personality and Social Psychology, 65,* 234–247.

40. Sheran, P., & McCarthy, E. (1992). Social structure, self-conception and well-being: An examination of four models with unemployed people. *Journal of Applied Social Psychology, 22,* 117–133.

41. Stewart, W., & Barling, J. (1996). Fathers' work experiences affect children's behaviors via job-related affect and parenting behaviors. *Journal of Organizational Behavior, 17,* 221–232.

42. See note 39.

43. Gunderson, E., & Rahe, R. (1974). *Life stress and illness.* Springfield, IL: Charles C. Thomas.

44. Roth, D. L., Wiebe, D. J., Fillingim, R. B., & Shay, K. A. (1989). Life events, fitness, hardiness, and health: A simultaneous analysis of proposed stress-resistance effects. *Journal of Personality and Social Psychology, 57,* 136–142.

45. Holmes, T. H., & Masuda, M. (1974). Life change and illness susceptibility. In B. S. Dohrenwend & B. P. Dohrenwend (eds.), *Stressful life events: Their nature and effects* (pp. 45–72). New York: Wiley.

46. Cohen, S., Tyrrell, D. A. J., & Smith, A. P. (1993). Negative life events, perceived stress, negative affect, and susceptibility to the common cold. *Journal of Personality and Social Psychology, 64,* 131–140.

47. Lazarus, R. S., Delongis, A., Folkman, S., & Gruen, R. (1985). Stress and adaptational outcomes: The problem of confounded measures. *American Psychologist, 40,* 770–779.

48. Weinberger, M., Hiner, S. L., & Tierney, W. M. (1987). In support of hassles as a measure of stress in predicting health outcomes. *Journal of Biological Medicine, 10,* 19–31.

49. Flett, G. L., Blankstein, K. R., Hicken, D. J., & Watson, M. S. (1995). Social support and help-seeking in daily hassles versus major life events stress. *Journal of Applied Social Psychology, 25,* 49–58.

50. Scheier, M. F., & Carver, C. S. (1993). On the power of positive thinking: The benefits of being optimistic. *Current Directions in Psychological Science, 2,* 26–30.

51. Scheier, M. F., Weinbtraub, J. K., & Carver, C. S. (1986). Coping with stress: Divergent strategies of optimists and pessimists. *Journal of Personality and Social Psychology, 51,* 1257–1264.

52. Nolen-Hoeksema, S. (1987). Sex differences in unipolar depression: Evidence and theory. *Psychological Bulletin, 101,* 259–282.

53. See note 26.

54. Anderson, N. B. (1989). Racial differences in stress-induced cardiovascular reactivity and hypertension: Current status and substantive issues. *Psychological Bulletin, 105,* 89–105.

55. Neff, J. A. (1985). Race and vulnerability to stress: An examination of differential vulnerability. *Journal of Personality and Social Psychology, 49,* 481–491.

56. Stroman, C. A., & Seltzer, R. (1991). Racial differences in coping with job stress: A research note. In P. L. Perrewe (ed.), *Handbook on job stress* (Special Issue). *Journal of Social Behavior and Personality, 6,* 309–318.

57. Krause, N., & Markides, K. S. (1985). Employment and psychological well-being in Mexican-American women. *Journal of Health and Social Behavior, 26,* 15–26.

58. Nezu, A. M., Nezu, C. M., & Blissett, S. E. (1988). Sense of humor as a moderator of the relation between stressful events and psychological distress: A prospective analysis. *Journal of Personality and Social Psychology, 54,* 520–525.

59. Anson, L., Carmel, S., Bonneh, D. Y., Levenson, A., & Maoz, B. (1991). Recent life events, religiosity, and health: An individual or collective effect. *Human Relations, 43,* 1051–1066.

60. Park, C., Cohen, L. H., & Herb, L. (1990). Intrinsic religiousness and religious coping as life stress moderators for Catholics versus Protestants. *Journal of Personality and Social Psychology, 59,* 562–574.

61. Frese, M. (1985). Stress at work and psychosomatic complaints: A causal interpretation. *Journal of Applied Psychology, 70,* 314–328.

62. See note 46.

63. Zakowski, S. G., McAllister, C. G., Deal, M., & Baum, A. (1992). Stress, reactivity, and immune function in healthy men. *Health Psychology, 11,* 223–232.

64. See note 46.

65. See note 35.

66. Seligman, M. E. P. (1975). *Helplessness: On depression, development and death.* San Fransisco: Freeman.

67. See note 14.

68. Driskell, J. E., & Salas, E. (eds.) (1996). *Stress and human performance.* Mahwah, NJ: Lawrence Erlbaum.

69. Motowidlo, S. J., Packard, J. S., & Manning, M. R. (1986). Occupational stress: Its causes and consequences for job performance. *Journal of Applied Psychology, 71,* 618–629.

70. Klein, G. (1996). The affect of acute stressors on decision making. In J. E. Driskell & E. Salas (eds.), *Stress and human performance* (pp. 49–88). Mahwah, NJ: Lawrence Erlbaum.

71. Beehr, T. A., & Newman, J. E. (1978). Job stress, employee health, and organizational effectiveness: A facet analysis, model and literature review. *Personnel Psychology, 31,* 665–699.

72. Maslach, C., & Jackson, S. E. (1984). Burnout in organizational settings. In S. Oskamp (ed.), *Applied social psychology annual,* Vol. 5 (pp. 135–154). Beverly Hills, CA: Sage.

73. Green, D. E., Walkey, F. H., & Taylor, A. J. W. (1991). The three-factor structure of the Maslach Burnout Inventory: A multicultural, multinational confirmatory study. *Journal of Social Behavior and Personality, 6,* 453–472.

74. Zohar, D. (1997). Predicting burnout with the hassle-based measure of role demands. *Journal of Organizational Behavior, 18,* 101–115.

75. Cordes, C. L., Dougherty, T. W., & Blum, M. (1997). Patterns of burnout among managers and professionals: A comparison of models. *Journal of Organizational Behavior, 18,* 685–701.

76. Lee, R. T., & Ashforth, B. E. (1991). Work-unit structure and processes and job-related stressors as predictors of managerial burnout. *Journal of Applied Social Psychology, 21,* 1831–1847.

77. Mickler, S. E., & Rosen, S. (1994). Burnout in spurned medical caregivers and the impact of job expectancy training. *Journal of Applied Social Psychology, 24,* 2110–2131.

78. Van Dierendonck, D. V., Schaufeli, W. B., & Buunk, B. P. (1996). Inequity among human service professionals: Measurement and relation to burnout. *Basic and Applied Social Psychology, 18,* 429–451.

79. Gaines, J., & Jermier, J. M. (1983). Emotional exhaustion in high stress organizations. *Academy of Management Journal, 26,* 567–586.

80. Seltzer, J., & Numerof, R. E. (1988). Supervisory leadership and subordinate burnout. *Academy of Management Journal, 31,* 439–446.

81. Clark, M. S., Ouellette, R., Powell, M. C., & Milberg, S. (1987). Recipient's mood, relationship

type, and helping. *Journal of Personality and Social Psychology, 53,* 93–103.

82. Medvene, L. J., Volk, F. A., Meissen, G. J. (1997). Communal orientation and burnout among self-help group leaders. *Journal of Applied Social Psychology, 27,* 262–278.

83. Van Yperen, N. W. (1996). Communal orientation and the burnout syndrome among nurses: A replication and extension. *Journal of Applied Social Psychology, 26,* 1995.

84. Turnipseed, D. L., & Turnipseed, P. H. (1991). Personal coping resources and the burnout syndrome. *Journal of Social Behavior and Personality, 6,* 473–488.

85. Jackson, S. E., Schwab, R. L., & Schuler, R. S. (1986). Toward an understanding of the burnout phenomenon. *Journal of Applied Psychology, 71,* 630–640.

86. Anderson, J. G. (1991). Stress and burnout among nurses: A social network approach. In P. L. Perrewe (ed.), *Handbook on job stress* (Special Issue). *Journal of Social Behavior and Personality, 6,* 251–272.

87. Frankenhaeuser, M., Lundberg, U., Fredrikson, M., Melin, B., Tuomisto, M., Myrstern, A., Hedman, M., Bergman-Losman, B., & Willin, L. (1989). Stress on and off the job as related to sex and occupational status in white-collar workers. *Journal of Organizational Behavior, 10,* 321–346.

88. Westman, M., & Eden, D. (1997). Effects of a respite from work on burnout: Vacation relief and fade-out. *Journal of Applied Psychology, 82,* 516–527.

89. Eastburg, M. C., Williamson, M., Gorsuch, R., & Ridley, C. (1994). Social support, personality, and burnout in nurses. *Journal of Applied Social Psychology, 24,* 1233–1250.

90. Van Dierendonck, D. V., Schaufeli, W. B., & Buunk, B. P. (1998). The evaluation of an individual burnout intervention program: The role of inequity and social support. *Journal of Applied Psychology, 83,* 392–407.

91. Ibid.

92. Bellarosa, C., & Chen, P. Y. (1997). The effectiveness and practicality of occupational stress management interventions: A survey of subject matter expert opinions. *Journal of Occupational Health Psychology, 3,* 247–262.

93. Lepore, S. J., Evans, G. W., & Schneider, M. L. (1991). Dynamic role of social support in the link between chronic stress and psychological distress. *Journal of Personality and Social Psychology, 61,* 899–909.

94. Brown, J. D., & Siegel, J. M. (1988). Exercise as a buffer of life stress: A prospective study of adolescent health. *Health Psychology, 7,* 341–353.

95. Rejeski, W. J., Thompson, A., Brubaker, P. H., & Miller, H. S. (1992). Acute exercise: Buffering psychosocial stress responses in women. *Health Psychology, 11,* 355–362.

96. Shepherd, R. J., Cox, M., & Corey, P. (1981). Fitness program participation: Its effect on workers' performance. *Journal of Occupational Medicine, 23,* 359–363.

97. Cox, M., Shephard, R., & Corey, R. (1981). Influence of an employee fitness program upon fitness, productivity and absenteeism. *Ergonomics, 24,* 795–806.

98. See note 3.

99. Ingledew, D. K., Hardy, L., & Cooper, C. L. (1997). Do resources bolster coping and does coping buffer stress? An organizational study with longitudinal aspect and control for negative affectivity. *Journal of Occupational Health Psychology, 2,* 118–133.

100. Ibid.

101. Alexander, C. N., Langer, E. J., Newman, R. I., Chandler, H. M., & Davies, J. L. (1989). Transcendental meditation, mindfulness and longevity: An experimental study with the elderly. *Journal of Personality and Social Psychology, 57,* 950–964.

Chapter 15

Getting Started: Choosing the Right Career

Career Choice: Some Key Factors
Career Decision Making: The Process and Resources
Searching for Jobs on the Internet: Using New Technology

Career Development: Staying on Track

Getting Help from Your Company: Benefiting from Human Resource Planning
Helping Yourself: Forming Your Own Plan for Career Development
The Changing Career: Is the Career Dead?
Protean Careers: Putting Yourself in Charge
A Relational Approach to Careers: The Importance of Relational Skills
360 Feedback: Getting a Broad Perspective

Careers: Changes over a Lifetime

Career Development and Life Stages
Career and Family
Women and Family: Some Special Challenges
Toward a Family-Friendly Workplace: A Little Flexibility

Special Sections

Human Relations in Action
What Is Your Occupational Type?

Ethics at Work
The Negative Side of Feedback

Guidelines for Effective Human Relations
Using What You've Learned

Experiential Exercise
How Flexible Is Your Company?

CAREER CHOICE AND DEVELOPMENT

Planning for Success

Learning Objectives

After reading this chapter, you should be able to:

1. List some of the major factors that play a role in career choice.

2. Understand the decision-making process involved in choosing careers.

3. Describe a more systematic approach to this process than most people seem to follow.

4. Explain how programs based on human resource planning can be of help to you in career development.

5. Outline the major steps in a systematic approach to personal career development.

6. Identify some new approaches to careers.

7. Define the term *career* and explain how changes in individuals' jobs and work-related experiences reflect different stages in their lives.

*S*tarbucks Coffee was founded in 1987 by Howard Schultz to provide a comfortable place for people to take a coffee break. It is now the largest coffee-bar chain in the United States. The central philosophy of Starbucks is that happy employees will make happy customers. This firm was the first company in the United States to provide its part-time employees with stock options and full health care benefits. Workers also receive a pound of free coffee every week. By treating its employees well, Starbucks hopes that they will have a high sense of self-esteem and a strong commitment to the company. As a result, they should be motivated to provide high-quality and friendly service to the customers. The Starbucks philosophy seems to work. It has one of the lowest attrition rates in the fast-food industry.[1]

*T*here are points in our lives when we have to make decisions about our careers. Certainly, the courses we take in school, our majors in college, and our grades will affect our options. Of course, even if we do well in school, it may be difficult for us to know what career best suits us. Furthermore, in the past when people entered a job, they often stayed in it for the rest of their working lives. Today, of course, the situation is radically different. Most persons realize that their first job is unlikely to be their last one. In fact, many would be quite upset if they suspected that this was the case. They expect change and look forward to progress. They anticipate promotions, rising status, growing income, and increasing autonomy. In short, they expect their careers to develop, and to do so along mainly positive lines. But—and here comes the paradox—while they expect such progress, they often do nothing to ensure it. They fail to engage in the careful planning that is essential to continued progress and ignore long-term trends that may affect the future of various careers. As a result, they miss out on golden opportunities, experience crushed hopes, and often end up in occupational blind alleys.

Can you personally avoid such difficulties? Our answer is "yes," but only if you adopt the right strategies. Good things sometimes happen in life without any effort on our part—we just sort of luck out. But usually they don't occur unless we take active steps to *make* them happen. This seems to be the rule with respect to successful careers. They don't appear out of thin air and drop softly into our laps. Rather, they are usually the result of careful planning plus a lot of hard work. How, then, can you plan for your own success? How can you make your own career rewarding and enjoyable? Unfortunately, we can't provide you with a simple, no-fail answer. The world of work is far too complex a place for this kind of luxury. But we don't have to leave you out in the cold, wondering, either.

In recent years, human relations experts have devoted growing attention to the topic of **careers**—how they develop, how they are pursued, and why, sometimes, they go on the rocks.[2] More formally, careers can be defined as *the sequence of attitudes and behaviors associated with work-related activities experienced by individuals over the span of their working lives.*[3] In this chapter, we focus on the rapidly growing body of knowledge such experts have acquired. Specifically, we examine three distinct but related issues. First, we delve into the question of how individuals *choose* their careers—why they select one field over others. Second, we turn to the ways that careers develop over time, both with and without careful long-range planning. Third, we analyze how career issues change over the course of our working careers. Finally, we examine how people become part of an organization—organizational socialization. Our hope, of course, is that armed with the information presented here, you will be better able to both plan and pursue a challenging and rewarding future.

$\mathcal{G}$ETTING STARTED: CHOOSING THE RIGHT CAREER

How many different jobs can you bring to mind? Probably you can think of dozens with little or no effort. Even if you listed hundreds, though, you would still only be scratching the surface. Today, there are literally thousands of careers we can pursue. The existence of this tremendous range of choices, in turn, raises an intriguing question: How do individuals ever zero in on a specific job? Why do some choose to become accountants, others carpenters, and still others doctors, farmers, or computer programmers? As you can readily guess, there are no simple answers to these questions. Rather, careful study of the way individuals choose their careers indicates that many factors play a role in this process.[4] In this discussion, we first examine some of the more important of these factors. We then suggest a useful technique for selecting an appropriate career—a technique based largely on detailed self-appraisal, careful study of the requirements of various jobs, and a search for a close match between the two.

Career Choice: Some Key Factors

If you stopped ten different people on the street and asked them how they ended up in their present job or career, you would probably receive ten different answers. This is hardly surprising, for people are unique, and their working lives reflect this fact. Sometimes people simply drift

careers   The sequence of attitudes and behaviors associated with work-related activities experienced by individuals over the span of their working lives.

into careers or end up in careers because of accidental experiences or connections. Some systematic factors, however, influence individual career choice.

The Intrinsic Appeal of a Job or Field.

Have you ever fantasized about becoming a surgeon, a movie star, or a great detective? If so, you are already familiar with one reason why individuals choose certain careers: They offer a high degree of excitement, challenge, and reward. Needless to say, not all fields are as attractive as the ones named above. But human beings, as you know, differ tremendously in their preferences. Thus almost any career you can imagine—no matter how dull it may seem to you—will appear wildly desirable to others. Clearly, one major factor in individual career choice, then, is personal interest. Because of their unique patterns of traits, abilities, and past experiences, specific persons are drawn to certain fields. And when they follow these preferences, they may embark on careers that occupy the rest of their working lives.

The Role of Social Influence.

As we noted in Chapter 7, people spend a lot of time and effort attempting to influence others. They often seek to change their attitudes, alter their behavior, or both. And they seek to accomplish these goals through persuasion and other tactics of social influence. Not surprisingly, these same processes often play a role in career choice. First, parents, teachers, and other adults may attempt to steer members of the younger generation into certain jobs or careers. In order to do so, they may dangle rewards in front of them for "correct" choices (for example, for deciding to pursue careers in law, medicine, engineering, or business). And they may withhold support (both social and financial) when a "difficult" daughter or son insists, instead, on selecting a field they do not favor. As you may already know, such pressure tactics often work—they do nudge many persons into careers that are perceived by their families as safe, conventional, and financially rewarding.

But direct persuasion is not the only way social influence affects career choice. Another and more subtle aspect of this process involves the impact of **social models.** At one time or another, almost all of us have had heroes or heroines—people we admire greatly and would like to emulate. Such individuals may not even be aware of our existence, let alone our admiration for them; they may be famous celebrities we never met, or even figures from history who lived centuries in the past. Yet, their impact on us can be powerful indeed. How many scientists were inspired to choose their careers by accounts of the lives of Albert Einstein and Marie Curie? How many musicians decided to take up their instruments after hearing the music of Beethoven or Mozart? It is impossible to tell, but research on the impact of social models suggests that the number is probably large.[5] It should be noted that such modeling effects are not in any way restricted to high-level or high-status careers. Many car-

social models Individuals who affect the behavior or attitudes of others through their words or deeds, often without any conscious desire to produce such effects.

penters, electricians, miners, and salespeople report having entered their fields because of early exposure to members of these occupations—members they liked or admired.

Personality.   Our interest in different types of careers is likely to be influenced by our own personal characteristics—our personalities, gender, and racial or ethnic group. Much research has examined the role of personality in careers. One of the most developed and widely used systems for classifying people in relation to their careers is that of Holland.[6] This system is the basis for the Strong-Campbell Inventory, which is often used to help individuals determine their career interests. Holland assumes that there are six different personality types. The *realistic* type is stable, practical, materialistic, and has mechanical skills but may be lacking in social skills. This person likes realistic jobs such as electrician, farmer, mechanic, and construction. The *investigative* type is analytical, rational, curious, methodical, and reserved. This type has mathematical and scientific ability but may lack leadership skills. This type of person would prefer investigative jobs such as anthropologist, biologist, geologist, or medical technologist. The *artistic* type is independent, imaginative, expressive, and nonconforming. This person has artistic skills and is disposed to such jobs as musician, actor, and writer. The *social* type is cooperative, sociable, and generous. This type has social skills and is inclined to jobs in teaching or counseling. The *enterprising* type is adventurous, confident, optimistic, and domineering. This person has leadership and speaking abilities and likes jobs in sales, promotion, and management. The *conventional* type is conscientious, practical, conforming, and efficient. This type has clerical and mathematical abilities and likes jobs such as accountant, banker, and financial analyst. Some of the items that represent each of the different personalities are listed in the *Human Relations in Action* section on pages 438–439.

Although many of us may fall clearly into one of these categories, we are likely to have a combination of traits. For example, we can be both social and enterprising or investigative and conventional. When you take the test based on this typology, you receive a code that indicates your three most important types. This code can then be used to select jobs that are best suited for this type of person. Holland has also divided work environments using the same typology system—realistic, investigative, artistic, social, enterprising, and conventional. Individuals presumably seek environments that are best suited to the expression of their skills and interests. Of course, a person may not know the typology of various jobs. This information is provided in the *Dictionary of Occupational Codes.*[7]

There are a number of other useful ways to categorize occupations in terms of the type of activity involved. One developed by Roe suggests the existence of eight basic occupational groups: service, business, managerial, technology, outdoor, science, arts, and culture transmission.[8] Furthermore, there are other factors that influence one's choice of occupation other than personality type.[9] We all differ in our inherited characteristics and abilities. Some of us certainly are better endowed for a career in basketball or opera than others. But there are also environmental conditions that can influence job opportunities. Where one lives, changes in technology, government policy, and the proximity of educational or training institutions can play an important role in one's ability to make career choices. Socioeconomic variables such as parental education, family size and stability, and family income are also likely to influence the job aspirations or range of choices one considers.[10] Positive experiences in one's activities in different environments (for example, public speaking) will also affect one's evaluation of careers that involve these activities. When individuals have opportunities to try out different skills and receive positive feedback about their performance, they have a basis for assessing their potential in various careers. Someone who is good at mathematical puzzles may decide on a career involving mathematical skills, such as finance or accounting. So it is important to have opportunities to develop different skills. If such opportunities are not easily available, a person may have to be assertive in finding them.

Human Relations in Action

What Is Your Occupational Type?

Holland's theory of careers suggests that different personalities are suited for different types of careers. The following items are representative of those used to determine interest in different types of activities.

Realistic Activities

Y N   Work on a car

Y N   Set up a stereo system

Investigative Activities

Y N   Find solutions to complex problems

Y N   Visit a science museum

Artistic Activities

Y N   Practice a musical instrument

Y N   Design furniture, clothing, or poster

Social Activities

Y N   Work for a charity

Y N   Train others to do a job

Gender and Racial/Ethnic Influences on Career Decision Making.   In the past, a great deal of gender segregation was observed in occupations (male engineers, female nurses) (see Figure 15.1 on page 440).[11] The increasing number of females who now enter computer programming is evidence of a trend toward a reduction in such segregation. Desegregation, however, can lead to an eventual new segregation, with women dominating a formerly male job such as real estate or editor. Sometimes this transformation is associated with a reduction in earnings. Women generally earn less than men, but it is not always clear whether this difference reflects discrimination, type of job, or degree of career investment.[12] Some of the differences may reflect basic biological differences related to empathy, spatial/visual ability, and the like. However, cultural factors are likely to play an important role. Most societies have developed socialization patterns that emphasize female involvement in domestic and nurturant activities and male involvement in mechanical and sport activities.[13] The different socialization patterns may affect both the skill levels and self-efficacy of

Enterprising Activities

Y N   Supervise the work of others

Y N   Operate your own service or business

These items represent only an abbreviated set of items from the Holland inventory. Go to your career counseling center for an assessment of your personality profile, using the *Self-Directed Search*. Your score on this test may be indicative of an interest pattern relevant to your career. For example, if you score high on Realistic Activities, you may enjoy a career that involves mechanical or athletic abilities, such as engineering or surveying. See the discussion in the text for additional discussion of these differing interest types.

Gender Bias in Careers: Evident in Many Settings

There appears to be a strong gender bias in career decision making. We see very few male kindergarten teachers.

males and females in different activities.[14] Even if skill or efficacy levels are comparable, women may be influenced by societal norms to choose certain types of careers.[15] Furthermore, there may be biases in those who do the hiring to select men for "masculine" jobs such as manager and women for "feminine" jobs such as secretary. In fact, women may be preferred for such jobs even if they are less qualified.[16] Of course, these systematic biases result in males and females having few successful role models in certain occupations, which in turn further influences career choice.

These same biases may also play a role in the career decision making of individuals belonging to different racial or ethnic groups.[17] For example, blacks are still greatly underrepresented on the professional golf tour. It is doubtful that this reflects any inborn lack of ability to hit a golf ball. Instead, a lack of opportunity to develop the skill is likely to be a major factor. With the success of Tiger Woods and with high-profile black athletes becoming increasingly visible in pro-amateur tournaments, increased interest in golf may be generated among younger blacks.

The choice behavior of women or minority groups is thus likely to be influenced by feelings of self-efficacy, self-concept, and accessibility of opportunities.[18] These are influenced by a variety of societal and environmental factors and may lead to significant differences in job aspirations based on gender and race. Moreover, differences in economic level may influence the degree to which individuals can explore various job opportunities or obtain training. Although certain religious and cultural traditions may incline some groups more to some careers than others, it is obviously important that all groups have opportunities to develop skills and make a broad range of career choices in order to tap their full potential. Counselors need to be sensitive to the career needs of different minority groups. Books and journals such as the *Journal of Multicultural Counseling* can provide help in these areas.[19]

Populations with Special Needs.   The Americans with Disabilities Act of 1990 made it illegal to discriminate against individuals with physical or mental disabilities. These are impairments that limit one or more life activities. There are more than 40 million Americans with such disabilities as epilepsy, muscular disorders, deafness, blindness, and accident injuries. Many of them have been unemployed in the past, but now employers are required to make reasonable modification of existing facilities to allow hiring of qualified disabled individuals. Furthermore, it is important to overcome stereotypes and misconceptions about the range of careers in which disabled individuals can be successful. Therefore, both career counselors and potential employees need to make sure that information about career options and opportunities is made available to disabled people.

Career Decision Making: The Process and Resources

Choosing a career is an important matter—one of the most crucial decisions we ever face. Ideally, then, it should be a rational systematic process. As noted earlier, though, it is not. Most persons seem to select a career largely on the basis of personal interests, social influence from others, or mere accident. But we don't simply flow in and out of careers. Most of us do some degree of analysis and evaluation as we contemplate our career choices. We will highlight some factors that may facilitate this process.

Educational Choices.   In the United States, the dominant educational track is one in which students go from high school to college. College degrees do prepare students for a variety of careers or additional study for more advanced degrees. But college may not be for everyone. There are other educational opportunities that can help students prepare for rewarding and well-paying careers.[20] Vocational schools can provide training in skills such as computer programming, carpentry, plumbing, and horticulture. There are also on-the-job training and apprenticeship programs provided by large corporations and government agencies. Correspondence courses or television courses and videos available in stores or libraries may be useful sources of information or training. Finally, the military service provides much training and education. This may be particularly helpful to those who do not have strong career or educational interests. Exposure to different types of jobs and training in the military may help resolve these uncertainties and open up future job opportunities.

Helpful Resources. How do we find out what the different job opportunities are? Most of us are exposed to people in different jobs or careers in the course of our everyday lives. We have contact with salespersons, secretaries, police, teachers, and doctors. So we have a fairly good idea what these jobs involve. There are also many jobs that most of us are unlikely to encounter or even hear about. Have you encountered or even heard of such jobs as actuary, librettist, or cytotechnologist? If not, how would you know whether you might be interested in those careers?

One way to overcome this gap in our experience is to look through books of information about jobs. The Department of Labor publishes a detailed interpretation of the job characteristics required for different occupations in the *Selected Characteristics of Occupations Defined in the Dictionary of Occupational Titles.*[21] This document provides information about physical demands, environmental conditions, mathematical and language development, and training time. Additional guidance about your suitability for different types of jobs can be found in the *Guide for Occupational Exploration.*[22] It provides information about work that matches the interests and abilities of job seekers. It is most helpful in a search for which jobs appear to be best suited for us.

Of course, when we discover we are well suited for a certain occupation, it would be useful to know whether the future prospects in this occupation are favorable. If there is an oversupply in one of your areas of interest, you may want to go in another direction that has better prospects. This information can be gleaned in part from the *Occupational Outlook Handbook.*[23] It provides information about more than 250 occupations. It describes duties, training requirements, earnings, and job outlook.

In addition to the sources we have described, there are a number of magazines and books that provide useful information about jobs. These can be found in your public or college library or the career counseling department at your institution. These locations may also have information about jobs that are available in the local area.

Searching for Jobs on the Internet: Using New Technology

The Internet has provided many new avenues in the job search process. Many employers advertise their open positions and information about their organization on the network. Professional groups may have electronic bulletin boards or networks that disseminate information about jobs or careers. These sites may help you become acquainted with professionals in a field, get job advice, and develop contacts for job opportunities.

In addition, some general sites may prove very useful for obtaining career information. Some of the ones you might consider are as follows:[24]

1. Job search guides and databases can be used to locate home pages of potential employers.

2. The *Online Career Center* has thousands of job listings and a résumé database and enables visitors to place job ads and add résumés. The site can be searched by area and occupation.

3. *Listservs* are subject-oriented e-mail discussion lists that are often associated with certain professions and may provide useful information about careers.

4. Many universities operate career centers that provide information on doing career searches, and some have their own career development pages on the Internet.

5. Classified ads from newspapers are now available on the Internet.

6. Résumé database services allow résumés to be posted by e-mail and updated when necessary.

7. Recruiting agencies have established sites on the Internet to advertise available positions.

To effectively use the Internet, you must be able to tap its job search resources and then design and submit an electronic resume. You also should keep a notebook describing the information you obtain and tracking where you have sent your resume.[25] Your college career center can probably help you get started in the search process, and you may want to rely on some books and friends in the early stages of your job hunt. It may take some time to learn the key skills needed for an Internet-based job search, but it will be worth the effort. Be aware, however, that the Internet is constantly changing. Its career search potential is not yet fully developed, and new avenues should be developed in the near future. Be sure to keep up with the latest developments on the Internet so that you can take advantage of them.

*C*AREER DEVELOPMENT: STAYING ON TRACK

Imagine that, for once, fate has smiled on you. After examining your own traits and interests and studying the requirements of many different jobs, you have found one that seems just about perfect. Through hard work and careful preparation, you have actually landed such a position with an excellent, growing company. What happens next? How do you launch your career with a bang, and then ensure that it stays on track? Fortunately, there are many things you can do to accomplish these goals. Since some of these involve getting help from your company, while others center on steps you can take yourself, we will divide them into these two major categories.

Getting Help from Your Company: Benefiting from Human Resource Planning

The world of the late 1990s has proved a tough place for organizations as well as individuals. Increased competition, rapid changes in technology, rising energy costs—these are only a few of the problems currently challenging even successful companies. In their efforts to cope with such conditions, many organizations have directed careful attention to the management of their financial and physical resources—closer attention to these matters than was paid in the past. But this is only part of the total picture. Companies have come to realize that human resources, too, are precious, and must be effectively managed.[26] The guiding principle behind this general approach—often known as **human resource planning**—is this: To operate at peak efficiency, organizations must put their human resources to the best possible use. That is, they must ensure that they have the *right* people with the *right* skills in the *right* jobs. This, in turn, requires three basic conditions. First, organizations must succeed in attracting and retaining a core of talented, motivated employees. Second, they must be able to foresee future personnel needs and plan as well as hire accordingly. Third, they must ensure that persons within the organization do not stagnate. On the contrary, they must assist employees to grow so that their knowledge and skills keep pace with the demands of an ever-changing and increasingly complex world.

As the importance of human resource planning has gained acceptance, a number of companies have developed special programs of **career development** for their employees. Such programs are designed to make remaining within the organization more attractive, and to assist individuals in acquiring new skills and competence. A wide range of specific techniques have been used for these purposes. For example, some organizations have provided employees with time off to attend college-level courses and have also paid any costs involved. Others have designed and conducted their own in-house training programs, often with the aid of outside consultants. By far the most popular techniques, however, have been based upon the use of detailed and constructive **performance appraisals**.[27] Such appraisals were once quite brief, consisting mainly of a few comments from a supervisor to the effect that an individual was doing a "good job" or, conversely, that he or she was in danger of losing his or her position. Within the last decade, however, informative appraisals have become widely viewed not simply as a means

human resource planning   Efforts by organizations to make the best possible use of the skills, abilities, and talents of their employees.

career development   The pattern of changes that occur during an individual's career.

performance appraisals   Steps undertaken by organizations to provide employees with feedback on their current performance. Detailed and constructive performance appraisals often form part of company-run programs of career management/career development.

of letting employees know where they stand, but also as a valuable tool for helping them develop in ways beneficial to both themselves and the company. Thus, currently, performance appraisals often include such features as (1) detailed and highly specific feedback on various aspects of job performance; (2) identification of special strengths and weaknesses shown by a particular individual; (3) the establishment of concrete objectives to be attained by the employee during the next evaluation period; and (4) a statement of each employee's career goals, along with concrete steps for moving toward them. As you can readily see, information of this type can often be helpful to employees in planning their future development and growth.

In sum, recent emphasis on human resource planning has led many companies to recognize the value of assisting their employees in career development. Of course, not every organization has seen the light in this respect—far from it. But if your organization (or one you join in the future) has such programs, try to take full advantage of them. Your participation will be duly noted and, one way or another, will contribute to your career.

Helping Yourself: Forming Your Own Plan for Career Development

Suppose that you interviewed one hundred individuals who had enjoyed outstanding careers and asked them to describe the factors that led to their success. Do you think you would uncover any common themes? The chances are excellent that you would. Further, we can even predict what the most important of these might be. Many of the individuals with whom you spoke would suggest that their success stemmed mainly from (1) understanding of their own strengths, weaknesses, interests, and motives; (2) having a good grasp of the internal workings of their organizations; (3) having clear and obtainable goals; and (4) developing concrete plans for reaching these objectives. Can you apply these principles to your own career? We believe you can. In fact, growing evidence suggests that to the extent you do, your chances of attaining success may be measurably enhanced. Given such potential benefits, each of these points is certainly worthy of a closer look.

Self-Knowledge Revisited.   Understanding yourself—knowing your own motives, interests, traits, and abilities—can be very helpful in choosing an appropriate career. It can also help you to develop your career along highly positive lines. There are several reasons for this beneficial effect.

First, unless you have a good grasp of your current strengths and weaknesses, it is difficult to know just where you need extra effort or require additional training. Thus, having an accurate grasp of where you stand right now is essential.

Second, consider this: Career development, by its very nature, suggests change and movement. It implies that a given individual is not standing still; rather, he or she is making progress, moving forward. But where, precisely, is this movement

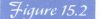 **Careers: A Variety of Motives**

Careers may be motivated by a variety of desires, such as power, wealth, or security. Which of these motives is most important to you?

directed? The answer depends, to a large degree, on a person's motives—what he or she is seeking. As you already know, tremendous differences exist with respect to this dimension. Some desire status and power, others focus on wealth, still others lust after fame, while many ask only security and stability (see Figure 15.2). Which of these motives is central to you? In short, which forms the core of your own *career motivation*?[28] Obviously, it is useful to know before setting out.

For these and other reasons, accurate self-knowledge is a valuable plus from the point of view of effective career development. Thus, an important step in this process—perhaps the first step you should take—is to determine as many of your traits and characteristics as possible. This knowledge is sure to come in handy in many ways.

Know Your Organization.   Individuals who seem to possess every trait needed for success often fail to live up to their bright promise. Instead of rising like rockets across the organizational sky, they fall flat on their faces, much to their own surprise and that of others around them. Many factors contribute to such disappointments. However, one of the most important is this: Such persons often lack what might be termed *career insight*.[29] Specifically, they do not seem to have a good grasp of just what makes their organization tick—how it really operates, apart from what the formal organizational chart dictates. For example, they lack insight into **organizational politics**—who holds power and how they use it. Similarly, they do not grasp the nature of *informal networks of communication*. As a result, they are

organizational politics   The process through which power and influence are exercised within a given organization. A clear understanding of such politics is necessary for effective career development.

often among the last to learn important information, and they fail to plug into one or more of the support groups that are essential to furthering their careers. They may be outstanding engineers, accountants, or programmers, but these technical skills do them little good. They simply don't know how to operate in the complex world of a modern organization.

Obviously, you want to do everything in your power to avoid sharing this fate. Thus, the second essential ingredient in your personal plan for success should be gaining good career insight. Unfortunately, we can't offer any simple guidelines for becoming skilled in this respect. In general, though, the best policy is to watch and listen as carefully as possible when you first join an organization. During the first few weeks or months, you will be given an opportunity to learn the ropes—to figure out how things should be done, what style is required, who really communicates with whom, and who really counts. Use this period of organizational socialization to maximum advantage.[30] Gather as much information as possible during this period and try to form the clearest picture you can of your department and organization. If you do your homework carefully in this general area, you will certainly help establish a firm base for your future career development.

Establish Clear-Cut Goals and Steps for Moving toward Them.   Now we come to the heart of any personal plan for career development. In essence, this consists of two major parts: (1) establishing clear-cut goals and (2) formulating concrete steps for their attainment. At first glance, these may seem like relatively simple tasks. Don't we all know what we want from our working lives? And isn't it clear how to get it? The answer on both counts is "no!" To see why this is so, let's consider these steps in order, one at a time.

First, what about goals? In most cases, it appears, individuals have only vague and poorly defined career objectives. If asked what they are seeking, they reply "success," "happiness," or "personal fulfillment." Certainly, no one could argue with the desirability of such outcomes, but no one could describe them very clearly, either. And vague goals have serious drawbacks. Usually, it is impossible to tell when—or whether—they have been reached. It is also often difficult to know just how to approach them. For these reasons, it is usually preferable, in developing your own career plan, to try to formulate specific goals. For example, try to determine just what promotions or other accomplishments you want to achieve during a given time period. Establishing such goals is no guarantee that you'll reach them—many factors influence your progress. But at least once they are determined, you'll know just where you are going and can gauge your own progress.

Setting the right goals, though, is only part of the process. In addition, you need to specify, as precisely and accurately as possible, just how to reach them. In short, you must outline a series of steps that, if carried out successfully, will lead you to your goals. Again, you need quite a bit of information about your organization and its policies to accomplish this task. For example, you must know precisely what

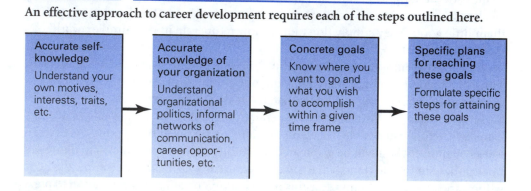

Figure 15.3   **Personal Career Development: Summing Up**

An effective approach to career development requires each of the steps outlined here.

Accurate self-knowledge	Accurate knowledge of your organization	Concrete goals	Specific plans for reaching these goals
Understand your own motives, interests, traits, etc.	Understand organizational politics, informal networks of communication, career opportunities, etc.	Know where you want to go and what you wish to accomplish within a given time frame	Formulate specific steps for attaining these goals

accomplishments are needed to gain a specific promotion. You must understand the organizational politics of promotions and other benefits—who has input into the process, who makes the final decision, and so on. Obviously, the precise series of steps needed to attain different goals will vary with the nature of the goals themselves and with countless features of your organization. Regardless of these factors, your strategy should remain the same: Determine just what you have to do to move from Point A (where you are now) to Point B (where you want to get) and beyond.

Personal Career Development: Summing Up.   Looking back over our comments in this section, you can probably see that the process we have described is almost like a personal program of *management by objectives*.[31] You begin by figuring out who and where you are. Then, you select concrete goals you wish to attain and devise specific steps for reaching them. And along the way, you continually gauge your progress and adjust the process to make sure you stay on track. (The major steps in this plan for career development are summarized in Figure 15.3.) Of course, we hasten to add that even this approach, as systematic and rational as it is, can offer no guarantee of ultimate success. There are simply too many personal, organizational, and external events that impinge on your career for this to be the case. The steps outlined here, however, will definitely accomplish one thing: They will get you thinking clearly and systematically about yourself, your organization, and your career. This, in itself, should give you an important edge and at least get you moving in the right (constructive) direction.

The Changing Career: Is the Career Dead?

Almost every day, the newspapers contain stories about companies that have laid off a large number of people because of a change in the market or a merger with another company. Other companies may constantly experiment with organizational structures and go through a reengineering process in which they try to become more efficient. Rapidly changing technology has prompted the development of many new small and large companies—but has led to the demise of others.[32] Partly as a result of this rather chaotic state of affairs, the possibility of developing one's entire career within a particular company is becoming rather slim.[33,34] Instead, most people are likely to move from one company to another. They may therefore need to constantly update or modify their skills so as to remain competitive in the job market.

Corporations are also changing the way that they are staffed. Temporary employees are often hired to cover periods involving extraordinarily heavy workloads. Employees are allowed to have more flexible job schedules or flex time. Sometimes job sharing—when two people divide a single full-time job—is possible. More jobs can now be done at home, and telecommuting has increased significantly (see Chapter 6). Today's companies want to maintain as much flexibility as possible so as to remain poised to adapt to their changing needs. Therefore, it is also important to have a flexible workforce.[35]

Protean Careers: Putting Yourself in Charge

The traditional career contract appears to be dead. So what will replace it? Hall, who has studied careers for most of his career, suggests that we should aim for more individualistic rather than organizational careers.[36,37] A **protean career** is one that is managed by the individual. The guiding forces for such a career are the person's own choices and search for personal fulfillment. As a result, the specific jobs and career directions may change as the person's needs change. Such flexibility requires a diversity of educational, training, and work experiences (see the *Experiential Exercise* on page 461).

The protean career does not follow a particular pattern or upward path because it is determined by the person's needs and changing circumstances. It also allows a person to take a more flexible perspective toward his or her career, by including family roles such as raising children or taking care of aging parents in career decisions. Working at home or flexible work schedules are also frequently a component of the protean career.

Although this approach may sound like the ideal career form, it does have some negatives. Not everyone likes the uncertainty and unpredictability involved in a protean career, especially individuals who lack the confidence or diverse skills to go it "alone." Still others may cherish their identity with a particular job, company, or career. Losing that connection at some later point in life may prove quite traumatic.[38]

How can you be successful in developing a protean career? First, you need a strong self-identity in which you have a clear sense of your values and goals in life. If you do not have this type of internal compass, it will be difficult to direct your own career. Second, a protean career

protean career   A career that is managed by the individual and guided by that person's own choices and search for fulfillment.

requires continuous learning to develop and maintain a broad variety of skills. One important skill is relational in nature—that is, the ability to work effectively with others and to appropriately encourage, coach, and lead them. Third, success requires the appropriate balancing of your life interests. If your work life reflects your values and interests, it is more likely to be compatible with your other identities, such as a parent, community leader, and participant in recreational activities. Therefore, it may be easier to balance your multiple roles, rather than succumb to overload or frustration because these roles are incompatible.

A Relational Approach to Careers: The Importance of Relational Skills

One consequence of the rapid changes and turnover in organizations is that models of long-term career development and mentoring are less applicable. Today, more work is done collaboratively in teams, and leadership tends to be less formal or hierarchical (see Chapter 9). The workplace also boasts a greater diversity in terms of gender, race, and ethnicity. It is therefore very important to develop interpersonal or relational skills at an early point in your career if you want to be successful.[39]

A *relational approach* to career development has the following requirements:

1. Relationships with mentors, supervisors, and peers must have some degree of mutuality and reciprocity. Development should be a two-way process, with both partners benefiting from the interactions.
2. There must be a willingness to focus on development and learning in personal relationships.
3. The types of interpersonal competencies that are needed for relational career development include self-reflection, active listening, empathy, and feedback.
4. Organizations can facilitate relational development by providing training, opportunities, mentoring, recognition, coaching, and feedback.

Such processes as listening, self-reflection, and self-disclosure on the part of both partners in a relationship can facilitate the development of competencies and self-concept for both participants.[40] Figure 15.4 provides an overview of the relational model of career development.

360 Feedback: Getting a Broad Perspective

Obtaining feedback from supervisors has long been a mainstay of the American workplace. The major concern of employees, not surprisingly, was to please their supervisors. This approach might not always be the best policy. The supervisor may

Figure 15.4	**A Relational Model of Career Development**

Career development requires the development of relational skills. Some features of this type of development are shown here.

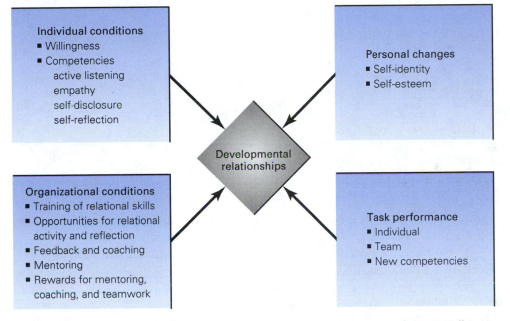

Kram, K. E. (1996). A relational approach to career development, Figure 5.1, p. 141. In D. T. Hall & Associates (eds.). *The career is dead—long live the career: A relational approach to career.* Copyright 1996 Jossey-Bass Inc., Publishers.

sometimes have very direct contact with an employee but be only one of many people who are exposed to a person's work habits and capabilities. To gain a more accurate picture of how well we are doing at work, then, we should receive feedback from a variety of people—our supervisor, our peers, our subordinates, and ourselves. This type of feedback process, called **three hundred sixty degree (360) feedback,** is increasing in popularity in organizations.[41] Although some organizations restrict 360 feedback to management or leadership development, it can also be incorporated into the general appraisal process. This type of feedback offers a number of potential benefits.[42] It helps employees identify their strengths and weaknesses and determine needs for development, and it may increase worker involvement and facilitate teamwork. Employees are encouraged to use the information to make changes or to seek further training, possibly with

360 feedback A method for getting job-related feedback from multiple sources, including peers, supervisors, and subordinates.

DILBERT reprinted by permission of United Features Syndicate.

the help of coaches, in the case of managers or executives. This step is particularly important in corporations that emphasize self-management.

Is 360 feedback more effective than other feedback procedures in increasing productivity and overall effectiveness? So far, no clear evidence supports its superiority. In fact, several problems are associated with the procedure (see Figure 15.5). When 360 feedback becomes evaluative rather than concerned with development, it may draw negative reactions.[43] Employees may feel threatened by the feedback that might be provided by their peers and subordinates—a particular problem for individuals who work in teams or who compete directly for rewards. Often one may know the source of the feedback, and hard feelings may arise. Not surprisingly, the type of feedback given reflects the extent to which the feedback is anonymous or evaluative.[44] Another problem is that ratings by different people often do not agree, so it may be difficult to determine which feedback is most valid.[45] Thus, while 360 feedback may prove useful in some situations, it may not be the best and most effective tool for providing feedback in all work settings (see also the *Ethics at Work* section).

*C*AREERS: CHANGES OVER A LIFETIME

During their work years (which typically span forty to fifty years), most individuals experience major shifts with respect to their work. The tasks they perform, the status they enjoy, the roles they play, their geographic location, the compensation they receive—all these features of working life, plus many others, can change radically as the decades slip by. As individuals move through various stages or portions of their careers, they are also moving from one stage of life to another. Youth is replaced by maturity, which gives way to middle age, and so on. This movement through the life-span, and the changes in family obligations and personal relationships it brings, is often closely linked to changes in individuals' careers. Thus it is impossible to consider one of these topics (careers) in isolation from the others (development during adult life). Recognizing this fact, we will call attention to links between careers and life events and change at several points.

Ethics at Work

The Negative Side of Feedback

We have discussed the importance of feedback in providing useful information about a person's effectiveness at work. 360 or multirater feedback can prove particularly helpful in providing a broad range of perspectives. Unfortunately, this type of rating system can be abused. If you wanted to get on the good side of your supervisor, you might be tempted to give generally positive responses instead of accurate ones. Of course, if the rater's identity is concealed from the supervisor, this "fudging" is less likely to occur. Alternatively, if you and a coworker are in competition for a promotion, you might give your coworker a less-than-glowing endorsement. This situation is especially likely to arise if coworkers do not know the identity of the person providing the feedback. Of course, such a selfish approach defeats the purpose of 360 feedback of promoting the development of employees and supervisors.

To be effective, development or feedback programs need to instill a sense of trust and caring among the employees. Some have called this understanding an "ethic of collaboration."[46] This ethic includes a number of elements:

1. **A sense of calling.** A need to serve others and to achieve self-fulfillment.
2. **A caring attitude.** A genuine concern for the welfare and success of one's coworkers.
3. **Conscientious stewardship.** The realization that one is benefiting from the efforts of others and that one should contribute to the future well-being of the organization.
4. **Creative energy.** The extent to which people strive to develop innovative solutions that go beyond the standard procedures.

To what extent does this type of collaborative ethic exist at your workplace? What do you think might be done to increase it? How can you personally help in this process?

Career Development and Life Stages

In our lifetimes we go through different maturational stages and changes in roles. Our job or career choices are strongly influenced by these factors. When we are in our teens and early twenties, we may be able to take low-paying jobs while we are receiving training or education for higher-level jobs. When we have family responsibilities, it is important to have a solid and steady income, and we may not take a chance on changing careers or have the opportunity for further education. When children leave the home, individuals may again reevaluate their career track and take some career risks.

Super has developed a career theory that focuses on the changes in the process over the life span.[47] As individuals develop in terms of values, self-concept, and skills, their suitability for various jobs or careers may change. **Career maturity** is the extent to which a person has acquired the physical, psychological, and social qualities to cope with career demands. Being a manager requires that a person have a strong self-concept and good human relations skills. Someone who has had little job and supervisory experience is not likely to be a successful manager. The career development process over one's lifetime may go through a series of life stages—growth, exploration, maintenance, and decline. However, each time we switch jobs by force or by choice, we go through a similar cycle in our new job. When we first start in a job, there is much to learn about it. When we have learned the basics, we may wish to explore more fully the different possibilities or roles available in the job. Once we have successfully developed our job role and skills, we are likely to maintain this job for a while. Eventually, we may feel we have outgrown the job and seek a new job or a career change. Job satisfaction depends on the extent to which a person finds an outlet for needs, values, interests, personality traits, and self-concepts in his or her work. As these change over our life span or our time in a particular job, job satisfaction may vary, and job or career transitions may occur.

The general predictions of this model seem to have reasonable support.[48] But it is also clear that one's career development is also strongly influenced by the social/environmental context. Changes in education, organization, and technology will affect the need for career changes. The advent of computers has changed the nature of many careers. For example, much accounting is now done with computer programs rather than by individual accountants. Family roles and responsibilities will have an impact on the extent to which individuals can take on roles that require travel or relocation. Finally, physical and psychological development processes will influence career decisions. When one has considerable physical stamina, the demands of climbing the corporate ladder may be an exciting challenge. In the later years, this excitement may have worn off, and there may be greater concern with the quality of life. A person may feel it is time to smell the roses and enjoy the fruits of past labors. Although it is

career maturity   The extent to which a person has acquired the physical, psychological, and social qualities to cope with career demands.

| Table 15.1 | **Life Stages: From Growth to Decline** |

At different stages of the life cycle, people encounter different issues as they go from growth to decline. At the end of each of these cycles, a person makes a transition into the next one.

Life Stage	Adolescence: 14–25 (years)	Early Adulthood: 25–45 (years)
Decline	Giving less time to hobbies	Reducing sports participation
Maintenance	Verifying current occupational choice	Making occupational position secure
Establishment	Getting started in a chosen field	Settling down in a permanent position
Exploration	Learning more about more opportunities	Finding opportunity to do desired work
Growth	Developing a realistic self-concept	Learning to relate to others

Life Stage	Middle Adulthood: 45–65 (years)	Late Adulthood: over 65 (years)
Decline	Focusing on essential activities	Reducing working hours
Maintenance	Holding own against competition	Keeping up what is still enjoyed
Establishment	Developing new skills	Doing things one has always wanted to do
Exploration	Identifying new problems to work on	Finding a good retirement spot
Growth	Accepting one's limitations	Developing nonoccupational roles

From Super, 1990, note 47; reprinted with permission.

difficult to make a precise prediction, it does appear that most of us will go through various cycles in our career lives (see Table 15.1).

Career and Family

Career and family are intertwined in many ways. One's family status and responsibilities affect the extent to which one can take advantage of educational and career opportunities. Single-parent families, especially those headed by women, are increasing in numbers. Requirements of child care and parenting often conflict with the needs for training, education, or a job. Single parents face many special challenges. Spending time with the children, coordinating schedules, dealing with sick children, monitoring children during after-school hours, and being unable to travel overnight are just a few. These concerns can limit choices of jobs or careers and be a significant source of stress. Affordable day care close to work environments and after-school activities are important to enable these parents to effectively deal with their many demands.

Dual career couples represent about 40 percent of the workforce.[49] Although this trend toward two-earner families represents in part increasing involvement and opportunities of women in the workforce, it also often represents a response to the economic needs of the family. These couples, of course, face some of the same problems as single parents in dealing with child care and monitoring. Travel is feasible if the couple is able to coordinate their travel schedules. The main problem faced by these couples is the division of family roles and responsibilities.[50] Cooking, housework, outside chores, child care, and finances are just a few of the activities that have to be coordinated. There may be a tendency to fall into traditional gender roles, with the man taking care of outside chores and finances and the woman handling the cooking, housework, and much of the after-work child care. Unfortunately, this is not likely to be a very equitable division of labor and can be a source of conflict and resentment. With luck, most couples will be able to develop a reasonable and fair distribution of the tasks. This balancing act may take a bit of communication and even some counseling from trusted friends or professionals. Even if there is a fair distribution of chores, the dual demands of work and home life may make it difficult to find opportunities to socialize.

There are a variety of solutions for couples who find that their dual careers are making their lives too stressful and demanding. One partner could work part-time or take a job that allows him or her to work at home. Some companies allow for job sharing, in which individuals can share a full-time job with another person. The two job sharers can determine how they wish to divide their work week. This provides a high degree of flexibility. Some families may decide to lower their economic aspirations and have one partner stay home with the children and take care of most of the household chores. Family leaves can provide opportunities to deal with personal or family crises.

Many companies are clearly increasing their sensitivity to the needs of the family. However, when professional football players are maligned by their coaches when they miss a game because they want to be part of the birth experience, it becomes apparent that our society still has a long way to go in learning to balance the needs of career and family. How would you handle conflicts between demands of your career and your family?

Women and Family: Some Special Challenges

As noted earlier, there has been a dramatic increase in participation of women in the workplace over the past few decades (see Figure 15.6). Despite family obligations, the majority of women now work outside the home when they are raising children. In 1994, women accounted for 46 percent of the labor force, and approximately 59 per-

Figure 15.6   **Working Women**

The percentage of women over 25 who are in the workforce or who work full-time has increased in recent decades.

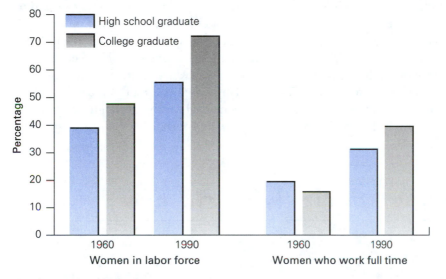

Based on Spain and Bianchi, 1996; see note 12.

cent of all women worked.[51] Women spend more time than men in housework, especially those who are part of a married couple.

To cope with family and employment, women adopt various strategies. They may postpone having children, have smaller families, or choose part-time work or a type of career that is easy to reenter. Child care is a major issue, with many seeking day-care services outside the home. Concerns have been raised, however, about the quality of child care and the importance of parental involvement in child rearing. Women may therefore face a tough balancing act if they are strongly interested in furthering their careers. As a result, dual career couples face special challenges in developing an effective means of dealing fairly with the household chores and providing optimum conditions for the development of their children. What they may need is family-sensitive workplaces.

Toward a Family-Friendly Workplace: A Little Flexibility

Many companies are sensitive to the conflicting demands of work and family life. In fact, 70 percent of large companies have developed so-called family-friendly policies.[52] They may provide flexible hours and schedules, part-time work, and job sharing. Large companies may provide child care, and many organizations offer extended leaves for family reasons, such as caring for sick children or parents.

Do such policies increase productivity? Some evidence indicates that long work hours and rigid schedules can reduce motivation and hinder productivity and that job sharers have a very high level of productivity.[53] Flexible work hours can lead to greater commitment and job satisfaction among employees.[54] On the other hand, some employees may fear that taking advantage of these flexible policies will hinder their career development.[55] There may be a feeling that doing so will be seen as a lack of commitment and thus hinder one's chances of advancement. It is therefore important for a company to communicate clearly its support for a flexible work policy. Flexible work should be seen as normal and beneficial for the overall functioning of the organization. It should also be supported by appropriate levels of compensation and benefits.

Guidelines for Effective Human Relations

Using What You've Learned

In this chapter, we examined a broad range of principles and findings about career development. Although few rules will apply to every situation, there are some general guidelines suggested by the various findings we have discussed. These are summarized below for your consideration. Remember, no rule works 100 percent in every situation. However, these guidelines should help you in your career selection and development.

■ Find out as much as you can about your own capabilities and traits. This information can guide you and counselors in selecting jobs or careers that should be most suitable for you.

■ Take some time to learn the characteristics of the jobs that seem to be best for you. Some of this information can be learned from books, but you should also visit with individuals who have such jobs.

■ Try to find out about the future prospects for different careers. Avoid committing to careers that seem to have declining prospects.

■ Realize that you can probably be successful in a number of different careers. So you may wish to keep your options open as long as possible before making a commitment to one career. One good strategy is to acquire as many skills and as much knowledge as possible in your areas of interest. Not only will this make you a more valuable employee, but it will also increase your flexibility in developing or changing careers.

Guidelines for Effective Human Relations (continued)

■ Keep learning. The one constant in life is change. To keep ahead of the game, you should keep taking courses and developing new skills. For example, engineers may want to take courses in business or management to enhance their promotion opportunities.

■ Be a career activist. Very few good careers come to those who simply wait around for them. Such careers have to be found, and they require significant preparation. Some careers can be created by those who combine skills or knowledge in a unique way. Remember, if the need exists for your talents, you have the upper hand.

■ Think small. Although we tend to think about careers with large corporations, most jobs are provided by small companies. This means that you will have to work hard to find the right company for you. Furthermore, it is not likely that they will find you unless you find them first.

■ You have to start somewhere. Don't expect your first or second job to meet all of your hopes for your career. Careers are a building process. Most successful individuals began their careers at the bottom of the ladder and rose to the top by hard work.

Wherever you are in your career development, we hope these guidelines may be of some help. Good luck!

Summary

Individuals seem to choose their careers largely on the basis of personal interests, social influence from others, and accident. A better approach involves efforts to obtain thorough knowledge of one's own traits, interests, and motives, plus systematic information on the requirements of various jobs. A final step involves seeking a career that offers a good match between these two sets of factors.

In recent years, many companies have begun to appreciate the importance of effective human resource planning—efforts to make the best possible use of their employees' skills and talents. Consistent with this shift, some organizations have established special programs of career management and development. One feature of these programs is often the provision of detailed performance appraisals to employees. In addition to relying on such help from their companies, individuals can contribute to their own career development through several steps. These steps include (1) increasing their knowledge of their own strengths and weaknesses, (2) forming a clear picture of the functioning of their organization (including its internal politics), (3) establishing concrete goals, and (4) devising specific steps to reach them.

The sequence of occupations and jobs that individuals hold during their working lives constitutes their careers. Crucial points in career planning occur at key times during an individual's life—for example, at about age thirty, during the early forties, and again in the late fifties. Marital status, the career of one's partner, and children also can have a strong impact on career development.

Careers are changing so that they are less controlled by organizations and depend more on the choices and interests of the individuals. Many careers also require the rapid development of interpersonal or relational skills. Feedback from multiple sources or 360 feedback can aid a person in developing such skills.

Key Terms

career development, p. 444

career maturity, p. 454

careers, p. 435

human resource planning, p. 444

organizational politics, p. 446

performance appraisals, p. 444

protean career, p. 449

social models, p. 436

360 feedback, p. 451

Experiential Exercise

How Flexible Is Your Company?

The protean career requires the development of a diverse set of skills and considerable flexibility on the part of the individual person and the corporation. Organizations today must provide an environment conducive to continuous learning in which employees are provided opportunities, resources, and feedback. It is particularly important to provide employees with challenging jobs throughout their careers and to support their efforts to grow and develop by providing opportunities for self-training and self-learning. This type of environment promotes employee development and enables companies to identify and assist the best employees. An example of one such company is Starbucks, as described in the introduction to this chapter.

How well does your current company (or one for which you have worked recently) support the development of this new type of career? Check all that apply.

_____ 1. People are rewarded for their skills, competencies, and adaptability.

_____ 2. Managers and supervisors are encouraged to coach or develop talent.

_____ 3. Employees receive feedback from coworkers as well as supervisors.

_____ 4. There is a focus on development of personal skills such as flexibility and effective communication.

_____ 5. Development of new job skills is encouraged.

_____ 6. People are encouraged to make lateral moves.

_____ 7. People are made aware of other opportunities in the organization.

_____ 8. The company is sensitive to educational and family needs.

_____ 9. Easy access is provided to other job opportunities in the organization.

_____ 10. Employees are encouraged to be self-directed.

A score of 8 or higher indicates that a company is sensitive to the individual's career needs. A score of 3 or lower indicates that the company needs to become more supportive on personal career needs.

Adapted from material in Hall, D. T., & Mirvis, P. H. (1996). The new protean career: Psychological success and the path with heart. In D. T. Hall & Associates (eds.). *The career is dead—long live the career: A relational approach to careers.* Copyright 1996 Jossey-Bass Inc., Publishers.

Notes

1. Hall, D. T., & Moss, J. E. (Winter, 1998). The new protean career contract: Helping organizations and employees adapt. *Organizational Dynamics,* 22–36.

2. Herriot, P. (1992). *The career management challenge: Balancing individual and organizational needs.* London: Sage.

3. Hall, D. T. (1987). *Careers and organizations.* Pacific Palisades, CA: Goodyear Publishing.

4. Montross, D. H., & Shinkman, C. J. (eds.). 1992. *Career development: Theory and practice.* Springfield, IL: Charles C. Thomas.

5. Liebert, R. M., Sprafkin, J. N., & Davidson, E. S. (1982). *The early window: Effects of television on children and youth* (2nd ed.). New York: Pergamon.

6. Holland, J. L. (1985). *Making vocational choices: A theory of vocational personalities and work environments* (2nd ed.). Englewood Cliffs, NJ: Prentice-Hall.

7. Gottfredson, G. D., & Holland, J. L. (1989). *Dictionary of Holland occupational codes* (2nd ed.). Odessa, FL: Psychological Assessment Resources, Inc.

8. Roe, A., & Lunneborg, P. (1990). Personality development and career choice. In D. Brown & L. Brooks (eds.), *Career choice and development* (2nd ed.) (pp. 68–101). San Francisco: Jossey-Bass.

9. Krumboltz, J. D. (1979). A social learning theory of career decision making. In A. M. Mitchell, G. B. Jones, & J. D. Krumboltz (eds.), *Social learning and career decision making* (pp. 19–49). Cranston, RI: Carroll Press.

10. Hotchkiss, L., & Borow, H. (1990). Sociological perspectives on career choice and attainment. In D. Brown, L. Brooks, and Associates (eds.), *Career choice and development: Applying contemporary theories to practice* (2nd ed.). San Francisco: Jossey-Bass.

11. Betz, N. E., & Fitzgerald, L. F. (1987). *The career psychology of women.* Orlando, FL: Academic Press.

12. Spain, D., & Bianchi, S. M. (1996). *Balancing act: Motherhood, marriage, and employment among american women.* New York: Russell Sage Foundation.

13. Astin, H. S. (1984). The meaning of work in women's lives: A socio-psychological model of career choice and work behavior. *Counseling Psychologist, 12,* 17–126.

14. Tomkiewicz, J., & Hughes, R. E. (1993). Women who choose business administration versus women who choose administrative services: How they differ. *Journal of Applied Social Psychology, 23,* 867–874.

15. Hacket, G., & Betz, N. E. (1981). A self-efficacy approach to the career development of women. *Journal of Vocational Behavior, 18,* 326–339.

16. Atwater, L. E., & Van Fleet, D. D. (1997). Another ceiling? Can males compete for traditionally female jobs? *Journal of Management, 23,* 603–626.

17. Brooks, L. (1990). Recent developments in theory building. In D. Brown, L. Brooks, and Associates (eds.), *Career choice and development: Applying contemporary theories to practice* (pp. 364–394). San Francisco: Jossey-Bass.

18. Gottfredson, L. S. (1981). Circumscription and compromise: A developmental theory of occupational aspirations. *Journal of Counseling Psychology Monograph, 28,* 545–579.

19. McDaniels, C., & Gysbers, N. C. (1992). *Counseling for career development: Theories, resources, and practice.* San Francisco: Jossey-Bass.

20. Ibid.

21. Employment and Training Administration, Department of Labor. (1981). *Selected characteristics of occupations defined in the dictionary of occupational titles.* Washington, DC: U.S. Government Printing Office.

22. Employment and Training Administration. (1984). *Guide for occupational exploration.* Department of Labor. (Stock no. 029-013-00080-2). Washington, DC: U.S. Government Printing Office.

23. Bureau of Labor Statistics. (1992). *Occupational outlook handbook* (1992–1993 ed.). Department of Labor. Washington, DC: U.S. Government Printing Office.

24. Lorenzen, E. A. (ed.)(1996). *Career planning and job searching in the information age.* Binghamton, NY: The Haworth Press.

25. Curry, J. (1998). Tapping the Internet's job search resources. *Business Communication Quarterly, 61,* 100–106.

26. Von Glinow, M. A., Driver, M. J., Brousseau, K., & Prince, J. B. (1983). The design of a career oriented human resource system. *Academy of Management Review, 8,* 23–32.

27. Greenberg, J., & Baron, R. A. (1994). *Behavior in organizations.* Boston: Allyn & Bacon.

28. London, M. (1983). Toward a theory of career motivation. *Academy of Management Review, 8,* 620–630.

29. See note 26.

30. Jones, G. (1983). Psychological orientation and the process of organizational socialization: An interactionist perspective. *Academy of Management Review, 8,* 464–474.

31. Kondrasuk, J. N. (1981). Studies in MBO effectiveness. *Academy of Management Review, 6,* 419–430.

32. Hall, D. T., & Associates (1996). *The career is dead—long live the career: A relational approach to careers.* San Francisco: Jossey-Bass.

33. See note 1.

34. Harkness, H. (1997). *The career chase: Taking creative control in a chaotic age.* Palo Alto, CA: Davies-Black.

35. Hall, D. T., & Mirvis, P. H.(1996). The new protean career: Psychological success and the path with heart. In D. T. Hall & Associates (eds.), *The career is dead—long live the career: A relational approach to careers* (pp. 15–45). San Francisco: Jossey-Bass.

36. See note 32.

37. See note 1.

38. See note 32.

39. Kram, K. E. (1996). A relational approach to career development. In D. T. Hall & Associates (eds.), *The career is dead—long live the career: A relational approach to career* (pp. 132–157). San Francisco: Jossey-Bass.

40. Ibid.

41. Waldman, D. A., Atwater, L. E., & Antonioni, D. (1998). Has 360 degree feedback gone amok? *Academy of Management Executive, 12,* 86–94.

42. Jones, J. E. (1996). 360-degree feedback: Strategies, tactics, and techniques for developing leaders. Amherst, MA: HRD Press.

43. Waldman, D. A., & Bowen, D. E. (1998). The acceptability of 360 degree appraisals: A customer supplier relationship perspective. *Human Resource Management, 37,* 117–129.

44. London, M., & Smither, J. W. (1995). Can multisource feedback change perceptions of goal accomplishment, self-evaluations, and performance related outcomes? Theory-based applications and directions for research. *Personnel Psychology, 48,* 803–839.

45. Borman, W. C. (1997). 360 degree ratings: An analysis of assumptions and a research agenda for evaluating their validity. *Human Resource Management Review, 7,* 299–315.

46. Haskins, M. E., Liedtka, J., & Rosenblum, J. (Spring, 1998). Beyond teams: Toward an ethic of collaboration. *Organizational Dynamics,* 34–49.

47. Super, D. E. (1990). A life-span, life-space approach to career development. In D. Brown, L. Brooks, and Associates (eds.), *Career choice and development: Applying contemporary theories to practice* (2nd ed.). San Francisco: Jossey-Bass.

48. Osipow, S. H. (1983). *Theories of career development* (3rd ed.). Englewood Cliffs, NJ: Prentice Hall.

49. Zedeck, S., & Mosier, K. L. (1990). Work in the family and employing organization. *American Psychologist, 45,* 240–251.

50. Sekaran, U., & Hall, D. T. (1989). Asynchronism in dual-career and family linkage. In M. B. Arthur, D. T. Hall, & B. S. Lawrence (eds.), *Handbook of career theory.* Cambridge, UK: Cambridge University Press.

51. See note 12.

52. Clay, R. C. (1998). Many managers frown on use of flexible work options. *Monitor, 29,* 11–12.

53. Googins, B. K. (1991). *Work/family conflicts: Private lives–public responses.* Westport, CT: Auburn House.

54. Scandura, T. A., & Lankau, M. J. (1997). Relationship of gender, family responsibility and flexible work hours to organizational commitment and job satisfaction. *Journal of Organizational Behavior, 18,* 377–391.

55. See note 52.

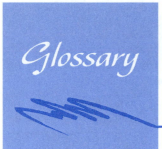

Glossary

achievement motivation   The desire to attain standards of excellence and accomplish tasks more successfully than others.

active listening   Attentive listening in which the listener reacts to communication with questions, feedback, or requests for elaboration.

additive tasks   Group tasks in which the individual efforts of several persons are added together to form the group's product.

affective commitment   A person's desire to stay with the organization because he or she agrees with its policies and wants to remain affiliated with the business.

aptitude tests   Tests that measure a person's capacities to benefit from certain types of training.

arbitration   A form of third-party intervention in disputes in which the intervening person has the power to determine the terms of an agreement.

arousal model of social facilitation   A theory stating that the presence of others increases arousal, which increases people's tendencies to perform the dominant response. If that response is well learned, performance will improve; if it is novel, performance will be impaired.

attitudes   Relatively stable clusters of feelings, beliefs, and predispositions to act directed toward some specific or abstract concept.

attitudinal politics   Holding an opinion so as to secure some strategic purpose.

bargaining   A process in which two or more sides exchange offers, concessions, and counteroffers in an attempt to resolve their disagreement; also called negotiating.

Big Five   Basic personality dimensions identified as universal in human nature. They are extroversion, agreeableness, conscientiousness, emotional stability, and openness.

brainstorming   A technique designed to enhance creativity in problem-solving groups by emphasizing the free exchange of novel ideas. These groups are not as effective as commonly thought.

burnout   A syndrome resulting from prolonged exposure to stress, consisting of physical, emotional, and mental exhaustion plus feelings of low personal accomplishment.

cardinal traits   Rare traits that, when they occur, dominate a person's personality.

career development   The pattern of changes that occur during an individual's career.

career identity   The degree to which people define themselves in terms of their work.

career insight   The clarity of an individual's career goals.

career maturity   The extent to which a person has acquired the physical, psychological, and social qualities to cope with career demands.

career motivation   A person's career plans, behaviors, and decisions.

career resilience   A person's ability to adapt to changing circumstances.

career-success orientation   An orientation found in cultures that emphasize acquisition of material possessions and individualism.

careers   The sequence of attitudes and behaviors associated with work-related activities experienced by individuals over the span of their working lives.

central route to persuasion   Persuasion that is accomplished through the impact of information. Involves thinking about the issue.

central traits   The relatively small number of traits that are highly characteristic of a person.

charismatic leaders   Leaders who exert powerful effects on their followers and to whom several special traits are attributed (such as possession of an idealized vision or goal, willingness to engage in unconventional behaviors to reach it).

coercive power   Power stemming from control over punishments and negative outcomes. The use of coercive power is discouraged in most work settings.

collective-effort model   A theory of social loafing that proposes that it occurs because of the uncertain connection between our efforts and outcomes in groups.

collectivist cultures   Cultures that emphasize interdependence, obedience, group goals, and harmony.

collectivist self-concept   A cultural emphasis on defining one's self as a part of a larger group or society.

common-knowledge effect   In group discussion, unique or unshared information tends to be repeated less than shared information.

communication   The process through which one person or group transmits information to another person or group.

comparison level (CL)   The outcome that people think they deserve in a relationship.

comparison level for alternatives (CLalt)   The outcome that people think can be obtained from the best available alternative.

compensatory expectations   Expectations that members of groups will "make up" for their stereotypically inconsistent behavior or the inconsistent behaviors performed by other group members.

concurrence seeking   The tendency of group members to strive for agreement on important issues.

conflict   Disagreements that occur because of differences in opinions or interests.

contingency theory   A theory suggesting that leader effectiveness is determined both by characteristics of the leader and the degree of situational control this person can exert over subordinates.

contingent relationship   A relationship in which a reward will be received only if a certain response occurs.

contingent work   Temporary employment involving short-time work.

continuance commitment   An individual's inclination to continue to work for the organization because he or she cannot afford to leave.

correlational method   A method of research in which two or more variables are carefully studied to determine whether changes in one are associated with changes in the other.

credibility   The perception that a communicator can be believed or trusted.

critical incident technique   A procedure used to study job satisfaction in which participants describe times in which they felt especially satisfied or dissatisfied with their jobs.

cross-functional teams   Teams that involve collaboration of members from different areas of an organization.

deficiency needs   In Maslow's need theory, lower-level needs that must be at least partially satisfied before higher-level growth needs can be activated.

dependent variable   A variable that is measured and potentially affected by the independent variable.

descriptive stereotype   Beliefs concerning how most people in a group behave and what they prefer.

diffusion of responsibility   The tendency of individuals to assume that others will take responsibility for needed actions.

discrimination   Negative actions directed toward an individual based on his or her group membership.

door-in-the-face technique   A tactic for enhancing compliance by beginning with a large request and, when it is rejected, backing down to a smaller one.

dual career ladders   Promoting people to new titles and ranks within an organization rather than promoting them to managerial positions. This practice is used to restructure corporations in a way that eliminates strict hierarchies of authority.

electronic communication   Recent technologic developments in communication, such as electronic mail and faxes, that provide a low-cost way to keep in touch with a broad network of individuals.

empowerment   The practice of giving as much authority and power as possible to those at the lowest ranks of the organization.

enhancement strategies   Impression management techniques that involve including statements of praise from others along with requests for feedback.

entitlement strategies   Impression management techniques that involve enhancing the credit received for positive outcomes.

equity theory   The theory stating that workers strive to maintain ratios of their own outcomes (rewards) to their own input (contributions) that are equal to the outcome-to-input ratios of other workers with whom they compare themselves.

equity   The condition in which a worker's outcome-to-input ratio is equal to that of another person who is used for comparison.

ERG theory   An alternative theory to Maslow's need hierarchy proposed by Alderfer, which asserts that three basic human needs exist: existence, relatedness, and growth.

esteem needs   In Maslow's need theory, the need to attain self-respect and the respect of others.

excuses   Impression management techniques designed to reduce the impression of responsibility for negative outcomes.

existence needs   Needs that are related to basic survival.

expectancy theory   The theory asserting that workers' motivation is based on their beliefs about the probability that effort will lead to performance (expectancy), multiplied by the probability that performance will lead to reward (instrumentality), multiplied by the perceived value (valence) of the reward.

experimentation   A method of research in which one or more factors (independent variables) are altered systematically to determine if such changes have an impact on one or more aspects of behavior (dependent variables).

expert power   Power based on the possession of special knowledge or skill.

fear appeals   Suggestions that failure to adopt your position will lead to negative outcomes.

figure-ground relationship   A principle of perception that states that our tendency is to organize sensory input into stimuli (figures) that stand out against a background (ground).

foot-in-the-door technique   A tactic for enhancing compliance by beginning with a small request and, when it is granted, moving to a larger one.

forewarning   Advance knowledge of the persuasive intent of a spoken, written, or televised message. When individuals know that attempts at persuasion are forthcoming, their ability to resist such appeals is often increased.

fundamental attribution error   The term used to describe our tendency to overemphasize the importance of internal causes for other persons' behavior.

goal setting   The process of determining specific levels of performance for workers to attain.

grapevine   An informal channel of communication based on social relations among employees.

great person theory   The view that leaders possess special traits that set them apart from others and that these traits are responsible for their assuming positions of power and authority.

group polarization   A process that occurs when groups of like-minded individuals discussing issues become more extreme in the direction of their initial attitudes and beliefs.

group   A collection of two or more interacting individuals with a stable pattern of relationships between them, who share common goals and who perceive themselves as being a group.

groupthink   The tendency of groups to make decisions without carefully evaluating alternative courses of action.

growth needs   Needs for developing one's human potential.

halo effect   When our overall impressions of others spill over into and influence our evaluations of their behaviors.

Hawthorne studies   A classic series of investigations that, taken together, demonstrated the impact of social factors on behavior in work settings.

heuristics   Mental shortcuts that allow us to make inferences in a rapid manner.

high-context culture   A culture in which the meaning of a communication depends greatly on nonverbal factors, such as eye contact and tone of voice.

human relations approach   An approach to work settings that pays attention to human needs, motives, and relationships.

human relations   A field that seeks to understand work-related aspects of interpersonal relations and apply its knowledge to help organizations and individuals in facing their goals.

human resource planning   Efforts by organizations to make the best possible use of the skills, abilities, and talents of their employees.

hygiene or maintenance factors   Work factors related to conditions surrounding jobs, such as working conditions and pay.

illusion of outgroup homogeneity   The tendency to view persons belonging to other groups as varying less than persons in our own group. In short, outgroup members are all perceived as being very much alike.

illusion of productivity   The tendency of individuals in brainstorming groups to perceive their performance favorably even though they typically perform more poorly than individuals in nominal groups.

illusory correlation   A phenomenon that occurs when we perceive a stronger relationship or association between two variables than actually exists.

impression formation   The process through which we combine diverse information about other persons into unified impressions of them.

impression management   The process by which we seek to control how others perceive us.

independent variable   A variable that is manipulated in an experiment so as to determine its effects on behavior.

individualist cultures   Cultures that emphasize individual achievement, rights, and independence.

individualistic self-concept   A cultural emphasis on defining one's self in terms of individual goals, desires, and characteristics, apart from one's group affiliations.

inequity   The undesirable condition in which a worker's outcome-to-input ratio is not equal to that of another person who is used for comparison. If this inequity favors a person, the result is *overpayment inequity,* which leads to feelings of guilt. If this inequity is to a person's disadvantage, the result is *underpayment inequity,* which leads to feelings of anger.

influence   The capacity to change others' behavior in some desired manner. In contrast to power, influence involves the consent of the target.

information dependence   A relationship in groups in which group members must exchange information to make decisions or complete a task.

informational influence   Movement in the direction of a group majority that is based on a belief that the majority view is correct.

ingratiation strategies   Impression management techniques that are motivated by the desire to get along with others.

initiating structure   A style of leadership focused mainly on productivity or successful task accomplishment. Leaders who rate highly on this dimension often engage in such actions as organizing work activities, setting deadlines, and assigning individuals to specific tasks; also called task orientation.

input   Workers' contributions to their jobs, such as their experience, qualifications, or amount of time worked.

inter-role conflict   Conflict that occurs when people from different parts of an individual's life have conflicting expectations about that person's role.

interactionist view   A view contending that how a particular member of a group becomes its leader depends both on the personal characteristics of the individual and on many situational factors.

interdependence   A state that exists when the actions, behaviors, and ideas of group members have important implications for one another.

interest tests   Tests that measure an individual's preference for engaging in certain kinds of activities.

job discrimination   Practices including a reluctance to hire, promote, or pay fairly based on a person's group membership.

job satisfaction   Individuals' degree of positive attitudes toward their current position or work.

law of effect   The law stating that the consequences of a response determine the probability of observing that response in the future.

law of proximity   A law of perceptual organization that states that objects that are near to one another, in either time or space, tend to be grouped together.

law of similarity   A law of perceptual organization that states that similar items within a field, whether people or objects, tend to be grouped together.

leadership prototypes   Assumptions we hold about the characteristics of effective leaders.

leadership   The exercise of influence by individuals within work or social groups over other members.

learning   The process through which lasting changes in behavior are made through experience with the world.

legitimate power   Power based on an individual's position or rank.

life satisfaction   Individuals' level of satisfaction with their lives away from work.

love   A strong, affectionate relationship between people.

low-context culture   A culture in which the meaning of communication comes primarily from the words spoken rather than nonverbal or other contextual factors.

mediation   A form of third-party intervention in disputes in which the intervener does not have the authority to dictate an agreement. Mediators simply attempt to enhance communication between opposing sides and to provide conditions that will facilitate acceptable agreements.

meditation   A technique for inducing relaxation in which individuals clear disturbing thoughts from their minds and then repeat a single syllable (mantra) over and over again.

mere exposure effect   Increased attraction to a stimulus based on repeated presentations of or exposure to stimulus.

metamorphic effect of power   The transformation that occurs in a persuader as a function of his or her success in changing others.

modern racism   The subtle and indirect forms of prejudice and discrimination that are characteristic of today's world.

motivation   An internal force or process that energizes, guides, and maintains behavior.

motivators   Work factors related to characteristics of the work itself, such as the growth opportunities it provides.

need hierarchy theory   Maslow's theory asserting that five levels of human needs (physiological, safety, social, esteem, and self-actualization) exist and these are arranged in such a way that lower, more basic needs must be satisfied before higher level needs become activated.

nonverbal communication   A silent form of communication involving facial expressions, eye contact, body movements, or dress.

normative influence   Movement in the direction of a group majority that is motivated by a desire to seek approval.

norms   Rules in task-performing or social groups that indicate how members of these groups should behave.

old-fashioned racism   Obvious forms of prejudice and discrimination, such as slavery and lynch mobs.

one-sided argument   A persuasion technique wherein you present only support for your own view.

optimism-pessimism   The personality dimension based on the outlook that individuals have on life. Those with a positive outlook are optimists, and those with a negative outlook are termed pessimists.

organizational citizenship behaviors   Behaviors that are important for organizations to run effectively but that are not required or compensated. Some categories of these behaviors are altruism, conscientiousness, sportsmanship, courtesy, and civic virtue.

organizational development   Techniques and procedures designed to produce planned change in an organization. Such change, in turn, is aimed at enhancing the organization's effectiveness and efficiency.

organizational politics   Tactics for gaining, holding, and using power in organizations.

organizational politics   The process through which power and influence are exercised within a given organization. A clear understanding of such politics is necessary for effective career development.

organizational spontaneity   Active behaviors that promote the survival and effectiveness of the organization and that go beyond the roles prescribed by the job.

organizational structure   The way in which an organization is put together—its departments, formal lines of communication, chain of command, and so on.

other-oriented lies   Lies that are motivated by a concern to maintain pleasant interactions.

outcome interdependence   A relationship in which group members have a mutual interest in the division of some scarce resources.

outcomes   The rewards a worker receives from his or her job, such as salary and recognition.

perception   The active process by which we interpret and organize information provided by our senses. It is through perception that we construct a representation of the world around us.

perceptual organization   Processes responsible for providing structure and order to our perceptual world.

performance appraisals   Steps undertaken by organizations to provide employees with feedback on their current performance. Detailed and constructive performance appraisals often form part of company-run programs of career management/career development.

peripheral route to persuasion Persuasion that is accomplished through the impact of cues unrelated to the issue. Sometimes called "mindless" persuasion.

person-role conflict Conflict between our own expectations and the expectations of others.

personality The unique pattern of traits and behaviors that define each individual.

persuasion Attempts to change the behavior or attitudes of others through convincing appeals and arguments.

physiological needs Basic biological needs, such as the need for food, water, or oxygen.

power The ability to affect the behavior of others regularly and strongly, and even against their will.

prejudice A negative attitude toward members of a social group.

prescriptive stereotype Controlling attitudes that tell members of groups how they should think, feel, and behave.

prosocial behavior Behavior designed to further the welfare of others or the organization. Helping behavior, organizational citizenship behaviors, and spontaneous behaviors are examples of such behavior.

protean career A career that is managed by the individual and guided by that person's own choices and search for fulfillment.

psychological reactance Going out of one's way to perform the behaviors that someone is trying to control or change.

qualitative overload The belief of an employee that he or she lacks the skills or abilities required to perform a specific job.

qualitative underload The lack of mental stimulation that accompanies many routine, repetitious jobs.

quality circle A small work group that comes together periodically to identify and resolve work-related problems. These groups are often part of a focus on the quality of work life in organizations.

quality circles (QCs) An approach to improving the quality of work life in which small groups of volunteers meet regularly to identify and solve problems related to the work they perform and the conditions under which they work.

quality of work life Techniques designed to make work more interesting and rewarding, and to make work settings better places in which to function.

quality-of-life orientation An orientation found in cultures that emphasize relationships among people and concerns about life quality.

quantitative overload A situation in which individuals are confronted with more work than can be completed in a given period of time.

quantitative underload A situation in which individuals have so little to do that they find themselves sitting around much of the time.

receiver The individual toward whom communication is directed.

reciprocity rule A societal norm that makes us feel a sense of indebtedness to repay what another person has given us.

referent power Power based on the personal attractiveness of the individual who possesses it.

reflexivity Thoughtful and careful analysis, planning, and action in the course of team activity.

reinforcers Response-contingent outcomes that strengthen preceding responses.

relatedness needs Needs for meaningful social relationships.

relaxation training Special training in which individuals learn to relax one group of muscles at a time. This, in turn, often causes them to experience a reduction in tension.

representativeness heuristic A heuristic for making judgments based on the extent to which a stimulus resembles our stereotypes.

response A measure of work performance, such as productivity.

reward power Power stemming from the ability to control various rewards sought by others.

rewards Things of value to an employee, such as pay or a promotion.

role Expectations that are held about a particular position.

rumor Information transmitted through the grapevine that has little or no basis in fact.

safety needs Needs to feel safe from threats to our physical or psychological well-being.

salience The extent to which a given stimulus stands out from other stimuli surrounding it.

sampling bias The tendency of groups to focus on information or knowledge that they have in common.

scientific management An early approach to management and behavior in work settings that emphasized the importance of good job design. It also directed attention to employee motivation and to the importance of selecting and training employees for their jobs.

secondary traits Relatively inconspicuous characteristics of people that are limited in influence.

self-actualization need The need to find out who we really are and to develop to our fullest potential.

self-centered lies Lies designed to maintain a positive impression.

self-deprecation Providing negative information about oneself to promote an image of modesty.

self-disclosure Offering personal information, even if it isn't requested, to foster the impression that one is honest and like the target person.

self-efficacy A person's belief that he or she possesses the necessary skills and abilities to accomplish a goal.

self-esteem An individual's positive or negative evaluation of himself or herself. A part of the self-concept.

self-leadership Being self-directed and motivated in your job.

self-managed teams Teams that have much freedom of choice in the conduct of their work.

self-managing work teams Teams that have much control over and responsibility for the conduct of their work.

self-presentation The effort to create a desired impression on others.

self-serving bias Our tendency to take credit for positive outcomes but attribute negative outcomes to external causes.

sender The individual who initiates communication by transmitting information to one or more people.

sensitivity training A group-interaction technique designed to increase interpersonal openness and communication accuracy.

sensitivity training An organizational development technique that seeks to enhance employees' understanding of their own behavior and its impact on others. Such insight can potentially reduce the interpersonal conflicts that interfere with organizational effectiveness.

sexual harassment An unwanted sexual communication or act.

showing consideration A style of leadership focused mainly on the establishment of positive relations between the leader and other group members; also called people orientation.

situational approach A view suggesting that the person who becomes the leader of a specific group is determined largely by situational factors (for example, the technical skill or knowledge needed for a particular task).

smiles-leniency effect Smiling wrongdoers are treated less severely than nonsmiling ones.

social categorization Tendency to divide people into groups.

social cognition The manner in which we process, store, and remember social information.

social equity The state in which one worker's outcome-to-input ratio is equivalent to that of another worker with whom this person compares himself or herself.

social loafing   The tendency for group members to exert less individual effort on an additive task as the size of the group increases.

social models   Individuals who affect the behavior or attitudes of others through their words or deeds, often without any conscious desire to produce such effects.

social needs   Needs to form friendships with others, to belong, and to love and be loved.

social perception   The process through which we come to know and understand other persons.

spamming   Bulk marketing of junk e-mail to many users.

status   The level of respect, prestige, and privilege assigned to a specific individual by other members of his or her group or organization.

stimulus   An event or object that elicits some type of response.

stress   The physical, psychological, and behavioral reactions experienced by individuals in situations where they feel that they are in danger of being overwhelmed—pushed beyond their abilities or limits.

stressors   Various aspects of the world around us that contribute to stress.

structural inertia   The organizational forces acting on employees that encourage them to perform their jobs in certain ways (for example, through a reward system), thereby making them resistant to change.

sublimunal persuasion   Persuasion that is accomplished by presenting a message to a person's subconscious.

superordinate goals   Goals shared by all members of an organization. When the parties to a conflict are made aware of these goals, the conflict may be resolved or lessened.

survey feedback   A technique of organizational development in which information about an organization is fed back to employees and plans are then formulated for dealing with specific identified problems.

team building   An organizational development technique in which employees discuss problems related to their work group's performance. On the basis of these discussions, specific problems are identified and plans for solving them are devised and implemented.

teams   Cooperative work groups that emphasize employee involvement and responsibility. Quality circles and self-managing teams are two examples of such work groups.

telecommuting   Doing work away from the work site by means of computer.

Theory Z   Ouchi's book contending that differences between Japanese and American management are responsible for differences in productivity levels in those countries.

360 feedback   A method for getting job-related feedback from multiple sources, including peers, supervisors, and subordinates.

transactional leadership   A leadership style based on providing rewards for accomplishments of subordinates.

transformational leadership   A leadership style that involves inspiration, intellectual stimulation, and individual consideration.

two-sided argument   A persuasion technique wherein you mention and refute opossing positions as well as offer support for your own view.

within-role conflict   Conflict that occurs when people in one area of an individual's life have different expectations.

Index

Absenteeism, 327–328, 332
Abusive organizations, 338
Accomplishment, low personal, 417
Accountability, 217
Achievement, 103–104, 113
Active listening, 171
Adaptability, 32
Additive tasks, 215–216
Adler, N. J., 320
Advertising, 184, 188–189
Affective commitment, 329–330
Agentic orientation, 289
Aggression
    anger and, 358–360
    causes of, 357–358
    controlling, 359–360
    culture and, 358
    incidence of, 356–357
    personal characteristics and, 358–359
    sexual assault, 350
    in work settings, 350, 358, 362
Alarm reaction, 399
Alderfer, Clayton, 127–128, 139
Allport, Gordon, 92–93
American Airlines, 300
American Express family initiatives, 66–67
American Management Association (AMA),
    110
Americans with Disabilities Act of 1990, 441
Amway Corporation, 182
Anger, aggression and, 358–360
Appeal of job or field, intrinsic, 436
Appreciation of employees, showing, 312–313
Aptitude tests, 111–112
Arbitration, 265
Arousal, 219–220
Arousal model of social facilitation, 220

Artistic occupational type, 437
AT&T, 299
Attention
    external factors affecting, 67–68
    internal factors affecting, 65–67
    motivation and, 66
    salience and, 69
    social perception and, 68–71
Attitudes. *See also* Discrimination; Job satisfaction;
        Prejudice
    appreciation of employees and, 312–313
    change in, 186–187
    components of, 313–314, 332
    guidelines for effective, 330–331
    about job, 314–329
        absenteeism and, 327–328, 332
        assessing, 324–325
        effects of, 326–329
        factors affecting, 314–318
        health and, 328–329, 332
        life satisfaction and, 327–328, 332
        motivation and, 322–323, 332
        stress and, 415
        turnover and, 327, 332
        variations in, 319–326
    organizational commitment and, 329–330, 332
    stress and, 413–414
    us-versus-them, 377–379, 382, 391
Attitudinal politics, 195
Attraction, 339–341, 362
Attractiveness, 183–185, 340
Attribution, 74–78, 86, 262
Attrition rates, 434
Avoidance, conflict, 259, 263–264

Baby boomers, 35
Baker, Bob, 300

Balancing work and family
    American Express initiatives and, 66–67
    expectancy theory and, 130–131
    interpersonal relations and, 354–356
    job sharing and, 98–99
    telecommuting and, 34–35
Bank-Wiring Room study, 13–15
Bargaining, 264–266, 271
Bay of Pigs fiasco, 232
Benefit plans, 131–132
Berscheid's three-factor theory of love, 343–344
Biases. *See also* Discrimination; Prejudice
    gender, 290, 439–441
    information, 229–231
    racial, 386–387, 439–441
    sampling, 230–231
    self-serving, 79, 86
Big Five dimensions, 93–94
Bigotry, 377, 388
Biofeedback, 424
Blake, R., 287, 289
Blocking of ideas, 222, 224
Brainstorming
    electronic, 223–225
    improving, 222–226, 239
    inhibition of, factors affecting, 221–222
    process of, 221
    social influence model of, 223
    verbal, 225–226
Brainwriting, 223, 225
Burnout
    causes of, major, 418–419
    countering, 420–421
    effects of, major, 419–420, 425
    fairness and, 418
    occurrence of, 417
    personal factors in, 419
    vacation and, 420

Cafeteria-style benefit plans, 131
Camouflage, 64–65
Cardinal traits, 92–93
Career centers, 443
Career changes
    case for studying, 333
    family and, 455–457
    flexibility and, 458, 461
    life stages and, 454–455
    types of, 452–454
    women's, 457

Career choices
    aptitude tests and, 111–112
    decision making about, 434, 439, 441–442
    educational choices and, 441–442
    factors in, key, 435–441, 460
        appeal of job or field, intrinsic, 436
        culture, 439–441
        gender, 439–441
        personality, 437–438
        social influences, 436–437
        special needs population, 441
    guidelines for effective, 458–459
    interest tests and, 111–112
    job searches and, 442–443
    occupational types and, 438–439
    steps in, crucial, 283
Career development
    goal setting and, 447–448
    guidelines for effective, 458–459
    human resource planning and, 444–445, 460
    needs and, 126–127
    organizational politics and, 446–447
    performance appraisals and, 444
    programs, 444
    protean careers and, 449–450
    relational approach to, 450–451
    screening and, 111–112
    self-knowledge and, 445–446
    summary of process of, 448
    technology and, 449
    three hundred sixty degree feedback and,
        450–452
    training and, 111–112, 441–442
    workplace changes and, 46–52, 448–449
        dual career ladders, 46–48
        job skills, transferable, 50–51
        social skills, 51–52
        temporary employment, 48–50, 449
Career identity, 120
Career insight, 120, 446
Career maturity, 454
Career motivation, 119–120, 139, 141, 446
Career resilience, 119–120
Careers, 435
Career-success orientation, 320
Career theory, 454–455
Carson, Johnny, 214, 232
Cases for studying
    career changes, 333
    persuasion, 208–209

Cases for studying *(continued)*
   sexism, 392–393
   workplace changes, 54–55
Causal attribution, 76–78
Central route to persuasion, 186–190
Central traits, 93
Challenger mission, 231–232
Change, 57–58. *See also* Career changes; Workplace changes
Charismatic leaders, 295–297, 304
Child-care dilemma, 355–356, 456
Cialdini, Robert, 190
Civic virtue, 251
CL_{alt}, 324–326, 332
CL, 323–326, 332
"Click, whirr" response, 190
Clinton, William, 166
Clothing. *See* Dress
Coercive power, 198
Cognitive appraisal, 399
Cognitive conflict, 261
Cognitive-oriented theories of personality, 96–97, 113
Cognitive social learning (Mischel theory of), 96–97
Cohesiveness, 252, 257
Collective-effort model, 217
Collectivist cultures, 19–20, 269
Collectivist self-concept, 108–109
Commitment, 329–330, 332
Common knowledge effect, 230–231
Common sense, 7–9, 21
Communal orientation, 289, 419
Communal versus exchange relationships, 343
Communication
   credibility and, 157
   deception and, 165–170
   downward, 149
   through dress, 162–164
   effective, 146, 170–171, 174
   electronic, 151–156
      brainstorming, 223–225
      computer-mediated, 153–155, 173
      e-mail, 152–153, 173
      Internet etiquette and, 152–153
      spamming and, 152
      telecommuting, 154–156
      trend toward, 151–152, 173
   face-to-face, 153–155
   faulty, 262, 262–263
   guidelines for effective, 172–173

honesty and, 167
listening and, 171
lying and, 165–170
nonverbal, 158–165
   application of, practical, 165
   culture and, 164
   dress, 162–164
   facial expressions, 159
   function of, 158–159, 173–174
   gazes, 161
   job interviews and, 165
   physical contact, 162
   smiling, 160–161
   stares, 161
   success and, 165
organizational structure and, 147–151
personal influences on, 156–157, 173
process of, 146–147, 173
receiver in, 147
sender in, 147
sensitivity training and, 170–171
style and, personal, 156–157
teamwork and, 146
upward, 149
verbal, 158, 225–226
Comparison level for alternatives (CL_{alt}), 324–326, 332
Comparison level (CL), 323–326, 332
Compensation, social, 218–219
Compensatory expectations, 374–375
Competition, 377–378, 391
Complementarity of skills, 257
Compliance
   "click, whirr" response and, 190
   compliance-gaming strategies and, 189–190, 207
   multiple requests and, 191–194
   resisting unwanted influence and, 194–196
   self-deprecation and, 191
   self-disclosure and, 191
   self-presentation and, 190–191
Compliance-gaining strategies, 189–190, 207
Compromising, 259
Computer group dynamics, 224
Computer-mediated communication, 153–155, 173
Concurrence seeking, 233
Conditioning, instrumental, 95
Conflict
   avoidance, 259, 263–264
   cognitive, 261
   creation, 260–261, 266–267

Conflict *(continued)*
  culture and, 269–270
  effects of, 267–268, 271
  fairness and, 264
  in groups, 246
  guidelines for effective management of,
      270
  informational, 258–261, 271
  interdependence and, 246, 258
  intergroup, 377
  interpersonal relations and, 262
  leadership and, 267
  management of
      assessing, 272
      culture and, 269–270
      personal, 263–267, 271
  occurrence of, 246, 258, 271
  personal, 261–267, 271
  prejudice and, 382
  reduction, 259–260, 264–266
  rewards and, 262
  role, 404, 406–407
  stereotypes and, negative, 267, 271
  stress and, 422–423
  two-tier workforce and, 49
Confrontational approach, 269
Conscientiousness, 251
Consensus information, 74–75
Contact, physical, 162
Contingency theory, 291–294, 304
Contingency work, 48–50, 449
Contingent relationship, 121–122
Continuance commitment, 329–330
Contrast effects, 80–81, 86
Conventional occupational type, 437
Coping style, 412, 426–427
Core Groups program, 370
Correlational method, 23–25
Country-club style of management, 287
Courtesy, 251–252
Creativity. *See* Brainstorming
Credentials, 81
Credibility, 157, 183–185
Critical incident technique, 322
Criticism, 263
Cross-functional teams, 254
Cues with lying, 169–170
Culture
  aggression and, 358

career choices and, 439–441
collectivist, 19–20, 269
conflict and, 269–270
diversity and, 19
human relations and, 18–20, 27
individualistic, 19–20, 269
intergroup contact and, 388–390
job interviews and, 386–387
job satisfaction and, variations in, 319–320,
    332
leadership and
    determining, 285–286
    style of, 290–291
nonverbal communication and, 164
social loafing and, 216
stress and, 413
values and, work, 124

Darwinian workplace, 32
Deception in communication, 165–170
Decision making. *See also* Groupthink
  about career choices and, 434, 439, 441–442
  in computer group dynamics, 224
  in groups, 226–236
      computer group dynamics and, 224
      defective, 234–235
      in democratic society, 226–227
      good, 236
      importance of, 214
      information biases and, 229–231, 239
      polarization and, 228–229, 239
      problems with, 227
      strength in numbers effect and, 227–228
  stress and, 416–417
  teamwork and, 304
Deficiency needs, 125
Department of Labor, 442
Dependent variable, 22–23
Depersonalization, 417
Descriptive stereotype, 372–373
Desegregation, 439
Devil's advocate, playing, 195–196, 260
Diamond International Corporation (DIC), 118,
    122
Dictionary of Occupational Codes, 437
Diffusion of responsibility, 249
Digital Equipment Corporation, 370
Direct pressure, 233
Dirty tricks, 205

Discrimination
    forms of, 375–376
    gender, 382–386, 392–393
    guidelines for avoiding, 390–391
    job, 376, 391
    prejudice versus, 370–371, 391
    racial, 386–387, 439–441
    reducing, 388–390, 392
    in work settings, 370, 381–387
Disposable workers, 48
Distinctiveness, 75
Diversity. See Culture
Dominant responses, 219–220
Door-in-the-face technique, 192–194
Downward communication, 149
Dress
    communication through, 162–164
    job interviews and, 24, 81
    stereotypes about, 163
Dual career couples, 354–355, 456
Dual career ladders, 46–48

Educational choices, 441–442
Effect, law of, 122
Electronic communication
    brainstorming, 223–225
    computer-mediated, 153–155, 173
    e-mail, 152–153, 173
    Internet and, 152–153, 173
    spamming and, 152
    telecommuting and, 154–156
    trend toward, 151–152, 173
E-mail, 152–153, 173
Emotional coping, 422
Emotions, controlling, 423–424
Employment tests, 111–112
Empowerment, 297–298
Encounter groups, 42–43
Enhancement strategies, 82–84
Enterprising occupational type, 437
Entitlement strategies, 83–84
Equity, 136. See also Fairness
Equity theory of motivation, 134–135, 140
ERG theory, 127–128, 139
Esteem needs, 125
Ethics at work
    disposable workers, 48
    lying, 168–169
    personality testing, 110

persuasion, subliminal, 188–189
    romance, office, 351
    self-presentation, 83–84
    three hundred sixty degree feedback, 453
    whistle-blowing, 248
Ethnic background. See Culture
Evaluation, 220–221. See also Performance appraisals
Evaluative concerns, 221
Exchange versus communal relationships, 343
Excuses, 84
Exercises, experiential
    change versus stability tendency, assessing, 57–58
    conflict management, assessing, 272
    coping style, checking, 426–427
    expressiveness, measuring own, 174–175
    family and group processes, analyzing, 240
    first impressions, forming, 87
    flexibility of company, assessing, 461
    groupthink at NBC, analyzing, 214, 239
    leadership styles, quiz for determining, 305
    managerial style, assessing, 56
    motivation, assessing, 141
    sexual harassment, assessing experience of, 363
Exhaustion, 399, 417
Existence needs, 127
Expectancy theory, 129–132, 139
Expectancy/valence theory, 129–132, 139
Experimentation, 21–23
Expert power, 199
Expressiveness, measuring own, 174–175
Eye contact, 161

Face-to-face communication, 153–155
Facial expressions, 159, 164
Facilitation, social, 219–221
Fairness
    burnout and, 418
    conflict and, 264
    motivation and, 133–138
    promotion of, 285–286
    rewards and, 136
Family. See also Balancing work and family
    career changes and, 455–457
    group processes and, analyzing, 240
    women and, 457
    work settings and, 458
Fear appeals, 186
Fear of unknown, 36–37

Feedback
  biofeedback, 424
  multirater, 299–300, 450–453
  negative, 263
  rewards and, 257
  suvey, 41–42
  teamwork's effectiveness and, 257
  three hundred sixty (360) degree feedback,
      299–300, 450–453
Fiedler's contingency model, 291–294, 304
Figure-ground relationship, 64–65
Fitness programs, employee, 422, 425
Flexibility
  in benefit programs, 132
  career changes and, 458, 461
  of company, assessing, 461
  workplace changes and, 32, 36
  in work schedules, 34, 449
  in work settings, 449, 458
Flex time, 34, 449
Foot-in-the-door technique, 191–192, 194
Forewarning, 195
Free ride, 221
Friendship, 339–341
Fundamental attribution error, 78, 86
Funder, David, 109

Gazes, 161
Gender. See also Sexual harassment
  biases, 290, 439–441
  career choices and, 439–441
  discrimination, 382–386, 392–393
  dual career couples and, 456
  harassment, 350
  job satisfaction and, variations in, 320–321,
      322
  leadership and
    determining, 283–285
    style of, 289–290
    transformational, 296
  self-concept and, 107–108, 113
  stress and, 413
Gender-role socialization, 289–290
General Aptitude Test Battery (GATB), 111–112
Generation X, 35
Globalization, 35
Goal setting
  career development and, 447–448
  guidelines for effective, 134–135

in human relations study, 10
  superordinate goals and, 266
  teamwork's effectiveness and, 257
Grapevine, 150–151
Great person theory, 279–280
Group pride, 218
Groups. See also Groupthink; Teamwork
  brainstorming in, 221–226
    electronic, 223–225
    improving, 222–226, 239
    inhibition of, factors affecting, 221–222
    process of, 221
    social influences model of, 223
    verbal, 225–226
  chosen, 264
  cohesiveness of, 257
  conflict between, 377
  conflict in, 246
  contact between different, 388–390
  decision making in, 226–236
    computer group dynamics and, 224
    defective, 234–235
    in democratic society, 226–227
    good, 236
    importance of, 214
    information biases and, 229–231, 239
    polarization and, 228–229, 239
    problems with, 227
    strength in numbers effect and, 227–228
  encounter, 42–43
  facilitation and, social, 219–221
  family and processes of, 240
  function of, 214–215, 239
  guidelines for effective, 238
  inner-circle, 264
  laboratory, 42–43
  minority, 285–286
  motivation in, 215–219, 239
  mutual admiration, 264
  nominal, 221–222
  orientation toward, assessing, 226–227
  polarization in, 228–229, 239
  productivity in, 215–219, 239
  rewards and, 257
  self-managing teams, 237, 255, 271
  social categorization and, 377–379, 391
  stability of, 215
  structure of, 257
  token, 264

Groups (continued)
  training of, 257
  types of, various, 214
  work teams, 43–44
Groupthink
  avoiding, 235–237
  concurrence seeking and, 233
  defective decision making and, 234
  evaluation of model of, 235–236
  examples of, 214, 231–233
  at NBC, 214, 232–233, 240
  pressure in, 233–234
  symptoms of, 233–235
  teamwork and, 237
Growth needs, 126–127
Grudges, 262
Guide for Occupational Exploration, 442

Habit, 37
Halo effect, 79–80, 86
Harmony, 269
Hassles Scale, 411
Hawthorne studies, 12–15, 27
Health
  fitness programs, employee, 422, 425
  job satisfaction and, 328–329, 332
  stress and, 415, 425
    in management of, 421
  Type A personality and, 100
Helpfulness. See Prosocial behavior
Helplessness, 415–416
Herzberg, F. H., 322–323, 332
Heuristics, 73
Hewlett-Packard, 146
High context culture, 164
High LPC (least preferred coworker) leaders,
    292–293
Historical perspective of human relations
  applications as guiding principle and, 16–17
  Hawthorne studies and, 12–15, 27
  international perspective and, 16
  science management and, 10–12, 27
  work settings as social systems and, 12–15,
    26–27
Hofstede, G., 319–320
Holland, J. L., 437–438
Honesty, 167
Hudson Institute, 35
Humanistic theories of personality, 95–96, 113

Human nature, recognizing assumptions about,
    70
Human relations. See also Interpersonal relations;
    specific components of
  in action
    common sense, assessing, 8–9
    goal setting, effective, 134–135
    groups, assessing orientation toward, 226–227
    human nature, recognizing assumptions
      about, 70
    illusion of outgroup homogeneity, under-
      standing, 380–381
    job satisfaction, assessing, 324–325
    occupational type, determining, 438–439
    organizational citizenship, assessing, 252
    power, measuring, 200–201
    self-concept, assessing own, 104–105
  application of, 6–7
    as guiding principle, 16–17
  common sense and, 8–9
  culture and, 18–20, 27
  definition of, working, 5–6
  example of, 4
  goals of, 5, 17, 27
  goals setting in study of, 10
  guidelines for effective
    attitudes, 330–331
    career choice and development, 458–459
    communication, 172–173
    conflict, 270
    discrimination and prejudice, 390–391
    groups, 238
    interpersonal relations, 361
    leadership, 302–303
    motivation, 138–139
    perception, 84–85
    personality, 112–113
    persuasion, 206
    prosocial behavior, 270
    stress, 424–425
    workplace changes, 52–53
  historical perspective of, 9–17
    applications as guiding principle and, 16–17
    Hawthorne studies and, 12–15, 27
    international perspective and, 16
    scientific management and, 10–12, 27
    work settings as social systems and, 12–15,
      26–27
  influence on, 25–27

Human relations *(continued)*
  knowledge from applied research on, 21–25
    correlational methods, 23–25
    experimentation, 21–23
    interpersonal relations and, 6–7
  life changes and, 4–5
  myth versus reality in, 7–9
  questions about, 5–6
  research process of, 21–25
  study of, 5
  success and, 7–8
  in work settings, 4, 9–10
Human relations approach, 15
Human resource planning, 444–445, 460
Hygienes or maintenance factor, 322

Illusion of outgroup homogeneity, 380–381
Illusion of productivity, 222
Illusory correlation, 73–74
Immediacy behaviors, 387
Impoverished style of management, 287
Impression, first, 87
Impression formation, 72, 87, 166
Impression management, 82–84, 86–87
Independent variable, 22–23
Individualist cultures, 19–20, 269
Individualistic self-concept, 108–109
Industrial Revolution, 32
Inequity, 136–138
Inference, social perception and, 72–74
Influence. *See also* Persuasion
  compliance-gaming strategies and, 189–190, 207
  on human relations, 25–27
  informational, 260
  normative, 260
  persuasion and, 196–197, 202–204
  power and, 196–197, 202
Informational conflict, 258–261, 271
Informational influence, 260
Information biases, 229–231
Information dependence, 258
Information exchange, 228, 239
Ingratiation strategies, 84
Ingroup, 377, 379, 391
Initiating structure, 286–289
Innovation in work teams, 256–257
Input, 135–136
Insecurity, economic, 36
Instrumental conditioning, 95

Integrative approach to love, 345
Interactions, human, 5. *See also* Human relations;
    Interpersonal relations
Interaction theories of leadership, 281–283
Interdependence, 246, 258
Interest tests, 111–112
Intergroup conflict, 377
Intergroup contact, 388–390
International perspective of human relations, 16
Internet, 34, 152–153, 442–443
Interpersonal relations. *See also* Human relations
  aggression and, 356–360, 362
    anger and, 358–360
    causes of, 357–358
    controlling, 359–360
    culture and, 358
    incidence of, 356–357
    personal characteristics and, 358–359
    sexual assault, 350
    in work settings, 350, 358, 362
  attraction and, 339–341, 362
  balancing work and family and, 354–356
  conflict and, 262
  examples of, 338
  guidelines for effective, 361
  human relations and, 6–7
  love and, 341–345, 362
  romance and, office, 346–354
    effects of, 349
    ethics of, 351
    features of, 346–348
    guidelines, 350
    motivation for, 347–348, 362
    occurrence of, 346, 362
    performance and, 348–349
    questions about, 346
    sexual harassment and, 350–354, 362
  social perception and, 63
  in work settings, 26–27, 63
Inter-role conflict, 404
Intervention, 248–250, 265, 271
Interviews. *See* Job interviews
Intrinsic motivation, 123
Investigative occupational type, 437
Isolation, 406–407

Janis, I. L., 233, 235
Japanese companies, 16
Job changes. *See* Career changes

Job discrimination, 376, 391
Job interviews
    culture and, 386–387
    dress and, 24, 81
    nonverbal communication and, 165
    social perception and, 80–81, 86
Job satisfaction
    absenteeism and, 327–328, 332
    assessing, 324–325
    effects of, 326–329
    factors affecting, 314–318
        external, 315–316, 318
        internal, 316–318
        variety of, 314
    health and, 328–329, 332
    life satisfaction and, 327–328, 332
    motivation and, 322–323, 332
    stress and, 415
    turnover and, 327, 332
    variations in, 319–326
        culture, 319–320, 332
        gender, 320–321, 332
        motivation-maintenance theory and,
            322–323
        occupation, 319, 332
        social exchange theory and, 323–326, 332
        stage of career, 319
Job searches, 442–443
Job sharing, 98–99, 449
Job skills, transferable, 50–51
Job stress
    isolation and, 406–407
    multiple roles and, 402–404
    occupational demands and, 401–402
    overload or underload and, 404–405, 408
    responsibility for others and, 405–406
    role conflict and, 404, 406–407
    unemployment and, 408–409
    working conditions and, 400–401

Karau, S. J., 217
Keeping Fit magazine case study, 54–55
Kelly Services, 49
K.I.S.S. (Keep It Short and Simple) principle, 157

Laboratory groups, 42–43
Langer, Ellen, 190
Lazarus, R. S., 411
Leader pressure, 234

Leadership
    conflict and, 267
    determining, 279–286
        culture and, 285–286
        gender and, 283–285
        interactionist theories, 281–283
        quiz for, 305
        situational theories, 280–281
        trait theories, 279–280
    directions in, new, 297–302
        development of leaders, 299–300, 303
        self-leadership, 300–302
        teamwork, 297–298, 304
        technology, 298–299
    effectiveness of, 278, 291–297, 303
        charismatic leadership and, 295–297, 304
        contingency theory and, 291–294, 303
        transactional leadership and, 294–295
        transformational leadership and, 295–297
    example of, 278
    great person theory and, 279–280
    management versus, 302
    prototypes, 283–284
    styles, 278, 286–291
        assessing own, 305
        burnout and, 419
        culture and, 290–291
        gender and, 289–290
        person-oriented, 286–290, 304, 360
        production-oriented, 286–290, 304
    variety of, 303
    in work settings, 278
Learning, 50, 94–95, 379–380
Learning-oriented theories of personality, 94–95,
    113
Least preferred coworker (LPC) leaders, 292–294
Legitimate power, 198
Leno, Jay, 214, 232
Letterman, David, 214, 232
Lewinsky, Monica, 166
Life changes, 4–5
Life events, 409–410
Life satisfaction, 327–328, 332
Life stages, 454–455
Lifestyle, 421–422
Liking, loving versus, 343
Limited resources, problem of, 261
Listening, 171
Listservs, 43

Loafing, social, 215–219, 221
Love, 341–345, 362
Low context culture, 164
Low LPC (least preferred coworker) leaders, 292–294
Lying, 165–170

McCauley, C. D., 320–321
Machiavelli, 93
Maintenance-oriented management, 289
Majority rule, 259
Malloy, John T., 162
Management, 56, 287–289, 302. *See also* Leadership
Management by objectives, 448
Manipulation of humans, 7
Manpower, 49
Mantra, 424
Marital status, 355
Maslow, Abraham, 124–127, 139, 322
Mayo, Elton, 13–15
Mediation, 265
Meditation, 424
Memory, social perception and, 71–72
Mental coping, 422
Mental states, stress on, 415
Mere exposure effect, 389
Metamorphic effects of power and persuasion, 202–203
Middle-of-the-road management, 287
Military service, training and, 441–442
Mindful persuasion, 186–190
Mindguards, 233
Mindless persuasion, 186–190
Minority groups, 285–286. *See also* Culture
Mischel's cognitive social learning theory, 96–97
Misperception, 234
Misumi, Jyuji, 289
MLQ, 295
Modern racism, 386–387
Mood, 251
Motivation
    achievement, 103–104, 113
    assessing, 141
    attention and, 66
    career, 119–120, 139, 141, 446
    collective-effort model and, 217
    components of, 118–119
    equity theory of, 134–135, 140
    fairness and, 133–138
    in groups, 215–219, 239
    guidelines for effective, 138–139
    inequity and, 136–138
    intrinsic, 123
    job satisfaction and, 322–323, 332
    needs and, 124–128
        ERG theory, 127–128, 139
        Maslow's theory, 124–128, 139, 322
    performance and, 132
    process views of, 128–133
        expectancy theory and, 129–132, 139
        function of, 128
        self-efficacy and, 132–133, 140
    rewards and, 120–123
        intrinsic motivation and, 123
        productivity and, 122–123
        reinforcement approaches, 121–122
        work quality and, 122–123
    for romance, office, 347–348, 362
    social equity and, 134–138
    social loafing and, 215–219, 221
    term of, using, 118–119
    in work settings, 118
Motivation-maintenance theory, 322–323, 332
Motivators, 322
Mouton, J., 287, 289
Multiculturalism. *See* Culture
Multifactor Leadership Questionnaire (MLQ), 295
Multiple careers, 34–35
Multiple requests, 191–194
Multiple roles, 402–404
Multirater feedback, 299–300, 450–453
Mutual admiration groups, 264

NBC television network, 214, 232–233, 240
Need hierarchy theory (Maslow), 124–128, 139
Needs
    achievement, 103–104
    career development and, 126–127
    for change, failure to recognize, 37
    motivation and, 124–128
        ERG theory, 127–128, 139
        Maslow's theory, 124–128, 139, 322
Negotiation, 264–266, 271
Netiquette, 152–153
Nominal groups, 221–222
Nominal group technique, 222–223
Noncontingent reward systems, 122

Nonverbal communication
    application of, practical, 165
    culture and, 164
    dress, 162–164
    facial expressions, 159, 164
    function of, 158–159, 173–174
    gazes, 161
    job interviews and, 165
    physical contact, 162
    smiling, 160–161
    stares, 161
    success and, 165
Nonverbal cues, 81
Normative influence, 260
Norms, 15, 257

Occupational demands, 401–402
Occupational Outlook Handbook, 442
Occupational types, 437–439
OD. *See* Organizational development
Office of Personnel Management, 34
Office romance. *See* Romance, office
Old-fashioned racism, 386
100 Club, 118, 122
One-sided arguments, 185–186
Online Career Center, 443
Optimism, 411–412
Oral messages, 158. *See also* Communication
Organizational citizenship behavior, 251–252
Organizational commitment, 329–330, 332
Organizational development (OD)
    effectiveness of, 46
    purpose of, 40–41, 53
    quality of work life and, 44–45
    sensitivity training in, 42–43
    survey feedback in, 41–42
    team building in, 43–44
Organizational politics, 203–205, 446–447
Organizational socialization, 435
Organizational spontaneity, 253
Organizational structure
    communication and, 147–151
    formal channels of, 148–150
    informal channels of, 150–151
    resistance to change and, 37–38
Other-oriented lies, 167
Ouchi, W. G., 16
Outcome interdependence, 258
Outcomes, 136

Outgroup, 378, 380–381, 391
Overload, 399, 404–405
Overpayment inequity, 136–138
Over-rewarded workers, 136

Participative management, 257
Passionate love, 343–44
Perception
    differences in, 62
    external factors affecting, 67–68
    first impression and, forming, 87
    guidelines for effective, 84–85
    impression management and, 82–84, 86–87
    internal factors affecting, 65–67
    of physical world, 63–68, 86
        organization of, 63–65
        selective nature of, 65–68
    of sexual harassment, 352
    social, 68–82
        attention and, 68–71
        attribution and, 74–78
        errors in, 78–79, 86
        halo effect and, 79–80
        inference and, 72–74
        interpersonal relations and, 63
        job interviews and, 80–81, 86
        memory and, 71–72
        performance appraisals and, 81–82, 86
        process of, 63, 68–69, 86
        in work settings, 79–82, 86
Perceptual organization, 63–65
Performance
    abilities and, 130
    inhibition of, 222
    motivation and, 132
    norms, 257
    pay based on, 122
    rewards and, 122–123, 130
    romance and, office, 348–349
    social loafing and, 217
    stress and, 416–417, 425
    Type A personality and, 101–102
    working conditions and, 400–401
Performance appraisals
    career development and, 444
    social perception and, 81–82, 86
    three hundred sixty degree feedback and, 299–300, 450–453
Performance-oriented management, 289

Peripheral route to persuasion, 186–190
Personal appearance. *See* Dress; Impression
     formation
Personal conflict, 261–263, 271
   managing, 263–267, 271
Personality
   approaches to, 92–97
      cognitive-oriented theories, 96–97, 113
      humanistic theories, 95–96, 113
      learning-oriented theories, 94–95, 113
      trait theories, 92–94, 113
   career choices and, 437–438
   guidelines for effective, 112–113
   of job, 92
   self-concept and, 104–109
      assessing own, 104–105
      collectivist, 108–109
      culture and, 108–109, 113
      development of, 104–106, 113
      foundations of, basic, 106
      gender and, 107–108, 113
      individualistic, 108–109
      as internal cause of job satisfaction, 316–317
      self-esteem and, 106–108
   testing, 109–112, 114
   in work settings, 98–104
      achievement motivation and, 103–104, 113
      importance of, 92, 98
      personality testing, 109–112, 114
      Type A versus Type B traits and, 99–103, 113
Personality Puzzle, The (Funder), 109
Person-oriented leaders, 286–290, 304, 360
Person-role conflict, 404
Person skills, 51
Persuasion
   advertising and, 184, 188–189
   case for studying, 208–209
   central route to, 186–190
   compliance and, 189–196
      "click, whirr" response, 190
      compliance-gaining strategies, 189–190,
         207
      multiple requests, 191–194
      resisting unwanted influences and,
         194–196
      self-deprecation and, 191
      self-disclosure and, 191
      self-presentation and, 190–191
   exposure to, everyday, 182

guidelines for effective, 206
hazards in, avoiding, 201–203
influence and, 196–197, 202–204
metamorphic effects of, 202–203
mindful, 186–190
mindless, 186–190
organizational politics and, 203–205
peripheral route to, 186–190
power and, 196–203
   hazards in, avoiding, 201–203
   individual, 197–200
   influence and, 196–197, 202–204
   measuring own, 200–201
   status and, 197
process of, 182–183
subliminal, 188–189
successful, 183–189
   attractiveness and, 183–185
   content of appeal and, 185–186
   credibility and, 183–185
   pathways, 186–190
   style and, 183–185
Pessimism, 411–412
Physical attractiveness, 340
Physical contact, 162
Physical fitness, 422, 425
Physical world, perception of
   organization of, 63–65
   selective nature of, 65–68
Physiological needs, 125
PM style of management, 289
Polarization, group, 228–229, 239
Police work, stressors of, 416
Politics, attitudinal and organizational, 195,
      203–205, 446–447
Position power, 292
Positive-negative nature of information, 80
Power
   function of, 207
   hazards in, avoiding, 201–203
   individual, 197–200
   influence and, 196–197, 202–204
   measuring own, 200–201
   metamorphic effects of, 202–203
   organizational politics and, 203–205
   sources, 197–200, 207
   status and, 197
   threats to existing balance of, 38
Pratto, F., 321

Prejudice
  components of, 371–372
  conflict and, 382
  discrimination versus, 370–371, 391
  explanations of, 376–381, 391
    competition, 377–378
    intergroup conflict, 377
    social learning, 379–380
    variety of, 380–381
  guidelines for avoiding, 390–391
  reducing, 388–390, 392
  stereotypes and, 372–374, 391
  types of, 383
  in work settings, 370, 381–387
Prescriptive stereotype, 373
Pressure in groupthink, 233–234
Price Waterhouse, 46
Principles of Scientific Management, The (Taylor), 11
Problem-focused coping, 412
Problem-solving, behavioral, 422–423
Process views of motivation
  expectancy theory, 129–132, 139
  function of, 128
  self-efficacy, 132–133, 140
Production-oriented leaders, 286–290, 304
Productivity
  Diamond International Corporation's program
    and, 118
  in groups, 215–219, 239
  Hawthorne studies and, 12–15
  illusion of, 222
  international perspective of, 16
  prosocial behavior and, 253–258, 271
  scientific management and, 10–12
  work quality and, 122–123
  work settings and, 10–12
Profit-sharing systems, 122
Prosocial behavior
  conflict and, 258–272
    avoidance of, 259, 263–264
    cognitive, 261
    creation of, 260–261, 266–267
    culture and, 269–270
    effects of, 267–268, 271
    fairness and, 264
    informational, 258–261, 271
    interdependence and, 246, 258
    intergroup, 377
    interpersonal relations and, 262

  leadership and, 267
  management of, assessing, 272
  occurrence of, 246, 258, 271
  personal, 261–267, 271
  prejudice and, 382
  reduction of, 259–260, 264–266
  rewards and, 262
  factors influencing, 250
  guidelines for, 270
  intervention, 248–250, 265, 271
  mood and, 251
  organizational citizen behavior and, 251–252
  productivity and, 253–258, 271
  range of, broad, 246–247, 271
  spontaneous behaviors, 253
  teamwork, 253–258, 271
  whistle-blowing, 248–250
  in work settings, 247–248
Protean career, 449–450
Prototypes, leadership, 283–284
Proximity, law of, 63–64
Psychological factors of resistance to change, 36–37
Psychological reactance, 202
Pulakos, E. D., 317
Putting in time, results versus, 34

Qualitative overload, 405
Qualitative underload, 405
Quality circles (QCs), 45, 254–255, 271
Quality-of-life orientation, 320
Quality of work life (QWL), 44–45, 254
Quantitative overload, 404–405
Quantitative underload, 405

Racism, 386–387, 439–441
Rate busters, 15, 251
Rationalization, 234
Reactance, 202
Realistic conflict theory, 377
Realistic occupational type, 437
Receiver in communication, 147
Reciprocity rule, 182, 205
Recruiting agencies, 443
Referent power, 198–199
Reflexivity, 256
Regulative approach, 269
Reinforcement-affect model, 342
Reinforcement approaches, 121–122
Reinforcers, 122

Relatedness needs, 127
Relational approach to career development, 450–451
Relaxation training, 423–424
Representativeness heuristic, 73
Resistance, 194–196, 399
Response, 121
Responsibility for others, 405–406
Results, putting in time versus, 34
Reward power, 197–198
Rewards
    collective-effort model and, 217
    conflict and, 262
    fairness and, 136
    feedback and, 257
    groups and, 257
    inequity of, 136
    instrumental, 129
    motivation and, 120–123
        intrinsic motivation and, 123
        productivity and, 122–123
        reinforcement approaches, 121–122
        work quality and, 122–123
    noncontingent system of, 122
    performance and, 122–123, 130
    types of, 121
    work quality and, promoting, 122–123
Role, 404
Role conflict, 404, 406–407
Romance, office
    effects of, 349
    ethics of, 351
    features of, 346–348
    guidelines, 350
    motivations for, 347–348, 362
    occurrence of, 346, 362
    performance and, 348–349
    questions about, 346
    sexual harassment and, 350–354, 362
Rumors, 150–151
Rusty halo, 80

Safety needs, 125
Salience, 67–71
Sampling bias, 230–231
Schmitt, N., 317
Scientific management, 10–12, 27
SCII, 111, 437
Screening, job, 111–112

Secondary traits, 93
Seductive behaviors, 350
Selected Characteristics of Occupations Defined in the Dictionary of Occupational Titles, 442
Self-actualization need, 125–126
Self-censorship, 233
Self-centered lies, 167
Self-concept
    assessing own, 104–105
    collectivist, 108–109
    culture and, 108–109, 113
    development of, 104–106, 113
    foundations of, basic, 106
    gender and, 107–108, 113
    individualistic, 108–109
    as internal cause of job satisfaction, 316–317
    self-esteem and, 106–108
Self-deprecation, 191
Self-disclosure, 191
Self-efficacy, 132–133, 140
Self-enhancing strategies, 82–83
Self-esteem, 106–108, 316, 405
Self-fulfilling nature, 371–372
Self-image. *See* Self-concept
Self-knowledge, 445–446
Self-leadership, 300–302
Self-managing teams, 237, 255, 271
Self-presentation, 82–84, 190–191
Self-realization need, 125–126
Self-serving bias, 79, 86
Selye, H., 399
Sender in communication, 147
Sensitivity training, 42–43, 170–171
Serve Rite Food Services Corporation, 62
Sexism, 382–386, 392–393
Sex-role socialization, 289–290
Sexual assault, 350
Sexual bribery, 350
Sexual coercion, 350
Sexual harassment
    ambient, 353
    dealing with, 353–354, 362
    experience of, assessing, 363
    gender discrimination and, 382–383
    perception of, 352
    physical contact and, 162
    romance in office and, 350–354, 362
    in work settings, 350–354, 362, 382–383
Shaffer, G. S., 320–321

Showing consideration, 286–289
Similarity, law of, 63–64
Single parents, 355–356
Situational theories of leadership, 280–281
Slime effect, 202
Smiles-leniency effect, 160
Smiling, 160–161, 164
Social categorization, 377–379, 391
Social cognition, 186
Social comparison process, 222, 228, 239
Social compensation, 218–219
Social competition, 378
Social conditions at work, 400
Social equity, 134–138
Social exchange theory, 323–326, 332
Social facilitation, 219–221
Social influence model of brainstorming, 223
Social influences on career choices, 436–437
Socialization, 289–290, 435
Social learning, 96–97, 379–380
Social loafing, 215–219, 221
Social models, 436
Social needs, 125
Social occupational type, 437
Social perception
    attention and, 68–71
    attribution and, 74–78
    errors in, 78–79, 86
    halo effect and, 79–80
    inference and, 72–74
    interpersonal relations and, 63
    job interviews and, 80–81, 86
    memory and, 71–72
    performance appraisals and, 81–82, 86
    process of, 63, 68–69, 86
    in work settings, 79–82, 86
Social relationships, threats to, 37
Social skills, 51–52
Social Skills Inventory, 51–52
Social support, lack of, 406–407
Society for Human Resource Management, 110
Spamming, 152
Special needs populations, 441
Spoken language, 158. See also Communication
Spontaneous behaviors, 253
Sportsmanship, 251
Stability, 57–58, 215
Starbucks Coffee, 434
Stares, 161

Status, 197
Stereotypes
    conflict and negative, 267, 271
    descriptive, 372–373
    about dress, 163
    prejudice and, 372–374, 391
    prescriptive, 373
    racial, 387
Stimulus, 121
Strength in numbers effect, 227–228
Stress. See also Burnout
    cognitive factors of, 399
    conflict and, 422–423
    decision making and, 416–417
    effects of, 414–421
        burnout, 417–421, 425
        health, 415, 425
        mental states, 415–416
        work behavior, 416
    emotions and, controlling, 423–424
    example of, 398
    guidelines for effective management of,
        424–425
    job, 400–409, 425
        isolation and, 406–407
        multiple roles and, 402–404
        occupational demands and, 401–402
        overload or underload and, 404–405, 408
        responsibility for others and, 405–406
        role conflict and, 404, 406–407
        unemployment and, 408–409
        working conditions and, 400–401
    job satisfaction and, 415
    managing, 421–426
    nature of, 399–400
    performance and, 416–417, 425
    personal factors affecting, 409–414
        attitude, 413–414
        culture, 413
        daily, 411
        gender, 413
        life events, 409–410
        resistance to, individual differences in,
            411–412
    physiological aspects of, 399
    stages of, 399
    stressors and, 399, 411, 416
    Type A personality and, 100–101
Stressors, 399, 411, 416

Strong-Campbell Interest Inventory (SCII), 111, 437
Structural inertia, 37
Style, personal, 156–157, 183–185
Subliminal persuasion, 188–189
Subordinate responses, 220
Super, D. E., 454–455
Superordinate goals, 266
Survey feedback, 41–42
Synectics, 223

Tacky power, 203
Task management, 287
Task performance strategies, 300–301
Taylor, Frederick W., 11–12
Team building, 43–44
Team management, 289
Teams, 253–254
Teamwork
    communication and, 146
    decision making and, 304
    effectiveness of, 257–258
    groupthink and, 237
    innovation in, 256–257
    leadership and, new directions of, 297–298, 304
    prosocial behavior and, 253–258, 271
    self-managed teams and, 237
Technology
    career development and, 449
    job searches on, 442–443
    job skills and, transferable, 50
    leadership and, new directions of, 298–299
    workplace changes and, 32
Telecommuting, 33–35, 154–156, 449
Temporary employment, 48–50, 449
Testing, personality, 109–112, 114
T-groups, 42–43
Theory Z (Ouchi), 16
Third-party intervention, 265, 271
Thought self-leadership strategies, 301
Threats, 37, 265
Three-factor theory of love (Berscheid), 343–344
Three hundred sixty (360) degree feedback, 299–300, 450–453
Token groups, 264
Touch, personal, 162

Training, job, 111–112, 257, 441–442
Trait theories
    of leadership, 279–280
    of personality, 92–94, 113
Transactional leadership, 294–295
Transference of emotions, 344
Transformational leadership, 295–297
Trustworthiness tests, 111–112
Turnover, 327, 332
Two-sided arguments, 185–186
Two-tier workforce, 49
Type A personality, 99–103, 113, 358, 415
Type B personality, 99–103, 113

Unanimity, illusion of, 234
Unanimity rule, 259
Underload, 404–405
Underpayment inequity, 136–138
Under-rewarded workers, 136
Unemployment, 408–409
Uniformity, pressure to, 233
Unspoken language. *See* Nonverbal communication
Upward communication, 149
USS Vincennes incident, 416–417
Us-versus-them attitudes, 377–379, 382, 391

Vacation, burnout and, 420
Valence, 129
Values, work, 124
Varca, P. E., 320–321
Variables, 22–23
Verbal communication, 158, 225–226
Violence. *See* Aggression
Virtual office, 33
Visual information, 81

Western Electric Company (Hawthorne plant), 12–15
Whistle-blowing, 248–250
Williams, J. E., 94
Williams, K. D., 217
Within-role conflict, 404
Word, C. O., 386–387
workandfamily@opm.gov Internet site, 34
Work context strategies, 30–301
Work and Family Program Center, 34
Workforce 2000, 35
Work group inertia, 38

Working conditions, 400–401. *See also* Work
    settings
Workplace changes
    adapting to, 32, 54–55
    career development and, 46–52, 448–449
        dual career ladders, 46–48
        jobs skills, transferable, 50–51
        social skills, 51–52
        temporary employment, 48–50, 449
    case for studying, 54–55
    failure of, previous, 38
    flexibility and, 32, 36
    in future, 33–36
    guidelines for effective management of, 52–53
    introducing, tactics for, 38–40
    magnitude of, 32
    organizational development and, 40–46, 53
        effectiveness of, 46
        purpose of, 40–41, 53
        quality of work life and, 44–45
        sensitivity training in, 42–43
        survey feedback in, 41–42
        team building in, 43–44
    resistance to, 36–38, 53
        organizational structure, 37–38
        overcoming, 38–40
        psychological factors, 36–37, 53
    technology and, 32
    telecommuting, 33–35
    types of, 32
Work quality, 122–123
Work schedules, flexible, 34, 449
Work settings. *See also* Balancing work and family;
        Ethics at work; Workplace changes
    aggression in, 350, 358, 362
    causal attribution and, 76–78
    discrimination in, 370, 381–387
    diversification of, 35
    family and, 458
    flexibility in, 449, 458

globalization of, 35
Hawthorne studies and, 12–15
humanizing, 44–45
human relations in, 4, 9–10
improving, 17, 40–41
international perspective of, 16
interpersonal relations in, 26–27, 63
leadership in, 278
motivation in, 118
organizational politics in, 203–205
personality in, 98–104
    achievement motivation and, 103–104, 113
    importance of, 92, 98
    testing, 109–112, 114
    Type A versus Type B traits and, 99–103, 113
prejudice in, 370, 381–387
productivity and, 10–12
prosocial behvior in, 247–248
racism in, 386–387
romance in, office, 346–354
    effects of, 349
    ethics of, 351
    features of, 346–348
    guidelines, 350
    motivations for, 347–348, 362
    occurrence of, 346, 362
    performance and, 348–349
    questions about, 346
    sexual harassment and, 350–354, 362
scientific management and, 10–12
sexism in, 382–386, 392
sexual harassment in, 350–354, 362, 382–383
social perception in, 79–82, 86
as social systems, 12–15, 26–27
women in, 457
Work teams, 43–44, 256–257
Work values, 124
Work versus family. *See* Balancing work and family
Written messages, 158

Photo Credits

Chapter 1:   p. 13, Courtesy of AT&T Archives; p. 17, National Archives; p. 18, © Eastcott/The Image Works.

Chapter 2:   p. 33, © 1996 PhotoDisc, Inc.; p. 49, © Spencer Grant/ Stock Boston.

Chapter 3:   p. 65, © Galen Rowell/Corbis; p. 87, left to right © Bob Daemmrich/The Image Works, © Holt Confer/The Image Works, © Bill Bachmann/The Image Works, © Skjold/The Image Works.

Chapter 4:   p. 95, © Bob Daemmrich/The Image Works; p. 104, © Michael Dwyer/Stock Boston.

Chapter 5:   p. 127, © Camilla Smith/Rainbow.

Chapter 6:   p. 152, © Robert Harbison; p. 163, left © Bob Daemmrich/Stock Boston, right © Brian Smith; p. 166, left Agence France Presse/Corbis, right Agence France Presse/Corbis.

Chapter 7:   p. 184, © Jon Burbank/The Image Works.

Chapter 8:   p. 216, © Anna Kaufman Moon/Stock Boston; p. 224, Courtesy of IBM; p. 232, NASA/The Image Works.

Chapter 11:   p. 315, left © Will Hart, right PhotoDisc, Inc.; p. 321, © Peter Menzel/Stock Boston; p. 328, © Dan McCoy/Rainbow.

Chapter 12:   p. 340, left © Tony Neste 1995, right © D. C. Head; p. 346, PhotoDisc, Inc.

Chapter 13:   p. 384, Corbis; p. 389, © Elizabeth Crews/The Image Works.

Chapter 14:   p. 401, left © Brian Smith, right Kelly-Mooney Photography/Corbis.

Chapter 15:   p. 440, © Jim Pickerell/Stock Boston; p. 446, left © Matthew McVay/Stock Boston, right © Tim Mosenfelder/Corbis.